Intermediate Microeconomics and Its Application

Intermediate Microeconomics and Its Application

Second Edition

Walter Nicholson
Amherst College

The Dryden Press
Hinsdale, Illinois

Preface

This book is intended for use by undergraduates in an intermediate microeconomics course. It provides an elementary but rigorous introduction to the tools that economists have developed for studying the allocation of resources. By covering a somewhat broader range of topics than does the usual text (for example, factor markets, welfare economics, public goods, and property rights) and by including a number of carefully integrated empirical examples, the book seeks to illustrate the variety and fascination of modern economics.

Formal prerequisites for using this book are minimal: Some knowledge of introductory economics and a familiarity with principles of algebra and graphing (which are reviewed early in the text) should suffice. Most "proofs" in the book are presented intuitively and graphically. Calculus is used only in a few footnotes.

New to the Second Edition

While retaining the general outline of the first edition, this second edition of *Intermediate Microeconomics and Its Application* incorporates a number of changes. Much of the theoretical presentation has been shortened and rewritten to improve its clarity of exposition; numerous empirical examples have been added as illustrations of the theoretical points being made; and the organization of some of the chapters has been altered. Perhaps of equal importance to these substantive changes are changes in format that have been made in the book: Empirical examples have been set off in a distinctive type face; important definitions and optimization principles have been highlighted for easy reference; and a large number of additional topic headers have been added. All of these changes should make the book a more effective learning aid. Finally, this edition includes many more problems, and these should also aid students in obtaining a thorough grasp of the subject.

Outline of the Book

There are twenty-one chapters in this book, divided into seven parts. Part I provides an introduction to what follows and reviews many basic concepts from elementary economics. Parts II, III, and IV develop the basic economic model of supply and demand and form the fundamental core of the book. Except for a few appendixes, these parts are integrally connected to the remainder of the book, and most instructors will choose to cover all of the chapters in them (that is, Chapters 3 through 12). The final three parts in the book may be covered more or less selectively. Part V analyzes pricing of factors of production, Part VI covers general equilibrium and welfare economics, and Part VII addresses economic roles of government. In my courses I have managed to cover all of those topics, but others may prefer a more leisurely and comprehensive pace. The book is intended to accommodate a variety of preferences in that regard.

Acknowledgments

In preparing this second edition I have benefited from thoughtful comments I have received from many users of the first edition. Similar helpful input to my thinking was provided by users of my *Microeconomic Theory,* Second Edition (Dryden, 1978). Since it is impossible to acknowledge here all of those contributors and since I wish to stay on good terms with each of them, discretion dictates that I refrain from specific attribution. Two Amherst College students from the class of 1978 provided substantial contributions to the present edition. William Adkinson helped me to develop the empirical examples. His insistence that I choose examples that make the right points was most appreciated. Eric Fornell developed many of the problems in the text, and he must share at least some of the responsibility for what passes for humor in them. Readers of my previous prefaces will surely know that Dorothy Ives typed the manuscript for this edition. I have about run out of superlatives for this amazing woman; I hope a simple thanks will suffice. At Dryden Press Nedah Abbott brilliantly shepherded this edition through all of its production phases. Her helpful suggestions and careful attention to detail improved the book in many ways. Finally, my children, Kate, David, and Tory, always like to see their names in print.

W. N.
Amherst, Amherst, Mass.
November 1978

Contents

vii

Part VI General Equilibrium and Welfare   459

Intermediate Microeconomics and Its Application

Introduction

The purpose of Part I is to provide some background material basic to the study of economics. In Chapter 1 we will investigate various definitions of "economics" and discuss the role that economic theory plays in understanding how real-world economies operate. Since this book is primarily concerned with the development of theoretical tools, it is important for us to begin with an understanding of the purpose to which these tools will be put. Chapter 1 also provides us with a general outline of the book and illustrates several important themes that occur frequently throughout the text.

Chapter 2 continues as an introduction to the book by presenting a brief historical treatment of economic analysis. In this chapter we will, first, discuss the way in which economic theory has evolved over time and, second, review the simple supply-demand model of price determination. The chapter therefore offers both historical perspective and a common background for the more detailed analysis of price determination that follows.

The Appendix to Chapter 2 summarizes a few elementary concepts from high-school algebra. We will be especially concerned with the relationship between algebraic functions and the graphical representations of these functions. Since we will be using graphic techniques a great deal throughout the book (and because they are widely used in the field of economics as a whole), readers uncomfortable with such concepts should carefully review this material.

Chapter 1

Economic Models

Definitions of Economics

Since several definitions of economics are in current usage, it should be useful for us to examine a few of them as an introduction to the subject. The most widely used definition describes economics as the *study of the allocation of scarce resources among alternative end uses*. Here we are introduced to two important aspects of society that are of concern to economists. First, productive resources are *scarce*—they are not able to satisfy all human wants. Any society is constrained in its production by the quantities of land, labor, and capital it has on hand and by the technology that exists for using those resources. Second, those productive resources that are available may be devoted to a variety of end uses. A society may choose to have television sets or automobiles or clean air or beautiful cities. In fact, a society is likely to choose some combination of all of those "ends," and economists have been particularly interested in studying the *alternatives* that are open to a society and in discovering the ways in which it makes its final choices.

A second definition builds directly on those ideas and describes economics as the *study of the ways in which a society makes choices*. Not only does a society as a whole make choices about the allocation of its resources, but the individuals in that society must also make a wide variety of choices. Individuals must choose the goods they will purchase with their incomes and decide how to spend their leisure time, for whom to vote, how many children to have, even whether to have children at all, and

3

so on. And beyond such personal matters, individuals also face various choices in connection with their occupations. A manager of a firm, for example, must make choices about the productive techniques to be used and the resources to be hired. *Microeconomics* centers attention on the choices that individuals make. By understanding the factors that influence the individual's choices and the ways in which the choices of many individuals interact, it becomes possible to understand how a society as a whole makes decisions in allocating its resources.

A final, somewhat facetious, definition describes economics as *what economists do*. The circularity in this definition points out the impossibility of classifying in any simple way the questions that interest economists. Economists are concerned with "large" questions, such as the relative merits of capitalism and socialism, or the proper role of government in a free market economy. They also study "small" questions, such as the effect of the development of hybrid corn on economic growth in the Midwest, or what rates an electric utility company should charge its customers. All such studies have, however, certain similarities in both the theories they employ and the methods by which the theories are focused on particular issues. The purpose of this book is, first, to guide the reader through a systematic development of the basic theoretical tools used by economists in their investigations; then, the reader will be shown, by means of numerous examples, how those theories can be applied.

Theoretical Models

The most striking feature of the structure of any developed economy is its overall complexity. Thousands of firms are engaged in producing millions of different goods. Millions of individuals work in numerous occupations and purchase a wide variety of products, ranging from peanuts to house trailers. All of those actions must in some way be coordinated. Wheat, for example, must be harvested at the right time; it must be shipped to a miller who, in turn, ships it to a baker who, in turn, must make certain that bread arrives at thousands of retail outlets in the proper quantities to meet individual demand. Obviously, to describe such features of an economy in complete detail would be impossible. Economists have, instead, chosen to abstract from the vast complexities of real-world economies and to develop rather simple *models* that capture the "essentials" of the economic process. Just as a road map is very useful even though it does not record every house, or every blade of grass, so too are economic models very useful for understanding reality even though they do not record every minute feature of the economy. In this book we will be studying the most widely used economic models; we will see that even though they are heroic abstractions from the true complexities of the economy, they nonetheless capture certain essentials that are common to all economic activities.

The use of models is widespread in both the physical and the social sciences. In physics the notions of a "perfect" vacuum or an "ideal" gas are abstractions that permit scientists to study real-world phenomena in simplified settings. In chemistry the idea of an atom or a molecule is in actuality a very simplified model of the structure of matter. Similarly, anthropologists use the concept of a "culture" in order to characterize and to simplify the structure of a society. Economists have also developed models as aids to understanding economic complexities, models that portray the way individuals make decisions, the way firms behave, and the way in which these two groups interact in "the market."

Verification of Models

Of course not all models prove to be "good." For example, the Ptolemaic model of planetary motion was eventually replaced as it proved incapable of explaining certain events. An important purpose of scientific investigation is to sort out the "bad" models from the "good." Two general methods have been used for the verification of economic models: (1) the *direct approach*, which seeks to establish the validity of the basic assumptions upon which a model is based; (2) the *indirect approach*, which attempts to establish validity by showing that a simplified model correctly predicts real-world events. To illustrate the basic differences in the two approaches we will briefly examine a model that we will use extensively in later chapters of this book—the model of a firm that has as its single goal of operation the maximization of profits.

The Profit Maximization Model

The model of a *profit-maximizing firm*, obviously a simplification of reality, abstracts from the personal motivations of a firm's managers and does not treat personal conflicts between the managers. It assumes that profits are the only relevant goal of a firm; other possible goals, such as obtaining power or prestige, are treated as unimportant. This simple model implies that a firm has sufficient information about its costs and the nature of the market to which it sells to be able to discover what its profit-maximizing decisions actually are. In most real-world cases, firms do not, of course, have this information readily available. Such shortcomings in the model are, however, not necessarily serious. As we have been suggesting, no model can exactly describe reality. The real question is whether this simple model has any claim to general validity.

Direct Test of Assumptions

Now let us test the model of a profit-maximizing firm by taking the direct approach and investigating its basic assumption: Do firms really seek maximum profits? Economists have made numerous frontal assaults on that question, most commonly by sending a questionnaire to executives asking them to specify what goals they pursue. The results of such studies have been varied. Businesspeople often mention goals other than profits, or claim they only do "the best they can" given their limited information. On the other hand, most respondents also mention a strong "interest" in profits and express the view that profit maximization is an appropriate goal. The direct approach to testing the profit-maximizing model by testing its assumptions has therefore proved to be inconclusive.

Indirect Empirical Tests

Some economists (most notably Milton Friedman[1]) object to the notion that a theory can be tested by inquiring into the "reality" of its assumptions. They argue that all theories are, almost by definition, based on "unrealistic" assumptions; the very nature of theorizing demands that we make certain abstractions. These economists conclude that the only way to determine the validity of a theory is to see whether it is capable of explaining and predicting real-world events. The ultimate test of an economic theory comes when it is confronted with data from the economy itself.

Friedman provides an important illustration of that principle. He asks what kind of a theory one should use to explain the shots an expert pool player will make. He argues that the laws of velocity, momentum, and angles from classical physics would be a suitable theoretical model. The pool player shoots shots *as if* he or she followed these laws. If we asked players whether or not they understood the physical principles behind the game of pool, they would undoubtedly answer that they did not. Nonetheless, Friedman argues, the physical laws provide very accurate predictions and should therefore be accepted as appropriate theoretical models.

That approach, then, provides the second way in which models can be tested. To return to the example of the profit-maximization hypothesis, a test of this model would be provided by trying to predict the behavior of real-world firms by assuming that these firms behave *as if* they were maximizing profits. If these predictions were reasonably in accord with reality, we might accept the profit-maximization hypothesis even though direct methods of verification yield ambiguous information regarding the "reality" of the basic assumption. The fact that firms respond to questionnaires by disclaiming any precise attempt at profit maximization is no more damaging to the validity of the basic hypothesis than is the pool player's disclaiming knowledge of the laws of physics. Rather, the ultimate test of either theory is in its ability to predict *real-world events*. Later on we will return to study the profit-maximization hypothesis in considerable detail, and we will show that in many ways the hypothesis does make predictions that accord well with real-world experience.

Uses of Empirical Examples

This book is about economic theories. But since our real objective is to learn something about the real world, we must be concerned with the validity of those theories. We will therefore use both of the methods of appraisal that we have been discussing. Occasionally we will try to establish the validity of a theory by pointing to the fact that it is based on "reasonable" assumptions. More often, however, we

---

[1]See M. Friedman, *Essays in Positive Economics* (Chicago: University of Chicago Press, 1953), chap. 1.

will examine examples from the real world which are in accord with the predictions that would be made from theory. (Some of these examples are highlighted in the text by a ■.) The purpose of including many examples in this book, then, is not only because they are interesting in their own right, but also because they provide empirical support for the theories being presented. The examples are therefore integral to developing an understanding of economics.

Positive-Normative Distinction

So far we have been talking primarily about the role of *positive* economic theories. Such "scientific" theories take the real world as an object to be studied, and they attempt to explain those economic phenomena that are observed. Positive economics seeks to determine how resources are *in fact* allocated in an economy. A somewhat different use of economic theory is for *normative* analysis. Such analysis takes a definite moral position on what *should be* done. Under the heading of normative analysis, economists have a great deal to say about how resources *should be* allocated. For example, an economist engaged in positive analysis might investigate why and how the American health care industry uses the quantities of capital, labor, and land that are currently devoted to providing medical services. The economist might also choose to measure the costs and benefits of devoting even more resources to health care. But when the economist advocates that more resources *should* be allocated to health, he or she has implicitly moved into normative analysis. An economist adopting the profit-maximization hypothesis because it seems to explain reality, is engaging in positive analysis. But an economist who argues that firms should maximize profits is taking a normative position.

Some economists believe that the only proper economic analysis is positive analysis. By drawing an analogy with the physical sciences, they argue that "scientific" economics should concern itself only with the description (and possibly prediction) of real-world events. To take moral positions and to plead for special interests is considered to be outside the competence of an economist acting as an economist. For example, one might argue that it is correct for an economist to measure the costs of alternative systems for delivering health services, but that the advocacy or choosing of a particular policy should be left to the political process.

Although this book is primarily "positive" in orientation, it does touch on many normative issues. We will investigate not only how the price system works but also how it should work. We will try to provide some framework for making decisions about what a government should and should not do in providing goods and services to its citizens. Finally, we will discuss the way in which an economy characterized by private property works, and we will speculate about what the proper role of private property in a society is. The position we will take is that there is no clear distinction between positive and normative questions in economics and that the methods of economic analysis can illuminate both types of issues. For that reason this book covers a somewhat broader range of topics than is usual in similar texts.

The treatment of normative issues presented here, however, does little more than raise some of the relevant questions; most answers are left to the reader.

Overview of the Book

This book is divided into seven parts. Each part is devoted to explaining a broad area of economic analysis, and each includes several closely related chapters. So that the reader may better understand the overall logic of the book, the contents of each part are briefly summarized here.

The purpose of Part I is to provide an introduction to the topics that follow later. The present chapter has provided an elementary discussion of some of the methodological issues arising in economic analysis. The purpose of Chapter 2, a brief history of the development of economics, is twofold. First, it places the theories in this book into an historical context. This permits us to view the current state of economics theory as one stage in the evolution of a series of investigations into the workings of an economy. Second, Chapter 2 reminds the reader of the *basic model of supply and demand*, which has been developed by economists to explain how prices are determined. That model, developed in the latter part of the nineteenth century, provides the framework for most of the analysis in the book.

In Parts II and III the actions of two important types of participants in the economic process are examined. Part II develops in detail the economic theory of individual behavior. Simply put, the purpose of this part is to explain how economists treat individuals' preferences and how these preferences affect decisions. A similar development is presented in Part III for the decisions that firms make. Part III quantifies important aspects of productive technology and shows how that technology affects costs.

Parts IV and V show how the preferences of individuals and the productive technologies of institutions interact to create markets and determine prices. The allocation of goods and resources takes place in these markets. Part IV specifically discusses the market for goods and investigates the various ways in which these markets are organized. A similar analysis is presented in Part V for the market for productive resources. Both parts build directly on the analysis of individuals' and firms' decisions presented in Parts II and III.

Parts VI and VII raise more general questions about the desirability of market operations. General concepts of social welfare are developed in Part VI, and a theoretically optimal exchange situation is described. Possible departures from this "ideal" are discussed in Part VII, and the role of government as an agent for dealing with these departures is investigated in some detail.

Recurrent Themes

Although numerous theories are discussed in this book, they are all, in one way or another, applications of a few simple ideas. Three themes are particularly relevant to a broad range of social issues. The following descriptions should be helpful as we will discuss these three themes throughout the book.

Beneficial Nature of Free Exchange

If Smith has something Jones wants and Jones has something Smith wants, then they both can be made better off by exchanging those goods. Many of the results in this book are specific applications of this common-sense idea.

Limitations of Exchange

In many situations, however, individuals left on their own to exchange goods freely will not produce socially desirable results. Therefore some coercion is necessary to direct the members of society to act for the good of society. It is, for example, unlikely that individuals left on their own would provide adequate mosquito control. Each person, acting in his or her own self-interest, would adopt the principle of "let the other guy do it," hoping to benefit from neighbors' expenditures. Since everyone (or almost everyone) would adopt that position, mosquitoes would never be controlled. Free exchange is not sufficient to guarantee a desirable allocation of resources, and there is room for governmental action.

Value of the "Maximization Hypothesis" in Explaining Behavior

In order to understand why economic agents (firms, individuals, labor unions, and others) act as they do, it is frequently useful to assume that these agents are rationally pursuing some goal. From among a number of possible actions, the agent will choose that one that best achieves (that is, maximizes) some goal. As we saw earlier, the most familiar example of this hypothesis is the assumption that firms act so as to maximize profits. From this one basic behavioral assumption a number of interesting implications about a firm's behavior can be derived, and these implications can then be tested in the real world. In this book similar assumptions will be made about most economic agents, and it will be shown that these assumptions can give considerable insights into the ways in which choices are made.

Suggested Readings

Friedman, M., *Essays in Positive Economics* (Chicago: University of Chicago Press, 1953), chap. 1.

Harrod, P. F., "Scope and Method in Economics," *Economic Journal* 48 (1938), pp. 383–412.

Knight, F. H., "The Limitations of Scientific Method in Economics," in *The Trend of Economics,* ed. R. G. Tugwell (New York: Appleton-Century-Crofts, 1930).

Lange, O., "The Scope and Method of Economics," in *Readings in the Philosophy of Science*, ed. H. Feigl and M. Brodbeck (New York: Appleton-Century-Crofts, 1953).

Machlup, F., "The Problem of Verification in Economics," *Southern Economic Journal* 22 (1955), pp. 1–21.

Nagel, E., "Assumptions in Economic Theory," *American Economic Review* 53 (May 1963), pp. 211–219.

Robbins, L., *An Essay on the Nature and Significance of Economic Science*, 2d ed. (London: Macmillan & Co., Ltd., 1935).

Chapter 2

A History of Economics

Introduction

Even prehistoric societies engaged in economic activities. Those early societies utilized the resources they had available to satisfy their basic needs. Two essential features of the economic organization of those societies were *specialization* and *exchange*. Rather than have every individual perform all the tasks necessary for the society's continuation, they came to recognize the benefits of specialization. Some individuals would engage in hunting and food-gathering activities; others would make tools and weapons; and still others would prepare food, care for children, and engage in other household activities. This specialization undoubtedly made primitive societies more productive than they would otherwise have been. Specialization could only exist together with the institution of exchange. Hunters exchanged game for the food gathered by others. Similarly, food-gatherers exchanged their food with craftsmen for tools and weapons, or with household workers in trade for their services. By means of the simple economic principles of exchange and specialization, early societies were able to survive and, eventually, to advance.

Although economic activity has been a central feature of all societies, it is surprising that these activities were not studied in any detail until fairly recently. For the most part, economic phenomena were treated as a basic aspect of human nature

11

that was not sufficiently interesting to deserve specific attention. It is, of course, true that individuals have always studied economic activities with a view toward making some kind of personal gain, but investigations into the analysis of these activities did not begin in any depth until the eighteenth century.[1]

We will survey the early history of the development of economics for two reasons. First, by examining the way that earlier economists tried to come to grips with the basic issues of economics, we will gain a greater understanding of the current nature of the subject. Just as the physical sciences have developed over time, so economics has made significant advances in understanding the features of the world it seeks to understand. But those advances did not come easily, and the accumulation of economic knowledge has not been smooth. One purpose of this chapter is to remind the reader of the simple supply and demand model of price determination that is used in elementary economics. By reviewing the theoretical precursors of this model it will be shown that this model is not only the culmination of several different strands of thought but also explains important phenomena that earlier economists were unable to explain.

A second reason for looking at the history of the development of economics is to impress upon the reader that all economic theories are historically relative. Economics is a constantly evolving subject, perpetually coming to grips with new and more difficult issues. Current theory has not been "proven" for all time but merely represents one stage in a long process of development. By seeing this process in its historical context, both the strengths of current theory and the possibilities for its future evolution can be more fully appreciated.

Theory of Value

Since this book is about economic theory as it stands today, not about the history of economic thought, the discussion of the evolution of this theory must be brief. Only one area of economic study will be examined in its historical setting: the *theory of value*, which has been of interest to economists—or their philosopher predecessors—from the earliest times to the present.

The theory of value, not surprisingly, concerns the determinants of the "value" of a commodity. The study of this subject is at the center of modern microeconomic theory and is closely intertwined with the subject of the allocation of scarce resources for alternative ends. One of our primary intentions is to develop this interconnection. Only recently have the theoretical interrelationships between the determinants of value and the optimal allocation of resources been made clear. Earlier economists were concerned primarily with explaining the determinants of "value," and these efforts are outlined in this chapter.

---

[1]This is not completely true. See the discussion that follows for a brief mention of earlier work. For a far more detailed treatment, see J.A. Schumpeter, *History of Economic Analysis* (New York: Oxford University Press, 1954), pt. II, chaps. 1, 2, and 3.

considering the physical analogy of a mountain. The slope of the ground on a mountain top must be 0. Otherwise you would not be on the top, since walking in the appropriate direction would increase your altitude. Only if the slope is 0 will it be impossible to make such a move. Since throughout this book we will be interested in maximum (that is "highest") points it is important to keep this physical analogy in mind. The fact that the slope of a function (or of its graph) must be 0 at a maximum point has many important economic applications.

Functions of Two or More Variables

Economists are usually concerned with functions of more than one variable. For example, a two-variable function might be denoted by

$$Y = f(X,Z) \qquad \text{[2A.10]}$$

That notation records the fact that the values Y takes on depend on the value of both X and Z. For example, equation 2A.10 might record the fact that an individual's weight (Y) depends not only on the calories he or she consumes (X) but also on the quantity of exercise (Z) he or she gets. We can readily expand the notation to have Y depend on the values of more than two variables. But since most of the points we will make here can be made by using the simple two-variable case, we will only analyze that case.

Economists use functions of two or more variables because they are interested in multiple causes. There is no real-world economic situation in which one variable depends only on one other variable. Any one "dependent" variable that is of interest undoubtedly depends on numerous other variables. For example, the quantity of wheat a farmer can produce depends not only on the size of the farm but also on the number of laborers used, the quantity of equipment employed, the amount of fertilizer, the weather, and so forth. Similarly the satisfaction an individual feels depends not only on the quantity of food eaten but also on the quantity and quality of housing, on how hard he or she has to work, and on numerous other physical and psychological variables. In order to deal with such relationships, economists use functions of several variables.[6]

As an example of a function of two variables, suppose the relationship between $Y, X,$ and Z is given by

$$Y = 100 - X^2 - Z^2 \qquad \text{[2A.11]}$$

Some values of this function are presented in Table 2A.2. For example, it is obvious from equation 2A.11 that if $X = 0$ and $Z = 0$, Y takes on the value 100. We can fill in

---

[6]Economists often analyze only a few variables that affect some other variable and hold all other causes fixed. This is an example of imposing the *ceteris paribus* assumption, which we will discuss more fully in Chapter 3.

Table 2A.2 / Some Values for the Function $Y = 100 - X^2 - Z^2$

X	Z	$Y = 100 - X^2 - Z^2$
0	0	100
5	0	75
0	5	75
4	3	75
3	4	75
−3	−4	75
−4	−3	75
2	1	95
1	2	95
7	0	51
0	7	51
10	0	0
0	10	0
9	3	10
9	−4	3
9	5	−6
5	−9	−6
12	0	−44

other entries in the table by substitution of suitable hypothetical values for X and Z into equation 2A.11. Notice in particular that Y may have the same value for several different combinations of values for X and Z. For instance, $Y = 75$ if $X = 0$ and $Z = 5$; if $X = 5$ and $Z = 0$; if $X = 3$ and $Z = 4$; if $X = -3$ and $Z = -4$; or for any other of an infinite number of combinations of X and Z.

Graphing Functions of Two Variables

In order for us to graph a function of the form 2A.10, we would require three dimensions: one axis would be needed for X, one for Z, and one for the values of Y.[7] To draw such three-dimensional functions in a two-dimensional book can be confusing. Not only must we be good artists, so that we somehow show depth in only two dimensions, but we must also have good imaginations to reinterpret the graph into the familiar three-dimensional world. Since economists are not necessarily good artists (and some would argue because economists lack imagination), they have chosen an alternative way of graphing functions of two variables. Because this treatment has many similarities to the techniques map makers use, we should consider this analogy as a starting point.

Map makers are also confined to working with two-dimensional drawings. However, they are able to depict a third dimension by making use of contour lines. These are lines of equal altitude that outline the physical features of the territory being mapped. For example, a contour line labeled "1000 feet" on a map shows all

---

[7]Of course, functions of more than two variables would require more than three dimensions for graphing. Since we live in a three-dimensional world it is hard even to visualize what such graphs might look like.

those points of land 1000 feet above sea level. By using a number of contour lines, map makers can show the heights and steepness of mountains and the depth of valleys and ocean trenches. Thus they add a "third dimension" to their two-dimensional map.

Similarly, economists make wide use of *contour maps*. Since we will be using such drawings throughout the text, let us develop a simple example using equation 2A.11. We will graph this equation in two dimensions (one each for the values of X and Z), and we will use contour lines to show the values of Y. That graph appears in Figure 2A.5, with contour lines for $Y = 100$, $Y = 75$, $Y = 51$, and $Y = 0$. For example, the circle labeled $Y = 75$ is simply a graph of either

$$75 = 100 - X^2 - Z^2 \qquad \text{[2A.12]}$$

or

$$X^2 + Z^2 = 25 \qquad \text{[2A.13]}$$

The other contour lines in Figure 2A.5 can be graphed in a similar way.

Of course, only a few of the contour lines of the function 2A.11 are shown in Figure 2A.5. There are in reality an infinite number. A three-dimensional graph of the function would look like an inverted ice cream cone with its point sticking out from the page and positioned over the origin of the X-Z axis. The contour lines are constructed by passing a cutting plane through this cone at different levels. These contour lines are circles that get larger as the cutting plane moves further from the point of the cone. Notice that there are many points on each contour line. For example, there are many alternative sets of X and Z for which $Y = 75$. The use of a contour map permits all of these combinations to be clearly shown.

Special Features of the Mathematical Tools Used in Economics

So far this appendix has been purely mathematical. The analysis we have used and the examples we have discussed have not been related in any particular way to the study of economics. In this section we will survey a few of the peculiarities that arise when we apply general mathematical tools to economic problems, and we will be offered a few warnings that should be kept in mind.

The first important aspect that we should note is that practically all the variables used in economic analysis can only take on positive values. Economists talk about prices, quantities of output, and quantities of factors of production. In most situations those variables are either positive or zero; a negative price or quantity would have no meaning.[8] Therefore most graphs in this book will show only the

---

[8]In more advanced areas of economic theory, both negative quantities and negative prices do have interesting uses; we will not encounter those here.

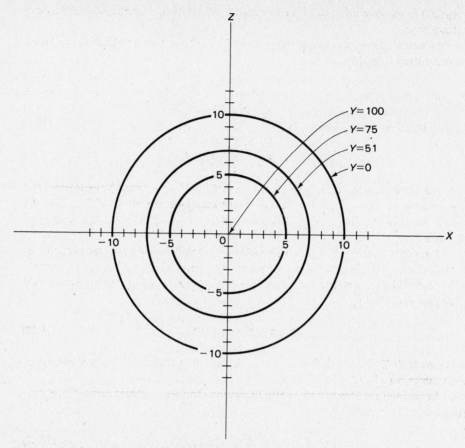

Figure 2A.5 / Contours of the Function $Y = 100 - X^2 - Z^2$

In three dimensions, the function $Y = 100 - X^2 - Z^2$ would look like an inverted ice cream cone with its point sticking out from the page. By cutting this cone with a plane at various heights, we can get the circular contour lines showing in the figure. For example, at $X = 0$, $Y = 0$ the value of $Y = 100$, and this is the very tip of the cone. There are many values of X and Z for which $Y = 75$, and these are shown by the circular contour line.

positive quadrant (quadrant I). In this quadrant both of the variables are always non-negative.

A second peculiarity is the economist's tendency to "reverse" the axes in a graph and to put the dependent variable on the horizontal axis. The most common occurrence of this is in supply and demand graphs, such as the one depicted in Figure 2.1. Economists usually assume that price is the independent variable in a supply-demand situation and that individuals and firms react to this price by choosing the quantities they will demand and the quantities they will produce, respectively. However, for reasons that should become apparent in Part III, economists have chosen to use the vertical axis to record the independent variable (price) in these relations and the horizontal axis to record the dependent variable (quantity).

Of course, the nature of an equation is not affected by which variables are put on which axes. The equation

$$Y = 2 + 2X \qquad \text{[2A.14]}$$

is identical to the equation

$$X = \tfrac{1}{2}Y - 1 \qquad \text{[2A.15]}$$

in the sense that the same set of points satisfy both equations. Nevertheless, the equations do look somewhat different (for example, the slope of 2A.15 is the *reciprocal* of the slope of 2A.14), and we should keep in mind this change in convention.

Finally, economists frequently wish to use more than two or three variables in their discussions, and to differentiate between variables they often use *subscripts*. Instead of adding letters to the familiar X, Y, and Z notation, economists simply denote variables by

$$X_1, X_2, X_3, \ldots, X_n, \qquad \text{[2A.16]}$$

where each X_i is regarded as a separate variable. In this way a large number of variables may be accommodated with a very compact notation.

Subscripts are particularly useful in writing long and complex sums. For example, instead of writing

$$Y = X_1 + X_2 + X_3 + X_4 + X_5 + X_6 \qquad \text{[2A.17]}$$

it is much more compact to write

$$Y = \sum_{i=1}^{6} X_i$$

where the symbol Σ means we are to add together all of those X's for which the subscript i is equal to the integers from 1 to 6. We will encounter this notation at several points in this book; it is nothing more than a compact way of showing addition.

Suggested Readings

Allen, R. G. D., *Mathematical Analysis for Economists* (New York: St. Martin's Press, Inc., 1938), chaps. 1-3.

Chiang, A. C., *Fundamental Methods of Mathematical Economics* (New York: McGraw-Hill, Inc., 1967).

Lewis, J. P., *An Introduction to Mathematics for Students of Economics* (New York: St. Martin's Press, Inc., 1969).

Yamane, T., *Mathematics for Economists* (Englewood Cliffs, New Jersey: Prentice-Hall, Inc., 1962).

Problems

2.1

Some practice with supply and demand curves:

a. Consider a demand curve of the form

$$Q_D = -2P + 20$$

where Q_D is the quantity demanded of a good and P is the price of the good. Graph this demand curve. Also draw a graph of the supply curve

$$Q_S = 2P - 4$$

where Q_S is the quantity supplied.

Be sure to put P on the vertical axis and Q on the horizontal axis. Assume that all the Q's and P's are nonnegative for 2.1 a, b, c.

At what values of P and Q do these curves intersect—that is, where does $Q_D = Q_S$?

b. Now suppose at each price that individuals demand 4 more units of output, that the demand curve shifts to

$$Q_D{}' = -2P + 24$$

Graph this new demand curve. At what values of P and Q does the new demand curve intersect the old supply curve—that is, where does $Q_D{}' = Q_S$?

c. Now, finally, suppose the supply curve shifts to

$$Q_S{}' = 2P - 8$$

Graph this new supply curve. At what values of P and Q does $Q_D = Q_S{}'$? At what values of P and Q does $Q_D{}' = Q_S{}'$?

You may wish to refer back to this simple problem when we discuss shifting supply and demand curves in later sections of this book.

2.2

Graph the demand curve

$$Q_D = -4P + 32$$

At what value of P does $Q_D = 0$? At $P = 0$ what is Q_D?

Now graph the demand curve

$$Q_D' = -2P + 16$$

Again, at what value of P does $Q_D' = 0$; what is Q_D' when $P = 0$? Call this value of Q_D', Q^*. Referring back to the demand curve Q_D, what are demanders willing to pay for Q^*? Call this price P^*. What is the product $P^* \times Q^*$? Can you give an economic interpretation to this figure?

Now consider all possible products of $P \times Q$ where both P and Q lie on the demand curve Q_D. Show that $P^* \times Q^*$ is the largest value of these products.

We will consider an example similar to this one in Chapter 8 when we discuss the concept of marginal revenue.

2.3

Consider the function

$$Y = \sqrt{X \cdot Z}$$

where $X > 0, Z > 0$

Draw the contour lines (in the positive quadrant) for this function for $Y = 4, Y = 5$, and $Y = 10$. What do we call the shape of these contour lines? Where does the line $10X + 10Y = 200$ intersect the contour line $Y = \sqrt{50}$?

2.4

Using the function $Y = \sqrt{X \cdot Z}$ from the previous problem, find that combination of X and Z for which Y is as large as possible and which also satisfies the following linear equations. Graph your results using contour lines for Y. (*Hint:* for this problem the slope of Y contour lines is given by $-Z/X$.)

a. $2X + Z = 20$

b. $X + Z = 20$

c. $X + 2Z = 40$

d. $X + 5Z = 100$

e. $2X + Z = 40$

f. $X + Z = 40$

2.5

Some practice with summation signs:

a. What does the sum

$$\sum_{i=0}^{5} X^i$$

mean? What is the value of this expression for $X = 2$?

b. Show that

$$\sum_{i=1}^{\infty} X^i = \frac{1}{1-X}$$

for $0 < X < 1$
c. Show that

$$\sum_{i=1}^{6} i = 21$$

d. Show that

$$\sum_{i=a}^{l} i = \frac{a+l}{2} \cdot (l-a+1)$$

where a and l are integers with $l > a$. Show that (c) is a special case of this formula.
e. Show that

$$\sum_{i=1}^{\infty} \left[\frac{1}{(1+a)} \right]^i = \frac{1}{a}$$

for $0 < a < 1$.
Several of these sums will be used in other parts of this book—especially in the Appendix to Chapter 16 on interest rates.

Demand

Introduction

In Part II we will be concerned with describing the way economists treat individuals' demands for the goods they buy. Our principal goal in this part will be to provide a rigorous development of the Marshallian demand curve for a product and to show why this demand curve is likely to be downward sloping. In getting to this final goal, we will take great care to show both how economists treat the way in which individuals make choices and how the choices of many individuals can be summarized by a market demand curve.

Economists explain consumer demand as the interaction of two forces: (1) consumers are assumed to have preferences or desires for commodities, and (2) they are assumed to have limited incomes that restrict their ability to purchase these commodities. It is the resolution of these conflicting forces in the mind of the consumer that determines which commodities he or she will purchase. The first force tells the consumer to buy a car (since a car provides desirable services) whereas the second warns not to (since there are many other uses for the income). Only if the right balance in expenditures is attained will the consumer satisfy as many desires as available income allows. Part II will demonstrate how this balance is reached and how changes in either preferences, income, or prices will affect an individual's demand for goods.

Chapter 3, the first of three in this part, describes the way economists formalize the consumer's decision problem. We will first define the concept of utility, which is used to represent a consumer's preference. The satisfaction that individuals receive from the goods they consume is called "utility." Of course, individuals differ in what they like, and economists seek to create models capable of dealing with these differences. In the first half of Chapter 3, therefore, we will develop the concept of an individual's tastes in a systematic way. These tastes reflect the first force that operates on consumers in making their demand decisions. In the second half of the chapter, we will analyze the assumption that individuals choose goods so as to achieve the greatest satisfaction possible, that is, to maximize their utility. This is the first example of the maximization hypothesis to be encountered in this book, and we will investigate the implications of the hypothesis in detail. It is at this point that income—the second of the two forces—is introduced as a constraint that restricts the utility that an individual can obtain. We will describe ways of formalizing this constraint and will show how it interacts with preferences to affect the choices individuals actually make.

Chapter 4 investigates how choices are altered in response to changes in the individual's income or in response to changes in market prices. This is the first example in the book of "comparative statics" analysis. In such an analysis we compare two hypothetical situations and ask how choices differ in these situations. Most economic analysis is of this type, and many interesting results are provided by such comparisons.

Chapters 3 and 4 describe the choices single individuals make. In Chapter 5 we show how a large number of individuals' actions can be "added-up" to provide a market demand curve. By building up to this market demand curve from a model of individuals' decisions we gain some insights into the nature of market demand. In particular, we are able to achieve a clear understanding of why most demand curves are downward sloping and why demand curves are likely to shift as the conditions facing consumers change. Market demand curves, and their theoretical underpinnings, provide the first building blocks for a study of price determination.

Chapter 3   Utility Maximization

Introduction

Any economic system is nothing more than a collection of individuals and a set of institutions that these individuals have established and currently operate. Economists therefore place the study of individuals' behavior at the center of their models. Desires of individuals are assumed to have a strong effect in determining what goods are demanded and ultimately produced; individuals, to a large extent, decide what levels of productive services they will supply; and, through their political activities, individuals influence the goals that a government will pursue. Hence each individual operates in the role of at least three economic agents. We will briefly discuss each role.

Each Individual is a Consumer

Individuals decide what goods and services they will purchase in the market. These goods may be immediately consumed (for example, a steak will be eaten soon after it is purchased), they may be used to provide services over several years (television sets and automobiles, for example), or they may be used in the home to produce other goods (stoves produce meals, washing machines produce clean clothes, and so on). All such activities provide benefits to individuals, and we will examine how choices between various goods are made.

Each Individual Provides Inputs into the Productive Process

Individuals make choices about the occupations they will pursue and the hours they will work. Through these decisions, they have important effects on what goods or services are produced. In a capitalist economy individuals also accumulate savings that provide capital equipment for use in production. Individuals also produce numerous goods in their homes for private consumption (child-care services, home repairs, brushing teeth). In all of these ways individuals supply inputs that are used in one way or another to produce economic goods.

Each Individual Participates in the Political Process

By voting and other political activities, individuals express their preferences for a variety of political goals. These include ways in which governments spend their revenues (on national defense, public parks, education), raise these revenues (through taxes of various types), and so on. More generally, individual participation in the political process provides direction for how the legal system of rights and responsibilities is structured. The consensus that emerges from the interaction of many individuals' political powers and preferences determines the framework within which the economic system operates.

It is important that we recognize that those roles cannot be separated from one another. Any decision an individual makes as a consumer, say to buy a new car, will undoubtedly have an effect on decisions as a provider of resources (he or she may save less or work harder) and on decisions as a voter (he or she may favor spending for new highways on which to drive the new car). Economic texts used to refer to "economic man" (*homo economicus*) and center attention on the individual's role as a consumer only. Most authors recognized other roles, but those were never explicitly discussed. Modern microeconomics explicitly recognizes this mixture of roles and has developed tools to aid in understanding the interrelationships.

In this book we will examine the economic theory that has been developed to explain the actions of individuals in various activities. In this part we concentrate on individuals as consumers of goods; in Part V we will investigate the role of individuals as suppliers of productive resources; and in Part VII we will examine the insights that economic analysis can provide into understanding the actions of individuals in the political process.

Definition of Utility

Economists have developed a useful apparatus whose purpose is to simplify their analysis of the consumer's decision problem. This apparatus involves a convenient formalization of the concepts of preferences and income, and it permits an algebraic or geometric description of these two forces that determine consumer demand. It is this conceptual apparatus more than anything else that underlies the thinking of economists and makes communication about difficult issues possible.

Preferences are formalized by the concept of *utility*.

Definition

Utility is the satisfaction that an individual receives from the various activities he or she pursues.

Obviously this concept is a very broad one and our concern in the next few sections will be to define it more precisely. To do so we will study the simple case of a single consumer who receives utility from just two commodities. We will eventually analyze how that individual chooses to allocate income between these two goods, but first we need to develop a better understanding of utility.

Ceteris Paribus Assumption

To identify all the factors affecting an individual's feelings of satisfaction would be a lifelong task for an imaginative psychologist; to measure these factors would be impossible. Consequently, economists have chosen to center their attention on basic, quantifiable economic magnitudes and to investigate how individuals choose among them. Economists clearly recognize that nonmeasurable factors (aesthetics, love, security, envy, and so forth) affect behavior, but they develop models in which such factors are conceptually held constant and are not specifically analyzed. Much economic analysis is therefore based on the *ceteris paribus* (other things being equal) assumption. When analyzing the choices an individual makes in consumption behavior, we simplify the analysis by assuming that satisfaction is affected only by changes in the choices being considered and that other effects on satisfaction remain constant. In this way we can isolate the economic factors that affect consumption behavior. It is important to emphasize again that such a narrowing of focus is not intended to imply that other factors affecting utility are "unimportant." Rather, we are conceptually holding these other factors constant so that we may study consumption choices in a simplified setting.

Utility from Consuming Two Goods

In this chapter we will be exclusively concerned with an individual's problem of choosing the quantities of two goods (X and Y) which he or she will consume.[1] To do

---

[1] Note 11 of this chapter provides some references that will permit the reader to investigate the analysis of the consumption of many goods. In many ways the many-good case is identical to the two-good case.

so we will assume that the individual receives utility from these goods and that this utility can be represented in functional notation by

$$\text{Utility} = U\ (X,\ Y;\ \text{other things}) \qquad [3.1]$$

Here the notation is intended to indicate that the utility an individual receives from consuming X and Y over some period of time depends on the quantities of X and Y consumed and on "other things." These "other things" might include easily quantifiable items such as the amounts of other kinds of goods consumed, the number of hours worked, or the amount of time spent sleeping. It might also include such unquantifiable items as love, security, and feelings of self-worth. The reason these other things appear after the semicolon in equation 3.1 is that we assume that they are held constant while we examine the choice between X and Y. Obviously if one of the other things should change, the utility from some particular amounts of X and Y might be very different than it was before.

For example, we will several times in this chapter return to consider the case of an individual choosing how many hamburgers (Y) and soft drinks (X) to consume during one period. Although this example uses seemingly trivial commodities, the analysis is quite general and will apply to any two goods. In analyzing the hamburger–soft drink choices, we will assume that all other factors affecting utility are held constant. The weather, the individual's tastes, the quantity of food eaten for breakfast, and everything else is assumed not to change during the analysis. If the weather, for instance, were to become warmer we might expect soft drinks to become relatively more desirable, and we wish to eliminate such effects from our analysis, at least for the moment.

We will usually write the utility function in equation 3.1 as

$$\text{Utility} = U\ (X, Y) \qquad [3.2]$$

with the understanding that other things are being held constant. All economic analyses always impose some form of *ceteris paribus* assumption so that the relationship between a selected few variables can be studied. The reader should try to identify the "important" things that are being held constant in any particular case.

Measurability of Utility

The first economists to deal with the concept of utility thought that it might be measurable. Indeed, some early psychological experiments on individuals' responses to various stimuli gave rise to premature hopes that all individual reactions were not only quantifiable but also of the same general type. If utility were measurable, many economic questions could be easily answered. Not only could we understand and predict individual consumer behavior, for example, but we could also produce a "fair" distribution of goods (and utility) among people.

Unfortunately, the obstacles to measuring utility have proved to be insurmountable. The major problems seem to be of two general types. The first of these is what to use for a unit of measurement. We have no very good psychological idea of what a *util* (that is, a unit of utility) might be. Similarly there is no way of determining how one person's utils compare to another's. The second class of problems arises in the attempts to impose the *ceteris paribus* assumption. Whereas in simple psychological experiments it may, to a first order of approximation, be possible to hold everything except the stimulus under question constant (that is, to provide an adequate "control"), in economics this has proven to be unfeasible. The myriad factors affecting an individual are impossible to list and quantify. To attempt to hold some of them constant while trying to measure an economically relevant concept of utility is out of the question.

Consequently, we must expect much less than measurability from a utility theory. All that can be assumed is that individuals rank bundles of commodities in some consistent way. To say that the utility of a bundle of goods A, $[U(A)]$, is greater than that of another bundle B, $[U(B)]$, only means that A is preferred to B. We cannot answer the question by "how much" A is preferred to B, since a hard-and-fast measure of utility is beyond our grasp. For example, we may be able to assert that an individual prefers a roast beef dinner to a fried chicken dinner, but we cannot say that he or she is "5 percent happier" with the roast beef or that the chicken provides "7 fewer utils." There are many things we can say about individual choices despite this problem, however. Most observable economic behavior can be explained without having to measure utility. In the next section we will examine the way that preferences can be described in a simple way.

Assumptions About Utility

In this section we shall develop a way of describing preferences that does not require utility measurement. We start by defining what it means to say that individuals' preferences are "consistent," and then we take up the issue of how preferences (utility) can be shown graphically. The principal goal of our analysis is to provide a way of demonstrating the trade-offs that individuals make in their consumption choices.

Consistency of Preferences

Although we cannot expect to be able to measure utility, we might expect individuals to order their preferences in a reasonably consistent manner. Between any two alternative consumption bundles, A and B, we would expect an individual to be able to state either "I prefer A to B," or "I prefer B to A," or "A and B are equally attractive to me." In this model, the individual is not paralyzed by indecision, but rather is able to state clearly how he or she feels about any potential consumption possibilities. In formal terms, individuals' orderings of the consumption possibilities they face are assumed to be *complete*. This rules out such situations as the mythical jackass who, finding himself midway between a pile of hay and a bag of oats, starved to death because he was unable to decide which way to go.

In addition to being complete we might also expect that an individual's preferences would not be self-contradictory. That is, we would not expect that an individual would make statements about his or her preferences that would conflict with each other. We can formalize this notion by assuming that preferences are *transitive*. If an individual reports that "I prefer A to B," and that "I prefer B to C," then he or she must also state "I prefer A to C." An individual who stated the contrary (that is, "I prefer C to A") would appear to be hopelessly inconsistent and we wish to rule out such behavior.[2]

More Is Better

The third assumption one might make about individual preferences is that more of a good is preferred to less. In Figure 3.1 all points in the shaded area are preferred to the amounts X^* of good X and Y^* of good Y. This assumes that individuals are not satiated (at least not in all goods). Movement from Point X^*, Y^* to any point in the shaded area is an unambiguous improvement, since the individual (at least) obtains more of one good without being forced to accept less of any other. This idea of preferences is implicit in a definition of "goods" as items that yield positive utility. It would be relatively simple to develop a theory of "bads" (garbage, termites, or lima beans) for which less is preferred to more.

Trades and Substitution

A more important aspect of individual taste that must be conceptualized is how individuals feel about getting more of some good when they must give up an amount of some other good. This would involve an ambiguous increase in utility. It is necessary to develop some additional terminology if one is to investigate such situations. We shall proceed to do just that in some detail, since ambiguous changes of this kind are very common in economics. Giving up units of one commodity to get back some other commodity is what trade and markets are all about.

---

[2]It is, of course, easy to find examples of non-transitivity in the real world. Everyone has seen "proofs," for example, that his or her school (say Podunk U.) could beat UCLA in football. Since Podunk beat team A, and team A beat team B, and team B beat team C . . . , and team X beat team Y, and team Y beat UCLA, Podunk must be able to beat UCLA. The problem with that logic is that football scores are subject to a large number of random influences and are not, therefore, transitive. In "Transitivity of Preferences" (*Journal of Political Economy* 76, March–April 1968, pp. 307–311), A. A. Weinstein reported on an experiment studying transitivity in individuals' choices among consumption bundles (such items as three Beetles records, a 15-inch pizza, or polka-dot bow ties). He found that most individuals exhibited transitivity in choices and that the extent of intransitivity was less for older subjects (for whom fewer than 7 percent of choices were not transitive) than for young ones (for whom more than 20 percent of choices were not transitive). The author concluded that rational behavior (that is, transitivity) is to some extent an acquired behavioral trait.

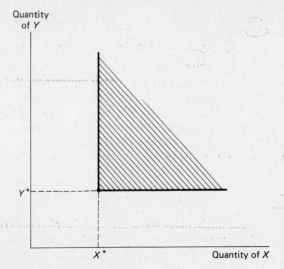

Figure 3.1 / More of a Good Is Preferred to Less

The shaded area represents those combinations of X and Y that are unambiguously preferred to the combination X^*, Y^*. In a sense this is why goods are called "goods": because, *ceteris paribus*, individuals prefer more of any good rather than less.

Marginal Rate of Substitution (*MRS*)

In order to analyze an individual's giving up some amount of one good to get some amount of another good, we will introduce the concept of an individual's *marginal rate of substitution*. The marginal rate of substitution (denoted by *MRS*) is used by economists to record how much of one good (say Y) an individual is willing to give up in order to get *one more unit* of some other good (say X). For example, suppose we let Y represent hamburgers and X represent soft drinks. Then if we say that the *MRS* is 2, we would mean that the person in question is willing to give up 2 hamburgers to get 1 additional soft drink in return. Similarly if we say that the *MRS* is ⅔, we would mean that the individual is willing to give up ⅔ of a hamburger only if he or she is compensated by receiving 1 additional soft drink. So that we maintain a consistent notation throughout our discussion, we will denote the marginal rate of substitution by *MRS* (of X for Y) to make clear that the individual is increasing X consumption by one unit and being asked to reduce Y consumption. Implicitly we are asking the question "how many units of Y is this individual willing to trade away to get one more X."

It seems reasonable to assume that an individual's *MRS* (of X for Y) will in some way depend on how many units of X and Y he or she is currently consuming. Surely the rate at which the individual will be willing to trade hamburgers for soft drinks will depend (among other things) on how many hamburgers and soft drinks are being consumed. Indeed, intuitively it is plausible that if the individual has eaten many hamburgers and few soft drinks, he or she will be willing to trade quite a few hamburgers away for the chance to have an additional soft drink. For example, if the

Definition

The *Marginal Rate of Substitution* (of *X* for *Y*) is the number of units of *Y* an individual is willing to give up to get one more *X*.

$$MRS \ (X \ \text{for} \ Y) = \frac{- \ \text{Change in } Y \text{ consumption}}{\text{Change in } X \text{ consumption}}$$

$$= - \ \text{Slope of Indifference Curve}$$

For the Hamburger/Soft Drink example:

$$MRS \ (\text{Soft Drinks for Hamburgers}) = \frac{- \ \text{Change in hamburger consumption}}{\text{Change in soft drink consumption}}$$

$$= - \ \text{Slope of Hamburger/Soft Drink} \\ \text{Indifference Curve.}$$

The minus sign is used because the slope of U_1 is negative but we wish the *MRS* to be defined as a positive number. This slight complication of definition should not, however, obscure the identical nature of the concepts: both record the number of hamburgers the individual will give up to get one more soft drink.

Diminishing Marginal Rate of Substitution

The *MRS* varies along the curve U_1. For points such as *A* the individual is well-endowed with hamburgers and is relatively willing to trade them for soft drinks. On the other hand, for consumption bundles such as those represented by point *D*, the individual has an abundance of soft drinks and is reluctant to give up any more hamburgers to get even more soft drinks. This increasing reluctance to trade away hamburgers accords well with the intuitive notion that the consumption of any good (here soft drinks) can be pushed too far. This is clearly exhibited by considering the trades that take place in moving from *A* to *B*, from *B* to *C*, and from *C* to *D*. The first trade involves giving up 2 hamburgers to get 1 soft drink, as we have already shown. The second involves giving up 1 hamburger to get an additional soft drink. For this trade, then, the *MRS* has declined to 1 reflecting the increased reluctance to trade away hamburgers. Finally, for the third trade (*C* to *D*), the individual is willing to give up a hamburger only if 2 soft drinks are received in return. For this final trade, then, the *MRS* is ½ (that is, the individual is willing to give up ½ a hamburger to get 1 soft drink); this again represents a decline from the *MRS* that prevailed in the previous trades.

The convex shape of the indifference curve U_1 therefore reflects a diminishing marginal rate of substitution. As we consider bundles of the two goods that contain increasing quantities of soft drinks (and diminishing quantities of hamburgers), the indifference curve becomes flatter. The slope of the curve (which is always negative) approaches zero. This then reflects another basic assumption that economists make about individuals' tastes: Individuals become increasingly reluctant to trade away an increasingly scarce good. Individuals prefer some balance in their consumption.[3] Because this point is sufficiently important, we will discuss it in more detail in the following section.

Balance in Consumption and the Assumption of a Diminishing *MRS*

We based the assumption of a diminishing *MRS* on the assumption that individuals tire of consuming too much of any one good. Another way of saying this is that individuals will prefer "balanced" consumption bundles to "unbalanced" ones. This fact is illustrated precisely in Figure 3.3. Here we have redrawn the indifference curve U_1 from Figure 3.2. For purposes of this discussion, we will examine the two extreme consumption bundles A and D. In consuming bundle A the individual receives 6 hamburgers and 2 soft drinks and would receive the same satisfaction by consuming bundle D (2 hamburgers and 6 soft drinks). Now consider a bundle of commodities (say E) midway "between" these extremes. With E (4

---

[3]If we are willing to assume utility is measurable we can provide an alternative analysis of a diminishing *MRS*. To do so we introduce the concept of the *marginal utility* of a good, X (denoted by MU_X). This is defined as the extra utility obtained by consuming one more unit of good X. The concept is only meaningful if utility can be measured.

If the individual is asked to give up some $Y (\Delta Y)$ to get some additional X (ΔX) the change in utility is given by

$$\Delta U = MU_X \cdot \Delta X + MU_Y \cdot \Delta Y \qquad \text{[i]}$$

That is, it is equal to the utility gained from the additional X less the utility lost from the reduction in Y. Since, along an indifference curve $\Delta U = 0$, we can use i to derive:

$$-\frac{\Delta Y}{\Delta X} = \frac{MU_X}{MU_Y} \qquad \text{[ii]}$$

That is, along an indifference curve, the negative of its slope is given by MU_X/MU_Y. But that slope is, by definition, the *MRS*. Hence we have

$$\boxed{MRS = MU_X/MU_Y.} \qquad \text{[iii]}$$

For example, if an extra hamburger yields 2 utils ($MU_Y = 2$) and an extra soft drink yields 1 util ($MU_X = 1$) the $MRS = \frac{1}{2}$ since the individual will be willing to trade away $\frac{1}{2}$ a hamburger to get an additional soft drink. If it is assumed that MU_X falls and MU_Y increases as X is substituted for Y, equation (iii) shows that the *MRS* will fall.

hamburgers and 4 soft drinks) the individual obtains a higher level of satisfaction (that is, the point E is northeast of the indifference curve U_1) than with either of the extreme bundles A or D. The reason for this should be geometrically obvious: All of the points on the straight line joining A and D lie above U_1. Point E is one of these points although, as the figure shows, there are many others. So long as the indifference curve obeys the assumption of a diminishing MRS, it will be convex; any "average" bundle will be preferred to two equally attractive extremes. Again it is clear that the assumption of a diminishing MRS can be seen to be consistent with the notion that some variety in consumption is desirable to individuals.

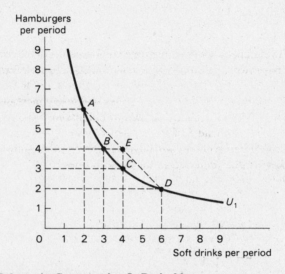

Figure 3.3 / Balance in Consumption Is Desirable

The consumption bundle E (4 hamburgers, 4 soft drinks) is preferred to either of the extreme bundles A and D. This is a result of the assumption of a diminishing MRS. Because individuals become progressively less willing to give up hamburgers as they move in a southeasterly direction along U_1, the curve U_1 will have a convex shape. Consequently all points on a straight line joining two points such as A and D will lie above U_1. Points such as E will be preferred to any of those on U_1.

Indifference Curve Maps

Figures 3.2 and 3.3 each show only one indifference curve. The positive quadrant is in reality full of such curves, each corresponding to a different level of utility. Since every conceivable combination of hamburgers and soft drinks must yield some level of utility, every point must have one (and only one) indifference curve passing through it. These curves are, as we said earlier, similar to the numerous contour lines that appear on topographical maps in that they each represent a different "altitude" of utility. In Figure 3.4 several of these curves have been drawn and are labeled U_1, U_2 and U_3. Of course, these are only three of the infinite number of curves that characterize an individual's entire indifference curve map. Just as we can conceive of a map's having many contour lines (say one for each inch of altitude), so too we should recognize that gradations in utility could be very fine, thus producing very closely spaced indifference curves. For graphical convenience, however, our analysis will generally deal with indifference curves that are relatively widely spaced.

The labeling of the indifference curves in Figure 3.4 has no special meaning except to indicate that utility increases as we move from combinations of goods on U_1 to those on U_2 and then to those on U_3. As we have repeatedly pointed out, there is no precise way to measure the level of utility associated with (say) U_2. Similarly, we have no way of measuring the amount of extra utility an individual receives from consuming bundles on U_3 instead of on U_2. All we know is that utility increases as the individual moves to higher indifference curves.

The indifference curve map shown in Figure 3.4, then, completely summarizes an individual's preferences about all possible combinations of the two goods being examined. The basic assumptions we have made about these preferences assure that the indifference curve map will exhibit the shape shown in the figure. First, the assumption that more is preferred to less implies that utility increases as we move from U_1 to U_2 to U_3. This can readily be seen by comparing the utility provided by commodity bundles C, E, and F. Second, the assumption of a diminishing *MRS* implies that the indifference curves will have the convex shape shown in the figure. Balanced bundles will be preferred to unbalanced ones.

We can now proceed to analyze an individual's consumption choices in detail.

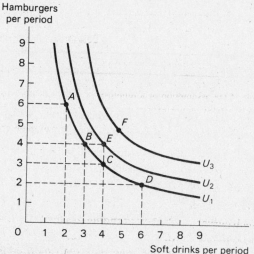

Figure 3.4 / Indifference Curve Map for Hamburgers and Soft Drinks

The positive quadrant is full of indifference curves each reflecting a different level of utility. Three such curves are illustrated. Combinations of goods on U_3 are preferred to those on U_2 which in turn are preferred to those on U_1. This is simply a reflection of the assumption that more of a good is preferred to less, as may be seen by comparing points C, E, and F.

Utility-Maximization Hypothesis: An Initial Survey

Economists assume that when an individual is faced with a choice from among a number of possible options, he or she will choose the one that yields the highest utility. As Adam Smith remarked more than two centuries ago: "We are not ready to suspect any person of being defective in selfishness."[4] In other words, individuals are assumed to know their own minds and to make choices consistent with their preferences. In this section we will briefly survey how such choices are made.

The most interesting feature of the utility-maximization problem is that it is a problem in *constrained maximization*. Individuals are constrained in what they can buy by the size of their incomes. Of those combinations of goods that an individual can afford, he or she will, by the utility-maximization assumption, choose the one that is most preferred. This most preferred bundle of goods will not, however, provide complete bliss; it may leave the individual in misery. It will, however, reflect the best use of limited income. All other bundles of goods that can be bought with that limited income would leave him or her even worse off. It is the limitation of income that makes the individual's problem of choice an "economic" one of allocating a scarce resource over alternative end uses.

The particular problem we will study in this section is how an individual will choose to allocate income in purchasing two goods so as to maximize utility. It is an example of *constrained maximization*, and it is the most fundamental analysis in all of economics. The result of this analysis can easily be stated at the outset.

Optimization Principle

In order to maximize utility given a fixed amount to spend on two goods, an individual will spend that entire amount and will choose a bundle of goods for which the Marginal Rate of Substitution between two goods is equal to the ratio of those goods' market prices.

The reasoning behind the first part of this principle is straightforward. Because of the "more is better" assumption an individual will spend the entire amount budgeted for the two items. In this problem the only alternative to spending is to throw the money away, and that alternative is obviously less desirable than the alternative of buying something.

To see the intuitive reasoning behind the second part of the proposition, consider again the hamburger–soft drink example. Suppose that an individual is currently consuming some combination of hamburgers and soft drinks for which the *MRS* is equal to 1; he or she is willing to trade away 1 hamburger in order to get an additional

---

[4]A. Smith, *The Theory of Moral Sentiments* (New Rochelle, N.Y.: Arlington House, 1969. First published 1759), p.446.

soft drink. Assume on the other hand that the price of hamburgers is $.20 and that of soft drinks is $.10. Consequently the ratio of their prices is $.10/$.20 = ½, and this states that the individual is able to obtain an extra soft drink in the market by giving up ½ of a hamburger. In this situation the individual's *MRS* is not equal to the ratio of the goods' market prices and we wish to show that there exists another bundle of goods that provides more utility.

This demonstration proceeds easily. Let the individual reduce consumption of hamburgers by 1. This frees $.20 in purchasing power. With this the individual can buy 1 more soft drink (at a price of $.10) and is now as well off as before since the *MRS* was assumed to be 1. However, there is now $.10 (= $.20 − $.10) unspent that can be spent on either soft drinks or hamburgers (or some combination of the two), thereby making the individual better off than in the initial situation.

Graphic Analysis

The numbers in the previous example were obviously arbitrarily chosen. Any time that the individual chooses a bundle of goods for which the *MRS* differs from the price ratio a similar beneficial reallocation can be made. This reallocation will continue until the *MRS* is brought into line with the price ratio. We now turn to presenting a more formal proof of this assertion.

Budget Constraint

We will assume that an individual has I dollars to allocate to the purchase of either good X or good Y. If P_X is the price of good X then $P_X \cdot X$ represents the total amount spent on X. Similarly, if P_Y is the price of good Y, then $P_Y \cdot Y$ is the amount spent on Y. Consequently the individual's *budget constraint* is given by

$$P_X \cdot X + P_Y \cdot Y = I \qquad [3.3]$$

This linear equation simply records the fact that the individual is constrained in choices of X and Y by the funds available. The budget constraint equation can be written in a somewhat more familiar form (with Y as a function of X) as

$$Y = -\frac{P_X}{P_Y} \cdot X + \frac{I}{P_Y} \qquad [3.4]$$

Although both equations 3.3 and 3.4 say exactly the same thing, equation 3.4 can be more directly graphed since it is in the simple linear form $Y = a + bX$, which we discussed in the Appendix to Chapter 2. Figure 3.5 shows this graph. The solid line in the figure represents the budget constraint, and the individual can choose only those combinations of X and Y that are in the shaded triangle in the figure. It is obvious from equation 3.4 that if the individual chooses to spend all available funds on Y (that is, if $X = 0$), he or she can buy I/P_Y units. That point is therefore the

Y-intercept in the figure. Similarly, a slight manipulation of the budget equation shows that if $Y = 0$, all income will be devoted to X purchases, and the X-intercept will be I/P_X. Finally, the slope of the budget constraint is given by $-P_X/P_Y$, and this shows the ratio at which Y can be traded for X in the market.

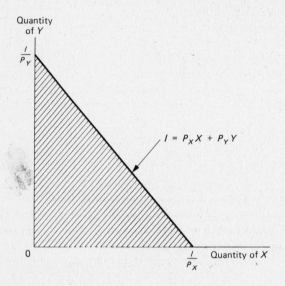

Figure 3.5 / Individual's Budget Constraint for Two Goods

Those combinations of X and Y that the individual can afford are shown in the shaded triangle. If, as we usually assume, the individual prefers more rather than less of every good, the outer boundary of this triangle is the relevant constraint where all of the available funds are spent either on X or on Y or on some combination of the two. The slope of this straight boundary is given by $-P_X/P_Y$.

To reinforce these elementary ideas we will return again to our hamburger–soft drink example. Remember that the price of hamburgers was assumed to be $.20 (that is, $P_Y = \$.20$) and the price of soft drinks was assumed to be $.10 ($P_X = \$.10$). Suppose also that total funds are $1.00. When the entire dollar is devoted to hamburger purchases, 5 hamburgers ($= I/P_Y = \$1.00/\$.20$) can be purchased. At the other extreme, if the dollar is spent on soft drinks, a total of 10 drinks ($= I/P_X = \$1.00/\$.10$) can be bought. As before, the ratio of the goods' prices ($.10/$.20 = ½) records the fact that 1 hamburger can be traded for 2 soft drinks in the market.

Utility Maximization

The individual can afford all bundles of X and Y that fall within the shaded triangle in Figure 3.5. From among these, the individual is assumed to choose the one that yields the greatest utility. The budget constraint can be imposed on the individual's indifference curve map to show this utility maximization process. Figure 3.6 illustrates the procedure. The individual would be irrational to choose a point such as *A*—he or she can get to a higher utility level just by spending some of the unspent portion of *I*. Similarly, by reallocating expenditures the individual can do better than point *B*. This is the case in which the *MRS* and the price ratio differ, and the individual can move to a higher indifference curve by choosing to consume less *Y* and more *X*. Point *D* is out of the question because *I* is not large enough to permit purchase of *D*. It is clear that the position of maximum utility will be at point *C* where the combination *X**, *Y** is chosen. This is the only point on indifference curve *U*₂ that can be bought with *I* dollars, and no higher utility level can be bought. *C* is a point of tangency between the budget constraint and the indifference curve. Therefore all funds are spent and:

$$\text{Slope of budget constraint} = \text{Slope of indifference curve} \qquad [3.5]$$

or

$$\frac{P_X}{P_Y} = MRS \text{ (of } X \text{ for } Y) \qquad [3.6]$$

The result is proved—for a utility maximum the *MRS* should equal the ratio of the prices of the goods. It is obvious from the diagram that if this condition is not fulfilled, the individual could be made better off by reallocating expenditures.[5] The reader may wish to try several other combinations of *X* and *Y* that the individual can afford in order to show that any of these provide a lower utility level than does combination *C*.

Figure 3.6 can be given a concrete interpretation by using the hamburger–soft drink example. Point *A* might represent a choice of two hamburgers and three soft drinks. This choice would be plainly inefficient since some part of the individual's dollar will not be spent. With the $.30 (= $1.00 − 2 × $.20 − 3 × $.10) that is left over it would be possible for the individual to buy more of either good and thereby increase utility. Point *B* (4 hamburgers, 2 soft drinks) is also inefficient, even though the entire dollar is spent. At this point relatively too much of the dollar has been allocated to hamburger purchases. The individual could enjoy a higher level of

---

[5]If we use the results of footnote 3 on the assumption utility is measurable, equation 3.6 can be given an alternative interpretation. Since,

$$P_X/P_Y = MRS = MU_X/MU_Y \qquad [i]$$

for a utility maximum, we have

$$\frac{MU_X}{P_X} = \frac{MU_Y}{P_Y}. \qquad [ii]$$

In words, the ratio of the extra utility provided by consuming one more unit of a good to its price should be the same for each good. Each good should provide the same extra utility per dollar spent. If that were not true, total utility could be raised by reallocating funds from a good that provided a relatively low level of marginal utility per dollar to one that provided a high level.

utility by trading hamburgers for soft drinks in the market. He or she would do so until reaching a point such as C (3 hamburgers, 4 soft drinks) at which the entire dollar is spent *and* the psychic rate of trade-off (*MRS*) between soft drinks and hamburgers is exactly equal to that rate that is provided in the market ($P_X/P_Y = \frac{1}{2}$). Notice that combinations such as D (4 hamburgers, 5 soft drinks), although preferred to point C, are unattainable because their total costs exceed $1.00.

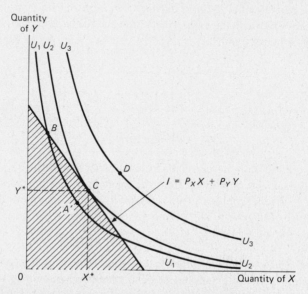

Figure 3.6 / Graphic Demonstration of Utility Maximization

Point C represents the highest utility that can be reached by the individual, given the budget constraint. The combination X^*, Y^* is therefore the rational way for the individual to allocate total purchasing power. Only for this combination of goods will two conditions hold: all available funds will be spent; and the individual's psychic rate of trade-off (*MRS*) will be equal to the rate at which the goods can be traded in the market (P_X/P_Y).

Importance of Diminishing Marginal Rate of Substitution

We have now shown that if the individual is to maximize utility subject to a budget constraint, he or she must choose consumption bundles that exhaust income and for which the *MRS* is equal to P_X/P_Y. Points of maximum satisfaction are characterized by a tangency between an individual's indifference curve map and the budget constraint. Not every such point of tangency must provide maximum satisfaction, however. Figure 3.7 illustrates this proposition. Here a point of tangency (C) is inferior to a point of nontangency (B). The true maximum is, as it must be, at another point of tangency (A). The failure of the tangency condition to produce an unambiguous maximum can be attributed to the peculiar shape of the indifference curves in Figure 3.7. If the indifference curves are shaped as are those in Figure 3.6, no such problem can arise. But it was shown previously that "normally" shaped indifference curves are a result of the assumption of a diminishing *MRS*. Therefore, if the *MRS* is assumed to be diminishing, the condition of tangency assures a true maximum. Without this assumption, we would have to be very careful in applying the tangency rule. Since we will in this book always assume a constantly diminishing *MRS*, we will not be particularly concerned with problems of the type illustrated in Figure 3.7.

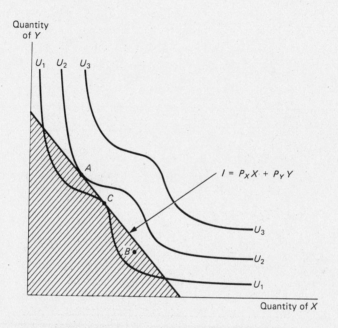

Figure 3.7 / Example of an Indifference Curve Map for Which the Tangency Condition Does Not Insure a Maximum

If indifference curves do not obey the assumption of a diminishing *MRS*, not all points of tangency (points for which *MRS* = P_X/P_Y) may truly be points of maximum utility. In this example tangency point *C* is inferior to many other points, which can also be purchased with the available funds. In order for the necessary conditions for a maximum (that is, the tangency conditions) also to be sufficient, we must assume that the *MRS* is diminishing.

A Numerical Example of Utility Maximization

We can give a numerical example of utility maximization if we are, for the moment, willing to assume that utility is measurable. Again let us suppose that an individual is choosing between hamburgers (*Y*) and soft drinks (*X*) and that the prices of these goods are P_Y = \$.20, P_X = \$.10. Assume also that the individual has \$2.00 to spend. Finally, suppose that the utility from consuming *X* and *Y* is given by

$$\text{Utility} = U(X, Y) = \sqrt{XY} \qquad [3.7]$$

We are therefore assuming not only that utility can be measured but also that its value is given by the square root (denoted by $\sqrt{}$) of the product of times Y. This particular utility function is suitable for our purposes because its indifference curves have the familiar convex shape.

Table 3.1 lists several possible ways in which the individual might spend $2.00 and calculates the utility associated with each choice. For example, if the individual buys 6 hamburgers and 8 soft drinks (totally exhausting the $2.00) utility will be 6.9 ($= \sqrt{48}$). The other entries in the table should be interpreted accordingly. Notice that we only consider combinations of X and Y that cost exactly $2.00. The individual cannot spend more than that, and it is irrational to spend less since, in this problem, unspent income just disappears.[6]

Table 3.1 / Alternative Combinations of X and Y That Can Be Bought with $2.00 and the Utility of Each Combination ($P_Y = \$.20$, $P_X = \$.10$)

Hamburgers Y	Soft Drinks X	$U(X,Y) = \sqrt{XY}$
0	20	$\sqrt{0} = 0$
1	18	$\sqrt{18} = 4.2$
2	16	$\sqrt{32} = 5.7$
3	14	$\sqrt{42} = 6.5$
4	12	$\sqrt{48} = 6.9$
5	10	$\sqrt{50} = 7.1$
6	8	$\sqrt{48} = 6.9$
7	6	$\sqrt{42} = 6.5$
8	4	$\sqrt{32} = 5.7$
9	2	$\sqrt{18} = 4.2$
10	0	$\sqrt{0} = 0$

From the table we can see that the combination $Y = 5$, $X = 10$ provides the maximum utility ($7.1 = \sqrt{50}$) of those combinations listed. Figure 3.8 shows that this is indeed a true maximum. With the budget constraint

$$\$.10X + \$.20Y = \$2.00 \tag{3.8}$$

the individual can just reach the indifference curve $U = \sqrt{50}$ at the single point $Y = 5, X = 10$. Any other choices which cost $2.00 or less yield a lower utility. At the point $Y = 5, X = 10$ the budget constraint is just tangent to the indifference curve;[7] the MRS is equal to the ratio of the goods' prices.

It should be stressed that this example is presented for pedagogic purposes only. Obviously we are not able to measure an individual's utility function; even if we

---

[6]We will briefly take up the subject of saving in Chapter 16.

[7]This indifference curve is a graph of $\sqrt{XY} = \sqrt{50}$ or, more simply, $XY = 50$.

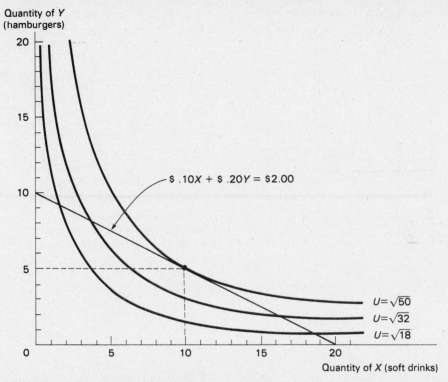

Quantity of Y
(hamburgers)

$ .10X + $ .20Y = $2.00

$U = \sqrt{50}$

$U = \sqrt{32}$

$U = \sqrt{18}$

Quantity of X (soft drinks)

Figure 3.8 / Graph of the Utility Maximization Example

If $P_X = \$.10$ and $P_Y = \$.20$, then the utility-maximizing choice for X and Y is $Y = 5, X = 10$. At this point, the budget constraint is just tangent to the indifference curve $U = \sqrt{XY} = \sqrt{50}$ (or $X \cdot Y = 50$), and this is the highest utility level obtainable.

were able to, it is highly unlikely it would take the simple form we have used. There are, however, economic maximization problems in which the function being maximized is (at least in principle) measurable. We will encounter examples of these in Part III when we discuss the technology of production.

Applications of the Utility Maximization Hypothesis

The model of utility maximization we have developed shows how individuals make choices in response to their economic circumstances and indicates the level of satisfaction that those choices yield. In this section we demonstrate how that model may be used to evaluate various policies that may affect an individual's well-being. Two specific policies, rationing and taxation, are investigated in detail. A few related policies are also mentioned.

Rationing

Because economic goods do not exist in quantities sufficient to satisfy all human wants, such goods must always in some way be allocated among individuals. The most common method of allocation is through reliance on the price system and the study of that process is the central focus of this book. At times, however, goods may be allocated by nonmarket means. Governmental rationing is one of the most common of these methods. Either because a society may not wish to allocate goods by price for ideological or humanitarian reasons (as, for example, is the case of rice allotments in China) or because temporary shortages arise that, it is believed, should be shared by all (as was the case in many countries during World War II), governments may choose to ration existing stocks of goods equally (or nearly equally) among individuals. Such a situation is illustrated in Figure 3.9. Given market prices and income, the individual wishes to consume the combination X^*, Y^*. But if rationing limits the quantity of X available to any individual to an amount X_R (which must still be purchased at the prevailing price), that preferred point will be unattainable. Rather, the effective budget constraint

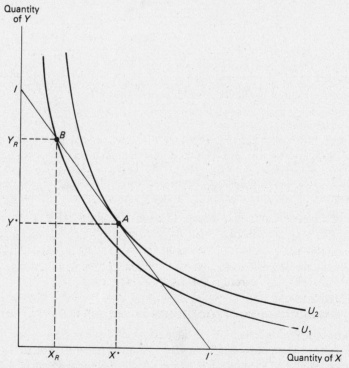

Figure 3.9 / The Effect of Rationing Is to Reduce Utility

Rationing that allows an individual to purchase only X_R reduces utility (if $X_R < X^*$) from U_2 to U_1. Rationing is more likely to affect the choices of high–income consumers than of low–income consumers.

then becomes the line $X_R BI$ and some other utility-maximizing point must be chosen. From the figure it is clear that point B provides maximum utility given this additional constraint. Rationing of X has reduced the individual's utility from U_2 to U_1 by forcing the purchase of less X (and more Y) than is desired.[8]

Two aspects of the solution pictured in Figure 3.9 might be highlighted. First, notice that rationing has an effect on the individual's choices only if $X_R < X^*$. If $X_R > X^*$, the individual is permitted to purchase more of good X than would be freely chosen and rationing is, for this individual, ineffective. Since, as we show in the next chapter, it is likely that X^* will be greater the higher is an individual's income, the probability that rationing will effectively limit choices is greater for high-income persons than for low-income persons. Table 3.2 illustrates this presumption for the

Table 3.2 / Ration Allotment of Food During World War II as a Percent of Peacetime Consumption by Income Class

	Country and Income Class								
	Germany			Poland			United Kingdom		
Food	Low Income	Medium Income	High Income	Low Income	Medium Income	High Income	Low Income	Medium Income	High Income
Bread	99.0	103.0	103.0	48.6	42.4	44.7	Not rationed		
Meat	71.8	45.9	32.9	34.9	22.7	15.5	91.3	55.3	43.8
Milk	150.0	109.1	96.8	71.4	45.5	31.3	500.0	168.2	94.6
Fats	75.0	47.6	36.6	NA	NA	NA	93.0	67.9	61.0

Source: *Wartime Rationing and Consumption*, League of Nations Intelligence Service (1941, IIa.2), pp. 58–59.

case of food rationing in Germany, Poland, and the United Kingdom during World War II. The table shows the wartime food allotment as a percent of peacetime consumption for food items: bread, meat, milk, and fats. Notice that for all items high-income consumers appear to have been more constrained than low-income consumers. In Germany, for example, meat allotments were nearly 72 percent of peacetime consumption for low-income families, but only about 33 percent of peacetime consumption for high-income families. Notice also that rationing had a much greater effect on those goods whose purchase might be expected to rise rapidly with family income (meat and fats) than on those whose purchase is relatively little affected by greater income (bread and milk).

A second feature of this problem concerns the stability of the rationed solution. Since the unrationed optimal choice (A) provides more utility than does the

---

[8]For example, rationing (both explicit and implicit) of most consumer goods during World War II in the United States caused the personal savings rate to triple (from around 7 to 8 percent of disposable income to nearly 25 percent). Constrained consumption choices meant that individuals made use of the only other available use for their incomes—additional savings. In fact, these savings were later used to finance the postwar boom in durable goods purchases.

rationed choice (B), there exist incentives for the individual to find some way of moving from B to A. The frequent appearance of "black markets" in rationed commodities attests to the strength of this incentive. Our observations also suggest that high-income individuals would be more likely to make black market purchases because they have more to gain by doing so.

Mandated Purchases

An argument formally identical to that presented for the case of rationing can be developed for the situation in which governments require minimum purchases of certain commodities. One example of such mandated purchases has occurred recently in product safety legislation (most notably in connection with characteristics of automobiles). Individuals have been, by law, required to purchase more safety features than they previously chose, and it is easy to show that the effect of such legislation is to reduce utility.[9] Our analysis suggests that such mandated purchases are more likely to affect low-income individuals than high-income individuals (since low-income individuals are less likely to choose the required amounts of safety features on their own) and that individuals will seek to increase their utility by "trading away" their excess safety equipment (perhaps by failing to keep it in good repair). Similar arguments can be made for laws that require use of lawyers' services when buying a house, purchase of certain municipal services (say, trash collection) through taxation, and the compulsory purchase of Social Security retirement benefits. In all of these cases, legal constraints that require certain purchases reduce individuals' utility relative to what it would be in the absence of such constraints.

Taxation and Lump-Sum Principle

The utility-maximization model can also be used to demonstrate that taxes on general purchasing power are "more efficient" than taxes imposed on individual goods (or on groups of goods). In that demonstration the term "more efficient" is taken to mean that if the two taxes yield equal governmental revenues, the general purchasing power tax can be shown to yield a higher level of utility than does the tax on a single commodity. The proof is shown in Figure 3.10. Initially the individual has I to spend and chooses to consume X^* and Y^* since that point obeys the budget constraint

$$I = P_X X^* + P_Y Y^* \qquad [3.9]$$

---

[9]This analysis may be a bit simplistic in its assumption of perfect knowledge. Advocates of requiring additional safety features argue that consumers of dangerous products are not generally aware of the risks involved and would purchase more safety if they were more knowledgable.

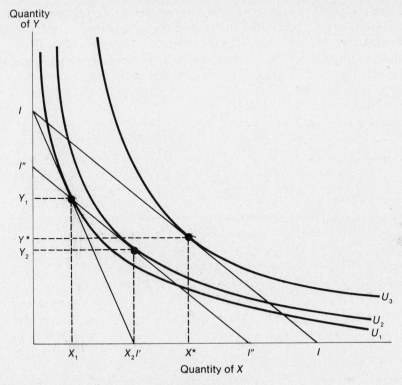

Figure 3.10 / The Efficiency of Lump Sum Taxes

A per-unit tax on good X causes the utility-maximizing point to shift to X_1, Y_1, and utility to fall from U_3 to U_1. A lump sum tax that collects the same revenue would shift the budget constraint to $I''I''$ and would reduce utility to U_2. The lump sum tax may therefore be preferred on efficiency grounds.

and the tangency condition for a maximum. A tax on good X of t dollars per unit would raise its price to $P_x + t$, and the budget constraint would become:

$$I = (P_x + t)X + P_Y Y. \qquad [3.10]$$

With that budget constraint (shown as line I'' in figure 3.10) the individual would be forced to accept a lower utility level and would choose to consume the combination X_1, Y_1. Total tax revenues (T) would be given by:

$$T = tX_1. \qquad [3.11]$$

A general purchasing power tax that also collected T dollars in revenue would leave the individual with $I - T$ dollars to spend, and the budget constraint would be given by

$$I'' = I - T = P_x X + P_Y Y. \qquad [3.12]$$

With that budget constraint[10] the individual will choose to consume X_2, Y_2 as shown in Figure 3.10. Notice that, even though the individual pays the same tax bill in both instances, the combination chosen under the purchasing power tax yields a higher utility than does the single commodity tax. An intuitive explanation of this result is based on the recognition that a single commodity tax affects an individual's well-being in two ways. It reduces general purchasing power and it directs consumption away from the taxed commodity. A purchasing power tax incorporates only the first effect and hence individuals are better off under it.

The analysis we have just presented provides a formal rationale for the belief that "lump sum" taxes (that reduce purchasing power on an across-the-board basis) are superior to equal revenue excise or sales taxes on individual items. One must be careful not to apply that argument uncritically, however. Lump sum taxes are more efficient only to the extent that they do not incorporate distorting price effects. The most commonly proposed real-world approximation to a lump sum tax is a general tax on income. That tax may not be free of price effects. As we show in detail in Chapter 15, an income tax affects an individual's hourly wage and may therefore affect his or her decisions about how many hours to work. Whether or not an income tax is the best available approximation to the lump sum principle then remains an open question.

Negative Income Taxes

The argument presented here for positive taxes applies to "negative taxes" (that is, income subsidies) as well. A general income subsidy can be shown to be a more effective way of raising utility than would be provision of some goods at below market prices. That conclusion (which is subject to the caveats raised previously about the lump sum properties of income taxes) has important policy implications for antipoverty programs. In recent years the most rapidly growing programs to aid the poor have been those that provide certain goods at subsidized prices. Food stamps, subsidized housing programs, and Medicaid are the most notable examples. Our analysis here suggests that antipoverty funds might be more effectively allocated (in terms of raising the utility of poor people) by a greater reliance on direct income grants. A number of current "welfare reform" plans suggest moving in that direction.

Summary

We have covered a lot of ground in this chapter. We first described the concept of utility and made precise the idea of the trades an individual would willingly make. This psychic trade-off rate between any two goods was called the marginal rate of

---

[10]The budget constraint given by Equation 3.12 must pass through the point X_1, Y_1 (as drawn in Figure 3.10). Since $T = (P_X + t)X_1 + P_Y Y_1$, it must be true that $I'' = I - tX_1 = P_X X_1 + P_Y Y_1$.

substitution (*MRS*), and we will make heavy use of this concept. The most important assumption we made about individuals' tastes was that the *MRS* (of *X* for *Y*) decreases as *X* is substituted for *Y* in consumption. This assumption seems entirely reasonable and is built on the general notion that individuals become satiated as they consume progressively more of a given item; that is, they prefer some balance in their consumption choices.

In the second half of the chapter we investigated the implications of the hypothesis that individuals make choices so as to obtain the highest level of utility possible given their limited incomes. The major conclusion of this investigation was that for a utility maximum an individual should choose that bundle of *X* and *Y* that exhausts total expenditures and for which the *MRS* (of *X* for *Y*) is equal to the ratio of the price of *X* to the price of *Y* (P_X/P_Y). Although this result was stated only for the case of two goods, it is quite general and applies to any number of goods.[11] Individuals in order to obtain a utility maximum should choose that combination of goods for which the psychic rate of trade-off between any two goods is equal to the rate at which these goods can be traded for one another in the market.

There are several general assumptions that underlie the utility-maximization principle, and they should be kept in mind:

1. The individual can rationally order his or her preferences and attempts to maximize utility.

2. The individual is assumed to have a diminishing *MRS* between any two goods. If this were not true our tangency solutions might not be true maximum points.

3. The *ceteris paribus* assumption holds constant all factors affecting individual welfare except those specifically being analyzed.

4. The individual is assumed to be a *price taker* in that he or she accepts market prices as given and adjusts behavior to them.

5. The individual has full information about those options open. If he or she had only partial information we would have to inquire how much he or she would be willing to pay to obtain further information.

Suggested Readings

Hicks, J. R., *Value and Capital*, 2d ed. (New York: Oxford University Press, 1946), pp. 1–25.

Lancaster, K. J., "A New Approach to Consumer Theory," *Journal of Political Economy* 74 (April 1966), pp. 132–157.

---

[11]To examine the case of more than two goods requires the use of mathematics since graphical techniques cannot be easily adapted to many dimensions. The reader interested in these mathematical derivations may wish to refer to W. Nicholson, *Microeconomic Theory: Basic Principles and Extensions,* 2d ed. (Hinsdale, Ill.: The Dryden Press, 1978), pp. 74–76, for a relatively simple treatment. For a more complex discussion, see Paul A. Samuelson, *Foundations of Economic Analysis* (Cambridge, Mass.: Harvard University Press, 1947), chap. 5.

Leibenstein, H., "Bandwagon, Snob, and Veblen Effects in the Theory of Consumers' Demand," *Quarterly Journal of Economics* 64 (May 1950), pp. 183–207.

Samuelson, P. A., *Foundations of Economic Analysis* (Cambridge, Mass.: Harvard University Press, 1947), pp. 90–97.

Stigler, G., "The Development of Utility Theory," *Journal of Political Economy* 58, pts. 1 and 2 (August–October 1950), pp. 307–327, 373–396.

Problems

3.1

Show that, given the assumptions of Chapter 3, it is impossible for an individual's indifference curves to intersect.

3.2

Graph the following utility functions and determine whether they have convex indifference curves (that is, whether they obey the assumption of a diminishing *MRS*):

a) $U = 3X + Y$
b) $U = \sqrt{X \cdot Y}$
c) $U = \sqrt{X^2 + Y^2}$
d) $U = \sqrt{X^2 - Y^2}$

Now sketch a budget constraint line on each of the graphs and state whether the point of tangency between the budget line and the indifference curve is a maximum or minimum for the utility function.

3.3

Oliver D. Dancefloor gets his utility by going to discos or rock concerts. His utility function is $U = \sqrt{D \cdot C}$, where D = the number of discos and C = the number of concerts he attends in a month. Draw the contour lines (in the positive quadrant) for this function for utility levels of 4, 5, and 10 (i.e. for $U = 4$, $U = 5$, and $U = 10$). What do we call the shape of these contour lines?

   If concert tickets are $4, the cover charge at the disco is $2 and Oliver's monthly entertainment budget is $64, his budget constraint is $2D + 4C = 64$. Where does this line intersect the utility function when $U = \sqrt{28}$?

3.4

Ms. Caffeine enjoys coffee (C) and tea (T) according to the function: $U(C, T) = 3C + 4T$. What does her utility function say about her *MRS* of coffee for tea? If coffee and tea cost $3.00 each and Ms. Caffeine has $12 to spend on these products, how much coffee and tea should she buy to maximize her utility? Draw the graph of her indifference curve and budget constraint, and show that the utility maximizing point is a boundary solution at which the usual utility maximizing condition does not hold. Under what condition would the usual condition hold? Would there be a unique maximizing point in that case?

3.5

Mr. A derives utility from martinis in proportion to the number he drinks, $U(M) = M$. Mr. A is very particular about his martinis, however: he only enjoys them made in the exact proportion of 2 parts gin to one part vermouth. Hence we can rewrite Mr. A's utility function as:

$$U(M) = U(G, V) = \text{Min} \left(\frac{G}{2}, V \right),$$

where "Min" means that utility is given by the minimum value of the two variables in the parentheses. Graph Mr. A's indifference curve in terms of G and V for various levels of utility. Show that regardless of the prices of the two ingredients, Mr. A will never alter the way he mixes martinis.

3.6

Assume consumers are choosing between housing services measured in square feet and consumption of other goods aggregated and measured in dollars.

a) Show the equilibrium position in a diagram.

b) Now suppose the government agrees to subsidize consumers by paying 50 percent of their housing cost. How will their budget line change? Show the new equilibrium.

c) Show in a diagram the minimum amount of income supplement the government would have to give individuals instead of housing subsidy to make them as well off as they were in situation b).

Appendix to	**Utility**
Chapter 3	**in Uncertain**
	Situations

Introduction

In Chapter 3 we implicitly assumed that individuals make decisions in an environment characterized by certainty. We assumed that when individuals purchase a good they know exactly what they are getting and how much utility it will yield. Once the allocation of the budget is determined, there is no uncertainty associated with the utility to be derived.

In a variety of real-world situations this assumption cannot be considered tenable. First, some goods that individuals purchase are in the nature of games or lotteries in which the outcome is uncertain. Racetrack bets, craps, insurance purchases, and stock market transactions all fit into this general category: The purchase of the good does not guarantee any particular outcome. A second way in which uncertainty affects an individual's behavior is in his or her dealings with others. Many encounters between individuals are in the form of a game in which the reward that anyone receives will depend on what the others do. This type of uncertainty is manifest in numerous situations ranging from poker games to the conduct of diplomacy.

Finally, individuals are confronted by uncertainty when they lack understanding or information concerning the problem they are trying to solve. An individual is not able to predict the weather with any degree of certainty, nor is he or she able to decide specifically which refrigerator offers the best quality for the money. In such situations individuals are faced by a lack of knowledge and might be willing to pay something for additional information.

Of these three types of uncertainty, the first is the most easily discussed and will be the only one we analyze in this appendix. We will be specifically concerned with showing why individuals are adverse to risk and how this may affect their behavior. We will make scattered references to the other types of uncertainty at other points in this book. In particular, we will discuss uncertainties faced by firms and the strategies they may adopt to cope with them in Chapter 12.

Probability and Expected Value

The study of individual behavior under uncertainty and the mathematical study of probability and statistics have a common historical origin in attempts to understand (and presumably to win) games of chance. The study of simple coin–flipping games, for example, has been unusually productive in the mathematics that has been developed from these games and in illuminating certain characteristics of human behavior that they exhibit. Two statistical concepts that originated in such games, and will be quite useful in the remainder of this appendix, are *probability* and *expected value*.

Probability

The *probability* of an event happening is, roughly speaking, the relative frequency with which it will occur. For example, to say that the probability of a head on the flip of a fair coin is ½ means that we would expect that, if a fair coin were flipped a large number of times, a head would appear in approximately ½ of the trials. Similarly, the probability of rolling a two on a single die is ¹/₆. In approximately one out of every six rolls a two will come up. Of course, before the die is rolled, an individual has no idea how many spots will come up. Hence, rolling a die involves an uncertain outcome.

Expected Value

The expected value of a game with a number of uncertain prizes (outcomes) is simply the size of the prize that the player will win, on average. As an example, suppose Jones and Smith agree to flip a coin once. If the coin comes up heads, Jones pays Smith $1; if the coin comes up tails, Smith pays Jones $1. From Smith's point of view there are two prizes (X_1 and X_2) in this game: If the coin is heads $X_1 = +\$1$; if it comes up tails $X_2 = -\$1$, where the minus sign indicates that Smith must pay. From Jones' point of view the game is exactly the same except that the signs of the outcomes are reversed. The expected value of the game is then:

$$\tfrac{1}{2}\,X_1 + \tfrac{1}{2}\,X_2 = \tfrac{1}{2}\,(\$1) + \tfrac{1}{2}\,(-\$1) = 0 \qquad \text{[3A.1]}$$

The game has expected value 0. If the game were to be played a large number of times, it is not likely that either player would come out very far ahead.

Now suppose the prizes of the game were changed slightly so that (again from Smith's point of view) $X_1 = \$10, X_2 = -\$1$. Smith will win \$10 if a head comes up but will lose only \$1 if it is a tail. The expected value of this game is

$$\tfrac{1}{2} X_1 + \tfrac{1}{2} X_2 = \tfrac{1}{2} (\$10) + \tfrac{1}{2} (-\$1) = \$5 - \$.50 = \$4.50 \qquad [3A.2]$$

If this game is played many times Smith will certainly end up the big winner. In fact, Smith might be willing to pay Jones something for the privilege of playing the game. He might even be willing to pay as much as \$4.50 for a chance to play. Games such as that in equation 3A.1, which have expected value 0, or games such as equation 3A.2, which do cost their expected values (here \$4.50) for the right to play, are called (actuarially) *fair games*. For such games, a player would expect to end up about even if he played the game a large number of times. A common observation is that, in many situations, people will refuse to play actuarially fair games. Because this point is central to an understanding of developments in the theory of uncertainty, we will take it up in the next section.

Fair Games and the St. Petersburg Paradox

People are generally unwilling to play fair games.[1] You may at times agree to flip a coin for small amounts of money, but if you were offered the chance to wager \$1000 on one coin flip you would probably refuse. Similarly, you would probably not be willing to pay \$4.50 for the right to participate in the game of equation 3A.2 even though this price is actuarially fair. An even more convincing example is the "St. Petersburg Paradox," which was first rigorously investigated by the mathematician Daniel Bernoulli in the eighteenth century.[2] In the St. Petersburg Paradox the following game is proposed: A coin is flipped until a head appears. If a head first appears on the nth flip, the player is paid $\$2^n$. This game has an infinite number of outcomes (a coin might be flipped from now until doomsday and never come up heads although the likelihood of this is small), but the first few can easily be written

---

[1]The games we will discuss here are assumed to yield no utility in their play other than the prizes. Hence, the observation that many individuals gamble at "unfair" odds (for instance, the game of roulette where there are 38 possible outcomes but the house only pays 36 to 1 for a winning number) is not necessarily a refutation of this statement. Rather, such individuals can reasonably be assumed to be deriving some utility from the circumstances associated with the play of the game. It is conceptually possible therefore to differentiate the consumption aspect of gambling from the pure risk aspect.

[2]The original Bernoulli article is well worth reading. It has been reprinted as D. Bernoulli, "Exposition of a New Theory on the Measurement of Risk," *Econometrica* 22 (January 1954), pp. 23–36.

down. If X_i represents the prize awarded when the first head appears on the ith trial, then

$$X_1 = \$2$$
$$X_2 = \$4$$
$$X_3 = \$8$$
$$\cdot$$
$$\cdot$$
$$\cdot$$
$$\text{[3A.3]}$$
$$X_n = \$2^n$$
$$\cdot$$
$$\cdot$$
$$\cdot$$

Equation 3A.3 simply records the payoff that an individual will receive under the various possible outcomes of the game.

The probability of getting a head for the first time on the ith trial is $\frac{1}{2}^i$; it is the probability of getting $(i - 1)$ tails and then a head. Hence the probabilities (π_i) of the prizes given in equation 3A.3 are:

$$\pi_1 = \frac{1}{2}$$
$$\pi_2 = \frac{1}{4}$$
$$\pi_3 = \frac{1}{8}$$
$$\cdot$$
$$\cdot$$
$$\text{[3A.4]}$$
$$\cdot$$
$$\pi_n = \frac{1}{2}^n$$
$$\cdot$$
$$\cdot$$
$$\cdot$$

The probability of getting a head on the first flip is $\frac{1}{2}$. The probability of getting the first head on say, the fifth flip would be the probability of getting 4 tails in a row ($\frac{1}{16}$) times the probability of getting a head on the fifth flip ($\frac{1}{2}$). Hence $\pi_5 = \frac{1}{32}$. The other entries in equation 3A.4 have been worked out in a similar way.

The expected value of the St. Petersburg Paradox game is infinite:

$$\text{expected value} = \sum_{i=1}^{\infty} \pi_i X_i = \sum_{i=1}^{\infty} 2^i \frac{1}{2^i}$$
$$\text{[3A.5]}$$
$$= 1 + 1 + 1 + \cdots + 1 \cdots = \infty$$

On the average, the game will have a very large payoff. Some introspection, however, should convince us that no player would pay very much (much less than infinity) to play this game. If you charged $1 billion to play the game, you would surely have no takers despite the fact that $1 billion is still considerably less than the expected value of the game. This, then, is the paradox—Bernoulli's game is in some sense not worth its (infinite) expected dollar value.

Expected Utility Hypothesis

In order to understand Bernoulli's solution to the St. Petersburg Paradox, we will first examine the prizes in the game a bit more carefully. Those prizes become quite large as longer and longer runs of tails are examined. For example, if it happened that 40 tails were flipped before a head occurred, the game's prize would be 2^{41}, which is a very large number indeed, exceeding the entire value of all property in the United States. Of course, the probability of getting 40 successive tails in flipping a coin is quite low, but Bernoulli centered his attention specifically on the large size of the prizes. He argued that the psychic value of an additional dollar of prize money declines as larger and larger prizes are considered. In the language of Chapter 3, Bernoulli's assertion is that the extra utility provided by additional prize dollars declines as larger prizes are considered.

Figure 3A.1 illustrates that assumption about individuals' tastes. There income is shown on the horizontal axis, and the utility derived from income appears on the vertical axis. The curve U records the level of satisfaction (that is, utility) derived from each income level. Notice the concave shape of the curve. This shape

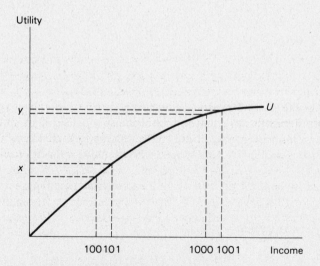

Figure 3A.1 / Bernoulli's Assumed Utility of Income

The curve U shows the utility value of different income levels. On the assumption that the additional utility provided by an extra dollar of income declines as income increases, the curve will have the concave shape shown in the figure. This is clearly shown by comparing interval x with interval y.

embodies the assumption that extra dollars of income mean less if income is high than if income is low. For example, the additional utility of an extra dollar of income if income is $100 is given by distance x on the vertical axis, whereas the additional utility of an extra dollar if income is $1,000 is given by y. The fact that x is considerably larger than y is an indication of what economists call the assumption of a *diminishing marginal utility* of income.

How does this assumption solve the St. Petersburg Paradox? Bernoulli argued that individuals base their decisions about playing the game on the psychic value of the game rather than on its monetary value. Since the psychic value of the game's large prizes is relatively smaller than these prizes' dollar values, Bernoulli argued that the psychic value of the game as a whole is far less than its (infinite) monetary value. Consequently, it is quite reasonable for an individual to refuse to pay a great amount for the right to play the game since the game in fact is not "worth" very much in utility terms.

In technical terminology, Bernoulli argued that individuals, in deciding on their behavior in uncertain situations, consider the *expected utility* of their various options rather than the expected dollar values of these options. It is the average utility value of a game that matters, not its average monetary value. Because the marginal utility of prize money diminishes for larger and larger prizes, this distinction can be quite important for games with large potential prizes (or, as we shall see below, for games with large losses). Even though Bernoulli hypothesized this aspect of behavior more than 200 years ago, it remains the fundamental assumption in the study of decision making in uncertain situations.[3] It is expected utility that guides individuals' actions, not expected dollar values. In the next section we will see that this observation carries with it implications about individuals' attitudes toward risk.

Risk Aversion

We started our discussion of the St. Petersburg Paradox with the observation that individuals are generally unwilling to play fair games. Individuals will refuse to play a game in which they will, on average, break even. In other words, individuals are averse to risk and would prefer to avoid taking chances. The reason for this again derives from Bernoulli's observations about the utility value of various prizes. A fair game that promises a gain of, say, $1,000 when you win and a loss of $1,000 when you lose is not "fair" in utility terms. The $1,000 loss brings more pain than the $1,000 gain brings pleasure. Consequently, individuals will refuse to play the game. Similarly, individuals will be more averse to playing fair games with big prizes than they will be to playing fair games with small prizes. If an individual has a diminishing marginal utility of income (as we have assumed), he or she will in this sense exhibit *risk aversion*.

---

[3]Modern aspects of the expected utility hypothesis are discussed in J. von Neumann and O. Morgenstern, *The Theory of Games and Economic Behavior* (Princeton, N.J.: Princeton University Press, 1949). See especially the discussion of axioms of rationality in the appendix.

to achieve a greater diversity in the number of securities owned than if these securities had to be purchased directly.

Mutual funds go even further in meeting the attitudes toward risk of individuals by tailoring their holdings to meet different demands. Some funds call themselves "growth" funds implying that they take above-average risks in their investments and hope for above-average returns. "Balanced" (or "income") funds, on the other hand, tend to hold low-risk securities and to achieve a commensurately lower return. In a study of 23 mutual fund portfolios, for example, D. E. Farrar[5] found that funds could be readily categorized by their relative riskiness and that more risky funds did indeed offer higher expected returns. He concluded that the funds studied did provide nearly "optimal" diversification for the degree of risk that particular investors were willing to accept.

Employment Decisions

Individuals' aversion to risk also is demonstrated in employment choices. Jobs that involve relatively uncertain earnings will be unattractive to potential employees. Average earnings on such jobs may therefore have to be higher than on "safe" jobs to compensate for the added risk. For example, Friedman and Kuznets[6] examined a number of surveys of professional employment that were conducted in the 1920s and 1930s. They concluded that individuals in independent practice earned considerably higher average incomes than those in a salaried practice. Table 3A.1 illustrates a few of their findings. Although the authors attribute income differences between independent and salaried practice to a number of factors (independent practitioners often have to buy their own equipment, for example),

Table 3A.1 / Average Annual Incomes in Independent and Salaried Professional Practice

	Average for Salaried Practice	Average for Independent Practice
Physicians		
AMA Survey (1928)	$5,428	$6,499
Lawyers		
New York County Survey (1933)	$4,316	$6,664

Source: M. Friedman and S. Kuznets, *Income from Independent Professional Practice* (New York: National Bureau of Economic Research, 1945), p. 299.

[5]D. E. Farrar, *The Investment Decision under Uncertainty* (Englewood Cliffs, N.J.: Prentice Hall Inc., 1962).

[6]M. Friedman and S. Kuznets, *Income from Independent Professional Practice* (New York: National Bureau of Economic Research, 1945).

one reason for the differences was clearly the more risky nature of independent practice. The higher average incomes earned in independent practice can be seen as in part compensating for that additional risk.

Summary: Uncertainty and Information

In this appendix we have examined two basic elements of the economic theory of decision making under uncertainty. First, we showed that individuals are concerned with the utilities from uncertain events. The dollar magnitudes of outcomes are important only in that they reflect utility. Second, individuals in general dislike uncertainty and may be willing to pay some amount to avoid being subjected to it. For example, individuals seem quite willing to buy insurance. When they do so they are, in effect, accepting a certain loss of income (the premium paid) in order to avoid the small probability of a substantial loss.

In a sense all uncertainty reflects a lack of information. If an individual knew a coin were going to come up heads when it was flipped there would be no uncertainty. Knowing what the weather will be tomorrow eliminates some of the uncertainty in deciding what to wear. Just as individuals are willing to pay something in order to avoid taking risks, they will also pay something for information. Presumably they will purchase additional information so long as the expected benefits from having such information exceed the costs of obtaining it. For example, expenditures on better weather forecasting techniques have undoubtedly been beneficial since the information provided has reduced the uncertainty associated with crop cultivation and mitigated the danger of living on the Gulf Coast. An individual consulting the publication of Consumers' Union is in a similar way gathering information about the nature of consumer products. He or she is investing some money and time in order to reduce the uncertainty associated with an intended purchase. Many other instances of this type make the study of the demand for information an important aspect of the analysis of behavior in uncertain situations.

Suggested Readings

Alchian, A., "The Meaning of Utility Measurement," *American Economic Review* 43 (March 1953), pp. 26–50.

Friedman, M., and L. J. Savage, "The Utility Analysis of Choices Involving Risk," *Journal of Political Economy* 56 (August 1948), pp. 279–304.

Luce, R. D., and H. Raiffa, *Games and Decisions* (New York: John Wiley & Sons, Inc., 1957), chap. 1 and 2.

Raiffa, H., *Decision Analysis* (Reading, Mass.: Addison-Wesley Publishing Company, Inc., 1968), chap. 1,2, and 10.

Von Neumann, J., and O. Morgenstern, *Theory of Games and Economic Behavior* (Princeton, New Jersey: Princeton University Press, 1944), chap. 1–3, Appen.

Chapter 4

Effects of Income and Price Changes

Introduction

In this chapter we will study the change in the quantity demanded of a particular good as a result of changed "conditions." In particular, the effect of changes in income, the effect of changes in the price of the good, and the effect of changes in the price of some other good will be investigated. We will be interested in comparing the new utility-maximizing choices that are made with those that prevailed before conditions changed. Because we are comparing these two optimal positions we will conduct an investigation of the type called *comparative statics* analysis.

At the outset we must be aware of two aspects of comparative statics analysis. First, the importance of the *ceteris paribus* assumption must be clearly recognized. We are only changing one variable at a time; everything else is being held constant. In particular, the tastes of the individual are being held constant. In graphic terms, we will be keeping the individual's *indifference curves fixed* and studying the effects of *shifting the budget constraint* to alternative positions.

Second, we must understand the general notion of changing "conditions." Ideally, we would like to explain why conditions have changed. Instead of hypothesizing that, say, the price of potatoes has risen, we would be more interested in asking *why* the price of potatoes has risen. This chapter is only a first step in answering this larger question, which we will not discuss in detail until Part IV.

Demand Functions

In Chapter 3 we showed that the quantities of X and Y that a utility-maximizing individual will choose depend on his preferences (that is, the shape of the indifference curve map) and on the budget constraint. It is convenient to summarize this dependence by *demand functions* (for X and Y) of the general form

$$X = D_X(P_X, P_Y, I; \text{tastes; other things}) \qquad [4.1a]$$
$$Y = D_Y(P_X, P_Y, I; \text{tastes; other things}) \qquad [4.1b]$$

where I (income) and P (prices of X and Y) are the *parameters* in the budget constraint. The notation indicates that the quantity, say, of X demanded depends on the parameters in the budget constraint, on tastes, and on other things such as the quantities of goods other than X and Y that are consumed. In most of the analysis of this chapter we will assume tastes and other things are held constant and consequently we will write equations 4.1a–b more simply as

$$X = D_X(P_X, P_Y, I) \qquad [4.2a]$$
$$Y = D_Y(P_X, P_Y, I) \qquad [4.2b]$$

This form is particularly useful because it exhibits the dependence of the quantity of X demanded on the three parameters P_X, P_Y, and I, and these are precisely the relationships we wish to investigate. Our strategy will be to look at the simple one-variable relationships between I and X, between P_X and X, and between P_Y and X while, in each of these investigations, holding the other two parameters fixed. This will permit us to develop a few "theorems" about the likely effect on the quantity of X demanded when only one of the parameters changes.

Homogeneity

Before starting this discussion, however, we can show an important "theorem," which was already demonstrated (at least implicitly) in Chapter 3: Demand functions are *homogeneous of degree 0* for proportional changes in P_X, P_Y, and I together.[1] If the prices of X and Y and income (I) were all to double (or to change by any identical percentage), the quantities of X and Y demanded would not be affected. The reason for this is quite simple. The budget constraint

$$P_X X + P_Y Y = I \qquad [4.3]$$

---

[1]Technically, a function $f(X, Y)$ is said to be homogeneous of degree "k" in X and Y if $f(tX, tY) = t^k f(X, Y)$ for any $t > 0$. The most important cases encountered in economics are functions homogeneous of degree 0 or 1. A doubling of X and Y for a function homogeneous of degree 0 leaves the value of f unchanged. A doubling of X and Y for a function homogeneous of degree 1 will exactly double the function. We will encounter functions of this second type in Part III.

is identical to the budget constraint

$$2P_X X + 2P_Y Y = 2I \qquad\qquad [4.4]$$

Graphically, equations 4.3 and 4.4 are exactly the same lines. Consequently, both budget constraints would be tangent to the individual's indifference curve map at precisely the same point. The quantities of X and Y demanded when the individual is faced by constraint 4.3 are the same as those demanded when the individual is faced by constraint 4.4. In the case of good X then, for example, we can write

$$X = D_X(P_X, P_Y, I) = D_X(2P_X, 2P_Y, 2I) \qquad\qquad [4.5]$$

Intuitively this says that the quantities an individual demands depend not on absolute prices nor on money income but, rather, on the relative prices of X and Y and on the "real" value of income. Proportional changes in the prices of X and Y and in income only change the units we count in and do not affect the physical quantities demanded. This tells us that individuals will not be hurt by a general inflation of prices if their incomes increase in the same proportion. They will be on exactly the same indifference curve both before and after the inflation. Only if inflation increases some individuals' incomes faster than others or if relative prices change will inflation have an effect on the quantities of goods demanded and on individuals' well–being.

We will now proceed to analyze changes in only one of the parameters in the demand function for X, while we assume the other two parameters to be constant. Such changes will alter the position of the budget constraint and will therefore change the utility maximizing choices of X and Y. We start by considering changes in income while holding P_X and P_Y constant.

Changes in Income

As total income rises, it might be expected that the quantity of each good purchased will also increase. This situation is illustrated in Figure 4.1. As income increases from I_1 to I_2 to I_3, the quantity of X demanded increases from X_1 to X_2 to X_3 and the quantity of Y increases from Y_1 to Y_2 to Y_3. Notice that the budget lines I_1, I_2, and I_3 are all parallel, which records that we are only changing income, not the relative prices of X and Y. The slope of the budget constraint is given by $-P_X/P_Y$; this ratio, by assumption, does not change in Figure 4.1. Since the budget constraints I_1, I_2, and I_3 are just tangent to the indifference curves U_1, U_2, and U_3, respectively, the MRS is the same at X_1, Y_1 as it is at X_2, Y_2 and X_3, Y_3. This common MRS is equal to the price ratio P_X/P_Y, as is required for utility maximization.

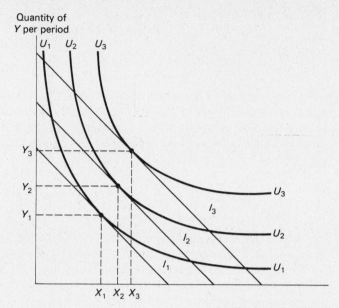

**Figure 4.1 / Effect of Increasing
Income on Quantities of X and Y Chosen**

As income increases from I_1 to I_2 to I_3 the optimal (utility-maximizing) choices of X and Y are shown by the successively higher points of tangency. Notice that the budget constraint shifts in a parallel way because its slope (given by $-P_X/P_Y$) does not change.

Engel Curves

By using the information from Figure 4.1 we can construct the *Engel curves*[2] in Figure 4.2. These curves record the relationship between the quantity of X purchased and total income. Notice that these curves are not necessarily straight lines. The demand for some "luxury" goods (such as Y) may increase proportionately more rapidly than income, whereas the demand for "necessities" (such as X) may grow proportionately less rapidly than income. The precise shape will depend on the individual's preferences for X and Y as reflected in the indifference curve map.

In Figures 4.1 and 4.2 both X and Y increase as income increases. This might be considered the usual situation, and goods that exhibit this property are called *normal goods*. Most goods seem to fit into this category—as incomes increase individuals tend to buy more of practically everything.

---

[2]The curves are named for the Prussian economist Ernst Engel (1821–1896) who was one of the first persons to study systematically the relation between the quantity of a good demanded and income.

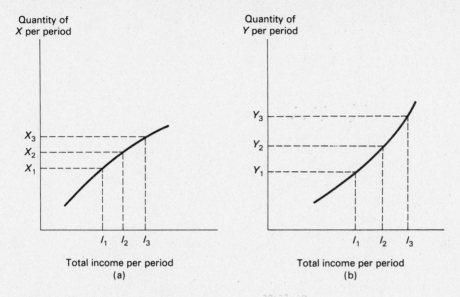

**Figure 4.2 / Engel Curves Derived
from the Individual's Indifference Curves**

Engel curves depict the relationship between total expenditures and the quantity of a particular good purchased. In 4.2a and b both goods are normal because the quantity purchased increases as income increases. The good pictured in 4.2a is, however, a "necessity" in the sense that the *fraction* of expenditures devoted to X declines as income increases. On the other hand, good Y 4.2b is a "luxury." The Engel curves were constructed directly from Figure 4.1.

Inferior Goods

There are goods, however, whose quantity decreases as income increases. Some examples of these goods might be rot-gut whiskey, potatoes, and second-hand clothing. A good for which quantity decreases as income increases is called an *inferior good*. This phenomenon is illustrated in Figure 4.3. In this diagram the good Z is inferior because as income increases less of it is actually chosen. Notice that indifference curves do not have to be "oddly" shaped to exhibit inferiority; although the curves shown in Figure 4.3 continue to obey the assumption of a diminishing MRS, they exhibit inferiority. Good Z is inferior because of the way it relates to the other goods available (good Y here), not because of a peculiarity unique to it. Purchases of rot-gut whiskey decline as income increases because there are other substitute goods (French wine for example) that an individual becomes increasingly able to afford. Contrary to the Engel curves shown in Figure 4.2, the Engel curves for an inferior good will be negatively sloped because quantity demanded declines as income increases. We have therefore developed the following definitions.

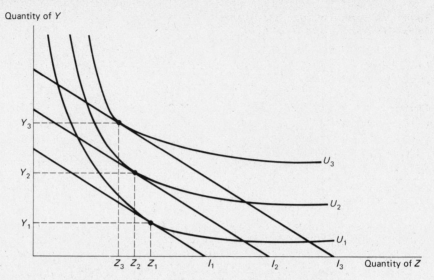

Quantity of Y

Figure 4.3 / Indifference Curve Map Exhibiting Inferiority

In this diagram good Z is inferior because the quantity purchased actually declines as income increases. Y is a normal good (as it must be if there are only two goods available), and purchases of Y increase as total expenditures increase.

Definition

If an increase in income leads an individual to buy more of some good, that good is a *normal good*. If the same individual buys less of a particular good, that good is an *inferior good*.

■ Examples of Engel Curves

The relationship between income and the consumption of specific items has been extensively studied by economists since the eighteenth century. Most commonly, expenditure data is collected from a sample of families and these data are then classified by income levels (or by "social class") to see if any important regularities are visible. Probably the most widely referenced sample data are those used by Engel in his original studies. An abbreviated set of these data is shown in Table 4.1. They refer to average budgetary allocations made by a sample of 153 Belgian families in 1853.

Engel's Law

Engel drew one major conclusion from these data: That the proportion of total expenditures devoted to food declines as incomes rise. In other words, food is a

**Table 4.1 / Percent of Total Expenditures
on Various Items by Belgian Families in 1853**

| | Annual Income | | |
Expenditure Item	$225–$300	$450–$600	$750–$1000
Food	62.0%	55.0%	50.0%
Clothing	16.0	18.0	18.0
Lodging, light, and fuel	17.0	17.0	17.0
Services (education, legal, health)	4.0	7.5	11.5
Comfort and recreation	1.0	2.5	3.5
Total	100.0	100.0	100.0

Source: Reproduced in A. Marshall, *Principles of Economics*, 8th ed. (London: Macmillan & Co., Ltd., 1920), p. 97. Some items have been aggregated.

necessity whose consumption rises less rapidly than does income. That hypothesis has come to be known as "Engel's Law," and it has been verified in hundreds of studies. It holds true not only within a particular geographic area: Cross-country comparisons also show that, on average, individuals in less developed countries spend a larger fraction of their incomes on food than do individuals in the industrial economies. Over time also the percentage of income spent on food tends to decline as incomes rise. For example, in nineteenth-century America individuals spent nearly 50 percent of their incomes on food. Today, as we show below, that figure has fallen to about 20 percent. Indeed, Engel's law appears to be such a consistent empirical finding that some economists have suggested the proportion of income spent on food as a useful indicator of poverty. Families that spend more than (say) 35 percent of their income on food might be regarded as "poor," whereas those who spend less than that percentage would not be so regarded.

Engel was cautious about drawing inferences from the other data in Table 4.1, and even today no other "laws" of consumption have as unanimous consent as does Engel's law of food consumption. For example, the data in Table 4.1 appear to indicate that shelter expenses are a constant fraction of income, but that conclusion has been hotly debated for many years—particularly in connection with the question of the incidence of property taxes on various income groups. Similarly, the data seem to indicate that spending on services rises more rapidly than income, but some care should be taken in interpreting this to mean that services are generally "luxury" goods (consider, for example, the case of medical care).

Recent Expenditure Data

Table 4.2 reports an updated version of Engel's data for the United States in 1972. Although there have been vast changes in the types of goods that individuals consume since 1853 (and therefore the categories in Tables 4.1 and 4.2 are not directly comparable), some of Engel's conclusions remain valid. Most importantly,

**Table 4.2 / Percent of Total Consumption
by Income Class for All U.S. Families, 1972**

Consumption Item	Annual Income		
	$3,000–$4,000	$7,000–$8,000	$12,000–$15,000
Food	24.5%	21.3%	19.7%
Clothing	7.1	7.6	8.1
Housing (incl. Furniture, Light, and Fuel)	34.7	30.7	29.9
Medical and Educational Services	7.8	7.3	6.8
Personal Care, Comfort, and Recreation	9.3	10.8	11.7
Transportation and Other	16.6	22.3	23.8
Total	100.0	100.0	100.0

Source: U.S. Dept. of Labor, Bureau of Labor Statistics Consumer Expenditure Survey Series, Report 455 (Washington, D.C., 1973), Table 1a.

Engel's Law continues to hold in the 1972 data. That is, higher-income individuals devote a smaller fraction of their expenditures to food than do those with lower incomes. Similarly, there is again some evidence that housing expenditures are a relatively constant proportion of the total, especially for incomes above the very lowest level. That finding is not so consistent as in Engel's original data, however. Transportation services are, on the other hand, new to the list of major expenditure items and there is some evidence in Table 4.2 that purchases of such services are an increasing proportion of total spending for higher-income people. This finding that transportation is a "luxury" is consistent with the data on automobile purchases, which we will discuss in Chapter 5.

One additional conclusion does emerge from most budgetary studies: The phenomenon of inferiority is confined to narrowly defined groups of commodities. For all of the broad groupings in Tables 4.1 and 4.2 total expenditures increase with income (although, for the case of food, the proportion of income spent declines). Only by investigating specific commodities (such as potatoes, used clothing, or, possibly, public-transit ridership) can items whose purchase declines with increasing income be identified.

Changes in a Good's Price

The effect of price change on the quantity of a good demanded is somewhat more complex to analyze than is the effect of a change in income. Geometrically this is because changing a price involves not only changing the level of the budget constraint but also changing its slope. Consequently, moving to the new utility-maximizing choice will involve not only moving to another indifference curve but will also necessitate changing the *MRS*. When a price changes, therefore, two analytically different effects come into play. One of these is a *substitution effect—*

even if the individual were to stay on the *same* indifference curve consumption would be reallocated in order to equate the *MRS* to the new price ratio. The second, the *income effect*, arises because a price change necessarily changes individuals' "real" purchasing power—they, in fact, will not stay on the same indifference curves on which they started. We can therefore define:

Definition

An individual's reaction to a price change can be analyzed as being composed of two effects. If utility is held constant, individuals will move along an indifference curve substituting the good that has become relatively cheaper for the one that has become relatively more expensive. That is the *substitution effect*. Movement to a new indifference curve indicates that the individual's real purchasing power has been affected by the price change. This second change is the *income effect*.

We will now investigate these effects in several different situations.

Substitution and Income Effects from a Fall in Price

Let us consider first the change in the quantity of X consumed in response to a fall in price that is illustrated in Figure 4.4. The individual is initially maximizing utility (subject to total income, I) by consuming the combination of X^*, Y^*. The initial constraint is $I = P_X{}^1X + P_YY$. Now suppose that the price of X falls to $P_X{}^2$. The new budget constraint is given by the equation $I = P_X{}^2X + P_YY$ in Figure 4.4. It should be clear that the new position of maximum utility is at X^{**}, Y^{**} where the new budget line is tangent to the indifference curve U_2. We can view the movement to this new point as being composed of two effects. First, the change in the slope of the budget constraint would have motivated the individual to move to point B even if it were necessary to stay on the original indifference curve U_1. The dashed line in Figure 4.4 has the same slope as the new budget constraint ($I = P_X{}^2X + P_YY$) but is drawn to be tangent to U_1 because we are conceptually holding his "real" income (that is, utility) constant. A relatively lower price for X causes the individual to move from X^*, Y^* to B if we do not allow him or her to be made better off as a result of the lower price. This movement is a graphic demonstration of the *substitution effect*. The further move from B to the optimal point X^{**}, Y^{**} is analytically identical to the kind of change exhibited in Figure 4.1 for changes in income. Because the price of X has fallen, and money income (I) has not, the individual has a greater "real" income and can afford a utility level (U_2) that is greater than could be attained previously. If X is a normal good the individual will demand more of it in response to this increase in purchasing power. This observation explains the origin of the term *income effect* for the movement. Consequently we have shown that both the substitution effect and the income effect operate to cause the individual to choose more X when the price of X declines.

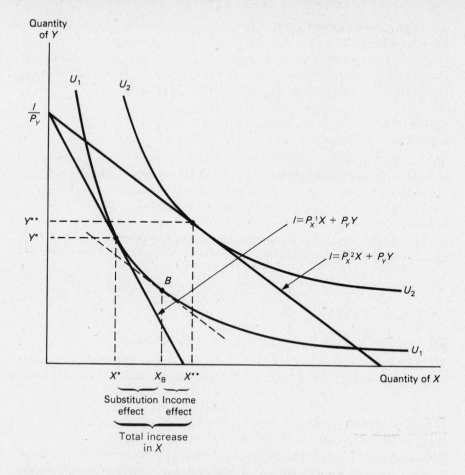

**Figure 4.4 / Demonstration of the Income
and Substitution Effects of a Fall in the Price of X**

When the price of X falls from $P_x{}^1$ to $P_x{}^2$, the utility-maximizing choice shifts from X^*, Y^* to X^{**}, Y^{**}. This movement can be broken down into two analytically different effects: first, a movement along the initial indifference curve to point B where the MRS is equal to the new price ratio (the substitution effect); second (the income effect), involves a movement to a higher level of utility since real income has increased. In the diagram both the substitution and income effects cause more X to be bought when its price declines. Notice that the point I/P_Y is the same as before. This is because P_Y has not changed, and the point I/P_Y appears on both the old and new budget constraints.

 It is important to realize that the individual does not actually move from X^*, Y^* to B and then to X^{**}, Y^{**}. We never observe the point B; only the two optimal positions are reflected in the individual's behavior. However, the notion of income and substitution effects is analytically valuable because it shows that a price change affects the quantity of X that is demanded in two conceptually different ways.

An Example of Substitution and Income Effects from a Price Decline

In order to reinforce this conceptual distinction let us return to the hamburger–soft drink example. Suppose that the price of soft drinks fell to $.05 (remember that previously soft drinks were assumed to sell for $.10). This price change has the effect of increasing the individual's purchasing power. For example, whereas earlier 10 soft drinks could be bought with a dollar, now a dollar can buy 20 of them. Individuals will probably not choose such unbalanced consumption bundles, but they could. Therefore the price decline represents an increase in welfare. The individual will, however, choose some different combination of hamburgers and soft drinks than before—if only because the previous selection (3 hamburgers, 4 soft drinks) now leaves $.20 extra in purchasing power. In moving to this new preferred consumption choice two different effects come into play. First, even if we conceptually hold constant the individual's "real income" (that is, if we *compensate* for the positive effect that the price change has on purchasing power), expenditures will be adjusted so that the *MRS* will be brought into line with the new price ratio (now 4 to 1). We call this compensated response the *substitution effect*. Even at a constant real income there is an incentive to substitute soft drinks for hamburgers. In actuality, real income has also increased; in order to assess the total effect of the price change on the demand for soft drinks, we must also investigate the *income effect*. Because the individual's real income has increased, this (assuming soft drinks are normal goods) would be another reason to expect soft drink purchases to increase.

Substitution and Income Effects from an Increase in Price

If the price of good X were to increase, we would use a similar analysis. In Figure 4.5 the budget line has been shifted inward because of an increase in the price of X from P_X^1 to P_X^2. The movement from the initial point of utility maximization (X^*, Y^*) to the new point (X^{**}, Y^{**}) can be decomposed into two effects. First, even if the individual could stay on the initial indifference curve (U_2) he or she would substitute Y for X and move along U_2 to point B. At this point the dashed line (with slope $-P_X^2/P_Y$) is just tangent to the indifference curve U_2. The movement from (X^*, Y^*) to B along U_2 is therefore the *substitution effect*. However, because purchasing power has been reduced by the rise in the price of X (since money income, I, has remained constant), the individual must move to a lower level of utility. This movement is again called the *income effect*. Notice in Figure 4.5 that both the income and substitution effects work in the same direction and cause the quantity of X demanded to be reduced in response to an increase in its price.

Summary of Substitution and Income Effects

Having discussed income and substitution effects, we are now in a position to summarize how the quantity of X demanded changes in response to changes in P_X.

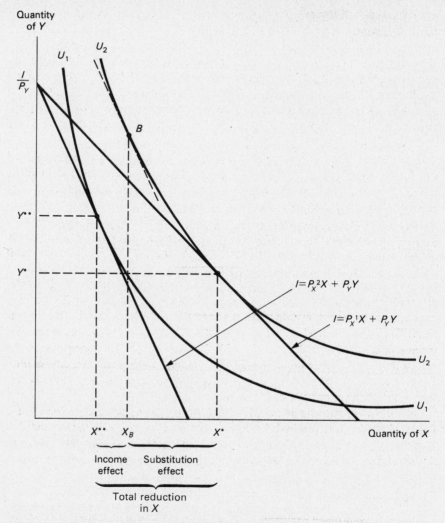

**Figure 4.5 / Demonstration of the Income and
Substitution Effects of an Increase in the Price of Good X**

When the price of X increases, the budget constraint shifts inward. The movement from the initial
utility-maximizing point (X^*, Y^*) to the new point (X^{**}, Y^{**}) can be analyzed as two separate effects.
The *substitution effect* would be depicted as a movement to point B on the initial indifference curve (U_2).
The price increase would, however, also create a loss of purchasing power and a consequent movement
to a lower indifference curve. This is the *income effect*. In the diagram, both the income and substitution
effects cause the quantity of X to fall as a result of the increase in its price. Again, the point I/P_Y is not
affected by the change in the price of X.

Insofar as the substitution effect is concerned, the quantity of X demanded always
moves in a direction opposite to the direction of price change. A *decrease* in P_X
lowers the price ratio P_X/P_Y, and to re-establish the conditions for utility maximization the MRS must also fall. In order to reduce the MRS (of X for Y) the individual

will substitute X for Y by moving in a southeasterly direction along the indifference curve. Consequently the quantity of X *increases* as a result of the substitution effect. This result is a direct consequence of the assumption of a diminishing *MRS*. Similarly, an *increase* in the price of X raises P_X/P_Y and requires the individual to move to a point on the indifference curve with a higher *MRS*. This is done by substituting Y for X; the quantity of X therefore *decreases*. The assumption of a diminishing *MRS* therefore assures that the substitution effect will always cause the quantity of X demanded to change in a direction opposite to the direction of the change in its price.

Substitution effects are, however, only part of the story. To determine the total effect of a change in P_X on the quantity of X demanded, we must also consider income effects. It is in examining income effects that the analysis becomes somewhat more complex. A change in the price of good X affects an individual's real income, and we must analyze how this income change affects quantity demanded. First, let us consider the case in which X is a normal good (that is, the quantity of X chosen increases as income increases). In this case (which is surely the most common one) income effects reinforce substitution effects: again, price and quantity move in opposite directions. For example, a decrease in P_X causes the individual's real income to rise, and therefore to choose to consume more X (this is a consequence of the assumption that X is a normal good). Consequently, the substitution effect is reinforced by the income effect. Similarly, when P_X increases, real income falls and, hence the quantity of X demanded falls; this also reinforces the substitution effect. For normal goods then, income and substitution effects reinforce each other, and both cause price changes to be met by changes in the quantity demanded of the opposite direction.

In both Figures 4.4 and 4.5 good X is a normal good. As we can see in these figures, both the substitution and the income effect cause the quantity demanded of X to move in a direction opposite to the assumed direction of change in P_X. Because this effect is probably the most important one in this chapter, let us restate it here:

Optimization Principle

The utility maximization assumption implies that, if X is a normal good, a fall in its price induces both substitution and income effects, causing the quantity demanded of X to increase. Similarly, a rise in the price of X induces both substitution and income effects, causing the quantity demanded of good X to fall.

An Example of the Substitution Effect: A Compensation Price Change for Gasoline

Substitution effects (that is, price-induced movements along an indifference curve) are sometimes termed "compensated price effects" to indicate that income (that is, utility) is being held constant. In other words, substitution effects reflect individuals' reactions to price changes after compensation has been made for the beneficial or adverse effect such changes have on purchasing power. The usefulness of this way of looking at price changes can be illustrated by examining a policy that was proposed (but never implemented) as a way of reducing U.S. gasoline consumption following the 1973 Arab oil embargo. At that time the U.S. government considered imposing a large excise tax (of at least 25 cents per gallon) on gasoline to discourage purchases. Since economic policy makers feared that such a tax would dangerously reduce consumer purchasing power (and add to recessionary pressures), it was also proposed that, on average,[3] revenues collected under the tax be returned to consumers as a tax rebate. This, then, was a policy to implement a "compensated" price change as a way of reducing gasoline sales.

The excise tax, tax rebate proposal is illustrated in Figure 4.6. There, gasoline purchases (X) are shown on the horizontal axis and purchases of all other goods (Y) are shown on the vertical axis. The initial budget constraint is given by I and the initial combination chosen is X^*, Y^*. Implementation of the excise tax alone would have shifted the budget constraint to I' and the combination X', Y' would have been chosen. Gasoline purchases would have been reduced from X^* to X' and utility would have been reduced from U_2 to U_1. Inclusion of the tax rebate as part of the proposal, however, would have shifted the budget constraint from I' to I'' and X'', Y'' would instead have been chosen. Gasoline consumption would increase slightly from what it would have been under the pure excise tax ($X'' > X'$), but the policy combination would result in a reduction of gasoline purchases over what they were originally, with no loss in utility.

We can use some empirical estimates of the determinants of gasoline consumption (which are discussed in more detail in Chapter 5) to indicate, in a rough way, the expected change in gasoline sales as a result of this policy combination. Historical data suggest that a 25-cent rise in gasoline price would reduce purchases of the average family by about 250 gallons per year. In equation format:

$$\text{Reaction to Tax} = X^* - X' = 250 \text{ gallons.} \qquad [4.6]$$

Since the average family consumed about 1000 gallons of gasoline in 1973, average excise tax collections amount to $250 (= \$0.25 \times 1000$). That is the extent to which real income would be reduced by the excise tax and represents the size of the average rebate check sent to each family under the plan. Since historical data also suggest that a $250 gain in annual income produces about a 20-gallon increase in annual gasoline purchases per family (gasoline is, as might be expected, a normal good), we have:

$$\text{Reaction to Rebate} = X'' - X' = 20 \text{ gallons.} \qquad [4.7]$$

---

[3]It was not proposed that each individual receive a rebate equal to the exact amount paid in gasoline taxes. In that case there would have been no actual price effect and (presumably) no change in consumption. Rather, the tax rebate proposal was intended only to compensate the "average" taxpayer.

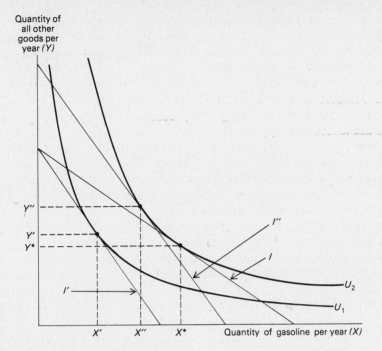

**Figure 4.6 / Illustration of the
Gasoline Excise Tax, Tax Rebate Proposal**

An excise tax that shifted the budget constraint from I to I' would reduce gasoline purchases from X^* to X' and utility from U_2 to U_1. Coupling the excise tax with a tax rebate would shift the budget constraint I' outward to I'' and restore utility to the U_2 level. Gasoline purchases would be reduced under the policy combination (from X^* to X'') because of the compensated price (or substitution) effect.

So, the overall effect of the excise tax, tax rebate plan would have been to reduce annual gasoline sales by 230 gallons per family (about 23 percent of previous sales). In fact, of course, that policy was never enacted (it was rather unpopular politically). The plan did, however, represent one of the clearest examples of the importance of considering both the substitution and income effects of a price change and of how it might be possible to compensate for the income effects of a price change.

Substitution and Income Effects for an Inferior Good

It is not possible to make an unambiguous statement about the effect of a price change on consumption when the good in question is an inferior good. In that case, the income and substitution effects induced by a price change have opposite effects on the quantity demanded. As always, the substitution effect causes price and quantity to move in opposite directions. When P_X rises individuals will substitute other goods for X, and the quantity of X chosen will tend to fall. Similarly when P_X falls individuals will substitute X for other goods and X will therefore tend to rise. However, when X is inferior, the income effect causes X to move in the *same* direction as the change in P_X. A rise in P_X causes real income to decline; because X is inferior, there is a tendency to buy more X. Similarly; when P_X falls the individual has a higher real income, and this creates a tendency for X purchases to be reduced. Consequently the income and substitution effects of a change in P_X work in opposite directions for an inferior good. The income effect now works against the substitution effect. For example, consider the effect that a rise in the price of rot-gut whiskey will have on its purchase. There will be first a substitution effect tending to discourage rot-gut whiskey purchases. Other beverages will be substituted for the now relatively more expensive rot-gut. However, the price rise will make the individual's real income lower; because rot-gut whiskey is inferior, the individual will have a tendency to increase purchases of it. Which of these two effects is stronger is an empirical question that cannot be answered unambiguously by theory. Purchases of rot-gut whiskey may either increase or decrease in response to a price rise.

In Figure 4.7 the income and substitution effects from a rise in P_X are shown for the case in which X is an inferior good. As the price of X rises from $P_X{}^1$ to $P_X{}^2$ there is

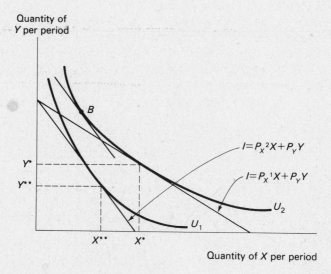

Figure 4.7 / Income and Substitution Effects Work in Opposite Directions for an Inferior Good

When the price of X rises to $P_X{}^2$ there is a substitution effect causing less X to be demanded (this is reflected by a movement to point B on the indifference curve U_2). However, because X is inferior (see Figure 4.3) the lower real income brought about by the price decline causes the quantity of X demanded to be increased from B to X^{**}. In this particular example, the substitution effect outweighs the income effect and $X^{**} < X^*$.

increase

a substitution effect that tends to cause the individual to decrease his purchases of X. This substitution effect is represented by a movement from the initial point (X^*, Y^*) to B. Because P_X has risen, however, the individual now has a lower real income and must move to a lower indifference curve, U_1. The final choice made is therefore the consumption choice X^{**}, Y^{**}. Notice that X^{**} represents a larger purchase of X than does point B. This is a reflection of the situation that good X is assumed to be an inferior good: as real income falls, the quantity of X demanded increases. Notice, however, that in the figure X^{**} is less than X^*: less X is ultimately demanded in response to the rise in P_X. However, this is only because the substitution effect has been sufficiently strong to outweigh the "perverse" income effect that arises because X is inferior. This need not be the case as we shall see in the next example.

Giffen's Paradox

If the income effect is strong enough, we might observe a change in P_X being met by a change in the quantity of X demanded in the *same* direction. For example, the English economist Robert Giffen is said to have observed the paradox that in nineteenth-century Ireland, when the price of potatoes rose, people consumed *more* of them.[4] This peculiar result can be explained by looking at the size of the income effect arising from a change in the price of potatoes. Potatoes were not only inferior goods but also made up a large portion of the Irish people's expenditures. A rise in the price of potatoes therefore reduced real income substantially. Because of this, the Irish were forced to cut back on "luxury" food consumption and, in fact, buy more potatoes. The possibility of quantity increasing in response to a price increase has come to be known as Giffen's Paradox. The paradox is illustrated graphically in Figure 4.8. In response to a rise in the price of good X more of it is demanded. Even though the substitution effect is (as always) negative, the "perverse" income effect is sufficiently strong to make the total effect of the price change positive. Real income *falls* and, since X is an inferior good, the demand for X *increases*. The occurrence of this paradox in the real world is extremely rare—not only must the good under consideration be inferior, but the positive income effect must also be large enough to outweigh the negative substitution effect. Such strong income effects will not occur unless the good in question occupies a major position in the individual's expenditures (as was the case for potatoes in Ireland) or the good is "extremely" inferior. We can therefore conclude that price and quantity will usually move in opposite directions, even when the good in question is inferior.

---

[4] Whether Giffen's Paradox was actually observed is subject to considerable debate. There is some evidence that the story is completely apocryphal. In any case, as George Stigler points out in *The Theory of Price*, 3d edition (New York: Macmillan and Company, pp. 24 and 62–63), it *could* have happened. The paradox does provide a useful example in understanding income and substitution effects, and perhaps the myth should be maintained for its pedagogic value.

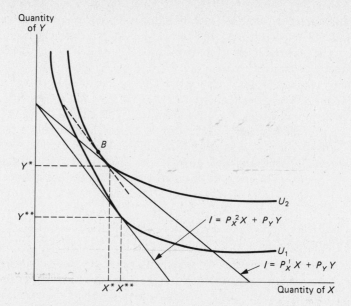

Figure 4.8 / Giffen's Paradox

The total effect of an increase in the price of X is to *increase* the quantity of X demanded. This happens because the negative substitution effect (the movement from X^*, Y^* to point B) is outweighed by a strong positive income effect resulting from the inferiority of good X (compare Figure 4.7). Not every inferior good need exhibit Giffen's Paradox.

Changes in the Price of Another Good

It is obvious from Figures 4.4, 4.5, and 4.7 that a change in P_X will also have an effect on the quantity of Y chosen. In Figure 4.4, for example, a fall in P_X not only causes the quantity of X chosen to increase, but the quantity of Y increases as well. We can explain this result by examining the substitution and income effects on the demand for Y associated with the decrease in P_X. First, as we see in Figure 4.4, the substitution effect causes less Y to be demanded. In moving along the indifference curve U_1 from X^*, Y^* to B, X is being substituted for Y because the lower ratio of P_X to P_Y requires an adjustment in the MRS. However, in this particular case the income effect from the decline in P_X is sufficiently strong to reverse this result. Since Y is a normal good, and since real income has increased, more Y is demanded; the individual moves from the point B to the point X^{**}, Y^{**}. Here Y^{**} exceeds Y^*, and consequently the total effect of the change in P_X is to cause more Y to be bought.

Of course, a slightly different set of indifference curves could have reversed this result. Figure 4.9 shows a relatively "flat" set of indifference curves. Here the substitution effect of a decline in P_X is very large. In moving from X^*, Y^* to B, a large amount of X is substituted for Y. The income effect on Y is not sufficiently strong to reverse the substitution effect, and in this case the quantity of Y finally

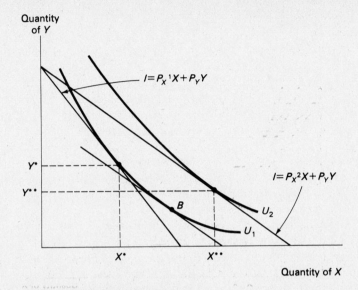

Figure 4.9 / Effect on Y of a Decrease in P_X

In this diagram (in contrast to Figure 4.4) the quantity of Y declines (from Y^* to Y^{**}) in response to a decrease in P_X. The reason is that the relatively flat indifference curves cause the substitution effect to be very large. Moving from X^*, Y^* to B involves giving up a substantial quantity of Y for additional X. This effect more than outweighs the positive income effect (from B to X^{**}, Y^{**}), and hence the quantity of Y demanded declines.

chosen (Y^{**}) is smaller than the amount before the price change. Consequently the effect that a change in P_X has on the quantity of Y demanded is ambiguous: It all depends on what the indifference curve map looks like. It is necessary to analyze the net result of income and substitution effects that (at least in the case of only two goods) work in opposite directions.

For example, let us consider once again the changing quantities chosen of hamburgers and soft drinks as the price of a soft drink falls from $.10 to $.05. We have already discussed the substitution and income effects that such a change will have on the number of soft drinks bought. Similar effects come into play when we examine the change in the number of hamburgers chosen. The substitution effect predicts that fewer hamburgers will be purchased. Since hamburgers are now relatively more expensive (that is, soft drinks are now relatively cheaper) the initial level of utility can be achieved at minimal cost by substituting soft drinks for hamburgers. However, to calculate the total effect on hamburger purchases the income effect of the price change must also be taken into account. As a result of the fall in the price of soft drinks the individual now has a higher real income and may use some of this increased purchasing power to buy more hamburgers. The total effect of the price change on hamburger purchases is therefore ambiguous. This substitution effect works to decrease hamburger purchases, whereas the income effect works to increase such purchases.

Substitutes and Complements

Economists use the terms *substitutes* and *complements* to describe the way individuals view the relationship between two goods. Intuitively, complements are goods that "go together" in the sense that individuals will increase their use of both goods simultaneously. Examples of complements might be coffee and cream, fish and chips, peanut butter and jelly, or brandy and cigars. Substitutes, on the other hand, are goods that may replace one another in consumption. Tea and coffee, hamburgers and hot dogs, or wheat and corn are pairs of goods that may exhibit such a relationship.

Although whether two goods are substitutes or complements is primarily a question of the shape of individuals' indifference curves, some attempts have been made to define such relationships by observing market behavior. Two goods are termed (gross) *complements* if an increase in the price of one causes a decrease in quantity consumed of the other. For example, an increase in the price of coffee might cause not only the quantity of coffee demanded to decline, but also the demand for cream to decrease because of the complementary relationship between cream and coffee. Similarly, coffee and tea would be called (gross) *substitutes* because an increase in the price of coffee might cause the demand for tea to increase as tea replaces coffee in use. In summary:

Definition

Goods X and Y are (gross) *complements* if an increase in the price of X causes less Y to be demanded. They are (gross) *substitutes* if an increase in the price of X causes more Y to be demanded.

The reason the word "gross" appears in those market-related definitions is that the response to a price increase reflects both income and substitution effects. It is only the combined result of the two effects that is observed in the market. Including both income and substitution effects in a definition of substitutes and complements can lead to problems. For example, it is possible for X to be classified as a complement for Y and at the same time for Y to be classified as a substitute for X. This asymmetry has led some economists to favor a definition of substitutes and complements that looks only at the direction of substitution effects. We will not, however, investigate that distinction in this book.[5]

---

[5] For a slightly more extended treatment of this subject, see W. Nicholson, *Microeconomic Theory: Basic Principles and Extensions*, 2d ed. (Hinsdale, Ill.: The Dryden Press, 1978), pp. 108–111. For a complete treatment, see J.R. Hicks, *Value and Capital* (London: Cambridge University Press, 1939), chap. 3 and the mathematical appendix.

Construction of
Individual Demand Curves

We have now completed our discussion of the individual's demand function for good X. We started by writing this relationship as

$$X = D_X (P_X, P_Y, I). \tag{4.8}$$

We have examined how changes in each of the factors P_X, P_Y, and I might affect an individual's decision to purchase good X. The principal purpose of this examination has been to permit us to derive individual demand curves in a rigorous way and to analyze those factors that might cause a demand curve to shift its position. In this section we will proceed to show how a demand curve can be constructed by using the utility maximization hypothesis, and in the next section we will turn to analyzing the reasons why this curve might shift.

An individual's *demand curve* shows the *ceteris paribus* relationship between the quantity demanded of a good (say X) and its price (P_X). It is important to stress the rather strong *ceteris paribus* assumptions that are in effect when we derive such a demand curve. Not only are tastes and "other" factors held constant (as they have been throughout our discussion), but the other parameters in the demand function (that is P_Y and I) are also held constant. Demand curves are therefore a special case of demand functions in which interest centers solely on the relationship between X and P_X.

Figure 4.10 shows the way in which we can construct an individual's demand curve for good X. In 4.10a the individual's indifference curve map is drawn together with three different budget constraints. These budget constraints differ only in that the price of X takes on three different values (P_X', P_X'', and P_X'''). The other parameters that affect the position of the budget constraint (P_Y and I) do not vary in the three budget constraints shown in the figure. In graphic terms, this means that all three constraints have the same Y-intercept (given by I/P_Y). Given the three separate budget constraints, the individual's utility maximizing choices of X are given by X', X'', and X'''. These three choices show that the quantity of X chosen increases as the price of X falls from P_X' to P_X'' to P_X''' on the general presumption that X does not exhibit Giffen's Paradox.

Shape of the Demand Curve

The information from Figure 4.10a can now be used to construct a demand curve, and this is done in 4.10b. Here the price of X is shown on the vertical axis, and the quantity demanded continues to be shown on the horizontal axis. The demand curve (D_X) is downward sloping showing that P_X and X move in opposite directions: When P_X rises the quantity of X demanded falls, and when P_X falls the quantity of X demanded increases. Of course, the precise shape and slope of the demand curve will be determined by the exact size of the income and substitution effects that come

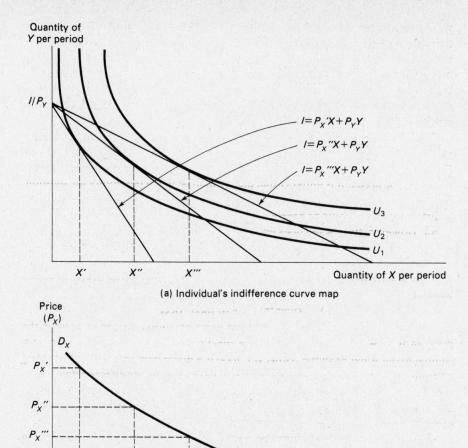

(a) Individual's indifference curve map

(b) Demand curve

Figure 4.10 / Construction of an Individual's Demand Curve

In 4.10a the individual's utility maximizing choices of X and Y are shown for three different prices of X (P_X', P_X'', and P_X'''). In 4.10b this relationship between P_X and X is used to construct the demand curve for X. The demand curve is drawn on the assumption that P_Y and I remain constant as P_X varies.

into play when P_X changes. An individual's demand curve may be either rather flat or quite steeply sloped depending on the nature of his indifference curve map. If X has many close substitutes, the indifference curves will be nearly straight lines (such as those shown in Figure 4.9), and the substitution effect from a change in P_X

will be very large. The quantity of X chosen may change substantially in response to the change in P_X; consequently the demand curve will be relatively flat. For example, consider an individual's demand for one particular brand of gasoline (say, brand X). Since any one brand has many close substitutes, the demand curve for brand X will be relatively flat. A rise in the price of brand X will cause individuals to shift to other brands of gasoline, and the quantity bought of brand X will be reduced significantly.

On the other hand, the individual's demand curve for some goods may be steeply sloped. This might be the case if the good in question had no very good substitutes. For example, consider an individual's demand for water. Because water satisfies many unique needs, it is unlikely that there would be much possibility for substituting other goods for water when the price of water rises. Technically, the individual's indifference curve would be nearly L-shaped, and substitution effects would be very small. However, since water does not make up a large portion of an individual's total expenditures, the income effect induced by the increase in the price of water would not be large. Consequently it is likely that the quantity of water demanded would not respond greatly to changes in its price; that is, the demand curve would be nearly vertical.

As a third possibility, consider the case of food. Because food as a whole has no close substitutes (although individual food items obviously do), an increase in the price of food will not induce important substitution effects. In this sense food is similar to our water example. However, food is a major item in an individual's total expenditures, and an increase in its price will have a significant effect on purchasing power. It is possible, therefore, that the quantity of food purchased may be reduced substantially in response to a change in its price, not because of the substitution effect of this price change but, rather, because of the income effect. Consequently the demand curve for food might be flatter (that is, more price responsive) than might have been anticipated by reference only to substitution effects.

The curve D_X therefore summarizes the *ceteris paribus* relationship between P_X and the quantity of X demanded. Changes in P_X induce income and substitution effects that cause the individual to move *along* his demand curve; conversely, the curve summarizes all there is to know about the simple relationship between P_X and X. On the other hand, if one of the factors (tastes, other things, P_Y, or I) that we have so far been holding constant were to change, the entire curve would shift to a new position. The demand curve remains in a fixed position only so long as the *ceteris paribus* assumption remains in effect. In the next section we will examine some of those factors that might cause a demand curve to shift.

Shifts in an Individual's Demand Curve

When one of the factors being held constant in Figure 4.10 does change, the entire demand curve will shift. Figure 4.11 shows the kinds of shifts that might take place. In 4.11a the effect of an increase in income is shown. On the assumption that X is a normal good, an increase in income causes more X to be demanded *at each price* (for an indifference curve proof see Figure 4.1). Reflecting this effect, the demand curve shifts outward. In 4.11b and c we have recorded two possible effects that an increase in P_Y might have on the demand curve for X. In 4.11b, X and Y are assumed to be gross substitutes (for example, coffee and tea). An increase in P_Y causes the individual to substitute X for Y in his consumption: More X is demanded at each price than was previously. Consequently, the demand curve for X shifts outward. On the other hand, if X and Y were gross complements (coffee and cream), an increase in P_Y would cause the demand curve to shift inward. Because X and Y "go together," less X will be demanded at each price than was previously the case. This shift in the demand curve is shown in Figure 4.11c.

Of course changes in P_Y or I are not the only factors that might cause the position of the demand curve D_X to shift. Changes in any of the other factors we have been holding constant would induce shifts similar to those pictured in Figure 4.11. For example, a sudden warm spell would undoubtedly shift the entire demand curve for soft drinks outward. More drinks would be demanded at each price. Similarly, the fashion for longer hair styles for men had the effect of shifting many individuals' demand curves for haircuts toward the origin. At each price an individual would buy fewer haircuts per year than he would have in the past. Again the effect of a change in some factor other than the price of the good caused the position of the entire demand curve to shift. In the next section we present some quantitative data about the size of such a shift in the demand curve for fish.

It is important that we keep the distinction between the shift in a demand curve and movement along a stationary curve clearly in mind. Changes in P_X lead to movements *along* the demand curve for good X. Changes in any other factor will cause the entire demand curve for X to *shift*. Consequently, if we wished to investigate how a change in the price of steak affects an individual's steak purchases, we would use a single demand curve and study movements along it. On the

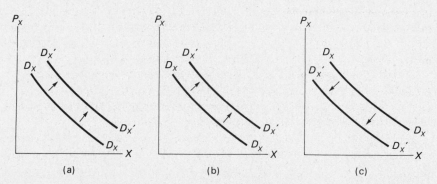

(a)   (b)   (c)

Figure 4.11 / Shifts in an Individual's Demand Curve

In panel (a) the demand curve shifts out because the individual has an increase in income. This causes more X to be demanded at *each* price. In panel (b) the demand curve shifts out because P_Y has increased, and the individual views X and Y as substitutes. In panel (c) the demand curve shifts inward as a result of the increase in P_Y, because X and Y are complements.

other hand, if we wished to know how a change in, say, income affects the quantity of steak purchased, we would have to study the shift in the position of the entire demand curve. Sometimes a movement downward along a stationary demand curve is referred to as an *increase in the quantity demanded*, whereas a shift outward in the entire curve is referred to as an *increase in demand*. It is important to be precise in using those terms; they are not interchangeable.

An Example of Shifts in Demand Curves: Religious Practices and Fish Consumption

Various practices of the Catholic Church require members to abstain from eating meat during certain periods of the year. Because fish is considered to be a good meat substitute, these practices have the effect of increasing the demand for fish during such periods. By using the results of a statistical study of the demand for fish by F. W. Bell, it is possible to show quantitatively the magnitude of such shifts.[6] Table 4.3 reports the estimated shifts in the demand curves in the New England states for four species of fish.

The effects of two religious practices are examined: abstinence from eating meat during Lent; and relaxation of the "meatless Friday" practice in December, 1966. For both examples the shifts in demand curves have been measured in a horizontal direction: that is, the figures report the total change in quantity of fish consumed as a result of the practices (summed over all individuals) holding price constant.[7] We will discuss the results for each practice separately and show how they illustrate more general principles about demand curves.

As Table 4.3 shows, the increase in demand for fish during Lent is substantial. There is clear evidence that during this period individuals substitute fish for meat thereby shifting their demand curves for various species of fish to the right. Such seasonal influences on demand are quite common. Other examples include increases in demand for ice cream and air conditioning during the summer months, turkeys at Thanksgiving, and wedding cakes in June. Since all of those shifts are reasonably predictable, it might be expected that firms would take them into account in planning their production and their inventory holdings.

In December 1966, American Catholic Bishops ended mandatory meatless Fridays and, as Table 4.3 shows, this had the effect of reducing the demand for various species as some individuals substituted meat for fish. Similar unexpected reductions in demand in recent years have been related to health concerns (cranberries, swordfish, and artificially sweetened beverages), political motivations (boycotting table grapes or certain textile manufacturers), or development of

---

[6]F. W. Bell, "The Pope and the Price of Fish," *American Economic Review*, LVIII, No. 5 (December 1968), pp. 1346–50.

[7]The original Bell study reported shifts in the vertical (price) direction and these have been recalculated for our purposes.

superior substitutes (slide rules and mechanical calculators being replaced by electronic calculators). In these cases the shifts were relatively permanent (rather than seasonal) and may have imposed hardships on some producers. In the case of fish, that outcome is ironic since one motivation of the original "meatless Friday" decree, more than one thousand years ago, was as an aid to the fishing industry.

Table 4.3 / Effects of Religious Practices on Fish Consumption in the New England States (shift in quantity demanded in thousands of pounds per month)

Species	Increase in Demand during Lent	Reduction in Demand after December 1966
Yellowtail Flounder	+17.8	−4.4
Large Haddock	+25.3	−7.1
Small Haddock (Scrod)	+13.3	−0.6
Cod	+29.0	−4.5

Source: F. W. Bell, "The Pope and the Price of Fish," *American Economic Review*, LVIII, No. 5 (December 1968), pp. 1346–50.

Summary

In this chapter we used our model of utility maximization to examine how individuals will react to changes in income or prices. We presented four major conclusions about the determinants of the demand for a good:

1. When income increases the demand for a good will increase unless that good is inferior;

2. A change in the price of a good will create substitution and income effects that reflect changes in consumption choices. Except in the unlikely case of Giffen's Paradox, a reduction in a good's price will cause more of it to be demanded and an increase in price will cause less of the good to be demanded;

3. A change in the price of some other good will affect the demand for a good. If two goods are complements, an increase in the price of one will reduce the demand for the other. If the goods are substitutes an increase in the price of one will increase the demand for the other;

4. The demand for a good is affected by a number of other influences (preferences, seasonality, information, and so forth). Although they may be of major significance in the real world, these influences are usually held constant under the *ceteris paribus* assumption in theoretical analysis.

Probably the most important tool developed in this chapter was the individual's demand curve, which shows the relationship between the quantity demanded of a product and its price (when all other influences are held constant). Demand curves are usually drawn downward sloping (in view of point 2 above) and their position would shift if one of the factors held constant (income, other prices, preferences) were to change. In the next chapter we will show how individuals' demand curves can be "added up" to yield a market demand curve.

Suggested Readings

Friedman, M., "The Marshallian Demand Curve," in *Essays in Positive Economics* (Chicago: University of Chicago Press, 1953).

Henderson, J. M., and R. E. Quandt, *Microeconomic Theory*, 2d ed. (New York: McGraw-Hill, Inc., 1971), chap. 2.

Hicks, J. R., *A Revision of Demand Theory* (Oxford: Clarendon Press, 1956).

Houthakker, H. S., "Revealed Preference and the Utility Function," *Economica* n.s.17 (May 1950), pp. 159–174.

Mishan, E. J., "Theories of Consumer Behavior: A Cynical View," *Economica* n.s.28 (February 1961), pp. 1–11.

Samuelson, P. A., "Consumption Theory in Terms of Revealed Preference," *Economica* n.s. 15 (November 1948), pp. 243–253.

———— *Foundations of Economic Analysis* (Cambridge, Mass.: Harvard University Press, 1948), chap. 5.

Stigler, G., *The Theory of Price*, 3d ed. (New York: Crowell-Collier and Macmillan, Inc., 1966).

Winch, D. M., "The Separation of Income and Substitution Effects," *Western Economic Journal* 1 (Summer 1963), pp. 172–190.

Problems

4.1

An indifference map is "vertically parallel" if the marginal rate of substitution is constant for every fixed level of X_1. Graphically this says that a vertical line cuts all indifference curves at points of equal slope (see Figure A).

a) What implications does this assumption have for individuals' behavior? Show that price and quantity must move in opposite directions.

b) Show that an indifference map is both "vertically parallel" and "horizontally parallel" (analogously defined) if and only if X_1 and X_2 are perfect substitutes (that is, the *MRS* is constant for all X_1 and X_2).

4.2

An indifference map is *homothetic* if any straight line through the origin cuts all indifference curves at points of equal slope: The *MRS* depends on the ratio X_2/X_1 (see Figure B).

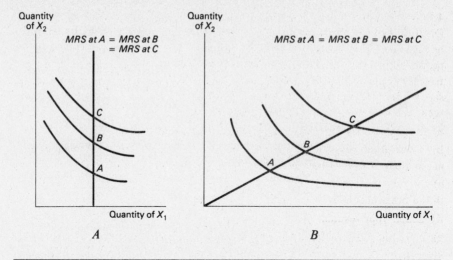

Indifference Maps for Problems 4.1 and 4.2

a) Prove that the Engel curves for a homothetic indifference map are straight lines.

b) Prove that if an individual's tastes can be represented by a homothetic indifference map, price and quantity must move in opposite directions.

4.3
Mr. Wright, a clothing salesman, is forced to spend a fixed amount of his income on clothing. Show that his utility level is lower than if he could freely allocate his income.

4.4
Suppose an individual is initially maximizing utility given P_X, P_Y, and I. Now assume that the budget constraint parameters change to P_X', P_Y', and I'. *Conceptually*, how might you define a level of income, I^*, such that I^* has as much "real" purchasing power when prices P_X' and P_Y' prevail as did I when the prices were P_X and P_Y? Is it legitimate now to compare I^* to I' to determine whether real income has improved?

4.5
Pete Moss buys 100 units of fertilizer and 80 units of grass seed along with quantities of other goods. Suppose the price of fertilizer rises by 40¢ per unit and the price of grass seed drops by 50¢ per unit; other prices and Pete's income remain unchanged. Will Pete buy more, less, or the same amount of fertilizer? Explain.

4.6
Show that if there are only two goods (X and Y) to choose from, both cannot be inferior goods.

4.7

David N. gets $3.00 per month as an allowance to spend any way he pleases. Since he only likes peanut butter and jelly sandwiches, he spends the entire amount on peanut butter (at $.05 per ounce) and jelly (at $.10 per ounce). Bread is provided free of charge by a concerned neighbor. David is a particular eater and makes his sandwiches with exactly 1 oz. of jelly and 2 oz. of peanut butter. He is set in his ways and will never change these proportions.

a) How much peanut butter and jelly will be bought with the $3.00?

b) Suppose the price of jelly were to rise to $.15 per ounce, how much of each commodity would be bought?

c) By how much should David's allowance be increased to compensate for the rise in the price of jelly?

d) Graph your results.

e) In what sense does this problem only involve a single commodity, peanut butter and jelly sandwiches? Graph the demand curve for this single commodity.

Chapter 5   Market Demand

Introduction

In Chapter 4 we demonstrated the way in which an individual's demand curve for a good can be constructed from an indifference curve map. There we showed that this demand curve will generally be downward sloping and that the position of the curve will shift when various factors change. In this chapter we will be primarily concerned with "adding-up" individual demand curves in order to derive a market demand curve. These market demand curves will then reflect the actions of many individuals and will permit us to analyze how these actions affect market price. We will also be concerned with defining a few means by which market demand curves can be described. We will introduce the concept of *elasticity*, and we will show why this concept provides a convenient way for recording the way in which the quantity of a good demanded changes in response to changes in the determinants of this demand. In the final section of the chapter we will review some empirical evidence relating to real-world demand curves, and we will show how this evidence can be used to predict changes in individuals' consumption patterns.

Market Demand Curves

For ease of exposition, let us assume that there are only two individuals in society. Let the first person's demand for X be given as

$$X_1 = D_X{}^1 (P_X, P_Y, I_1) \tag{5.1}$$

and the second person's demand for X be given as

$$X_2 = D_X{}^2 (P_X, P_Y, I_2) \tag{5.2}$$

Although equations 5.1 and 5.2 are just generalizations of equation 4.2a to allow for two individuals, there are two important features of these functions that we should emphasize. First, both individuals are assumed to face the same prices (P_X and P_Y). Each person is a price-taker who must accept the prices prevailing in the market. Second, each person's demand depends on his or her own income. Each individual is bound by a budget constraint that determines how much can be bought.

The total demand for X is simply the sum of the amounts demanded by the two individuals. Obviously this market demand will depend on P_X, P_Y, I_1, and I_2. Mathematically,

$$\text{total } X = X = X_1 + X_2 = D_X{}^1 (P_X, P_Y, I_1) + D_X{}^2 (P_X, P_Y, I_2) \tag{5.3}$$

$$\text{total } X = MD_X (P_X, P_Y, I_1, I_2) \tag{5.4}$$

where the function MD_X represents the market demand for good X. We can now construct the *market demand curve* for X in a way similar to the method we use to derive individual demand curves—by holding P_Y, I_1, and I_2 fixed and graphing the relationship between X and P_X. If we assume that each person's demand curve for X is downward sloping, the market demand curve also will be: A decrease in price will increase the total quantity demanded in the market.

Construction of the Market Demand Curve

Figure 5.1 shows the construction of the market demand curve for X. For each price, the point on the market demand curve is found by summing the quantities demanded by each individual. For example, at a price of $P_X{}^*$ individual 1 demands $X_1{}^*$ and individual 2 demands $X_2{}^*$. The total quantity demanded in the market at $P_X{}^*$ is therefore the sum of these two amounts: $X^* = X_1{}^* + X_2{}^*$. Consequently the point X^*, $P_X{}^*$ is one point on the market demand curve MD_X. The other points on the curve are derived in a similar way. The market curve is simply the "horizontal sum" of each individual's demand curve.

Shifts in the Market Demand Curve

The market demand curve, then, summarizes the *ceteris paribus* relationship between X and P_X. If the factors underlying the construction of this curve do not change, the position of the curve will remain fixed. If we are to analyze the reasons why a market demand curve might shift, we must first examine how individual demand curves shift and then see how the horizontal summation of these new

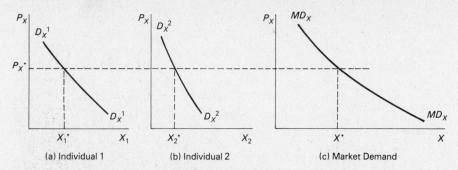

(a) Individual 1   (b) Individual 2   (c) Market Demand

**Figure 5.1 / Construction of a Market
Demand Curve from Individual Demand Curves**

A market demand curve is the horizontal sum of each individual's demand curve. At each price the quantity demanded in the market is the sum of the amounts each individual demands. For example, at P_X^* the demand in the market is $X_1^* + X_2^* = X^*$.

demand curves compares to the old market demand. In some cases the direction in which the market demand curve will shift is reasonably unambiguous. For example, if both individuals' incomes increase and if both regard X as a normal good, then each person's demand curve would shift outward, and the market demand curve would also shift outward. At each price more would be demanded in the market because each person's income had increased. This situation is illustrated in Figure 5.2.

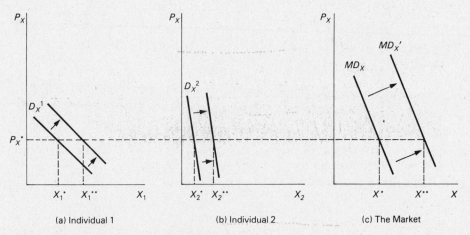

(a) Individual 1   (b) Individual 2   (c) The Market

**Figure 5.2 / Increases in Each Individual's
Income Causes the Market Demand Curve to Shift Outward**

An increase in income for each individual causes each demand curve for X to shift out (assuming X is a normal good). For example, at P_X^* individual 1 now demands X_1^{**} instead of X_1^*. Consequently the market demand curve shifts out to MD_X'. At P_X^* previously X^* was demanded, now X^{**} ($= X_1^{**} + X_2^{**}$) is demanded.

Other cases may, however, be more complex. If some individuals' demand curves shift outward while others' shift inward, the resultant effect on market demand will be ambiguous. For example, suppose that I_1 increases and I_2 decreases. The total effect on the location of the market demand curve will then depend on the relative shifts that these income changes induce in individuals' demand functions. It is possible that the total demand curve could shift inward even though the increase in I_1 exceeded the decrease in I_2 if the reaction of the second person's demand response to income was great and the first person's was small. The effect of changes in total income on market demand will therefore depend greatly on how the income changes are distributed among individuals.

Figure 5.3 illustrates one possible situation in which the market demand curve shifts to a different position because of the way in which income gains are distributed among individuals. Here, because individual 2's curve shifts inward to a greater extent than individual 1's shifts outward, the net result of the income changes is to shift the market demand curve inward to MD_X'. This result could have easily been reversed by a rather different distribution of the income changes. If personal income in the United States were to rise, the implications of this rise for the demand curve for pizza would depend greatly on whether the income gains went to people who love pizza or to people who never touch it.

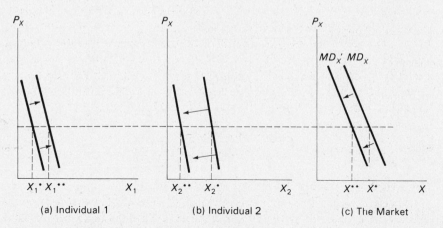

(a) Individual 1   (b) Individual 2   (c) The Market

Figure 5.3 / Effect of Income Changes on Market Demand Will depend on How These Changes Are Distributed

It is assumed here that individual 1's income has increased, whereas 2's has decreased. The net result of these particular changes is to shift the market demand curve inward to MD_X'.

Similar comments apply when discussing the effect that a change in the price of some other good (Y) will have on the market demand for X. If P_Y rises, for example, the market demand for X would shift outward if X and Y are regarded by "most" people as being substitutes. On the other hand, an increase in P_Y will cause the market demand curve for X to shift inward if most people regard the two goods as complements.

A Word On Notation

Often in this book we will be looking only at one market. In order to simplify the notation we will use the letter Q to refer to the quantity of the particular good demanded in this market, and we will use P to denote its price. As always, when we draw a demand curve in the Q-P plane, the *ceteris paribus* assumption is in effect. If some outside factor should change, the demand curve would probably shift to a new location.

Concept of Elasticity

Economists frequently wish to summarize the way in which changes in one variable, say A, affect some other variable, say B. For example, an economist might be interested in measuring how the change in the price of a good affects the quantity demanded or how a change in income affects total expenditures. One problem that arises in attempting to develop a useful definition of such effects is that consumption goods are measured in different units. For example, steak is typically sold *per pound* whereas oranges are sold *per dozen*. We might know (from historical data, say) that a \$.10 per pound rise in the price of steak causes consumption to fall by 2 pounds per week and that a \$.10 per dozen rise in the price of oranges causes orange purchases to decrease by ½ dozen per week. But, because the commodities are measured in different units, we have no way of comparing these two facts about demand to determine which item is more price responsive. As a solution to this problem, economists have developed the concept of *elasticity*. In general, the elasticity of variable B with respect to variable A (denoted by $E_{B,A}$) is defined as the percentage change in B brought about by a 1 percent change in A. Using the notation Δ to represent "change in," this definition can be stated precisely as

$$E_{B,A} = \frac{\text{percent change in } B}{\text{percent change in } A} = \frac{\Delta B/B}{\Delta A/A} \qquad [5.5]$$

The reason this concept is useful is that it is unit-free: It compares only one percentage to another. In our orange-steak example, we might know that a 1 percent change in the price of steak leads to a 2 percent change in the quantity bought, whereas a 1 percent change in the price of oranges leads to a 1 percent change in the quantity bought. Consequently we could conclude that steak purchases were more responsive to price. The fact that steak and oranges are measured in different units no longer presents a problem because we are dealing only in percentage changes that are unit free.

Price Elasticity of Demand

Although we will come across many different applications of the concept of elasticity in this book, probably the most important is that of the *price elasticity of demand*. Changes in the price of a good (*P*) will lead to changes in the quantity purchased (*Q*), and the price elasticity of demand is intended to measure this response. Applying formula 5.5, the price elasticity of demand would be defined as:

Definition

The price elasticity of demand ($E_{Q,P}$) is the percentage change in the quantity of a good demanded induced by a 1 percent change in its price. Mathematically:

$$E_{Q,P} = \frac{\text{percent change in } Q}{\text{percent change in } P} = \frac{\Delta Q/Q}{\Delta P/P} \qquad [5.6]$$

This elasticity, then, records how *Q* changes (in percentage terms) in response to a percentage change in *P*. Since *P* and *Q* move in opposite directions (except in the case of Giffen's Paradox), $E_{Q,P}$ will usually be negative.[1] For example, a value of $E_{Q,P}$ of −1 would mean that a 1 percent rise in price leads to a 1 percent decline in quantity, whereas a value of $E_{Q,P}$ of −2 would record the fact that a 1 percent rise in price causes quantity to decline by 2 percent.

Values of the Price Elasticity of Demand

A distinction is often made among values of $E_{Q,P}$ that are less than, equal to, or greater than −1. Specifically, the terminology used is as shown in Table 5.1. For an elastic curve, a price increase is met by a more than proportionate quantity decrease. For a unit elastic curve, the price increase and the quantity decrease are of identical proportional magnitudes. For an inelastic curve, price increases proportionally more than quantity decreases. If a curve is elastic, price therefore affects quantity "a lot"; if a curve is inelastic, price does not have as much of an effect on quantity demanded. We might classify goods by their elasticities of demand. For example, the quantity of medical services demanded is undoubtedly very inelastic. The

Table 5.1 / Terminology for a Curve to Distinguish the Three Values of $E_{Q,P}$

Value of $E_{Q,P}$ at a Point on Demand Curve	Terminology of Curve at this Point
$E_{Q,P} < -1$	Elastic
$E_{Q,P} = -1$	Unit Elastic
$E_{Q,P} > -1$	Inelastic

[1] Sometimes the elasticity of demand is defined as the absolute value of the definition in equation 5.6. Consequently, under this alternative definition, elasticity is never negative; curves are classified as elastic, unit elastic or inelastic depending on whether $E_{Q,P}$ is greater than, equal to, or less than 1. The reader should recognize this distinction in examining empirical work, since there is no consistent usage in economic literature.

market demand curve may be almost vertical in this case, indicating that the quantity demanded is not responsive to price. On the other hand, it is likely that price changes will have a great effect on the quantity of candy bought (the demand is elastic). Here the market demand curve would be relatively flat. If market price were to change even slightly the quantity demanded would change significantly.

The price elasticity of demand therefore provides a convenient, unit-free way of comparing the responsiveness of the quantity of a good demanded to changes in its price. By referring back to our discussion of income and substitution effects in Chapter 4, we can provide some theoretical basis for judging what the size of the demand elasticity for particular goods might be. Goods with many close substitutes (particular brands of cereal, types of small cars, brands of electronic calculators, and so on) exhibit large substitution effects in response to a price change. For such goods there is the presumption that demand will be relatively elastic ($E_{Q,P} < -1$). On the other hand, goods for which there are few substitutes (water, insulin, salt) have small substitution effects; it is likely that demand for such goods will be inelastic with respect to price changes ($E_{Q,P} > -1$). Of course, as we mentioned previously, price changes also induce income effects, and we must consider these in any complete assessment of the likely size of demand elasticities. Although food as a whole, for example, has few if any substitutes, income effects associated with changes in the price of food will be large. Demand for food may not, therefore, be so price-inelastic as we might presume on the basis of substitution effects alone.

Price Elasticity and Total Expenditures

The price elasticity of demand can be used to record how total expenditures on a good change in response to a price change. Total expenditures on a good are simply the product of the price of the product (P) times the quantity purchased (Q). If demand is elastic ($E_{Q,P} < -1$) a price decline will cause total expenditures to increase, since the percentage decline in price is more than counterbalanced by the increase in quantity it causes. For example, suppose individuals are currently buying 1 million automobiles at $2,000 each. Consequently total expenditures on automobiles amount to $2 billion. Suppose also that the elasticity of demand for automobiiles is -2.0. Now, if the price declines to $1,800 (a 10 percent drop) the quantity purchased would rise to 1.2 million cars (a 20 percent increase). Total expenditures would now be $2.16 billion. Because demand is elastic, a price decline has caused total expenditures to increase. This argument can be easily reversed to show that if demand is elastic a price *rise* will cause total expenditures to *fall*.

If demand is unit elastic ($E_{Q,P} = -1$) total expenditures stay constant whenever prices change. A movement of P in one direction causes an exactly opposite proportional movement in Q, and the product $P \cdot Q$ stays fixed. Finally, when demand is inelastic ($E_{Q,P} > -1$), a price reduction will cause total expenditures to fall. There is not sufficient additional demand generated by the price fall to keep the product of $P \cdot Q$ from falling. A price rise in an inelastic situation does not cause a very large reduction in quantity, and total revenues will increase. For example, suppose individuals buy 100 million bushels of wheat per year at a price of $3.00 per bushel. Total expenditures on wheat therefore amount to $300 million. Suppose also that the price elasticity of demand for wheat is −0.5 (demand is inelastic). If the price of wheat rose to $3.60 per bushel (a 20 percent increase) quantity demanded would fall by 10 percent (to 90 million bushels). The result of these actions would be to increase total expenditures on wheat to $324 million. Because the quantity of wheat demanded is not very responsive to changes in price, total revenues are increased by a price rise. A similar argument could be used to show that, in the inelastic case, total revenues are reduced by a fall in price. This result for inelastic, demanded products explains what is sometimes called the "paradox of agriculture." When weather is bad, farm prices are high and total expenditures on farm products (and hence farm incomes) are high. Bad weather (in moderation) is therefore good for farmers. Good weather, on the other hand, results in lower prices and lower total expenditures. For farmers good weather can be a disaster.

Because we will in later chapters make use of these relationships between price elasticity and total expenditures, they are summarized in Table 5.2. The reader should think through the logic of each entry in the table to obtain a working knowledge of the elasticity concept.

Table 5.2 / Relationship Between Price Changes and Changes in Total Expenditure

If Demand Is	In Response to an Increase in Price PQ Will	In Response to a Decrease in Price, PQ Will
Elastic	Fall	Rise
Unit Elastic	Not change	Not change
Inelastic	Rise	Fall

Income Elasticity of Demand

Another type of elasticity frequently encountered in the study of consumption is the *income elasticity of demand* ($E_{Q,I}$). This concept records the relationship between income changes and quantity changes and is another application of the general definition given in equation 5.5.

Definition

The income elasticity of demand for a good is the percentage change in the quantity of the good consumed in response to a 1 percent increase in income. Mathematically:

$$E_{Q,I} = \frac{\text{percent change in quantity}}{\text{percent change in income}} = \frac{\Delta Q/Q}{\Delta I/I}$$

[5.5]

For a normal good, $E_{Q,I}$ is positive since increases in income lead to increases in purchases of the good. For an inferior good, on the other hand, $E_{Q,I}$ would be negative, implying that income increases lead to quantity decreases. Among normal goods there is considerable interest about whether $E_{Q,I}$ is greater than or less than 1. Goods for which $E_{Q,I} > 1$ might be called luxury goods in the sense that purchases of these goods increase more rapidly than income. For example, if the income elasticity of demand for automobiles is 2.0, then a 10 percent rise in income will lead to a 20 percent increase in automobile purchases. On the other hand, a good such as food probably has an income elasticity of less than 1. If the income elasticity of demand for food were 0.5, then a 10 percent rise in income would result in only a 5 percent increase in food purchases. [2] Considerable research has been undertaken to determine the actual values of income elasticities for various items, and the results of some of these studies are reported in the final section of this chapter.

Forms of Demand Curves

A straight-line demand curve is certainly the easiest to draw, and it is the type that appears most frequently in textbook graphs. In a sense this is unfortunate because the behavior implied by a straight line demand curve seems unrealistic. Along a straight line $\Delta Q/\Delta P$ is constant. This means that a price change from, say, \$.25 to \$.50 (a doubling of price) will have the same effect on Q as a change from \$5.00 to \$5.25 (an increase of 5 percent). Behavior of this type would seem unreasonable on the basis of the information we have about market reactions.

Linear Demand Curves and Elasticity

This problem with straight-line demand curves can be rephrased to state that the price elasticity of demand ($E_{Q,P}$) is not constant along a straight line demand curve. At low price levels demand is inelastic; at high price levels it is elastic.

We can observe this result geometrically. Figure 5.4 illustrates a straight-line demand curve. We can investigate the elasticity of this curve by asking what happens to total expenditures as P falls. At a very high price, a fall in P will increase total expenditures ($P \cdot Q$). The size of the $P \cdot Q$ rectangle increases as price moves downward from the P-intercept of the demand curve in Figure 5.4. Consequently, from our previous discussion, we know that the demand curve is elastic in its upper

---

[2] It seems obvious that not every good can have an income elasticity greater than 1. Individuals cannot, in total, increase their expenditures by more than their incomes rise. In general, it can be shown that goods for which $E_{Q,I} > 1$ must be roughly balanced by those for which $E_{Q,I} < 1$.

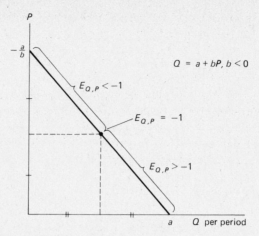

**Figure 5.4 / Elasticity of Demand
Varies Along a Straight-line Demand Curve**

A straight-line demand curve may be inappropriate for empirical work because it implies individual behavior in reaction to price changes that is difficult to believe.

ranges. The rectangle $P \cdot Q$ reaches its maximum size at a price midway between 0 and the intercept on the vertical axis. This is a familiar result from plane geometry, and we will not prove it explicitly here. For price declines below this midpoint, the total revenue rectangle actually decreases in size. Demand is therefore inelastic in the lower section of the demand curve.

Constant Elasticity Curves

Economists generally feel that it may be more reasonable to deal with demand curves that have a constant elasticity along their entire length. This assumes that individuals respond to proportionate rather than absolute changes in price. A curve that does have a constant elasticity along its entire length is

$$Q = aP^b \qquad [5.8]$$

where $b < 0$ and $P \neq 0$.

Another useful way of writing this functional relationship between P and Q is[3]

$$\log Q = \log a + b \log P \qquad [5.9]$$

---

[3]The term "log" used in equation 5.9 refers to the mathematical concept of logarithms usually discussed in high school algebra. Equations that are linear in logarithms have the same elasticities along their entire length whereas, as we have shown, simple linear equations do not.

This curve is graphed in Figure 5.5 The curve resembles a hyperbola and never meets either the P or Q axes. Along the curve

$$E_{Q,P} = b \qquad\qquad [5.10]$$

That is, the elasticity is simply given by the exponent of P and does not vary. For example, if $b = -1.5$, then a 1 percent rise in price is always met by a 1.5 percent fall in quantity demanded. Although proving that equation 5.10 is generally true does require some use of mathematics,[4] it is easy to see that it holds for the simple case $b = -1$. If $b = -1$, then the demand curve is

$$Q = aP^{-1} \text{ or } P \cdot Q = a \qquad\qquad [5.11]$$

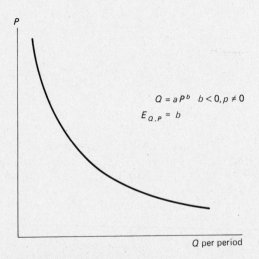

$$Q = aP^b \quad b < 0, p \neq 0$$
$$E_{Q,P} = b$$

Q per period

Figure 5.5 / Constant Elasticity Demand Curve

A curve of this mathematical form (or, equivalently, one that is linear in the logarithms of P and Q) exhibits a constant elasticity of demand along its entire length. This feature may make such curves more suitable for empirical work since demand functions of this form seem to fit historical data rather well.

But 5.11 just says that the product of $P \cdot Q$ remains constant along the demand curve. Our previous discussion of total expenditures showed that in that case $E_{Q,P} = -1$, and that is what we set out to show.

Ultimately the choice of functional forms for a demand curve cannot be made on purely theoretical grounds. Usually the only two candidates are the linear curve and the constant elasticity curve. Both of these are easy to work with, and frequently the

---

[4]To see that this function does have constant elasticity requires some simple calculus. First, in calculus notation, $E_{Q,P}$ is defined as $dQ/dP \cdot P/Q$. Consequently, if $Q = aP^b$, then $E_{Q,P} = baP^{b-1} \cdot P/Q = baP^b/aP^b = b$.

one that "best fits" the data is chosen. There may be some slight preference for the constant elasticity curve because it does exhibit somewhat more desirable theoretical properties, but for relatively small variations in P and Q, the differences between the two curves do not seem to be great.

Empirical Studies of Demand: Some Selected Elasticities

Economists have for many years been interested in studying the demand for various goods. Some of the earliest studies looked at the expenditure patterns of a small sample of families and attempted to generalize from those empirical regularities that were observed.[5] Probably the most widely quoted result of those early studies was Engel's Law (see Chapter 4). This law stated that the percentage of income families spent on food declined as families with increasingly higher incomes were examined. The conclusion drawn was that the income elasticity of the demand for food, although positive, was considerably less than 1.[6]

Estimating Demand Curves

More recent studies have examined a wide variety of goods and have attempted to estimate both income and price elasticities. Although it is not possible for us to discuss here the statistical techniques used in such studies, it should be useful to suggest in an intuitive way how economists have proceeded. The first important problem faced in any empirical investigation is how to implement the *ceteris paribus* assumption. In examining the relationship between the price of a good and the quantity demanded, for example, our theory requires that we hold income, other prices, and all other factors constant. Otherwise, if income and other prices are not held constant, observed combinations of P and Q will lie on many different demand curves. Conceptually it is possible to envision finding several individuals identical in every respect except that each faces a different price for the single good in question. We could then plot the price each individual faces together with the quantity demanded at this price on a graph such as that shown in Figure 5.6. If we

---

[5]For an interesting survey of some of the early empirical work in demand analysis see George J. Stigler, "The Early History of Empirical Studies of Consumer Behavior," *Journal of Political Economy* (April 1954), pp. 95–113.

[6]There is an important leap in logic here that should be recognized. Remember that demand theory is developed by observing how a single individual reacts to differing budget constraints. On the other hand, most empirical studies look at different individuals at one point of time, each faced by a different budget constraint. To draw inferences about one individual's behavior from such a cross-section requires the assumption that, in some sense, rich individuals are "just like" poor ones except that, at the time of the survey, they have more income. Many controversies have arisen in economics over how results of cross-section studies should be interpreted and what they in fact show about individual economic behavior.

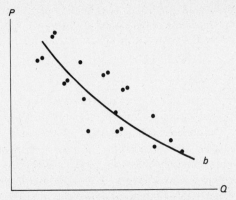

Figure 5.6 / Fitting a Demand Curve to Empirical Observations

The points in Figure 5.6 show observed combinations of P and Q. It is important that these points be observed while holding constant the other factors that affect the demand for Q. The curve shown is a constant elasticity curve of the form $Q = aP^b$. This curve seems to fit the data "reasonably well." The parameter b provides an estimate of the price elasticity of demand.

were careful to assure that our individuals were in fact identical, the points in Figure 5.6 would indeed reflect the *ceteris paribus* influence of price on quantity.

Of course, it would be impossible for us to impose the *ceteris paribus* principle in this way in practice. Identifying a group of individuals identical in every respect but one is impossible. It may be possible in the experimental sciences to isolate such a single factor, but economists must rely on the real world for their data. Consequently, they have instead adopted statistical techniques for imposing the *ceteris paribus* assumption. The most widely used technique is "multiple regression analysis";[7] while we will not examine this technique here, it is the technique that was used to estimate all of the elasticities we will discuss below.

Once the problem of dealing with the *ceteris paribus* assumption has been resolved, there remains the issue of how to find a curve that "fits" the data points fairly well. Since it appears that a large number of possible curves could be used to represent the points in Figure 5.6, we must develop some criteria for choosing which curve is the best. Again this is a statistical problem that we cannot investigate in detail here. Usually the choice made will depend on which form of curve best fits the data (that is, comes closest to the observed points) and on which curve seems most intuitively plausible. For example, in Figure 5.6 a constant elasticity curve (of the form $Q = aP^b$) is drawn through the observed P,Q points. Because, as was discussed previously, such a curve makes sense from a behavioral point of view and because, as is shown in the figure, the curve fits the data reasonably well, this curve

---

[7]Multiple regression analysis, instead of looking only at the simple relationship $Q = a + bP$, attempts to estimate a relationship of the form $Q = a + bP + cI + dP' +$ other terms. Once this relationship is estimated, all the terms other than P can be held constant while the partial relationship between Q and P is examined. This is precisely what is required by the *ceteris paribus* assumption.

would be acceptable as an estimate of the demand curve. The curve provides an estimate (*b*) of the price of the elasticity of demand.

Some Elasticity Estimates

Table 5.3 lists a few income and price elasticities of demand that economists have estimated. Although these estimates come from a variety of sources, they do exhibit certain similarities. The income elasticities for "necessities" (food and medical services) are considerably below those for "luxuries" (automobiles). This is in accord with *a priori* expectations about the way in which the purchases of these types of goods respond to income changes. A second observation is that most of the price elasticities are fairly low (although, as we expected, they are all negative). Price changes do not induce substantial proportional changes in quantities.

Interestingly, the demand for electricity is responsive to changes in price and that may explain the slowdown in the growth of electricity demand in the mid-1970s

Table 5.3 / Representative Income and Price Elasticities

Item	Income Elasticity	Price Elasticity
Food	0.28	−0.21
Medical Services	0.22	−0.20
Automobiles	3.00	−1.20
Housing		
Rental	1.00	−0.18
Owner Occupied	1.20	−1.20
Gasoline	1.06	−0.54
Electricity	0.61	−1.14
Giving to charity	0.70	−1.29
Beer	0.93	−1.13
Marijuana	0	−1.50

Source: Food—H. Wold and L. Jureen, *Demand Analysis* (New York: John Wiley & Sons, Inc., 1953), p. 203. Medical Services—income elasticity from R. Andersen and L. Benham, "Factors Affecting the Relationship Between Family Income and Medical Care Consumption"; price elasticity from G. Rosenthal, "Price Elasticity of Demand for Short-Term General Hospital Services"; both in *Empirical Studies in Health Economics*, ed. Herbert Klarman (Baltimore: Johns Hopkins Press, 1970). Automobiles—Gregory C. Chow, *Demand for Automobiles in the United States* (Amsterdam: North-Holland Publishing Co., 1957). Housing—income elasticities from F. deLeeuw, "The Demand for Housing," *Review of Economics and Statistics* (February 1971); price elasticities from H.S. Houthakker and L.D. Taylor, *Consumer Demand in the United States* (Cambridge, Mass.: Harvard University Press, 1970), pp. 166–167. Gasoline—Data Resources, Inc., "A Study of the Quarterly Demand for Gasoline." A Study Prepared for the Council on Environmental Quality, December 1973. Electricity—R.F. Halvorsen. "Residential Demand for Electricity," unpublished Ph.D. dissertation, Harvard University, December 1972. Giving to charity—M. Feldstein and A. Taylor, "The Income Tax and Charitable Contributions," *Econometrica* 44, No. 6 (November 1976), pp. 1201–1222 Beer—T.F. Hogarty and K.G. Elsinger, "The Demand for Beer," *Review of Economics and Statistics* 54, No. 2 (May 1972), pp. 195–198. Marijuana–T.C. Misket and F. Vakil, "Some Estimates of Price and Expenditure Elasticities among UCLA Students," *Review of Economics and Statistics* 54, No. 4 (November 1972), pp. 474–475.

when price rose sharply. Similarly, charitable contributions seem to respond to the net cost of making them, and this indicates that tax policy favoring such contributions may have a substantial effect on prompting individuals to give. On the other hand, the demand for gasoline is not very responsive to price changes, indicating that it would take relatively large increases in prices to restrict consumption. A 50 percent increase in the price of gasoline (perhaps brought about by an excise tax such as that considered in Chapter 4) would reduce purchases only by about 27 percent $[= 0.5 \cdot E_{Q,P} = 0.5 \cdot (-0.54)]$.

Applications of Elasticity Estimates

Of course, the data in Table 5.3 are not the final word on income and price elasticities. As better data and more sophisticated estimation techniques are developed, different (and hopefully better) estimates will be made. Such estimates will provide not only a better understanding of consumer behavior, but also the information necessary to predict the results of public policies. We shall examine three such issues: (1) National Health Insurance; (2) the effects of income tax rebates; and (3) Federal tax benefits associated with home ownership.

National Health Insurance

Most countries have some type of national health insurance program and a number of different plans have been proposed for the United States. A major issue in predicting what the cost of various alternative plans will be concerns how individuals will react to being covered by medical insurance. Because insurance lowers the out-of-pocket cost that any demander of medical service must pay, there is the expectation that national health insurance would increase the demand for medical care. The empirical question is how large that increase will be. To answer this question requires knowledge of the price elasticity of demand for medical care. The estimate provided in Table 5.3 suggests that this elasticity is relatively low $(-.20)$, but even this low elasticity implies a large increase in demand if insurance reduces out-of-pocket prices substantially (perhaps even to zero). Consequently, many health insurance proposals contain cost-sharing provisions (such as requiring patients to pay 20 percent of costs) that moderate their price-reducing features. In addition, many plans exclude from coverage those medical services known to have relatively elastic demands (dentistry and psychiatric care). Price elasticity estimates have therefore, at least implicitly, played a major role in shaping health insurance legislation.

Income Tax Rebates

Temporary income tax rebates have been used on a number of occasions in the United States to provide a stimulus to the economy. One way of assessing the possible effects of these rebates on product markets is by using estimates of the income elasticities of various goods (since tax rebates increase spendable income). For example, the estimates in Table 5.3 suggest that tax rebates will have relatively major impacts on the demand for automobiles, housing, gasoline, and even beer. On the other hand, demands for food and medical service would be only slightly affected. For example, if a tax rebate increased disposable incomes by ½ of 1 percent ($50 for a family with a $10,000 income), the estimates imply that automobile purchases would increase by 1.5 percent (= ½ × 3.0) whereas food purchases would increase only by about 0.15 percent (= ½ × 0.3). Of course, for such a policy one would want to use a somewhat more sophisticated analysis than this example employs. It would be particularly important to take account of both how the tax rebate is distributed among families of different types, and the possibility that individuals may respond differently to temporary tax rebates than to changes in their normal income patterns.

Federal Tax Benefits to Homeowners

As a final example of using elasticity estimates, suppose we wished to know how current federal tax benefits to individuals living in their own homes affect the demand for owner-occupied housing. Federal tax policy does make it more advantageous to own rather than rent housing because an owner can deduct mortgage payments and property taxes from his or her taxable income whereas a renter (who presumably pays these same costs to his or her landlord) cannot. There is a benefit to homeowners to the extent that mortgage payments and property taxes make up the total costs of owning or renting. Most authors estimate that these two costs in fact make up about 70 percent of total gross rents. Consequently it is argued that homeowners are permitted by law to deduct 70 percent of true "rental" costs from their income before they pay taxes whereas renters are not able to do so. The value of this benefit will, of course, depend on the income tax rate that particular families pay. If, for example, a home-owning family pays 20 percent of its income in federal taxes then essentially the government pays 14 percent of true rental costs (= 70 percent deduction times 20 percent tax rate). The deductibility of mortgage payments and property taxes causes the government to be subsidizing the price of an owner's house to the extent of 14 percent. The effective price is 14 percent lower than it would be in the absence of preferential treatment. Of course, this subsidy may or may not be in some sense desirable from the viewpoint of national policy, but the effect on the demand for housing is clear cut: individuals will respond to the lower price by demanding more owner-occupied housing. In fact we can use the price elasticity for housing reported in Table 5.3 (there it is given as −1.20) to estimate that the 14 percent reduction in price will lead to approximately a 17 percent (= 14 percent times 1.20) increase in the quantity of owner-occupied housing demanded. The effect of the governmental subsidy is, then, to provide a considerable impetus to home ownership. For families facing a higher tax rate, the subsidy (and the impetus to own their homes) would be even greater. We could investigate other governmental tax and subsidy in a similar manner by obtaining information on the relevant elasticities.

Summary

In this chapter we used the individual demand curves constructed in Chapter 4 to construct a market demand curve. That curve shows how individuals as a group respond to changes in prices when other factors are held constant. Developing the market demand curve from its basic foundations (as we have done) permits an understanding of why it is likely to be downward sloping and of how it will shift when other factors change.

As a way of measuring the responsiveness of demand to various influences, we introduced the concept of elasticity. The two most important examples of that concept were the price elasticity of demand (which records the proportionate change in quantity in response to a 1 percent change in price) and the income elasticity of demand (the responsiveness of quantity to proportionate changes in income). Both of these concepts (together with some of the empirical estimates presented in this chapter) will be used later in this book to show how economic analysis can be used to predict real-world occurrences.

Suggested Readings

Baumol, W. J., *Economic Theory and Operations Analysis*, 2d ed. (Englewood Cliffs, New Jersey: Prentice-Hall, Inc., 1965), chap. 10.

Brown, A., and A. Deaton, "Surveys in Applied Economics: Models of Consumer Behavior," *Economic Journal* 82 (December 1972), pp. 1145–1236.

Ferber, R., "Consumer Economics, A Survey," *Journal of Economic Literature* 11 (December 1973), pp. 1303–1342.

Harberger, A. C., ed., *The Demand for Durable Goods* (Chicago: University of Chicago Press, 1960), pp. 3–14.

Houthakker, H. J., and L. D. Taylor, *Consumer Demand in the United States*, 2d ed. (Cambridge, Mass.: Harvard University Press, 1970).

Schultz, H., *The Theory and Measurement of Demand* (Chicago: University of Chicago Press, 1938), chap. 2–5.

Stigler, G., *The Theory of Price*, 3d ed. (New York: Crowell-Collier and Macmillan, Inc., 1966), chap. 3.

Wold, H., and L. Jureen, *Demand Analysis* (New York: John Wiley & Sons, Inc., 1953).

Working, E., "What Do Statistical 'Demand Curves' Show?" *Quarterly Journal of Economics* 41 (1927). pp. 212–235.

Problems

5.1

Imagine a market for X's that is composed of four individuals: Mr. Pauper (P), Ms. Broke (B), Mr. Average (A), and Ms. Rich (R). All four have the same demand function for X: it is a function of income (I), P_X, and the price of an important substitute (Y) for X:

$$X = \frac{IP_Y}{2P_X}.$$

a) What is the market demand function for X? If $P_X = P_Y = 1$, and $I_P = I_B = 7, I_A = 14$, and $I_R = 100$, what is the total market demand for X?

b) If P_X doubled, what would be the new level of X demanded? If Mr. Pauper lost his job and his income fell 50 percent, how would that affect the market demand for X? What if Ms. Rich's income were to drop 50 percent? If the government imposed 100 percent tax on Y, how would the demand for X be affected?

c) If $I_P = I_B = I_A = I_R = 32$, what would be the total demand for X? How does that figure compare with your answer to a)? Answer b) for these new income levels and $P_X = P_Y = 1$.

d) If Ms. Rich found Z's a necessary complement to X's, her demand function for X's might be described by the function:

$$X = \frac{I P_Y}{2P_X P_Z}.$$

What is the new market demand function for X? If $P_X = P_Y = P_Z = 1$ and income levels are those described by a), what is the demand for X? What is the new level of demand for X if the price of Z rises to 2? Notice Ms. Rich is the only one whose demand for X drops.

5.2

Suppose the quantity of good X demanded by individual 1 is given by:

$$X_1 = 10 - 2P_X + 0.01\, I_1 + 0.4\, P_Y$$

and the quantity of X demanded by individual 2 is:

$$X_2 = 5 - P_X + 0.02\, I_2 - 0.2\, P_Y .$$

What is the market demand function for total X ($= X_1 + X_2$) as a function of P_X, I_1, I_2, and P_Y? Graph the two individual demand curves (with X on the horizontal axis, P_X on the vertical axis) for the case $I_1 = 1000$, $I_2 = 1000$, and $P_Y = 10$.

Using these individual demand curves construct the market demand curve for total X. What is the algebraic equation for this curve?

Now suppose I_1 increases to 1100 and I_2 decreases to 900. How would the market demand curve shift? How would the individual demand curves shift? Graph these new curves.

Finally, suppose P_Y rises to 15. Graph the new individual and market demand curves that would result.

5.3

Suppose ham and cheese are pure complements—they will always be used in the ratio of one slice of ham to one slice of cheese to make a sandwich. Suppose also that ham and cheese sandwiches are the only goods that consumers can buy and that bread is free.

Show that if the price of a slice of ham equals the price of a slice of cheese:

a) the price elasticity of demand for ham is $-1/2$;

b) the cross-price elasticity of a change in the price of cheese on ham consumption is also $-1/2$.

c) How would your answers to a) and b) change if a slice of ham cost twice as much as a slice of cheese?

5.4

Given that the price elasticity of demand for crude oil in the United States is .25, and that the current consumption of oil in the United States is 38 million barrels a day, how much oil would be demanded if the controlled price of $9.60 per barrel were allowed to rise to the world price of $13 per barrel? How much more will be spent on oil in this situation?

5.5

A *luxury* is defined as a good for which the income elasticity of demand is greater than 1. Show that for a two-good economy, both goods cannot be luxuries. (*Hint*: What happens if both goods *are* luxuries and income is increased by 10 percent?)

5.6

If $E_{X, P_X} = -.6$ and $E_{X, P_Y} = -.8$ in a two-good economy, what is $E_{X, I}$? (*Hint*: A 10 percent increase in income can be seen as a 10 percent drop in all prices.)

5.7

For the linear demand curve shown in Figure A (see next page) show that the price elasticity of demand at any point (say, point E) is given by minus the ratio of distance X to distance Y in the figure. (*Hint*: What is the equation for a linear demand curve? Use this equation in the definition of price elasticity.)

Figure A

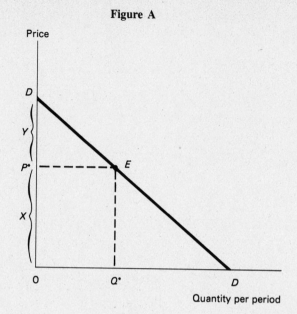

Part III

Production and the Firm

Introduction

In this part we examine the production of economic goods. These goods are produced by combining various inputs (land, labor, capital, and so forth) using the best available technology. Institutions that coordinate this transformation of inputs into outputs are called *firms*. They may be large institutions (such as General Motors, IBM, or the U.S. Defense Department) or small ones (such as "Mom and Pop" stores or self-employed individuals). They may pursue differing goals (IBM may seek maximum profits; a Soviet collective farm may seek to make members of the collective as well off as possible). But all firms must make certain basic choices in the production process. The purpose of Part III is to develop some methods of conceptualizing those choices.

In Chapter 6 we will introduce the concept of a *production function*, which is used by economists to represent the physical relationship between the inputs that a firm employs and the outputs that are produced. By using the production function approach economists are able to summarize existing technologies and to illustrate those choices that are feasible for a firm to make. In a sense, production functions represent the constraints imposed by nature on ways in which firms may carry on production. Of course, technology changes over time as new productive techniques are developed. In the appendix to Chapter 6 we briefly discuss some ways of conceptualizing these changes.

In Chapter 7 the production function is used to discuss the economist's notion of costs. After carefully defining what economists mean by "costs," we turn to considering how the costs of production are affected by the input choices that a firm makes. Our final goal in the chapter is to develop a set of curves that show the relationship between the quantity that a firm produces and the costs of producing that quantity. Those curves will be very useful in our development of the theory of price determination in Part IV. A brief appendix to Chapter 7 presents a numerical example of a production function and shows how cost curves can be derived from that function. The appendix therefore provides an example of how Chapters 6 and 7 fit together.

Chapter 8 discusses the goals of a firm and centers attention on the profit maximization hypothesis. In the chapter we show why there is a need for some theory of what a firm tries to do, and we demonstrate that the hypothesis that firms seek maximum profits (suitably defined) is the most acceptable of the simple alternatives that have been proposed. We discuss the implications of the assumption of profit maximization in some detail.

By drawing an analogy to the development of Part II, it might be thought that the discussion of the theory of the firm developed in this part would end by deriving a market supply curve. Unfortunately this is not the case. In many respects supply is a more complex subject than demand, and we must be more careful in analyzing it. For this reason, we do not discuss supply curves until Part IV, when we show how the demands of individuals and the costs of firms interact in the market to determine price.

Chapter 6

Technology of Production

Production Functions

The activity pursued by all firms is to turn inputs into outputs. Because economists are interested in the choices that the firm makes in accomplishing this goal, and because they wish to avoid many of the engineering intricacies involved in actual production decisions, they have chosen to construct an abstract model of production. In this model the relationship between inputs and outputs is formalized by a *production function* of the form

$$Q = f(K, L, M, \ldots)$$ [6.1]

where Q represents the output of a particular good[1] during a period, K represents the machine (that is, capital) usage during the period, L represents hours of labor input,[2]

---

[1] The term "output of a particular good" is used here to indicate that we are only considering productive processes that produce identical goods. For example, "cheap" shoes and "good" shoes are two different goods and, presumably, have different production functions. We shall see in later chapters that it may be difficult in some productive processes to specify exactly what output is (for example, consider the problem of defining the output of a hospital).

[2] Capital and labor inputs are assumed to be homogeneous. This is a great simplification since there are in reality numerous kinds of labor and many types of machines. The recognition that these inputs are in fact inhomogeneous raises many technical problems in the theory of aggregation that cannot be elaborated here.

131

M represents raw materials used, and the notation indicates the possibility of other variables affecting the production process.[3] The function 6.1 is assumed to provide, for any conceivable set of inputs, the engineer's solution to the problem of how best to combine those inputs to get output. For example, the production function might represent a farmer's output of wheat during one year as being dependent on the amount of labor used on the farm that year, the quantity of capital equipment employed during the year, the amount of land under cultivation, and so forth. The function records the fact that there are many different ways in which, say, 100 bushels of wheat could be produced. The farmer could use a very labor-intensive technique with only a small amount of mechanical equipment; alternatively, the 100 bushels could be produced by using huge amounts of equipment with very little labor. Similarly, techniques that were very land-intensive might be adopted to produce the 100 bushels of wheat; or relatively little land could be used together with great amounts of labor, equipment, and fertilizer. All of those possible techniques are represented by the general production function in equation 6.1. For any possible choices of land, equipment, and labor input, the function records the maximum of wheat output that can be produced from those given inputs. In this sense the eocnomist's production already represents a set of technically efficient production processes. The important question from an economic point of view is how the levels of Q, K, L, and M are chosen by the firm. We take this question up in detail in the next several chapters.

This chapter will not touch on the questions of optimal choice. Rather our intention is to describe a few concepts that have been developed for the purpose of understanding the relationship between inputs and outputs. The chapter centers on purely physical relationships in contrast to later chapters, which will concentrate on costs and profit maximization. Production functions represent physical constraints on the activities of producers that are imposed by the existing technology. Our purpose is to examine the way in which these constraints can be formalized. For the purposes of this examination (and indeed for most of the purposes of this book) it will be more convenient to write equation 6.1 as:

$$Q = f(K,L)$$
[6.2]

with the understanding that all inputs other than K and L are being held constant during the analysis. Most of the analysis to be presented will hold true for any two inputs that might be investigated. For example, if we wished to examine the effects of rainfall and fertilizer usage on crop production, it would be appropriate to examine a production function using those two inputs while holding other inputs (quantity of land, hours of labor input, and so on) constant. Similarly, if we were interested in the production function that characterizes a school system, it would be

---

[3] In a purely formal way technical progress can be accommodated within the formulation of equation 6.1 by assuming that variable "time" enters into the production function (see Appendix to Chapter 6 for an elaboration of this point).

appropriate for us to examine the relationship between the "output" of the system (say, academic achievement) and the inputs used to produce this output (teachers, buildings, learning aids). For the theoretical development, however, it is convenient for us to use the two general inputs "capital" and "labor" since we will frequently wish to show these inputs on a two-dimensional graph.

Marginal Physical Productivity

A first question we might ask about the relationship between inputs and outputs is how much extra output is provided by adding one more unit of an input to the production process. As a formal measure of this relationship, we define:

Definition

The *marginal physical productivity* of an input is the quantity of extra output provided by employing one additional unit of that input while holding the level of usage of all other inputs constant. For the two principal inputs we are using:

$$\text{marginal physical product of capital} = MP_K = \frac{\text{change in } Q}{\text{change in } K} \qquad [6.3]$$

$$\text{marginal physical product of labor} = MP_L = \frac{\text{change in } Q}{\text{change in } L} \qquad [6.3]$$

As a physical example of these definitions, let us consider the case of a farmer hiring one more person to harvest a crop while holding all other inputs constant. The extra output produced by this person is the marginal physical productivity. The marginal physical productivity of this labor input is measured in physical quantities (such as bushels of wheat, crates of oranges, or heads of lettuce). We might, for example, observe that 50 workers on a farm are able to produce 100 bushels of wheat per year whereas 51 workers (with the same land and equipment) can produce 102 bushels. The marginal physical product of the fifty-first worker is then 2 bushels per year.

Diminishing Marginal Physical Productivity

We might expect that the marginal physical productivity of an input depends on how much of that input is used. Labor, for example, cannot be added indefinitely to a given field (while keeping the amount of equipment, fertilizer, and so forth fixed) without eventually exhibiting some deterioration in its productivity. This possibility is illustrated in Figures 6.1a and 6.1b. The relationship between the quantity of a particular input (labor) and total output is recorded in Figure 6.1a as TP_L. For small amounts of L, output increases rapidly as additional L is added. However, because *other inputs are held constant*, eventually the ability of additional labor to generate

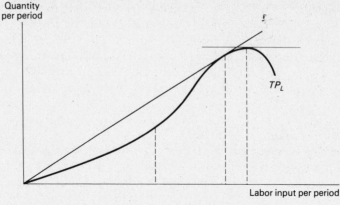

(a) Total Product of Labor Curve

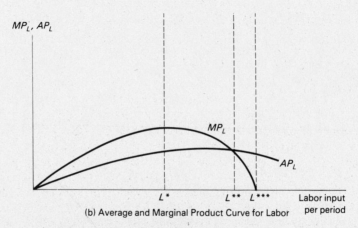

(b) Average and Marginal Product Curve for Labor

**Figure 6.1 / Deriving Average and Marginal
Product of Labor Curves from the Total Product Curve**

These curves show how the average and marginal product of labor curves can be derived from the total product curve. The curve TP_L in 6.1a represents the relationship between labor input and output, on the assumption that all other inputs are held constant. The slope of this curve is the marginal product of labor (MP_L), and the slope of a chord joining the origin to a point on the TP_L curve gives the average product of labor (AP_L). The relationship between the AP_L and the MP_L curves is geometrically obvious from the figures.

additional output begins to deteriorate. Finally, at L^{***} output reaches its maximum level. Any additional labor added beyond this point actually decreases output. Beyond L^{***} additional laborers get in each other's way to such an extent that total output begins to decline.

The TP_L curve shown in Figure 6.1a therefore embodies the assumption that labor's marginal physical productivity eventually declines as more labor is added to the production of a good while holding other inputs constant. This assumption is an extremely important one in economic analysis. Intuitively it seems clear that if a firm adds additional labor to a production process it must eventually run into diminishing returns. The inputs that are being held fixed will eventually become "overutilized," and a decline in productivity will set in. Thomas Malthus, for example, argued that additional labor cannot be constantly added to a fixed supply of land without the productivity of labor in food production eventually beginning to diminish.[4] Since the quantity of land is, in the long run, absolutely fixed, the principle of a diminishing marginal productivity of labor implied, to Malthus, serious problems for man's future. Malthus's prediction that the diminishing productivity of labor would eventually lead to a situation in which population growth outpaced the growth in food production, in fact caused economics to be called the "dismal science." Most modern economists would agree that Malthus did not adequately recognize the possibilities for increases in capital equipment and for technical advances to prevent the decline of labor's productivity in agriculture. Nevertheless, the basic observation that the marginal productivity of labor (or any other factor) declines when *all other inputs* are held constant is still recognized by economists as an empirically valid proposition.

Marginal Physical Product Curve

From the total labor productivity curve, both average and marginal productivity curves can be constructed. The marginal physical product of labor is simply the slope of the curve TP_L. This should be clear from definition 6.3: The slope of the TP_L curve just shows how output expands as additional labor is added, and this is what is required by the definition of the marginal physical product of labor. In Figure 6.1b the marginal product curve (MP_L) is drawn. Notice that MP_L reaches a maximum at L^* and declines as labor input is added beyond this point. This is a reflection of the assumption of a diminishing marginal product of labor. MP_L is equal to 0 at the point L^{***} for which TP_L reaches a maximum. Beyond L^{***} further additions of labor input actually reduce output. Production will not take place beyond L^{***} since using more labor (which is presumably costly) will result in less output for the firm.

Average Physical Product Curve

In common usage the term "labor productivity" usually means *average productivity*. When it is said that a certain industry has experienced productivity increases, this is taken to mean that output per unit of labor input has increased. Although this concept of average productivity is not nearly so important in theoretical economics as is marginal productivity, it receives a great deal of attention in popular discussions. Because it is easily measured (say, as so many bushels of wheat

---

[4]A somewhat facetious "proof" of the diminishing marginal productivity of an input argues that if it were not true that marginal productivities diminish, the entire world food supply could be grown in a single flower pot if a sufficient quantity of labor were applied to the pot. Since this situation is obviously absurd, the marginal product of labor must, after some point, diminish.

per hour of labor input), it is often used as a measure of efficiency. It is a simple matter to derive average productivity relationships from the total product curve. This is also done in Figure 6.1. We define

Definition

The *average productivity* of any input is the total output per unit of that input employed. For the case of labor input, average productivity (AP_L) is given by:

$$AP_L = \frac{\text{output}}{\text{labor input}} = \frac{Q}{L}.$$ [6.4]

Geometrically, the value of AP_L for any quantity of labor input is the slope of the chord drawn from the origin in Figure 6.1a to the relevant point on the TP_L curve. This is true since the slope of such a chord is simply Q/L. By drawing a series of chords through the origin to various points on the total product curve (TP_L), the average product of labor curve (AP_L) can be constructed. This curve is shown in Figure 6.1b. From the diagram it can be seen that the average and marginal productivities of labor are equal at L^{**}. For this level of labor input, the chord through the origin in 6.1a is just tangent to the TP_L curve. Hence the average and marginal products of labor are equal. Also at L^{**} the average product of labor is at its *maximum value*. This feature of the curve can be demonstrated as follows: for levels of labor input less than L^{**}, the marginal product of labor (MP_L) exceeds its average product (AP_L). Consequently adding one more worker will raise the average productivity of all workers since the increment to output from hiring this additional worker exceeds that which was being produced by the average worker previously. An analogous situation would occur if a baseball team with a team batting average of .260 acquired a .300 hitter: the team average would rise. A similar argument would show that for labor input greater than L^{**}, the average productivity of labor is falling. Beyond L^{**}, labor's average productivity exceeds its marginal productivity so average productivity is falling. Adding a worker to the production process causes output to rise by less than the average that previously prevailed. Consequently the average productivity of labor will fall. In our baseball analogy, adding a .200 hitter to the team will indeed cause the team average to fall.

We have shown that to the left of L^{**} the AP_L curve is rising, to the right of L^{**} it is falling. Therefore the average product of labor reaches its maximum value at L^{**}. Labor added beyond this point will cause the average productivity of labor to fall.

Physical Productivity Curves
and the *Ceteris Paribus* Assumption

Figure 6.1, then, records all the available information about the way in which varying labor input (or any other input) affects output. It is important to remember the assumption that lies behind the construction of these curves: All productive inputs other than labor are being held constant at some specified levels. The MP_L curve records the *ceteris paribus* productivity of additional units of labor input, and the AP_L curve similarly records the *ceteris paribus* average productivity of various levels of labor input. If the firm were to hire more of some other input (say, more machines) all of the curves pictured in Figure 6.1 would move to new positions. For example, if a farmer were to double the land under cultivation and the use of machinery, we would expect that both the MP_L and the AP_L curves would shift to the right. With increased levels of complementary inputs more labor can be used before diminishing returns begin to appear.

Although the curves in Figure 6.1 are useful for pedagogic purposes, it is the *ceteris paribus* assumption implicit in their construction that limits their applicability to the study of real-world production processes. Most firms we are likely to observe will be using different levels of both labor and machines. Similarly, over time a single firm will vary all of its inputs. We will therefore never observe a neat tracing out of a single total product of labor curve but, rather, a series of Q, L points that lie on a number of different curves. Before we describe a way of illustrating the entire production function to avoid these problems, it may be interesting to examine some productivity data from the real world.

An Example: Average Productivity in Steel Production

Table 6.1 reports data on the average productivity of labor in steel during the period 1970–1976 for three producing areas: the U.S., Japan, and the European Coal and Steel Community (ECSC). Entries in the table represent the output of steel (measured in metric tons) per 100 hours of labor input. A number of interesting conclusions emerge from comparing the various figures contained in the table. First, there is clear evidence of an upward trend in average productivity during the period covered. Increasing amounts of capital used in steel production

Table 6.1 / **Average Physical Productivity in Steel Production 1970–1976 (Metric Tons of Finished Steel per 100 Labor-Hours)**

Year	United States	Japan	European Coal and Steel Community
1970	7.4	5.7	5.2
1971	7.9	5.6	5.2
1972	8.2	6.4	5.8
1973	9.3	8.0	6.4
1974	9.4	8.1	6.9
1975	8.1	7.5	6.7
1976	8.6	8.1	6.5

Source: Calculated from Council on Wage and Price Stability Report to the President on Prices and Costs in the United States Steel Industry, Washington, D.C., October 1977, Appendix Table No. 20.

together with the spread of improved steel-making technology (such as wider adoption of the basic oxygen process) probably accounted for this trend. Productivity rose more rapidly in Japan during the period than in the United States or in the ECSC and that may also be related to the more rapid adoption of new technologies in that country. The recent economic problems of U.S. steelmakers and demands in the United States (and in Europe) for increased tariff protection against imported steel indicate that these productivity trends are of more than academic concern.

A final fact illustrated by the table concerns the behavior of labor productivity over the business cycle. Each of the producers involved experienced a fall in the average productivity of labor in steel production during 1975—a year of worldwide recession. This pattern can better be explained as the reaction of steel firms to a downturn in demand than as a shift in the underlying productivity relationships. When orders for steel fall off (as they do in a recession) firms are reluctant to lay off workers immediately. Adopting a quick layoff policy would impose current costs on firms (such as having to make "severance payments" to laid-off workers) and might make it hard for the firms to hire their skilled workers back when demand conditions improve. Consequently, firms may "hoard" labor during temporary recessions. Since output (Q) falls and the workforce (L) stays relatively constant, average productivity (Q/L) falls during such periods. In judging overall productivity trends in an industry (or in the entire economy) some care must therefore be taken not to attribute any great importance to short-term, cyclical movements.

Isoquant Maps and the Rate of Technical Substitution

One way to picture the entire production function in two dimensions is to use its *isoquant map*. We will again use a production function of the form $Q = f(K, L)$ with the understanding that "capital" and "labor" are simply convenient examples of any two inputs that might happen to be of interest. We seek a way of showing alternative combinations of these inputs that might be used to produce a given output level. To do so we introduce:

Definition

An isoquant (from the Greek *iso* meaning equal) shows alternative combinations of capital and labor input that can be used to produce a particular level of output.

For example, all those combinations of K and L that fall on the curve labeled "$Q = 10$" in Figure 6.2 are capable of producing 10 units of output per period. This isoquant, then, records the fact that there are many alternative ways of producing 10 units of output. One way might be represented by point A: We would use L_A and K_A

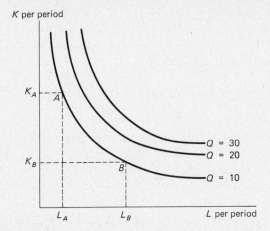

Figure 6.2 / Isoquant Map

Isoquants record the alternative combinations of inputs that can be used to produce a given level of output. The slope of these curves shows the rate at which L can be substituted for K while keeping output constant. The negative of this slope is called the (marginal) rate of technical substitution ((RTS). In the figure, the RTS is positive, and it is diminishing for increasing inputs of labor.

to produce 10 units of output. Alternatively, we might prefer to use relatively less capital and more labor and would therefore choose a point such as B. The isoquant map clearly demonstrates the different ways in which a firm can produce 10 units of output.

There are infinitely many isoquants in the K-L plane. Each isoquant represents a different level of output. Isoquants record successively higher levels of output as we move out in a northeasterly direction. Presumably using more of each of the inputs will permit output to increase. Several other isoquants (for $Q = 20$ and $Q = 30$) are shown in Figure 6.2. These record those combinations of inputs that can produce the required output. The reader will probably notice the similarity between an isoquant map and the individual's indifference curve map discussed in Part II. These are indeed similar ideas, since both represent "contour" maps of the particular function of interest. For isoquants, however, the labeling of the curves is measurable (an output of 10 units has a quantifiable meaning), and we will therefore be somewhat more interested in studying the shape of these curves than we were in examining the exact shape of indifference curves.

Rate of Technical Substitution

The slope of an isoquant shows how one input can be traded for another while holding output constant. Examining the slope will give us some information about the technical possibility for substituting labor for capital. Because of this, the slope of an isoquant (or, more properly, its negative) is called the *marginal rate of technical substitution* (*RTS*) of labor for capital. More formally,

Definition

The *rate of technical substitution* of labor for capital is the amount by which capital input can be reduced while holding quantity produced constant when one more unit of labor input is used. Mathematically,

Rate of Technical Substitution (of labor for capital)

$$= RTS \text{ (of } L \text{ for } K)$$

$$= - \text{ (slope of isoquant)} \qquad [6.5]$$

$$= - \frac{\Delta K}{\Delta L} \text{ (for } Q \text{ constant)}$$

The particular value of this trade-off rate will depend not only on the level of output but also on the quantities of capital and labor being used. Its value depends on the point on the isoquant map at which the slope is to be measured. At a point such as A (in Figure 6.2), relatively large amounts of capital can be given up if one more unit of labor becomes available. At A therefore the RTS is a high positive number. On the other hand, at B the availability of an additional unit of labor does not permit a very large reduction in capital input; therefore the RTS is relatively small.

Marginal Productivities and the Rate of Technical Substitution

In order to examine the shape of production function isoquants we should prove the following result: The RTS (of L for K) is equal to the ratio of the marginal product of labor (MP_L) to the marginal product of capital (MP_K). We can show the proof of this assertion by considering the addition of some extra labor (ΔL) to the productive process while at the same time reducing capital usage by ΔK (that is, ΔK is negative). The additional output produced by the extra labor is simply $\Delta L \cdot MP_L$: It is the marginal productivity of labor times the amount of additional labor hired. Similarly, the loss in output from the decreased use of capital is given by $\Delta K \cdot MP_K$. Now, along an isoquant, output is constant. Consequently the net result of adding labor and reducing capital should be to leave output unchanged.

This means that

$$\Delta L \cdot MP_L + \Delta K \cdot MP_K = 0 \qquad [6.6]$$

or

$$\Delta L \cdot MP_L = - \Delta K \cdot MP_K \qquad [6.7]$$

or, by rearranging terms,

$$- \frac{\Delta K}{\Delta L} \text{ (} Q \text{ constant)} = \frac{MP_L}{MP_K} = RTS \text{ (of } L \text{ for } K) \qquad [6.8]$$

which is the result that we wished to show. The rate at which labor can be substituted for capital in the productive process (while holding output constant) is given by the ratio of the marginal productivity of labor to the marginal productivity of capital.

A numerical proof of this proposition may be more convincing. Suppose that the marginal productivity of labor in wheat production is 2 bushels of wheat per hour; that is, the additional output provided by a person working for one more hour on a given field is 2 bushels of wheat. Similarly, suppose that the marginal product of capital is 1 bushel per hour; that is, using the available farm machinery for one more hour would produce an extra bushel of wheat. Now suppose 1 hour of human labor were added to the production of wheat. By how much could the usage of machinery be reduced while keeping output constant? The answer is clear: Since the extra labor yields 2 bushels of wheat, the machinery input can be reduced by 2 hours. In this way the lost output from cutting back on machine time would exactly compensate for the additional output provided by the extra worker. Consequently, 2 machine hours can be traded for 1 labor-hour while keeping output constant: The *RTS* is 2/1. This is simply the ratio of MP_L to MP_K, and we have therefore provided an intuitive "proof" of equation 6.8.

Rate of Technical Substitution and the Shape of Isoquants

We can use the result of equation 6.8 to see that those isoquants that we observe must be negatively sloped. Since both MP_L and MP_K will be positive (no firm would choose to produce where a marginal productivity is negative), the *RTS* will also be positive. Because the negative of the *RTS* is the slope of an isoquant, the slopes of those isoquants that are observed must be negative.[5] An increase in L must be met by a decrease in K if output is to be held constant. If both L and K had to be increased to keep output constant, one of the inputs would of necessity have a negative marginal productivity.

The isoquants in Figure 6.2 are drawn not only with a negative slope (as they should be) but also as convex curves. Along any one of the curves the *RTS is diminishing*. For high ratios of K to L the *RTS* is a large positive number indicating that a great deal of capital can be given up if one more unit of labor becomes available. On the other hand, when a lot of labor is already being used, the *RTS* is low, signifying that only a small amount of capital can be traded for an additional unit of labor if output is to be held constant. This shape seems intuitively reasonable: The more labor (relative to capital) that is used, the less able labor is to substitute for capital. In some sense labor becomes less potent as a substitute as more of it is used. Since this idea seems reasonable, it would be nice if it could be derived as a fundamental rule built on some more basic foundation. For example,

---

[5] It is possible for an isoquant to have a positive slope: It is easy to dream up functions that do. The importance of this discussion is to indicate that such positively sloped portions will not be observed in the relevant range of production.

using equation 6.8, it might be thought that the convex shape of the isoquants could be derived as a corollary to the assumption that the marginal productivity of an input is likely to be decreasing for increases in the use of that input. Unfortunately, no such general rule can be derived.[6] Nevertheless, the assumption of a diminishing *RTS* is an intuitively reasonable formalization of the notion that the use of a particular input can be pushed "too far." Firms will not want to use "only labor" or "only machines" to produce a given level of output but will probably stop short of adopting such extremes in input usage. They will choose a more balanced input mix. In Chapter 7 we will see exactly how an "optimal" mix of inputs might be chosen. For the purposes of the present chapter we are only interested in providing a demonstration of those alternatives that are feasible.

Returns to Scale

Because production functions represent tangible productive processes, economists have paid more attention to the particular form of these functions than they have to characterizing the shape of an ethereal utility function. Knowledge of the shape and properties of a firm's productive function is important for a variety of policy reasons. Such information may, for example, suggest how research funds might best be spent on developing technical improvements, or how government regulators should decide on the wisdom of allowing large-size plants. In the next few sections we will develop some terminology to aid in examining such issues.

The first important question we might ask about production functions is how does output respond to increases in all inputs together? For example, suppose all inputs were doubled, would output then double or would the relationship not be quite so simple? This is a question of the *returns to scale* exhibited by the production function that has been of interest to economists ever since Adam Smith intensively studied the production of pins. Smith identified two forces that came into operation when the conceptual experiment of doubling all inputs was performed. First, a doubling of scale permits a greater division of labor; Smith was intrigued by the skill of people who made only pin heads, pin shafts, or who stuck the two together. Hence there is some presumption that efficiency might increase—production might more than double. The possibility of specializing in production may lead to efficiency as the scale of production is increased. Smith did not, however, envision that these benefits to large-scale operation would be available throughout all possible

---

[6]An incorrect argument based on equation 6.8 would proceed as follows. In moving along an isoquant more labor and less capital are being used. Assuming that each factor exhibits a diminishing marginal productivity it might be argued that MP_L would decrease (since the quantity of labor has increased) and that MP_K would increase (since the quantity of capital has decreased). Consequently the *RTS* ($= MP_L/MP_K$) should decrease. The fallacy in this argument is that both factors are changing together, and it is not possible to make such simple determinations about changes in the marginal productivities. What will happen to the *RTS* as K and L change will also depend on how MP_L responds to changes in K and how MP_K responds to changes in L.

ranges of output. He recognized that large productive enterprises may encounter inefficiencies in managerial direction and control. Coordination of production plans may become more difficult when there are many layers of management. Which of those two effects of scale is more important is then an empirical question. To investigate this question properly we should have a precise definition of returns to scale.

Providing a mathematically precise definition of returns to scale is a misleadingly simple exercise. Given the production function $Q = f(K, L)$, then we say that this function exhibits *constant returns to scale* if

$$f(2K, 2L) = 2f(K, L) = 2Q \qquad [6.9]$$

That is, if all inputs are doubled, output is also doubled. Similarly a production function exhibits *decreasing returns to scale* if

$$f(2K, 2L) < 2f(K, L) = 2Q \qquad [6.10]$$

and *increasing returns to scale* if

$$f(2K, 2L) > 2f(K, L) = 2Q \qquad [6.11]$$

For a constant-returns-to-scale production function, then, a doubling of K and L will cause output to double. A similar doubling for a decreasing-returns-to-scale production function, however, will cause output to be less than double. For some reason, increasing all inputs does not lead to a proportionate increase in output. Finally, for an increasing-returns-to-scale production function, a doubling of K and L causes output to more than double. Perhaps, as Adam Smith theorized, a proportionate increase in all factors of production brings about the possibility of a greater division of labor and this permits output to increase more than proportionally. The definitions then are clear cut, and it would seem to be quite important (and relatively easy) to determine what kind of production function characterizes any particular productive process.

The simplicity of those definitions may be somewhat misleading, however, when it is recognized that inputs other than K and L enter into the production function. What is to be done with the inputs when K and L are doubled? Does it make sense to talk of doubling "all" inputs, or must some necessarily be regarded as fixed? For example, suppose climatic conditions are an important element in a production function. What sense could be made out of the stipulation that we "double the weather"? Alternatively, if we hold the weather "constant," we have violated the rigorous definition of returns to scale that requires that all inputs increase proportionately.

Such "problem" inputs are both difficult to deal with conceptually and extremely important in empirical investigations. However, because the methods used will depend on the particular productive process under investigation, the subject will not be pursued here. In later chapters (notably Chapter 7) we will see how a slightly different notion of returns to scale is sometimes used in dealing with policy questions.

Cobb-Douglas Production Function

One particular production function has been widely used to examine the question of returns to scale. That function assumes that the relationship between inputs (capital and labor) and output is given by:

$$Q = AK^a L^b \qquad [6.12]$$

where A, a, and b are all positive constants. Because this function was first investigated by C. W. Cobb and P. H. Douglas in the 1920s, it is called the *Cobb-Douglas Production Function*.[7] To see how the function can be used to investigate returns to scale, consider two possible combinations of K and L that might be used: (1) K_1, L_1; and (2) $2K_1$, $2L_1$. Notice that combination (2) uses exactly twice the amount of inputs as does combination (1) and we are interested in whether such an increase in inputs permits a doubling of output. Using the Cobb-Douglas to record output (Q_2) provided by input combination (2) gives

$$Q_2 = A \ (2K_1)^a \ (2L_1)^b = 2^{a+b}AK_1^a \ L_1^b. \qquad [6.13]$$

If $a + b = 1$, Q_2 will be exactly twice the output that can be produced using combination (1). In other words, if $a + b = 1$, the function would exhibit constant returns to scale. On the other hand, if $a + b < 1$, a doubling of inputs would result in less than a doubling of outputs and the function would exhibit decreasing returns. If $a + b > 1$ there would be increasing returns to scale.

A widely used research technique then is to gather industry data on Q, K, and L and use those to estimate the constants a and b.[8] Once these estimates are available, it is a simple matter to form the sum $a + b$ and check whether the industry appears to be characterized by increasing ($a + b > 1$), constant ($a + b = 1$) or decreasing ($a + b < 1$) returns to scale. We now turn to examine some evidence that has been gathered in that way.

---

[7]See P. H. Douglas, *The Theory of Wages* (New York: The Macmillan Company, 1924), pp. 132–135. Douglas had a long and distinguished career as a U.S. Senator from Illinois, being a major architect of much of the social legislation in the 1930s and 1940s.

[8]The Cobb-Douglas Production Function is useful for empirical work because it is linear in logarithms. Taking logs of equation 6.12 yields $\log Q = \log A + a \log K + b \log L$. Using this form, relatively simple statistical procedures permit estimates of a and b to be made.

Examples of Returns to Scale

There are many reasons why it is important to know whether production functions exhibit constant, increasing, or decreasing returns to scale. All of the reasons share a common policy interest in finding out whether large-scale production of a certain good (or group of related goods) leads to efficiencies or to inefficiencies. From the point of view of economic historians, for example, there is considerable interest in knowing how much of the growth in the output produced by the United States economy can be attributable to increases in factors of production and how much can be attributed to the economies made possible by large-scale operations. To government regulators the question of returns to scale is an important one because they must make judgments about the desirable size for certain firms to be. If there are substantial economies of scale it may be desirable to permit firms to attain a very large size and then regulate them to prevent monopolistic practices.[9] Similarly, the governments of underdeveloped countries are interested in the question of returns to scale so that they may adopt intelligent investment strategies. It is very difficult for a small country to compete with the large industrialized countries in the production of goods that exhibit substantial scale economies. Rather, a more successful strategy may be to promote investment in those industries for which small-scale production is relatively efficient.

Unfortunately, there has been some lack of precision in economists' discussions of economies of scale. Some economists use the term "returns to scale" to refer to a technical property of the production function. This is also the sense in which we have introduced the term. Other economists judge returns to scale by looking at the shape of firms' or industrywide cost curves. In this section we will discuss only results of those analyses that look directly at production functions; that is, we will look only at investigations that study the functional relationship between inputs and outputs. In Chapter 7 we will discuss cost curves and will examine some of the empirical evidence on their shapes.

The Economy as a Whole

P. H. Douglas, in his pioneering study of production in the United States economy between 1899 and 1922,[10] found the value of b in the Cobb-Douglas function to be approximately .75 and a to be about .25. Consequently, he concluded that $a + b$ was very close to unity. That is, the production function for total United States output exhibits constant returns to proportional increases in the factors of production. Numerous other authors have followed Douglas's suggestions and examined aggregate production functions for various national economies. Although the specific values of a and b calculated from those studies have varied considerably,

---

[9]We discuss this subject at length in Chapter 11.

[10]P. H. Douglas, *The Theory of Wages*, p. 134.

generally the sum of those parameters has been reasonably close to 1. Thus, while it is impossible to survey all of those studies here,[11] most empirical findings are in agreement with Douglas's original results that economywide production functions exhibit constant returns to scale.

Particular Industries

For particular industries there is also some evidence that constant returns to scale is a widespread phenomenon. In a 1967 study, for example, J. R. Maroney used data on a large number of industries to estimate Cobb-Douglas Production Functions.[12] In most of the industries examined it was not possible to reject the hypothesis that production functions exhibited constant returns. The first column of Table 6.2 illustrates these findings for 8 specific industries. Only for 3 of these industries (Food and Beverages, Furniture, and Chemicals) were there estimated to be statistically significant returns to scale. Even for these, the sum of the Cobb-Douglas exponents was reasonably close to 1 and hence the benefits of large-scale operation were not substantial.

Table 6.2 / Estimated Economies of Scale and Range in Plant Sizes for 8 Industries, 1957

Industry	Estimated Economies of Scale $(a + b)$	Value Added in Smallest Plant ($1,000)	Value Added in Largest Plant ($1,000)
Food and Beverages	1.07	192	775
Textiles	1.00	203	2,278
Lumber	1.04	41	201
Furniture	1.11	85	727
Paper and Pulp	0.98	360	5,157
Chemicals	1.09	366	6,414
Transport Equipment	1.02	194	5,196
Instruments	1.04	148	1,529

Source: J. R. Maroney, "Cobb-Douglas Production Functions and Returns to Scale in U.S. Manufacturing Industry," *Western Economic Journal,* 6, no. 1 (December 1967), pp. 46, 49.

Maroney employed a second technique to examine returns to scale that also suggested the widespread occurrence of constant returns. If increasing returns to

---

[11]For a survey of much of the literature on Cobb-Douglas production functions see A. A. Walters, "Production and Cost Functions: An Econometric Survey," *Econometrica* 31, nos. 1–2 (January–April 1963), pp. 1–66.

[12]J. R. Maroney, "Cobb-Douglas Production Functions and Returns to Scale in U.S. Manufacturing Industry," *Western Economic Journal* 6, no. 1 (December 1967), pp. 39–51. In this article the author used three factors of production: capital, production workers, and nonproduction workers. For ease of exposition we have combined the final two categories into the single input, "labor."

scale were important, it might be expected that all plants would be of a uniformly large size to take advantage of such economies. On the other hand, under constant returns, no one scale of operation is more efficient than any other and hence plants would be expected to occur in a wide range of sizes. To differentiate between those possibilities the author gathered data on the largest and smallest plant in each of the industries studied. His data are presented in the second and third columns of Table 6.2. These data showed that a wide range of plant sizes could be found in each of the industries. The author therefore concluded that a wide range in scale of operation was economically viable for each industry and that these data provided additional confirmation of the presence of constant returns to scale. Although other authors have, at times, found that industries are characterized by increasing or decreasing returns to scale, most reach conclusions similar to those of Douglas and Maroney. It appears that most industries (in the United States at least) experience constant returns to scale over a broad range of input-output possibilities. In Chapter 7 we will return to examine this question again for a few specific industries and will show that, although the constant returns to scale conclusion is generally upheld, there are a number of important cases in which it might be modified.

Input Substitution

Another important characteristic of the production function is how "easy" it is to substitute capital for labor. This is essentially a question of the shape of a single isoquant rather than a question about the whole isoquant map. Along one isoquant we have assumed that the rate of technical substitution will decrease as the capital-labor ratio decreases (that is, as K/L decreases), and we wish to define some way to measure this degree of responsiveness. If the RTS does not change at all for changes in K/L we might say that substitution is easy (we will see in Chapter 7 exactly why the term "easy" is used), whereas if the RTS changes rapidly for small changes in K/L we would say substitution is difficult. In this section we will examine the isoquant maps of three specific production functions that exhibit a wide range in the ease with which one input may be substituted for another.[13]

An Infinitely Substitutable Production Function

For the isoquant map pictured in Figure 6.3, the RTS is constant along the entire length of an isoquant. Labor may be freely substituted for capital at a constant trade-off rate (that is, without running into a diminishing relative marginal productivity). In fact, the isoquant map shows that any given output level could be

---

[13]Technically, the ease of input substitution is measured by the *elasticity of substitution*, which is defined as the ratio of the percentage change in K/L to the percentage change in the RTS along an isoquant. The three production functions to be examined have values for this elasticity of ∞, 0, and 1, respectively.

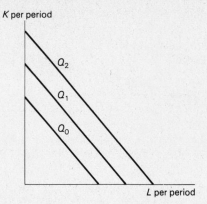

**Figure 6.3 / Isoquant Map for an
Infinitely Substitutable Production Function**

Here the *RTS* is constant over all choices of *K* and *L*. Capital and labor may be freely substituted for one another without affecting the trade-off between these inputs. This view of production is unrealistic because it assumes *only* capital or *only* labor can produce any output level.

produced using *only* capital or *only* labor simply by pushing factor substitution far enough. Such a possibility seems unlikely in the real world. Surely every machine requires some labor complement (if only to press buttons), and every laborer requires some capital equipment, however modest. Hence, although the isoquant map pictured in Figure 6.3 is a useful pedagogic device for illustrating the polar case of "easy" substitution, it has little relevance to real-world production processes.

Fixed-Proportions Production Function

Figure 6.4 demonstrates a case where no substitution is possible. This is a case opposite to the one we have just discussed. Here the isoquants are *L*-shaped, indicating that machines and labor must be used in absolutely fixed proportions. Every machine has a fixed complement of workers, and this cannot be varied. For example, if K_1 machines are available, these require L_1 workers if they are to produce output level Q_1. Employing more workers than L_1 would not increase output (the Q_1 isoquant is horizontal beyond the point K_1, L_1). In other words, the marginal productivity of labor is 0. On the other hand, using fewer workers would result in excess machines. If only L_0 workers were hired, for instance, only Q_0 units could be produced, but this could be accomplished with only K_0 machines. When L_0 workers are hired, therefore, there is an excess of machines of an amount given by $K_1 - K_0$.

This discussion indicates why the production function whose isoquant map is shown in Figure 6.4 is called a "fixed-proportions production function." Only if a combination of *K* and *L* that lies along the ray through the vertices of the isoquants is chosen will both inputs be fully employed. Otherwise there will be an excessive use of one input in the sense that its use could be cut back without restricting output.

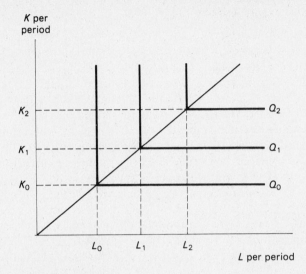

Figure 6.4 / Isoquant Map for
Fixed-Proportions Production Function

The isoquant map shown here has no substitution possibilities. Capital and labor must be used in fixed proportions if neither is to be redundant. For example, if K_1 machines are available, L_1 units of labor should be used. If L_2 units of labor are used there will be excess labor since no more than Q_1 can be produced from the given machines. Alternatively, if L_0 laborers were hired, machines would be redundant to the extent $K - K_0$.

Similarly, if a firm with such a production function wishes to expand, it must increase all inputs simultaneously so that none of the inputs become redundant.

In contrast to the first polar case we discussed, the fixed-proportions production function has a wide variety of applications to real-world production techniques. Many machines do require a fixed complement of workers, and any excess is superfluous. For example, consider combining capital and labor to mow a lawn. Here the lawn mower will always take one person for its operation, and a worker needs one lawn mower in order to produce any output. Output can be expanded (that is, more lawns can be mowed) only by adding capital and labor to the productive process in fixed proportions. It is possible that many types of machines, once built, are of this type; hence the fixed-proportions model is in many ways appropriate for production planning.[14]

---

[14]The lawn mower example points up another possibility, however. Presumably there is some leeway in choosing what size of lawn mower to buy. Hence, prior to the actual purchase, the capital-labor ratio in lawn mowing can be considered variable. Any device, from a pair of clippers to a gang mower, might be chosen. Once the mower is purchased, however, the capital-labor ratio becomes fixed.

Several authors have adopted this general "putty-clay" view of productive processes. In the planning stage there may be substantial possibilities for substituting capital for labor. Once investment decisions have been made (the "putty" has hardened into "clay"), the machines have to be used with a specified amount of labor.

Cobb-Douglas Production Function

The Cobb-Douglas production function (which we discussed previously) exhibits a
degree of input substitutability that is somewhere between the two polar cases we
have just presented. Its isoquant map is shown in Figure 6.5. These isoquants
resemble rectangular hyperbolas and exhibit a diminishing *RTS* (for the actual
construction of the isoquants of a Cobb-Douglas production function, see the
appendix to Chapter 7). That is, as labor is substituted for capital the *RTS* falls,
making even further substitution more "difficult" (in terms of the additional labor
required to permit a reduction in capital usage). But, contrary to the fixed proportions case, substitution is possible and firms might be expected to alter their
input proportions if they had an economic incentive to do so. Of course, the
Cobb-Douglas production function is not the only one with an isoquant map similar
to the one shown in Figure 6.5. Economists believe that most real-world production
processes exhibit some degree of substitutability and hence have isoquant maps
that have a diminishing *RTS*. We now turn to examine some evidence on this
question.

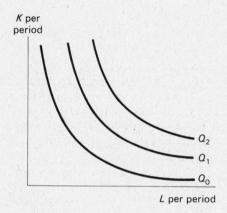

**Figure 6.5 / Isoquant Map for
Cobb-Douglas Production Function**

The isoquants for the Cobb-Douglas function resemble rectangular hyperbolas. Along these the *RTS*
falls as the ratio of *K* to *L* falls thus implying that it becomes increasingly difficult to substitute *L* for *K*.
In this sense the Cobb-Douglas case provides an intermediate case between the two polar examples of
substitutability illustrated in Figures 6.3 and 6.4, respectively.

Evidence on Input Substitutability

The question of the relative ease with which one input can be substituted for another
is of considerable interest to economists. The shape of a firm's isoquant map
provides a measure of the relative ease with which different industries can adapt to

the changing availability of productive inputs. For example, over the past 100 years there has been a great shift in the composition of output in the American economy away from agricultural production and toward the manufacturing and service industries. This shift in the composition of demand has necessitated a movement of factors of production (notably labor) out of agriculture and into other industries. If production were relatively flexible in terms of input substitutability, the inputs released from agriculture could be easily accommodated in new industries. On the other hand, if production were closer to fixed proportions it might have been difficult to absorb the inputs in exactly the proportions released by agriculture. To take an unrealistically simple example, let us suppose that the capital-labor ratio in manufacturing was 2 to 1; that is, it always took 2 machines to equip 1 worker. Suppose, on the other hand; that the capital-labor ratio in agriculture was 1 to 1. Now if demand shifted so that agricultural production must be reduced and manufacturing output increased, problems could arise. A reduction in agricultural output would have released capital and labor in the ratio of 1 to 1. However, manufacturing could only absorb capital and labor in the ratio 2 to 1. It must get 2 machines from the agricultural sector in order to be able to employ 1 more worker. In this simple example it would appear that one-half of the workers released by the agricultural sector would have been unemployed. On the other hand, the released labor could have easily been absorbed if the capital-labor ratio in manufacturing could have changed. To assess the effects of such an intersectoral shift in demand, therefore, it is important to know how flexible production techniques are.

A similar problem that arises in the American economy (and most other economies) is that the stock of capital available for production generally grows more rapidly than the labor force. Consequently, the productive techniques used by firms must become more *capital intensive* (K/L must rise). If it is relatively easy to substitute capital for labor, this process can be smoothly accomplished. But inflexible techniques would require major disturbances in order to absorb the additional capital.

In a seminal article written in 1961, K. J. Arrow, H. B. Chenery, B. S. Minhas, and R. M. Solow demonstrated a new production function that permitted the ease of input substitution to be determined from real-world data.[15] The Cobb-Douglas and fixed-proportions functions are special cases of this new production function. Although we will not discuss this function here in any technical detail, it is the one that has been used in most recent studies of the flexibility of production.

The 1961 article provided considerable evidence that for the United States economy as a whole production is neither so flexible as implied by the Cobb-Douglas production function nor so inflexible as in the fixed-proportions case. The American economy seems to be characterized by some possibilities for substituting one factor for another, but this substitutability is by no means perfect.

---

[15] K. R. Arrow et al., "Capital Labor Substitution and Economic Efficiency," *Review of Economics and Statistics* 43 (August 1961), pp. 225–250.

The evidence on differences in the flexibility of production among industries is quite inconclusive.[16] There are some indications that production functions in the agriculture, lumber, and primary metals industries are relatively flexible, whereas machinery production is characterized by a low degree of substitutability.

Some authors have suggested that an inflexibility in input substitution is a serious problem facing underdeveloped countries.[17] Since small, less developed countries are subject to rather sudden changes in the demand for the products they export, and since these countries are experiencing a movement of their labor forces from rural to urban areas, this lack of flexibility can have serious repercussions. For example, it has been claimed that the substantial unemployment found in the urban areas of many less developed countries is a direct result of an inability to substitute labor for capital in these countries' industries. Because these countries often must use capital equipment produced in the developed countries, it is often the case that this equipment is not suited for the abundant labor supplies these countries have. A careful analysis of such issues can suggest ways in which productive techniques might be modified to ameliorate the problem.

■ Other Applications of Production Functions

In addition to being a useful way of quantifying the relationship between inputs and outputs in physical production processes, the production function concept can be illuminating in other contexts as well. For situations in which there is interest in analyzing how certain actions have certain results, the production function idea provides a useful unifying device. For example, we might want to study how the various pieces of equipment used by a police force are combined to produce "public safety," how a court system produces law and justice, or how public health programs produce good health in a population. Similarly we might wish to study how labor input, appliances, and time are combined in the home to produce a variety of outputs that are never traded in any market. One major difficulty in making most such studies is developing some adequate measure of the output of the process under consideration. Defining public safety, justice, good health, or even a "good" meal is no simple task. If this problem can be solved, however, the

---

[16]For a summary of many studies see M. Nerlove, "Recent Empirical Studies of the CES and Related Production Functions," in *The Theory and Empirical Analysis of Production*, ed. M. Brown, National Bureau of Economic Research Studies in Income and Wealth (New York: Columbia University Press, 1967).

[17]This problem was first explored in detail by R. S. Eckaus in "The Factor-proportions Problem in Underdeveloped Areas," *American Economic Review* 45 (1955), pp. 539–565. Some evidence that possibilities of substitution are relatively low in a particular less developed country is provided by J. R. Behrman, "Sectoral Elasticities of Substitution between Capital and Labor in a Developing Economy: Time Series Analysis in the Case of Postwar Chile," *Econometrica* 40 no. 2 (March 1972), pp. 311–326.

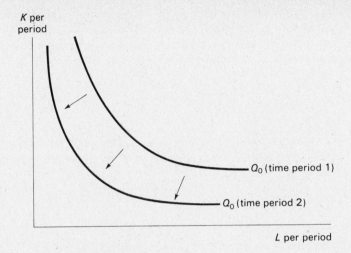

**Figure 6A.1 / Technical Progress
Shifts the Isoquants of a Production Function**

Over time, technical progress causes isoquants to move toward the origin. A given level of output (here Q_0) can be produced with fewer physical inputs than it could be in previous periods.

we will consider various ways in which this technical change may have taken place. Here we will be particularly concerned with the way in which inputs have improved in quality over time. Finally, we will investigate the determinants of technical progress, and we will discuss the way in which innovations in productive technology are spread throughout an economy.

Quantitative Importance of Technical Progress

Mathematics of Growth

Before analyzing the specific ways in which the production function might shift, we will present some data that indicate the importance of technical progress. In order to understand these data, we must first demonstrate the simple mathematical relationship between growth in output and growth in inputs. For this purpose, we will assume that the production function for the economy under study is given by

$$Q = A(t) f(K, L) \qquad \text{[6A.1]}$$

where Q is output, K and L are inputs of capital and labor, and the term $A(t)$ represents shifts in the production function due to technical progress. For example, if the term $A(t)$ grows at 1 percent per year, equation 6A.1 shows that Q would also be growing at 1 percent per year even if K and L stayed constant in each year. This is what we mean by technical progress: more output can be produced from unchanged physical quantities of inputs. The isoquant map of the production function 6A.1 would be very similar to that already diagrammed in Figure 6A.1.

Recording Growth Rates

In order to simplify the discussion, we will introduce some notation to indicate growth rates. By the symbol G_X we mean the growth rate (in percent per year) of the variable X. That is

$$G_X = \text{percent change in } X = \frac{\text{change in } X}{X} = \frac{\Delta X}{X} \qquad \text{[6A.2]}$$

where the change in X is recorded over a one-year period.

Growth rates obey certain simple algebraic rules. The growth rate of the product of two variables (X and Y) is simply the sum of each variable's growth rate:

$$G_{X \cdot Y} = G_X + G_Y \qquad \text{[6A.3]}$$

For example, consider GNP statistics. Suppose real GNP (Q) is growing at 5 percent per year. Suppose also that prices (P) are rising at 3 percent per year. Then money GNP, $(P \cdot Q)$, will, by equation 6A.3, be rising at 8 percent ($= 5 + 3$) per year. The reader should recognize that this sort of calculation is frequently made in everyday statements.

It is similarly easy to show that the rate of growth of the ratio of two variables is given by the difference in the growth rates of the two variables:

$$G_{X/Y} = G_X - G_Y \qquad \text{[6A.4]}$$

For example, if real GNP is growing at 5 percent per year and if population (L) is increasing at 2 percent per year, then real GNP per capita, (Q/L), is growing at 3 percent ($= 5 - 2$ percent) per year. Again this type of calculation is frequently encountered.

Measuring Technical Progress

Using this notation we are now ready to discuss changes in output over time. It is possible to show that, if the production function is given by equation 6A.1, the rate of growth in real output (G_Q) is given by

$$G_Q = G_A + E_{Q,L}G_L + E_{Q,K}G_K \qquad \text{[6A.5]}$$

where $E_{Q,L}$ and $E_{Q,K}$ are the elasticities of output with respect to labor and capital inputs, respectively.[1] Equation 6A.5 says that the growth rate in output is simply the sum of the growth rates of the determinants of Q. The elasticity terms appear in the equation to indicate how responsive Q is to increases in the inputs used in its production.

Equation 6A.5 provides a way of estimating the relative importance of technical progress (G_A) in determining the growth of output. For example, in a study of the United States economy over the period 1909–1949, R. M. Solow records the following values for the terms in equation 6A.5:[2]

$$G_Q = 2.75 \text{ percent per year}$$
$$G_L = 1.00 \text{ percent per year}$$
$$G_K = 1.75 \text{ percent per year}$$
$$E_{Q,L} = 0.65$$
$$E_{Q,K} = 0.35$$

Consequently

$$
\begin{aligned}
G_A &= G_Q - E_{Q,L}\, G_L - E_{Q,K}\, G_K \\
&= 2.75 - 0.65(1.00) - 0.35(1.75) \\
&= 2.75 - 0.65 - 0.60 \\
&= 1.50
\end{aligned}
$$

The conclusion reached, then, is that technology advanced at a rate of 1.5 percent per year over the period 1909–1949. More than one-half of the growth in real output can be attributed to technical change rather than to growth in the physical quantities of the factors of production. That figure becomes even more impressive when the sources of growth in per capita income are examined. Using equation 6A.5 and Solow's estimates for $E_{Q,L}$ and $E_{Q,K}$ we have

$$G_Q = G_A + 0.65\, G_L + 0.35\, G_K \qquad\qquad \text{[6A.6]}$$

Subtracting G_L from both sides gives

$$G_Q - G_L = G_A + 0.35\, (G_K - G_L) \qquad\qquad \text{[6A.7]}$$

---

[1]The proof of this assertion requires calculus and is not presented here. It can be found in W. Nicholson, *Microeconomic Theory: Basic Principles and Extensions,* 2d ed. (Hinsdale, Ill.: The Dryden Press, Inc. 1978), p. 21.

[2]R.M. Solow, "Technical Progress and the Aggregate Production Function," *Review of Economics and Statistics* 39 (August 1957), pp. 312–320. The data in the text are abstracted from Table I and have been rounded off for convenience. The figures for $E_{Q,L}$ and $E_{Q,K}$ are taken from Solow's data on the shares of income accruing to labor and capital. In later chapters (particularly Chapter 13) we will show why such data are relevant to determining the elasticity of output.

or, using rule 6A.4

$$G_{Q/L} = G_A + 0.35G_{K/L} \qquad \text{[6A.8]}$$

That is, the rate of growth in per capita output is equal to the sum of the rate of technical change plus some fraction of the rate of growth in the capital-labor ratio. Again Solow's figures give

$$G_{Q/L} = G_Q - G_L = 2.75 - 1.00 = 1.75$$
$$G_{K/L} = G_K - G_L = 1.75 - 1.00 = 0.75 \qquad \text{[6A.9]}$$

Consequently, output per capita grew at approximately 1.75 percent per year, and more than 80 percent of this growth (1.5/1.75) is attributable to technical change. Increases in the stock of capital per worker played only a minor role in per capita output growth between 1909 and 1949.[3]

How Technical Progress May Have Taken Place

Classifying Technical Progress

The term $A(t)$ and its rate of growth really tell us very little about the mechanism by which technical progress comes about. All we know is that a substantial part of the growth in output is not explained by growth in inputs; this unexplained residual is a "measure of our ignorance." Recognizing the importance of technical progress in explaining economic growth, economists have spent a great deal of effort in trying to understand its determinants. Most of the initial work in this area attempted to determine whether technical progress affected only the stock of machines, or affected only the labor force, or was "neutral" in the sense that it affected both inputs equally. This distinction can be made conceptually with the following production function

$$Q = A(t)f[a(t)K, b(t)L] \qquad \text{[6A.10]}$$

Changes in $A(t)$ over time represent neutral technical progress. If, for example, $A(t)$ is growing at 1 percent per year, fixed quantities of K and L can produce 1 percent

---

[3]We must be careful in inferring from Solow's results that increases in capital are somehow "unimportant" for growth. First, increases in the capital stock are needed in order to equip new workers entering the labor force. Second, it may be that technical change can only occur when it is embodied in new capital equipment (see the discussion of the embodiment hypothesis in this appendix). Finally, some authors have questioned the way in which Solow (and most other economists) chose to measure the capital stock claiming that the methods used tend to minimize the role of capital in the growth process.

more output each year. On the other hand, if technical progress is *capital augmenting*, $a(t)$ increases over time. For example, if $a(t)$ is growing at 2 percent per year then a given capital stock becomes effectively 2 percent larger each year; that is, the capital stock becomes more productive over time. Finally, changes in $b(t)$ signify improvements in the labor force: The labor force may become more productive over time if technical progress is *labor augmenting*.

E. F. Denison's study of the American economy was the first major work to attempt to determine whether the unexplained residual in the growth of GNP was neutral or could more properly be attributed to improvements in the stocks of capital or labor.[4] While it is impossible to survey here all of Denison's conclusions or any of the further analysis his work engendered, we will mention two central findings. First, Denison found that a substantial part (about 40 percent) of the residual could be explained by improvements in the quality of the labor force. This result indicated the strong role that education can have in the growth process. Since Denison's work there have been numerous empirical attempts to understand better the relationship between education and economic growth.

Second, he was relatively unsuccessful in demonstrating the importance of improvements in capital to the growth process. Since many economists believe that improvements in capital equipment are a major means by which new techniques become adopted, this conclusion provided a serious challenge for future analysis. The most interesting models to emerge from his study involve the "embodied" nature of technical progress, and we now turn to consider this hypothesis.

Technical Progress and the Capital Stock

The *embodiment hypothesis* of technical progress starts with the observation that the stock of machinery in an economy at any point in time is in reality a collection of equipment of various ages. Some machines are new and exemplify the latest in modern techniques while other machines were built many years ago. The view of capital augmenting technical progress expressed in equation 6A.10 assumes that all of the capital stock shares equally in technical progress, that is, that both old and new machines become more productive over time. Proponents of the embodiment hypothesis object to this all-encompassing view of technical progress. They argue that technological advances are only manifested in the latest additions to the capital stock and that the productivity of old machines remains more or less constant. This view holds that it is new investment that provides the major method by which technical change is introduced. Consequently, capital accumulation becomes far more important than is implied by studies that do not take the embodied nature of technical change into account. For example, an interesting study by Solow found

---

[4]E. F. Denison, *The Sources of Economic Growth in the United States and the Alternatives before Us*. (New York: Committee for Economic Development, 1962). Denison has also examined growth rates in Europe in *Why Growth Rates Differ: Postwar Experience in Nine Western Countries* (Washington, D.C.: The Brookings Institution, 1967).

that new capital equipment improves at the surprisingly fast rate of 5 percent per year.[5] In terms of productive ability, machines introduced during the current year are 5 percent more effective than were machines produced the previous year. Using this estimate of the improvement experienced by the capital stock, Solow concludes that most of the unexplained growth in output found in earlier studies can be attributed to the embodiment of improved technology in latest additions to the capital stock.

Technical Progress and Labor

Although most investigations of the embodiment hypothesis have involved the importance of improved technology to the capital stock, there is no inherent reason why the same arguments cannot be applied to the labor force as well. The composition of the labor force changes each year as some workers retire and new workers are added. If the new workers entering the labor force are equipped with better skills than those already at work, technical progress is indeed embodied in these new workers. Simply counting labor input in people-hours will miss this qualitative improvement. Another interesting possibility is that workers will learn how to perform a given job more efficiently the longer they remain on it. This "learning curve" was first observed in the manufacture of airframes,[6] but many authors believe it to be an important phenomenon in any precision manufacturing industry. If such learning effects are an important factor in technical progress, we would need to know not only the educational and training levels of the groups of workers who make up the labor force, but also how long each worker had been pursuing his current job. Only from such complete information could we obtain an adequate picture of the effectiveness of the labor force.

There can be no doubt that recognizing the quality of inputs of different "vintages" has been an important step toward a more realistic theory of technical progress. After all, technical progress does not descend like manna from heaven upon all the factors of production in an economy at one time. Technical advances are implemented through more or less conscious decision. The increase in descriptive realism provided by the embodiment hypothesis is not, however, without costs. The principal cost is a great increase in analytical complexity. We can no longer speak of general inputs called "capital" and "labor." We must rather, understand that there

[5] R. M. Solow, *Capital Theory and the Rate of Return* (Amsterdam: North-Holland Publishing Co., 1964), chap. 3.

[6] See for example A. A. Alchian, "Reliability of Progress Curves in Airframe Production," *Econometrica* 31 (October 1963), pp. 679–693. Most estimates of the airframe industry have reported a "learning factor" of about .8. This means that only about 80 percent of the labor input needed to produce one unit of output in an initial period is needed after workers have been at work two periods. A more general discussion of the learning phenomenon can be found in K. J. Arrow, "The Economic Implications of Learning by Doing," *Review of Economic Studies* 29 (June 1962), pp. 155–173.

are many different ages of machines in use at any one time and many workers with different levels of formal education and learning. Developing tools to deal with this additional number of factors of production and assembling adequate data to permit accurate measurement is an important area for future research in the determinants of technical progress.

Causes of Technical Progress

So far in this appendix we have studied the problem of defining and measuring technical progress. We have not, however, discussed the causes of technical progress. Changes in production functions are not random phenomena. Rather, they reflect the results of innovative activities that are somehow generated within the economic system. Economists are therefore not only interested in measuring how production functions have changed, but are also concerned with discovering the ways by which new knowledge is produced and spread throughout the firms in an economy. In studying the nature of technical progress it is customary to make a distinction between *invention*, *innovation*, and *the spread of innovation*. "Invention" is the discovery of new productive techniques; "innovation" is the first commercial application of these techniques; and the "spread of innovation" refers to how new techniques are adopted by different firms. All of these causes of technical progress are affected in important ways by the economic system, and it is important to understand these relationships.

Invention

Thomas Edison said that inventive genius is 1 percent inspiration and 99 percent perspiration. Even without checking the accuracy of those figures, they do make an important point. Invention is in some way related to the inputs into inventive activity. In fact, some economists have discussed the concept of a production function for invention that records the combining of labor (in varying degrees of genius) with capital inputs to produce "new knowledge." Looked at in this way, we might ask several interesting questions about the production function. How much substitution is there among inputs: Can computers substitute for workers? Can average inventors with substantial quantities of equipment be substituted for inventors of true genius? Are there economies of scale in the production of new knowledge: Are the "think-tanks" of large corporations highly productive, or do diseconomies of scale (primarily problems in managerial overseeing) become apparent as research departments expand? Finally (a bit facetiously), we might ask whether there can be technical progress in the production function for inventions: Has the process of invention speeded-up in recent years? All of those questions are just beginning to be asked by economists, and there is as yet very little quantitative information on how knowledge is produced.

Innovation

Besides asking how new knowledge is produced, economists have also investigated the incentives to apply scientific knowledge to the production of economic goods. Two general incentives for innovation have been discussed. First is the role of demand. Demand pressures can create an environment in which inventions and product innovations can be commercially successful. We need only look at the success of the Xerox and Polaroid corporations to observe the possible profit available from innovating to meet a previously unfulfilled demand. Second is the desire to decrease production costs. Such innovation may be of a "neutral" nature in that it saves on the use of all inputs equally, or it may be "biased" in the sense that it economizes relatively more significantly on the use of one particular input. Several economists have suggested that much invention in the United States is biased toward labor-saving techniques since labor is a relatively scarce productive input. Estimating such a bias in the direction of innovation raises difficult theoretical and statistical issues.[7]

Spread of Innovation

It is costly for a firm to adopt a new productive technique. Not only are there the financial costs of adoption to be considered, but there are also the costs of taking the risk of using a new process, the costs of getting information about the invention, and the psychic costs that reflect general resistance to change. All of those factors will go into determining whether a firm will be the first to adopt a new technology and how the use of this new technology will spread among firms. In Chapter 10 we will discuss the basic economics involved in the decision to adopt a new technique. Here we will discuss briefly two general findings about the spread of innovation among firms.

Several authors have found that the spread of innovation can be pictured as an S-shaped (technically, a logistic) curve. In the curve shown in Figure 6A.2, the percent of firms adopting a particular innovation is shown on the vertical axis, and time appears on the horizontal axis. The shape of the curve records that most innovations gain initial acceptance slowly, then undergo a period of rapid growth in acceptance, and finally level off at some upper level of acceptance. A particularly interesting study of this type of spread of an innovation was a paper on the spread of hybrid corn throughout American farm states by Z. Griliches.[8] He found that the shape of each state's S-curve depended on the relative profitability of hybrid corn production there. In a state such as Iowa where hybrid corn was especially suitable,

---

[7]The major issue is how to differentiate between labor-saving innovations and simple substitution of capital for labor (along the isoquant of a fixed production function) in response to changing relative input prices.

[8]Z. Griliches, "Hybrid Corn: An Exploration in the Economics of Technical Change," *Econometrica* 25 (October 1957), pp. 502–522.

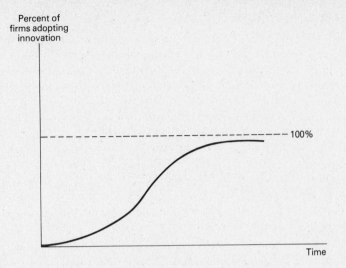

Figure 6A.2 / The S-Shaped Curve of the Spread of Innovation

This curve shows that most innovations exhibit a slow initial acceptance, a period during which many firms adopt the innovation, and a final stage in which adoption ceases (at perhaps less than 100 percent). The shape of the curve may differ among countries, among industries, or even among particular innovations. Economists generally believe that the shape of the curve is determined by the profitability of making innovations.

acceptance of the new technique was quite rapid and adoptions quickly exceeded 90 percent of all farms. In states far from the "Corn Belt" (Alabama, for example) conditions were not so suited to hybrid adoptions and there the spread of innovation was quite slow. These findings add support to an economic theory of innovation and its spread.

A second question asked by economists concerns the speed with which innovation spreads and whether there are significant differences in speed among countries. Since most knowledge (in the absence of patent restrictions) is more or less available to all firms simultaneously, differences in the spread of best-practice techniques can lead to substantial differences in the overall technological level of production in a country. In particular, there is some evidence that the "knowledge gap" between firms in the United States and in Western Europe is more a result of different speeds of innovative spread than a reflection of some basic difference in best-available techniques.[9]

---

[9]A summary of the evidence on this situation and several other interesting observations about current research on technical progress, can be found in C. Kennedy and A. P. Thirwell, "Surveys in Applied Economics: Technical Progress," *Economic Journal* 82: 325 (March 1972), pp. 11–72.

Suggested Readings

Brown, M., *On the Theory and Measurement of Technological Change* (New York: Cambridge University Press, 1968), Chap. 1, 2, and 10.

Denison, E. F., *The Sources of Economic Growth in the United States and the Alternatives before Us* (New York: Committee for Economic Development, 1962).

Kennedy, C., and A. P. Thirwell, "Surveys in Applied Economics: Technical Progress," *The Economic Journal* 82 (March 1972), pp. 11–72.

Mansfield, E., *The Economics of Technical Change* (New York: W. W. Norton and Company, Inc., 1968).

Schmookler, J., *Invention and Economic Growth* (Cambridge, Mass.: Harvard University Press, 1966).

Schumpeter, J., *Capitalism, Socialism, and Democracy* (New York: Harper & Row, Publishers, 1947).

Solow, R. M., "Technical Change and the Aggregate Production Function," *The Review of Economics and Statistics* 39 (August 1957), pp. 312–320.

definitior
accounta
hiring on

Capital

In the cas
of costs (
price of t
arbitrary
to charge
"sunk co:
we will
Economi
would be
rate for tl
itself, the
pay for it:
the rate t
whether t
machine

Entrepre

The conc(
cies that a
of what a
economis
payment
would arg
defined a:
of the ent
firm earns
conclude
many bus
case migh
Economis
owners o1

²In most oth
often confu
chosen here
³An interes
over wheth(

Chapter **7**   Costs

Introduction

Having developed some concepts that describe the technical aspects of production, we can now discuss the firm's costs of production in a rigorous way. We will investigate two basic questions in this chapter. First, how should the firm choose its inputs so as to produce any given level of output as cheaply as possible? Second, how will this process of cost minimization differ between the *short run* and the *long run?* In a sense these questions are still of a technical nature. There will be no mention of demand in this chapter. We are still skirting the crucial issue of how a firm chooses the level of output it will supply. A development of the theory of costs is, however, a necessary prerequisite to any understanding of the nature of the supply decision.

Defining Costs

Before we can discuss the theory of costs some conceptual difficulties about the proper definition of "costs" must be cleared up. At least three different concepts of costs can be distinguished: opportunity cost, accounting cost, and "economic" cost. For economists the most important of these is *social*, or *opportunity*, *cost*. Because resources are limited, any decision in our economy to produce some good necessitates doing without some other good. When an automobile is produced, for example, an implicit decision has been made to do without the, say 15 bicycles that

this alternative earnings possibility should be counted as a cost of their being in the gift shop business. If, for example, the owners of the shop could earn $7,500 if they were employed elsewhere, economists would conclude that the economic profits on the shop are $-\$2,500$. Here is a situation in which accounting profits are positive whereas true economic profits are negative.

Assumption about Economic Costs

In this book, not surprisingly, we will use the economist's definition of cost. This is not meant to imply that the accountant's concepts are irrelevant to economic behavior, however. Indeed, bookkeeping methods are integrally important to any manager's decision-making process because they can greatly affect the rate of taxation to be applied against profits. Accounting costs also have the desirable property of being readily available sources of data. Since the "economic profits" and "costs" of General Motors are never calculated (perhaps not even unambiguously defined), it is usually necessary to use some accounting concepts for empirical work. The economist's definitions do, however, have the desirable features of being broadly applicable to all firms[4] and of forming a conceptually consistent system. They are therefore best suited for a general theoretical analysis.

Two simplifications will initially be made in this chapter about the inputs a firm uses. First, we will assume, as before, that there are only two inputs: worker labor (L, measured in worker hours) and capital (K, measured in machine hours). Cases of more than two inputs can be handled in an analogous way to that used here—most of the proofs carry over directly. The use of only two inputs is simply a graphic convenience.

Second, we will assume that the inputs to the firm are bought in perfectly competitive markets. Firms can buy (or sell) all the labor or capital they want at the prevailing rental rates (w and v). In graphic terms the supply curve for these resources that the firm faces is horizontal at the prevailing factor prices. Both w and v are treated as "parameters" in the firm's decisions; there is nothing the firm can do to affect them. These conditions will be relaxed in later chapters (notably Chapter 14), but for the moment the perfectly competitive assumption is a convenient and useful one to make.

Cost-Minimizing Input Choice

Because of the assumptions we have made so far, the total costs for the firm are given by

$$\text{total costs} = TC = wL + vK \qquad [7.1]$$

---

[4]In fact, in recent years accountants have moved toward economists' definitions in their work. For example, the conceptual model of economic costs has been applied to several topics in depreciation accounting and to the calculation of the profits of life insurance companies.

In other words, total costs are given by the number of labor hours hired (L) times labor's wage (w) plus the number of machine hours hired (K) times capital's rental rate (v). The problem for the firm if it is to operate at minimal cost is to choose quantities of capital and labor so that total costs are minimized for *any* output level. Before we present a graphic analysis of this problem, we should examine an intuitive argument.

Intuitive Analysis

In order to minimize the cost of producing a given level of output, say Q_0, a firm should choose that point on the Q_0 isoquant for which the rate of technical substitution of L for K is equal to the ratio w/v: It should equate the rate at which K can be traded for L in the productive process to the rate at which they can be traded in the market place. Suppose this were not true. In particular, suppose the firm were producing output level Q_0 using $K = 10, L = 10$; assume that the RTS were 2 at this point. Assume also that $w = \$1, v = \$1$, and hence that $w/v = 1$ (which is unequal to 2). At this input combination the cost of producing Q_0 is \$20. It is easy to show this is not the minimal input cost. Q_0 can also be produced using $K = 8$ and $L = 11$; the firm can give up two units of K and keep output constant at Q_0 by adding one unit of L. But at this input combination the cost of producing Q_0 is \$19, and hence the initial input combination was not optimal. A proof similar to this one can be demonstrated any time the RTS and the ratio of the factor costs differ. Therefore we have shown:

Optimization Principle

To minimize the cost of producing any particular output level (Q_0), the firm should choose a combination of inputs (L and K) that is technically capable of producing Q_0 and for which the rate of technical substitution is equal to the ratio of the inputs costs (w/v). In mathematical terms, along the Q_0 isoquant:

$$RTS \text{ (of } L \text{ for } K) = \frac{\text{wage rate}}{\text{rental rate for capital}} = \frac{w}{v} \qquad [7.2]$$

Graphic Presentation

This principle is demonstrated graphically in Figure 7.1. The isoquant Q_0 shows all the combinations of K and L that are able to produce Q_0. We wish to find the least costly point on this isoquant. From equation 7.1 it is easy to see that those combinations of K and L that keep total costs constant lie along a straight line with slope $-w/v$. Consequently, all lines of equal total cost can be shown in Figure 7.1 as a series of parallel straight lines with slopes $-w/v$. Three lines of equal total cost are shown in Figure 7.1: $TC_1 < TC_2 < TC_3$. It is clear from the figure that the minimum total cost for producing Q_0 is given by TC_1 where the total cost curve is just tangent to the isoquant. The cost-minimizing input combination is L^*, K^*. This point will be a true minimum if the isoquant is convex (if the RTS diminishes for increases in

L/K). We have therefore shown that for a cost minimum the slope of the isoquant should equal $-w/v$: at that point of tangency the rate at which the firm is technically able to trade L for K (the RTS) is equal to the rate at which the firm can trade L for K in the market.

Derived Demand for Inputs

Figure 7.1 exhibits the formal similarity between the firm's cost-minimization problem and the individual's utility-maximization problem. In both cases we took prices as fixed parameters and derived the tangency conditions. In Chapter 4 we then asked the question of how the utility-maximizing choice of goods would change if a price were to change. The analysis of this change permitted the construction of the familiar downward–sloping demand curve. An interesting question is whether an analogous development could be made here for the firm's demand for an input. Could we change some input price (change the slope of the TC curves) and then trace out the effects of this price change on the quantity of the factor demanded? The analogy to the individual's utility-maximization process can be misleading at this point. In order to analyze what happens to K^*, say, as v changes, we also have to know what happens to Q_0. The demand for K is a *derived demand* based on the demand for the firm's output. We cannot answer questions about K^* without looking at the goods market. While the analogy to the theory of

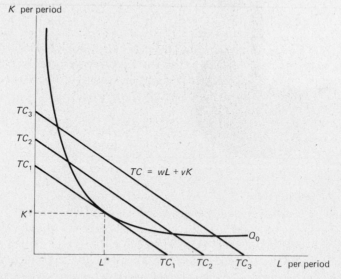

Figure 7.1 / Minimization of Costs Given Q = Q$_0$

A firm is assumed to choose K and L to minimize total costs. The condition for this minimization is that the rate at which K and L can be technically traded (while keeping $Q = Q_0$) should be equal to the rate at which these inputs can be traded in the market. In other words, the RTS (of L for K) should be set equal to the price ratio w/v. This tangency is shown in the figure; costs are minimized at TC_1 by choosing inputs K^* and L^*.

individual behavior is useful in pointing out basic similarities, it is not an exact analogy—the derivation of a firm's demand for an input is considerably more complex. An analysis of the firm's demand for inputs is presented in Part V.

Alternative Interpretation

By using a result from Chapter 6, we can give the cost-minimizing condition an interesting interpretation. In that chapter we showed that the *RTS* (of *L* for *K*) is equal to the ratio of the marginal product of labor to that of capital. Therefore, for a cost minimum

$$RTS \text{ (of } L \text{ for } K) = \frac{MP_L}{MP_K} = \frac{w}{v} \qquad [7.3]$$

or

$$\frac{MP_L}{w} = \frac{MP_K}{v} \qquad [7.4]$$

What equation 7.4 says is that for a cost minimum each input should provide the same additional output per dollar spent on that input. For example, suppose we are studying the production of shoes and $MP_L = 3$ shoes and $MP_K = 8$ shoes. That is, an additional unit of labor will produce 3 more shoes per hour whereas an additional unit of capital produces 8 more shoes. Now suppose $w = \$1$ per unit and $v = \$2$ per unit. It is clear that capital is the "better buy" in this situation, since it provides 4 shoes per dollar spent whereas labor provides only 3 shoes per dollar. The firm could reduce costs by substituting capital for labor. Another way of phrasing this result is that, if costs are to be minimized, an additional unit of output should cost the same amount for the firm regardless of whether it decides to produce this output with additional labor or additional capital. If either input were capable of producing an extra unit of output more cheaply, the firm should substitute this input in its production process.

Firm's Expansion Path

A firm can perform an analysis, such as the one we just performed, for each level of output. For each Q it finds that input choice that minimizes the cost of producing Q. If input costs (w and v) remain constant for all amounts the firm may demand, we can easily trace out this locus of cost-minimizing choices. This procedure is shown in Figure 7.2. The ray *OE* records the cost-minimizing tangencies for successively higher levels of Q. For example, the minimum cost for producing output level Q_1 is given by TC_1, and inputs K_1 and L_1 are used. Other tangencies in the figure can be interpreted in a similar way. The locus of these tangencies is called the firm's *expansion path* because it records how input usage expands as output expands while holding the prices of the inputs constant.

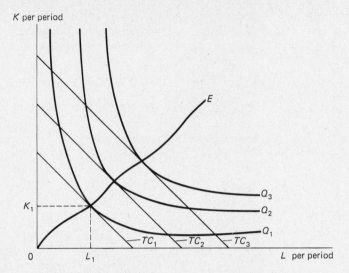

Figure 7.2 / Firm's Expansion Path

The firm's expansion path is the locus of cost-minimizing tangencies. On the assumption of fixed input prices, the curve shows how input usage increases as output increases.

As shown in Figure 7.2, the expansion path need not be a straight line. The use of some inputs may increase faster than others as output expands. Which inputs expand more rapidly will depend on the shape of the production isoquants. Since cost minimization requires that the *RTS* always be set equal to the ratio w/v, and since the w/v ratio is assumed to be constant, the shape of the expansion path will be determined by where a particular *RTS* occurs on successively higher isoquants. In later chapters we will see that the expansion path is an important analytic tool for studying both the firm's output decision and the firm's demand for inputs.

Inferior Inputs

It would seem reasonable to assume that the expansion path will be positively sloped, that successively higher output levels will require more of both inputs. This need not be the case, however, as Figure 7.3 illustrates. Increases of output beyond Q_2 actually cause the quantity of labor used to decrease. In this range labor would be said to be an *inferior input*.[5] The occurrence of inferior inputs is then a theoretical possibility that may happen even when isoquants have their usual convex shape.

Much theoretical discussion has centered on the analysis of factor inferiority. Whether inferiority is likely to occur in real-world production functions is a difficult empirical question to answer. It seems unlikely that such comprehensive mag-

---

[5]Inferior inputs have many graphic similarities to inferior consumption goods, for example, compare Figures 4.3 and 7.3.

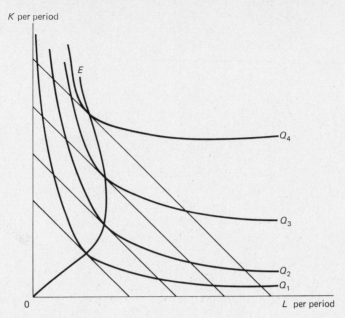

Figure 7.3 / Factor Inferiority

With this particular set of isoquants, labor is an inferior input since less L is chosen as output expands beyond Q_2.

nitudes as "capital" and "labor" could be inferior, but a finer classification of inputs may bring inferiority to light. For example, the employment of "unskilled labor" may decline as output increases. In this book we will not be particularly concerned with the analytical complications raised by this possibility.

Distinction Between the Short Run and the Long Run

It has been traditional in economics to make a distinction between the *short run* and the *long run*. These terms are used in order to denote the length of time over which a firm has a chance to alter its decisions, and they are useful terms for studying market responses to changed conditions. If only a short period is allowed, it may be necessary for a firm to treat some of its inputs as being fixed. It may be technically impossible to change the level of employment of those inputs on short notice. For example, if a time interval of only one week is chosen, it would be necessary to treat the size of a firm's plant as absolutely fixed. Similarly, an entrepreneur may be committed to a particular business in the short run, and it would be impossible (or extremely costly) to retire. In the short run, therefore, the entrepreneur's input to the production process is essentially fixed. Over a longer period, however, a firm might not want to treat either of those inputs as being fixed since it is clear that a firm's size of plant can be altered and that an entrepreneur can indeed quit the business. The distinction to be made then is between a period over which the levels of some inputs' usage are fixed and a longer period over which all inputs become variable. By so doing, we will be able to study the different types of responses that a firm might make.

Short-Run Production Function

There are several possible ways of introducing the short-run, long-run distinction into the analysis of the firm we have so far presented. Probably the easiest method (and the one we will use here) is to assume that one of the productive inputs is held constant in the short run. Specifically we will assume that capital input is held constant at a level of K_1 and that (in the short run) the firm is only free to vary its labor input. As a result of this assumption, we may write the short-run production function as

$$Q = f(K_1, L) \tag{7.5}$$

where this notation explicitly shows that capital inputs may not vary. Of course the level of Q may still be changed by the firm by altering its use of labor. We have already studied this possibility in Chapter 6 when we examined the marginal productivity of labor. Here we are interested in analyzing the way in which changes in a firm's output level in the short run are related to changes in total costs.

A Note on Input Flexibility

Before turning to this question, we should comment on the method of analysis we have chosen. It is obvious that any firm uses far more than two inputs in its production process. The level of usage of some of these inputs may be changed on rather short notice. Firms may ask workers to work overtime hours, hire part-time replacements from an employment agency, or rent equipment (such as power tools or automobiles) from some other firm. It may take a somewhat longer time for the level of usage of other inputs to be adjusted; for example, to hire new, full-time workers is a relatively time-consuming (and costly) process. Similarly, ordering new machines designed to unique specifications may involve a considerable time lag. At the most lengthy extreme, plant size may be changed, new managers may be recruited and trained, and raw material supplies may be discovered and extraction may have begun. To cover all such variations of input types in any detail is an impossibility. Consequently we will proceed by using only the two-input model we have been analyzing, and we will hold the level of capital input fixed. Such a treatment should not be taken to imply that in some way labor is a more flexible input than is capital. As we have just pointed out, this need not be the case. Rather, all we wish to do is to make a distinction between fixed and variable inputs, and this approach will enable us to do so. We could substitute any other appropriate input names for "capital" and "labor" in the discussion that follows.

Short-Run Total Costs

Total cost for the firm continues to be given by

$$TC = vK + wL \qquad [7.6]$$

for our short-run analysis, but now capital input is fixed at K_1. To denote this fact we will write

$$STC(K_1) = vK_1 + wL \qquad [7.7]$$

where the addition of S makes it clear that we are analyzing the short run and the notation also records the level of capital usage that is being held constant. The two types of input costs in equation 7.7 are given special names. The term vK_1 is referred to as (short-run) *fixed costs;* since K_1 is constant, these costs will not change in the short run. The term wL is referred to as (short-run) *variable costs* since labor input can indeed be varied in the short run. Using the symbols $SFC(K_1)$ for short-run fixed costs and $SVC(K_1)$ for short-run variable costs we have

$$SFC(K_1) = vK_1$$
$$SVC(K_1) = wL \qquad [7.8]$$

and therefore

$$STC(K_1) = SFC(K_1) + SVC(K_1) \qquad [7.9]$$

We have therefore classified short-run total costs as:

Definition

In the short run, costs of fixed inputs are called *fixed costs*. Costs of variable inputs are called *variable costs*. Short-run total costs are the sum of these two components.

What we wish to do now is to examine how short-run total costs change as the firm's output changes.

Short-run Fixed and Variable Cost Curves

In the short run, fixed costs are obviously "fixed." They do not change as the level of output changes. This relationship is shown in Figure 7.4a. The $SFC(K_1)$ curve is simply a horizontal line representing the cost of the fixed amount of capital being employed. Figure 7.4b records one possible relationship between short-run variable costs and output. The assumption made here is that initially the marginal productivity of labor is rising as labor is added to the production process. Since there is

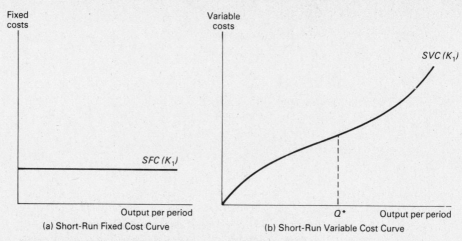

Figure 7.4 / Fixed and Variable Costs in the Short Run

The curve $SFC(K_1)$ in 7.4a shows that fixed costs do not vary in the short run. They are determined by the fixed input of capital (here K_1) being used. Variable costs do change as the output increases. The shape shown in 7.4b assumes that initially labor exhibits an increasing marginal productivity but that, after some point, the marginal productivity of labor diminishes, thus causing short-run costs to rise rapidly.

a fixed input of capital initially this capital is "underutilized," and labor's marginal productivity rises as the amount of labor available to work with this fixed amount of capital increases. Because the marginal product of labor is increasing, short-run variable costs rise less rapidly as output expands—in its initial section, the $SVC(K_1)$ curve is concave downward. Beyond some output level, say Q^*, however, the marginal product of labor will begin to decline. Because capital input is constant at K_1, the ability of labor to generate extra output will diminish; since the per-unit cost of labor is assumed to be constant, costs of production will begin to rise rapidly. Beyond Q^* the $SVC(K_1)$ curve becomes concave upward to reflect this diminishing marginal productivity of labor. For output levels to the right of Q^*, existing capital inputs are being "overutilized." What we have shown, therefore, is that the shape of the $SVC(K_1)$ curve shown in Figure 7.4b is in general agreement with the initial hypotheses we made about the marginal productivity of labor in Chapter 6 (see especially Figure 6.1).

Short-Run Total Cost Curve

We should now be able to construct the short-run total cost curve by summing the $SFC(K_1)$ and $SVC(K_1)$ curves, as is required by the definition given in equation 7.9. This total cost curve is shown in Figure 7.5. Two features of the figure should be pointed out explicitly. First, notice that when output is 0 total costs are given by fixed costs, $SFC(K_1)$. Since capital input is fixed, it must be paid its rental rate even if no production takes place. The firm cannot avoid these fixed costs in the short run.

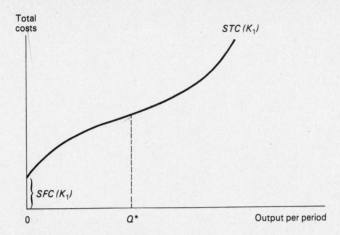

Figure 7.5 / Short-run Total Cost Curve

This curve simply represents the summation of the two curves shown in Figure 7.4. Short-run fixed costs determine the zero-output intercept for the curve, whereas the short-run variable cost curve determines the total cost curve's shape.

It can, of course, avoid all variable costs simply by hiring no labor. A second important feature of the graph is that the shape of the curve is solely determined by the shape of the short-run variable cost curve. It is the way in which changes in output affect costs that determines the shape of the curve; since fixed costs are constant, they play no role in determining the shape of the $STC(K_1)$ curve other than determining its zero-output intercept.

Input Inflexibility and Cost Minimization

It is important to understand that the costs shown in Figure 7.5 are not the minimal costs for producing the various output levels shown. Because we are holding capital fixed in the short run, the firm does not have the flexibility in input choice that was assumed when we discussed cost minimization earlier in this chapter. Rather, to vary its output level in the short run, the firm will be forced to use "nonoptimal" input combinations: the RTS will not be equal to the ratio of the input prices. This is shown in Figure 7.6. In the short run, the firm is constrained to use K_1 units of capital. To produce output level Q_0 it will therefore use L_0 units of labor. Similarly, it will use L_1 units of labor to produce Q_1, and L_2 units to produce Q_2. The total costs of these input combinations is given by TC_0, TC_1, and TC_2, respectively. Only for the input combination K_1, L_1 is output being produced at minimal cost. Only at that point is the RTS equal to the ratio of the input prices. From Figure 7.6 it is clear that Q_0 is being produced with "too much" capital in this short-run situation. Cost minimization should suggest a southeasterly movement along the Q_0 isoquant indicating a substitution of labor for capital in production. Similarly Q_2 is being produced with "too little" capital, and costs could be reduced by substituting

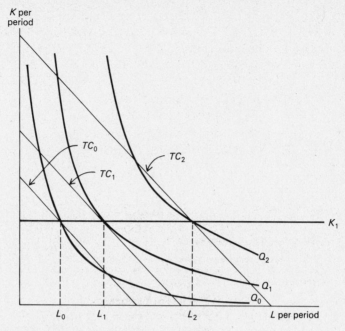

Figure 7.6 / "Nonoptimal" Input Choices Must Be Made in the Short Run

Because capital input is fixed at K_1 in the short run, the firm cannot bring its *RTS* into equality with the ratio of input prices. Given the input prices, Q_0 should be produced with more labor and less capital than it will be in the short run, whereas Q_2 should be produced with more capital and less labor than it will be.

capital for labor. Neither of these substitutions is possible in the short run. However, over a longer period the firm will be able to change its level of capital input and will adjust its input usage to the cost-minimizing combinations. We have already discussed this flexible case earlier in this chapter, and will return to it when we analyze long-run cost curves.

Per Unit Short-Run Cost Curves

The short-run total cost curve summarizes the relationship between output levels and total costs in the short run. Since this is precisely the information relevant to firms' short-run output decisions, it would be feasible to proceed simply to analyze those decisions. Frequently, however, we will find it more useful to analyze costs on a per-unit of output basis rather than on a total basis, and therefore we will delay our discussion of firms' decisions in order to construct such curves. The two most important per-unit curves that can be derived from the short-run total cost curve are the short-run average total cost curve and the short-run marginal cost curve. These concepts are defined as:

Definition

Short-run average costs (SATC) are defined to be total costs per unit of output. *Short-run marginal costs* (SMC) are defined as the change in total costs brought about by a one-unit increase in output. Mathematically:

$$SATC(K_1) = \frac{\text{total costs}}{\text{total output}} = \frac{STC(K_1)}{Q}$$

[7.10]

$$SMC(K_1) = \frac{\text{change in total costs}}{\text{change in output}} = \frac{\Delta STC(K_1)}{\Delta Q}$$

In these definitions we have continued to record the level of capital input, which is fixed in the short run. We now wish to show how these two cost concepts can be derived from the total cost curve.

Short-Run Marginal Cost Curve

In Figure 7.7a the short-run total cost curve has been redrawn. Short-run marginal costs are given by the slope of this total cost curve, since the slope reflects how costs change when output changes. Because of the shape of the $STC(K_1)$ curve, marginal costs initially fall. The cost of producing one more unit falls because the marginal productivity of labor is initially increasing. At Q^* the $STC(K_1)$ curve has a point of inflexion—it changes from being concave downward to concave upward. Beyond Q^*, therefore, marginal costs begin to increase. Again this records that beyond Q^* the marginal productivity of labor is diminishing. Because of the assumed shape of the short-run total cost curve, the marginal cost curve in Figure 7.7b has a U-shape. Initially marginal costs fall. But after a point diminishing marginal productivities set in (because some inputs are fixed in the short run), and this causes marginal costs to rise.

Short-Run Average Cost Curve

The short-run average cost curve is constructed from the total cost curve by drawing a chord through the origin to each point on the $STC(K_1)$ curve. The slope of this chord will be the ratio of short-run total costs to Q, and this is required by the definition of short-run average costs. For example, at Q_0 the slope of the chord is given by STC_0/Q_0, and this is the required average cost figure. By using some geometric intuition it is easy to see that the slope of this chord (that is, average costs) declines up to output level Q^{**} and increases thereafter. Consequently the $SATC(K_1)$ curve will also have a U-shape. The curve is shown in Figure 7.7b.

Figure 7.7b shows that at Q^{**} average and marginal costs are equal; the SMC curve passes through the low point of the $SATC$ curve. That this is the case is geometrically obvious from Figure 7.7a. Average costs reach a minimum at Q^{**}, and there the slope of the chord through the origin is exactly equal to the slope of the

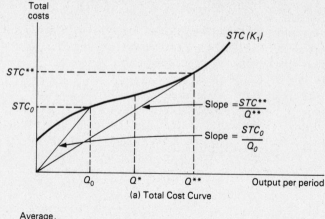

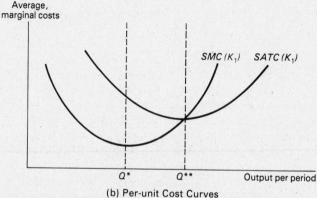

(b) Per-unit Cost Curves

Figure 7.7 / Construction of Short-run Average and Marginal Cost Curves from a Firm's Short-run Total Cost Curve

The short-run marginal cost curve reflects the slope of the *STC* curve. The curve has a U-shape because of the assumptions about total costs that we have made. The short-run average curve also has a U-shape. Average and marginal costs are equal at Q^{**} since this is the low point of the *SATC* curve.

STC curve itself. By definition, therefore, average and marginal costs are equal. For output levels below Q^{**}, marginal cost is less than average cost; producing one more unit will reduce average costs. Hence average costs must be falling. Conversely, for output levels in excess of Q^{**}, marginal costs exceed average costs; this will have the effect of causing average costs to rise. At Q^{**}, therefore, the marginal cost curve passes through the low point of the *SATC* curve.[6] When $SMC = SATC$, average costs are not changing, and therefore the slope of the *SATC* curve is 0.

---

[6] An analogy may help here. If on your most recent quiz (that is your marginal quiz) you received a lower grade than your previous average, that average must be falling. On the other hand, if your most recent quiz score exceeded your average, the average must be rising. When the marginal and average grades are identical, your average will not change.

Other Short-Run Cost Curves

Occasionally it is useful to divide short-run average total costs into two components: average *fixed* costs and average *variable* costs.

Definition

Short-run average fixed costs (SAFC) are defined as total short-run fixed costs per unit of output. Similarly, *short-run variable costs* are defined as total short-run variable costs per unit of output. In algebraic terms:

$$SAFC(K_1) = \frac{\text{total fixed costs}}{\text{output}} = \frac{SFC(K_1)}{Q}$$

[7.11]

$$SAVC(K_1) = \frac{\text{total variable costs}}{\text{output}} = \frac{SVC(K_1)}{Q}$$

These two components sum exactly to total short-run average costs because all costs have been categorized as being either fixed of variable in the short run.

Although we will not show the derivation of these curves in detail, the curves are drawn in Figure 7.8, together with the marginal and average total cost curves we have already derived. The *SAFC* curve is simply a hyperbola reflecting that as Q increases, fixed costs are being divided by a larger and larger number. The *SAVC*

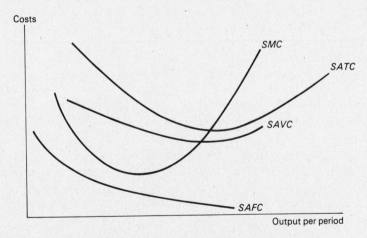

Figure 7.8 / Short-run Average Fixed and Variable Cost Curves

The *SAFC* curve is simply a hyperbola since fixed costs are being divided by a progressively higher output level. The *SAVC* curve reflects the results of subtracting average fixed costs from average total costs. The *SAVC* curve therefore approaches the *SATC* curve at high output levels. In the diagram we have omitted the fixed capital input notation, but the reader should remember that capital is being held constant in this short-run figure.

curve has a shape generally similar to the *SATC* curve but always falls below it to the extent of average fixed costs. At high levels of output the *SATC* and *SAVC* curves get very close together since average fixed costs become small. By an argument similar to the one we presented for the average total cost curve, we can show that the short-run marginal cost curve also passes through the low point of the average variable cost curve. This is also shown in Figure 7.8. In later chapters we will make considerable use of the *SATC* and *SMC* curves. The *SAFC* and *SAVC* curves will be of less use, although they will enter the analysis on one or two occasions.

Examples of Short-Run Cost Curves

The reason economists examine short-run cost curves is to gain some insight into how costs change in response to short-run fluctuations in output. This (as we shall see in Chapter 9) in turn provides information about the nature of the supply response that firms can make to changes in demand. *A priori* there is a strong expectation that both marginal and average costs will increase in response to increases in output. This belief stems from the view that firms are usually operating "near capacity" and that increasing output will raise costs as some variable inputs are added to the productive process while others must be held fixed. By imagining a suitably large increase in the employment of variable factors, it seems that average costs must indeed start to rise, if only because workers would begin to interfere with each other. The important question is whether such increasing costs can be brought about by the relatively small fluctuations in output that occur in a firm's normal experience, and this is the question to which most short-run cost curve studies have been addressed.

A majority of those studies fail to show sharply increasing average or marginal costs. In fact, the common conclusion is that marginal and average costs are approximately constant over a relatively broad range of output levels. J. Dean, for example, found this to be true in such diverse firms as a leather belt shop, a department store, furniture production, and a hosiery mill.[7] Other authors have found similar results for steel production, cement production, and grocery retailers.

Given the problems inherent in analyzing cost curves, and in view of the "reasonableness" of the increasing marginal cost assumption, economists have not been greatly convinced by those studies. Many other pieces of evidence suggest that marginal costs of production do increase for modest increments to output. For example, prices seem to rise in most markets in response to short-run shifts in demand. As we will see in Chapter 9, the most obvious explanation for this is that marginal costs rise as firms attempt to expand output to meet the new demand. Other supporting evidence comes from engineering studies that show

---

[7]The Dean studies are summarized in Johnston, *Statistical Cost Functions*. The references are also given in A.A. Walters, "Production and Cost Functions: An Econometric Survey," *Econometrica* 31, nos. 1–2 (January–April 1963), pp. 1–66.

that optimal operating rates for certain types of machines occur in rather narrow ranges of output. Attempting to obtain increased output from these machines by using them more intensively in the short run causes marginal costs to rise because of both decreased operating efficiency and an increased frequency of machine malfunctions. In view of these observations, we must regard the results from statistical studies of short-run curves as ambiguous. Until better data and better statistical models become available, we are forced to accept the assumption of increasing short-run average and marginal costs because of its intuitive "reasonableness" rather than because it is firmly established by empirical observation.

Increasing Costs from Congestion

One area in which the phenomenon of increasing cost is unambiguous is the case of traffic congestion. The demand placed on transportation facilities (for example, expressways) during peak travel hours can be viewed as an increase in output (vehicle miles) in the short run. Because some inputs (the size of the roadway) are held fixed when such output increases occur, there is the expectation that costs will rise. These increased costs will be primarily experienced by travelers in the form of increased time delays, although it is possible that other costs (such as the costs of road maintenance) may increase as well. Anyone who has driven on a busy urban expressway at 8:00 A.M. or tried to land at a major airport at 4:00 P.M. knows that these costs can be substantial.

Some evidence on rising costs as a result of congestion is presented in Table 7.1. Two situations are reported: (1) costs of automobile travel on San Francisco Bay Area expressways; and (2) costs of landing at LaGuardia Airport in New York City. Both sets of figures refer to the marginal cost incurred by having one more

Table 7.1 / Increasing Marginal Time Costs During Peak Travel Hours

Time Period	San Francisco Expressways		LaGuardia Airport	
	Marginal Costs (Cents per vehicle mile)	Actual Hours of the Day	Marginal Costs (Dollars per arriving flight)	Actual Hours of the Day
Peak Hours	38.1¢	7–8 AM, 5–6 PM	$1025	3–5 PM
Near Peak Hours	8.9¢	6–7, 8–9 AM, 4–5, 6–7 PM	$670	1–3, 5–7 PM
Off Peak Hours	7.7¢	Other times	0–$200	Other times

Sources: *Expressways*: T. E. Keeler and K. A. Small, "Optimal Peak-Load Pricing, Investment, and Service Levels on Urban Expressways," *Journal of Political Economy* 85, No. 1 (February 1977), pp. 1–26; figures are calculated from equation 16 and from Table 5, p. 18.

LaGuardia Airport: A. Carlin and R. F. Park, "Marginal Cost Pricing of Airport Runway Capacity," *American Economic Review* LX, No. 3 (June 1970), pp. 310–319. Figures are averaged from Table 2, p. 314.

"unit of output" (that is, respectively, one more vehicle mile or one more arriving flight). As the table shows, such costs increase markedly during hours of peak travel demand. For both facilities peak hour marginal costs represent a more than four-fold increase over those incurred at off-peak hours. These data show that individuals who choose to travel during peak hours impose considerable costs (primarily in terms of time delays) on their fellow travelers. In Part VII we will return to this example to show how the use of tolls during peak hours might provide incentives to individuals to use such transportation facilities in more "optimal" ways.

Long-Run Total Cost Curve

You will remember that we defined the "long run" as a period over which all (or almost all) productive inputs are variable. In the long run, then, plant sizes may be altered and entrepreneurs may enter or leave an industry. In this section we will examine how a firm's long-run input choices are related to their short-run input choices, and we will derive a long-run curve that relates total costs to output level.

Because of the assumptions we have made about the two-input nature of the production function, we can easily study long-run behavior. All we need to do is permit the firm to adjust its capital input usage in order to minimize long-run total costs. Actually we have examined this process earlier in this chapter when we showed that in order to minimize costs, the firm must produce any given output level with that combination of inputs for which the RTS is equal to the ratio of the inputs' prices. This process permits the construction of the expansion path, which shows how input choices (and hence total costs) change as output changes. Here we will present a rather different analysis that arrives at exactly the same conclusion regarding cost-minimizing input choices.

Choice of Capital Input in the Long Run

Let us suppose that a firm has decided to produce output level Q_1 in the long run. How will it choose the "correct" quantity of capital to use in the production of Q_1 so as to minimize total costs? One possible method would be for the firm to examine the short-run total cost curve for each possible level of capital input. Three such short-run total cost curves are shown in Figure 7.9. Here the total cost curve $STC(K_0)$ refers to the total cost curve that prevails for a fixed capital input of K_0; $STC(K_1)$ refers to that which prevails when capital input is K_1; and $STC(K_2)$ depicts the total cost curve for a capital input level of K_2. It is obvious from Figure 7.9 that K_1 is the lowest cost level of capital input that might be used to produce output level Q_1. Using K_0 would not be appropriate since to produce output level Q_1 using K_0 causes far too much labor to be used relative to this amount of capital. The upward slope of the $STC(K_0)$ curve at Q_1 indicates that strong diminishing returns to labor

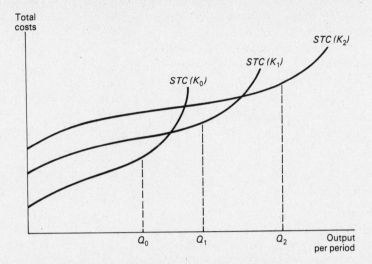

Figure 7.9 / Long-run Cost-minimizing Choice of Capital Input

In the long run, the firm may choose its capital input so as to minimize total costs. This would require a choice of K_0 to produce output level Q_0; K_1 to produce output level Q_1; and K_2 to produce Q_2. The cost-minimizing choice implied by this diagram is identical to that shown in Figure 7.1. In both diagrams, firms have complete flexibility in choosing both K and L to minimize the costs of producing any output level.

input have set in. On the other hand, K_2 represents "too much" capital being used for the production of Q_1. With K_2 units of capital input, fixed costs are very high; this fact makes K_2 nonoptimal for producing Q_1. Of course, if the firm wanted to produce a relatively small output in the long run (say Q_0), then K_0 might be an appropriate level of capital input. Similarly, if the firm desired a high output level (say Q_2), then K_2 would be the correct level of capital input. Clearly the cost-minimizing choice of K will depend on how much output the firm wishes to produce.

Construction of the Long-Run Total Cost Curve

Although Figure 7.9 shows only three short-run total cost curves reflecting three possible levels of capital input, there are in reality an infinite number of such short-run total cost curves, one for every conceivable level of capital input. In order to construct the *long-run total cost curve* (*LTC*), we must consider all of those short-run curves and choose the lowest one for producing *each* possible output level. For any Q we must find the "correct" amount of capital for producing this output level, and it is possible to do so by referring to the entire set of short-run curves. The locus of all these cost-minimizing choices is called the long-run total cost curve because it summarizes the relationship between costs and output when all inputs are variable.

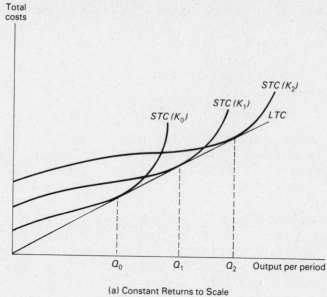

(a) Constant Returns to Scale

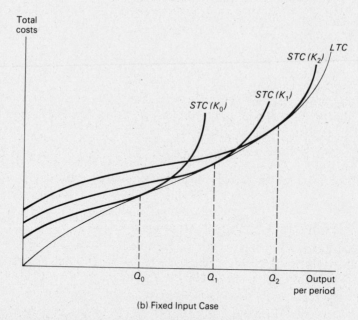

(b) Fixed Input Case

Figure 7.10 / Two Possible Shapes for Long-run Total Cost Curves

By considering all possible levels of capital input, the long-run total cost curve (LTC) can be traced out. In 7.10a the underlying production function exhibits constant returns to scale—in the long run, total costs are proportional to output. In 7.10b the production function contains a factor that is fixed even in the long run. For this reason, costs rise rather slowly initially but rise rapidly for high output levels as diminishing marginal productivities to both K and L occur.

The construction of two differently shaped long-run total cost curves is shown in Figure 7.10. In 7.10a we have assumed that the production function is characterized by constant returns to scale. This implies that costs will be proportional to output in the long run—the *LTC* curve is a straight line. Since an increase in output for a constant returns to scale production function requires a proportional increase in all inputs, costs will also rise by this proportion.[8] Figure 7.10b shows an alternative shape for the *LTC* curve. Here we have assumed that there is some fixed factor in the production process that cannot be changed even in the long run.[9] For example, it may not be possible for a firm to change the quantity of land it uses even over the very long term, or it may have to treat the services of its manager-owner as fixed over the long run. The presence of such a fixed input will cause the firm's *LTC* curve to have a shape that resembles that of a short-run curve. For low levels of *Q* the fixed factor is underutilized, and costs do not rise very rapidly as *Q* expands. Beyond some point, however, the presence of the fixed factor causes other factors to exhibit diminishing marginal productivities (this is analogous to the case of labor in short-run analysis), and costs will begin to rise rapidly. The presence of a fixed factor therefore causes the *LTC* curve to have a shape very different from that which characterizes a constant returns to scale production function. In the next section we will derive long-run average and marginal cost curves for the two long-run total cost curves shown in Figure 7.10, and we will show why discovering the shape of long-run cost curves is an empirical question that has important implications for public policy.

Per Unit Long-Run Cost Curves

The *LTC* curve summarizes the relationship between quantity produced and total cost when long-run adjustments in capital input are permitted. It is a simple matter to derive long-run average and marginal cost curves from the total cost curve. As before, we define

---

[8]This can be easily shown with simple algebra. Suppose that the cost-minimizing combination of K and L necessary to produce 1 unit of output is given by K_1, L_1. Hence $Q = 1 = f(K_1, L_1)$, and the costs of one unit of output are $TC_1 = vK_1 + wL_1$. Now, to produce m units of output requires $m \cdot L_1$ units of labor and $m \cdot K_1$ units of capital. Therefore $TC_m = v \cdot m \cdot K_1 + w \cdot m \cdot L_1 = m \cdot TC_1$. Hence long-run total costs rise proportionally with output. For an example, see the numerical example that follows later in the text.

[9]The perceptive reader will note that this explanation marks a departure from our assumption that K and L are the only inputs in the productive process. An alternative approach would be to assume that the production function itself initially exhibits increasing returns to scale, then constant returns to scale, and finally decreasing returns to scale. Most of the reasons that have been put forward for a production function's having such a shape usually resort to some form of fixed factor argument. It is perhaps best to present this approach explicitly rather than to introduce the production function shape as some undefined attribute of "nature."

Definition

Long-run average cost (LATC) is defined to be the ratio of long-run total cost to the quantity produced. Long-run marginal cost is defined to be the change in long-run total costs for a one-unit increase in output. Mathematically:

$$LATC = \frac{\text{total costs}}{\text{output}} = \frac{LTC}{Q}$$

[7.12]

$$LMC = \frac{\text{change in total costs}}{\text{change in output}} = \frac{\Delta LTC}{\Delta Q}$$

Our construction of the *LATC* and *LMC* curves from the total cost curve proceeds in exactly the same way as did our construction of the short-run curves. In Figures 7.11 and 7.12 long-run curves derived from the hypothetical long-run total cost curves shown in Figure 7.10 are presented. Both Figures 7.11 and 7.12 also show three sets of short-run curves that correspond to the three short-run total cost curves sketched in Figure 7.10. What we wish to examine is the relationship between the long-run curves and the short-run curves.

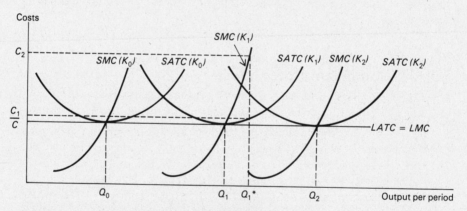

Figure 7.11 / Long-run Average and Marginal Cost Curves for the Constant Returns to Scale Case

This figure is derived from the long-run curves shown in Figure 7.10a. Because the underlying production function exhibits constant returns to scale, long-run average and marginal costs will be constant (and equal) over all output ranges. In this figure, three sets of short-run curves are also shown for three different levels of capital input.

Constant Returns to Scale Case

The average and marginal cost curves in Figure 7.11 correspond to the constant returns to scale case shown in Figure 7.10a. Since the *LTC* curve is a straight line in Figure 7.10a, average and marginal costs will be constant (and equal) in the long run. Because of the constant returns nature of the underlying production function, producing one more unit will cost exactly the same no matter how much is produced. The $LATC$ and LMC curves are therefore the same horizontal line in Figure 7.11, and this line represents the long-run per-unit cost of production. In Figure 7.11 three short-run sets of curves are shown for different levels of capital input. Each of the short-run average cost curves is tangent to the long-run average cost curve at that output level for which the short-run choice of capital input reflected by the curve is appropriate in the long run as well. For example, long-run cost minimization requires that K_1 units of capital input be used to produce output level Q_1, and the short-run average cost curve associated with K_1 is tangent to the $LATC$ curve at Q_1. Figure 7.11, then, clearly shows that although per-unit costs are constant in the long run, short-run output fluctuations may cause costs to rise rather steeply. A firm initially producing output level Q_1 would incur an average cost of $\overline{C}$. If the firm wished to expand production to $Q_1{}^*$ because of an increased demand for its product, it would incur an average cost of C_1 and a marginal cost of C_2. Because capital is fixed at K_1 in the short run, cost rises rapidly as output is adjusted away from Q_1. In later chapters we will wish to analyze this short-run cost response and its implications for pricing. It is important to recognize that, in this constant returns to scale case, the increased costs associated with producing $Q_1{}^*$ are strictly short-run phenomena. In the long run, average and marginal costs will again fall to $\overline{C}$. The firm will be able to increase its capital inputs, and this will bring costs down to their constant per-unit level.

Fixed Input Case

The long-run average and marginal cost curves shown in Figure 7.12 have the familiar U-shapes that we saw in the case of short-run curves. Such a shape reflects the shape of the LTC curve in Figure 7.10b, and this was in turn derived from the assumption that some productive input must be treated as being fixed in the long run. Average costs fall initially as more variable inputs are added to this fixed input. Beyond some point, however, average costs rise as diminishing marginal productivities to the variable inputs set in. Long-run average costs reach a minimum at Q_1. We might therefore say that the optimum long-run output level is Q_1. In later chapters we will show that it is quite important to know how large the optimum output level is for a firm. If this level is "large" relative to the potential demand for the firm's product, only a few firms will be able to coexist in the market. The economies that arise from large-scale operation will permit one or two firms to drive their competitors out of business. On the other hand, if the minimum $LATC$ output is "small" relative to total market demand, many firms may be able to coexist in the market. Each firm can produce at minimum average cost and still supply only a small portion of total demand. Of course, this whole discussion of optimal sizes of firms relies on the assumption

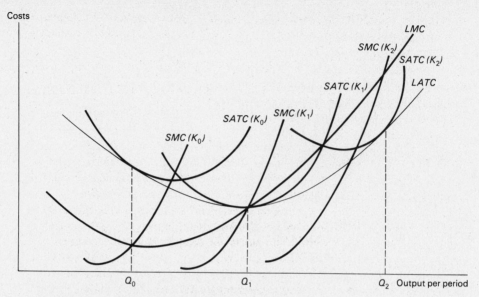

**Figure 7.12 / Long-run Average and
Marginal Cost Curves for the Fixed Input Case**

This set of curves is derived from the total cost curves shown in Figure 7.10b. The *LATC* and *LMC* curves have the usual U-shapes, reflecting the effects of a factor of production that is fixed in the long run. At Q_1, long-run average costs are minimized. The configuration of curves at this minimum point is quite important.

that the *LATC* curve is U-shaped. If the curve for a particular firm were horizontal (the constant returns to scale case shown in Figure 7.11), the firm would be able to produce any output level at the same minimum *LATC*; that is, no one output level would be superior to any other.

Minimum Point of the *LATC* Curve

Because the minimum point of the *LATC* curve plays an important role in the theory of long-run price determination, it is important to note the various curves that pass through this point in Figure 7.12. First, as is always true for average and marginal cost curves, the *LMC* curve passes through the low point of the *LATC* curve. At Q_1 long-run average and marginal costs are equal. Associated with Q_1 is a certain level of capital input (say K_1), and the short-run average cost curve for this level of capital input [$SATC(K_1)$] is tangent to the *LATC* curve at its minimum point. The $SATC(K_1)$ curve also reaches its minimum at output level Q_1. For movements away from Q_1, the *LATC* curve is much flatter than the $SATC(K_1)$ curve, and this reflects the greater flexibility open to firms in the long run. Short-run costs rise rapidly because capital inputs are fixed. In the long run, such inputs are not fixed, and diminishing marginal productivities do not occur so abruptly. Finally, because the $SATC(K_1)$ curve reaches its minimum at Q_1, the short-run marginal cost curve [$SMC(K_1)$] also passes through this point. The minimum point of the *LATC* curve therefore brings together the four most important per-unit costs we have been analyzing. At this point

$$LATC = LMC = SATC(K_1) = SMC(K_1) \qquad\qquad [7.13]$$

For this reason, as we will show in Chapter 10, the output level Q_1 is an important equilibrium point for the firm in the long run.

Examples of Long-Run Cost Curves

Economists study long-run cost curves in order to discover something about the appropriate scale of operation for various industries. They are particularly interested in estimating the output level (or range of levels) for which long-run average cost reaches its minimum value. The location of this point of minimum long-run average cost is indicative of whether or not the industry in question is appropriate for the development of large-scale firms. If the point of minimum long-run average cost occurs at an output level that is small relative to the total industry output, economists would argue that it is efficient for such an industry to contain many small firms. For the American economy this observation has been made most often for the agricultural industry, where it appears that long-run average costs reach a minimum for farms of a relatively small size (400–800 acres). On the other hand, there are industries for which long-run average cost curves seem to be downward sloping over a broad range of output levels; that is, the point of minimum average cost occurs at an output level that represents a substantial portion of total industry production. Economists sometime refer to such industries as exhibiting "increasing returns to scale," as indicated by their negatively sloped *LATC* curves. Usually that term is not meant in the strict production function sense of "returns to scale," which we discussed in Chapter 6, although there are situations in which the two definitions coincide. Whatever term is attached to the phenomenon of declining long-run average costs, this possibility does present serious problems for resource allocation in an economy because industries dominated by a few large firms may not operate efficiently. In Chapters 11 and 12 we will examine such industries, and we will outline the problems in resource allocation that they pose.

Some General Findings on Long-Run Average Costs

Most studies of long-run cost curves have found that average costs decrease up to some particular output level and then remain relatively constant. Average cost curves therefore have a modified L-shape such as that shown in Figure 7.13. The industries studied might therefore be said to exhibit "increasing returns to scale" up to some point, but there is no strong evidence that long-run average costs begin to rise after some point. Adam Smith's hypotheses about the difficulties of managing large-size firms do not appear to be supported by the data.

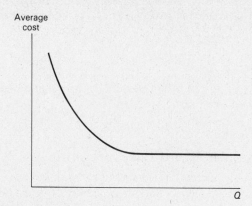

**Figure 7.13 / Long-run Average
Cost Curve Found in Many Empirical Studies**

In most empirical studies the *LATC* curve has been found to have this modified L-shape. Average costs decline up to a point, then remain constant. There is no strong evidence that, after some output level is reached, average costs start to rise.

Table 7.2 reports some representative results of studies of long-run average cost curves for six industries: banking, electric power, hospitals, life insurance, railroads, and trucking. Entries in the table represent the long-run average cost in the industry for a firm of a particular size (small, medium, or large) as a percentage of the minimum cost firm in the industry. For example, the data for hospitals indicate that small hospitals have average costs that are about 29.6 percent greater than average costs for large ones. Hospitals are therefore one industry for which there do appear to be some cost advantages to larger–scale operations. For most other industries a picture similar to that illustrated in Figure 7.13 emerges. Average costs are lower for medium and large firms than for smaller ones. In most cases, however, these cost advantages are not great and for at least one case (trucking) smaller firms seem to operate with lower costs. Clearly there is no overwhelming evidence of substantial benefits to large-scale operation. Of course, far more information has been gathered about the cost curves of the industries listed in Table 7.2 than is suggested by that brief summary. We will now examine three of these industries in some additional detail.

Electric Generation

In an important study of electricity generation, M. Nerlove examined a cross section of 145 privately owned utilities.[10] He found strong indications of decreasing long-run average costs, although the benefits from increasing in size

---

[10]M. Nerlove, "Returns to Scale in Electricity Supply" in *Measurement in Economics*, ed. C. F. Christ et al. (Stanford, Calif.: Stanford University Press, 1963), pp. 167–198.

Table 7.2 / Long-Run Average Cost Estimates for Six Industries (Average Cost as a Percent of Minimal Average Cost)

Industry	Firm Size		
	Small	Medium	Large
Commercial Banking			
Demand Deposits	116.1	104.7	100.0
Installment Loans	102.4	101.5	100.0
Electric Power Generation	113.2	101.0	101.5
Hospitals	129.6	111.1	100.0
Life Insurance (Canada)	113.6	104.5	100.0
Railroads			
East	100.0	127.9	119.9
South	100.0	100.0	100.0
West	106.9	108.4	100.0
Trucking	100.0	102.1	105.6

Sources: *Banking*: F. W. Bell and N. B. Murphy, *Costs in Commercial Banking* (Boston: Federal Reserve Bank of Boston Research Report No. 41, 1968); *Electric Power*: L. H. Christensen and W. H. Greene, "Economies of Scale in U.S. Power Generation," *Journal of Political Economy* 84 (August 1976), pp. 655–676; *Hospitals*: H. A. Cohen, "Hospital Cost Curves" in H. F. Klarman (ed.), *Empirical Studies in Health Economics* (Baltimore: Johns Hopkins Press, 1970), pp. 279–293; *Life Insurance*: R. Geehan, "Returns to Scale in the Life Insurance Industry," *The Bell Journal of Economics* 8, No. 2 (Autumn 1977), pp. 497–516; *Railroads*: G. Borts, "The Estimation of Real Cost Functions," *Econometrica* 28 (January 1960), pp. 108–131; *Trucking*: R. Koenka, "Optimal Scale and the Size Distribution of American Trucking Firms," *Journal of Transport Economics and Policy* (January 1977), pp. 54–67.

seemed somewhat greater for small firms than for large ones. This may occur because of difficulties in managing multiplant electric firms, since large firms typically have several generating stations. Indeed, Nerlove's results do show considerably smaller returns to scale on the firm level than do reports by other authors on individual generating plants. One particularly interesting problem that Nerlove had to face in his study was that input costs were not identical for the firms in his cross section. Wage rates and fuel costs varied greatly among firms, being generally higher in the northeastern states than in the southern and western states. But Nerlove developed several ingenious analytical tools for dealing with the price differences. His work provided important guidelines for future developments in the use of cross-section data for examining long-run cost curves.

Although Nerlove's study focused on the question of declining average costs at the firm level, it might be argued that it is more appropriate to focus on individual generating units. Some economists have proposed separating the generating and distribution functions of electric utilities and have favored greater competition among generating units. One recent study[11] suggests that the efficiency gains from operation of multiple generating units are small: that is, average costs for

---

[11]L. R. Christenson and W. H. Greene, "Economies of Scale in U.S. Electric Power Generation," *Journal of Political Economy* 84 (August 1976), pp. 655–676.

firms that operate several generating units are not much different from those that operate only one. Hence, the authors conclude that "policies to promote competition cannot be faulted in terms of sacrificing economies of scale."[12]

Railroads

A 1960 study by G. Borts looked at long-run cost curves for American railroads.[13] Borts examined 61 *class I* railway firms. He defined the "output" of a railway to be either the number of car loadings or the mean length of haul. Using such a definition, he found that railways in the West exhibited slightly decreasing long-run average costs but that those in the East exhibited increasing average costs. Borts attributed that to the higher traffic density experienced by the Eastern railroads. The author's technique of examining railways in different parts of the country separately indicates the necessity of trying to hold some factors constant when analyzing a cross section of rather different firms.

More recently, the question of "excess capacity" of railroads has been examined. Because various regulatory agencies require railroads to retain little-used lines, it is possible that they are not minimizing long-run average costs: They may be operating with too much capital given prevailing output levels. For example, T. E. Keeler[14] estimated a series of short-run cost curves for American railroads and used those cost curves (much as we did earlier in this chapter) to calculate a long-run cost curve. He concluded that railroads currently possess an enormous amount of excess capacity (over 200,000 miles of track) and that adoption of a more appropriately sized rail network might save over $2.5 billion in annual operating costs.

Commercial Banking

A study by F. W. Bell and N. B. Murphy provides a comprehensive analysis of cost curves for commercial banks.[15] After looking at nearly 300 banks, the authors conclude that most banking functions (that is, demand and time deposit creation, business loans, real estate loans, and so forth) exhibit declining average costs. For example, they show that the average cost of granting a business loan is about $46 for a bank having an annual volume of 300 loans, whereas the average cost is $35 for a bank granting 8000 loans. Bell and Murphy then investigate the source of

---

[12]Ibid., p. 656.

[13]G. Borts, "The Estimation of Rail Cost Functions," *Econometrica* 28 (January 1960), pp. 108–131.

[14]T. E. Keeler, "Railroad Costs, Returns to Scale, and Excess Capacity," *Review of Economics and Statistics* 56 (May 1974), pp. 201–208.

[15]F. W. Bell and N. B. Murphy, *Costs in Commercial Banking: A Quantitative Analysis of Bank Behavior and Its Relation to Bank Regulation*, Federal Reserve Bank of Boston, Research Report No. 41 (Boston, 1968).

these scale economies and conclude that the availability of more advanced types of data processing equipment to large banks is in part responsible for those results. The authors also show, however, that the tendency of a bank to open more branch offices as it grows can mitigate many of these positive scale effects, primarily because of the additional workers needed to staff such offices.

Shifts in Cost Curves

We have shown how the cost curves for a firm's output are derived from its cost-minimizing expansion path. Any change in economic conditions that affects this expansion path will affect the shape and position of the cost curves. Two kinds of economic changes are likely to have such effects: changes in input prices and technological innovations. We will now examine both of these.

Changes in Input Prices

A change in the price of a productive input will tilt the firm's total cost lines and will thereby alter the expansion path. A rise in wage rates will, for example, cause firms to produce any output level with relatively more capital and relatively less labor. To the extent that such a substitution of capital for labor is possible (remember substitution possibilities depend on the shape of the isoquant map), the entire expansion path of the firm will rotate toward the capital axis. This movement in turn implies a new set of cost curves for the firm: A rise in the price of labor input has caused the entire relationship between output levels and costs to be altered. Presumably all cost curves would be shifted upward with the extent of the shift depending both on how "important" labor is in production and on how successful the firm can be in its attempt to substitute other inputs for labor.

As an historical example of the effects of changing input prices on cost curves, consider the effect that the opening of major coal fields in Pennsylvania and West Virginia in the nineteenth century had on the cost curves of iron producers. The development of the new fields had the effect of sharply reducing the price of coal. Iron producers consequently substituted coal for wood as a fuel. The cost curves for iron output were therefore shifted downward in response to the substitution. The downward shift in costs had important implications for the price of iron, which also fell (we will analyze this effect precisely in Chapters 9 and 10).

Technological Innovation

A second economic change that can have important effects on cost curves is the development of new technologies. Since technical advances will have the effect of altering a firm's production function (see the discussion in Appendix to Chapter 6), isoquant maps will be shifted as will be the firm's expansion path. For example, an advance in knowledge might simply shift all isoquants toward the origin with the result that any output level could then be produced with a lower level of input usage (and therefore at lower cost). Alternatively, technical change might be "biased" in the sense that it saves only on the use of one input ("automation" might be implemented to save on labor costs for instance). The end result of such a process will again be to alter isoquant maps, shift expansion paths, and finally affect the shape and location of a firm's cost curves.

An example of this kind of technical advance occurred in the New England textile industry during the period 1815–1825 after the power loom was introduced. The new production technique had the effect of sharply reducing textile costs and made American firms more able to compete against British imports. And the development of a viable domestic textile industry had beneficial consequences for the economic growth of the United States in that period.

Although in this section we have not analyzed cost curve shifts in great detail, we have attempted to show how such an analysis should be approached. Only by carefully sorting out the effects of technical change from those of input price changes can the reasons for such shifts be thoroughly understood. This understanding is important if we are to analyze why supply conditions in an industry might change.

Summary

One assumption underlies most of the analysis in this chapter: Firms choose inputs so as to minimize the cost of producing any particular output level. Given this assumption, we proceeded to derive the firm's expansion path from the isoquant map of its production function. The path shows how input usage (and hence cost) changes as output expands. Using the expansion path we were then able to develop the long-run set of cost curves to be used in analyzing the firm's behavior. Similarly, by holding one productive input constant, we were able to derive the firm's short-run cost curves. The development of these concepts repeatedly emphasized that the precise shape of a firm's cost curves depends on the nature of the production function for its product. It is essentially the technology of production that determines how costs and output are related. In particular, the assumption that short-run average and marginal costs increase as output expands derives from the assumption of diminishing returns to the increased use of variable inputs in the short run. Because some inputs are fixed in the short run, it is not possible to expand output substantially without encountering those rising costs. In the long run, on the other hand, the firm has considerably greater flexibility in meeting demands for increased output. Because all (or most) inputs may be varied, diminishing returns will not be as important a determinant of the shape of the cost curves as in the short run. Rather, the form of the entire production function will be the principal determinant of the shape of long-run cost curves. These curves in turn may suggest the "optimal" scale of operations for specific firms.

Presenting a rigorous development of cost curves from the underlying production function has the additional advantage of providing insights into why the positions of these curves might shift. Any change in economic conditions that affects the expansion path will affect cost curves. Changes in the cost of an input, for example, will alter the firm's cost-minimizing input choices and will cause cost curves to shift. Similarly, technical progress will shift a firm's isoquant map, and the relationship between output and total cost will be affected. By examining shifts in cost curves and deciding on the reasons for these shifts, economists can both explain past price behavior and make reasonably good guesses about the future.

In the next chapter we will discuss the profit-maximization hypothesis. It should be clear that cost minimization is an obvious necessary condition if profits are to be at a maximum. If the costs of producing a certain level of output can be reduced by a firm's actions, it is not maximizing profits in the first place. On the other hand, the assumption that a firm minimizes costs does not imply that it has opted for maximum profits. As we will see, a firm may minimize costs and still choose the "wrong" level of output. Consequently the cost-minimization assumption is considerably broader than the profit-maximization hypothesis and may well apply to firms (such as hospitals, schools, or government agencies) that have no interest in profits. Such nonprofit institutions will also have cost curves, and economists have applied the tools we discussed in this chapter to the study of these as well as to the study of the cost curves of profit-making firms.

Suggested Readings

Clark, J. M., *The Economics of Overhead Cost* (Chicago: University of Chicago Press, 1923), Chaps. 4 and 5.

Dean, J., "Statistical Cost Curves," *Journal of the American Statistical Association* 32 (March 1937), pp. 83–89.

Johnston, J., *Statistical Cost Analysis* (New York: McGraw-Hill, Inc., 1960).

Knight, F. H., "Cost of Production and Price over Long and Short Periods," *Journal of Political Economy* 29 (April 1921), pp. 304–335.

Marshall, A., *Principles of Economics*, 8th ed. (New York: Crowell-Collier and Macmillan, Inc., 1920), book 5, chaps. 8–11.

Stigler, G. J., *The Theory of Price*, 3d ed. (New York: Crowell-Collier and Macmillan, Inc., 1966), chap. 6.

Viner, J., "Cost Curves and Supply Curves," *Zeitschrift für Nationalökonomie* 3 (September 1931), pp. 23–46. Reprinted in *Readings in Price Theory,* American Economic Association (Homewood, Ill.: Richard D. Irwin, Inc., 1952).

Walters, A. A., "Production and Cost Functions," *Econometrica* 31 (January–April 1963), pp. 1–66.

Problems

7.1

Show that for an infinitely substitutable production function, the cost-minimizing input ratio, if it is unique, will require the use of only capital or only labor. In such a situation what will be the firm's expansion path? What will the shape of its marginal and average cost curves depend upon? How will these cost curves shift as the price of the input that is utilized rises?

7.2

Is it possible that isoquants might have positive slopes? Can you interpret this occurrence? Show that positively sloped sections of isoquants will never be observed because they do not represent cost-minimizing positions.

7.3

Professor Smith and Professor Jones are going to produce a new introductory textbook. As true scientists they have laid out the production function for the book as:

$$Q = S^{1/2} J^{1/2}$$

where Q = the number of pages in the finished book, S = the number of working hours spent by Smith and J = the number of hours spent working by Jones.

Smith values his labor at \$3 per working hour. He has spent 900 hours preparing the first draft. Jones, whose labor is valued at \$12 per working hour, will revise Smith's draft to complete the book.

a) How many hours will Jones have to spend to produce a finished book of 150 pages? of 300 pages? of 450 pages?

b) What is the marginal cost of the 150th page of the finished book? of the 300th page? of the 450th page?

7.4

An enterprising entrepreneur purchases two firms to produce widgets. Each firm produces identical products and each has a production function given by

$$Q_i = \sqrt{K_i L_i} \qquad i = 1, 2.$$

The firms differ, however, in the amount of capital equipment each has. In particular, firm 1 has $K_1 = 25$ whereas firm 2 has $K_2 = 100$. The marginal product of labor is $MP_L = 5/(2\sqrt{L})$ for firm 1 and $MP_L = 5/\sqrt{L}$ for firm 2. Rental rates for K and L are given by $w = v = \$1$.

a) If the entrepreneur wishes to minimize short-run total costs of widget production, how should output be allocated between the two firms?

b) Given that output is optimally allocated between the two firms, calculate the short-run total and average cost curves. What is the marginal cost of the 100th widget? the 125th widget? the 200th widget?

c) How should the entrepreneur allocate widget production between the two firms in the long run? Calculate the long-run total and average cost curves for widget production.

d) How would your answer to part c) change if both firms exhibited diminishing returns to scale?

7.5

Suppose a firm's production function requires it to use capital and labor in a fixed ratio of 2 workers per machine and that the rental rates for capital and labor are given by $v = 1$, $w = 3$.

a) Calculate the firm's long-run total and average cost curves.

b) Suppose K is fixed at 10 in the short run. Calculate the firm's short-run total and average cost curves. What is the marginal cost of the 10th unit? the 25th unit? the 50th unit? the 100th unit?

7.6

In a famous article [J. Viner, "Cost Curves and Supply Curves," *Zeitschrift für Nationalökonomie* 3 (September 1931, pp. 23–46)] Viner criticized his draftsman because he could not draw a family of *SATC* curves whose points of tangency with the *LATC* curve were also the minimum points on each *SATC* curve. The draftsman protested that such a drawing was impossible to construct. Who would you support in this debate? Are there cases in which either might be correct?

7.7

A wombat manufacturer determined that the lowest average production costs were achieved when 8 wombats were produced at an average cost of $1000 each. If the marginal cost curve is a straight line intersecting the origin, what is the marginal cost line for producing the 9th wombat?

A Numerical Example of Production Functions and Cost Curves

Introduction

In this appendix we will examine a simple numerical example of a production function and its associated cost curves. The purpose of providing such an example is to illustrate in detail the precise way in which cost curves are derived from production functions. The appendix may therefore serve as an aid to understanding how the two concepts are related. It should be pointed out, of course, that the example we have chosen is not necessarily a "realistic" one: it is presented primarily for pedagogic purposes.

The Production Function

For our simple example we will assume that there are only two factors of production (again represented by K and L) and that the production function is given explicitly by

$$Q = 10\sqrt{K \cdot L} \qquad [7A.1]$$

where Q represents output per period and K and L represent input usage per period.

We can also write this function as

$$Q = 10K^{1/2}L^{1/2} \qquad\qquad [7A.2]$$

which makes clear that it is a Cobb-Douglas production function with constant returns to scale (since the exponents sum to 1). Hence it is of a type widely used in economic studies. Table 7A.1 shows that the production function does indeed exhibit constant returns to scale: As the inputs are increased proportionally, output also increases in the same proportion.

Table 7A.1 / Values of $Q = f(K, L) = 10\sqrt{K \cdot L}$ for Proportionate Increases in K and L

K	L	$Q = 10\sqrt{K \cdot L}$
1	1	10
2	2	20
3	3	30
4	4	40
5	5	50
6	6	60
7	7	70
8	8	80
9	9	90
10	10	100

Marginal and Average Productivities

In Tables 7A.2 and 7A.3 we show the total product of labor, the marginal product of labor, and the average product of labor for two alternative values of K (for $K = 4$ and for $K = 9$). Two features of those tables are immediately clear. First, the marginal product and average product of labor both decline in each table as the quantity of labor used increases. This is a reflection of the fact that the quantity of K is held constant in the tables. Although when both factors are increased together the production function exhibits constant returns to scale, holding one factor constant causes the other to exhibit a diminishing marginal productivity. Because the marginal productivity of labor is always less than the average productivity and the marginal productivity is falling, the average is falling also. Since an extra worker produces less than the average per worker output that previously prevailed, the addition of this extra worker to the productive process causes the overall average to fall.

Second, the marginal and average productivities of labor are all higher in Table 7A.3 than they are in Table 7A.2. This simply reflects that the entries in the latter table have a higher level of capital input than do those in the former. Even though the marginal productivity of labor declines in both cases, labor is more productive in Table 7A.3 because it has more of the other input with which to work.

Table 7A.2 / Total, Marginal, and Average
Product of Labor for $Q = 10 \sqrt{K \cdot L}$ when $K = 4$

L	K	$Q = 10\sqrt{K \cdot L} = 20\sqrt{L}$	MP_L	$AP_L = \dfrac{20\sqrt{L}}{L} = \dfrac{Q}{L}$
1	4	20.0		20.0
2	4	28.3	8.3	14.2
3	4	34.6	6.3	11.5
4	4	40.0	5.4	10.0
5	4	44.7	4.7	8.9
6	4	49.0	4.3	8.2
7	4	52.9	3.9	7.6
8	4	56.6	3.7	7.1
9	4	60.0	3.4	6.7
10	4	63.2	3.2	6.3

Table 7A.3 / Total, Average, and Marginal
Product of Labor for $Q = 10\sqrt{K \cdot L}$ when $K = 9$

L	K	$Q = 10 \sqrt{K \cdot L} = 30\sqrt{L}$	MP_L	$AP_L = \dfrac{30\sqrt{L}}{L} = \dfrac{Q}{L}$
1	9	30.0		30.0
2	9	42.4	12.4	21.2
3	9	52.0	9.6	17.3
4	9	60.0	8.0	15.0
5	9	67.1	7.1	13.4
6	9	73.5	6.4	12.3
7	9	79.4	5.9	11.3
8	9	84.8	5.4	10.6
9	9	90.0	5.2	10.0
10	9	94.9	4.9	9.5

The Isoquant Map

As a final exercise in using the simple production function given by equation 7A.1, we shall construct its isoquant map. Of course, there are infinitely many isoquants that might be drawn (one for each conceivable output level), but we will only consider two—for $Q = 50$ and for $Q = 100$.

For the $Q = 50$ isoquant, we are interested in those possible combinations of K and L for which

$$Q = 50 = 10\sqrt{K \cdot L} \qquad\qquad \text{[7A.3]}$$

Manipulating this expression we get

$$\frac{Q}{10} = 5 = \sqrt{KL} \text{ or } KL = 25 \qquad [7A.4]$$

or

$$K = \frac{25}{L} \qquad [7A.5]$$

Holding Q constant therefore implies a relationship between K and L, and we wish to graph that relationship. In Table 7A.4 we have calculated those values of K that combine with integral values of L (from 1 to 10) to produce 50 units of output. These are calculated directly from equation 7A.5. For each input combination we have also calculated the RTS as the ratio of the change in capital input to the change in labor input. From the information in Table 7A.4, the $Q = 50$ isoquant is drawn in Figure 7A.1. The isoquant records those combinations of K and L that are able to produce 50 units of output. As is clearly shown by Table 7A.4, the isoquant exhibits a diminishing RTS (of L for K) and resembles those we have been drawing throughout this chapter.

Table 7A.4 / Construction of the $Q = 50$ Isoquant for $Q = 10\sqrt{K \cdot L}$

L	$K = \dfrac{25}{L}$	ΔL	$-\Delta K$	$RTS = -\dfrac{\Delta K}{\Delta L}$
1	25.0	1		
2	12.5	1	12.5	12.5
3	8.3	1	4.2	4.2
4	6.3	1	2.0	2.0
5	5.0	1	1.3	1.3
6	4.2	1	0.8	0.8
7	3.6	1	0.6	0.6
8	3.1	1	0.5	0.5
9	2.8	1	0.3	0.3
10	2.5	1	0.3	0.3

The construction of Table 7A.5 for the $Q = 100$ isoquant proceeds in an identical manner. By an algebraic manipulation similar to that shown previously it is an easy matter to calculate that those combinations of K and L that can produce 100 units of output satisfy the relation

$$K = \frac{100}{L} \qquad [7A.6]$$

Table 7A.5 / Construction of the $Q = 100$ Isoquant for $Q = 10\sqrt{K \cdot L}$

L	$K = \dfrac{100}{L}$	ΔL	$-\Delta K$	$RTS = -\dfrac{\Delta K}{\Delta L}$
1	100.0	1		
2	50.0	1	50.0	50.0
3	33.3	1	16.7	16.7
4	25.0	1	8.3	8.3
5	20.0	1	5.0	5.0
6	16.7	1	3.3	3.3
7	14.3	1	2.4	2.4
8	12.5	1	1.8	1.8
9	11.1	1	1.4	1.4
10	10.0	1	1.1	1.1

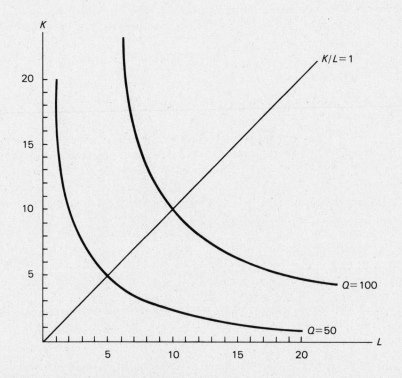

**Figure 7A.1 / Graph of the $Q = 50$ and
$Q = 100$ Isoquants for the Production Function $Q = 10\sqrt{K \cdot L}$**

These isoquants are taken directly from Tables 7A.4 and 7A.5. They show those combinations of K and L that can produce 50 and 100 units of output respectively. The isoquants clearly display a diminishing RTS.

Some of those combinations are shown in Figure 7A.1. Again the isoquant exhibits a diminishing *RTS*. On the two isoquants we can see that the *RTS* depends only on the ratio of K to L (as is true for any constant returns to scale production function). For example, at the point $K = 5$ on the $Q = 50$ isoquant, $L = 5$, the K/L ratio is 1 to 1, and the *RTS* is also approximately 1. Similarly on the $Q = 100$ isoquant, at the point $K = 10, L = 10$, the K/L ratio is also 1 to 1, and the *RTS* is also approximately 1. Consequently this example shows that for a constant returns to scale production function, the *RTS* depends only on the ratio K/L, not on the absolute values of K and L. The isoquants are simply radial blowups of one another. Unfortunately the *RTS*'s do not agree exactly in Tables 7A.4 and 7A.5, but this reflects that we are studying "large" changes in K and L rather than the infinitesimal changes that are actually required by the definition of the *RTS*. If we had calculated such infinitesimal changes, the agreement would have been exact.

Cost Minimization

In order to discuss the firm's cost minimizing input choices we must, of course, know the costs of capital and labor. Suppose that both inputs have rental rates of $1 per hour; that is, assume that $v = \$1$ per hour and $w = \$1$ per hour. Consequently total costs are given by

$$TC = \$1 \cdot K + \$1 \cdot L \qquad [7A.7]$$

Now suppose we want to minimize the total costs of producing, say, 50 units of output. Remember that there are many possible ways of producing 50 units of output, and those possible combinations of K and L lie on the $Q = 50$ isoquant. The first two columns of Table 7A.6 repeat some of those combinations of K and L that can produce 50 units of output listed in Table 7A.4. In the third column of the table, we have computed the total costs of each of those input combinations. As the table makes clear, the cost-minimizing way to produce 50 units of output is by using 5 units of capital input and 5 units of labor input. These will cost $10.00, and this is the lowest cost attainable. That $K = 5, L = 5$ is the cost-minimizing input combination should have been obvious from our previous discussion, which showed that the *RTS* on the $Q = 50$ isoquant is 1 for this input combination. But this is exactly the ratio of w/v—consequently at $K = 5, L = 5$ the *RTS* is equal to the ratio of the inputs prices, and this is what must be true for cost minimization.

A Graphic Proof

In Figure 7A.2 we have redrawn the $Q = 50$ isoquant in the K–L plane together with the $TC = 10$ line. Notice that for $K = 5, L = 5$ total costs are indeed $10, and all other input combinations capable of producing 50 units of output cost more than $10. It should be also clear from the figure that had the ratio w/v been other than 1

Table 7A.6 / Costs of Various Input Choices for $Q = 50 = 10\sqrt{K \cdot L}$

L	K	$TC = \$1 \cdot K + \$1 \cdot L$
1	25.0	$26.00
2	12.5	14.50
3	8.3	11.30
4	6.3	10.30
5	5.0	10.00
6	4.2	10.20
7	3.6	10.60
8	3.1	11.10
9	2.8	11.80
10	2.5	12.50

some other capital-labor combination would have been chosen. For example, if w had been $2 instead of $1, the ratio w/v would be 2; the firm would have used more capital and less labor in producing $Q = 50$. It is not hard to show that such an input price ratio would cause the firm to use about 3.5 units of labor and 7.0 units of

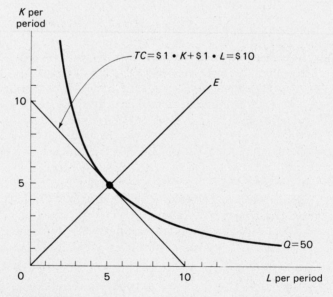

Figure 7A.2 / Cost-Minimizing Input Choice for $Q = 50 = 10\sqrt{K \cdot L}$

Using 5 units of capital and 5 units of labor is the minimal cost input combination that can be used to produce 50 units of output. For this input choice, the *RTS* (of L for K) is equal to the factor price ratio w/v. In other words, the slope of the $Q = 50$ isoquant at $K = 5$, $L = 5$ is -1.

capital if it wanted to produce 50 units of output most cheaply. Total costs would then be $14 [= $2 ·(3.5) + $1 ·(7.0)], which is the lowest level of costs attainable given the new input prices.

The Expansion Path

We can also compute the firm's expansion path, so long as w and v stay constant. We have already shown that if $w = \$1$ and $v = \$1$ then the cost-minimizing input choice is $K = 5$, $L = 5$, because at this point the *RTS* is equal to the input price ratio. We also know that for a constant returns to scale production function (such as the one we are using) the *RTS* depends only on the K/L ratio, not on the level of production. Consequently the *RTS* will always be 1 along the ray $K/L = 1$. Since w/v is also always equal to 1, for any level of output the cost-minimizing choices of K and L will be those input combinations for which $K/L = 1$ or, more simply, those where $K = L$. The firm's expansion path is then just the ray through the origin along which $K/L = 1$; this is labeled $0E$ in Figure 7A.2. Table 7A.7 calculates the firm's expansion path for output levels ranging from $Q = 10$ to $Q = 100$. It also computes the (minimum) total cost for producing each of these output levels. The table clearly reflects the constant returns to scale nature of the production function—total costs are exactly proportional to output. Along the expansion path, output costs exactly $.20 per unit.

Table 7A.7 / Expansion Path for $Q = 10\sqrt{K \cdot L}$

Q	L	K	$TC = \$1 \cdot K + \$1 \cdot L$
10	1	1	$ 2.00
20	2	2	4.00
30	3	3	6.00
40	4	4	8.00
50	5	5	10.00
60	6	6	12.00
70	7	7	14.00
80	8	8	16.00
90	9	9	18.00
100	10	10	10.00

Short-Run Cost Curves

For the purpose of conducting a short-run analysis of costs, let us assume that capital inputs are fixed at 4 units. Consequently, the short-run production function is given by

$$Q = 10\sqrt{K \cdot L} = 10\sqrt{4 \cdot L} = 20\sqrt{L} \qquad [7A.8]$$

Similarly, short-run fixed costs are simply $4:

$$SFC(K = 4) = \$1 \cdot K = \$1 \cdot 4 = \$4 \qquad [7A.9]$$

Variable costs are given by

$$SVC(K = 4) = w \cdot L \qquad [7A.10]$$

but, by equation 7A.8, the short-run relationship between Q and L is

$$\frac{Q}{20} = \sqrt{L} \qquad [7A.11]$$

or

$$L = \frac{Q^2}{400} \qquad [7A.12]$$

Consequently we can write our expression for variable costs as:

$$SVC(K = 4) = w \cdot L = \$1 \cdot L = \$1 \cdot \frac{Q^2}{400} \qquad [7A.13]$$

Short-run total costs therefore are:

$$STC(K = 4) = SFC(K = 4) + SVC(K = 4) = \$4 + \$1 \cdot L$$

$$= \$4 + \$1 \cdot \frac{Q^2}{400} \qquad [7A.14]$$

and this provides a relationship between Q and total costs for a fixed input of 4 units of capital. In Table 7A.8 we have calculated short-run total costs for output levels ranging from 10 to 100. It is important to notice two features of the table. First, total costs increase rapidly as output gets large. This is a reflection of the diminishing marginal productivity of labor input when it is applied to a fixed level of capital input. The second and related observation is that all but one of the entries in the table exceed those in Table 7A.7. The fact that K is fixed at 4 units causes all the input combinations except $K = 4$, $L = 4$ to be more costly than they need be if both capital and labor can be adjusted. Only when the "correct" amount of labor (here 4 units) is being used with the available capital will costs be truly minimized. A comparison of the tables, therefore, indicates the kinds of adjustments that a firm would like to make in the long run when all inputs become variable.

Short-Run Average and Marginal Costs

In Table 7A.9 we have used the total cost information from Table 7A.8 to calculate short-run average and marginal costs. In this particular example marginal costs are

Table 7A.8 / Short-run Total Costs for $Q = \sqrt{K \cdot L}$ when $K = 4$

Q	K	$L = \dfrac{Q^2}{400}$	$STC = \$1 \cdot K + \$1 \cdot L$
10	4	0.25	\$4.25
20	4	1.00	5.00
30	4	2.25	6.25
40	4	4.00	8.00
50	4	6.25	10.25
60	4	9.00	13.00
70	4	12.25	16.25
80	4	16.00	20.00
90	4	20.25	24.25
100	4	25.00	29.00

Table 7A.9 / Short-run Average and Marginal Costs for $Q = \sqrt{K \cdot L}$ when $K = 4$

Q	STC	$SATC = \dfrac{STC}{Q}$	ΔSTC	$MC = \dfrac{\Delta STC}{10}$
10	\$4.25	\$0.425		
20	5.00	0.250	\$0.75	\$0.075
30	6.25	0.208	1.25	0.125
40	8.00	0.200	1.75	0.175
50	10.25	0.205	2.25	0.225
60	13.00	0.217	2.75	0.275
70	16.25	0.232	3.25	0.325
80	20.00	0.250	3.75	0.375
90	24.25	0.269	4.25	0.425
100	29.00	0.290	4.75	0.475

always increasing.[1] The marginal product of labor is always decreasing here, and there is no interval of increasing marginal productivity. So long as marginal costs are below average costs, average costs decline. Consequently average costs decline from \$.425 each to \$.20 each as output expands from 10 to 40 units. For output expansions beyond 40 units, however, marginal costs exceed average costs; therefore average costs rise. At output levels of 100 units, average costs are rising quite rapidly.

Because we will want to use this example in our discussion of the long run, it is

---

[1] Again, here the marginal cost figures do not reflect small changes as they should. Rather, for pedagogic purposes, marginal costs have been recorded for rather large changes in output (10 units). For this reason, marginal and average costs are not equal at the minimum point of the $SATC$ curve (that is, at 40 units of output). Had the figures been computed exactly, $SATC$ and SMC would be identical (\$.20) at $Q = 40$. This is shown in Figure 7A.3.

useful here to graph the cost curves recorded in Tables 7A.8 and 7A.9. These graphs are presented in Figure 7A.3. The total cost curve is simply a quadratic function in Q with an intercept of \$4 (this reflects the cost of the 4 units of capital). The average cost curve in the figure has the familiar U-shape and reaches a minimum at 40 units of output. The marginal cost curve passes through this minimum and, in this example, is simply a straight line. All of the curves in Figure 7A.3, then, clearly

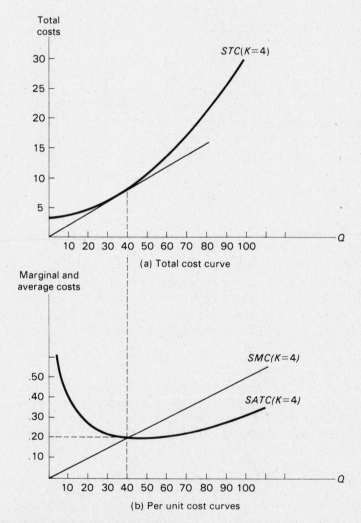

(a) Total cost curve

(b) Per unit cost curves

Figure 7A.3 / Short-run Total, Average, and Marginal Cost Curves for $Q = 10\sqrt{K \cdot L}$ when $K = 4$

These curves are derived from Tables 7A.8 and 7A.9. They show that for our example the total, average, and marginal cost curves more or less resemble those we drew on the basis of *a priori* theory in Chapter 7.

show the effect that holding capital constant in the short run has on costs. Since producing extra output requires the addition of labor input, this process runs into diminishing marginal productivities, and costs rise rapidly.

Long-Run Cost Curve

In this section we will make one final use of our simple numerical production function ($Q = 10\sqrt{K \cdot L}$. Here we will derive the long-run cost curves for this production function, and we will show how the long-run curves are related to the short-run curves that we derived previously. In Table 7A.7 we have already derived the expansion path for the production function, and this provides us with the necessary information for constructing long-run cost curves. We derived the expansion path on the assumption that both capital and labor inputs may be freely varied, and this is precisely what is required for long-run analysis. Table 7A.10 repeats this relationship between output level (Q) and (long-run) total costs. From these data it is a simple matter to derive average and marginal costs, and we have done so in Table 7A.10. For this example, long-run average and marginal costs are constant at $.20 per unit. This, of course, reflects the constant returns to scale nature of the production function we are analyzing.

Table 7A.10 / Long-run Costs for $Q = 10\sqrt{K \cdot L}$

Q	LTC	$LATC$	ΔLTC	$LMC = \dfrac{\Delta LTC}{10}$
10	$2.00	$0.20	$2.00	$0.20
20	4.00	0.20	2.00	0.20
30	6.00	0.20	2.00	0.20
40	8.00	0.20	2.00	0.20
50	10.00	0.20	2.00	0.20
60	12.00	0.20	2.00	0.20
70	14.00	0.20	2.00	0.20
80	16.00	0.20	2.00	0.20
90	18.00	0.20	2.00	0.20
100	20.00	0.20	2.00	0.20

Relationship of Long-Run and Short-Run Cost Curves

In Table 7A.11, three different short-run cost curves are derived: for $K = 1$, $K = 4$, and $K = 9$. For $K = 4$, the table merely repeats the information derived in Table 7A.9, and the data for $K = 1$ and $K = 9$ have been derived in an analogous manner. The most important observation to be made about the table is that all of the short-run average cost curves are U-shaped and all reach a minimum value of $.20 per unit. This minimum occurs when K and L are used in a ratio of one-to-one, and such points occur on the long-run average cost curve.

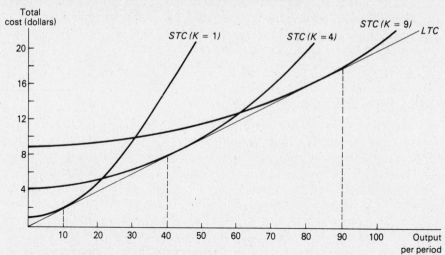

**Figure 7A.4 / Short- and Long-run Total
Cost Curves for $Q = 10\sqrt{K \cdot L}$ when $w = v = \$1$**

Because the production function $Q = 10\sqrt{K \cdot L}$ possesses constant returns to scale, the LTC curve is a straight line. The short-run curves for $K = 1$, $K = 4$, and $K = 9$ lie above this line except at output levels $Q = 10$, $Q = 40$, and $Q = 90$, respectively. At these output levels, the constant short-run level of K is also appropriate for long-run cost minimization. Hence at these output levels, the short- and long-run total cost curves are tangent.

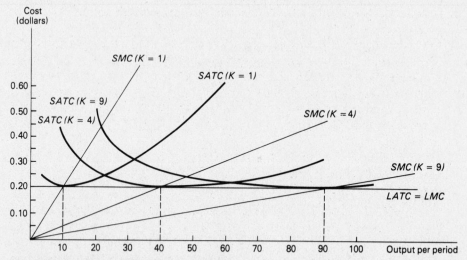

**Figure 7A.5 / Short- and Long-run Average
and Marginal Cost Curves for $Q = 10\sqrt{K \cdot L}$ when $w = v = \$1$**

For the production function $Q = 10\sqrt{K \cdot L}$, $LATC$ and LMC are constant over all ranges of output. Since $w = v = \$1$, this constant average cost is $\$.20$ per unit. The short-run average cost curves do, however, have a general U-shape since K is held constant in the short run. The $SATC$ curves are tangent to the $LATC$ curves at output levels $Q = 10$, $Q = 40$, and $Q = 90$.

Table 7A.11 / Short-run Costs for
$Q = 10\sqrt{K \cdot L}$ when $K = 1$, $K = 4$, and $K = 9$

Q	STC ($K = 1$)	SATC ($K = 1$)	STC ($K = 4$)	SATC ($K = 4$)	STC ($K = 9$)	SATC ($K = 9$)
0	$1.00		$4.00		$9.00	
10	2.00	$0.20	4.25	$0.42	9.11	$0.91
20	5.00	0.25	5.00	0.25	9.44	0.47
30	10.00	0.33	6.25	0.21	10.00	0.30
40	17.00	0.43	8.00	0.20	10.78	0.27
50	26.00	0.52	10.25	0.21	11.78	0.24
60	37.00	0.62	13.00	0.22	13.00	0.22
70	50.00	0.71	16.25	0.23	14.44	0.21
80	65.00	0.81	20.00	0.25	16.11	0.20+
90	82.00	0.91	24.25	0.27	18.00	0.20
100	101.00	1.01	29.00	0.29	20.11	0.20+

Figure 7A.4 is a graph of the information on short-run and long-run total costs. There the LTC curve has a straight line, and each of the STC curves is tangent to the LTC curve at that output level that is appropriate for the level of capital input reflected by the short-run curve. The vertical axis intercepts of the STC curves reflect fixed costs. These are the costs of the capital input that must be paid even if no output is being produced. In the long run, there are no fixed costs; the LTC curve passes through the origin.

Finally, Figure 7A.5 depicts the average and marginal cost curves that can be derived from Tables 7A.10 and 7A.11. This configuration of curves resembles that which was shown in Chapter 7 for the general theoretical case. Again the curves show that costs may rise rapidly in the short run even though the long-run cost curves are horizontal. Only at the "appropriate output levels" are short- and long-run average costs equal.

Summary

This exhaustive analysis of our simple example therefore shows how, once input costs are known, all of a firm's cost curves can be derived directly from its production function. Because of the cost minimization assumption it is always possible to obtain information about a firm's cost curves from its production function and vice versa. Of course, the mathematics associated with such a process may not always be so simple as in the example presented here, but the approach used would be identical. The references to this appendix list a few empirical studies of production in which this relationship between the two concepts is used to derive important conclusions about the nature of production in various industries.

Suggested Readings

Christensen, L. H. and Greene, W. H., "Economies of Scale in U.S. Power Generation," *Journal of Political Economy* 84 (August 1976), pp. 655–676.

Keeler, T. E., "Realized Costs, Returns to Scale, and Excess Capacity," *Review of Economics and Statistics* 56 (May 1974), pp. 201–208.

Nerlove, M., "Returns to Scale in Electricity Supply" in *Measurement in Economics*, ed. C. Christ *et al*. (Stanford, Cal.: Stanford University Press, 1963), pp. 167–198.

Chapter **8**

Firms' Goals: Profit Maximization and Alternatives

Introduction

In Chapter 7 we studied the way in which a firm chooses the cost-minimizing input combination for any particular output level. In this chapter we will be concerned with how the firm decides how much output to produce. But before we examine possible hypotheses about the firm's output choice, we should discuss the decision to treat the firm as a single decision-making unit in this investigation. Seldom is a firm run completely by one person. Rather, management is a diffuse process with individuals at different levels having special talents, special interests, and varying amounts of information. Consequently, one way to study a firm's decisions might be to identify the goals of each employee, to study the authority relations between employees, and to "add up" all the factors to reach a conclusion on how a firm's goals are set. While some economists have adopted such a "behavioral" approach, most economists have found this method too cumbersome for general analytical purposes. Whereas a behavioralist would study each firm as a separate unit made up of unique individuals, most economists have adopted a "holistic" theory of the firm, which treats a firm as a single unit. Sometimes it is convenient to assume that a firm is run by a manager who has complete discretion over how the firm acts. This was the way we treated firms in Chapter 7 when cost minimization was discussed, and we will continue to do so here.

For the major part of this chapter we will further simplify our discussion by assuming that the manager of the firm has only one goal: achieving maximum profits for the firm. Consequently, we are avoiding, for the moment, a discussion of other goals that a manager might reasonably be expected to pursue. The desires of the manager for power, prestige, a lavish office, or just a good life are all assumed to be subjugated to the goal of profit maximization.

The assumption that firms operate in a manner so as to maximize profits has a long history in economic literature. The assumption has much to recommend it. It seems intuitively reasonable; it is simple; it has been analytically productive; and, perhaps most important, it has never been unambiguously disproved. Nonetheless, the assumption has been attacked on a number of fronts, and we will be discussing some of these attacks. In addition, we will briefly examine the behavior of "non-profit" firms to determine what goals they might pursue. First, however, we will explore some of the implications of the profit-maximization assumption for the behavior of a firm.

Profit Maximization and Marginalism

If firms are strict profit maximizers, they will make decisions in a "marginal" way. The entrepreneur will perform the conceptual experiment of adjusting those variables under his or her control until it is impossible to increase profits further. This involves, say, looking at the incremental (or "marginal") profit obtainable from producing one more unit of output, or the additional profit available from hiring one more laborer. So long as this incremental profit is positive, the firm will produce the extra output or hire the extra laborer. When the incremental profit of an activity becomes 0, the entrepreneur has pushed that activity far enough and it would not be profitable to go farther.

The Output Decision

This relationship between profit maximization and marginalism can be most clearly demonstrated if we examine the output level that a firm will choose to produce in attempting to obtain maximum profits. First we must define "profits." In its activities a firm sells some level of output, Q, and from these sales receives revenues, $R(Q)$. The amount of revenues received obviously depends on how much output is sold. Similarly, in producing Q certain (economic) costs are incurred, $C(Q)$, and these also will depend on how much is produced. Profits are therefore defined as:

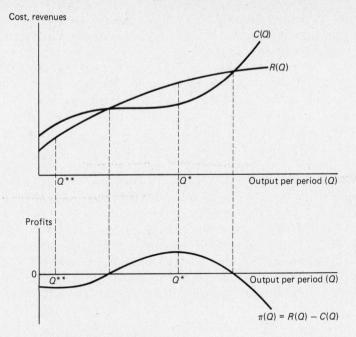

**Figure 8.1 / Marginal Revenue Must
Equal Marginal Cost for Profit Maximization**

Since profits are defined to be revenues (R) minus costs (C), it is clear that profits reach a maximum when the slope of the revenue function (marginal revenue) is equal to the slope of the cost function (marginal cost). This equality is only a necessary condition for a maximum, as may be seen by comparing points Q^* (a true *maximum*) and Q^{**} (a true *minimum*).

Definition

The economic profit, $\pi(Q)$, from producing a particular output level is defined to be the difference between the revenues obtained from selling that output level and the economic costs of producing it.[1] In mathematical terms:

$$\pi(Q) = R(Q) - C(Q) \qquad [8.1]$$

In deciding on how much to produce, the firm will choose that Q for which $\pi(Q)$ is as large as possible. This process is illustrated in Figure 8.1. There the curve $C(Q)$ is

---

[1]Remember, here we are using the term "costs" in the economists' sense. Consequently profits (revenues − costs) are also intended to be defined in the economists' sense, and this definition may differ from the "profits" reported by accountants. In particular, as we pointed out in Chapter 7, much of what accountants term "profits" economists would call "entrepreneurial costs" or "capital costs" since they reflect what the firm's entrepreneur or the firm's capital could earn in an alternative employment.

drawn with the same general shape as the total cost curves we introduced in Chapter 7. The curve $R(Q)$, which represents total revenue, is drawn so that greater revenues are provided from selling more output.[2] Profits can then be calculated by looking at the vertical distance between the $R(Q)$ and $C(Q)$ curves, and profits are shown explicitly in the bottom panel of the figure. It is clear that profits reach a maximum at Q^*. For outputs either larger or smaller than Q^*, profits are smaller than they are at Q^*. We wish to examine those conditions that must hold at Q^* if profits are to be a maximum.

The Marginal Revenue–Marginal Cost Rule

For output levels below Q^* an increase in output brings in more in additional revenue than producing this additional output costs. Consequently a firm interested in maximizing profits would never stop short of Q^*. Similarly a firm that decided to increase output beyond Q^* would be reducing its profits. The additional revenues yielded by increasing Q fall short of the additional costs incurred in expanding output. What we have shown, therefore, is that at Q^* the additional costs of producing an infinitesimal amount more are exactly equal to the additional revenues that this extra output will bring in. Economists would say that at Q^*, *marginal cost* (we have already met this concept in Chapter 7) is equal to *marginal revenue* (that is, the extra revenue provided by the sale of one more unit—this term is discussed at greater length below); this indicates profit maximization.[3] We have therefore derived the following:

Optimization Principle

In order to maximize profits, a firm should produce that output level for which the marginal revenue obtained from selling one more unit of output is exactly equal to the marginal cost of producing that unit of output. More succinctly, the profit maximization condition is given by:

$$\text{Marginal Revenue} = \text{Marginal Cost} \qquad [8.2]$$

or

$$MR = MC \qquad [8.3]$$

[2]We will examine the exact shape of the $R(Q)$ curve when we reintroduce demand curves. For the moment, the curve $R(Q)$ is rather arbitrarily drawn.

[3]This result can be shown in two other ways. First, mathematically, we wish to find that Q for which $\pi(Q)$ is a maximum. In calculus it is shown that a necessary condition for a function of one variable to attain a maximum at some point is that its derivative be 0 at that point. Using equation 8.1 this says that

This principle is so important for the theory of the firm (and for the analysis of supply) that it deserves further elaboration. A firm seeking maximum profits might perform the following conceptual experiment: Start at an output level of 0 and increase output one unit at a time. So long as marginal revenue exceeds marginal cost, the firm should continue in this procedure because each additional unit it produces will add something to its profits. It can, however, push things too far. Eventually marginal costs will start to rise. As soon as they reach marginal revenue, the firm has gone far enough. Further increases in output would entail reducing profits since the cost of producing such output would exceed the revenue it brings in. In each period the firm can conduct a similar conceptual experiment and thus decide on a profit-maximizing output level.

Marginalism in Input Choices

Although we have so far developed a firm's marginal decision rules as they relate to output choices, we can make a similar argument for input choices as well. Hiring additional labor, for example, entails some increase in costs, and a profit-maximizing firm should balance the additional costs against the extra revenue brought in by selling the output produced by the extra labor. A similar analysis holds for the firm's decision on the proper number of machines to rent. Additional machines should be hired only so long as their marginal contributions to profits are positive. As the marginal productivity of machines begins to decline, the ability of machines to yield additional revenue also declines. Consequently the firm will reach a point at which the marginal contribution of an additional machine to profits is exactly zero, and it should not expand the rental of machines beyond this point. In later chapters we will denote the profit-maximizing conditions for input choices by

$$MR_L = MC_L$$

[8.4]

$$MR_K = MC_K$$

where the subscripts L and K indicate that we are interested in the effects of hiring additional labor and capital inputs on revenue and costs. This notation will be quite convenient when we turn (in Part V) to discuss a firm's demand for inputs. For the moment, however, our attention will be centered on a firm's output choice and,

---

$$\pi'(Q) = R'(Q) - C'(Q) = 0$$

or

$$R'(Q) = C'(Q)$$

This is precisely the condition that marginal revenue equals marginal cost but written in calculus notation.

The second way of seeing the result is geometric. The distance between any two curves is greatest when the slopes of the curves are equal. For the $R(Q)$ and $C(Q)$ curves, this geometric fact again proves that $\pi(Q)$ is a maximum when marginal revenue equals marginal cost.

$MR = MC$.

therefore, on the profit-maximizing condition 8.3. Since we have already discussed the concept of marginal cost in detail, we can go on to a brief analysis of the notion of marginal revenue.

Marginal Revenue

It is the revenue obtained from selling one more unit of output that is relevant to the profit-maximizing firm. If the firm can sell all it wishes without affecting market price (that is, if the firm is a *price taker*), the market price will indeed be the extra revenue obtained from selling one more unit. Phrased in another way, if a firm's output decisions will not affect market price, marginal revenue is equal to price. We can easily demonstrate this result. Suppose a firm were selling 50 widgets at $1 each. Then total revenues would be $50. If selling one more widget does not affect price, that widget will also bring in $1 and marginal revenue will be $1 (= $51 − $50). Hence for a firm that takes market price as given:

$$MR = P \qquad [8.5]$$

Marginal Revenue for a Downward-sloping Demand Curve

A firm may not, however, always be able to sell all it wants at the prevailing market price. If it faces a downward-sloping demand curve for its product, it can sell more only by reducing price. In this case marginal revenue will be less than market price. To see why, assume that the sale of the 51st widget causes market price to fall to $.99. Total revenues are now $50.49 (= $.99 × 51) and marginal revenue is only $.49 (= $50.49 − $50). Even though the 51st widget brought in revenues of $.99, its sale caused the price on the "first" 50 widgets sold to fall by $.01. Hence, the net result of selling the 51st widget was a gain of only $.49 (a $.99 gain on the 51st widget less a $.50 reduction in revenue from the first 50). When selling one more unit causes market price to decline, we have shown that marginal revenue is less than market price:

$$MR < P \qquad [8.6]$$

We have therefore developed an elaborated definition of marginal revenue:

Definition

Marginal revenue is the extra revenue that a firm obtains by selling one more unit of output. If the firm is a price taker, that sale has no effect on market price and marginal revenue is equal to price. If the firm faces a downward-sloping demand curve, sale of one more unit will require a reduction in price and marginal revenue will be less than price.

A Numerical Example

The result that marginal revenue is less than price for a downward-sloping demand curve is shown again in Table 8.1. There we have recorded P, Q, $P \cdot Q$, and MR for a simple linear demand curve of the form

$$Q = 10 - P \qquad [8.7]$$

Table 8.1 / Total and Marginal Revenue for the Demand Curve $Q = 10 - P$

P	Q	$P \cdot Q$	MR
10	0	0	
9	1	9	9
8	2	16	7
7	3	21	5
6	4	24	3
5	5	25	1
4	6	24	-1
3	7	21	-3
2	8	16	-5
1	9	9	-7
0	10	0	-9

Notice that total revenue reaches a maximum at $Q = 5$, $P = 5$ and that for $Q > 5$, total revenues decline. Increasing Q beyond 5 actually causes marginal revenue to be negative.

Marginal Revenue and Price Elasticity

In Chapter 5 we introduced the concept of the price elasticity of demand ($E_{Q,P}$), which we defined as

$$E_{Q,P} = \frac{\text{percent change in } Q}{\text{percent change in } P} \qquad [8.8]$$

We also showed that the price elasticity of demand provides some information about how total expenditures ($P \cdot Q$) change when price changes. A fall in price will increase total expenditures if demand is elastic ($E_{Q,P} < -1$), but such a fall will decrease total expenditures if demand is inelastic ($E_{Q,P} > -1$). The concept of marginal revenue, on the other hand, is concerned with changes in quantity, not price. However, since for a negatively sloped demand curve increases in Q imply decreases in P, it is clear that the two concepts are closely related. In particular, attempting to sell one more unit may require a firm to reduce its price slightly. What will happen to total revenues (that is, to total expenditures, $P \cdot Q$) will depend on the elasticity of demand. From our previous discussion it is easy to see that if demand is elastic, selling one more unit will increase revenues: The marginal revenue of the last unit sold will be positive. Since demand is price responsive, selling one more unit will not necessitate a "very large" fall in price; consequently total revenues will increase. On the other hand, if demand is inelastic the firm would have to reduce price substantially if it wanted to sell one more unit of output. This price decline will be so large that total revenues will be reduced by the sale: Marginal revenue is negative.[4] As an intermediate case, demand might be of unitary elasticity ($E_{Q,P} = -1$), in which case total revenues are constant. Selling one more unit will bring about a price decline of the exact magnitude to keep $P \cdot Q$ constant. In that case the marginal revenue yielded from the sale of one more unit is 0.

We can now summarize this relationship between marginal revenue and elasticity by referring to Table 8.2.

Table 8.2 / Relationship between Marginal Revenue and Elasticity

Demand Curve	Marginal Revenue
Elastic ($E_{Q,P} < -1$)	$MR > 0$
Unit elastic ($E_{Q,P} = -1$)	$MR = 0$
Inelastic ($E_{Q,P} > -1$)	$MR < 0$

More specifically, it can be shown that[5]

$$MR = P \left(1 + \frac{1}{E_{Q,P}} \right) \tag{8.9}$$

The relationships in Table 8.2 can be derived from equation 8.9. The reader should try to show this. As another use of the equation, suppose that a firm knew that the elasticity of demand for its produce was -2. It might derive this figure from historical data that show that a 10 percent decline in price has usually led to an

---

[4]In this light it might be pointed out that so long as marginal costs are positive a profit-maximizing firm will not produce at a point on the demand curve for which demand is inelastic. In such a case marginal revenue (negative) could not be equated to marginal cost (positive).

[5]The proof requires calculus:

$$MR = \frac{d(P \cdot Q)}{dQ} = P + Q \cdot \frac{dP}{dQ}$$

but

$$E_{Q,P} = \frac{dQ}{dP} \cdot \frac{P}{Q} \text{ so } \frac{P}{E_{Q,P}} = Q \cdot \frac{dP}{dQ}$$

Substituting this into the expression for MR gives

$$MR = P + \frac{P \cdot 1}{E_{Q,P}} = P \left(1 + \frac{1}{E_{Q,P}} \right)$$

which is what we wanted to show.

increase in sales of 20 percent. Now assume that the price of the firm's output is $10 and the firm wishes to know how much additional revenue the sale of one more unit of output would yield. The additional output will not yield $10 since the firm faces a downward-sloping demand curve: To sell the unit requires a reduction in its overall selling price. The firm can, however, use equation 8.9 to calculate that the additional revenue yielded by the sale will be $5 (= $10 · (1 + 1/−2) = $10 · ½). The firm will produce this extra unit if marginal costs are less than $5; that is, if *MC* < $5 profits will be increased by the sale of one more unit of output. Although firms in the real world may use more complex means to decide on the profitability of increasing sales (and thereby lowering price), our discussion in this section illustrates in a simple way the kind of logic these firms must use. They must recognize how changes in quantity sold affect price and how these price changes affect total revenues.

Marginal Revenue Curve

Any demand curve has a marginal revenue curve associated with it. It is sometimes convenient to think of a demand curve as an *average revenue curve* in that it shows the revenue per unit (in other words, the price) yielded by alternative output choices. The marginal revenue curve, on the other hand, shows the extra revenue provided by the last unit sold. In the usual case of a downward-sloping demand curve, the marginal revenue curve will lie below the demand curve for the reasons we analyzed earlier.[6] In Figure 8.2 we have drawn such a curve together with the demand curve from which it was derived. Notice that for output levels greater than Q_1 marginal revenue is negative. As Q increases from 0 to Q_1, total revenues ($P \cdot Q$) increase. However, at Q_1 total revenues ($P_1 \cdot Q_1$) are as large as possible; beyond this output level, price falls proportionately faster than output rises.[7]

In Chapter 5 we talked in detail about the possibility of a demand curve's shifting because of changes in factors other than price that go into determining individuals' choices. Whenever a demand curve does shift, its associated marginal revenue curve also shifts. This should be obvious since a marginal revenue curve cannot be calculated without referring to a specific demand curve. In later analysis we will have to keep in mind the kinds of shifts that marginal revenue curves might make.

This concludes our introductory analysis of the concept of marginal revenue. We have shown that if a firm is to maximize profits it must make marginal calculations relating to the last unit sold: It must proceed to the point at which marginal revenue is equal to marginal cost. In order to make such calculations, the firm must have substantial information about the nature of the demand curve it faces (for example,

---

[6]Notice that if demand is infinitely elastic (that is, if the demand curve is a horizontal line at some price), the average and marginal revenue curves coincide. Selling one more unit has no effect on price, therefore marginal and average revenue are equal.

[7]Another way of saying this is that beyond Q_1 demand is inelastic. This is confirmed by Table 8.2.

conflicting methodological views may never be achieved. Clearly, both views have elements of truth, and each can be valuable for certain applications. The position we will take here is that the profit-maximization hypothesis is the single most accept- able starting point for a theory of firm behavior. We will also show in later chapters that firms that operate in a profit-maximizing way (or firms that are forced to do so by the state) may perform the task of production in an efficient manner. Hence, for a theoretical overview of microeconomic behavior, profit maximization seems a reasonable and useful assumption to make.

Simple Alternatives to Profit Maximization

Although no simple alternative to the profit-maximization hypothesis has won widespread acceptance, several have been proposed and a brief discussion of a few of these will suggest the general flavor of the debate. A first, rather obvious, generalization of the marginalist approach is to assume firms act so as to maximize "long-run" profits. Under this hypothesis the observation, say, that firms build luxury office buildings is not taken as evidence that disproves the profit- maximization hypothesis. Rather, the cultivation of a suitable image is viewed as integral to a strategy of maximizing long-run profits. Similarly, charitable contri- butions by firms certainly do not increase short-run profits, but, in a more general sense, they may maximize long-run profits by building up a favorable public climate. The objection to the long-run maximization hypothesis is that it is too general; it is not able to be refuted by any evidence. Any conceivable behavior might be consistent with very long-run maximization goals.

Constrained Profit Maximization

A second variation on the profit-maximization hypothesis is the assumption that firms seek to maximize profits subject to constraints. These constraints keep firms from operating in a strictly marginalist way since any constraint, if it is effective, will lower the maximum profit achievable. For example, it has been proposed that firms may maximize profits subject to the constraint of maintaining their share of the market.[11] They may therefore, in the interest of maintaining market share, continue to produce unprofitable items, or may introduce new lines that are not immediately profitable. Other constraints that have been suggested are maximization of profits subject to a liquidity constraint (this applies mainly to banks); maximization of profits subject to the desire of the entrepreneur to maintain control of the company (high profits may attract some greedy, unwanted merger partner); or profit maximi- zation subject to the desire to keep the firm a "nice place to work." Each of these

---

[11]It has also been suggested that maintaining market share is a reasonable long-run profit-maximizing strategy in an uncertain market environment.

assumptions undoubtedly has explanatory ability in some situations. To the extent that these constraints are effective, the firm may not satisfy the marginal conditions of Equations 8.3 or 8.4.

Revenue Maximization

A third alternative hypothesis has been proposed by William J. Baumol.[12] In his consulting work Baumol noticed that most managerial incentives are tied to increasing sales rather than profits. For example, higher salaries are paid to the managers of the largest corporations (ones with a high volume of sales) than to managers of the most profitable ones. Other pieces of evidence (for example, that bank credit is more easily available to large firms) also suggested to Baumol that sales volume might be the relevant goal. A strictly revenue-maximizing firm would produce that quantity of output for which marginal revenue equals 0 (the quantity Q^{**} in Figure 8.3).[13] Output will be expanded so long as any additional revenue is obtainable.

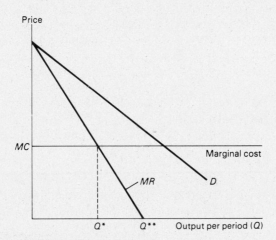

Figure 8.3 / A Comparison of Profit Maximization and Revenue Maximization

For simplicity it has been assumed that each unit of output can always be produced at a cost of MC. A profit-maximizing firm will therefore produce output level Q^* for which $MR = MC$. If the firm were devoted to the goal of revenue maximization, however, it would proceed to output level Q^{**}, since at this level of output *marginal* revenue is 0.

Baumol suggests that a firm may not go this far in pursuing sales volume, but may in fact be bound by a profit constraint imposed by the firm's owners. Hence Baumol's

---

[12] A clear statement of this hypothesis is found in chap. 6 of William J. Baumol, *Business Behavior, Value and Growth*, rev. ed. (New York: Harcourt, Brace & World, Inc., 1967).

[13] In the figure it has been assumed for simplicity that marginal costs are constant at level MC.

firm would probably produce some quantity between that which a profit maximizer would (Q^*) and that which a revenue maximizer would (Q^{**}).

■ An Example: Full Cost Pricing

Major corporations (and minor ones also) use neither the terminology nor the analytical techniques that we have introduced in this chapter. Even though firms may profess to be seeking maximum profits, the methods they use are considerably different. In this section we shall examine the most common management technique, *full-cost pricing*,[14] and we shall see how this technique compares to the simplified model we have developed.

The full-cost pricing technique works as follows. Management first computes the average total costs of producing some "normal" level of output. To this cost is added a profit markup to arrive at the good's selling price. Usually the profit markup is taken to be a fixed percent of the selling price of the good. Consequently, selling price is simply a multiple of average total costs. This pricing technique raises two questions relevant to the simple profit-maximizing model we have developed. First, how does the idea of a price-setting firm relate to our model in which output is the choice variable: Are these just two ways of looking at the same phenomenon? Second, does the full-cost markup technique yield maximum profits in the same way that the marginal revenue equals marginal cost rule does? Will the full-cost rule incorporate any information about demand? We take up these questions in turn below.

Full-Cost Pricing and Output Choices

In making its decisions a firm may choose the "most favorable" point on the demand curve for its product. In the analysis of this chapter we have chosen to use output as the firm's choice variable, but most of the analysis would carry through equally well if we had instead considered firms as price setters. The marginal revenue–marginal cost rule, for example, can be developed with price rather than quantity being the decision variable used by the firm. The profit-maximizing P, Q combination would be the same no matter which approach we take. Of course, the firm is always constrained by the demand curve for its product: It may choose either Q or P but not both. Since treating firms as quantity setters is convenient for the analytical results that follow, we shall continue to use this approach. Most conclusions could be rephrased by assuming firms to be price setters.

---

[14]The use of this method of pricing in particular corporations is discussed in A. D. H. Kaplan, J. B. Dirham, and R. F. Lanzillotti, *Pricing in Big Business: A Case Approach* (Washington, D.C.: Brookings Institution, 1958).

Full-Cost Pricing and Demand

A more interesting question about the full-cost pricing policy is whether or not it is consistent with profit maximization. Taken at face value it seems that the policy cannot possibly lead to maximum profits, since it pays no attention to demand. To see that this is so, let us consider the markup that would be required in order to maximize profits. In general, the markup (m) is given by

$$m = \frac{P - ATC}{P}.$$ [8.10]

That is, m is simply the percent by which price exceeds average total cost (expressed as a percent of price). For example, suppose that $m = 0.25$ (that is, the markup is 25 percent). This means that the difference between a good's price and its average cost of production is one-fourth of the market price. In other words, price is 1.33 ($= 1/0.75$) times the average production cost of the item.

Now let us assume that the firm is planning on an output level that corresponds to the low point on its long-run ATC curve. At this "optimal" output level ATC is equal to marginal cost. Therefore

$$m = \frac{P - MC}{P}.$$ [8.11]

But for profit maximization, marginal cost should equal marginal revenue. Consequently,

$$m = \frac{P - MR}{P}.$$ [8.12]

By using equation 8.9 we can finally write

$$m = -\frac{1}{E_{Q,P}}.$$ [8.13]

This final result says that the markup a profit-maximizing firm will aim for should vary inversely with the elasticity of the demand curve facing the firm. Firms faced by an elastic demand curve will have to settle for a smaller markup than will firms faced by an inelastic demand curve. Similarly, within a single multiproduct firm, we would expect to see higher markups for those items for which demand is relatively inelastic. A final implication is that profit maximization should lead to varying markups over the business cycle. In periods of economic boom, demand curves may be relatively inelastic and hence markup should be high. On the other hand, during recessions, demand may be relatively elastic and profit margins will be low.[15] All of these implications suggest that in order to test the consistency of the

---

[15] Actually the setting of profit margins over the business cycle is far more complex than this. Short-run demand fluctuations may cause output levels to move away from the minimum point on the ATC curve, and in this case the markup formula 8.13 does not have such a simple interpretation. In addition, over the

markup method of pricing with the profit-maximization hypothesis we should study the nature of firms' profit-margin decisions.

Markups in Major Corporations

Most available evidence concludes that major corporations do take demand into account in their pricing policies. For example, in their study of the pricing policies of U.S. Steel Corporation, Kaplan, Dirlam, and Lanzillotti found that the markup on steel products varied inversely with the elasticity of demand for these products. Margins were high on steel rails, for example, since this was a product line in which U.S. Steel faced little competition. On the other hand, margins were low in stainless steel and tin plate, since these are products for which competition from aluminum and lumber producers was strong. The authors found similar results for many major corporations, including E. I. DuPont de Nemours, Standard Oil Company of New Jersey, and Aluminum Company of America.[16] In all of them, target profit margins seemed to vary inversely with the elasticity of demand, just as profit maximization requires. In a study of Danish firms, B. Fog also found that target profit margins vary with demand conditions. He reports that many companies respond to questions about how profit margins are set by noting they will "charge what the traffic will bear" or that "market conditions determine the price."[17] In other words, markups are determined in a profit-maximizing way.

Retail Markups

In their study of retailing, R. M. Cyert and J. G. March spend considerable effort in analyzing the feedback that the market provides for the pricing of a product. Even though prices and profit margins may initially be set without adequate reference to demand, the reaction of the market provides information on the true demand situation, and prices are adjusted accordingly. Cyert and March apply their model to the examination of a department store's markdown policy and conclude that the prices of items are adjusted over time to meet demand conditions.[18] Any experienced bargain hunter knows that retailers adjust the prices of unpopular items downward much more rapidly than they adjust the prices of "hot" items. Such behavior is clearly consistent with the notion that markups are set with profit-maximization goals in mind.

---

business cycle strategic decisions have to be made by firms, and these are too complex to be captured by the simple models presented here. For a more complete analysis of these issues, see F. M. Scherer, *Industrial Market Structure and Economic Performance* (Chicago: Rand McNally & Company, 1970), especially chaps. 8, 12, and 13.

[16]Kaplan, Dirlam, and Lanzillotti, *op. cit.*, pp. 172–174.

[17]B. Fog, *Industrial Pricing Policies* (Amsterdam: North-Holland Publishing Co., 1960), p. 104 and see especially chap. 6.

[18]R. M. Cyert and J. G. March, *A Behavioral Theory of the Firm* (Englewood Cliffs, N.J.: Prentice-Hall, Inc., 1963), chap. 7.

Applications to Nonprofit Organizations

Many firms are organized on a not-for-profit basis. Examples of such organizations include government bureaucracies, most hospitals and schools, philanthropic foundations, and some labor-managed firms (for example, agricultural communes). For such organizations the hypothesis of profit maximization may be inappropriate and some other specification of the firm's goals may be required. Although a complete discussion of these alternatives is outside the scope of this book, we shall present a few examples to indicate the kinds of analysis of nonprofit organizations that have been undertaken.

Hospitals

Most hospitals operate on a not-for-profit basis and there is considerable interest in comparing their behavior to that which would characterize a profit-maximizing hospital. A first step in this investigation is to decide what goal (or goals) a non-profit hospital pursues. It might be hypothesized, for example, that a hospital seeks to maximize the health status of the average citizen served given the resources at its disposal; or that it maximizes the number of lives saved; or that it pursues some other health-oriented goal. A somewhat less philanthropic hypothesis has been proposed by Newhouse, who assumes that hospitals seek to maximize the utility of the doctors who govern them.[19] One implication of this hypothesis is that nonprofit hospitals will have a bias (relative to profit-maximizing hospitals) toward high-quality, high-technology care and away from "bargain" care (such as emergency room facilities). Some empirical data tend to support this hypothesis.

Regulatory Agencies

The rapid growth in government regulation of business in recent years has focused increased attention on the operations of agencies charged with this activity. An important set of investigations has attempted to identify precisely the agencies' goals and to measure the extent to which those goals have been met. For example, in one of the first investigations of this type, Stigler examined the goals of the U.S. Securities and Exchange Commission.[20] Two frequently mentioned goals of security market regulation were postulated: (1) The protection of "innocent" investors; and (2) The creation of an efficient securities market. Stigler examined a variety of data to determine if the SEC had any effect in its pursuit of these goals. After a series of careful analyses, the author concluded that

---

[19]J. P. Newhouse, "Toward a Theory of Nonprofit Institutions: An Economic Model of a Hospital," *American Economic Review* 60 (March 1970), pp. 64–74.

[20]G. J. Stigler, "Public Regulation of the Securities Market," *Journal of Business* 37 (April 1964), pp. 117–142.

no such effect could be detected. Given the substantial resources devoted to SEC activities, one must conclude either that the Commission performed ineffectively, or that it in fact pursued goals other than those postulated. Other possible goals include: protection of the industry from "unfair competition"; increasing the power (or budget) of the SEC itself; or maximizing the utility of SEC employees. Stigler offers no evidence with which to differentiate among these hypotheses, however.[21]

Labor-Managed Firms

In a variety of organizations workers make the principal production decisions. Agricultural and craft communes, Yugoslavian manufacturing plants, and (to some extent) university faculties are examples of this sort of management. Recent trends toward "worker participation" suggest that this mode of decision making will increase in importance. Economists have adopted two alternative approaches to the study of labor-managed firms. Under the first, workers are viewed as owning the firm's capital and (like any other owners of capital) desiring maximum profits from its use. Results of analyzing firms that operate in this way differ little from those concerning profit maximization analyzed elsewhere in this chapter. A rather different assumption adopted by some writers is that the labor-managed firm seeks to maximize the output (or, more properly, the "value added") per worker. In the terminology of Chapter 6, the firm will produce where the average product of labor is a maximum (at labor input L^{**} in Figure 6.1). Such decisions may differ substantially from those made by profit-maximizing firms, and the nature of the differences has been the subject of considerable analysis and controversy.[22]

Summary

This chapter has been concerned primarily with the hypothesis that firms seek to maximize profits. In such a situation we showed that a firm will choose the variables under its control in a marginal way. That is, it will increase each variable up to the point at which further increases add nothing to profits. The most important example of this process is the firm's choice of output level. A firm will produce units of output up to the point at which the increment to revenue provided by the last unit sold (marginal revenue) is precisely equal to the cost of producing it (marginal cost).

---

[21] In Chapter 19 we will briefly examine some other empirical evidence on governmental bureaucracies.

[22] For a summary, see J. Vanek, *The General Theory of Labor-Managed Market Economies* (Ithaca, N.Y.: Cornell University Press, 1970).

Similar results apply for the hiring of inputs or for any other decision that firms must make.

In the chapter we also summarized various objections that have been voiced about the profit-maximization hypothesis and examined a few alternatives. Although those alternatives were shown to have many important applications (particularly in the case of nonprofit institutions), none has the intuitive appeal and widespread applicability of the profit-maximization hypothesis. The assumption of profit maximization, therefore, seems a logical basis for the theories of supply and price determination we shall develop in the next parts of the text.

Suggested Readings

Baumol, W. J., *Business Behavior, Value, and Growth*, rev. ed. (New York: Harcourt Brace Jovanovich, 1967), chap. 6.

Boulding, K. E., "The Theory of the Firm in the Past Ten Years," *American Economic Review* 32 (1942), pp. 791–802.

Cyert, R. M., and March, J. G., *A Behavioral Theory of the Firm* (Englewood Cliffs, N.J.: Prentice-Hall, Inc., 1963), chap. 7.

———, and Hedrick, C. L., "Theory of the Firm: Past, Present, and Future: An Interpretation," *Journal of Economic Literature* 10 (1972), pp. 389–412.

Edwards, E. O., "An Indifference Approach to the Theory of the Firm," *Southern Economic Journal* 28 (1961), pp. 123–129.

Encarnación, J., "Constraints and the Firm's Utility Function," *Review of Economic Studies* 31 (1964), pp. 113–120.

Ferguson, C. E., "Static Models of Average-Cost Pricing," *Southern Economic Journal* 23 (1957), pp. 272–284.

Fog, B., *Industrial Pricing Policies* (Amsterdam: North-Holland Publishing Co., 1960), chap. 6.

Friedman, M., "The Methodology of Positive Economics," in *Essays in Positive Economics* (Chicago: University of Chicago Press, 1953).

Griliches, Z., "Are Farmers Rational?" *Journal of Political Economy* 68 (1960), pp. 68–71.

Kaplan, A. D. H., Dirlam, J. B., and Lanzillotti, R. F., *Pricing in Big Business: A Case Approach* (Washington, D.C.: Brookings Institution, 1958).

Machlup, F., "Theories of the Firm: Marginal, Behavioral, Managerial," *American Economic Review* 47 (1957), pp. 1–33.

Newhouse, J. P., "Toward a Theory of Non-profit Substitutions: An Economic Model of a Hospital," *American Economic Review* 60 (1970), pp. 64–74.

Scitovsky, T., "A Note on Profit Maximization and Its Implications," *Review of Economic Studies* 11 (1943–1944), pp. 57–60.

Simon, H. A., "New Developments in the Theory of the Firm," *American Economic Review*, Papers and Proceedings, 52 (1962), pp. 1–15.

Problems

8.1

Suppose a firm can sell all the output it can produce at a price of P. Show the total revenue curve for such a firm and demonstrate geometrically (using a graph similar to Figure 8.1) that in this case the profit-maximizing output level occurs where marginal cost is equal to P.

8.2

Would a lump-sum profit tax affect the profit-maximizing quantity of output? How about a proportional tax on profits? How about a tax assessed on each unit of output?

8.3

Suppose that a firm faces a constant elasticity demand curve of the form

$$Q = 256 \, P^{-2}$$

and has a *marginal cost* curve of the form

$$MC = .001Q$$

a) Graph these demand and marginal cost curves.

b) Calculate the marginal revenue curve associated with the demand curve; graph this curve. [*Hint*: Use equation 8.9 for this part of the problem.]

c) At what output level does marginal revenue equal marginal cost?

8.4

Suppose Mr. Entrepreneur is the only decision maker in his firm. The profits of this firm depend solely on the amount of time Mr. Entrepreneur spends on the job:

$$\pi = f(H)$$

where H is the number of hours on the job. However, Mr. E. is a harsh boss and gets on everyone's nerves if he is around too long. Hence π reaches a maximum long before H reaches twenty-four hours per day.

Suppose also that Mr. E. has a utility function for profits and leisure ($L = 24 - H$) of the form:

$$U = U(\pi, L).$$

a) In this situation will the number of hours of work corresponding to profit maximization be the same number that maximizes Mr. E.'s utility? What special condition must hold for this to be true? Is this condition "reasonable"?

b) In fact, profits (?) should, according to Marshall, be defined to exclude that portion of entrepreneurial income necessary to keep Mr. E. in the business. Hence economic profits $= \pi' = \pi - w$, where w is the amount of income necessary to keep

Mr. E. in the business (that is, the wage to make him indifferent between working and staying home). Clearly w depends on H.

With this new definition of profits, will the profit-maximizing position agree with Mr. E.'s utility-maximizing position? Show that in order for this to be true Mr. E. must have indifference curves where there is no income effect in the demand for hours worked.

8.5
A firm faces a demand curve given by:

$$Q = 100 - 2P.$$

Marginal and average costs for the firm are constant at $10 per unit.

a) Use a graphic or tabular proof to show that, for this demand curve, $MR = 50 - Q$.

b) What output level should the firm produce to maximize profits? What are profits at that output level?

c) What output level should the firm produce to maximize revenues? What are profits at that output level?

d) Suppose the firm wishes to maximize revenues subject to the constraint that it earn $12 in profits for each of the 64 machines it employs: what level of output should it produce?

e) Graph your results.

8.6
Universal Widget produces high quality widgets at its plant in Gulch, Nevada, for sale throughout the world. The cost function for total widget production (Q) is given by

$$\text{Total Costs} = .25\, Q^2$$
$$\text{Marginal Costs} = .50\, Q$$

Widgets are demanded only in Australia (where the demand curve is given by $Q = 100 - 2P$) and Lapland (where the demand curve is given by $Q = 100 - 4P$). If Universal Widget can control the quantities supplied to each market, how many should it sell in each location in order to maximize total profits?

8.7
A hospital produces services that can be quantified in two dimensions: quantity (Q) and quality (C). It faces infinitely elastic market demands for these aspects of service: prevailing prices are $P_Q = 10$, $P_C = 4$. The hospital's costs are given by:

$$\text{Total Cost} = .1\, Q^2 + .2\, C^2 - 125$$
$$\text{Marginal Cost of } Q = .2\, Q$$
$$\text{Marginal Cost of } C = .4\, C$$

a) If the hospital wishes to maximize profits how much Q and C should be produced? What will profits be?

b) Suppose the hospital is managed by a nonprofit foundation. The utility of the foundation's president depends on the hospital's outputs. In particular, the president requires that $C = Q$ and that both be as large as possible. If the hospital is now constrained to have the same total costs as in the profit-maximizing case, what levels of Q and C will be chosen to maximize the foundation president's utility? What will "profits" be in this case?

Part **IV**

Pricing in the Goods Market

Introduction

In the previous sections of this book we have discussed various aspects of individuals' demands and productive technologies. In this part we will bring these two strands of analysis together to discuss how the prices of goods are determined. In many respects the analysis here is simply an elaboration of the Marshallian supply-demand analysis we first mentioned in Chapter 2, and a principal purpose of this part is to make the Marshallian approach more precise.

There are several assumptions that underlie the analysis of Part IV. First, we will only be looking at the market for one good. We are consciously ignoring the secondary effects that in fact spread through the economy whenever conditions in one market change. The analysis is therefore of a "partial equilibrium" nature; we will study "general equilibrium" analysis in Part VI.

Second, we will assume that there are a large number of individuals demanding the good under examination. Although the actions of demanders as a group have a great deal to do with the market price of a good, we will assume here that no one individual is able to have any effect on price by his or her own actions. Each individual therefore takes the price of the good as given: There is nothing he or she can do about the price except to adjust consumption patterns to it. This is the assumption we made throughout Part II, and therefore the analysis of individual and market demand carries over here.

While this assumption of individual "impotence" may be justified in a large and complex economy, an analogous assumption cannot be made about the supply side

241

of the market. It is an obvious fact of economic life that there are many goods that are produced by only a few sellers. The behavior of General Motors, for example, certainly has an effect on the price of cars. And a major purpose of Part IV is to investigate the differences in the behavior of markets characterized by "one," "few," or "many" sellers. We will conclude that most real-world situations cannot be characterized as either having one or many sellers but that the case of few sellers is by far the most prevalent. Unfortunately, the case of a few sellers is difficult to analyze; we will often have to rely on the two other polar cases for insights.

In this introductory section we will develop some vocabulary that will be useful in our discussions of various market types. Our aim is to provide a firm methodological foundation on which to build the analysis of pricing in this part. First we will discuss the notion of *product differentiation* and we will see that it is important to make a distinction between markets for homogeneous and for differentiated products. Next we will discuss general concepts about the ways in which markets work, and then we will turn to some definitions of specific market types. A final section of this introduction provides an overview of Part IV.

Homogeneous and Differentiated Products

In order to analyze pricing in the goods market we must first describe what is meant by the terms *good* and *market*. For example, how precisely is the notion of a good to be defined? Possible definitions extend from the very general ("consumption," "investment") to the uniquely specific ("1 pound of 10X confectioner's cane sugar delivered at 9:00 A.M. on January 21, 1979, in Amherst, Massachusetts"). Obviously neither of those extremes is a useful definition for the purpose of studying pricing. The first is too general a definition: Individuals' and firms' decisions on total consumption are in reality a multitude of decisions on more specifically defined goods. If we used such an aggregate we would obscure any understanding of market interactions. But the other very specific definition is also useless because it represents a unique transaction that will never again take place. Clearly some middle ground must be chosen, and the particular choice made will depend on the interests of the investigator.

We will therefore define goods to be either "homogeneous" or "differentiated." All suppliers of a *homogeneous good* produce the identical good. Individuals are indifferent about which firm they will buy from. In this case (assuming perfect knowledge and costless mobility of goods), the market for this good must obey the *law of one price*. All trades of the good between seller and buyer must be conducted at the same price. If the price for a homogeneous good were to differ between firms, everyone would flock to the less expensive seller. Hence only a single price can prevail. Examples of strictly homogeneous goods are hard to find. Some tentative examples might be steel girders, concrete pipe, work clothes, gasoline, and club soda.[1]

---

[1] Even for those goods firms make valiant efforts to differentiate their products by providing "service" or "brand identification."

For *differentiated products*, on the other hand, it does make a difference which firm one buys from. The goods produced are not identical (although the differences may be more apparent than real), and firms may strive to differentiate their products from those of their competitors. Most consumer goods fall in this category. This creates some problem for us in defining exactly what we mean by a good. For example, suppose we wished to study the demand for automobiles. Several questions then arise about the exact products we should include in the study. Should station wagons be included? How about jeeps? Or pickup trucks? Or taxis? And so on. Even in the category of what are usually considered automobiles, there is a huge variation of possible models. Should all these be considered the same basic good?

This line of questions could be extended indefinitely, but the point should now be clear. In order to get some theoretical grasp of the factors that influence pricing, we must of necessity make some simplification about what we mean by a good. And we will assume that it is possible to delimit a well-defined good and its respective market. Homogeneous goods, because they can be most easily handled, will occupy the major portion of our analysis, but we will occasionally mention the complications presented by differentiated products.

Organization of Markets

A *market* is a hypothetical "place" where the producers of a good (suitably defined) get together with the demanders to haggle about price.[2] In order to analyze the behavior of the agents entering into these bargains, we must look at matters through their eyes. For individuals this is easy. Individuals are so numerous that any one of them can have no effect on the outcome of the price-setting process. Each is a *price taker*, being forced to accept the price that the market dictates. The actual quantities that any one individual (and that individuals as a group) will demand depends on this price.

The way a firm looks at the market is not so simple. If there are so many firms that any particular one of them feels that it must accept the price of its product as given by the market, then the firm believes it is faced by a horizontal demand curve. It can sell all it wants at the prevailing price because its actions, if taken alone, will have no effect on price. In this case the firm too is a *price taker*.

At the other extreme, if a firm is the only producer of some good it will face the entire market demand. Its actions will obviously affect price. If the market demand curve is downward sloping it will have to charge a lower price to get people to buy a high level of output than it would if it produced less.

Between those two possibilities lies the case of a market with a "few" sellers. In that case it is difficult to say exactly what kind of a demand curve faces the firm. The

---

[2]This is, of course, a simplification. In reality, most trading is through middlemen such as supermarkets, department stores, trading companies, or automobile dealerships. The buyer of a good purchases the services of these middlemen together with purchasing the actual product.

firm's actions will have some effect on price, so it is not a price taker. On the other hand, its competitors are also absorbing some of the total demand for the product, so the total market demand curve is not relevant either. The demand curve facing the firm is therefore uncertain. The firm must make decisions while being in some ignorance about what its competitors will do. Analyzing firm behavior in such situations raises challenging and interesting problems.

Taxonomy of Market Types

As our previous discussion makes clear, to study pricing in the market for a good we must first ask how the market is organized. The approach we take in explaining a firm's actions will depend on how many other firms there are in the market: It will depend on the type of *demand curve which faces the firm*. Markets are usually classified by whether there are many, few, or one producer. A cross-classification is also made about whether the good under investigation is homogeneous or differentiated. There are therefore six possible market types (although we will see below that one of these is not relevant). The names that have been given to these types are recorded in Table IV.1 and are discussed below.

Table IV.1 / Market Types

Number of Firms	Type of Product	
	Homogeneous	Differentiated
Many	Perfect competition	Differentiated or monopolistic competition
Few	Homogeneous oligopoly	Differentiated oligopoly
One	Monopoly	(Not used)

Perfect Competition

A perfectly competitive market is characterized by a large number of firms each producing an identical product. None of the firms is large relative to the market as a whole. Hence each firm in a perfectly competitive industry operates as if it were faced by a horizontal (that is, infinitely elastic) demand curve. Its individual decision on output will not affect price. Entry into the industry by other firms is assumed to be costless. In the long run, new firms will be able to enter the market in response to opportunities for profit. Perfect competition is the prototype for a major portion of economic analysis. Although it is difficult to identify a market that is perfectly competitive in a strict sense, the closest example is provided by the market for most agricul-

tural crops. Whether many other markets can be understood by using the competitive model is a question we will investigate in detail in this part.

Differentiated Competition or Monopolistic Competition

A market characterized by a large number of producers in which each producer supplies a good slightly different from his competitors' is termed monopolistic competition.[3] Although each firm in such a market is small relative to total demand, because it sells a slightly different product, its actions will affect the price it receives. The firm is therefore faced by a negatively sloped demand curve. It must be careful in its decisions, however, because there are many close substitutes for its product that are offered by competitors. Again, entry into the market is assumed to be costless, and it is presumed that new firms will be brought into the market by the prospect of profits. An example of a monopolistically competitive market is provided by the construction industry. There are many relatively small firms in this industry, and the product of each is slightly different from that of its competitors principally because of locational advantages. There are obvious limits on the ability of firms in this industry to take advantage of any beneficial location they might have.

Homogeneous Oligopoly

A market in which relatively few[4] firms produce a homogeneous product is termed a homogeneous oligopoly. A firm in an oligopoly market can, because it produces a large share of the total output, have some effect on the price it will receive. However, to give a precise idea of the kind of demand curve one firm faces is difficult. This is so not only because there are close substitutes (indeed the identical product) being produced by others, but also because the firm must explicitly take account of how its competitors will react to any decisions that it makes. This feature of the market makes decision making in oligopoly markets subject to great uncertainties. Most observed behavior can be rationalized as a reaction to these uncertainties. Consequently, the analysis of these markets has a certain lack of precision and an absence of definitive results. Nonetheless, since numerous markets (steel, aluminum, glass, chemicals to name a few) can be classified as pure oligopolies, such studies are extremely important to any understanding of the details of how the United States economic system works.

---

[3]The term "monopolistic competition" was made widely known by E. Chamberlin in *The Theory of Monopolistic Competition* (Cambridge, Mass.: Harvard University Press, 1933).

[4]The meaning of "few" is necessarily ambiguous and will vary from case to case. Entry into the market by others can be assumed to be either impossible or relatively costly. If the latter assumption is made (as would usually be the case) then those firms already in the market will not only pay attention to the actions of their rivals but they may also adopt strategies that discourage potential entrants.

Differentiated Oligopoly

Most ordinary consumer products (toothpaste, soft drinks, frozen food, automobiles—the list is endless) are produced in markets that can be described as differentiated oligopolies: there are a relatively few firms each producing a slightly different product. All of the comments made about homogeneous oligopoly markets also apply to this case. In this type of market firms have the additional strategy of product differentiation available. Whereas it may be hard to impart a special identity to brands of concrete pipe, this is not the case for deodorants or toothpastes. For these products much effort goes into developing "product identification" and "brand loyalty." Any model that seeks to explain behavior in markets dominated by differentiated oligopolies must take into account these additional choices open to firms.

Monopoly

A monopoly market is one in which there is only a single supplier. This single firm then faces the entire market demand. It has relative freedom in its pricing policies because there are no other firms to worry about. The monopoly is in a general competition for the consumer's dollar, but this does not lead to the great uncertainties that are present in oligopolies. Entry into a monopoly market is difficult, perhaps entailing high initial investment costs. Nonetheless, most monopolies are aware of the possibility of entry and may adopt strategies that make it more difficult. For example, companies that obtain monopoly power in a market by owning patents may not strive for huge profits for fear of attracting successful imitators.

Overview of Part IV

In Part IV we will not investigate all of those market types in detail. Rather, we will center attention on the polar cases of perfect competition and monopoly since most real-world markets represent a mixture of these two types. In Chapter 9 we will discuss the theory of short-run, perfectly competitive pricing. In the short run, the number of firms in an industry is fixed: No entry by new firms is possible. This is the model most often used in supply-demand analysis. Appendix to Chapter 9 analyzes how equilibrium prices are established and whether a new equilibrium can be established when either supply or demand conditions change.

In Chapter 10 we take up the study of long-run price determination in a competitive industry. In the long run, new firms are lured into an industry by the availability of profits; the entry of these new firms changes supply conditions. By combining the material in Chapters 9 and 10, a complete picture of the competitive model of price determination is provided. This model is not only a complete view of a simplified theoretical model, but it also provides an excellent starting place for the analysis of real-world markets. Only by understanding how demand, costs, and the possibility of the entry of new firms interact in a simple model can we understand how those factors may be affected by real-world impediments.

In Chapter 11 we take up the theory of monopoly. The primary purpose of the chapter is to illustrate the misallocation of resources that monopolies may bring about. The chapter also discusses some ways in which this misallocation might be measured and analyzes both theoretical and practical problems in regulating monopolies.

Chapter 12 provides a brief introduction to the ways in which economists have tried to evaluate real-world markets. By drawing on material discussed in Chapters 9, 10, and 11, we will show how actual behavior can be contrasted to that predicted by simplistic models. We make a considerable effort to provide insights into the strategic relationships among the firms in an industry with only a "few" competitors. We will briefly discuss the Prisoner's Dilemma and the tool of game theory in an attempt to illustrate those interrelationships. The Appendix to Chapter 12 discusses two formal models of interfirm strategy that have been developed.

In short, then, Part IV is about supply and demand. Although markets may diverge from the perfectly competitive "ideal," a natural place to start any analysis is by quantifying demand and cost conditions. The insights provided by even a cursory examination of such factors can be great. At the same time, we should be aware of the limitations of simple supply-demand models and should recognize the extensions of these models that have been made. The purpose of this part and, indeed, of the remainder of this book, is to demonstrate those limitations and extensions.

Chapter 9

Perfectly Competitive Pricing in the Short Run

Introduction

In this chapter we will discuss short-run, perfectly competitive price determination. The theory we will develop is an elaboration of the Marshallian supply-demand analysis; conversely, Marshallian analysis is strictly appropriate only for short-run analysis of perfectly competitive markets. One final result of this chapter will be the development of the familiar upward-sloping short-run supply curve. We will see how such a curve is derived from the assumption that profit-maximizing firms exhibit increasing marginal costs in the short run.

Timing of a Supply Response

In the analysis of pricing it is important to decide the length of time that is to be allowed for a *supply response* to changing demand conditions. The establishment of equilibrium prices will be different if we are talking about a very short period of time during which supply is absolutely fixed or if we are envisioning a very long-run process in which it is possible for entirely new firms to enter an industry. For this reason, it has been traditional in economics to discuss pricing in three different time periods: (1) very short run, (2) short run, and (3) long run. While it is not possible to give these terms an exact chronological definition, the essential distinction being made concerns the nature of the supply response that is assumed to be possible. In the *very short run* there is no supply response: Quantity supplied is absolutely fixed.

even though no new production takes place. A similar analysis would follow for many types of durable goods such as antiques, used cars, back issses of the *National Geographic,* or corporate shares, all of which are in nominally "fixed" supply. We are more interested in examining how demand and production are related, and we will not analyze those other cases in detail.

Short-Run Supply

In short-run analysis the number of firms in an industry is fixed. It is assumed that firms do not have sufficient flexibility either to enter or to leave a given industry. However, those firms in the industry are able to adjust the quantity they are producing in response to changing conditions. They will do this by altering levels of employment for those inputs that can be varied in the short run, and we will investigate this supply decision here. Before beginning the analysis, we should perhaps repeat the assumptions of the perfectly competitive model. The most important assumption of perfectly competitive analysis is that there are a large number of small, profit-maximizing firms in an industry; each firm produces an identical product. Related to this assumption is the assumption that each firm knows the prevailing market price of the good it produces and believes that its decision will have no effect on this price. Every firm is therefore a *price-taker.* We also assume that there are a large number of demanders of the good so that no one purchaser can have a disproportionate influence on the market in question. Finally, an implicit assumption in our analysis is that transactions are costless. Buyers and sellers incur no special costs from their meeting in the market place. In the appendix to this chapter we will discuss reasons why real-world transactions may be costly and examine the implications that these costs have for the analysis of supply and demand.

Firms' Supply Decisions

In Chapter 8 we saw that a profit-maximizing firm should produce that level of output for which marginal revenue is equal to marginal cost. Because of the assumptions of the perfectly competitive model, each firm regards its marginal revenue curve as being a horizontal line at the prevailing market price. The firm believes that the revenue yielded by selling one more unit of output is given by the price of the good, since the firm's decisions have no effect on this price. Under these assumptions the firm's desire to maximize profits then dictates that it should produce that quantity for which *marginal cost equals price.* In the short run it is the short-run marginal cost curve that is relevant to this decision.

Figure 9.2 shows the individual firm's short-run decision. The market price is given by P^*. The demand curve facing the firm is therefore a horizontal line through P^*. This line is labeled $P = MR$ to remind the reader that an extra unit can be sold by the perfect competitor without affecting market price. Output level q^* provides maximum profits, since at q^* price is equal to marginal cost. The profits earned by the firm in the short run can be read off Figure 9.2 as the area $P*EAC$. This is simply the amount by which price exceeds average cost (EA) times the total quantity produced ($q*$).

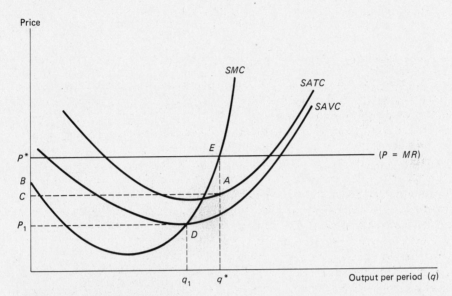

Figure 9.2 / Short-run Equilibrium for a Perfectly Competitive Firm

In the short run, the firm will produce that quantity for which price is equal to short-run marginal cost. The short-run marginal cost curve is therefore the firm's supply curve. Should price fall below P_1, however, the firm will choose to produce nothing, since at such prices it is not even covering its variable costs.

A geometric proof that profits are a maximum at $q*$ would proceed as follows. For output levels slightly less than $q*$, price ($P*$) exceeds short-run marginal cost. Consequently reducing output below $q*$ would cut back on revenues more than on costs. Profits would fall. Similarly, for output levels greater than $q*$, marginal costs exceed $P*$. Producing more than $q*$ would cause costs to rise more rapidly than revenues. Again profits would fall. Consequently if a firm produces either more or less than $q*$ it will lower its profits. Only at $q*$ are profits a maximum. Notice that at $q*$ the marginal cost curve has a positive slope. This is required if profits are to be a true maximum. If $P = MC$ on a negatively sloped section of the marginal cost curve, this is not a point of maximum profits, since increasing output would yield more in revenues (price times the amount produced) than this production would cost (marginal cost would decline if the MC curve had a negative slope). Consequently, profit maximization requires both that $P = MC$ and that at this point marginal cost be increasing.

Firms' Supply Curves

The positively sloped portion of the short-run marginal cost curve is therefore the *short-run supply curve* for a perfectly competitive firm. The curve shows how much the firm will produce for every possible market price. One exception must be made to this statement, however. Should market price fall below P_1, the profit-maximizing decision would be to produce nothing. Prices less than P_1 do not cover variable costs: There is a loss on each unit produced in addition to the loss of all fixed costs. By shutting down production the firm still must pay fixed costs, but it avoids the loss incurred on the units produced. Since, in the short run the firm cannot leave the industry and avoid all costs, its best decision is to produce no output. On the other hand, a price only slightly above P_1 will cause production to take place. Even though profits may be negative (which they will be if price falls short of average total costs), so long as variable costs are covered, the profit-maximizing decision is to continue production. Fixed costs must be paid in any case, and any price that covers variable costs will provide revenue as an offset to the fixed costs. The conclusion of these observations then is:

Optimization Principle

The profit-maximization assumption implies that the short-run supply curve for a perfectly competitive firm will be the positively sloped section of its short-run marginal cost curve above the point of minimum average variable cost.

Construction of the Short-Run Market Supply Curve

The quantity of output supplied to the entire market in the short run is simply the sum of the quantities supplied by each firm. Since each firm uses market price to determine how much to produce, the total amount supplied by all firms to the market will obviously depend on price. Hence we have:

Definition

The *short-run supply curve* shows the total quantity that all firms will supply at each possible market price.

Figure 9.3 illustrates the construction of the curve. For simplicity there are assumed to be two firms, A and B. The short-run supply (that is, marginal cost) curves for firms A and B are shown in 9.3a and 9.3b. The market supply curve shown in 9.3c is the horizontal sum of these two curves. For example, at a price of P_1, firm A is willing to supply q_1^A and firm B is willing to supply q_1^B. Therefore at this price the total supply in the market is given by Q_1, which is equal to $q_1^A + q_1^B$. The other points on the curve are constructed in an identical way. Because each firm's supply curve has a positive slope, the market supply curve will also have a positive slope. The positive slope reflects the fact that short-run marginal costs increase as firms attempt to increase their outputs.

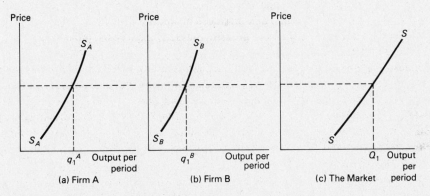

Figure 9.3 / Short-run Market Supply Curve

The supply (marginal cost) curves of two firms are shown in 9.3a and 9.3b. The market supply curve 9.3c is the horizontal sum of these curves. For example, at P_1 firm A supplies $q_1{}^A$, firm B supplies $q_1{}^B$, and total market supply is given by $Q_1 = q_1{}^A + q_1{}^B$.

Slope of the Supply Curve

Although the construction shown in Figure 9.3 used only two firms, actual market supply curves represent the horizontal summation of many firms' supply curves. Again the market supply curve will have a positive slope because of the positive slope in each firm's underlying marginal cost curve. This market supply curve summarizes the production functions used by all firms, the prices of the inputs they use, and their profit-maximizing decisions.

There is a second reason why the short-run supply curve may have a positive slope. Although each firm takes input prices as given in making its decisions, those prices may not remain constant as output for the industry as a whole expands. It is posoutput will increase the demand for scarce inputs thereby bidding up the prices of those inputs. For example, expansion of professional sports leagues in the 1960s had the effect of bidding up players' salaries, and that raised teams' costs. Such *interaction effects* may cause the short-run market supply curve to be more steeply sloped than a simple sum of firms' short-run marginal cost curves would suggest. Expansion in output raises firms' marginal costs both because of diminishing marginal productivity and because rising factor prices may increase overall costs. The short-run supply curve summarizes both effects and, as we show in the next section, permits an examination of how these factors interact with market demand to determine price.

Short-Run Price Determination

We are now ready to combine demand and supply curves to demonstrate the establishment of equilibrium prices in the market. Figure 9.4 shows this process. Looking first at 9.4b, we see the market demand curve D (ignore for the moment D') and the short-run supply curve S. The two curves intersect at a price of P_1 and a quantity of Q_1. This price-quantity combination represents an *equilibrium* between the demands of individuals and the supply decisions of firms. As before, at that point there is a precise balancing of the forces of supply and demand. Equilibrium will tend to persist from one period to the next unless one of the factors underlying the supply and demand curves should change. Here the equilibrium price P_1 serves two important functions. First, this price acts as a *signal* to producers by providing them with information with which to decide how much should be produced. In order to maximize profits, firms will produce that output level for which marginal costs are equal to P_1. In the aggregate, then, production will be Q_1. A second function of the price is to *ration* demand. Given the market price P_1, utility-maximizing individuals will decide how much of their limited incomes to devote to buying the particular good. At a price of P_1, total quantity demanded will be Q_1, and this is precisely the amount that will be produced. This is what economists mean by an equilibrium price-quantity combination. No other P, Q combination represents such a balancing of supply and demand.

The implications of the equilibrium price (P_1) for a typical firm and for a typical individual are shown in Figures 9.4a and 9.4c, respectively. For the typical firm, the price P_1 will cause an output level of q_1 to be produced. The firm earns a small profit

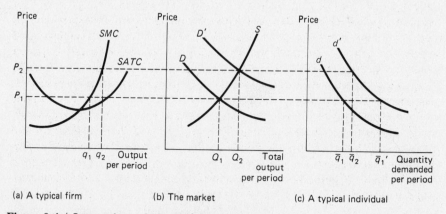

(a) A typical firm   (b) The market   (c) A typical individual

**Figure 9.4 / Interactions of Many Individuals
and Firms Determine Market Price in the Short Run**

Market demand curves and market supply curves are each the horizontal sum of numerous components. These market curves are shown in 9.4b. Once price is determined in the market each firm and each individual treat this price as a fixed parameter in their decisions. Although individual firms and persons are impotent in determining price, their interaction as a whole is the sole determinant of price. This is illustrated by a shift in an individual's demand curve to d'. This will not affect market price if only one individual reacts in this way. However, if everyone exhibits an increased demand, market demand will shift to D'; in the short run, price will rise to P_2.

at this particular price because short-run average total costs are covered. The demand curve d (ignore d' for the moment) for a typical individual is shown in 9.4c. At a price of P_1, this individual demands $\overline{q}_1$. By adding up the quantities that each individual demands at P_1 and the quantities that each firm supplies, we can see that the market is in equilibrium. The market supply and demand curves provide a convenient way of making such a summation.

An Individual's Demand Has No Effect on Price

The three panels in Figure 9.4 can be used to show two important facts about short-run market equilibrium: the individual's "impotence" in the market, and the nature of short-run supply response. First, suppose a single individual's demand curve were to shift outward to d', as shown in 9.4c. Since it was assumed that there are many demanders, this shift will have practically no effect on the market demand curve. Consequently, market price will be unaffected by the shift to d'; that is, price will remain at P_1. Of course, at this price the person for whom the demand curve has shifted will consume more ($\overline{q}_1'$), as is shown in 9.4c.[1]

Effect of an Increase in Market Demand

If many individuals experience shifts outward in their demand curves, the entire market demand curve may shift. Figure 9.4b shows the new demand curve D'. The new equilibrium point will be at P_2, Q_2: At this point, supply-demand balance is re-established. Price has increased from P_1 to P_2 in response to the demand shift. Notice also that the quantity traded in the market has increased from Q_1 to Q_2. The rise in price has served two functions. First, as in our previous analysis of the very short run, it has acted to ration demand. Whereas at P_1 a typical individual demanded $\overline{q}_1'$, now at P_2 only $\overline{q}_2$ is demanded. The rise in price has also acted as a signal to the typical firm to increase production. In 9.4a, the firm's profit-maximizing output level has increased from q_1 to q_2 in response to the price rise. That is what we mean by a *short-run supply response:* An increase in market price acts as an inducement to increase production. Firms are willing to increase production (and to incur higher marginal costs) because price has risen. If market price had not been permitted to rise (suppose, for example, government price controls were in effect) firms would not have increased their outputs. At P_1 there would have been an excess (unfilled) demand for the good in question. If market price is allowed to rise, a supply-demand equilibrium can be re-established so that what firms produce is

---

[1] It might properly be asked where the extra quantity $\overline{q}_1' - \overline{q}_1$ comes from since nothing has happened to cause firms to change their output decisions. If, prior to the increase in demand, supply and demand were in balance, now there will be a shortage. The answer to this question lies in the extremely small magnitude $\overline{q}_1' - \overline{q}_1$ represents when compared to the market as a whole. It is not literally true that nothing changes when one individual's demand curve shifts, but for all practical purposes that will be the case. The effect of one individual on market price is inconsequential.

again equal to what individuals demand at the prevailing market price. Notice also that at the new price, P_2, the typical firm has increased its profits. This increasing profitability in the short run will be important to our discussion of long-run pricing in Chapter 10.

Shifts in Supply and Demand Curves

In previous chapters we have analyzed many of the reasons why either demand or supply curves might shift. Such shifts may be caused by changes in prices in other markets, changes in tastes, or changes in productive technologies. It seems likely that these types of changes are constantly occurring in real-world markets. When either a supply curve or a demand curve does shift, equilibrium price and quantity will change. In this section we will investigate briefly the relative magnitudes of such changes, and we will show that the outcome depends on the shapes of the curves. This is an additional example of comparative statics analysis: We will be comparing equilibria at two different points in time. Appendix Chapter 9 presents a brief discussion of how prices move from one equilibrium level to another.

Shifts in Supply Curves:
Importance of the Shape of the Demand Curve

Let us consider first a shift upward in the short-run supply curve for a good. Such a shift might, for example, have resulted from an increase in the prices of inputs used by firms to produce the good. Whatever the cause of the shift, it is important to recognize that the effect of the shift on the equilibrium level of P and Q will depend on the shape of the demand curve for the product. Figure 9.5 illustrates two possible situations. The demand curve in 9.5a is relatively price-elastic; that is, a change in price substantially affects quantity demanded. For this case, a shift in the supply curve from S to S' will cause equilibrium prices to rise only moderately (from P to P') whereas quantity is contracted sharply (from Q to Q'). Rather than being "passed on" in higher prices, the increase in the firms' input costs is met primarily by a decrease in quantity (a movement down the firms' marginal cost curves)[2] and only a slight increase in price.

This situation is reversed when the market demand curve is inelastic. In 9.5b, a shift in the supply curve causes equilibrium price to rise substantially whereas quantity is little changed. The reason for this is that individuals do not reduce their demands very much if prices rise. Consequently, the shift upward in the supply curve is passed on to demanders almost completely in the form of higher prices.

---

[2]Notice, for example, that on the supply curve S', the marginal cost of producing output level Q is considerably higher than the marginal cost of producing Q'.

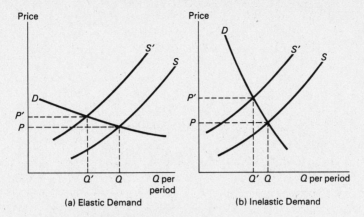

**Figure 9.5 / Effect of a Shift in the Short-run
Supply Curve Depends on the Shape of the Demand Curve**

In 9.5a the shift upward in the supply curve causes price to increase only slightly, whereas quantity contracts sharply. This results from the elastic shape of the demand curve. In 9.5b the demand curve is inelastic; price increases substantially with only a slight decrease in quantity.

Shifts in Demand Curves: Importance of the Shape of the Supply Curve

In a manner identical to that we just used, we can show that a given shift in a market demand curve will have different implications for P and Q depending on the shape of the short-run supply curve. Two illustrations are shown in Figure 9.6. In 9.6a the supply curve for the good in question is very steep. As quantity expands, firms' marginal costs rise rapidly, and this gives the supply curve its slope. Using the terminology we developed in Chapter 5, we might say that supply is relatively inelastic with respect to changes in price. In this situation, a shift outward in the market demand curve (caused, for example, by an increase in income) will cause prices to increase substantially. On the other hand, the quantity traded increases only slightly. Intuitively what has happened is that the increase in demand (and in Q) has caused firms to move up their steeply sloped marginal cost curves. The concomitant large increase in price serves to ration demand.

Figure 9.6b shows a relatively elastic short-run supply curve. Such a curve would occur for an industry in which marginal costs do not rise steeply in response to output increases. For this case an increase in demand produces a substantial increase in Q. However, because of the nature of the supply curve, this increase is not met by great cost increases. Consequently, price rises only moderately.

These examples again demonstrate Marshall's observation that demand and supply determine price and quantity simultaneously. Recall our analogy from Chapter 1: Just as it is impossible to say which blade of a scissors does the cutting, so too is it impossible to attribute price solely to demand or to supply characteristics. Rather, the effect that shifts in either a demand curve or a supply curve will have

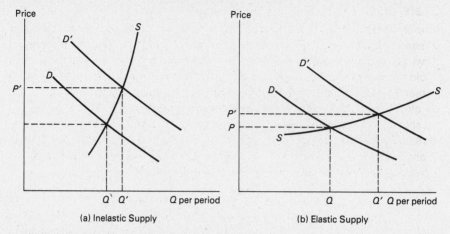

(a) Inelastic Supply

(b) Elastic Supply

**Figure 9.6 / Effect of a Shift in the Demand
Curve Depends on the Shape of the Short-run Supply Curve**

In 9.6a supply is inelastic; a shift in demand causes price to increase greatly with only a small concomitant increase in quantity. In 9.6b, on the other hand, supply is elastic; price only rises slightly in response to a demand shift.

depends on the shapes of both of the curves. In predicting the effects of shifting supply or demand conditions on market price and quantity in the real world it is necessary to consider this simultaneous relationship. We will examine some examples in the next section.

Examples of the Use of Empirical Data to Study Shifts in Demand Curves

Although the examples we outlined in the previous section show how shifts in supply and demand curves might be analyzed graphically, they do not provide us any precise guidance about how actual calculations might be made from real-world data. In this section we will show how such calculations might be made in a very rough way. But before we begin our analysis, it is necessary to introduce an equation that shows the implications that a shift in a demand curve or a supply curve will have for the new equilibrium market price. Since the new equilibrium price will be determined by the intersection of the demand curve with the market supply curve, the equation involves both the price elasticity of demand (denoted by $ED_{Q,P}$, which is defined as the percent change in quantity demanded in response to a 1 percent change in market price) and the short-run price elasticity of supply (denoted by $ES_{Q,P}$, which is defined as the percentage change in quantity produced in the short run in response to a 1 percent increase in price).

Quantitative Result of a Shift in Demand

Now let us consider a shift in the demand curve so that 1 percent more quantity is demanded *at each price.* Such a shift is shown in Figure 9.7. Now, if the supply curve were infinitely elastic (such as that represented by S) equilibrium price would not change. Consequently, by our assumption, quantity demanded would increase by 1 percent. This would be reflected by a movement from Q* to Q**. On the other hand, if the supply curve were positively sloped (curve S' in Figure 9.7), the shift in demand would cause a rise in price; for this reason, quantity would not increase by the full 1 percent. Rather, the new equilibrium would occur at a price of P' and a quantity of Q' (where Q' < Q**). We can show that the 1 percent shift outward in the demand curve will cause market price to rise by [3]

$$\text{Percent change in price} = \frac{1}{ES_{Q,P} - ED_{Q,P}} \qquad [9.1]$$

That is, the percent change in market price induced by a 1 percent shift outward in the demand curve is given by the reciprocal of the difference between the elasticities of supply and demand (remember $ED_{Q,P}$ is usually negative).

This result can be used to show several of the results that we have derived previously. Suppose that the price elasticity of demand is −2. Now consider various alternative elasticities of supply. If supply is infinitely elastic (for example, curve S in Figure 9.7), equation (9.1) records the fact that a proportional shift outward in demand will not cause price to increase at all. If the elasticity of supply is +2, however, equation (9.1) records the fact that a 1 percent shift outward in the demand curve will cause price to rise by ¼ = 1/(2 + 2) of 1 percent. This would be similar to the increase of price from P* to P' in Figure 9.7. Finally, if supply were totally inelastic ($ES_{Q,P} = 0$), equation (9.1) records the fact that price would have to rise by ½ of 1 percent to restore equilibrium. This price rise (because the elasticity of demand is −2) would exactly compensate for the 1 percent outward shift in the demand curve and would cause quantity demanded to remain unchanged (as it must since supply has not changed). The shift outward in the demand curve

---

[3]This can be proved as follows: Suppose the market demand curve has a constant elasticity form given by $Q_D = a\,P^b$, where $b < 0$ and this is the price elasticity of demand. Suppose also that the market supply curve has a constant elasticity form given by $Q_s = c\,P^d$, where $d > 0$ and this is the elasticity of supply. Setting $Q_D = Q_s$ yields an equilibrium price (P_E) for which

$$aP_E{}^b = cP_E{}^d$$

or

$$P_E{}^{d-b} = \frac{a}{c}$$

or

$$P_E = \left(\frac{a}{c}\right)^{1/(d-b)}$$

Consequently, a 1 percent shift in the demand curve (that is, 1 percent shift in a) will cause P_E to increase by $[1/(d - b)]$ percent. This is the result given by equation (9.1).

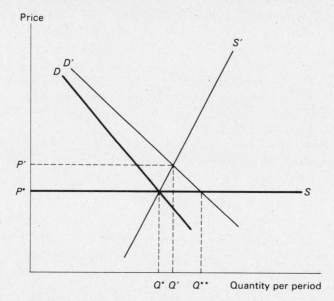

**Figure 9.7 / Proportional Shift in a
Demand Curve and Its Effect on Market Price**

The demand curve in this figure has shifted proportionally outward from D to D'. For any price, 1 percent more is demanded with D' than was with D. If supply is perfectly elastic (curve S) quantity will increase by 1 percent also, since this is the way in which the shift was defined. If the supply curve is positively sloped, however, price will rise in response to the demand shift. The extent of this rise in price is given by equation (9.1). The price rise will cause a movement upward along D', and Q will increase by less than 1 percent.

causes quantity demanded to increase by 1 percent, whereas the movement along the new demand curve occasioned by the price rise causes quantity to fall by 1 percent.

We now turn to examine how equation (9.1) might be used in conjunction with other information to predict the outcome of shifts in real-world demand curves.

Effect of an Income Tax Surcharge on Automobile Purchases

In the late 1960's a 10 percent income tax surcharge was imposed by the United States government in an effort to restrain consumer demand and to control inflation. Government forecasters were anxious to know what effect this surtax might have on consumer purchases in general and on automobile purchases in particular. A simple analysis of this problem might proceed as follows. The surtax reduces disposable income by about 2 percent. Assuming that the income elasticity of demand for automobiles is about 2.0, this implies that automobile purchases would be reduced by 4 percent.

Although there are many reasons why such an analysis is extremely superficial, we will only analyze one here.[4] The tax surcharge causes the demand curve for automobiles to shift inward. This would exactly reverse the process shown in Figure 9.7: The surcharge causes the demand curve to shift from D' to D. If supply were infinitely elastic, quantity would in fact fall by 4 percent (from Q^{**} to Q^*). However, if the supply curve is positively sloped, the shift in the demand curve may cause equilibrium price to fall (from P' to P^*). For example, automobile dealers may reduce their selling prices in an effort to attract new buyers because of the slackness introduced by the surtax. This fall in price will have a stimulating effect on demand, and the decline in quantity will be mitigated. Suppose, for example, that the price elasticity of demand for automobiles is -2 and that the supply elasticity is $+2$. Then, by equation (9.1), each 1 percent shift inward in the demand curve will cause a ¼ of 1 percent fall in equilibrium price. Since the surtax causes the demand curve to shift inward by 4 percent, price can be predicted to fall by one percent (= 4 percent × ¼). This 1 percent fall in price would, other things being equal, cause demand to increase by 2 percent since the price elasticity of demand was assumed to be -2.

We are now ready to provide a slightly more sophisticated analysis of the effect that the income tax surcharge would have on automobile purchases. First, the reduction in income has the direct effect of causing automobile purchases to be reduced by 4 percent. However, this shift in demand induces a fall in price that stimulates purchases (by causing a movement *along* the new demand curve) to the extent of 2 percent. The net result, then, is a decrease of automobile sales of 2 percent (= 4 percent − 2 percent). Because dealers are willing to reduce their prices in a time of slack demand, they have moderated the decline in sales; this should be taken into account in any attempt at a complete analysis of the effects of the income tax surcharge.

Effect of Devaluation of the Dollar on United States Exports

As a second example of simple numerical manipulations with supply and demand curves, we will consider the effect that the 1971 devaluation of the dollar had on United States exports. During the period April 1971 to December 1971 the United States dollar was devalued by about 10 percent vis-à-vis other world currencies.[5] One ostensible purpose of this devaluation was to increase sagging United States exports (and to restrict imports, but that's another story). The purported effect of

---

[4]An important factor that should be considered in any actual attempt at estimating the effect of the surtax is that automobile purchases are probably based on a longer term concept of income than simply earnings in a single year. A one-year surtax will not therefore reduce automobile purchases nearly to the extent that a permanent decline in income of the same amount would.

[5]The figures in this example are generally abstracted from W. H. Branson. "The Trade Effects of the 1971 Currency Realignments." *Brookings Papers on Economic Activity* 1 (1972), pp. 15–58.

devaluation can also be shown by Figure 9.7. Here the dollar price of American exports is on the vertical axis and the quantity of American exports bought by foreign nationals is shown on the horizontal axis. Prior to devaluation, foreigners' demand for exports is given by the curve *DD*. Although the curve *DD* relates the quantity of exports to their dollar price, it is important to remember that foreigners really care very little about the dollar price of American goods. Rather, they are interested in the prices of goods in their own domestic currency (that is, in marks, pounds, francs, and so forth). After the devaluation of the dollar, foreign nationals can buy more dollars with their currencies. Whereas previously a dollar might cost 4 marks, after the devaluation it may only cost 3.6. Consequently, at each dollar price for United States exports, more goods will be demanded: Foreign demand will shift to *D'D'* as a result of the devaluation. We now wish to analyze the extent of this shift and its implication for pricing.

As before, in order to assess the effect of the shift in demand, we need information about the elasticities of supply and demand for United States exports. Although there is considerable controversy surrounding the actual values of these elasticities, we will assume that the price elasticity of demand for exports is -1.5 and that the supply elasticity of American exports is about 10.0.[6] Consequently each percent shift outward in the demand curve brought about by the devaluation will have the effect of raising the dollar price of United States exports by 0.085 (= 1/11.5) percent. In general, then, because the supply elasticity is rather high, dollar prices of exports will not rise by much. However, the effects should be taken into account.

Now we must ask how large a shift in foreign nationals' demand curve for American exports has been induced by the 10 percent devaluation of the dollar. Suppose we conceptually hold the dollar price of exports constant. Because the dollar has been devalued by 10 percent, exports will now cost 10 percent less in foreign currency. Therefore, since the elasticity of demand is -1.5, the quantity demanded at the constant dollar price will increase by 15 percent. This then is the answer we need: The demand curve in Figure 9.7 has shifted outward by 15 percent as a result of the devaluation.

We are now ready to compute the total effect of the devaluation on American exports. If the supply curve were infinitely elastic (curve *S* in Figure 9.7), quantity demanded would increase by 15 percent as a result of the devaluation with no change in the dollar price of exported goods. However, supply is not infinitely elastic; consequently, the equilibrium dollar price of American-produced goods will rise by about 1.3 percent (= 15 × 0.085). This, in turn, will cause quantity to decline by 1.9 percent (= -1.5 × 1.3) because of the movement along the *D'* curve. The total effect of the devaluation, therefore, will be to cause an increase in the quantity of American exports by 13.1 percent (a 15 percent increase because of the shift outward in the demand curve less a 1.9 percent decrease arising from the increase in the dollar cost of producing exports). In order to predict accurately

---

[6]See Branson, "Effects of 1971 Currency Realignments," pp. 21, 22.

the effects of the devaluation it is therefore necessary to examine not only how foreign demand for United States exports will be affected but also how the dollar prices of these exports will be affected as United States firms move along their supply curves. As always, to study the effect of some action on equilibrium price and quantity we must analyze both supply and demand curves.

The Arab Oil Embargo

Effects of shifts in the supply curve can be analyzed in a manner similar to the one we have just used to study demand shifts. An inward shift in supply (caused, say, by a rise in input prices) will have the effect of raising market price and the extent of this increase will depend on the price elasticities of demand and supply. In fact, it is relatively easy to show that a one percent inward shift in the supply curve has an identical effect on the equilibrium price that a one percent outward shift in demand has.[7] The size of such a shift is again "predicted" by equation 9.1. Of course, although the implications for equilibrium *price* are the same for an outward shift in demand and an inward shift in supply, the implications for the equilibrium *quantity* are quite different. A shift outward in demand will increase equilibrium quantity as firms respond to the higher price by moving along their supply curves. A shift inward in supply, on the other hand, will cause equilibrium quantity to fall as individuals react to the price increase by buying less.

As an application of these principles, consider the case of the oil embargo placed on the United States in October 1973 by the Arab members of the Organization of Petroleum Exporting Countries (OPEC). Since U.S. oil imports from Arab nations totaled about 20 percent of total supply, this action had the effect of shifting the oil supply curve inward by 20 percent; at each price, 20 percent less oil was available to meet demand. It would be expected that such a restriction would raise the price of oil in the United States and we wish to estimate the extent of this price increase. To do so requires estimates of short-run price elasticities of supply and demand for oil.

Most estimates of the demand for oil suggest that it is quite price-inelastic in the short run. A figure for $ED_{Q,P}$ of -0.2 is fairly representative of the empirical data that have been calculated. Similarly, most empirical work suggests that the short-run supply of oil is also price-inelastic. A value of $ES_{Q,P}$ of 0.2 is a typical estimate.[8] Using these values, equation (9.1) "predicts" that each one percent inward shift in supply will increase market price by 2.5 percent

---

[7]For a proof see footnote 3 of this chapter.

[8]For some references on the price elasticity of supply for oil see the discussion of long-run supply in Chapter 10. Long-run supply elasticities are probably higher than short-run elasticities because the long-run effect of an increase in price may be to prompt firms to discover additional reserves. Even with a fixed level of reserves, however, there are a number of ways in which firms may increase output in the short run. These include: more intensive pumping, use of lower grade (and more expensive to refine) crude oil, and adoption of "tertiary" recovery methods such as steam and water injection.

$(= \dfrac{1}{0.2 - (-0.2)} = \dfrac{1}{.4} = 2.5)$. Hence, the Arab embargo would be expected to increase price by 50 percent (= 20 × 2.5) in the short run and that is approximately the price increase recorded during the period the embargo was in effect. Our model also shows that the 20 percent shortfall in supply was accommodated in two ways. First, the price rise reduced demand by 10 percent (= 50 × $ED_{Q,P}$ = 50 × −0.2). Second, the price rise also increased supply from non-Arab sources by 10 percent (= 50 × $ES_{Q,P}$ = 50 × 0.2). These rather simple calculations therefore provide some insights into the way in which the oil market adjusted to the embargo.[9] Figure 9.8 illustrates that adjustment. Initial equilibrium in the oil market was at the point P^*, Q^* where the demand and (short-run) supply curves for oil intersect. Onset of the embargo shifted the supply curve inward to S'. If the market price remained at P^* there would have been a shortage given by the distance Q^*-Q_2 amounting to about 20 percent of total demand. That shortage did not occur, however, because of the rise in price in the short run from P^* to P. This price rise equilibrated the market in two ways: firms increased their output by an amount $Q_1 -Q_2$ in response to the higher price, and individuals reduced their demand for oil from Q^* to Q_1 by moving along the demand curve as price rose. The market was therefore brought into equilibrium by the responses of both firms and individuals to rising prices.

Summary

In this chapter we brought together the analyses of demand, technology, and costs presented in previous chapters to develop a model of competitive price determination in the short run. That model is the familiar Marshallian supply-demand cross, and it represents the single most useful tool for economic analysis. Our development in this chapter showed why the assumption of increasing marginal costs (and the possibility that input prices are bid up as industry output expands) leads to positively sloped short-run supply curves. We also examined in detail how shifts in either the supply or the demand curve might affect equilibrium prices and showed how estimates of demand and supply elasticities can be used to predict the size of such effects.

Throughout the chapter, we used only short-run cost curves and held the number of firms constant. Such restrictions were valuable in permitting us to focus on market reactions to relatively short-term influences. Such analysis does not, how-

---

[9]Of course, this discussion abstracts from a number of important additional determinants of pricing in the oil market such as the effects of: monopoly power by OPEC members; price and allocation controls imposed by the U.S. government in response to the embargo; and the possibility that demand or supply curves may have shifted during the period because of other economic factors (such as the onset of a recession in the U.S.). For these reasons, the calculations should be accepted for pedagogic purposes only.

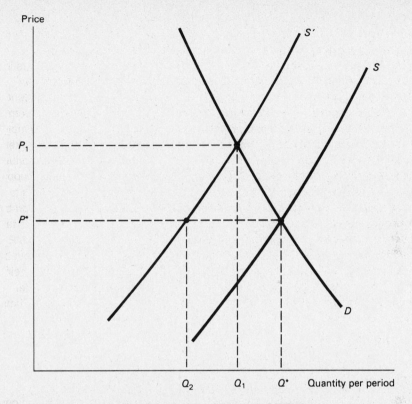

Figure 9.8 / Effect on the U.S. Oil Market of the Arab Oil Embargo

The oil embargo by the Arab members of OPEC in 1973–74 had the effect of shifting the supply curve for oil consumed in the United States inward. This caused market price to rise from P^* to P_1, and this equilibrated the market in the short run at a lower output level (Q_1). Actual reactions in the oil market were more complex than indicated in the figure, however.

ever, provide a complete explanation of equilibrium price determination since, over the longer term, markets have additional flexibility in the types of adjustments they can make. Most important, firms may adjust all of their inputs (long-run cost curves therefore enter the analysis) and firms may enter or leave an industry. We shall examine these additional adjustments in the next chapter.

Suggested Readings

Branson, W. H., "The Trade Effects of the 1971 Currency Realignments," *Brookings Papers on Economic Activity* 1 (1972), pp. 15–58.

Henderson, J. M., and Quandt, R. E., *Microeconomic Theory,* 2d ed. (New York: McGraw-Hill Book Company, Inc., 1971), chap. 4.

Khusro, A. M., "The Pricing of Food in India," *Quarterly Journal of Economics* 81 (1967), pp. 271–285.

Knight, F. H., *Risk, Uncertainty and Profit* (Boston: Houghton Mifflin Company, 1921), chaps. 5 and 6.

Machlup, F., *Economics of Seller's Competition* (Baltimore: Johns Hopkins Press, 1952), pp. 79–125.

Marshall, A., *Principles of Economics,* 8th ed. (New York: Crowell-Collier and Macmillan Co., 1920), book 5, chaps. 1–3.

Nordhaus, W., and Shoven, J., "Inflation 1973: The Year of Infamy," *Challenge* (May/June 1974), pp. 14–22.

Robinson, J., "What Is Perfect Competition?" *Quarterly Journal of Economics* 49 (1934), pp. 104–120.

Samuelson, P. A., *Foundations of Economic Analysis* (Cambridge, Mass.: Harvard University Press, 1947), chap. 9.

Stigler, G. J., "Perfect Competition, Historically Contemplated," *Journal of Political Economy* 65 (1957), pp. 1–17.

Problems

9.1

Assume the price of an input, say labor, increases. Using the isoquant map for a typical firm, show how a new set of cost curves might be constructed for the firm. Show how these new cost curves imply a new short-run industry supply curve. What will happen to price and quantity in the short run? What factors does the size of these changes depend on?

9.2

A perfectly competitive market has 1,000 firms. In the very short run each of the firms has a fixed supply of 100 units. The market demand is given by

$$Q = 160,000 - 10,000P$$

a. Calculate the equilibrium price in the very short run.

b. Calculate the demand schedule facing any one firm in the industry.

c. Calculate what the equilibrium price would be if one of the sellers decided to sell nothing or if one seller decided to sell 200 units.

d. At the original equilibrium point, calculate the elasticity of the industry demand curve and the elasticity of the demand curve facing any one seller.

Suppose now that in the short run each firm has a supply curve that shows the quantity the firm will supply (q_1) as a function of market price. The specific form of this supply curve is given by

$$q_i = -200 + 50P$$

Using this short-run supply response, supply new solutions for **a–d** above.

9.3
Suppose there are one hundred identical firms in a perfectly competitive notecard industry. Each firm has a short-run total cost curve of the form:

$$C = 0.0033\,Q^3 + 0.2\,Q^2 + 4\,Q + 10.$$

and marginal cost is given by

$$MC = .01\,Q^2 + .4\,Q + 4.$$

a. Calculate the firm's short-run supply curve with Q (the number of crates of notecards) as a function of market price (P).
b. On the assumption that there are no interaction effects between costs of the firms in the industry, calculate the industry supply curve.
c. Suppose market demand is given by $Q = -200\,P + 8000$. What will be the short-run equilibrium price-quantity combination?
d. Suppose everyone starts writing more research papers, and the new market demand is given by $Q = -200\,P + 10,000$. What is the new short-run price-quantity equilibrium? How much profit does each firm make?

9.4
Suppose there are 1000 identical firms producing diamonds and that the total cost curve for each firm is given by:

$$C = q^2 + wq$$

and marginal cost is given by:

$$MC = 2q + w$$

(where q is the firm's output level and w is the wage rate of diamond cutters).

a. If $w = 10$ what will be the firm's (short-run) supply curve? What is the industry's supply curve? How many diamonds will be produced at a price of 20 each? How many more diamonds would be produced at a price of 21?
b. Suppose that the wages of diamond cutters depend on the total quantity of diamonds produced and that the form of this relationship is given by

$$w = .002\,Q$$

(where Q represents total industry output, which is 1000 times the output of the typical firm).

In this situation show that the firm's marginal cost (and short-run supply) curve depends on Q. What is the industry supply curve? How much will be produced at a price of 20? How much more will be produced at a price of 21? What do you conclude about the shape of the short-run supply curve?

9.5

Suppose that the quantity of chicken demanded (Q) depends on the price of chicken (P), the price of beef (P'), and income (I). Suppose also that the price elasticity of demand for chicken ($E_{Q,P}$) is -1.0; that the cross-price elasticity of demand for chicken ($E_{Q,P'}$—that is, the percent change in the quantity of chicken demanded in response to a 1 percent rise in the price of beef) is $+1.0$; that the income elasticity of demand ($E_{Q,I}$) is $+0.5$; and that the short-run elasticity of supply for chicken is $+2.0$. Initially, the price of chicken is \$.50 per pound, the price of beef is \$1.50 per pound, and total personal income is \$800 billion. At these prices and incomes, 2 billion pounds of chicken are bought per year.

Now suppose that the price of beef rises to \$1.80 per pound and that personal incomes increase to \$960 billion.

a. How will the demand curve for chicken shift?

b. By how much will the price of chicken rise in the short run? What will the new equilibrium price of chicken be?

c. What will be the final effect of all of these changes in the quantity of chicken bought? How much (in pounds) will now be bought?

d. Draw an approximate graph of your results.

9.6

Demand curves and supply curves are never absolutely fixed for any period. Rather, they are constantly shifting in response to changing tastes and technologies. Use this observation to discuss the notion of a "teacher shortage," which was widely publicized in the early 1960s (although more recently "teacher glut" might be a better term), and to analyze the U.S. housing "shortage." How would you interpret the concept of shortage in the usual static framework?

9.7

A common empirical problem is to estimate the demand curve for a good from data on its price and quantity. Since price and quantity are in fact jointly determined by the interaction of supply and demand, obtaining an unambiguous estimation of a demand curve from such data is very difficult. In order to be certain that the price-quantity combinations that are observed do represent a demand curve, the assumption must be that either the demand curve is fixed and has no random component or, since the first condition is quite unlikely, the supply curve, during the period of observation, shifted around "a lot" relative to the demand curve. Use a simple supply-and-demand diagram to discuss these aspects of the "identification problem."

Appendix to Chapter 9	**Short-Run Supply-Demand Dynamics**

Introduction

In Chapter 9 we discussed a number of examples of what we have called "comparative statics analysis." The conditions of supply-demand equilibrium for a particular situation were demonstrated and then we asked what new equilibrium would emerge as a result of changed conditions. There was always the implicit assumption that price and quantity would move promptly to their new short-run equilibrium[1] levels whenever a movement from one equilibrium to another was necessary. While this assumption may be suitable in an elementary analysis a more detailed investigation raises several difficult issues. For example, how is it that suppliers and demanders are able to settle on a new equilibrium price? The only information available to them must come from the market, and no trading is permitted except at equilibrium prices. It would seem that some crucial element of the ajdustment process has been left out of the analysis. Unless an omniscient figure is overseeing the operation of markets, it is hard to envision exactly how a new equilibrium is established. It is the purpose of this appendix to discuss briefly the ways in which economists have attempted to formalize those economic adjustment processes that are necessary to any complete supply-demand model.

---

[1]This appendix discusses only the establishment of short-run equilibrium prices. Since the functioning of markets in the long run is a succession of short-run equilibria, the analysis to be presented is also relevant to that case.

Adjustment Processes: Basic Concepts

The problem we will investigate can be stated most precisely in a mathematical way. Consider a demand function in which quantity depends on price, $D(P)$, and a (short-run) supply function in which quantity also depends on price, $S(P)$. An equilibrium price, P^*, has the property that:

$$D(P^*) = S(P^*) \text{ or } D(P^*) - S(P^*) = 0 \qquad \text{[9A.1]}$$

That is, at P^* the quantity demanded is equal to the quantity supplied.

Suppose, now, that the price initially starts at P_0 (perhaps this was an equilibrium before conditions changed, but that is not a necessary condition of the problem). Are there economic forces that cause the market price to move from P_0 to P^*? Related to this basic question are several others such as: How long will it take for price to get to P^*? Will prices "midway" between P_0 and P^* be observed in the market? What meaning are we to assign to any nonequilibruim prices that do occur? Only the initial question will be answered in any detail; the others will be discussed in a cursory manner at the end of the appendix.

The Impartial Auctioneer

To explain the movement of price to its equilibrium level, economists have relied on the fictitious notion of an *impartial auctioneer*. The auctioneer is charged with calling out prices and recording the actions of buyers and sellers. Only when the auctioneer calls a price for which the quantity demanded is identical to that which is supplied will he permit trading to take place.[2] Presumably the auctioneer will use information about the market supply and demand curves to guide his pricing decisions, but precise rules for this operation are seldom spelled out.

The abstract idea of an auctioneer seems too far removed from reality to be an acceptable representation of the way in which prices are actually set. There have been numerous attempts, therefore, to give this fictional concept a behavioral interpretation. One such interpretation is the idea of *recontracting*. Buyers and sellers are assumed to enter into provisional contracts before the exchange of goods actually takes place. Each of these provisional contracts is voided if it is discovered that at the agreed upon price the market is not in equilibrium. Only when market clearing prices for all markets are discovered will exchange take place. Recontracting is then a form of haggling over price.

---

[2]Real-world analogies to this notion are rare. One interesting Middle Eastern custom has an auctioneer sit between buyer and seller holding the hand of each. The auctioneer then calls off prices and the buyer and seller indicate their willingness to trade at these prices by pressing the hand of the auctioneer. When the auctioneer calls a price to which both parties agree, he announces that the trade has been completed.

Walrasian Price Adjustment

A second suggestion, which is similar to recontracting, was proposed by L. Walras. In this scheme equilibrium prices are a goal toward which the market gropes. Changes in price are motivated by information from the market about the degree of *excess demand* at any particular price.[3] Although the Walrasian model is essentially mathematical, it is possible to give an intuitive explanation. Walras assumes that

$$\begin{aligned}
\text{Change in price} &= k[\text{excess demand}] \\
&= k[D(P) - S(P)] = k[ED(P)] \qquad k > 0 \qquad \text{[9A.2]}
\end{aligned}$$

where $ED(P)$ is used to represent excess demand at price P. Equation 9A.2 says that price will increase if there is positive excess demand, and decrease if excess demand is negative.

Figure 9A.1 shows the Walrasian process of adjustment schematically. For the supply and demand curves shown in the figure, P^* is an equilibrium price. For

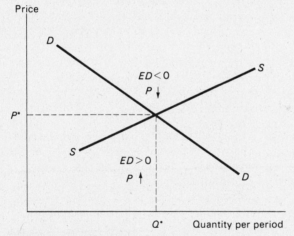

Figure 9A.1 / Schematic Representation of the Walrasian Adjustment Process

For prices above P^*, supply exceeds demand. Such a price may set into motion a chain of events that cause price to fall. For prices less than P^*, the quantity demanded exceeds what is supplied. In reaction, price may rise.

prices less than P^*, there will be an excess demand for this good. At such bargain prices individuals will demand more than firms would be willing to supply. Crowds will descend on stores and buy all of this good off the shelves. Walras assumed that this behavior would be translated in the market into an increase in price and this

[3]L. Walras, *Elements of Pure Economics,* trans. W. Jaffé (Homewood, Ill.: Richard D. Irwin, Inc., 1954).

increase in price will serve to equilibrate supply and demand. In Figure 9A.1 the upward-pointing arrow indicates that movement in price in response to excess demand. A similar argument follows for prices above P^*. At such prices, the quantity supplied will exceed that which is demanded. Firms will be producing more than individuals demand, and the inventory of the good will begin to accumulate in the firms' warehouses. Eventually this will lead to a fall in price that will again equilibrate supply and demand. The downward-pointing arrow in the figure indicates that result.

Marshallian Quantity Adjustment

The adjustment process we have just discussed views price as the motivating force in the adjustment of markets to equilibrium. Individuals and firms respond to price changes by moving along their respective demand and supply curves until an equilibrium price-quantity combination is reached. A somewhat different picture of the adjustment process was suggested by Marshall in his classic *Principles of Economics*.[4] There Marshall theorized that individuals and firms should be viewed as adjusting quantity in response to imbalances in demand and supply, and that price changes follow from these changes in quantity. If we let $D^{-1}(Q)$ represent the price that demanders are willing to pay for each quantity and $S^{-1}(Q)$ represent the price that suppliers require for each quantity (that is, their marginal cost), then the Marshallian adjustment mechanism can be represented by:

$$\text{Change in Quantity} = k[D^{-1}(Q) - S^{-1}(Q)] = k[ED^{-1}(Q)] \quad k > 0. \quad \text{[9A.3]}$$

In words, movements in quantity toward equilibrium are motivated by discrepancies between the price individuals are willing to pay and what firms wish to receive. When those two figures coincide, quantity adjustment ceases.

Quantity adjustment is illustrated in Figure 9A.2. For quantities below equilibrium (Q^*), demand price exceeds supply price. Quantity produced and consumed therefore increases. For quantities above equilibrium, supply price exceeds demand price and that provides incentives for quantity reduction. As was the case for the price-adjustment mechanism pictured in Figure 9A.1, the Marshallian mechanism pictured in Figure 9A.2 implies that the price-quantity equilibrium is a stable one. Starting from any initial position, forces come into play that move economic agents toward equilibrium. The precise mechanism by which the movement comes about, however, differs between the Walrasian and Marshallian models.

The Importance of Economic Factors in the Adjustment Process

Movement to an equilibrium price-quantity combination will usually involve changes in both price and quantity. The important questions concern which of those

---

[4]A. Marshall, *Principles of Economics*, 8th ed. (London: Macmillan & Co., Ltd., 1920), pp. 287–288.

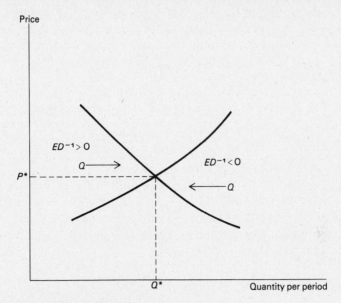

Figure 9A.2 / Marshallian Quantity

Under Marshallian adjustment, a difference between demand and supply prices sets up incentives for economic agents to alter output levels. If demand price exceeds supply price ($ED^{-1} > 0$), Q will rise. If supply price exceeds demand price ($ED^{-1} < 0$), Q will fall. The adjustment mechanism shown in the figure is stable, since Q converges to Q^*.

variables is adjusted by economic agents, and how do these agents perceive the need to make such adjustments. Although economists are only beginning to investigate these questions, the general approach to be followed is clear. Any theory of the adjustment process must focus on the costs to demanders and suppliers of changing their behavior. Those costs derive both from problems associated with gathering information about the true supply-demand configuration and from difficulties in adapting to this new information once it is acquired. Given a quantification of these various costs, it might be hypothesized that price-quantity adjustments are made in ways that minimize them. Later in this appendix we shall summarize a few models of this sort of behavior. First, however, we shall investigate another model of the adjustment process, which shows in a formal way how disequilibrium prices might arise.

Cobweb Model of Price Adjustment

One problem that interferes with the specification of a realistic price adjustment process is that the traditional model pictures supply and demand decisions as being made simultaneously. There are two equations (the supply and demand curves) to be solved for two unknowns (price and quantity).

Imagining how this solution is discovered presents conceptual difficulties. If it were possible to assume that the supply decision preceded the demand decision, this problem would be simplified. For example, if firms based their current output decisions on the market price occurring in the previous period, then output in the current period could be regarded as fixed; there will be no current period supply response. The analysis of pricing in the "very short run" would then be the relevant model to study. The mechanisms for pricing in such situations are relatively well understood (auctions[5] are the primary example). Here price acts only as a rationing device for demand; it has no influence on production in the current period. In the next period the market price established in the previous period will be the one relevant to output decisions and there is thus some (lagged) response of output to price changes.

Supply-Demand Assumptions

These ideas can be shown most clearly by a simple *cobweb model* of price determination. Suppose firms' supply decisions in period t depend only on the market price that prevailed in period $t - 1$:

$$\text{Supply in period } t = Q_t^S = a + bP_{t-1} \qquad [9A.4]$$

For example, this equation may represent the supply decision of farmers planting a crop. At the time the crop is planted only the previous year's price is known. Farmers must make their decisions based on that price. Once the crop is harvested, it represents the current year's supply. The supply will not, however, respond to the current year's price. The total quantity supplied will then be sold in the market for whatever it will bring. Market demand depends on current price:

$$\text{Demand in period } t = Q_t^D = c - dP_t \qquad [9A.5]$$

and equilibrium in the market at time t necessitates that

$$Q_t^S = Q_t^D \qquad [9A.6]$$

That view of the market assumes the following sequence of events: Firms decide how much they will produce by referring to the previous period's price (P_{t-1}). They produce this output during the current period and sell it in the market for what demanders are willing to pay. Demanders then bid for this output (perhaps in auctions, such as the way in which the prices of crops are set); in so doing they establish the current market price (P_t). It is this price, then, that enters into firms' production decisions in period $t + 1$. In this way there is a lagged response of suppliers to the actions of demanders in determining price.

---

[5]For an interesting survey of a variety of auction techniques and the institutional peculiarities of these systems, see R. Cassady, Jr., *Auctions and Auctioneering* (Berkeley, Calif.: University of California Press, 1967).

A Graphic Analysis

Figure 9A.3 illustrates the working of the cobweb model. There P^* is an equilibrium price because the quantity demanded at this price is exactly equal to that which is supplied.[6] The price P^* can persist from one period to the next since firms, by referring to the previous period's price (which is also P^*), produce Q^*; this is what demanders are willing to buy at P^* in the current period.

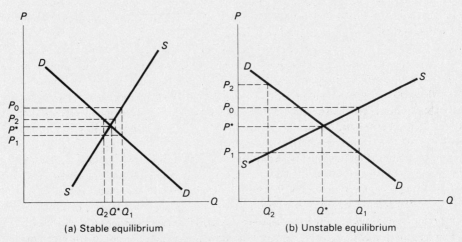

(a) Stable equilibrium   (b) Unstable equilibrium

Figure 9A.3 / Cobweb Model of Price Determination

In the cobweb model of lagged response to price by firms, a theory of nonequilibrium pricing can be established. Whether these prices will approach an equilibrium level will depend on the relative slopes of the demand and supply curves. In the configuration shown in 9A.3a convergence will take place, whereas in 9A.3b it will not. A third possibility (not shown) would be for the supply and demand curves to have slopes so that the price perpetually oscillates at about P^*.

We can easily see why this model is called the "cobweb" by analyzing the sequence of events that follows if price starts from a nonequilibrium position. Suppose, for example, that price starts at P_0 and consider first Figure 9A.3a. In period 1, firms will produce output level Q_1 by referring to P_0. For example, P_0 might represent the average price of wheat from the 1978 grain harvest, and farmers use this information to decide the number of acres to be planted in 1979. Once Q_1 is produced, however, it must be sold in the market for whatever it will bring. Since Q_1 represents a relatively large output level, a low price must prevail in the market in period 1 (call this price P_1) to get demanders to buy this amount. In the grain harvest example, the price of wheat will fall substantially in 1979 from its 1978 level because of the "overproduction" in 1978.

In period 2, firms will base their output decisions on P_1. They will therefore produce a relatively low output level (Q_2). Demanders will bid for this output level

---

[6]Simple algebra can be used to solve equations 9A.4 and 9A.5 for $P^* = (c - a)/(b + d)$.

Transaction Costs and Market Adjustments

Many economists believe that markets are usually out of equilibrium. Demand and supply curves constantly shift as tastes and costs change, and markets never have a chance to adjust completely to a particular supply-demand configuration. In explaining why markets do not adjust immediately to changing conditions, economists have tended to stress *transactions costs*. Bringing suppliers and demanders together is not so simple a process as the Marshallian diagram suggests: There may be significant costs involved. such costs not only consist of the direct costs of finding a "place" in which to transact business but, more important, they also include the costs to the participants of gaining information about the market. For demanders, all prices are not perfectly known. Rather, they must invest some time in search procedures that permit them to learn market prices.[10] They must also spend some effort in analyzing the quality of the products they intend to buy. Similarly, suppliers face costs in making transactions. The most important of these is the need to find out something about the demand for their product. Since production takes time, the absence of such information can lead to serious mistakes in the quantity a firm chooses to produce. Firms must also consider the random nature of demand over a short period. For example, no retailer knows exactly when he or she will sell shirts of particular sizes. One of the costs incurred in selling shirts is the necessity of maintaining an inventory and making adjustments in that inventory.

That discussion illustrates that the competitive assumption of zero transaction costs is not likely to be fulfilled in the real world. Although supply and demand analysis will provide information about equilibrium prices and about the direction of change in prices, various costs will prevent markets from adjusting promptly. Consequently we should observe in the real world examples of not only the systematic influence of supply and demand but also *disequilibria* caused by the existence of transactions costs. Here we shall discuss three specific illustrations.

Unemployment

Probably the most important example of market disequilibrium is the persistently high level of unemployment experienced in the American economy.[11] If a simple

---

[10]Existence of such transactions costs may result in markets falling to obey the law of one price. Rather, it is possible that several different prices for the identical commodity may coexist (even in equilibrium). For example, one study found that the price of regular gasoline exhibited an average price range of 4.5 cents per gallon in 20 U.S. cities. The price range was lower in cities where use of gasoline was greater (and hence costs of gaining price information may have been lower). See H. Marvel, "The Economics of Information and Retail Gasoline Price Behavior," *Journal of Political Economy* 84 (1976), pp. 1033–1059.

[11]See, for example, A. Alchian, "Information Costs, Pricing, and Resource Unemployment," in *Microeconomic Foundations of Employment and Inflation Theory,* ed. E. Phelps et al. (New York: W. W. Norton & Company, Inc., 1970), pp. 27–52.

supply-demand model adequately represented the labor market, there would be little unemployment: The wage rate would be adjusted to ensure that every worker who wanted to work would be able to get a job. This does not happen, however, because there is always some "frictional" unemployment. Demands for labor are constantly shifting, and workers released by one firm will take time to find a job at another firm. Similarly, new workers enter the labor force and spend time searching for a job. Finally, workers may voluntarily quit one job in order to look for a better one. All those factors cause a temporary mismatch between the supply of labor and the demand for labor, and this shows up in the unemployment statistics.[12]

Inventory Behavior

Similar results occur in the supply and demand for industrial products. An increase in demand, for example, may not always lead to an adjustment in price. Rather, the demand shift will first show up in firms' inventory positions. As inventories are depleted, firms may adjust prices upward toward the new supply-demand equilibrium. Inventory fluctuations and lags in price adjustments are therefore an important type of market disequilibria. These may result from transactions costs. It is costly for a firm to analyze the demand for its produce precisely, and watching inventory levels may be a relatively inexpensive method for doing so. Changing input levels also may be costly, and this may keep firms from making input adjustments until some "threshold level" is passed. One example of this is the tendency of firms to "hoard" labor in the initial phase of a recession in order to reduce special costs associated with laying off workers.

Queueing

A final important sign of market disequilibrium is queueing. Waiting lines for doctor appointments, ski lifts, and theater tickets reflect a failure of price to respond to short-run demand fluctuations. In the long term, some adjustment in price (or perhaps the entry of new firms) would be expected. However, in the short run, queues reflect the inability of price to act as an effective rationing device.

---

[12]This frictional unemployment might be differentiated from unemployment that arises from a lack of "aggregate" demand. This other type of unemployment is usually studied in macroeconomics courses and will not be analyzed here. It should be pointed out, however, that the microeconomic determinants of such "Keynesian" unemployment are not well understood. Some authors, in fact, believe that Keynesian economics should be interpreted as a short-run, disequilibrium model of competitive markets in which information is low and transactions costs are high. See, for example, A. Leijonhufvud, *On Keynesian Economics and the Economics of Keynes* (London: Oxford University Press, 1968), especially pp. 67–80.

A Concluding Note

It is important to repeat that these examples do not invalidate the supply-demand models we have developed. Knowing equilibrium prices and quantities can provide good information on where the market is heading. However, because transactions costs of various types interfere with the instantaneous attainment of equilibrium, some analysis of disequilibrium pricing is also needed to understand real-world phenomena.

Suggested Readings

Arrow, K. J., "Limited Knowledge and Economic Analysis," *American Economic Review* 64 (March 1974), pp. 1–10.

————, and Capron, W. M., "Dynamic Shortages and Price Rises: The Engineer-Scientist Case," *Quarterly Journal of Economics* 73 (May 1959), pp. 292–308.

Harlow, A. A., "The Hog Cycle and the Cobweb Theorem," *Journal of Farm Economics* 42 (November 1960), pp. 842–853.

Henderson, J. M., and Quandt, R. E., *Microeconomic Theory,* 2d ed. (New York: McGraw-Hill Book Company, Inc., 1971), pp. 132–149.

McCallum, B. T., "Competitive Price Adjustments: An Empirical Study," *American Economic Review* 64 (March 1974), pp. 56–65.

Phelps, E. S., et al., *Microeconomic Foundations of Employment and Inflation Theory* (New York: W. W. Norton & Company, Inc., 1970).

Stigler, G. J., "The Economics of Information," *Journal of Political Economy* 69 (June 1961), pp. 213–225.

Chapter 10 Perfectly Competitive Pricing in the Long Run

Introduction

In this chapter we will examine how long-run equilibrium prices are established in perfectly competitive markets. The analysis will differ in two ways from that presented in Chapter 9. First, we will be using long-run cost curves because these reflect the input flexibility that firms have in the long run. Second, we must also allow for the entry and exit of firms from an industry in response to profit opportunities in the long run. These actions will have important implications for pricing. We begin the chapter with a description of the long-run equilibrium for a competitive industry and then will show how that equilibrium changes when conditions change. The final sections of the chapter show how the model of competitive pricing in the long run can be applied.

Equilibrium Conditions

A perfectly competitive market is in equilibrium when no firm has an incentive to change its behavior. Such an equilibrium has two components: firms must be content with their output choices (that is, they must be maximizing profits) and firms must be content to stay in (or out of) the industry. We will discuss each of these components separately.

Profit Maximization

As before, we assume that firms pursue the goal of maximum profits. Because each firm is a price taker, profit maximization requires that the firm produce where price is equal to (long-run) marginal cost. This first equilibrium condition, $P = LMC$, therefore illustrates both the firm's output choice and its adaptation of inputs so as to minimize costs in the long run.

Entry

We must also consider a second feature of long-run equilibrium: the possibility of the entry of entirely new firms into the industry, or the exit of existing firms from the industry. The perfectly competitive model assumes that there are no special costs of entering and exiting from an industry.[1] Consequently, new firms will be lured into any market in which (economic) profits are positive. Similarly firms will leave any industry in which profits are negative. The entry of new firms will cause the short-run industry supply curve to shift outward, since there are now more firms producing than there were previously. Such a shift will cause market price (and industry profits) to fall. The process will continue until no firm contemplating entering the industry is able to earn an economic profit.[2] At that point, entry will cease and an equilibrium number of firms will be in the industry. A similar argument can be made for the case in which some of the firms in an industry are suffering short-run losses. Some firms will choose to leave the industry, and this will cause the supply curve to shift to the left. Market price will rise thus restoring profitability to those firms remaining in the industry.

Long-Run Equilibrium

For the purposes of this chapter we will assume that all the firms in an industry have identical cost curves; that is, we will assume that there are no special resources or technologies controlled by any one firm.[3] Because all firms are identical, the equilibrium long-run position requires that every firm earns exactly zero economic profits. In graphic terms, this means that long-run equilibrium price must settle at the low point of each firm's long-run average total cost curve. Only at this point do the two equilibrium conditions $P = LMC$ (which is required for profit maximization) and $P = LATC$ (which is the required zero profit) hold. Hence we can summarize our discussion by:

---

[1] In Chapter 12 we will discuss some barriers to entry that may make this assumption inappropriate in certain situations.

[2] Remember, we are using the economists' definition of profits here. These profits represent a return to the owner of a business in excess of that which is strictly necessary to keep him or her in the business.

[3] The important case of firms having different costs is discussed in Chapter 13. In that chapter we will see that very low cost firms can earn positive, long-run profits.

Optimization Principle

An industry composed of many identical firms will be in *long-run equilibrium* when price is equal to the firms' minimum long-run average total costs. At that point firms will be maximizing profits and, since economic profits are zero, there will be no incentives for firms to enter or leave the industry.

It is important to emphasize, however, that these two equilibrium conditions have rather different origins. Profit maximization is a goal of firms. The $P = LMC$ rule therefore derives from the behavioral assumptions we have made about firms and is similar to the output decision rule used in the short run. The zero-profit condition is not a goal for firms. Firms would obviously prefer to have positive profits. The long-run operation of the market, however, forces all firms to accept a level of zero economic profits ($P = LATC$) because of the willingness of firms to enter and to leave an industry. While the firms in a perfectly competitive industry may either earn positive or negative profits in the short run, in the long run only a level of zero profits will prevail.

As an example that may make this short-run, long-run distinction clear, consider the market for wheat. Suppose that the market demand for wheat increases as a result of a change in individuals' tastes. In the short run, the effect of this increase in demand will be to increase the market price of wheat. As a result of this increase in price, farmers' profits will also increase. Each farmer may respond to this increased profitability by increasing output (the farmer may, for example, work harder and thereby provide more labor input); in the short run, the farmer is limited in terms of the types of adjustment that can be made. When the view shifts to the long run, several additional possibilities for adjustment must be considered. First, individual farmers can decide to increase the land they have under cultivation. They may also buy additional farm equipment. In other words, those farmers already in the industry can adjust all the inputs under their control. The possibility of profits may also lure other farmers into the wheat-growing business. The entry of these new "firms" will have a depressing effect on price, and entry will continue until the possibility for profit disappears. The industry will be in long-term equilibrium only when it has fully adjusted to the initial increase in demand.

Long-Run Supply: Constant Cost Case

In order to discuss long-run pricing in detail, we must make some assumption about how the entry of new firms into an industry affects the costs of inputs for firms already in the industry. The simplest assumption we might make is that entry has no effect on the costs of those inputs. Under this assumption, no matter how many firms enter (or leave) an industry, every firm will retain the same set of cost curves with which it started. There are many important cases in which the constant input cost assumption may not be tenable, and we will analyze these in the next section. For the moment, however, we wish to examine the equilibrium conditions for a *constant cost industry.*

Market Equilibrium

Figure 10.1 demonstrates long-run equilibrium for an industry. For the market as a whole (10.1b) the demand curve is given by D and the short-run supply curve by SS. The short-run equilibrium price is therefore P_1. The typical firm (10.1a) will

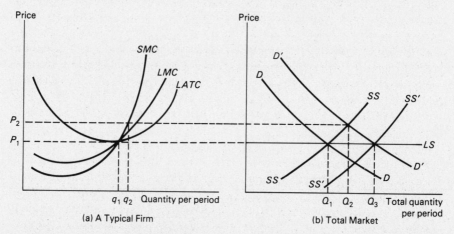

Figure 10.1 / Long-run Equilibrium for a Perfectly Competitive Industry: Constant Cost Case

An increase in demand from D to D' will cause price to rise from P_1 to P_2 in the short run. This higher price will create profits in the industry and new firms will be drawn into the market. If it is assumed that the entry of these new firms has no effect on the cost curves of the firms in the industry, new firms will continue to enter until price is pushed back down to P_1. At this price economic profits are 0. The long-run supply curve (LS) will therefore be a horizontal line at P_1. Along LS output is increased by increasing the number of firms each producing q_1.

produce output level q_1 since at this level of output price is equal to short-run marginal cost (SMC). In addition, with a market price of P_1, output level q_1 is also a long-run equilibrium position for the firm. The firm is maximizing profits since price is equal to long-run marginal costs (LMC). When all possible long-run variations in input usage are considered, q_1 remains the optimal level of output for a profit-maximizing firm. There is a second long-run equilibrium property implied by 10.1a: Price is equal to long-run average total costs ($LATC$). Consequently, economic profits are zero and there is no incentive for firms either to enter or to leave the industry. The market depicted in 10.1b is therefore in both short-run and long-run equilibrium. Firms are in equilibrium because they are maximizing profits, and the number of firms is stable because economic profits are zero. This equilibrium will tend to persist until either supply or demand conditions change.

A Shift in Demand

Suppose now that tastes change. Specifically, assume that the market demand curve shifts upward to D'. If SS is the relevant short-run supply curve for the industry, then in the short run, price will rise to P_2. The typical firm will, in the short run, choose to produce q_2, and will earn profits on this level of output. In the long run, these profits will attract new firms into the market. Because of the constant cost assumption, this entry of new firms will have no effect on cost curves. Costs of factors of production are not affected by the new firms that enter the industry. New firms will continue to enter the market until price is forced down to the level at which there are again no pure economic profits. The entry of new firms will therefore shift the short-run supply curve to SS' where the equilibrium price (P_1) is re-established. At this new long-run equilibrium, the price quantity combination P_1, Q_3 will prevail in the market. The typical firm will again produce at output level q_1, although now there will be more firms than there were in the initial situation.

Long-Run Supply Curve

By considering all possible shifts in demand we can examine long-run pricing in this industry. Our discussion suggests that, no matter how demand shifts, economic forces will come into play that cause price to return to P_1. Hence, all long-run equilibria will occur along a horizontal line at P_1. Connecting these equilibrium points indicates the long-run supply response of the industry. This locus of points is labeled LS in Figure 10.1. Hence we can define:

Definition

The *long-run supply curve* for a perfectly competitive industry is the locus of long-run equilibrium points for the industry for all possible shifts in demand.

For a constant cost industry composed of identical firms, the supply curve is a horizontal line at the low point of the firms' long-run average total cost curves.[4] If the constant cost assumption is relaxed the supply curve may, however, have a variety of shapes, as we now show.

---

[4]These equilibrium conditions also point out what seems to be, somewhat imprecisely, an "efficient" aspect of the long-run equilibrium in perfectly competitive markets: The good under investigation will be produced at minimum average cost.

Shape of the Long-Run Supply Curve

In the previous section we pointed out that, contrary to the short-run case, long-run analysis has very little to do with the shape of the (long-run) marginal cost curve. Rather, the zero-profit condition centers attention on the low point of the long-run average cost curve as the factor most relevant to long-run price determination. In the constant cost case the position of this low point does not change as new firms enter the industry. Consequently, only one price can prevail in the long run regardless of how demand shifts. The long-run supply curve is horizontal at this price. Once the constant cost assumption is abandoned, this need not be the case. If the entry of new firms causes average costs to rise, the long-run supply curve will have an upward slope. On the other hand, if entry causes average costs to decline it is even possible for the long-run supply curve to be negatively sloped. We will now discuss these possibilities.

Increasing Cost Industry

There are several reasons why the entry of new firms may cause the average cost of all firms to rise. New firms may compete for scarce inputs, thus driving up their prices. New firms may impose "external costs" on existing firms (and on themselves) in the form of air or water pollution. And new firms may place strains on governmental services (police forces, sewage treatment plants, and so forth), and these may show up as increased costs for all firms. Figure 10.2 demonstrates market equilibrium in such an *increasing cost industry*. The initial equilibrium price is P_1. At this price the typical firm produces q_1, and total industry output (shown in Figure 10.2c) is Q_1. Suppose now that the demand curve for the industry shifts outward to D'. In the short run, price will rise to P_2, since this is where D' and the industry's short-run supply curve (SS) intersect. At this price, the typical firm will produce q_2 and will earn a substantial profit. It is this profit that attracts new entrants into the market and shifts the short-run supply curve outward. Suppose that this entry of new firms causes the cost curves of all firms to rise. The new firms may compete for scarce inputs and thereby drive the prices of these inputs up. A typical firm's new (higher) set of cost curves is shown in Figure 10.2b. The new long-run equilibrium price for the industry is P_3 (here $P_3 = LMC = LATC$), and at this price Q_3 is demanded. We now have two points (P_1, Q_1 and P_3, Q_3) on the long-run supply curve.[5] All other points on the curve can be found in an analogous way by considering all possible shifts in the demand curve. These shifts would trace out the long-run supply curve LS. Here LS has a positive slope because of the increasing cost nature of the industry. Notice that the LS curve is somewhat flatter than the short-run supply curves. This indicates the greater flexibility in supply response that is possible in the long run.

---

[5]Figure 10.2 also shows the short-run supply curve associated with the point P_3, Q_3. This supply curve has shifted to the right because there are more firms producing now than there were in the initial situation.

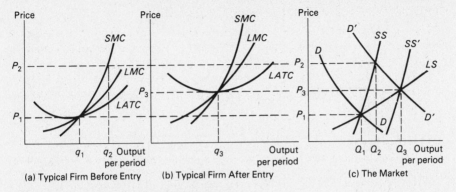

**Figure 10.2 / An Increasing Cost Industry
Has a Positively Sloped Long-run Supply Curve**

Initially the market is in equilibrium at P_1, Q_1. An increase in demand (to D') causes price to rise to P_2 in the short run, and the typical firm produces q_2 at a profit. This profit attracts new firms into the industry. The entry of these new firms causes costs to rise to the levels shown in 10.2b. With this new set of curves, equilibrium is re-established in the market at P_3, Q_3. By considering many possible demand shifts and connecting all the resulting equilibrium points, the long-run supply curve (LS) is traced out.

Decreasing Cost Industry

Not all industries must exhibit constant or increasing costs, however. There are reasons why the entry of new firms may in fact reduce the costs of firms in an industry. For example, the entry of new firms may provide a larger pool of trained labor to draw from than was previous available, thus reducing the costs associated with the hiring of new workers. Similarly, the entry of new firms may provide a "critical mass" of industrialization that permits the development of more efficient transportation and communications networks. Whatever the exact nature of the cost reductions, the final result is illustrated in the three panels of Figure 10.3. The initial market equilibrium is shown by the price quantity combination P_1, Q_1 in 10.3c. At this price the typical firm produces q_1 and earns exactly zero in economic profits. Now suppose market demand shifts outward to D'. In the short run, price will increase to P_2 and the typical firm will produce q_2. At this price level, positive profits are being earned. These profits cause new entrants to come into the market. If this entry causes costs to decline, a new set of cost curves for the typical firm might resemble those shown in 10.3b. Now the new equilibrium price is P_3; at this price, Q_3 is demanded. By considering all possible shifts in demand, the long-run supply curve, LS, can be traced out. This curve has a negative slope because of the decreasing cost nature of the industry.

A Summary

We have therefore shown that the long-run supply curve for a perfectly competitive industry may assume a variety of shapes. The principal determinant of that shape is the way in which entry of firms into the industry affects costs. In the constant cost

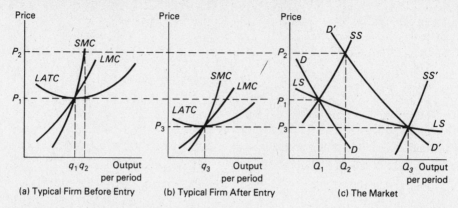

Figure 10.3 / A Decreasing Cost Industry Has a Negatively Sloped Long-Run Supply Curve

Initially the market is in equilibrium at P_1, Q_1. An increase in demand to D' causes price to rise to P_2 in the short run, and the typical firm produces q_2 at a profit. This profit attracts new firms to the industry. If the entry of these new firms causes costs to fall, a set of new cost curves might look like those in panel 10.3b. With this new set of curves, market equilibrium is re-established at P_3, Q_3. By connecting such points of equilibrium, a negatively sloped long-run supply curve (LS) is traced out.

case entry or exit has no effect on costs and hence the long-run supply curve is horizontal. If costs increase as new firms enter the industry, the long-run supply curve will have a positive slope reflecting those cost increases. In the event that entry of new firms causes costs to fall, on the other hand, long-run supply curves may be negatively sloped.

Some Theoretical Examples of Long-Run Perfectly Competitive Analysis

The analysis of long-run equilibrium in perfectly competitive markets is very precise. Given the underlying assumptions of this type of market structure, the tools that have been presented permit exact answers to be given for interesting economic questions. Here we will present three examples of such long-run analysis. In the first we assume that the industry in question exhibits constant costs, and we investigate the long-run incidence of a specific tax on a firm's output. In the second we will examine the economic factors affecting the adoption of new, lower-cost equipment. In the final example we discuss the infant industry argument for tariff protection in an underdeveloped country. The analyses in this section are primarily theoretical. In later sections we will examine some real-world evidence on long-run pricing.

Effect of a Specific Tax

A *specific tax* is a tax of a fixed amount per unit of output on a firm's production. It is a cost per unit of output that is (in appearance) paid by the firm to the government. If a per-unit specific tax of t dollars is levied, the total costs of a firm are therefore increased by tq. The average and marginal cost curves of the firm are similarly shifted upward by t. There is, however, another way of analyzing a specific tax that will be more convenient here. The demand curve relevant to an industry's behavior is in fact an "after-tax" demand curve. A specific tax merely shifts the demand curve that is relevant to the firms in the industry downward by the amount t. Any quantity that is produced will sell at some market price P, but the after-tax amount received by firms in the industry will be $P - t$. The after-tax demand curve is labeled D' in Figure 10.4. This is the demand curve on which industry output decisions will

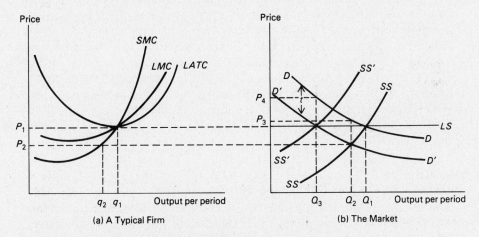

Figure 10.4 / Effect of the Imposition of a Specific Tax on a Perfectly Competitive, Constant Cost Industry

A specific commodity tax of amount t lowers the after-tax demand curve to D'. With this "new" demand curve Q_2 will be produced in the short run at an after-tax price of P_2. The market price will be P_3. In the long run, firms will leave the industry and the after-tax price will return to P_1. The entire amount of the tax is shifted onto consumers in the form of a higher market price (P_4).

be based, although the market price of any output produced will still be determined by the original market demand curve D.

The initial equilibrium in the market is given by the intersection of the long-run supply curve (LS) and the market demand curve. At this initial point, market price is P_1, the quantity exchanged in the market is Q_1, and the typical firm will produce output level q_1. With the imposition of the tax, the after-tax demand curve becomes D'. In the short run, industry output will be determined by the intersection of the curve D' with the industry short-run supply curve SS. This intersection occurs at output level Q_2 and price P_2. The after-tax price received by the firm is now P_2, and the typical firm will (assuming P_2 exceeds average variable cost) produce output level q_2. In the market, total output Q_2 will sell for P_3. Notice that $P_3 - P_2 = t$. In the short run, then, the tax is borne partially by the consumers of the good (market price has risen from P_1 to P_3) and partially by the firms in the industry who are operating at a short-term loss.

In the long run, firms will not continue to operate at a loss. Some firms will leave the industry bemoaning the role of an oppressive government in bringing about their demise. The industry short-run supply curve will therefore shift leftward as fewer firms remain in the market. A new long-run equilibrium will be established at Q_3 where the after-tax price received by the firm enables it to earn exactly 0 in economic profits. Those firms left in the industry will return to producing output level q_1. The price paid by individuals in the market will now be P_4. In the long run the entire amount of the tax has been shifted into increased prices. Even though the firm ostensibly "pays" the tax, in fact the burden is borne by individuals.[6]

This analysis is perhaps the simplest example of tax incidence theory. It clearly shows that in order to determine who ultimately pays a tax, it is necessary to investigate market responses. It is incorrect to argue that the agent who writes a check to the government actually bears the burden of the tax. Two other interesting possibilities of tax shifting occur in the cases of the corporate income tax and in employers' contributions for social security. Even though firms "pay" both taxes it has been argued that the true burden of the profits tax is shifted to consumers in the form of higher prices and that the burden of the social security tax is shifted onto workers in the form of lower wages. Each of these assertions deserves empirical investigation.

Introduction of Low-cost Equipment

Suppose a new productive technique is developed that is characterized by a lower *LATC* than that currently prevailing. In the long run it is clear that this new technique will displace the previous one, and the lower *LATC* minimum will set the long-run price. However, in the short run, this may not be the case. The older, high-cost firms are "stuck" in the industry. There is nothing they can do with their now outmoded techniques, except to continue producing. This situation is pictured in Figure 10.5. In 10.5a the older, higher cost firms' cost curves are drawn; 10.5c shows the cost curves for the low-cost firms. Suppose that the initial market equilibrium is given by the price-quantity combination P_1, Q_1. Assume that the low-cost firms can enter the industry freely and in a much shorter time interval than those already in can get out. Low-cost firms will be lured in so long as they envision a long-run profit—so long as price exceeds P_2. Entry will therefore continue until price falls to P_2. If P_2 exceeds the average variable cost for the high-cost firms they will continue to produce as indicated by their short-run supply curve SS. At P_2 they are, in the short run, willing to supply Q_2 (the typical firm produces q_2). But at P_2 total demand calls for Q_3, and

---

[6]It should be emphasized that this result depends crucially on the assumptions of perfect competition and free entry and exit. If either or both of these do not hold, the result must be modified. Similarly, the prediction that price will rise by exactly the amount of the tax depends on the assumption of constant costs. If the industry is characterized by increasing costs, price will ultimately rise by less than t, and will rise by more than t in the decreasing cost case. Why?

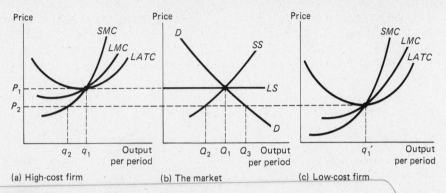

Figure 10.5 / Introduction of Low-cost Techniques into a Perfectly Competitive Industry

With the entry of new low-cost firms, market price will be forced down to P_2. At this price, Q_3 is demanded in the market. Since the high-cost firms are stuck in the industry, they will continue to produce; their total output will be Q_2. The remaining output ($Q_3 - Q_2$) will be supplied by the low-cost firms. In the very long run, all firms will adopt the low-cost techniques.

therefore the amount $Q_3 - Q_2$ will be supplied by the new low-cost firms. The low-cost firms cannot produce more than this. If they did, price would fall below P_2 and they would suffer a loss. In the very long run, the high-cost firms will be forced to adapt to the new technology.[7] In the short run, however, their production serves the useful function of providing output during this transitional phase.

Infant Industry Case for Tariff Protection

Industries in underdeveloped countries frequently exhibit high production costs. They must absorb the expense of training workers, contend with a poor internal monetary system, and make do with poorly developed transportation facilities and inefficient public utilities. Faced with those costs, such industries frequently cannot compete at prevailing world prices. For example, the cost curves for the firms in an underdeveloped economy might resemble those in Figure 10.6a. Since the minimum point on the $LATC$ curve (P_1) exceeds the world price (P_w), a policy of free trade will cause the good in question to be imported: a domestic industry will not develop.

In an effort to protect their industries, many underdeveloped countries adopt tariffs that have the effect of raising the price for imports above P_1. Given the shield of the

---

[7]The reader may wish to apply this analysis to his or her decision to purchase a new car (or any durable good) to replace an older, higher-cost one. If you are not tempted by Detroit's advertising prowess, you will not buy the new car until the average total cost of its operation is less than the average variable cost of the old junker.

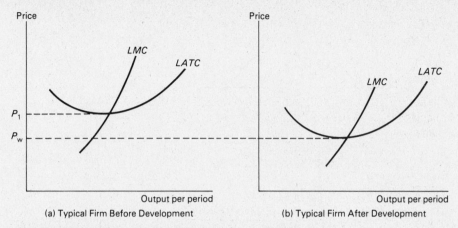

Figure 10.6 / Infant Industry Argument for Tariff Protection

The firms in an underdeveloped country may have high costs as shown in 10.6a. The firms cannot compete at world prices (P_w). A tariff that raises price above P_1 will permit the firms to sell in the domestic market, and their growth may bring about the development of a more efficient economic network. That development may lower firms' costs so that they may now compete at the world price without tariff protection.

tariff, the domestic industry can now sell in its home market. If this were the end of the story, many economists would object to the imposition of the tariff on the grounds that residents of the country are being forced to pay more for the good than would be necessary in a free trade situation.[8] However, it is possible that temporarily protecting the "infant" industry will permit the development within the country of a better-trained labor force and the construction of more efficient transportation, communication, and utility facilities. If that happens, cost curves in the industry may be lowered so that firms may eventually compete in world markets. Such a lowering of costs is shown in Figure 10.6b. Once costs have been reduced, the tariff can be removed, having served its purpose of nurturing the domestic industry.

Long-Run Supply Elasticity

As we showed previously in this chapter, the long-run supply curve for an industry is constructed by considering all possible shifts in the demand curve. In order to predict the effects that increases in demand will have on market price it is therefore important to know something about the shape of that supply curve. A convenient measure for summarizing the shape of long-run supply curves is the *long-run*

---

[8]The economic case for free trade is discussed in more detail in Chapter 18.

elasticity of supply. This concept records how proportional changes in price affect quantity supplied, once all long-run adjustments have taken place. More formally:

Definition

The *long-run elasticity of supply* ($E_{Q,P}^{LS}$) is the percentage increase in long-run quantity supplied in response to a one percent increase in price. Mathematically:

$$E_{Q,P}^{LS} = \frac{\text{Percent change in } Q}{\text{Percent change in } P}$$

[10.1]

A value of $E_{Q,P}^{LS}$ of 10, for example, would indicate that a 1 percent increase in price would result in a 10 percent increase in the long-run quantity supplied. We would say that long-run supply is price-elastic: the long-run supply curve would be nearly horizontal. A principal implication of such a high price-elasticity is that long-run equilibrium prices would not increase very much in response to outward shifts in the market demand curve.

A small value for $E_{Q,P}^{LS}$ would have a quite different implication. If $E_{Q,P}^{LS}$ were 0.1, for example, a 1 percent increase in price would increase quantity supplied by only 0.1 percent. In other words, the supply curve would be nearly vertical and shifts outward in demand would result in rapidly rising prices without significant increases in quantity.

Some Examples of Estimated Long-Run Supply Elasticities

Table 10.1 reports a number of long-run supply elasticity estimates that have been gathered from a variety of sources. Many of these concern natural resources since economists have, from the time of Thomas Malthus, been interested in the effects of increasing demand for resources on their price. Other estimates are for agricultural crops and for housing. We will now briefly illustrate the implications of some of these numbers.

Agricultural Production

The estimated elasticities for agricultural products are "acreage elasticities": That is, they reflect how acres planted in a particular crop respond to that crop's price. Assuming a constant yield per acre, these then can be translated directly into the supply-elasticity concept. All of the reported elasticities are relatively low (all are less than 1). But all are positive, indicating that increases in prices do lead to increases in output.

Table 10.1 / Selected Estimates of Long-Run Supply Elasticities

Agricultural acreage:	
Cotton	0.67
Wheat	0.93
Corn	0.18
Aluminum	Nearly infinite
Chromium	0–3.0
Coal (eastern reserves)	15.0–30.0
Natural gas (U.S. reserves)	0.20
Oil (U.S. reserves)	0.76
Urban housing:	
Density	5.3
Quality	3.8

Sources: Agricultural acreage: M. Nerlove, "Estimates of the Elasticities of Supply of Selected Agricultural Commodities," *Journal of Farm Economics* 38, No. 2 (May 1956), pp. 496–509; Aluminum and chromium: estimated from U.S. Department of Interior, *Critical Materials Commodity Action Analysis* (Washington, D.C., 1975); Coal: estimated from M. B. Zimmerman, "The Supply of Coal in the Long Run; The Case of Eastern Deep Coal" (Cambridge, Mass.: MIT Energy Laboratory Report No. MITEL 75–021, September 1975); Natural gas: based on estimate for oil (see text). See also J. D. Khazzoom, "The FPC Staff's Econometric Model of Natural Gas Supply in the United States," *The Bell Journal of Economics and Management Science,* Spring 1971; Oil: E. W. Erickson, S. W. Millsaps, and R. M. Spann, "Oil Supply and Tax Incentives," *Brookings Papers on Economic Activity* 2 (1974), pp. 449–478; Urban housing: B. A. Smith, "The Supply of Urban Housing," *Journal of Political Economy* 40, No. 3 (August 1976), pp. 389–405.

Because the estimates follow our development of the concept of long-run supply by holding technology constant, however, they may substantially understate the "overall" responsiveness of agricultural output to increases in price. Indeed the history of the past 20 years has been one of stable relative food prices in response to large increases in demand. Whereas some have attributed this to the favorable weather experienced during the period, others have conjectured that the true, long-run elasticity of agricultural supply (when technological changes induced by higher prices are taken into account) is considerably greater than unity, and may be close to the infinite-supply elasticity that characterizes the constant cost case.

Natural Resources

Two different types of supply elasticity are reported for natural resources in Table 10.1. For aluminum and chromium the figures refer to the relationship between annual production and market price. They show that the long-run supply of aluminum is nearly infinitely elastic at current market prices. This results from the fact that alumina deposits are reasonably accessible given current technology. On the other hand, the supply elasticity for chromium is considerably lower—primarily because it would require large price increases to make most existing deposits economically attractive.

For coal, natural gas, and oil, supply elasticities refer to the responsiveness of economically accessible reserves to price. In order to relate these elasticities directly to the notion of current production, one would also need a theory of firms' profit-maximizing output decisions from existing resource stocks.[9] The data show that coal reserves are far more price responsive than are oil and natural gas reserves. That result derives primarily from geological features of the additional reserves' accessibility. Natural gas has a particularly low elasticity because it is usually found in conjunction with oil, but has a much lower value per well than does its associated oil. For example, at present market prices, the oil produced from the typical oil-gas well is worth four times the value of the gas produced from such a well. Hence the effect of an increase in natural gas price alone on drilling is only about one-fourth the effect of an increase in the price of oil. Some geologists expect that most natural gas that will be discovered in the future in the United States will not be found with oil, however. If that expectation is borne out, the future supply-elasticity for natural gas may be higher than is indicated in the table.

Housing

The final estimates in Table 10.1 refer to two aspects of the supply of urban housing. They show that "more housing" can be produced in two ways: by increasing residential density, while holding house quality constant; and by increasing quality, while holding density constant. Both of these output measures seem to be reasonably responsive to price. That is, increases in the demand for housing will not result in sharply increased costs and prices in the long run.

Price Controls and Shortages

In our model of competitive pricing in the long run, price increases played the crucial role of providing firms with the incentive to increase production in response to increases in demand. Governmental controls over prices may short-circuit this process and deter any long-run supply responses. That possibility is illustrated in Figure 10.7. Initially the market is in equilibrium at the point P_1, Q_1 where the market demand curve D, and the long-run supply curve, LS, intersect. Consider now the reaction to a shift in the market demand curve to D'. In the absence of price controls, price would rise to P_2 in the short run and firms would increase output to Q_2. Supply would increase further (to Q_3) in the long run as new firms enter the industry in response to profit possibilities. Imposition of price controls prevents both of these supply responses. If price is not allowed to rise above P_1, firms will continue to produce Q_1 even though demand has increased. At a price of P_1 individuals demand Q_4 (with the demand curve D') but only Q_1 is produced. Hence there is a shortage in the market given by the distance $Q_4 - Q_1$. That shortage will

---

[9]For a brief discussion of such a theory see Chapter 16.

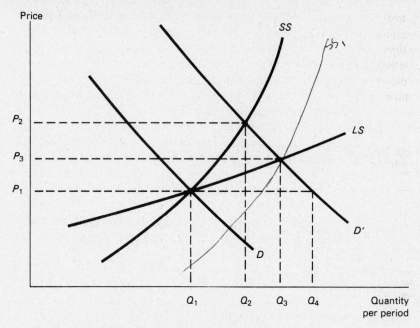

Figure 10.7 / Price Controls Inhibit Supply Responses

This market is initially in equilibrium at P_1, Q_1. A shift in demand to D' would cause price to rise to P_2 in the short run and to P_3 in the long run. Quantity would increase to Q_2 and Q_3, respectively. Price controls which held price at P_1 would inhibit this process since firms would continue to supply Q_1. At P_1 there is a long-run shortage given by $Q_4 - Q_1$.

persist so long as price controls continue to retard supply response. Notice that the shortage is exacerbated by the fact that more is demanded at the artificially low controlled price (Q_4) than would be demanded at the long-run market clearing price (Q_3).

The model depicted in Figure 10.7 therefore makes two predictions about the impact of price controls: (1) they will cause shortages; and (2) they will result in somewhat lower prices for those who are able to buy the good (for the increasing cost case illustrated in the figure). We will now examine two important cases, rent control and controls on the price of natural gas in the United States, where these predictions have been proved accurate.

◼ Two Examples of Price Controls

Rent Controls

During World War II many American cities adopted controls on rents in order to stop rising housing prices that were occurring as a result of increased demand. Many cities (notably New York) and several European countries still retain such controls. These are usually rationalized on the grounds that landlords (who are assumed to be rich) should not reap profits that occur as new demanders (who are assumed to be poor) enter a market. Without examining the facts behind such asserted principles of equity, the economic implications of controls are clearly predicted by the competitive model: shortages will result. Table 10.2 provides some evidence on such shortages in the city of Stockholm during the 1950s. The

**Table 10.2 / Waiting Time
(in Months) for an Apartment in Stockholm**

Year	Wait	Year	Wait
1950	9	1955	23
1951	15	1956	30
1952	21	1957	35
1953	24	1958	40
1954	26		

Source: S. Rydenfelt, "Rent Control Thirty Years On" in *Verdict on Rent Control* (London: Institute for Economic Affairs, 1972), p.65.

data show the average period (in months) that families had to wait to obtain an apartment. The data clearly show that this period lengthened greatly during the 1950s as postwar increases in income sharply increased the demand for housing, and rent controls retarded long-run supply responses. Existing tenants may have benefited from lower rents, but it is clear that substantial costs were imposed on families who had to wait more than three years to find a place of their own in which to live.

The effects of rent controls may show up in many other ways. In addition to the shortfall in the quantity of housing, the quality of housing may also deteriorate as landlords find it unprofitable to make repairs. For example, one study[10] found that repair expenditures in 1967 on rent-controlled apartments in New York City averaged only about one half of the expenditures on similar apartments that were not subject to rent controls. "Elective" repairs (that is, those in excess of minimal requirements for health and safety) were particularly unlikely to be made in the rent-controlled apartments. Finally, tenants of rent-controlled apartments may sometimes find they can take advantage of their possession of a good for which there is excess demand. It is a common practice in some cities, for example, to require that new tenants pay "key money" to existing tenants for the right to take over their leases. Similarly, rent-controlled apartments are passed down among family members as if they were valuable heirlooms.

---

[10]G. Sternlieb, *The Urban Housing Dilemma* (New York Housing and Development Administration, 1972), p. 202.

Natural Gas

A 1954 Supreme Court decision required the Federal Power Commission to begin regulating the wellhead price of natural gas sold through interstate pipelines in the United States. The effects of that decision were predicted at the time in a dissent by Justice Douglas: "The effect is certain to be profound . . . sales price determines profits and (these profits) have profound effects on the rate of production, the old wells that are continued in production, and the new ones explored."[11] By the mid-1970s, natural gas shortages induced by price controls were readily apparent. Many industries in the Northeast and North Central states were not able to obtain all the gas they wanted at prevailing prices and were forced to adopt more expensive and less suitable substitute fuels. Few natural gas utilities permitted hook-ups to new residential customers. By some estimates the shortfall of supply was, in 1977, as high as 20 to 25 percent of total demand.[12]

At the time of this writing the Congress is close to adopting a program of "phased deregulation" for natural gas prices. Over the period 1979–1985 natural gas prices would be permitted to rise from present, controlled levels of $1.45 per 1000 cubic feet, to an estimated market-clearing price of $2.50 by 1985. This policy offers some prospect of eliminating such bizarre results of natural gas price controls as the flocking of gas-using industries to Louisiana and Texas (since gas sold in the intrastate market is not price controlled), and the rush to import liquefied natural gas at prices above $4.00. Opponents of decontrol have focused on the costs of rising prices to present users of natural gas (estimated to be as high as $20 billion per year by 1985). Such a calculation, of course, ignores the costs of present price regulation of demanders who are not able to obtain gas because of production shortages. By some estimates these costs exceed by a substantial margin those that would be imposed on present users by price decontrol.[13]

Summary

In long-run analysis we must take into consideration the possibility of the entry (and exit) of firms into (and out of) an industry. Since, in the perfectly competitive model, entry costs are assumed to be zero, new firms will enter an industry until economic profits are driven to zero. At this zero-profit point, price will equal *LATC* and will also equal *LMC;* therefore, profits are being maximized. The entry or exit of firms may have some effect on the costs of all firms in the industry. The precise way in which entry (or exit) affects costs will determine the

---

[11]*Phillips Petroleum Company v. Wisconsin* 347 US 690, 1954.

[12]P. W. MacAvoy and R. S. Pindyck, *Price Controls and the Natural Gas Shortage* (Washington: American Enterprise Institute, 1975), p. 38.

[13]*Ibid.*, p. 54.

shape of the industry's long-run supply curve. Positively sloped long-run supply curves are probably the most important types empirically, but other shapes (including negatively sloped curves) are possible.

This chapter completes the development of the perfectly competitive model of supply and demand. Most of the analytical properties of this model are well known and for this reason it represents a "standard" against which other industrial structures can be judged. For example, the assumption of no entry costs is a crucial one for this chapter. If there were costs associated with entering an industry it would not in general be true that long-run profits would be forced to zero by the entry of new firms. Rather, firms already in an industry may continue to earn profits so long as the value of these profits does not exceed the costs of entry. The examination of pricing when there are costs of entry would yield rather different conclusions, as we shall see in the next two chapters. There are, of course, many other ways in which industries may depart from the perfectly competitive "ideal"; for each of these cases, comparison to the competitive model can provide insights that may suggest both analytical principles and proper public policy.

Suggested Readings

Knight, F. H., *Risk, Uncertainty and Profit* (Boston: Houghton Mifflin Company, 1921), chaps. 5 and 6.

Marshall, A., *Principles of Economics,* 8th ed. (New York: Crowell-Collier and Macmillan, Inc., 1920), book 5, chap. 5.

Meade, J. E., "External Economies and Diseconomies in a Competitive Situation," *Economic Journal* 62 (March 1952), pp. 54–67.

Nordhaus, W., "The Allocation of Energy Resources," *Brookings Papers on Economic Activity* 3 (1973), pp. 529–570.

Reynolds, L. G., "Cut-Throat Competition," *American Economic Review* 30 (December 1940), pp. 736–747.

Scitovsky, T., "Two Concepts of External Economies," *Journal of Political Economy* 17 (April 1954), pp. 143–151.

Stigler, G. J., *Price Theory,* 3d ed. (New York: Crowell–Collier and Macmillan, Inc., 1966), chap. 10.

Problems

10.1

Suppose there is a fixed, one-time cost for all firms attempting to enter an industry. Otherwise both new entrants and firms already in an industry are identical. How (if at all) would this entry cost affect the long-run analysis presented in Chapter 10?

10.2

A perfectly competitive painted-necktie industry has a large number of potential entrants. Each firm has an identical cost structure such that long-run average cost is minimized at an output of twenty units ($q_i = 20$). The minimum average cost is $10 per unit. Total market demand is given by:

$$Q = 1500 - 50\,P$$

a. What is the industry's long-run supply schedule?

b. What are: the long-run equilibrium price (P^*); the total industry output (Q^*); the output of each firm (q_i^*); the number of firms; and the profits of each firm?

c. The short-run total cost curve associated with each firm's long-run equilibrium output is given by:

$$C = .5\,q^2 - 10\,q + 200$$

where $MC = q - 10$.

   Calculate the short-run average and marginal cost curves. At what necktie output level does short-run average cost reach a minimum?

d. Calculate the short-run supply curve for each firm and the industry short-run supply curve.

e. Suppose now painted neckties become more fashionable and the market demand function shifts upward to $Q = 2{,}000 - 50P$. Using this new demand curve, answer b. for the very short run when firms cannot change their outputs.

f. In the short run use the industry short-run supply curve to recalculate the answers to b.

g. What is the new long-run equilibrium for the industry?

10.3

Suppose the demand for stilts is given by:

$$Q = 1500 - 50\,P$$

and that long-run total operating costs of each stilt-making firm in a competitive industry are given by

$$C = .5\,q^2 - 10\,q$$

where $MC = q - 10$.

   Entrepreneurial talent for stiltmaking is scarce. The supply curve for entrepreneurs is given by

$$Q_S = .25\,w$$

where w is the annual wage paid.

Suppose also that each stilt firm requires one (and only one) entrepreneur (the quantity of entrepreneurs hired is equal to the number of firms). Long-run total costs for each firm are hence given by

$$C = .5\, q^2 - 10\, q + w$$

a. What is the long-run equilibrium quantity of stilts produced? How many stilts are produced by each firm? What is the long-run equilibrium price of stilts? How many firms will there be and how many entrepreneurs will be hired? What is their wage?

b. Suppose the demand for stilts shifts outward to

$$Q = 2{,}428 - 50\, P$$

Answer the questions posed in part a.

c. Sketch your results. Show the approximate shape of the long-run supply curve. Why does the curve have this shape?

10.4
A specific tax imposed on a competitive, decreasing-cost industry will, in the long run, raise market price by more than the amount of the tax. Show why this is so and explain your result intuitively.

10.5
As output in the steel industry expands, the cost of iron ore is bid up. This causes the industry to exhibit increasing costs. Suppose one steel firm owns its own iron ore supply. Do that firm's costs increase when industry output expands? Why can't that firm keep its costs lower than its competitors and earn large profits?

10.6
Suppose average costs for each firm in the calculator industry are given by the function

$$AC_i = f(q_i,\ w,\ v,\ t)$$

where q_i is the output of the firm, w and v are the rental rates of labor and capital, and t is time. Suppose also that technical progress causes average costs to decline over time. Assuming the industry is perfectly competitive:

a. If the industry exhibits constant costs, what must happen to market price and the number of firms over time? What will the rate of increase in output depend upon?

b. Assume that labor costs (w) are bid up as industry output expands. How will this affect your conclusion in part a?

c. Suppose demand for calculators also increases over time. How will this affect your answers to parts a and b?

10.7

Suppose the long-run average cost curves for the firms in a perfectly competitive industry are horizontal over a broad range of output levels (hence within those ranges, average and marginal costs are equal).

a. Show that, in such an industry, firms may exhibit a wide variability in the quantity of output produced in equilibrium (that is, some firms may produce large amounts, others only small amounts).

b. Suppose demand for the industry's product fell. What factors would determine which firms were the first to leave the industry?

Chapter **11**   Pricing in Monopoly Markets

Introduction

The market for a particular good is described as a monopoly if there is only one producer of the good.[1] This single firm faces the entire market demand curve. Using its knowledge of this demand curve, the monopoly makes a decision on how much to produce. Unlike the perfectly competitive firm's output decision (which has no effect on market price), the monopoly's output decision will, in fact, determine the good's price. In this sense monopoly markets are the opposite, polar case from markets characterized by perfect competition. Some authors treat monopolies as having the power to set price; in a sense, monopolies do have this power. Technically, a monopoly can choose that point on the market demand curve at which it prefers to operate. It may choose either market price or quantity (but not both). In this chapter it will be convenient for us to assume monopolies choose that quantity of output that maximizes profits. It would be a simple matter to rephrase the discussion in terms of price setting, although the wording of some results would be more complex.

---

[1] It should be recognized at the outset that no monopoly is totally without competition. The good in question will always have some substitutes available, if only because it is in competition for the consumer's dollar.

Causes of Monopoly

The reason monopolies exist is that other firms find it unprofitable or impossible to enter the market. *Barriers to entry* are therefore the source of all monopoly power. If other firms could enter the market, there would, by definition, no longer be a monopoly. There are two general types of barriers to entry: technical barriers and legal barriers.

Technical Barriers to Entry

A primary technical barrier is that the production of the good in question may exhibit decreasing marginal (and average) cost over a wide range of output levels. The technology of production is such that relatively large-scale firms are efficient. In this situation one firm may find it profitable to drive others out of the industry by price-cutting. Similarly, once a monopoly has been established, entry will be difficult because any new firm must produce at relatively low levels of output and therefore at relatively high costs. It is important to stress that the range of declining costs need only be "large" relative to the market in question. Declining costs on some absolute scale are not necessary. For example, the manufacture of concrete does not exhibit declining marginal costs over a broad range of output when compared to the total United States market. However, in any particular small town declining marginal costs may permit a monopoly to be established. The high costs of transportation in this industry tend to isolate one market from another.

Another technical basis of monopoly is special knowledge of a low-cost productive technique. The problem for the monopoly fearing entry is to keep this technique uniquely to itself. When matters of technology are involved this may be extremely difficult, unless the technology can be protected by a patent (see below). Ownership of unique resources (mineral deposits, land locations) or the possession of unique managerial talents may also be a lasting basis for maintaining a monopoly.[2]

Legal Barriers to Entry

Many pure monopolies are created as a matter of law rather than as a matter of economic conditons. One important example of a government-granted monopoly position is in the legal protection of a productive technique by a patent. Situations of this sort are numerous; Xerox machines and Polaroid cameras are the most notable

---

[2]High costs of entry into a market are sometimes mentioned as a basis for monopoly. Whereas there are undoubtedly cases in which this is correct, it is important to be careful in distinguishing these cases. In a world of certainty and perfect capital markets a firm would enter a market so long as the present discounted value of future profits exceeded the fixed costs of entry. In the real world, uncertainty (particularly about the behavior of the firm already in the industry) and imperfect capital markets undoubtedly make high entry costs a real barrier.

examples. Because the basic technology for these products was uniquely assigned to one firm, a monopoly position was established. The defense made of such a governmentally granted monopoly position is that the patent system makes innovation more profitable and therefore acts as an incentive to technical progress. Whether or not the benefits of such innovative behavior exceed the costs of having technological monopolies is an open question.[3]

A second example of a legally created monopoly is in the awarding of an exclusive franchise to serve a market. These franchises are awarded in cases of public utility (gas and electric) service, communications services, the post office, some airline routes, some television and radio station markets, and a variety of other situations. The argument usually put forward in favor of creating these franchised monopolies is that having only one firm in the industry is somehow "more desirable" than permitting open competition. In that this rationale has an economic basis, the one usually proposed is that the industry in question is a *natural monopoly:* Marginal cost is diminishing over a broad range of output levels and minimum average cost can be achieved only by organizing the industry as a monopoly. The argument in the early part of this section may convince the reader that a monopoly might emerge in such a market even without the legislative sanction of a franchise. The public utility and communications industries can be considered representative of these natural monopolies. It would seem to be extremely undesirable to have two overlapping telephone or electricity distribution systems. Other cases of government franchises (certain airline routes, the post office) do not appear to be clearcut natural monopolies, and it is more difficult to specify the rationale for franchising in these instances. Whatever the rationale of the government franchise, it serves the function of eliminating the possibility of entry into the market in question. Frequently the pricing policy of the franchised monopoly is regulated by the government to make up for this lack of actual or potential competition. In the final section of this chapter we will discuss briefly the issues raised by such price regulation.

Profit Maximization

In order to maximize profits a monopoly will choose to produce that output level for which marginal revenue is equal to marginal cost. Since the monopoly, in contrast to a perfectly competitive firm, faces a negatively sloped market demand curve, marginal revenue will be less than price. To sell an additional unit the monopoly

---

[3]Some economists have argued that inventors should be rewarded directly by the government and that the invention should then be made available to all firms at no cost. Ideally the prize to inventors would provide the incentive that the patent system currently provides without creating the monopolies that arise under patents. In practice, however, it would be very difficult to decide how much a particular invention is "worth."

must lower its price on all units to be sold, if it is to generate the extra demand necessary to absorb this marginal unit. Hence we have the following:

Optimization Principle

In order to maximize profits a monopoly should produce that level of output for which marginal revenue is equal to marginal cost. Since the monopolist's demand curve is downward sloping (that is, marginal revenue is less than price), this will result in the firm's producing an output level for which market price exceeds marginal cost.

The profit-maximizing output level for a firm is then the level Q^* in Figure 11.1.[4] At that level marginal revenue is equal to marginal costs, and profits are maximized. If a firm produced slightly less than Q^*, profits would fall, since the revenue lost from

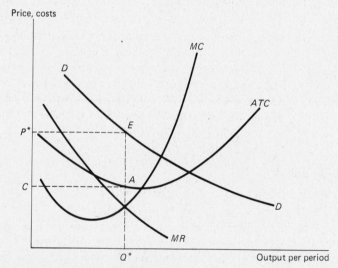

Figure 11.1 / Profit Maximization and Price Determination in a Monopoly Market

A profit-maximizing monopolist produces that quantity for which marginal revenue is equal to marginal cost. In the diagram this quantity is given by Q^*, which will yield a price of P^* in the market. Monopoly profits can be read as the rectangle P^*CAE.

---

[4]In Figure 11.1, and in the other diagrammatic analyses of this chapter, no distinction is made between the behavior of a monopoly in the short run and in the long run. The analysis is the same in both cases, except that different sets of cost curves would be used depending on the possibilities for adjustment that are assumed to be feasible for the firm. Notice though that in the long run a monopoly will not in general choose that plant size for which long-run average cost is a minimum. The only situation in which this would occur would be if MR and LMC happened to intersect at the low point of the $LATC$ curve.

this cutback (MR) would exceed the decline in production costs (MC). A decision to produce more than $Q*$ would also lower profits since the additional costs from increased production exceed the incremental revenues yielded by selling the extra output in the market. Consequently, profits are at a maximum at $Q*$, and a profit-maximizing monopoly will choose this output level.

Given the monopoly's decision to produce $Q*$, the demand curve D indicates that a market price of $P*$ will prevail. This is the price that demanders as a group are willing to pay for the output of the monopoly. In the market, an equilibrium price-quantity combination of $P*$, $Q*$ will be observed.[5]

Monopoly Supply Curve

In the theory of perfectly competitive markets we presented earlier, it was possible to speak of an industry supply curve. We constructed this curve by allowing the market demand curve to shift and observing the supply curve that was traced out by the series of equilibrium price-quantity combinations. This type of construction is not possible for monopoly markets. With a fixed market demand curve, the supply "curve" for a monopoly will be only one point, namely, that quantity for which $MR = MC$. If the demand curve should shift, the marginal revenue curve would also shift, and a new profit-maximizing output would be chosen. However, to connect the resulting series of equilibrium points on the market demand curves would have little meaning. This locus might have a very strange shape, depending on how the market demand curve's elasticity (and hence its associated MR curve) changes as the curve is shifted. In this sense the monopoly firm has no well-defined supply curve.

Monopoly Profits

Economic profits earned by the monopolist can be read directly from Figure 11.1. These are shown by the rectangle $P*CAE$ and again represent the profit per unit (price minus average cost) times the number of units sold. These profits will be positive if market price exceeds average total cost. Since no entry is possible into a monopoly market, these monopoly profits can exist even in the long run. For this reason some authors refer to those profits that a monopoly earns in the long run as *monopoly rents*. These profits can be regarded as a return to that factor that forms the basis of the monopoly (a patent, a favorable location, a dynamic entrepreneur), hence another possible owner might be willing to pay that amount in rent for the right to the monopoly. We will now examine some evidence on the value of such rights.

---

[5]This combination will be on an elastic section of the demand curve. This will be true because $MC > 0$ implies that for a profit maximum $MR > 0$. Hence $E_{q,P} < -1$, since we have shown that $MR = P(1 + 1/E_{q,P})$. One conclusion of this observation is that industries that are estimated to be operating along an inelastic portion of the demand curve for their product cannot be regarded as exercising strong monopoly power.

■ Examples of the Market Value of Monopoly Profits

Occasionally ownership rights to a monopoly are sold to another owner in the market. Such a sale provides an opportunity to obtain a measure of the value of those rights. Table 11.1 lists a few examples of sale prices for various types of monopoly rights in the taxicab, sports, brokerage, television, and trucking industries. These figures represent only the costs of franchise ownership rights. Costs of equipment and other physical capital have been excluded. Hence the sales prices provide a pure measure of the present value of economic profits. Although the data indicate a definite positive value for monopoly ownership, some prices exhibit a wide range for similar assets and that reflects differential demand conditions facing particular monopoly firms. The New York Yankees baseball franchise is obviously more profitable than is the Montreal Expo franchise. Similarly, a television station in Los Angeles has a considerably greater profit potential than one in Bismarck, North Dakota.

Interestingly, all of the monopoly franchises reflected in Table 11.1 were created either explicitly or implicitly through government regulation. Taxicab licenses are issued by many city governments as a way of restricting entry. Television station licenses and truck operating rights are issued by federal agencies (the Federal Communications Commission and Interstate Commerce Commission, respectively). Those agencies also stipulate the general conditions under which the franchises can be transferred from one owner to another. In the cases of professional sports and the New York Stock Exchange, on the other hand, monopoly rights were created implicitly through exemption from antitrust prosecution for those industries. This exemption has been somewhat less

Table 11.1 / Values of Monopoly Rights in Selected Industries

	Value (Dollars)	Year
Chicago Taxicab Licenses	$15,000	1969
Sports Franchises:		
National Basketball League Teams	$1–$3 Million	1971
American Baseball League Teams	$4–$10 Million	1971
National Baseball League Teams	$6–$11 Million	1971
Seats on the New York Stock Exchange	$145,000–$300,000	1971
Television Station License	$2–$50 Million	1973
Trucking Operating Rights	$5,000–$300,000	1972

Sources: Taxicab Licenses: F. W. Kitch, M. Isaacson, and D. Kasper, "Regulation of Taxicabs in Chicago," *Journal of Law and Economics* 14, No. 2 (October 1971), pp. 285–350; Sports Franchises: R. G. Noll, ed., *Government and the Sports Business* (Washington: The Brookings Institution, 1974); Stock Exchange Seats: The New York Stock Exchange, *1976 Fact Book* (New York: New York Stock Exchange, 1976); Television Station License: R. G. Noll, M. J. Peek, and J. J. McGowarn, *Economic Aspects of Television Regulation* (Washington: The Brookings Institution, 1973); Trucking: M. Kafoglis, "A Paradox of Regulated Trucking," *Regulation,* September/October 1977, pp. 27–32.

successful in assuring monopoly profits for franchise owners than has the explicit awarding of monopoly franchises. Uncontrolled entry by new firms (as in the case of the establishment of rival sports leagues) has at times eroded the value of some "monopoly" franchises. Similarly, governmental attacks on price-fixing agreements (as in the case of stock exchange commissions and, more recently, the pricing of legal services by local bar associations) has had the effect of promoting competition and reducing the possibilities for monopoly profits. We will now examine an example.

The Changing Value of a Monopoly Right: Stock Exchange Seats

The value of a monopoly depends on the value of the profits it is able to generate. Those profits will, in turn, depend on the location of the demand curve for the monopolist's product. Shifts in demand affect potential profits and the market value of the monopoly itself. Table 11.2 illustrates this for the case of sales prices for seats on the New York Stock Exchange. These prices have fluctuated widely over time. They reached their peak value in 1929 in response to the huge stock trading activity (and brokerage profits) in that year. Prices were relatively low throughout the Depression and during World War II. In the 1960s trading activity in stocks picked up and this was again reflected in the market value of exchange seats. Although trading volume continued high in the 1970s, a number of factors during that decade reduced monopoly profits available from Stock Exchange membership. Most important among these was the fact that a growing proportion of stock trades came to be executed off the New York Exchange as improved methods of communication reduced the need for a central marketplace. In a related development, after several years of prodding by the Securities and Exchange Commission, the New York Stock Exchange eliminated fixed commission rates on May 1, 1975. The occurrence of these pro-competition developments was reflected in the sales price for Exchange

Table 11.2 / Changing Values of Monopoly Rights: Stock Exchange Seats (Selected Years)

Year	Price of an Exchange Seat (in $ Thousands)
1905	72
1925	99
1929	625
1945	49
1960	135
1970	130
1975	55
1977	42

Source: *The New York Stock Exchange Fact Book, 1976* (New York: The New York Stock Exchange, 1976), pp. 58 and 82. 1977 data supplied by the author. All prices are the lowest bid price in a given year.

memberships, which by 1977 had fallen to a level less than one-tenth of what it was in 1929. That contrast is even more dramatic when it is recognized that the overall price level increased more than fourfold between 1929 and 1977.

Market Separation and Price Discrimination

It may sometimes be the case that a firm will have a monopoly position in two different markets for the same good. If these markets are effectively separated so that buyers cannot shift from one market to the other there may be the possibility for the monopolist to increase his profits further by practicing *price discrimination*. The profit-maximizing decision would be to produce that quantity in each market for which marginal revenue equals marginal cost. This may lead to different prices for the same good in the two markets; if the markets are effectively separated, these price differentials can persist even though they are unrelated to production costs. We have therefore defined:

Definition

A firm with a monopoly in two separated markets is said to practice *price discrimination* if it charges different prices for its output in the two markets that are not commensurate with differences in costs (if any).

A Graphic Analysis

Such a situation is shown graphically in Figure 11.2. The figure is drawn so that the market demand (and marginal revenue) curves in the two separated markets share the same vertical axis. For simplicity it also assumes that marginal cost is a constant over all levels of output. The profit-maximizing decision for the monopoly is to produce Q_1^* in the first market and Q_2^* in the second market. The prices in these two markets will then be given by P_1 and P_2, respectively. It is clear from the figure that the market with the more inelastic demand curve will have the higher price in this price-discriminating example.[6] The price-discriminating monopolist will charge a higher price in that market in which quantity purchased is less responsive to price changes. Although the analysis in Figure 11.2 assumes that marginal costs are constant, an identical result would hold in the more realistic case of increasing marginal costs. The price discriminator would charge higher prices in the market in which demand is less elastic with respect to changes in price.

---

[6]*Proof:* Since $MR = P(1 + 1/E)$, $MR_1 = MR_2$ implies $P_1(1 + 1/E_1) = P_2(1 + 1/E_2)$. If $E_1 > E_2$ (if the demand in market 1 is less elastic), then P_1 must exceed P_2 for this equality to hold.

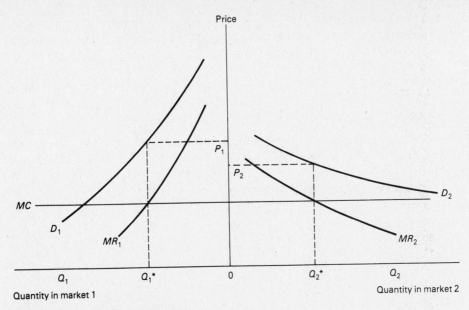

Figure 11.2 / Separated Markets
Raise the Possibility of Price Discrimination

If two markets are separate, a monopolist can maximize profits by selling his product at different prices in the two markets. This would entail choosing that output for which $MC = MR$ in each of the markets. The diagram shows that the market that has a less elastic demand curve will be charged the higher price by the price discriminator.

Examples of Price Discrimination

There are many examples in the real world of a firm selling an identical product in different markets at different prices. For example, bulk chemical producers will charge less to large buyers than to small ones; electric utilities usually charge lower rates to industrial and commercial users than to consumers; and supermarkets may charge higher prices to central city purchasers than to suburban buyers. Each of those situations presents the firm with the possibility of separating markets to maximize profits. Similarly, the results that emerge might have been predicted by the simple price discrimination model: Large chemical buyers presumably have a more elastic demand because they can more easily take their business elsewhere or even go into the production business themselves; industrial and commercial users of electricity have a more elastic demand because they use electricity on a scale where it might be profitable for them to generate their own; and central city residents are generally less mobile than their suburban counterparts and may therefore have a less elastic demand for the services of a particular supermarket. Nonetheless, these situations are not exactly analogous to the textbook price-discriminating model. The markets are not pure monopolies as we have defined them, and entry is possible in a number of ways. Marginal costs may differ between the two markets; these cost differentials could lead to differing prices, regardless of whether the markets were monopolistic or perfectly competitive. Finally, some of these markets are not so perfectly separated as is required for successful price discrimination. For example, although there may be some costs involved, central city residents can buy from stores in the suburbs. To draw any definitive conclusions about price discrimination from such simple *a priori* arguments can therefore be unwarranted. A careful investigation of demand and cost data is required before making such an assessment.

What's Wrong with Monopoly?

Firms that occupy a monopoly position in a market are frequently damned for a variety of reasons. It has been argued that monopolies earn "excess" profits; give poor, unresponsive service; "exploit" their employees; stifle technical progress; and distort the allocation of resources. Although each of these complaints undoubtedly has some analytic truth to it, only two of the claims will be discussed here: the profitability of monopoly and the effect of monopoly on resource allocation. Some of the other claims will be investigated in other sections of this book.

"Excess" Profitability

Since perfectly competitive firms earn no pure profits in the long run, it is true that a firm in a monopoly market can earn higher profits than if the market were competitive. This does not imply, however, that monopolies necessarily earn huge profits. Two equally "strong" monopolies may differ greatly in their profitability.

To see this, we must define what is meant by a strong monopoly. One definition, proposed by A. P. Lerner, defines the *degree of monopoly* to be

$$D = \frac{\text{price} - \text{marginal cost}}{\text{price}} \qquad [11.1]$$

The distinguishing characteristic of monopoly is a divergence between price and marginal cost, and Lerner's definiton measures this divergence.[7] Notice that for a perfectly competitive firm $D = 0$ since, in this case, marginal cost is equal to price.

---

[7]A. P. Lerner, "The Concept of Monopoly and the Measurement of Monopoly Power," *Review of Economic Studies* 1 (June 1934), pp. 157–175. For a profit-maximizing monopoly $MR = MC$ and therefore Lerner's definition becomes

$$D = \frac{P - MR}{P} = -\frac{1}{E_{Q,P}}$$

The closer $E_{Q,P}$ is to -1, the closer D will be to 1, which is its maximum value (in view of footnote 5 of this chapter). In empirical work it is frequently assumed that marginal and average costs are equal. In this case, Lerner's definition reduces to simply measuring profits as a percent of sales.

For two firms with similar degrees of monopoly power (as measured by Lerner's criterion), the degree of profitability may differ greatly. The level of profits will depend on the relative positions of the average cost curve and the demand curve but not necessarily on the degree of monopoly. Figure 11.3 exhibits the cost and demand possibilities for two firms with essentially the same degree of monopoly power (that is, the divergence between price and marginal cost is the same in the two panels). The monopoly in 11.3a earns a high level of profits, whereas the one illustrated in 11.3b actually earns zero in profits. The primary objection to monopoly profits, then, is not based on the inevitability of huge profits but, rather, rests on an objection to the *distributional effects of monopoly profits*. If these profits go to relatively wealthy owners at the expense of less well-to-do consumers, there may be valid objections to monopoly profits no matter what their size. This may not necessarily be the case. For example, consider the decision of Navajo blanket makers to form a monopoly in the sale of their products to tourists. This is clearly a situation in which monopoly profits would make the income distribution more equal.[8]

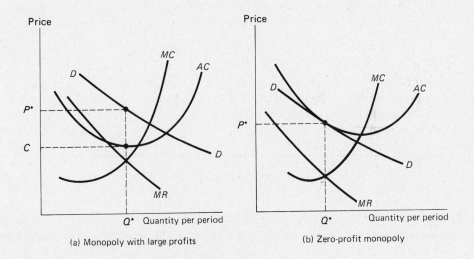

(a) Monopoly with large profits   (b) Zero-profit monopoly

Figure 11.3 / Monopoly Profits Depend on the Relationship Between the Demand and Average Cost Curves

Both of the monopolies in this figure are equally "strong," if by this we mean they produce similar divergences between market price and marginal cost. However, because of the location of the demand and average cost curves, it turns out that the monopoly in 11.3a earns high profits, whereas that in 11.3b earns no profits. Consequently, the size of profits is not a measure of the strength of a monopoly.

[8]Some observers have noted that early U.S. antitrust policy (especially in the period 1890–1910) was more directly aimed at attacking the distributional harm caused by monopolies than it was related to allocational issues.

Distortion of Resource Allocation

A second objection to monopolies is that their existence distorts the allocation of resources. Monopolies intentionally restrict their level of output in order to maximize profits. The discrepancy between price and marginal cost reflects that at the monopoly's preferred output level consumers are willing to pay more for one more unit of output than it would cost to produce that output. From a social point of view, therefore, output is too low. Figure 11.4 illustrates this observation by comparing the output that will be produced in a market characterized by perfect competition with the output that will be produced in the same market when there is only one firm in it. The figure assumes that the monopoly produces under conditions of constant marginal cost and that the competitive industry exhibits constant costs with the same minimum long-run average cost as the monopolist. In this situation a perfectly competitive industry would choose output level Q^*, where price is equal to average and marginal cost. A monopoly would choose output level Q^{**}, for which marginal revenue is equal to marginal cost. The restriction in output $(Q^* - Q^{**})$ is then some measure of the allocational harm done by monopoly. Because of the way in which the market is organized, fewer resources are being devoted to the production of the good than the demand curve warrants. Individuals would be willing to pay P^{**} for additional output, and this would only cost MC.

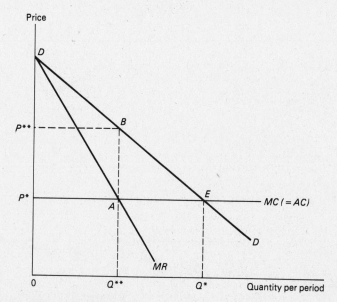

**Figure 11.4 / Differential Effects of
Perfect Competition and Monopoly in a Market**

A perfectly competitive industry would produce output level Q^*, for which price equals marginal (and long-run average) cost. A monopoly, by recognizing the downward slope of the demand curve, would produce Q^{**} where marginal revenue equals marginal cost. This output reduction is a measure of the allocational "evil" of monopolies. In some cases it may be possible to place a value on this loss in output.

However, the monopolist's market control prevents the additional resources from being drawn into the industry to fill this demand.

Measuring Monopolistic Distortions

We have demonstrated that monopolies cause an artificial restriction in output and thereby distort the allocation of resources. In order to evaluate this distortion (in dollar terms), economists have devised a way of measuring how much the total output of a good is "worth" to the consumers of the good. By using such a measure, it is possible to place an approximate value on monopolistic output restrictions.

Perfect Price Discrimination

In Figure 11.5 we have drawn a downward-sloping demand curve for a good, Q. Suppose that Q^* is currently being consumed. What we wish to measure is the total value of Q^* to consumers. One way to investigate this question is to ask how much in total revenues a *perfect price discriminator* could collect for Q^*. If the market were organized so that the producer of Q could dole out one unit at a time to that consumer who would pay the highest price for that unit, we wish to know how much in total revenue would be collected. This will be our measure of the total value of

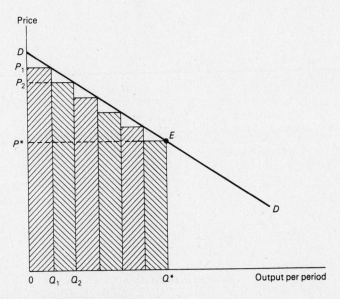

Figure 11.5 / Consumer's Surplus

A perfect price discriminator could collect a total revenue of DOQ^*E for output level Q^*. Because most goods sell at a single price, however, consumers pay only P^*OQ^*E. Consequently, consumers receive a "surplus" given by area DP^*E.

Q^*; it represents the maximum amount that can be collected from consumers in exchange for Q^* units of output.

Figure 11.5 illustrates the perfect price-discrimination procedure. If the producer initially puts Q_1 on the market, it will bring a price of P_1; total revenues will be given by the area of the rectangle P_1, Q_1. After this sale, the producer can now put some more of the good on sale $(Q_2 - Q_1)$. This additional amount will have a price of P_2, and total revenues are given by the rectangle $P_2, Q_2 - Q_1$ in the figure. It should be clear that, by continuing in this manner, the producer can eventually collect a total revenue equal to the area under the demand curve from $Q = 0$ to $Q = Q^*$. This total revenue (given by DOQ^*E in Figure 11.5), then, represents the total value that individuals place on output level Q^*: It is the *maximum amount* that consumers would be willing to pay for Q^* if forced to buy it one unit at a time.

Consumer's Surplus

It is not usually possible for a producer to practice the kind of perfect price discrimination that we have just described. Most firms cannot successfully discriminate among individual buyers, and firms are therefore unable to charge the maximum amount each individual will pay. Rather, the firm will usually treat all buyers as a group and will in any period sell its output at a single price to this group. A firm that is faced by the demand curve D in Figure 11.5 will, if it sells Q^* without practicing discrimination among buyers, obtain a price of P^* on the sale. It is the "marginal buyer" who determines this price. Intramarginal buyers (perhaps those who were, say, willing to pay P_1 for an output of Q_1) receive a "bonus" through the workings of the market. They can buy Q at a lower price than they would have to if the firm practiced perfect price discrimination. This bonus is called *consumer's surplus* and can also be seen in Figure 11.5. If the firm adopts a one-price policy, consumers will pay total revenues of P^*OQ^*E for the output they buy: However, as we have shown, the total value of this output is given by DOQ^*E. Consequently, because of the one-price policy, consumers receive a bonus; the value of this bonus is given by the triangle DP^*E. This is the difference between the total value of Q^* and what individuals actually pay for it. It is this triangle that is termed consumer's surplus.[9]

Having shown how to measure the benefits that consumers derive from consuming a particular output level, we are now in a position to evaluate monopolistic

---

[9]For a more rigorous discussion of the concept of consumer's surplus, see J. R. Hicks, "A Rehabilitation of Consumer's Surplus," *Review of Economic Studies* 8 (February 1941), pp. 108–116. Using the notion of consumer's surplus, it has sometimes been claimed that perfect price discrimination may be desirable. By being a perfect discriminator a firm is able to expropriate all (or almost all) the "value" of its product. If perfect price discrimination were possible, therefore, the good might be provided even though cost considerations could prevent its being provided if the firm had to obey a one-price pricing policy. For example, it might be argued that the ability of small-town doctors to practice price discrimination among their patients is beneficial because otherwise there would be no medical service at all.

distortions. We shall show that the monopolization of a market leads to a loss of consumer's surplus, and we shall show how this loss can be measured.

Monopolistic Effect on Allocation and Distribution

In Figure 11.4 we demonstrated the nature of the output reduction brought about by the monopolization of a market. Now we can use the notion of consumer's surplus to place a value on that reduction. Figure 11.6 repeats our previous illustration of monopolistic output restriction. When the market is competitively organized, Q^* is produced at a price of P^*. The total value to consumers of this output level in Figure 11.6 is given by the area under the demand curve (that is, by area DOQ^*E), for which they pay P^*OQ^*E. Consequently, total consumer's surplus is given by the triangle DP^*E. Under a monopoly only Q^{**} is produced, and the price of this output is P^{**}. The restriction in output has had several effects. The total value of this good

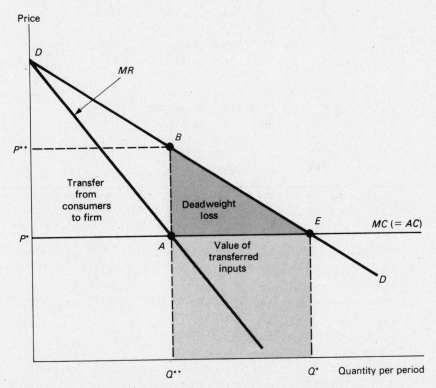

Figure 11.6 / Allocational and Distributional Effects of Monopoly

This figure repeats Figure 11.4 and can be used to show the effects of monopolization. Consumer expenditures and productive inputs worth $AQ^{**}Q^*E$ are reallocated into the production of other goods. Consumer surplus equal to $P^{**}P^*AB$ is transferred into monopoly profits. There is a deadweight loss given by BAE.

that consumers receive has been reduced in Figure 11.6 by the area $BQ^{**}Q^*E$. This reduction is not a total loss, however, since consumers previously had to pay $AQ^{**}Q^*E$ for these goods, and they may now reallocate the expenditures elsewhere. Resources released through monopolization of the market will be used to produce those other goods. The loss of consumer's surplus given by the area BAE is, however, an unambiguous reduction in welfare as a result of the monopoly. Some authors refer to the triangle BAE as the *deadweight loss* from a monopoly. It is the best single measure of the allocational harm caused by monopoly.

In addition to the allocational effect of monopolization of a market, there is a distributional effect, and this can also be seen in Figure 11.6. At the monopoly's output level of Q^{**}, there exist monopoly profits given by the area $P^{**}P^*AB$. In the case of perfect competition this area was part of the consumer's surplus triangle. If the market is a monopoly, that portion of a consumer's surplus is redistributed into monopoly profits. The area $P^{**}P^*AB$ in Figure 11.6 does not represent an unambiguous loss of welfare. It does measure the redistributional effects of a monopoly, and these may be undesirable. In order to make such an assessment, however, we would have to introduce an explicit concept of equity so that the welfare of the firm's owners and consumers could be weighed. But it is not necessary to introduce such concepts of equity in order to demonstrate the nature of the allocational loss represented by area BAE. That is an unambiguous loss occasioned by monopolization of the market. If the market were competitive, output would expand to Q^*, and overall welfare would increase by the extent of area BAE.

■ An Application:
Measurement of Real-World Distortions

Using the kind of analysis we have just discussed, A. Harberger was able to estimate the allocational losses from monopolization of markets in the U.S. economy.[10] Harberger's method was rather simple. First, he assembled cost and profit data for 73 different industries. For each industry he then estimated the percent by which price exceeded average cost. This is equivalent to measuring the distance $P^{**} - P^*$ in Figure 11.6. For example, Harberger found that prices in the cement industry exceed average costs by 8.4 percent. Next, Harberger calculated the expansion in demand ($Q^* - Q^{**}$) that would occur by lowering prices to the competitive level. By assuming an elasticity of demand for cement of -1.0, the quantity of cement demanded would be increased by 8.4 percent if competitive prices prevailed. Using those two figures, the author then calculated the area of the triangle BAE [$= \frac{1}{2} \times (P^{**} - P^*)(Q^* - Q^{**})$] as a measure of the

---

[10] A. Harberger, "Monopoly and Resource Allocation," *American Economic Review* 44 (May 1954), pp. 77–87.

welfare loss from monopoly. For the case of cement, this loss amounted to $420,000 for the period under investigation (1924–1928). By making similar calculations for the other 72 industries in his sample, Harberger concluded that the total welfare loss from monopolies was about $150 million. This amounted to about 0.1 percent of Gross National Product during the period.

Most economists were quite surprised by the relatively modest level of distortions that Harberger calculated. Both the legal and the rhetorical emphasis given to antimonopoly activity would seem to indicate that monopolistic distortions had a much greater quantitative importance. Of course, there has been considerable controversy over Harberger's methods, and they are by no means widely accepted by economists. More recent studies of the same subject have, however, failed to refute the impression that the overall welfare loss from monopoly is a relatively small percentage of total output. For example, in a 1974 article by J. J. Siegfried and T. K. Tiemann,[11] the authors show that, in 1963, monopolistic distortions amounted to less than 0.1 percent of national income. Three industries (motor vehicles, plastics, and petroleum refining and extraction) accounted for more than 60 percent of the total value of monopolistic distortions. Even in those industries, however, the authors express some doubt that there is much to be gained by pursuing some type of antimonopoly policy.

Regulation of Monopoly

The regulation of monopolies is an important subject in applied economic analysis. The utility, communications, and transportation industries are highly regulated in most countries, and devising regulatory procedures that cause these industries to operate in a desirable way is an important practical problem. Here we will briefly investigate a few of the questions that have been raised in studying the regulation of monopoly.

Marginal Cost Pricing

By analogy to the perfectly competitive model, many economists believe it is important for the prices charged by a monopoly to reflect marginal costs of production. In this way the welfare loss from monopolization of the market may be minimized. Considerable effort has gone into defining marginal costs for various industries and into describing ways in which marginal cost pricing might be implemented. One problem raised by such a policy is that it may require monopolies to operate at a loss. We now examine that possibility.

---

[11]J. J. Siegfried and T. K. Tiemann, "The Welfare Cost of Monopoly: An Inter-Industry Analysis," *Economic Inquiry* 12, No. 2 (June 1974), pp. 190–202.

The "Natural" Monopolies Dilemma

"Natural" monopolies, by definition, exhibit decreasing average costs over a broad range of output levels. The cost curves for such a firm might look like those shown in Figure 11.7. In the absence of regulation, the monopoly would produce output level Q_A and receive a price of P_A for its product. Profits in this situation are given by the rectangle $P_A CBA$. A regulatory agency might instead set a price of P_R for the monopoly. At this price, Q_R is demanded, and the marginal cost of producing this output level is also P_R. Consequently, marginal cost pricing has been achieved. Unfortunately, because of the declining cost nature of the firm's cost curves, the price $P_R (=$ marginal cost) falls below average costs. With this regulated price the monopoly must operate at a loss of $GP_R EF$. Since no firm can operate indefinitely at a loss, this poses a dilemma for the regulatory agency: Either it must abandon its goal of marginal cost pricing or it must subsidize the monopoly forever.

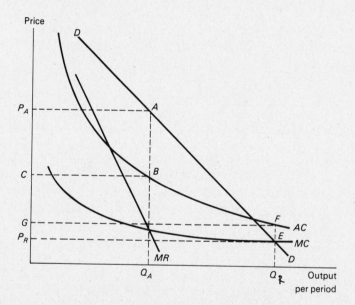

Figure 11.7 / Price Regulation for a Decreasing Cost Monopoly

Because natural monopolies exhibit decreasing costs, marginal costs fall below average costs. Consequently, enforcing a policy of marginal cost pricing will entail operating at a loss. A price of P_R, for example, will achieve the goal of marginal cost pricing but will necessitate an operating loss of $GP_R EF$.

Two-Tier Pricing Systems

One way out of the marginal cost pricing dilemma is the implementation of a two-part pricing system. Under such a system the monopoly is permitted to charge some users a high price while maintaining a low price for marginal users. In this way the demanders paying the high price in effect subsidize the losses of the low-price customers. Such a pricing scheme is shown in Figure 11.8. Here the regulatory commission has decided that some users will pay a relatively high price, P_1. At this price, Q_1 is demanded. Other users, presumably those who would not buy the good at the P_1 price) are offered a lower price, P_2. This lower price generates additional demand of $Q_2 - Q_1$. Consequently, a total output of Q_2 is produced at an average cost of A. With this two-part pricing system, the profits on the sales to high-price demanders (given by the rectangle P_1ABD) balance the losses incurred on the low-priced sales ($BCEF$). Furthermore, for the "marginal user," the marginal cost pricing rule is being followed: It is the "intramarginal" user who subsidizes the firm so that it does not operate at a loss. Although it may not in practice be so simple to establish pricing schemes that maintain marginal cost pricing and cover operating costs, many regulatory commissions do use multipart tariff schedules that charge higher prices to some users than to others.

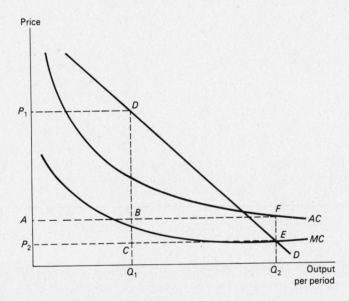

Figure 11.8 / Two-Part Pricing Schedule

By charging a high price (P_1) to some users and a low price (P_2) to others, it may be possible for a regulatory commission to: (1) enforce marginal cost pricing and (2) create a situation where the profits from one class of user (P_1ABD) subsidize the losses of the other class ($BCEF$).

An Example: Electricity Pricing

Many regulated electric utilities follow a "declining block" pricing schedule such as that illustrated in Table 11.3. One intention of such a schedule is to approximate the theoretical goals illustrated in Figure 11.8. That is, the marginal price of electricity is an approximation to the marginal cost of producing it.

**Table 11.3 / Typical Monthly Residential
Electricity Rate Schedule Showing Declining Block Structure**

Usage	Price
First 12 KWH	$2.25
Next 338 KWH	$.0455 per KWH
Next 650 KWH	$.0260 per KWH
All over 1000 KWH	$.0200 per KWH

(KWH = Kilowatt-hours)

Source: Author's electric bill.

One problem with this approach is in defining what "marginal cost" means. For a single residential customer, the decision, say, to turn on a toaster probably has a low marginal cost to the electric system as a whole. But the decision of many customers to use their toasters at the same time or, more importantly, of a major industrial user to open its factory for the work day, may place a substantial incremental demand on the electric system. Because it is not generally possible to store electricity for when it is needed, these large incremental demands create the need for the construction of additional power generation facilities. Viewed in this way, marginal "peak load" demand is very costly to produce. For this reason several electricity-pricing reform proposals suggest moving toward a system of "peak load pricing" under which incremental capital costs would generally be paid by additional charges to peak period users. A number of experimental pricing plans of this type are currently under examination in the United States and are in current use in several European countries (notably France[12]). To the extent that peak period users respond to these higher prices by shifting their demands to off-peak periods it may be possible for the overall stock of electricity generation equipment to be reduced.

Other Effects of Regulation

Although economic analysis of regulation has tended to focus on price-setting and on the relationship of price to marginal cost, it is clear that regulatory agencies affect the behavior of the firms they regulate in many other ways. For example, many regulatory agencies employ a "fair rate of return" criterion in determining the "profit" that firms will be permitted to earn on their capital investment. Because this permitted rate of return may differ from the market rental rate on capital (what we denoted by v in Chapters 6 and 7), regulatory procedures may affect firms' cost-

---

[12]For example, under the French "Green Tariff," electricity prices during peak winter hours are about four times the price during periods of normal demand. See R. Meek, "An Application of Marginal Cost Pricing: The Green Tariff in Theory and Practice," *Journal of Industrial Economics*, November 1963, pp. 45–63.

the firm's choice of inputs? How would it affect the firm's output level? During a period of inflation, how might a lag in allowing utilities to raise prices affect these outcomes?

11.7
Suppose that the market for taxi rides is perfectly competitive and exhibits constant costs in the long run. Let the long-run equilibrium price of rides be given by P^* and the number of rides by Q^*. Assume now that the government licenses cabs and issues only enough licenses to provide Q_L rides (where $Q_L < Q^*$). Graph this situation. What will be the new long-run equilibrium price? Will firms with licenses be able to earn a long-run profit? If licenses are transferable, what will determine their price?

Chapter 12

Industrial Organization: A Brief Survey

Introduction

Most real-world markets can be classified as being somewhere "between" the polar cases of perfect competition and monopoly. In studying real-world markets we might follow two strategies. For the first we would follow a pattern we employed earlier by seeking to develop a few simplified models that capture "essential" aspects of market behavior. For the second strategy, we would adopt a descriptive mode of analysis and attempt to summarize what economists have to say about real-world industrial structures. Although the appendix to this chapter does discuss two simple models of price determination (the Cournot and Stackelberg models), our discussion in Chapter 12 itself will follow the second strategy. The vocabulary and mode of analysis we will use is called the *theory of industrial organization*. In recent years this field has expanded rapidly, and this chapter can only hint at the sophisticated and thought-provoking questions that have been raised. The purpose of these investigations, in a broad sense, has been to evaluate the performance of certain industries. The standards by which these industries are to be judged vary from study to study, but they generally fall into two categories: *static efficiency* and *dynamic efficiency*.

Static Efficiency

By "static efficiency" we usually mean how closely an industry in question approximates the perfectly competitive model. Questions that are raised include:

How close is price to marginal cost? Are prices flexible in response to changing demand conditions? Is entry relatively costless (are there long-run forces that assure that the low point on the average cost curve will be approached)? Finally, the general issues of private versus social costs in production, and whether markets are providing a socially desirable allocation of resources are of concern. These investigations use the competitive model as a standard against which to measure actual performance. An industry that approximates the perfectly competitive ideal is sometimes described as being "workably competitive."

Dynamic Efficiency

The concept of dynamic efficiency has no such clearly defined standards. Rather, this category represents a catch-all for many difficult real-world problems of evaluation. A brief taste of this sort of analysis was presented in the previous chapter when we discussed Schumpeter's views of the innovative potential of monopoly. It is not clear whether perfect competition or monopoly (or some combination of the two) is more amenable to technical innovation, and empirical research must be used to investigate this issue. Similar problems occur when attempting to evaluate the desirability of product differentiation (Can there be too many kinds of toothpaste?) or of advertising (Is it persuasive or informative?). We must of necessity step beyond the perfectly competitive model (and perhaps beyond the traditional bounds of economics) to answer such questions. Another departure from the competitive model's stress on allocative efficiency is the study of what H. Leibenstein has termed *X-efficiency*.[1] Leibenstein uses this term to refer to the ability of firms' managements to lessen costs within the confines of existing technology. Examples of this would include entrepreneurial organizational ability, increases in worker motivation, and other sources of productivity increase that are not easily handled by the usual methods of concentrating on the productivity of specific factors.

Concentration in Markets

A first question we might pose about industrial structure is, which markets[2] are generally characterized by a small number of firms and which by a large number? One concept that is commonly used for measuring this is the *concentration ratio:*

---

[1]H. Leibenstein, "Allocative Efficiency v. X-Efficiency," *American Economic Review* 56 (June 1966), pp. 392–415.

[2]Economists have been most interested in concentration within one market. This is the relevant consideration for questions about pricing strategy and related allocational matters. Sociologists and political scientists, on the other hand, have had considerable interest in the question of the general concentration of manufacturing industry. For example, much analysis has been devoted to examining what has been happening to the percent of manufacturing assets controlled by the top 200 corporations.

Definition

The *concentration ratio* measures the percentage of an industry's output produced by the largest firms: The *Four Firm Concentration Ratio* records the percentage produced by the four largest firms; The *Eight Firm Concentration Ratio* records the percentage produced by the eight largest firms.

Numerical values of these ratios for a few selected markets are shown in Table 12.1. Generally the ratios are quite variable. Markets such as those for automobiles, telephone and telegraphic equipment, and cigarettes have four-firm concentration ratios above 80 percent. For machinery, tools and dies, and women's dresses, on the other hand, the ratios are 10 percent or lower.

Table 12.1 / Selected Concentration Ratios in U.S. Manufacturing, 1970

Industry	Percent Produced by Four Largest Firms	Percent Produced by Eight Largest Firms
Blast furnaces and steel mills	47	65
Motor vehicles	92	98
Motor vehicle parts	60	68
Petroleum refining	33	57
Baking	29	39
Miscellaneous machinery	7	12
Aircraft engines	68	81
Tires and inner tubes	72	89
Telephone and telegraphic equipment	94	99
Cigarettes	84	99
Special tools and dies	7	9
Sawmills	16	20
Women's dresses	10	13
Soap and detergents	70	79
Canned fruits and vegetables	21	33

Source: Selected entries from Table 1233, *Statistical Abstract of the United States* (Washington, D.C.: U.S. Government Printing Office, 1974), pp. 720–722.

It is important to point out that one should be very careful in interpreting concentration ratios. For example, imports are not considered in the published figures. Imports may have significant effects on particular markets (for example, consider

---

Although there is no general agreement on the direction of the trend in the level of overall concentration, nor in the meaning to be attached to any trend that is finally determined, the discussion has engendered much debate.

the cases of automobiles and primary steel production, both "highly concentrated" industries), and the published concentration ratios may overestimate the strength of firms in the market. Low concentration ratios need not imply lack of market power. We have already mentioned the case of ready-mixed concrete as an example of an industry that appears to be unconcentrated on a national scale: in fact, many firms in this industry occupy strong local monopolies. Similarly, the toilet preparations market appears to be relatively unconcentrated (a four-firm ratio of 38 percent was reported in 1967). Yet some segments of that market (toothpaste and deodorants, for example) are far more highly concentrated. Additional problems in interpretation are raised by firms that sell in more than one product market and by licensing arrangements (as in the soft-drink market) that are not represented in the available data. Consequently, published figures on concentration must be regarded as indicative rather than as a definitive scheme for locating markets on the continuum between perfect competition and monopoly.

Economic Implications of Concentration

In view of the unsatisfactory nature of the available data on market concentration it is not surprising that there have been few specific findings about the behavior of firms in concentrated markets. For example, although there is some agreement that firms in highly concentrated markets are more profitable than firms in unconcentrated ones, there is wide disagreement about the extent of these differences.[3] There are many markets that appear to be concentrated in which profitability is below average. Another question that has not been answered satisfactorily is whether concentrated industries produce goods (or services) of a quality that is inferior to that produced in unconcentrated markets. Again, there is evidence on both sides. Many questions about pricing and price flexibility in concentrated markets are similarly unsettled. We shall discuss these later in this chapter.

The question can properly be raised: If concentration is so hard to define, and if those ratios that can be calculated are able to tell us very little about behavior, then why bother about the concept in the first place? There are two possible answers, one pragmatic and the other theoretical. On pragmatic grounds the data currently available on concentration ratios, although far from perfect, are about all that we have on industrial structure. It is necessary to use those data that are available until something better comes along.

Concentration and Interfirm Behavior

From a theoretical point of view, concentration ratios may in fact indicate the types of interactions among firms that prevail in a market. In highly concentrated industries actions by one firm cannot be taken without regard to possible reactions by

---

[3]See G. Stigler, *Capital and Rates of Return in Manufacturing Industry* (Princeton, N.J.: Princeton University Press, 1963).

rivals. On the other hand, firms in less concentrated markets may regard possible reactions of other firms as being of secondary importance and may omit the consideration of the reactions in their decisions. Hence concentration ratios may be quite useful in indicating the proper method of analysis to be used in the study of any particular market. For example, an analysis of an automobile company's decisions to produce a small car might be very different from an analysis of a dress company's decision to produce a new line of low-cost dresses. In the former case we might want to consider feedback effects: The decision to produce a small car will undoubtedly cause the producer's rivals to adopt some competitive strategy (they, too, might enter the small-car field) that would affect the demand curve facing the firm. For the dress firm these feedback effects may be small. Because there are many small firms in the industry, there will not be a general reaction to the decisions of a single firm.

Other Choice Variables

In Part III we talked about the choices that a profit-maximizing firm must make. There we analyzed in detail only two types: choice of output level and choice of the mix of inputs to use in production. Since we assumed that every firm produced a product identical to its competitor and that demanders were perfectly knowledge-able about the products they buy, there was no place in the model for considering product differentiation or advertising. In most real-world situations, however, firms must make important choices about the level of those other activities they will pursue. In this section we will briefly analyze the way in which a firm might make such choices, and we will then discuss the effects that product differentiation and advertising may have.

Product Differentiation

If firms are strict profit maximizers they will pursue any activity up to the point at which the marginal gain from further increases is equal to the marginal cost of such increases. This result holds also for possible product differentiation or advertising strategies a firm might undertake. For example, a firm may have some options open to it that permit it to differentiate its product from that of its competitor. It may provide special services to purchasers, use slightly higher quality ingredients, wrap the product in an attractive (and perhaps reusable) container, or offer special prizes to potential buyers. Each of those results in making the firm's product different from other firms', and such differences may cause the demand curve facing the firm to shift outward. The firm will then weigh the additional revenues generated by such shifts against the costs of differentiating its product when deciding on the optimal strategy to pursue.

Advertising

A similar argument holds for advertising. A firm advertises with the intention of increasing the demand for its output. Advertising informs potential buyers of the existence of a firm's product, it identifies the differences between the firm's product and that of its competitors (thus aiding in product differentiation), or it may simply create the impression that the firm's product is superior to others in the market even though by some objective criteria all products are in fact identical. All such effects will operate on the demand curve facing a firm. The firm will allocate funds to an advertising budget so long as an additional dollar spent on advertising brings in more than a dollar of net profits. The profit-maximization assumption, therefore, provides a framework within which these other choices open to firms in imperfectly competitive markets can be analyzed. We will now examine each of these choice variables in more detail.

Advertising

As for any area of economic investigation, it is useful to distinguish between positive and normative questions about advertising. Economists who study positive issues related to advertising are primarily concerned with assessing the extent to which advertising expenditures affect the demand curve facing a firm. Knowledge of the size of this effect permits an evaluation of how advertising affects the allocation of resources. Those who study normative questions about advertising are, on the other hand, primarily concerned with advertising's informational content, and with whether advertising "distorts" the allocation of resources. We will now briefly summarize these two areas of investigation.

The Economic Effects of Advertising

There must be some truth to the hypothesis that advertising affects consumption choices. Since some firms obviously spend a great deal on advertising, it would imply a peculiar lack of rationality if these expenditures were being made without having any effect. Unfortunately, empirical evidence on the precise effect of advertising is not available.[4] There seems to be general agreement that advertising can affect choices among goods that are close substitutes, but whether it has any effects on overall consumption choices is difficult to determine. For example, it is widely (but not universally) believed that advertising of cigarettes can have a major effect on individuals' choices of brands. However, there is no good evidence that cigarette advertising has substantially increased the demand for cigarettes as a whole or that it has had any effect on overall consumption expenditures. In a 1972 article,[5] for example, J. L. Hamilton estimated that advertising expenditures had no effect on the short-run demand for cigarettes and that a 10 percent increase in such

---

[4]For a summary of several empirical studies see P. Doyle, "Economic Aspects of Advertising: A Survey," *Economic Journal* 78 (September 1968), pp. 570–602.

[5]J. L. Hamilton, "The Demand for Cigarettes: Advertising, the Health Scare, and the Cigarette Advertising Ban," *Review of Economics and Statistics,* LIV, 4 (November 1972), pp. 401–411.

expenditures would increase long-run sales by less than 2 percent. This finding was further supported by the failure of cigarette purchases to fall off sharply following the banning of radio and television advertising of cigarettes in 1970.[6] Similar results have been found for the effects of advertising expenditures on the demand curves for other industries.

False Advertising

Economists have posed two normative questions about the informational content of advertising. The first of these concerns the necessity of regulating false or misleading advertising. It has been argued that the government should monitor advertising to ensure that the information provided is accurate. By insisting that advertising claims must be validated, the government is protecting individuals from incurring the costs of making decisions based on false information. Of course, defining what "truth in advertising" means in specific instances poses difficult problems in legal interpretation, and most current controversy has centered on such ambiguities.

Allocation of Resources to Advertising

The second question is whether or not there is "too much" advertising. Analyses that support such a view are based on two related observations. First, it has been noted that the "market" for advertising messages is not separated from the market for the good being advertised. When someone purchases a box of laundry soap, he or she also pays for the advertising messages that the soap maker provides. In other words, a good and its associated advertising are *joint products*. This technical property of the way in which advertising messages are supplied may cause too many messages to be produced. Firms will produce additional advertising messages up to the point at which the marginal revenue brought from the additional demand generated by a message is equal to the message's cost. This additional revenue being generated reflects individuals' willingness to pay both for the goods being bought and for the information provided by the advertising message itself. Looking at the advertising message alone, it is clear that individuals must be evaluating it at less than its production cost (since the good itself must have some value). If the information contained in the advertisement had been marketed separately, its market price would not have exceeded its production cost. The fact of joint production causes too many advertising messages to be produced.

The second observation that suggests that there may be too much advertising derives from a distinction (first made by A. Marshall) between *constructive* and *combative* advertising. Constructive advertising conveys useful information and by so doing may increase the total demand for a product. Combative advertising, on the other hand, merely reflects competition between different brands for a share of a

---

[6]Hamilton finds that whatever negative effect the ban had was more than offset by the positive effect on cigarette demand of the reduction in anti-smoking advertisements that accompanied the ban.

fixed market. This kind of advertising is "defensive" in that any one firm is forced to do it because all the others do. An across-the-board reduction of advertising by all firms would not affect total demand at all, whereas a reduction by any one firm would be harmful to that firm. A governmentally imposed reduction in such combative advertising would free resources that could be productively employed elsewhere. In this sense there may again be too much advertising.

Although those arguments are suggestive, they are by no means widely accepted. Each of the observations poses a variety of questions that can be answered only by a detailed examination of the production of advertising in the real world. Several economists have attacked these *a priori* arguments about excessive advertising, and no clearcut consensus has emerged.[7]

Product Differentiation

Although the issues of advertising and product differentiation are closely related, far more analytical effort has been devoted to the former. Generally it has proved to be very difficult to make any broadly acceptable statement about product differentiation. Although it is known that some differentiation efforts are very costly and therefore affect market prices (see the example later in this section), it is hard to arrive at a consensus on the normative question of what too much differentiation might be. Individuals do purchase 50 or so different brands of toothpaste, and it is unclear how such choices should be limited as a matter of policy. Different individuals will hold different views with regard to the desirability of particular brands, and any limitation may make some individuals worse off. On the other hand, resources saved from the restriction of "wasteful" differentiation can be productively employed elsewhere, thus raising general well-being. As is generally the case in economics, there are no clearcut rules for dealing with situations in which some individuals gain and others lose, since these involve complex issues of equity.

■ An Example: Automobile Model Changes

One of the most important examples of product differentiation is the practice of annual model changes by U.S. (and, increasingly, most foreign) makers of automobiles. This strategy serves three basic functions for firms in the highly concentrated automobile industry. First, the annual model change differentiates this year's model from last year's and thereby provides consumers with an incentive to switch from used cars to new ones. Second, the strategy provides each firm with the possibility of out-guessing its rivals and garnering a larger share of the market. The importance of this motive is illustrated by the great secrecy that

---

[7]Some of these analyses (together with a wealth of empirical information) are reviewed in R. Schmalensee, *The Economics of Advertising* (Amsterdam: North-Holland Press, 1972), chap. 1.

surrounds the designing of new models and the advertising that accompanies their unveiling. Finally, some authors have argued that the annual model change provides an important barrier to entry in the automobile industry. Because of economies of scale associated with the model change-over, new firms are not able to compete successfully and firms in the industry are able to earn profits above the competitive level.

Costs of annual automobile model changes are quite high. In a study of automobile costs in the 1950s, for example, F. M. Fisher, Z. Griliches, and C. Kaysen estimated that the total costs averaged $3–$5 billion per year and amounted to nearly 25 percent of the total cost (including gasoline) of a car.[8] The authors' principal findings are presented in Table 12.2 for the years 1950–1960. The major cost item (labeled "Direct Costs" in the table) refers to the extent to which production costs exceeded what it would have cost to produce a car with the same characteristics as a 1949 model. The figures therefore reflect the tendency, throughout the 1950s, of consumers to buy heavier cars with more horsepower and various optional equipment (power steering and brakes, automatic transmissions, and so forth). Other components of the annual model change cost included retooling costs associated with making the required changes in capital equipment and costs of the extra gasoline consumed by the new models.

Table 12.2 / Costs of Annual Automobile Model Changes 1950–1960 (in millions of dollars)

Year	(1) Direct Costs	(2) Retooling Cost	(3) Gasoline Costs	(4) Total Costs	(5) Total Passenger Car Production (000)	(6) Total Costs per Car (dollars)
1950	−27	20	13	6	6,659	1
1951	267	45	36	348	5,331	65
1952	460	82	102	644	4,337	148
1953	436	246	161	844	6,135	138
1954	1,072	264	240	1,576	4,359	362
1955	2,425	469	372	3,266	6,201	527
1956	3,040	336	590	3,966	6,295	630
1957	4,048	772	806	5,626	6,218	905
1958	2,354	626	949	3,924	4,256	922
1959	3,675	532	1,147	5,354	5,568	962
1960	3,456	537	1,346	5,339	6,011	888

Source: F. M. Fisher, Z. Griliches, C. Kaysen, "The Cost of Automobile Model Changes Since 1949," *Journal of Political Economy*, LXX, No. 5 (October 1962), pp. 433–451. Columns (1)–(4) from Table 8, p. 448. Column (5) from Table 2, p. 437. Column (6) = Col. (4) ÷ Col. (5).

[8]F. M. Fisher, Z. Griliches, and C. Kaysen, "The Cost of Automobile Model Changes Since 1949," *Journal of Political Economy*, 70 (October 1962), pp. 433–451.

Clearly the dollar amounts in Table 12.2 are quite large: they exceed the total sales of many other industries during the period. The direct and retooling costs were presumably reflected in the prices of cars. Assessing the social desirability of these costs is difficult, however. On the one hand it might be argued that the model change expenses were defensive and strategic in nature. Absence of such "wasteful" competition would release resources that could better be used elsewhere. On the other hand, consumers during the 1950s generally had the option of choosing automobiles with 1949 model characteristics, but they did not do so. It is therefore possible that resources invested in the model changeover provided more utility than they would have in an alternative use.

Entry

The possibility of new firms entering an industry plays an important part in the development of the theory of perfectly competitive price determination. That possibility assures that any long-run profits will be eliminated by new entrants and that firms will produce at the low points of their long-run average cost curves. Under conditions of oligopoly, the first of these forces continues to operate. To the extent that entry is possible, long-run profits are constrained. If entry is completely costless, long-run economic profits will be zero (as in the competitive case).

Whether firms in an oligopoly industry will be directed to the low point of their average cost curves depends on the nature of the demand curve facing them. If firms are price takers the analysis given for the competitive case carries over directly: Since $P = MR = LMC$ for profit maximization and since $P = LATC$ if entry is to result in zero profits, production will take place where $LMC = LATC$ (that is, at minimum average cost).

If oligopoly firms have some control over the price they receive (perhaps because each produces a slightly differentiated product), each firm will face a downward-sloping demand curve and the competitive analysis will not hold. Entry may still reduce profits to zero, but now production at minimum average cost is not assured. This situation is illustrated in Figure 12.1. Initially the demand curve facing the firm is given by dd and economic profits are being earned. New firms will be attracted by these profits and their entry will shift dd inward (because there are now a larger number of firms to contend with a given market demand curve). Indeed, entry can reduce profits to zero by shifting the demand curve to $d'd'$. The level of output that maximizes profits with this demand curve (q') is not, however, the same as that level at which average costs are minimized (q_m). Rather, the firm will produce less than that "efficient" output level and will exhibit "excess capacity" given by $q_m - q'$. Some economists have hypothesized that this outcome characterizes industries such as service stations, convenience stores, and fast-food franchisers, where product differentiation is prevalent but entry is relatively costless.

Of course, entry into oligopoly industries need not be free and hence economic profits need not be driven to zero. Many of the barriers to entry discussed in

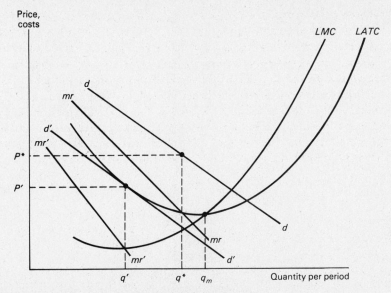

Figure 12.1 / Entry Reduces Profitability in Oligopoly

Initially the demand curve facing the firm is dd. Marginal revenue is given by mr, and q^* is the profit-maximizing output level. If entry is costless, new firms attracted by the possibility for profits may shift the firm's demand curve inward to $d'd'$, where profits are zero. At output level q' average costs are not a minimum, and the firm exhibits excess capacity given by $q_m - q'$.

connection with monopoly (Chapter 11) can exist under oligopoly as well. Other barriers that should also be mentioned include those arising from product differentiation, economies of scale, and pricing policies.

Product Differentiation

Consumers faced with uncertainty rely heavily on brand identification to judge quality. It may be difficult for new firms to break through this attachment. The possibility of product differentiation is not always unfavorable to entry, however, and some firms have been very successful in gaining entry to a market by satisfying a demand not currently being met by those firms already in the market. Volkswagens and the variety of small electronic calculators currently available are prominent examples.[9]

---

[9]The classic treatment of the entry issue is presented by J. S. Bain in *Barriers to New Competition* (Cambridge, Mass.: Harvard University Press, 1956). Bain estimates that a new product in a differentiated market may have to sell for 10–25 percent less than one already established in the market in order to win customer acceptance.

Economies of Scale

Economies of scale may be a significant barrier to entry. This is probably a factor limiting entry in such cases as the automobile and primary aluminum markets. In those industries the total market size permits only a few optimally sized plants. It is important, however, to be careful in assigning great importance to this barrier to entry. Often barriers that appear to be related to economies of scale are in fact caused by an inability of an entrant to differentiate its product successfully from that of an existing firm or by a high cost of capital to potential entrants. Recent diversification by "conglomerate" firms may indicate the failure of economies of scale to be an effective barrier to entry in many markets where this was previously thought to be the case.

Pricing Policies

Frequently mentioned as a possible barrier to entry is that the firms already in a particular market may settle for less than maximum profits in order to discourage potential entrants. For example, firms may pursue maximum sales rather than profits in the short run in order to maintain control over a share of the market. In a similar vein, firms may adopt a strategy of *limit pricing*—charging a price below that which would result in profit maximization in order to discourage entrants. Certainly limit pricing would seem to be a more successful method for discouraging entry than would be, say, engaging in wasteful business practices to keep profits low. The latter strategy would only encourage the entry of more efficient firms, whereas limit pricing combined with efficient operations may be a true barrier to entry. Empirical research on limit pricing has served to clarify many issues in the theory of entry by new firms, but there is no hard evidence of the widespread use of this technique.

Pricing in Oligopoly Markets

Neither the Marshallian supply-demand analysis nor the simple monopoly model is strictly appropriate for analyzing pricing in markets characterized by a few firms. Although these models may yield some insights (certainly demand and cost conditions have some relevance to pricing in any market), the absence of any notion of interaction among firms severely limits these models' predictive ability in the real world. Unfortunately, there are no generally applicable models of oligopoly pricing. Rather, several models have been proposed as explanations of certain aspects of observed oligopoly behavior, but none of these has won widespread acceptance. In this section we shall investigate only one such model: the *kinked demand* curve model. Because this model has features common to many oligopoly pricing models, it can be considered to be generally representative. Two additional duopoly (two-firm) models are discussed in the appendix to this chapter.

Kinked Demand Curve Model

The ki... ...loped by P. M. Sweezy in 1939 to
... tended to be inflexible.[10] It was
...t by changes in market prices and
...ligopoly markets, these changes
...explained these observations by
...firm in an oligopoly market. He
...cautious and pessimistic way.
...lieves all its rivals will follow.
...elastic for price decreases. If a
...assumes that the firm believes
..., therefore, the firm will find
...competitors' products whose
...rve possibility is labeled D in

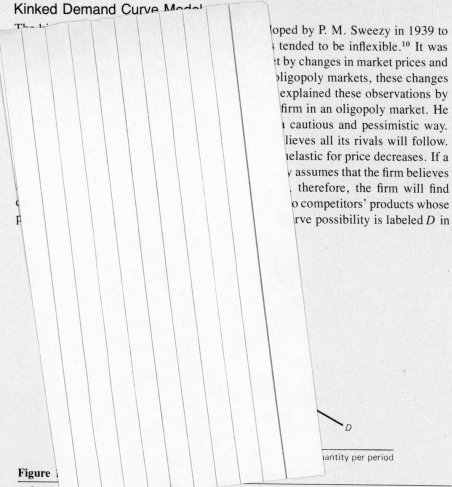

...antity per period

Figure ...

A firm in ... ...may believe it is faced by a demand curve (D) with a kink at the
prevailing price (P*). If the firm considers raising its price, others would not follow: demand would
appear to be very elastic since customers would shift to its competitors. Conversely, the firm may believe
that if it lowered price, all its competitors would do the same. Demand would be relatively inelastic
below P*. The kink at P* means that the MR curve will be discontinuous at this point. Therefore firms
may not respond to shifts in their marginal cost curves.

Figure 12.2. The prevailing market price is P^*, and the firm sells quantity q^*.
Quantity sold would not be increased greatly by lowering price (since rivals are
assumed to follow) but would be decreased markedly by attempting to raise price.

[10]P. M. Sweezy, "Demand Under Conditions of Oligopoly," *Journal of Political Economy* 47 (August
1939), pp. 568–573.

If the firm believes that it is faced by a kinked demand curve, it may not react to small changes in costs. This can be seen by examining the marginal revenue curve associated with the kinked demand curve. Notice that the MR in Figure 12.2 is discontinuous at q^*, reflecting the kinked nature of the assumed demand curve. Suppose that marginal cost were initially MC and that cost increases have shifted this curve to MC'. With this new marginal cost curve there will be no incentive to change either price or quantity because marginal revenue is still "equal to" marginal costs and profits are being maximized. Hence prices will tend to remain fixed until some unifying event can get all firms to raise prices in concert.

Price Leadership

This view of oligopoly pricing tends to accord with many real-world observations. For example, in some markets *price leadership* is a prevalent phenomenon. In such markets one firm or group of firms is looked upon as the leader in pricing, and all firms will adjust prices when the leader does. These general price changes are relatively infrequent but are generally of substantial magnitude. The price leadership technique can then be seen as a way of creating market discipline and as a way of providing a signal to firms (which believe they are faced by a kinked demand curve) when the "right" time to raise prices has arrived. Two examples of price leadership are the steel industry (where U.S. Steel or Bethlehem plays the role of a leader) and the commercial banking industry (where the prime rate tends to be determined by the major New York City banks). In both of those industries cost changes are not manifested by price changes until the leaders decide to move.

There is one major theoretical weakness of the kinked demand curve model: It gives no real guidance about where prices will settle if they are disturbed from the "kink." Similarly, if price changes are assumed to be initiated by a leader, it is not clear how a leader is chosen nor why other firms may not initiate price increases if the leader has been successful in the past. The theory must at least be made more complete if it is to represent a general theory of oligopoly pricing.

Empirical Evidence on Oligopoly Pricing

Empirically, a closer examination of oligopoly pricing behavior reveals a surprising lack of rigidity. For example, whereas the banking prime rate may change only occasionally, other conditions associated with borrowing (the riskiness of those loans granted, the balance a borrower must hold with the bank, and so on) tend to be far more flexible in responding to changing cost conditions. In manufacturing industries rigidity of list prices is by no means indicative of actual market prices. There is considerable evidence that various forms of discounts from list prices vary greatly in response to supply and demand conditions in the market.[11] From this

---

[11] See G. J. Stigler and J. K. Kindahl, *The Behavior of Industrial Prices* (New York: National Bureau of Economic Research, distributed by Columbia University Press, 1970).

discussion it should be clear that any theory that attempts to explain pricing in oligopoly markets must be a hybrid of simpler economic theories. As always, a reasonable place to start is with a careful analysis of market demand and cost conditions. The specific content of any theory will then be determined by the particular institutional setting under investigation.

Decision Making in Oligopoly Markets: Strategy and the Theory of Games

Probably the most interesting aspect of the behavior of industries having only a few firms is that every firm must take other firms' actions and reactions into account. Because no firm can know with certainty what its competitors will do, it must make decisions in a world of uncertainty. Many of the most prominent features of oligopoly markets are a direct result of this uncertainty. In the 1930s and 1940s economists devoted considerable effort to understanding the strategic relationships among firms in an attempt to analyze such oligopoly markets. The principal tool that was developed for this purpose was *game theory*. The basic structure of game theory consists of specifying the number of players in a game (or the number of firms in an industry), the strategies available to each player, and the outcomes that accrue to each player once a particular choice of strategies has been made. Obviously, a complete treatment of game theory is beyond the scope of this book.[12] However, since even an elementary discussion can provide many insights into real-world strategic choices, we will here briefly study the simplest type of games—two-person games.

A Simple Game Situation

More specifically, our discussion of two-person games will involve two firms (call them A and B) that must choose how much to spend on advertising. Suppose each firm has only two choices: It may adopt either a small advertising budget or a large one. We will denote A's strategies by a_1 (a low advertising budget) and a_2 (a high budget). Similarly, B's strategies will be denoted by b_1 (low budget) and b_2 (a high budget). We will study several different games in which these strategies might be used.

Zero-sum Games

The first two games we consider will be *zero-sum games*. In such games A and B are directly competitive: What A "wins" B "loses" and vice versa. This would be the

---

[12]The central work in the field is, of course, J. von Neumann and O. Morgenstern, *The Theory of Games and Economic Behavior* (Princeton, N.J.: Princeton University Press, 1949). A more intuitive coverage is provided in R. D. Luce and H. Raiffa, *Games and Decisions* (New York: J. Wiley & Sons, Inc., 1957).

case, for example, if total demand for the output of the two firms were absolutely fixed and consequently advertising would only affect the distribution of sales between them. The *payoff matrix* for the first zero-sum game we will consider is shown in Table 12.3. In this table A's strategies are shown vertically and B's

Table 12.3 / Payoff Matrix for Equilibrium Zero-sum Game

		B's Strategies	
		b_1 (low budget)	b_2 (high budget)
A's Strategies	a_1 (low budget)	A: + 5 B: − 5	A: − 5 B: + 5
	a_2 (high budget)	A: 0 B: 0	A: 0 B: 0

strategies are recorded horizontally. The entries in the table record the outcomes (in terms of dollars of profits) that accrue to A and B when the particular strategy choices are made. For example, the upper left hand corner of the matrix records the fact that when A "plays" a_1 and B "plays" b_1, A receives profits of 5 and B receives profits of −5. Similarly, when both firms have high advertising budgets, profits for each are 0. The other entries in the table are to be interpreted in the same way. Notice that total profits for the industry are always 0 thus indicating that the game is truly "zero-sum."

Equilibrium Solution

Assuming that both A and B fully understand the outcomes of the game, it is possible to examine how they might decide on which strategy to pursue. First, notice that for firm B, strategy b_2 dominates b_1: No matter what A does, B can do best by playing b_2. Against a_1, that strategy promises a gain of 5 and against a_2 it promises 0 profits. A, on the other hand, has no dominant strategy: against b_1, strategy a_1 is preferred whereas against b_2, strategy a_2 is preferred. There are numerous ways in which A might choose a strategy in this situation. One method would be for A to adopt the *pessimistic* assumption that "no matter what I do, B will choose the strategy that harms me the most." Under this assumption, A should choose that strategy for which the worst possible outcome is as good as possible.[13] Here that choice would be a_2. By choosing a_2, A can assure itself 0 profits no matter what B does. On the other hand, choosing a_1 runs some risk of getting a profit of −5.

---

[13]This pessimistic way of choosing a strategy is called a "maximin" (or sometimes "minimax") decision rule.

Consequently A chooses a_2, B chooses b_2, and both end up earning 0 profits. The choice a_2, b_2 is, in this situation, an *equilibrium* pair of strategies. If either A or B knew ahead of time what its competitor were going to do, it would not affect its decision: Knowing B will choose b_2 does not alter A's determination to choose a_2 and vice versa.[14]

Nonzero-sum Games

Most interesting oligopoly situations are not zero-sum. It is not usually the case that what one firm gains the other loses but, rather, that a variety of outcomes is possible depending on the strategies that are actually chosen. A particularly fascinating nonzero-sum game might resemble that shown in Table 12.4. This table is to be

Table 12.4 / Nonzero-sum Game: The Prisoner's Dilemma

		B's Strategies	
		b_1 (low budget)	b_2 (high budget)
A's Strategies	a_1 (low budget)	A: + 7 B: + 7	A: + 3 B: +10
	a_2 (high budget)	A: +10 B: + 3	A: + 5 B: + 5

interpreted in exactly the same way that the previous one was, except that the outcomes no longer sum to a constant value. In this game, strategy a_2 dominates a_1 for firm A: No matter what B does, A is better off with a_2. Similarly, b_2 dominates b_1 for firm B. Consequently both firms will choose to have high advertising budgets and will each receive a profit of $+5$. Notice, however, that an ironclad agreement by both firms to pursue low advertising budgets would result in a profit level of $+7$ for each. The difficulty with this twin low-budget strategy choice is that it is unstable. If A knows that B will choose b_1, it is to A's advantage to choose a_2 and increase its profits from $+7$ to $+10$. Similarly, if B knows A will choose a_1, B too has an incentive to cheat. Consequently, both firms by pursuing their own self interest will choose their second strategies even though, in a broader sense, rationality would suggest the twin low-budget strategy.

---

[14]Not all two-person zero-sum games have such equilibrium solutions. It can be shown, however, that most such games do have equilibrium solutions in which each opponent plays each strategy with a certain fixed probability (that is, say, each firm might adopt each of its advertising strategies in half the plays of the game). For a discussion, see Luce and Raiffa, *Games and Decisions, op. cit.,* Appendix 2.

The Prisoner's Dilemma

The game shown in Table 12.4 is one example of what has come to be known as the *prisoner's dilemma.*[15] The dilemma arises because the best choice of strategies is unstable and provides great incentives to cheat. Faced with the uncertainty inherent in the game, both players end up making a second-best choice. This problem arises in many real-world market situations. The example of advertising budgets may actually occur. Much advertising may be merely "defensive" in the sense that a mutual agreement to reduce expenditures would be profitable to both parties. However, such an agreement would be unstable because one firm could increase its profits even further by cheating on the agreement. Similar situations arise in the tendency for airlines to show in-flight movies (there would be larger profits if all firms stopped showing movies, but such a solution is unstable); in the instability of farmers' agreements to restrict output (it is just too tempting for the individual farmer to try to sell more milk); or in the banking industry's move to "free" checking accounts (keeping service charges is more profitable, but this is unstable since one bank can greatly increase its deposits by offering free checks). As those examples show, the difficulty of enforcing agreements may be very detrimental to the profits of an industry.

■ An Example: The OPEC Cartel

Many of these game-theoretic issues in oligopoly theory are illustrated by the oil production cartel composed of the members of the Organization of Petroleum Exporting Countries (OPEC). Although that cartel was not the first group to have a

---

[15]This game was first discussed by A. W. Tucker in the 1940s. The origin of the title stems from the following game situation. Two men are arrested for a crime. The district attorney has little evidence in the case and is anxious to extract a confession. She separates the suspects and tells each "If you confess and your companion doesn't, I can promise you a reduced (6-month) sentence, whereas your companion will, on the basis of your confession, get 10 years. If you both confess you will each get a 3-year sentence." Each suspect also knows that in the absence of either one of them confessing, the lack of evidence will cause them to be tried for a lesser crime for which they will receive 2-year sentences. The payoff matrix of the game is therefore

		B	
		Confess	Not confess
A	Confess	A: 3 years B: 3 years	A: 6 months B: 10 years
	Not confess	A: 10 years B: 6 months	A: 2 years B: 2 years

Notice how closely this game resembles that shown in Table 12.4. The "confess" strategy dominates for both A and B. However, an agreement by both not to confess would reduce their terms from 3 to 2 years. This "rational" solution is not stable, and there is an incentive for either man to cheat.

substantial monopolizing effect on an important market (indeed, cartels of natural resource producers existed in Biblical times), OPEC has proved to be one of the most profitable and durable cartels ever formed. In this section we briefly examine the reasons for OPEC's success and then demonstrate some of the problems OPEC must solve if its success is to continue.

Figure 12.3 illustrates the OPEC example in a simplified setting. In that figure the demand curve for oil is given by *DD*, and this demand curve is relatively price

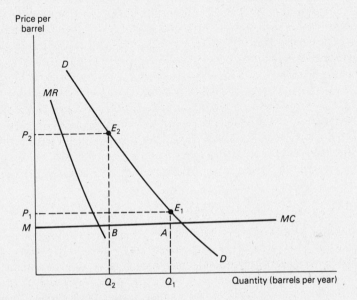

Figure 12.3 / Effects of the OPEC Cartel

Strengthening of the OPEC cartel in late 1973 caused market prices to rise from P_1 to P_2 together with a similar increase in producers' profits. These profits presented problems for the cartel both in deciding how they should be allocated among members and in providing an incentive to chisel.

inelastic. The marginal costs of oil production are assumed to be constant over all output levels. Although OPEC was founded in the early 1960s, it had relatively little effect on the petroleum market for the first ten years of its existence. The observed market equilibrium was at E_1. Because of the highly concentrated nature of the industry, market price was somewhat above the competitive level (and output was correspondingly lower), but price was far below monopoly price. With the onset of the October 1973 oil embargo. OPEC came to recognize its economic power and raised price toward its monopoly level.[16] In moving from E_1 to E_2, OPEC managed to increase the price of oil more than fourfold from about $2.50 to about

---

[16]Since there are many non-OPEC oil producers, the complete monopoly position was not attainable.

$12.00 per barrel. Profits (which mainly, though not solely, accrued to the OPEC members) rose sharply from area P_1E_1AM to area P_2E_2BM. This increase in profits represented a vast transfer of income (as much as $75 billion per year) from consumers to producers. Many of the OPEC countries, particularly those with relatively small populations, entered the ranks of the world's most affluent nations.

Apportioning OPEC Profits

OPEC's profits also created major internal problems, however. First, it was necessary to decide how those profits should be divided up among OPEC members. Since the cartel did not wish to make explicit side payments among its members, this then required that the desired output reduction $Q_1 - Q_2$ be apportioned in a way so that each member would be content with its assigned share. By geological accident it happened that the country with the largest oil reserves (Saudi Arabia) was also in the best position to restrain production (because its small population did not "need" major increases in oil profits). Hence Saudi Arabia (and, to a lesser extent, other Arab states) supported the OPEC cartel by holding back output. This made it unnecessary for the less affluent and more populous OPEC member countries (Indonesia, Nigeria, and Venezuela) to produce below maximal levels.

Chiseling and the Prisoner's Dilemma

OPEC's long-run success is by no means assured, however. The large discrepancy that now exists between the market price of oil and its marginal production cost creates an incentive for each member country to try to gain additional sales by shaving prices. As our discussion of the prisoner's dilemma pointed out, although such "chiseling" on price appears attractive to each cartel member, it is ultimately destructive to the market power and profitably of the cartel as a whole. So far, chiseling among OPEC members has been minimal: Only a few countries have (covertly) cut prices to gain business. In addition, many governments and some of the major oil companies have made enforcement of price discipline among OPEC members relatively costless by making purchase price information widely available. Whether OPEC will fall victim to the price-cutting behavior that has destroyed most other cartels or whether the unique political and geological characteristics of oil will permit it to remain a virtual monopoly remains an open question.

Summary

Many real-world markets resemble neither of the polar cases of perfect competition or monopoly. Rather, such markets are characterized by some degree of concentration (hence individual firms have some effect on market price—they are not price takers), but no single firm exercises complete market control. In these circumstances there is no generally accepted model of market behavior. Aspects of both competitive and monopoly theory must be used together with particular institutional details of the market in question in order to develop a realistic picture of behavior. Several specific issues that must be addressed in developing such a model are the following:

1. The degree of market concentration and the importance of feedback effects;

2. The importance of nonprice methods of competition such as product differentiation and advertising;

3. Entry conditions in the market and the constraints that potential entry places on attaining monopoly profits;

4. The uncertainty faced by individual firms and the strategies they may adopt to cope with it;

5. The potential benefits from monopolization of a market and the costs associated with maintaining such a cartel.

Suggested Readings

Bain, J. S., *Barriers to Competition* (Cambridge, Mass.: Harvard University Press, 1956).

Bishop, R. L., "Duopoly: Collusion or Welfare?" *American Economic Review* 50 (1960), pp. 933–961.

Chamberlain, E. H., *The Theory of Monopolistic Competition* (Cambridge, Mass.: Harvard University Press, 1950).

Dorfman, R., and Steiner, P. O., "Optimal Advertising and Optimal Quality," *American Economic Review* 44 (1954), pp. 826–836.

Doyle, P., "Economic Aspects of Advertising: A Survey," *Economic Journal* 78 (1968), pp. 570–602.

Kaplan, A. D. H., Dirlam, J. B., and Lanzillotti, R. G., *Pricing in Big Business: A Case Approach* (Washington, D.C.: The Brookings Institution, 1958).

Modigliani, F., "New Developments on the Oligopoly Front," *Journal of Political Economy* 66 (June 1958), pp. 215–232.

Schmalensee, R., *The Economics of Advertising* (Amsterdam: North-Holland Press, 1972), chap. 1.

Sherer, F. M., *Industrial Market Structure and Economic Preference* (Chicago: Rand McNally & Co., 1971).

Stigler, G. J., *Capital and Rates of Return in Manufacturing Industry* (Princeton, N.J.: Princeton University Press, 1963).

———, "Price and Non-Price Competition," *Journal of Political Economy* 76 (January–February 1968), pp. 149–154.

Telser, L. G., "Advertising and Competition," *Journal of Political Economy* 72 (December 1964), pp. 541–546.

Problems

12.1

A monopolist can produce at constant average (and marginal) costs of $AC = MC = 5$. The firm faces a market demand curve given by: $Q = 53 - P$.

(a) Calculate the profit-maximizing price-quantity combination for this monopolist. Also calculate the monopolist's profits.

(b) Suppose a second firm enters the market. Let q_1 be the output of the first firm and q_2 the output of the second. Market demand is now given by:

$$q_1 + q_2 = 53 - P.$$

On the assumption that this second firm has the same costs as the first, calculate the profits of firms 1 and 2 as functions of q_1 and q_2.

(c) Suppose (after Cournot) that each of these two firms chooses its level of output so as to maximize profits on the assumption that the other's output is fixed. Calculate each firm's "reaction function" that expresses desired output of one firm as a function of the other's output.

(d) On the assumption in Question (c), what is the only level for q_1 and q_2 with which both firms will be satisfied (what q_1, q_2 combination satisfies both reaction curves)?

(e) With q_1 and q_2 at the equilibrium level specified in Question (d) what will be the market price, the profits for each firm, and the total profits earned?

(f) Suppose now that there are n firms in the industry. If each firm adopts the Cournot strategy toward all its rivals, what will be the profit-maximizing output level for each firm? What will the market price be? What will the total profits earned in the industry be? (All these will depend on n.)

(g) Show that when n approaches infinity, the output levels, market price, and profits approach those which would "prevail" in perfect competition.

12.2

Some industries exhibit "price leadership." That is, there is a clearly designated firm that sets the industry price and all other firms take that price as given. To develop a model of this method of pricing:

a. Show how the price leader could construct the demand curve it faces from the market demand curve and the total supply curve for all the firms other than the leader.

b. Using the demand curve facing the price leader, show its profit-maximizing output (and price) choice. How will this choice compare to that which would prevail under perfect competition?

c. How might alternative behavior by the "minor" firms affect the success of the leader's plans?

12.3

Use Marshall's distinction between constructive and combative advertising to show how the prisoner's dilemma might arise among firms making decisions on their advertising budgets. Show that profits might be larger if advertising in the industry were completely banned. How might you apply your argument to the present ban on cigarette advertising on TV and radio?

12.4

Use the analysis developed in this chapter and elsewhere in this part to explain the following price behavior:

a. Doctors charge poor patients less for identical services than they charge rich patients.

b. Banks announce a widely publicized "prime rate" and change it only occasionally.

c. Blacks pay more than whites for identical houses.

d. Insurance companies continue to solicit automobile insurance business in spite of their plea that "we lose money on every policy we write."

e. Seats on the New York Stock Exchange are very expensive. They also fluctuate greatly in price.

f. A certain brand of beer used to be sold in cans and returnable bottles (with a deposit required). It was less expensive to buy beer in bottles and throw them away than to buy the beer in cans.

12.5

Some critics contend that U.S. automobile companies pursue a strategy of "planned obsolescence": that is, they produce cars that are intended to become obsolete in a few years. Would that strategy make sense in a monopoly market? How might the production of obsolescence depend on the characteristics of market demand? How would oligopolistic competition affect the profitability of the strategy?

12.6

Recently the Federal Trade Commission has challenged the breakfast cereal industry for violating antitrust law by operating as a "shared monopoly." It is not argued that the firms explicitly coordinate their marketing practices, but rather that they independently take actions that result in their obtaining monopoly profits available to the industry. How might the cereal companies pursue such a strategy (say through product differentiation or advertising)? What barriers to entry might their competition create? Would the "shared monopoly" strategy be stable and insure monopoly profits in the long run?

12.7

A major issue in current antitrust litigation concerns definition of "the market" for a product so that concentration within that market can be measured. In theoretical terms how would you define "the market" for computers? What is a "computer"? How should computer peripheral equipment be included? How about programming and other support services? Who makes "computers"? What are the geographic boundaries of the computer market you have described? How would you judge whether, say, the IBM Corporation had a monopoly position in the market you have described?

Appendix to Chapter 12	**Duopoly Models**

Introduction

Economists have developed several formal models that attempt to capture the interdependent nature of output decisions in oligopoly markets. These models range from simple two-firm (*duopoly*) models, through complex models that portray several different decisions being made by an arbitrary number of firms.[1] Each of these has as a central concern the construction of a model that is both analytically compact and flexible enough to incorporate strategic interactions among firms. While none of the models has won the widespread acceptance that the monopoly and perfectly competitive models have, some of them are useful pedagogic tools for demonstrating the nature of interdependence in a simple setting. In this appendix we will not attempt an exhaustive survey of oligopoly models. Rather, we will only develop a simple duopoly model that demonstrates market interdependence. A concluding section to the appendix suggests a few ways in which generalizations might be made.

---

[1]For a survey of many of these models see K. J. Cohen and R. M. Cyert, *Theory of the Firm: Revenue Allocation in a Market Economy* (Englewood Cliffs, N.J.: Prentice-Hall, Inc., 1965), chaps. 11 and 12.

Basic Model: Monopoly Situation

Suppose the demand function for a good is given by

$$Q = 120 - P \qquad\qquad [12A.1]$$

This curve is shown in Figure 12A.1. Assume also that there are no costs of production.[2] Consequently, profit maximization requires that any firm produce that output level for which revenues are as large as possible. That is, output should be expanded to the point at which marginal revenue is 0 (which then is equal to

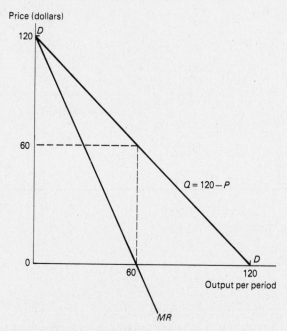

Figure 12A.1 / Monopolist's Output Choice

Given the market demand curve $Q = 120 - P$, a zero-cost monopolist would produce that output (60) for which marginal revenue is equal to 0. At this output a price of $60 would prevail and profits would be $3,600. Notice that $MR = 0$ at an output level $= \frac{1}{2} Q_0$ (where Q_0 is the quantity demanded at $P = 0$). This result holds for any linear demand curve.

marginal cost). If there is only one firm facing the demand curve 12A.1, or if two firms decide to coordinate their decisions, this monopoly will choose to produce 60 units of output. At this output level, P will be $60 and the monopoly's profits (and revenues) will be $3,600 (= 60×60). For the future development of the duopoly

---

[2]The assumption of zero costs is for convenience only. The models to be presented can be easily generalized to include any general cost function. To do so, however, would require the use of calculus.

point of intersection of R_1 and R_2 is the only *equilibrium* that can prevail in this two-firm market. It is easy to find this point of intersection by simply substituting 12A.5 into 12A.4 to get

$$Q_1 = \frac{120 - Q_2}{2} = \frac{120 - (120 - Q_1)/2}{2}$$

$$= \frac{120 - 60 + (Q_1)/2}{2} = 30 + \frac{Q_1}{4} \qquad [12A.6]$$

or

$$4Q_1 = 120 + Q_1 \qquad [12A.7]$$

or

$$Q_1 = 40 \qquad [12A.8]$$

Substituting this into 12A.5 gives

$$Q_2 = \frac{120 - Q_1}{2} = 40 \qquad [12A.9]$$

In equilibrium both firms will produce 40, total output will be 80, and the market price will be $40 (= 120 - 80)$. Profits for each firm will therefore be $1,600 (= \$40 \times 40)$, and total industry profits will be $3,200.

The Cournot equilibrium solution is stable in the sense that each firm has adjusted its output to the output level being produced by the other firm. Notice that total industry profits in the duopoly case ($3,200) are lower than under the monopoly case ($3,600). This is a result of the failure of the firms in the duopoly situation to coordinate their actions. Only if the firms collude will they be able to achieve the highest profits possible from the given demand curve. It is possible, however, that one of the duopoly firms can increase its profits by recognizing the way in which the other firm reacts to its output level. We take up this possibility in the next section.

Stackelberg Leadership Model

Suppose firm 1 recognizes that firm 2 follows a reaction function given by equation 12A.5. If firm 2 faithfully follows such a reaction function, firm 1 can increase its profits by making use of its knowledge of the function. Substituting the reaction function into the demand equation 12A.3 gives

$$Q_1 = 120 - Q_2 - P = 120 - \frac{120 - Q_1}{2} - P$$

$$= 60 + \frac{Q_1}{2} - P \qquad [12A.10]$$

or

$$2Q_1 = 120 + Q_1 - 2P$$

therefore

$$Q_1 = 120 - 2P \qquad \text{[12A.11]}$$

By knowing firm 2's reaction function, we have been able to derive the demand curve facing firm 1 as a function of Q_1 only. Now, using the profit-maximizing rule, firm 1 should produce

$$Q_1 = 60 \qquad \text{[12A.12]}$$

since this is the output level at a price of 0 divided by 2 (= 120/2). Now if firm 1 produces 60 and firm 2 is a faithful follower of its reaction function, it will produce

$$Q_2 = \frac{120 - 60}{2} = 30 \qquad \text{[12A.13]}$$

Consequently, industry output will be 90 and market price will be $30. The profits earned by firm 1 will be

$$\pi_1 = \$30 \times 60 = \$1,800 \qquad \text{[12A.14]}$$

whereas the profits earned by firm 2 will be

$$\pi_2 = \$30 \times 30 = \$900 \qquad \text{[12A.15]}$$

By using its knowledge of firm 2's reaction function firm 1 has been able to increase its profits. Of course the profits of firm 2 have been seriously eroded in the process.

Price Leadership

This model of a leader-follower relationship was first proposed by the German economist Heinrich von Stackelberg.[5] One ambiguous feature of the model is how to decide which firm will be the leader and which the follower. If each firm assumes the other is a follower, each will produce 60 and will be disappointed at the final outcome (with total output of 120, market price will, in the present example, fall to 0). On the other hand, if each acts as a follower the situation will revert to the Cournot equilibrium discussed in the previous section. That equilibrium is, however, unstable: Each firm can perceive the benefits to being a leader and may try to

---

[5]H. von Stackelberg, *The Theory of the Market Economy,* trans. A. T. Peacock (New York: Oxford University Press, 1952), pp. 195–204.

Table 12A.1 / Payoff Matrix for the Stackelberg Model (Profits for Each Firm under Various Strategies)

| | | Firm 2's Strategies | |
		Leader	Follower
Firm 1's Strategies	Leader	1: 0 2: 0	1: $1,800 2: $ 900
	Follower	1: $ 900 2: $1,800	1: $1,600 2: $1,600

choose its output accordingly. The various outcomes from strategic choices by each firm are shown in Table 12A.1. Notice how closely this matrix resembles that of the prisoner's dilemma we discussed in Chapter 12. Because of the uncertainty and interdependence inherent in the model, each firm will try to be a leader, and this will have disastrous consequences for the profits of both. An ironclad agreement between the firms with each promising to adopt the follower strategy would lead to

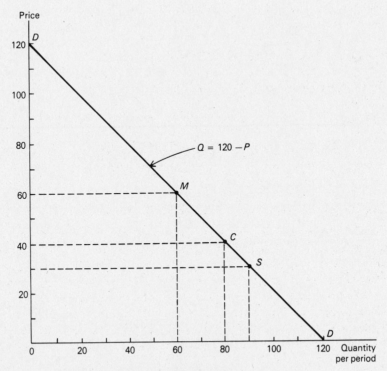

Figure 12A.3 / Solutions to the Duopoly Problem

Given the demand curve $Q = 120 - P$ the points M, C, and S represent, respectively, the monopoly, Cournot, and Stackelberg solutions to the duopoly problem.

larger industry profits than those which arise when one or both of the firms try to adopt the leader strategy.[6]

Comparison of the Models: Approaching the Competitive Solution

We have consequently presented three solutions to the simple duopoly problem posed at the beginning of this appendix: (1) the monopoly solution; (2) the Cournot solution; and (3) the Stackelberg solution. These solutions are denoted by the points M, C, and S, respectively, on the demand curve in Figure 12A.3. Notice that these points of market equilibrium approach the competitive solution (where $P = MC = 0$) as the more sophisticated models of duopoly behavior are examined. Indeed, as we showed in the previous section, if both firms attempt to take Stackelberg leadership roles the competitive solution will be attained. In a sense then, the uncertainty inherent in the duopoly model may provide a substitute for competition among many firms. There exist a number of more complex models of interdependent firm behavior for which that result also holds. Whether uncertainty in oligopolistic industries in the real world can provide an adequate substitute for competition, however, remains an open question.

Suggested Readings

Bishop, R. L., "Duopoly: Collusion or Warfare," *American Economic Review* 50 (December 1960), pp. 933–961.

———— "The Theory of Monopolistic Competition after Thirty Years: The Impact on General Theory," *American Economic Review* 54 (May 1964), pp. 33–43.

Chamberlin, E. H., *The Theory of Monopolistic Competition* (Cambridge, Mass.: Harvard University Press, 1932).

Cohen, K. J., and R. M. Cyert, *Theory of the Firm* (Englewood Cliffs, New Jersey: Prentice-Hall, Inc., 1965), chap. 12.

Ferguson, L. E., *Microeconomic Theory,* 3d ed. (Homewood, Ill.: Richard D. Irwin, Inc., 1972), chaps. 10 and 11.

Robinson, J., *The Economics of Imperfect Competition* (London: Collier-Macmillan, Ltd., 1933).

---

[6]Of course, if we permit ironclad agreements, it is most profitable for the firms to coordinate their strategies completely and to act as a monopolist.

Part V   Pricing in the Factor Market

Introduction

Factors of production also have prices. Labor services are purchased for a wage rate per hour, machines have rental rates, and something must be paid for the use of land. In this part we will investigate how those prices are determined. As a starting point it might be assumed that those prices (as is the case for the prices of goods) are established by the forces of supply and demand. Individuals supply labor services and these services are demanded by firms. Owners of capital and land are similarly willing to rent these resources to a firm for a price. In some way, then, prices are determined by the operation of the market.

In Chapter 13 we will discuss the perfectly competitive model of factor pricing. There are several ways in which this model differs from the perfectly competitive model of pricing in the market for goods, and we will analyze these differences in detail. The most important difference is that the demand for a factor of production is a *derived demand:* The demand for the factor depends indirectly on the demand for the good that the factor produces. For example, the demand for the labor services of airline pilots depends on the demand for air travel. If the demand curve for air travel were to shift, the demand curve for pilots would also shift.

A second important concept introduced in Chapter 13 is *economic rent.* Simply defined, any factor of production is said to earn rents when the factor is paid more than the amount necessary to keep the factor in its present employment. The most important example of such economic rent is the rent paid for the use of land. Since, to

363

a first approximation, the supply of land is absolutely fixed, any payment to landowners is an economic rent in the sense that the payment does not induce additional supply. Early economists (most notably Ricardo) intensively studied the phenomenon of land rent, and in many respects their investigatioins provided a foundation for the *marginal productivity theory of factor pricing.* This theory underlies much of the analysis of Chapter 13.

Chapter 14 presents a brief discussion of factor pricing in imperfectly competitive markets. Here we show that there are several different ways in which the market for a factor of production can be noncompetitive. Each of these departures from the competitive model has important implications for factor pricing.

The development of Chapters 13 and 14 is quite general in that it applies to any factor of production. In Chapters 15 and 16 we take up several issues specifically related to pricing in the labor and capital markets. Chapter 15 discusses three particular aspects of the supply and demand for labor services. First we analyze the simple labor supply decision for a single individual and develop a market supply of labor curve in much the same way we developed a market demand curve in Part II. Next we briefly discuss occupational choice and the concept of *compensating wage differentials.* Finally, in Chapter 15, we take note of the fact that important portions of the labor market are characterized by the presence of unions, and we show how these organizations can be incorporated into the general theory of factor pricing.

In Chapter 16 the market for capital is analyzed. The central purpose of the chapter is to emphasize the interconnection between capital and the study of the allocation of resources over time. An economy's stock of capital represents some output that was produced in the past but was not consumed, and we will analyze the choices that were made in this process. Some care is also taken to integrate the theory of capital into the models of firms' behavior we developed in Part III. Appendix to Chapter 16 presents some useful mathematical results about interest rates.

In *The Principles of Political Economy and Taxation* Ricardo wrote:

> The produce of the earth . . . is divided among three classes of the community, namely, the proprietor of the land, the owner of the stock of capital necessary for its cultivation, and the laborers by whose industry it is cultivated. To determine the laws which regulate this distribution is the principal problem in Political Economy.[1]

The purpose of Part V is to analyze how the prices of those factors of production are determined. An understanding of this pricing mechanism not only provides insights into how the market distributes income among the various factors of production but also suggests how this distribution might change over time. In this part we will, however, stop somewhat short of developing a complete theory of the distribution of income. We will take up some of the basic elements that might enter into such a theory in Chapter 21.

---

[1]D. Ricardo, *The Principles of Political Economy and Taxation* (1817; reprinted, London: J. M. Dent and Son, 1965), p. 1.

Chapter 13

Pricing in Perfectly Competitive Factor Markets

Introduction: Supply and Demand in Factor Markets

A reasonable way to start a discussion of pricing in factor markets is to assume that prices are established by the interaction of supply and demand. Figure 13.1 depicts this Marshallian concept. The factor supply curve (S) is drawn positively sloped on the assumption that higher factor rewards (v) will induce suppliers to offer more factor services (F) in the market place. Similarly the demand curve for the factor (D) is drawn with a negative slope on the assumption that demanders (principally firms) will hire a smaller quantity of the factor at higher levels of v. The price v^* is therefore an equilibrium price at which the total quantity of factor services supplied is exactly equal to the quantity that is demanded. At a price above v^* supply would exceed demand and there would be "unemployment"; for a price below v^* there would be excess demand for the factor.

Assumptions about Supply

The curves in Figure 13.1 are rather casually drawn. As in our examination of pricing in the goods market, the most interesting aspects of the analysis arise when we inquire into the more basic determinants of the shape of these curves. In this chapter we will be primarily interested in the demand side of the market; therefore, initially, it might be useful to discuss the supply assumptions that will be made here.

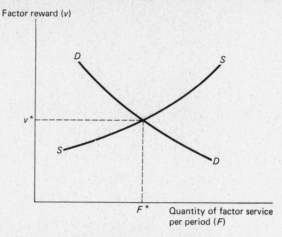

Figure 13.1 / Supply and Demand in the Factor Market

By analogy to the theory of pricing in the goods market, the supply and demand curves for a productive factor (F) have been drawn. It has been assumed that the quantity of the factor service supplied is an increasing function of the factor payment (v) and that the quantity demanded is a decreasing function of v. The factor reward v^* is an equilibrium price, since at this price the quantity supplied is equal to the quantity demanded.

Basically it will be assumed that there are a large number of suppliers of the resource in question. No single supplier can affect the price to be received, and therefore he or she will treat factor price as a fixed parameter in making decisions. The market supply curve can assume a wide variety of possible shapes. For example, the supply curve for land might be assumed to be very inelastic, whereas the supply of certain other factors might be very elastic. It is at least a theoretical possibility that the supply curve for a factor may be negatively sloped. Whatever the shape of the factor supply curve, we will usually assume that its position remains fixed throughout our analysis. In later chapters (notably Chapters 15 and 16) we will return to examine the question of factor supply in more detail.

Derived Demand

The demand curve in Figure 13.1 was drawn with a negative slope: A lower price for the input causes firms to demand more of it. To understand why a firm would hire more of an input in response to a fall in its price, we must recognize that a firm's demand for any factor of production is a *derived demand*. Firms hire labor, capital, and land in order to produce output, and the quantities they will hire obviously depend on how much output they are able to sell. General Motors' demand for production workers, for machinery, and for land and buildings depends on how many cars it can market. If the price of an input were to fall, the firm would increase its use of that input for two reasons. First, it would then be able to produce *any* output level more cheaply by using relatively more of this input. For example, a decline in wages might cause General Motors to use more workers and fewer machines on its assembly line. Second, if the firm, in response to the fall in the factor price, chose to produce more output, it would demand even more inputs. In the General Motors example, for instance, costs of manufacturing cars would fall, and the firm might find it profitable to produce more of them and to hire more labor to do so. Later in this chapter we will analyze this sequence of events in more detail. For the moment, the discussion is sufficiently precise to indicate why a firm's demand curve for an input will be negatively sloped. We can now proceed to analyze in more detail the supply-demand equilibrium pictured in Figure 13.1. In particular we will investigate the question of the "rent" earned by factors of production.

Economic Rent

The notion of "rent" plays an important role in the analysis of factor pricing. Because this term is used in a variety of contexts it is important to be precise about its economic meaning:

Definition

The *economic rent* earned by any factor of production is the extent to which payments to that factor exceed the minimal amount required to retain it in its present use.

One example of economic rent that we have already examined is the long-run profits earned by a factor of production that creates a monopoly. To the extent these profits exceed the factor's potential remuneration in an alternative employment, economic rent is created. In Figure 13.2 the concept is illustrated as a general case. Since the supply curve records that amount of factor service that would be supplied at each price, the total dollar amount necessary to retain the level F^* in this occupation is given by the area SOF^*E. If firms could perfectly discriminate among factor suppliers by hiring one unit at a time at an amount necessary to draw *that unit* into employment, total factor payments would be SOF^*E.[1] Perfectly competitive markets, however, do not work in this manner. Rather, all units of a productive input are paid the same price, and this price (v^*) is determined by what firms have to pay the last unit hired. Because all other units receive a return of v^*, but would settle for somewhat less and still remain in their current employment, these "intramarginal" suppliers receive an economic rent. Total factor payments in the competitive case are given by v^*OF^*E, and hence, total economic rents are given by the shaded area v^*SE.

---

[1] This analysis is very similar to that presented in Chapter 11 when the notion of consumer's surplus was discussed.

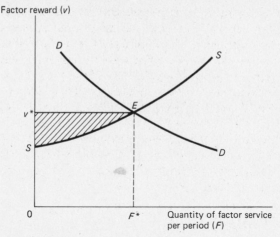

Figure 13.2 / Economic Rent

The shaded area represents total factor payments that exceed those necessary to keep F^* in its current employment. This quantity is the difference between total factor payments (v^*OF^*E) and those payments a perfectly discriminating hirer might pay (SOF^*E).

It is easy to see that the flatter (that is, the more elastic) the supply curve for a factor is, the smaller the area that represents economic rent is. If a supply curve were infinitely elastic (a horizontal line at the prevailing price), there would in fact be no economic rent. At the other extreme, all of the return to a factor that is in fixed supply is in the nature of an economic rent.[2] The factor payments in such a situation are determined solely by demand, and there is no notion of sacrifice on the part of the supplier of this fixed factor. It will always be supplied no matter what factor reward is offered. Any return that is received is a result of the "accident" of where the demand curve happens to be.

Economic Rent and Opportunity Cost

It is important to recognize the relationship between the concepts of "economic rent" and "opportunity cost." A factor production that has many alternative uses will have a very elastic supply curve to any one employment. Since this factor can receive almost as high a price elsewhere, quantity supplied will be reduced sharply if an employer reduces its price offer even slightly. In such a case, economic rents would be small because the factor earns only slightly in excess of what it might earn elsewhere. For example, clerical workers have numerous employment opportunities, all of which offer approximately the same wage. The earnings of a clerical

---

[2]Some authors make a distinction between short-run and long-run rents. In the short run, when supply curves tend to be more inelastic, rent is referred to as "quasi-rent" to indicate that it may disappear when long-run supply response is permitted. The profits of perfectly competitive firms in the short run would be one example of quasi-rent.

worker in, say, a life insurance firm represent virtually no economic rent, then, since he or she could earn almost exactly the same amount in employment by some other firm. On the other hand, there are factors of production that are uniquely suited to one employment and have considerably lower productivity elsewhere. In that case, their supply curve to this employment is inelastic, reflecting the fact that a lower price would not cause a marked reduction in supply. Most of the earnings of such a factor would be called economic rent and would be measured by the difference between the factor's earnings and its opportunity cost in its next best employment. The high wages paid to players in the professional basketball leagues, for example, might be considered, in large part, as economic rent in the sense that the alternative earnings possibilities of these individuals (in occupations outside basketball) may be relatively low.

Land Rent

The most commonly encountered example of this analysis of economic rent is in the case of a fixed land supply. This situation is represented in Figure 13.3 by the vertical supply curve at the existing level of land (T_0). No matter what the level of demand is, this supply will be fixed. If demand were given by curve D the rental rate on the land would be v_0, and the total return to the owner of the land would be $v_0 O T_0 E$. If, on the other hand, demand were given by the curve D', the equilibrium rental rate would be v_1, and total rentals would be $v_1 O T_0 E'$. It is clear that the increase in price from v_0 to v_1, although it does ration the available land among demanders, has no effect on increasing supply. The nineteenth-century American

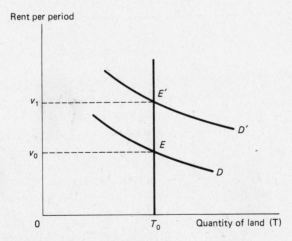

Figure 13.3 / All Returns to a Fixed Supply of Land are Economic Rent

With land in absolutely fixed supply (at T_0) the rental rate will be determined solely by demand conditions. A lump-sum tax on landowners would not affect the quantity of land supplied.

economist H. George[3] noted this fact and proposed that those rents accruing to such fortunate landowners be taxed at a very high level, since this taxation would have no effect on the quantity of land provided. While there are numerous complications in this proposal, George's idea of a single tax on land still has many adherents, particularly in the British Labour Party.

Although there are important historical reasons why the examination of economic rent centers on the returns to owners of land, we have seen that there is little economic reason for such a narrow view. Any factor of production for which alternative uses are slight will have a relatively inelastic supply to its most favorable employment. Most of the total return to this factor will represent economic rent, and this could be taxed away without creating a major reduction in supply. The price paid for rental of a favorably located parcel of land in Manhattan is largely economic rent in the same sense that the price Elizabeth Taylor receives for a picture is. In both cases supply may be quite inelastic, and demand conditions will play a major role in determining price.

Ricardian Rent

In examining the rents earned on different parcels of land, one of the most important observations made by classical economists was that more fertile land tended to command a higher rent. Ricardo, for example, carefully analyzed the way in which differential rents were related to land's fertility and to the demand for crops grown on the land.[4] Ricardo theorized that additional land of inferior quality would be cultivated up to the point at which the last acre planted earned exactly zero in economic rents. More fertile acres would earn positive rents, however, and these would represent a return based on the land's higher quality. Since the market price of any particular crop is determined by costs of the marginal producer and since, for this marginal producer, rents are zero, Ricardo concluded that economic rent cannot properly be considered a determinant of market price. Rather, prices are determined solely by the market demand for crops and by the availabilities of fertile land.

Graphic Presentation of Ricardo's Analysis

Ricardo's argument can be most readily demonstrated using a graphic analysis. Assume there are many parcels of land suitable for growing wheat. These parcels range from very fertile (low costs of production) to rather poor quality (high cost). The long-run supply curve for wheat can be constructed as follows: At low prices only the best land is cultivated; as price rises, production continues on the fertile land and additional crops are planted on land of poorer quality; at still higher prices

---

[3]See Henry George, *Progress and Poverty: An Inquiry into the Cause of Industrial Depressions and of Increase of Want with Increase of Wealth* (New York: Henry George, 1881).

[4]See Ricardo, *Political Economy and Taxation*, chaps. 2 and 32.

it will be profitable to utilize lower quality land in production. The market equilibrium is pictured in Figure 13.4. At the equilibrium price P^* owners of low-cost land parcels earn large economic profits (rent); those less favorably situated earn smaller rents; the marginal farm earns 0 in rents. If it were possible to earn any rents on additional pieces of land, these would be brought into cultivation. Those acres that are left unplanted must be of lower quality than those of the marginal farm. Notice that the equilibrium described in Figure 13.4 is stable in the long run. It is

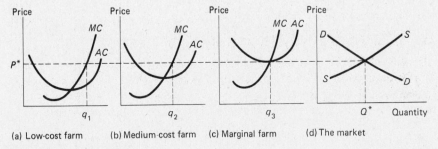

(a) Low-cost farm   (b) Medium-cost farm   (c) Marginal farm   (d) The market

**Figure 13.4 / Creation of
Ricardian Rent on Land of Differing Fertility**

Because land differs in quality, farms with the most fertile land will have lower costs. Since price will be determined by the costs of the marginal supplier, low-cost firms will earn pure economic profits. These profits might be called rent and will persist even in the long run since fertile land is in fixed supply.

impossible for new entrants to earn a profit even though those farms already in the market, by virtue of controlling the best land, are able to do so. This analysis shows how the demand for land is a demand derived from the product market; the location of the market demand curve determines how much land can be profitably cultivated and how much income in the form of rent will be generated. It might be argued that the rents earned by low-cost farmers should be accounted as implicit costs since this is what someone else would pay for the right to farm the land. Hence all farms in reality have the same cost curves: Those of low-cost producers have a large element of implicit rental cost. This is a purely semantic distinction and would not change the analysis of the way in which superior fertility determines rent.

Generalizations of Ricardian Analysis

This analysis of Ricardian rent can be generalized to any situation in which differing productivities of resources result in differing cost curves for the firms that own those resources. Other cases of land rents reflecting cost differences include: high rental values of especially favorable locations for retail businesses; higher prices for homes located near transit lines (or simply near the central city); and the tendency of identical houses to sell for more in towns with low property taxes. For the case of natural resource deposits a similar analysis would hold: those deposits from which resources can be obtained at low cost will command a rent relative to less accessible deposits. A major controversy over deregulation of natural gas prices in the United States, for example, concerned the distinction between "old" gas (that is gas produced from older, lower-cost wells) and "new" gas produced in more recent and costly locations. It was argued that "old" gas should continue to be produced under controlled prices so that owners of those low-cost wells would not gain "windfall" profits (that is, rents) as a result of rising prices that reflected production costs from new wells. Hence, Ricardo's analysis continues to provide insights into a number of important current policy issues.

Marginal Productivity Theory of Factor Demand

Ricardian rent theory was an important predecessor of the development of "marginalist" economics. Ricardo's hypothesis that price is determined by the costs of the marginal producer, in many ways, represents the seed from which modern price theory grew. One major generalization of this hypothesis took place in the development of the marginal productivity theory of factor demand. Since this is in many respects the theory of factor pricing, we will investigate it in detail for the rest of this chapter.

The basic concept of the marginal productivity theory of factor demand has already been stated in Chapter 8 when we discussed profit maximization. There we showed that one implication of the profit-maximization hypothesis is that the firm will make marginal input choices. More formally, we showed:

Optimization Principle

A profit-maximizing firm will hire units of any input up to the point at which the additional revenue from hiring one more unit is exactly equal to the cost of hiring that unit.

If markets are assumed to be perfectly competitive, this principle can be given a more specific interpretation. Suppose the firm uses two inputs, capital (K) and labor (L), and is able to rent these at constant per-unit costs of v and w, respectively. The profit-maximizing firm will therefore hire capital and labor up to the point at which the additional revenue yielded by hiring one more unit is equal to these costs.

Marginal Value Product

To analyze the additional revenue yielded by hiring one more unit of an input is a two-step process. First we must ask how much additional output the additional input can produce. As we discussed in Chapter 7, this magnitude is given by the input's marginal physical productivity. For example, if a firm hires one more worker to make shoes, the worker's marginal physical productivity is simply the number of additional pairs of shoes produced per period by that worker.

Once the additional output has been produced, it must be sold in the market. Assessing the value of that sale is the second step in analyzing the revenue yielded by hiring another input. In this chapter we will assume that the firm sells its output in a perfectly competitive market at a price P. Consequently, the extra revenue provided is simply P times the extra output produced. In the shoe example, it is the price of a pair of shoes times the number of extra shoes produced. More formally, we have:

Definition

The *marginal value product* (*MVP*) of an input is the market value of the extra output produced by hiring one more unit of that input. It is the product of the input's marginal physical productivity (*MP*) times the market price of the output (*P*). Mathematically, for the two inputs capital and labor:

$$MVP_K = P \cdot MP_K$$

[13.1]

$$MVP_L = P \cdot MP_L$$

Returning again to the shoe example, suppose an additional worker can produce 400 pairs per year and that the shoes sell for $20 each. Then the worker's marginal value product is $8,000 (= $20 \times 400). In deciding how many workers to hire, a shoe firm will compare this number to the wages of shoemakers to decide whether hiring another would be profitable. We will now analyze this application of our optimization principle.

Profit-Maximizing Input Choice under Perfect Competition

Because of the perfectly competitive assumptions we have made, the profit-maximizing input principle can be stated more precisely as:

Optimization Principle

With competitive markets, a profit-maximizing firm will hire any input up to the point at which its marginal value product is equal to its market rental rate. For the inputs capital and labor this requires that

$$MVP_K = P \cdot MP_K = v$$

[13.2]

$$MVP_L = P \cdot MP_L = w$$

To see why this principle is a necessary condition for profit maximization,[5] suppose the wage for shoemakers is $7,000 per year. The shoe firm's manager will compare this figure to a shoeworker's *MVP* to decide whether to hire another worker. In our previous example the *MVP* was $8,000 per year and hence hiring the additional worker will increase profits (by $1,000 per year in this case). As the firm hires more workers the *MVP* will fall because workers' marginal physical productivity declines as labor input is increased. Additional workers will be hired up to the point at which their marginal physical productivity has fallen to 350 pairs of shoes per year. At that point an additional worker's *MVP* is $7,000 ($= 350 \times \$20$) and that is exactly what it would cost to hire the workers. Hiring would not proceed beyond this point. A further fall in workers' marginal physical productivity, say to 300 pairs per year, would imply that the worker's wage ($7,000) exceeds his or her *MVP* ($6,000 $= 300 \times \$20$) and hiring the worker would result in a reduction in profits.

A Graphic Demonstration

Figure 13.5 shows this result graphically. The horizontal axis in the figure records the level of labor inputs hired, and the vertical axis shows the *MVP* for each of these levels.[6] We can construct an *MVP* curve for labor directly from the marginal physical product of labor curve (MP_L) we introduced in Chapter 6 by simply multiplying MP_L by the market price of the firm's output. The resulting MVP_L is shown in Figure 13.5. The negative slope of that curve reflects the assumption of a diminishing marginal physical productivity: the more labor hired the lower will be labor's marginal physical productivity and the lower will be the marginal value product.

The firm's profit-maximizing labor input is shown by recording labor's wage rate (w) on the vertical axis. At that wage, profit maximization requires hiring L^* workers. Only for this level of labor input does $w = MVP_L$. For levels of labor input less than L^* (say L') labor's *MVP* will exceed the market wage and it would be profitable to hire more workers. Quantities of labor input greater than L^* (say L''), on the other hand, have an *MVP* that falls short of w and profits would be increased by cutting back on employment. Only at L^* is the cost of hiring an extra worker

---

[5]Notice that equations (13.2) imply cost minimization. Dividing the two gives:

$$\frac{P \cdot MP_L}{P \cdot MP_K} = \frac{MP_L}{MP_K} = \frac{w}{v}$$

but in Chapter 6 we showed that *RTS* (of L for K) $= MP_L/MP_K$. Consequently a firm that pursues a marginal productivity approach to input demand will equate

$$RTS \text{ (of } L \text{ for } K) = \frac{w}{v}$$

and this is what is required for cost minimization.

[6]Although here we analyze only the case of labor input, it should be clear that an analysis of the demand for capital input would proceed in exactly the same way.

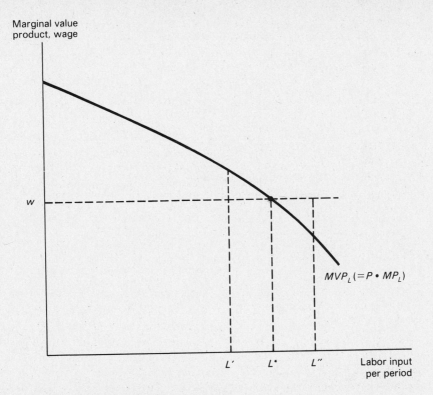

Figure 13.5 / Profit-Maximizing Input Choice

The marginal value product curve for labor (MVP_L) is constructed by multiplying labor's marginal physical productivity times the market price of the firm's output. The curve is downward sloping because of the assumption that labor exhibits a diminishing marginal physical productivity. At a wage of w, profit maximization requires that L^* units of labor input be hired.

exactly equal to the revenue that hiring the worker provides to the firm: only at L^* is the firm maximizing profits.

Of course, if w were to change we would expect the profit-maximizing quantity of labor input to change. We will examine that possibility in the next section.

Responses to Changes in Input Prices

Suppose the price of labor (w) were to fall. Earlier we showed why it seems "reasonable" to predict that firms will demand more labor in response to such a change. In this section we will provide a detailed analysis of why this is so.

Single-Input Case

As a simple first case, let us assume that a firm uses only labor to produce its output. The firm's MVP_L curve is shown in Figure 13.6. At a wage of w_1 the firm's

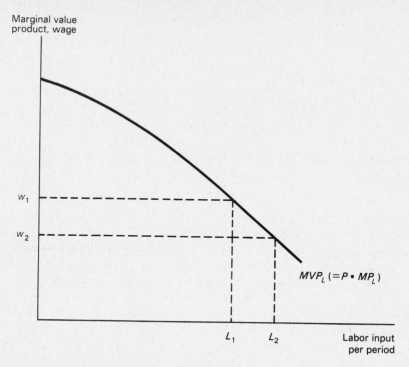

**Figure 13.6 / Change in Labor
Input When Wage Falls: Single-Input Case**

At a wage rate w_1, profit maximization requires that L_1 labor input be hired. If the wage rate falls to w_2 more labor (L_2) will be hired because of the assumed slope of the MVP_L curve.

profit-maximizing choice of labor input is given by L_1. The firm will persist in hiring L_1 units of labor so long as the conditions it faces do not change.

If the wage rate were to fall to W_2, more labor (L_2) would be demanded. At such a lower wage, more labor can be hired because the firm can "afford" to have a lower marginal physical productivity from the labor it employs. If it continued to hire only L_1, the firm would not be maximizing profits since, at the margin, labor would now be capable of producing more in additional revenue than hiring additional labor would cost. Consequently we have shown that, for the single-input case, the assumption of a diminishing marginal productivity of labor insures that a fall in the price of labor will cause more labor to be hired.[7] A similar analysis would hold for any other case of a single input that obeys these assumptions.

---

[7]Since the marginal productivity of labor is positive, hiring more labor also implies that output will increase when w declines.

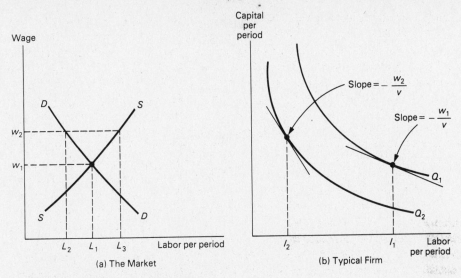

(a) The Market   (b) Typical Firm

Figure 13.8 / Effects of a Minimum
Wage in a Perfectly Competitive Labor Market

Initially a wage rate of w_1 is set by the forces of supply and demand. At this wage rate a typical firm chooses to use l_1 units of labor. The imposition of a minimum wage (w_2) causes the firm to reduce labor usage to l_2 because it will both substitute capital (and other inputs) for labor and cut back output. All firms' demands will be reduced to L_2 at the new wage rate. Individuals wish to supply L_3, however, and there will be unemployment of $L_3 - L_2$.

equilibrium wage rate, w_1, is established in the market. At this wage, a typical firm hires l_1 and this choice of input is shown on the firm's isoquant map in 13.8b. Suppose now that a minimum wage of w_2 ($> w_1$) is imposed by law.[11] This new wage will cause the firm to reduce its demand for labor from l_1 to l_2. The reduction comes from two effects. First, the increase in the price of labor causes the firm to substitute capital for labor along the Q_1 isoquant. In addition to this substitution effect, there is a negative output effect since the increase in costs has caused the firm's output to be reduced from Q_1 to Q_2. Consequently, the typical firm will reduce its demand for labor from l_1 to l_2. Similar actions by many firms will be reflected in a movement along the market demand for labor curve from L_1 to L_2. At the same time, more labor (L_3) will be supplied at w_2 than was supplied at the lower wage rate. The imposition of the minimum wage will therefore result in an excess of the supply of labor over the demand for labor of $L_3 - L_2$. This excess supply is what we mean by "unemployment." At the new prevailing wage more individuals want to work than are able to find jobs. The extent of this unemployment will depend on the size of the substitution and output effects that come into play as firms are affected by the new wage. We now examine one particular labor market where those effects are probably quite large.

---

[11]The imposition of a minimum wage of less than w_1 would have no effect since the competitively determined wage already exceeds this level.

Minimum Wages and Teenage Unemployment

There is some empirical evidence that changes in the minimum wage law have had serious effects in increasing teenage unemployment. Teenagers are the labor market participants most likely to be affected by minimum wage laws, since they usually represent the lower end of the spectrum of skills. An increase in minimum wages may cause employers to substitute capital and skilled labor for what has become more expensive, unskilled teenage labor; it may also cause large negative output effects, since the products produced by teenage employees (services, for example) usually have a fairly high price elasticity. In recent years teenage unemployment has increased rapidly. Particularly hard hit have been teenage minority group members, for whom unemployment rates often exceed 30 percent. Although there are several factors that may account for such statistics (unstable employment opportunities, discrimination in employment, long periods of searching for jobs), many economists assign an important role to statutory changes in the minimum wage. For example, one study[12] found that each 1 percent increase in the minimum wage resulted in a reduction of 0.3 percent in teenagers' share of total employment. A particularly important example of this reduction is in the changing employment patterns of "fast-food" chains in response to rising minimum wages. These businesses are highly labor-intensive and sell a product (eating out) the demand for which is relatively price-responsive. Hence the firms may find their sales falling off substantially in response to price rises stemming from minimum wage increases. In addition, the firms may attempt to substitute capital equipment (automatic hamburger turners) for teenage workers, thereby further reducing their demand for workers. In response to the 1977 minimum wage increase, for example, the McDonald's Corporation (reputedly the largest hirer of teenage workers in the United States) adopted a new program of research on labor-saving technology and adopted several changes in their teenage hiring practices.[13]

Effects of Expanding Minimum Wage Coverage

Although periodic increases in the minimum wage have undoubtedly had a negative effect on teenage employment, those increases have not exceeded increases in wages in general. The minimum wage has remained relatively constant at about 45 percent of the average wage in manufacturing over the past 40 years. The percent of employment covered by minimum wage legislation has, however, been greatly expanded in recent years. Some analysts believe that this expansion has had even more significant effects than has the rise in the minimum wage itself. These effects show up both in reduced employment in industries newly covered by the minimum wage law, through the process illustrated in Figure

---

[12]F. Welch, "Minimum Wage Legislation in the United States," *Economic Inquiry* 12, No. 3 (September 1974), pp. 285–318.

[13]See "Fast Food Chains Act to Offset the Effects of Minimum Pay Rise," *The Wall Street Journal*, December 22, 1977, page 1.

13.8 and in lower wages for individuals who work in uncovered industries (because of the increased supply of workers seeking such jobs). Since much of the employment in uncovered industries is not officially recorded, however, it is difficult to estimate the magnitude of that second effect.

Summary

In this chapter we investigated the marginal productivity theory of factor demand as it applies to perfectly competitive markets. We demonstrated that a profit-maximizing firm will hire additional units of any productive input up to the point at which the value of this factor's marginal productivity is equal to its market price. When a factor price increases, our theoretical development showed that two effects come into play (the substitution and output effects) both of which cause the quantity of that factor demanded to decline. Separating firms' responses into these two effects permits an investigation of the degree to which firms will respond to such an input price change. In addition, the theoretical development provides insights into the ways in which the demand for any factor of production is derived from the goods market. Wages for labor and rental rates for capital equipment are to a major extent determined by the demands for the goods these inputs produce. The marginal productivity theory neatly ties together theories of pricing in the goods market with theories of the derived demand for inputs, and it provides a comprehensive picture of the way in which resources are allocated in a market economy.

Although the marginal productivity theory of factor pricing is the most fully articulated theory of how factor rewards are determined, it is not the only one. In the next chapter, for example, we shall examine several cases in which the presence of imperfect competition causes factor prices to differ from marginal value products. In such situations supply and demand conditions get general bounds within which factor payments will fall; actual payments observed in the market will, however, depend on such factors as the bargaining power of the parties involved, the goals toward which each party aspires, and the degree of information about the market that each individual has. The marginal productivity theory is a reasonable place to start a detailed analysis, but some recognition must be given to those other important factors.

Suggested Readings

Brozen, Y., "The Effect of Statutory Minimum Wage Increases on Teenage Employment," *Journal of Law and Economics* 12 (April 1969), pp. 109–122.

Douglas, P. H., *The Theory of Wages* (New York: Crowell-Collier and Macmillan, Inc., 1934).

Ferguson, C. E., " 'Inferior Factors' and the Theories of Production and Input Demand," *Economica*, n.s., 35 (1968), pp. 140–150.

Hicks, J. R., *The Theory of Wages* (London: Collier-Macmillan, Ltd., 1932).

————, *Value and Capital,* 2d ed. (Oxford: Clarendon Press, 1946), pp. 78–111.

Kosters, M., and Welch, F., "The Effects of Minimum Wages on the Distribution of Changes in Aggregate Employment," *American Economic Review* 62 (June 1972), pp. 323–332.

Reder, M., "Alternative Theories of Labor's Share," in *The Allocation of Economic Resources,* ed. Abramovitz, M., et al. (Stanford, Calif.: Stanford University Press, 1959), pp. 180–206.

Samuelson, P. A., *Foundations of Economic Analysis* (Cambridge, Mass.: Harvard University Press, 1947), pp. 57–89.

Stigler, G. J., "Production and Distribution in the Short Run," *Journal of Political Economy* 47 (1939), pp. 305–327.

Worcester, D. A., "A Reconsideration of the Theory of Rent," *American Economic Review* 36 (June 1946), pp. 258–277.

Problems

13.1

Suppose the demand for labor is given by

$$L = -50w + 450$$

and the supply is given by

$$L = 100w$$

where L represents the number of people employed and w is the real wage rate per hour.

a. What will be the equilibrium levels for w and L in this market?

b. Suppose the government wishes to raise the equilibrium wage to $4 per hour by offering a subsidy to employers for each man hired. How much will this subsidy have to be? What will the new equilibrium level of employment be? How much total subsidy will be paid?

c. Suppose instead the government declared a minimum wage of $4 per hour. How much labor would be demanded at this price? How much unemployment would there be?

d. Graph your results.

13.2

Suppose there are only two industries in an economy with a perfectly competitive labor market. Assume that a minimum wage (which exceeds that presently prevailing) is imposed by law on one of the industries. How will this policy affect wages and employment in the covered and uncovered industries? What information would you need to predict the effect of the minimum wage on total employment?

13.3

A landowner has three farms, A, B, and C, of differing fertility. The levels of output for the three farms with one, two, and three laborers employed are as given:

	Farm A	Farm B	Farm C
1 laborer	10	8	5
2 laborers	17	11	7
3 laborers	21	13	8

For example, if three laborers were hired, one for each farm, the total output would be $10 + 8 + 5 = 23$. This would represent a poor allocation of labor, however, since by assigning the Farm C laborer to help on Farm A the total output would be $17 + 8 = 25$.

If market conditions were such as to make the employer hire 5 laborers, what would be the most productive allocation of that labor? How much would be produced? What is the marginal product of the last worker?

If we assume that farm output is sold in a perfectly competitive market with one unit of output priced at $1.00, and we assume that labor market equilibrium occurs when 5 workers are hired, what wage is paid? How much profit does the landowner receive?

13.4

Explain each of the following observations about the labor market by using a supply-demand analysis.

a. Women are often paid less than men for the same job.

b. Wages of doctors and construction workers have risen rapidly in recent years, whereas general manufacturing wage rates have not.

c. The United States in the early 1960s had a "shortage" of engineers and scientists.

d. There now appears to be a "surplus" of persons in the academic job market.

13.5

Assume that the quantity of envelopes licked per hour by Sticky Gums, Inc. is $Q = 10,000 \sqrt{L}$ where L is the number of laborers hired per hour by the firm. Assume further that the envelope-licking business is perfectly competitive with a market price of $.01 per envelope. The marginal product of a worker is given by

$$MP_L = \frac{5000}{\sqrt{L}}$$

a. How much labor would be hired at a competitive wage of $10? $5? $2? Use your results to sketch a demand curve for labor.

b. Assume that Sticky Gums hires its labor at an hourly wage of $10. What quantity of envelopes will be licked when the price of a licked envelope is $.10, $.05, $.02? Use your results to sketch a supply curve for licked envelopes.

Chapter 14

Pricing in Imperfectly Competitive Factor Markets

Introduction

Departures from the perfectly competitive model may affect factor pricing in three different ways. First, the firm hiring a particular factor may sell its output under imperfectly competitive conditions. If the factor market is itself competitive, this aspect of imperfect competition can easily be handled as an extension of the analysis of the previous chapter. Second, the factor market may diverge from the perfectly competitive assumption if there are only a few [or perhaps only one] demanders of the factor. This is the case of *oligopsony or monopsony* in the factor market. Third, a departure from the competitive model can occur if the sellers of a factor are able to form an effective monopoly. In this case, the analysis is much the same as that we developed in Chapter 11 for any monopoly seller. In this chapter we will examine the first and second departures from perfect competition.

Imperfect competition can occur in any factor market. For simplicity we will, in this chapter, use the labor market as an example; the analysis to be presented applies equally well to any other factor of production. In Chapters 15 and 16 we will take up questions uniquely related to the labor and capital markets, respectively.

Imperfect Competition in the Goods Market

The first way in which imperfect competition affects factor pricing results from the possibility of monopoly in the goods market. Remember that a profit-maximizing firm will hire any input, say labor, up to the point at which the extra revenue from hiring one more unit of labor is equal to its extra cost. If it is assumed that the labor market is perfectly competitive, the extra cost of an additional unit of labor is the wage rate: The firm is faced by a horizontal supply-of-labor curve. It can hire as much labor as it needs at the prevailing market wage (w). However, if the firm sells its output in an imperfectly competitive market, the analysis differs slightly from the one given in the previous chapter. Hiring an additional unit of labor will permit the firm to produce some extra output (MP_L). This extra output is then sold in the market for the extra (that is, marginal) revenue it will yield (MR). The net result of these two steps will determine how much extra revenue is yielded by hiring the extra worker. Hence we have defined:

Definition

The addition to revenue yielded by hiring one more unit of an input is called the *Marginal Revenue Product* (*MRP*). Its value is given by the product of the input's marginal physical productivity times the marginal revenue the firm obtains on its output. For the case of labor,

$$MRP_L = MR \cdot MP_L \qquad [14.1]$$

This concept is just a generalization of the Marginal Value Product concept introduced in Chapter 13. In that chapter we assumed that the firm sells its output in a perfectly competitive market, and that the firm is a price taker and has no effect on market price. In this case $MR = P$, and the definition of marginal revenue product given in Equation 14.1 simply reduces to the marginal value product definition (see Equation 13.1). All we have done here is to allow for the noncompetitive case in which the firm faces a downward-sloping demand curve for its product.

p. 373

Profit-Maximizing Input Choice

We have therefore discussed the effect of a firm's hiring one more worker on both its revenues and its costs. Our conclusion is:

Optimization Principle

A firm that hires its inputs in a perfectly competitive market but sells its output under conditions of imperfect competition can maximize its profits by hiring additional inputs up to the point at which the input's marginal revenue product is equal to its market rental rate. For the case of labor, the firm should hire workers up to the point at which

$$MRP_L = MR \cdot MP_L = w \qquad [14.2]$$

If $MRP_L > w$ profits could be increased by hiring more workers at a wage of w, whereas if $MRP_L < w$ too many workers have been hired and profits could be raised by cutting back on employment. Again notice the similarity between this optimization principle and the one presented in Chapter 13 (see Equation 13.2). If competition prevails in the goods market, $MR = P$ and the two equations are identical.

p. 373

Responses to Changes in the Price of an Input

We can construct the firm's demand curve for labor for the case presented here in much the same way as we did in Chapter 13. Again a change in w will induce both substitution and output effects. The sum of these two effects will determine what happens to the quantity of labor demanded. Figure 14.1 illustrates such a comparative statics analysis. A reduction in w will cause the optimal input combination to shift from point A on the Q_1 isoquant to point B in Figure 14.1a. As before, this is the substitution effect. An analysis of the output effect is somewhat different from that presented previously because now we must consider the possibility of a negatively sloped demand curve for the firm's output. Such a curve is drawn in Figure 14.1b together with its associated marginal revenue curve. The initial profit-maximizing output is Q_1 where $MR = MC$. A reduction in w will, however, shift this MC curve. Because w has fallen, the curve will shift downward to MC'. At MC' the new profit-maximizing output is Q_2, and this output will be produced with the input combination C shown in 14.1a. The substitution and output effects work in the same direction causing an increase in L in response to a decrease in w. Consequently, any firm that acts as a price taker in the labor market (even if it sells its output in an

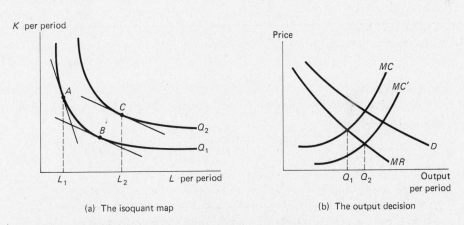

(a) The isoquant map

(b) The output decision

Figure 14.1 / Substitution and Output Effects of a Change in w when Output Is Not Sold in a Perfectly Competitive Market

This figure is identical to 13.7 except that the firm faces a negatively sloped demand for its output. The profit-maximizing choice of L in response to a decrease in w changes from L_1 to L_2. The output effect differs slightly from that presented previously because the firm now recognizes that marginal revenue is less than market price.

imperfect market) will have a negatively sloped demand curve for labor.[1] This curve will be the locus of (w, L) combinations for which the profit-maximizing condition of equation 14.2 holds.

Monopsony in the Labor Market

There are many situations in which the supply curve of labor faced by a firm is not a horizontal line at the prevailing wage rate. It may frequently be necessary for the firm to offer a wage above that currently prevailing if it is to attract more employees. In order to study such situations it is most convenient to examine the polar case of *monopsony* (a single buyer) in the labor market. If there is only one buyer in the labor market this firm faces the entire market supply curve. In order to increase its hiring of labor by one more unit it must move to a higher point on this supply curve. This will involve paying not only a higher wage to the last worker hired but also additional wages to those workers already employed. The marginal cost of the extra unit of labor therefore exceeds its wage rate. To denote this fact we define:

Definition

The *marginal expense* of hiring one more unit of an input is the increase in total costs as a result of that hiring. For a monopsonist facing an upward-sloping supply curve for the input, the marginal expense will exceed the market price of the input. For labor input, for example, the marginal expense (MC_L) exceeds the market wage (w).[2]

Notice the similarity between the concept of the marginal expense of an input and the marginal revenue for a monopolist. Both concepts are intended to be used when firms possess market power and their choices have an effect on prices. In such

---

[1] In a sense it might be said that a firm faced by a negatively sloped demand curve for its product has a "less elastic" demand for labor than if this output were traded in a competitive market. This can be seen in Figure 14.1 because an increase in output means a decrease in MR, whereas in the perfectly competitive case MR is constant at the prevailing market price. The output effect is then "smaller" in the case illustrated in Figure 14.1 than it was in Figure 13.7.

[2] For example, suppose a firm is currently hiring L_1 labor hours at a wage of w_1. Total labor costs are therefore $w_1 L_1$. Now assume the firm wishes to hire one more man-hour, and to do so it must raise wages to w_2 ($> 2_1$). The total labor bill is now $w_2(L_1 + 1)$. The cost of hiring the extra labor is

$$MC_L = w_2(L_1 + 1) - w_1 L_1 = (w_2 - w_1) L_1 + w_2$$

This will exceed w_2 because of the higher wages $(w_2 - w_1)$ that have to be paid to the previously employed workers.

situations firms can no longer be treated as price takers. Instead, firms will recognize that their actions affect prices and will use this information in making decisions.

Monopsonist's Input Choice

As for any profit-maximizing firm, a monopsonist will hire any input up to the point at which the additional revenue and additional cost of hiring one more unit are equal. Our final application of this marginal principle is therefore:

Optimization Principle

A profit-maximizing monopsonist will hire any input up to the point at which the marginal expense of hiring an additional unit is exactly equal to that unit's marginal revenue product. For the case of labor this requires:

$$MC_L = MRP_L \qquad [14.3]$$

In the special case of an infinitely elastic labor supply ($MC_L = w$) Equations 14.2 and 14.3 are identical. However, if the firm faces a positively sloped labor supply curve, Equation 14.3 dictates a different level of input choice as we will now show.

A Graphic Analysis

The monopsonist's choice of labor input is illustrated in Figure 14.2. The firm's demand curve for labor (D) is drawn negatively sloped, as we have shown it must be. Here also the MC_L curve associated with the labor supply curve (S) is constructed in much the same way that the marginal revenue curve associated with a demand curve can be constructed. Because S is positively sloped, the MC_L curve lies everywhere above S. The profit-maximizing level of labor input for the monopsonist is given by L_1, for at this level of input the condition of equation (14.3) holds. At L_1 the wage rate in the market is given by w_1. Notice that the quantity of labor demanded falls short of that which would be hired in a perfectly competitive labor market (L^*). The firm has restricted input demand by virtue of its monopsonistic position in the market. The formal similarities between this analysis and the monopoly analysis we presented in Chapter 11 should be clear. In particular, the "demand curve" for a monopsonist consists of a single point. In Figure 14.2 this point is given by L_1, w_1. The monopsonist has chosen this point as the most desirable of all those points on the supply curve S. A different point will not be chosen unless some external change (such as a shift in the demand for the firm's output or a change in technology) affects labor's marginal revenue product.

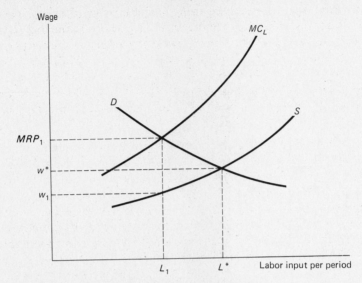

Figure 14.2 / Pricing in a Monopsonistic Labor Market

If a firm faces a positively sloped supply curve for labor (S) it will base its decisions on the "marginal expense" of labor curve (MC_L). Because S is positively sloped, MC_L lies above S. The curve S can be thought of as an "average cost of labor curve," and the MC_L curve is marginal to S. At L_1 the equilibrium condition $MC_L = MRP_L$ holds and this quantity will be hired at a market wage rate w_1.

Monopsonistic Exploitation

In addition to restricting its input demand, the monopsonist also pays inputs less than their marginal revenue product. This result is also illustrated in Figure 14.2. At the monopsonist's preferred choice of labor input (L_1) a wage of w_1 prevails in the market. But for this level of input demand, labor's marginal revenue product is equal to MRP_1: this is the amount of extra revenue that hiring another worker would provide to the firm. Hence, at L_1 the monopsonist pays workers less than they are "worth" to the firm. In the absence of effective competition the monopsonist can persist in this behavior. Some authors refer to this gap between an input's MRP and its market price as (monopsonistic) *exploitation*. It should be clear from Figure 14.2 that the extent of this exploitation will be greater the more inelastic the supply of labor is to the monopsonist.

Examples of Monopsony

To practice monopsonistic exploitation a firm must possess considerable power in the market for a particular input. If the market is reasonably competitive, monopsonistic exploitation cannot occur because other firms will recognize the profit potential reflected in the gap between MRP's and input costs. They will therefore bid for these inputs, driving their prices to equality with marginal revenue products. Under such conditions the supply of labor to any one firm will be nearly infinitely elastic (because of the alternative employment possibilities available) and monopsonistic exploitation will be impossible. Our analysis therefore suggests monopsonistic behavior will be observed in real-world situations in which, for some reason, effective competition for inputs is lacking. We will now examine three causes of such an absence of competition: geography, specialized employment, and monopsonistic cartels.

Geography

Some firms may occupy a monopsonistic position by being the only source of employment in a small town. Because moving costs for workers are high, alternative employment opportunities for local workers are unattractive and the firm may be able to exert a strong effect on wages paid. This possibility may, in part, explain the low wage rates that prevailed in the southern United States prior to World War II. Many small southern towns had isolated labor markets that were dominated by one or two firms. The term "company town" originated in this situation and carried a connotation of exploitation that may have been appropriate. A number of factors have been at work since World War II, however, that have tended to undermine these monopsonistic positions. The population has become more willing to relocate in response to wage rate differences. Similarly, the entry of new firms into southern labor markets (together with improved methods of commuting to work) has further improved workers' alternative earnings possibilities. Finally, "noncompetitive" forces, such as increasing unionization and the expansion of the minimum wage law, have probably also had an effect on monopsonistic practices.

Specialized Employment

It may sometimes be the case that only one firm hires a particularly specialized type of input. If the alternative earnings prospects for that input are unattractive, its supply to the firm will be inelastic, thereby presenting the firm with the opportunity for monopsonistic behavior. For example, marine engineers with many years of experience in designing nuclear submarines must work for the one or two companies that produce such vessels. Because other jobs would not make use of their specialized training, alternative employment is not particularly attractive. Similarly, experienced telephone circuit designers find they have to work for AT&T if they wish to capitalize on their skills. As a nonlabor example, the McDonald's Corporation for many years bought more than 50 percent of all frozen french fried potatoes produced in the United States; the corporation probably occupied a monopsonistic position in that market.

These examples suggest that monopsonistic hiring of specialized inputs is often associated with a monopoly position in the sale of an output (nuclear submarines, telephone service, french fries, and so forth). A particularly prevalent example of this relationship is in hiring by the Federal government. Since the government occupies a monopoly position in the production of a number of goods requiring specialized inputs (space travel, armed forces, and national political offices, to name a few), it would be expected to be in the position to exercise monopsony power. Because it is very difficult to define and measure the marginal revenue product of labor in some of these occupations, however, it is impossible to test empirically for the presence of such behavior.

■ An Example of Monopsonistic Cartels: The Case of Professional Baseball

Our discussion of production cartels in Chapter 12 suggested that firms may be able to obtain monopoly profits by coordinating their output decisions. An identical argument can be made about firms' input decisions. If firms can coordinate their hiring, they can behave monopsonistically even though each firm individually has limited market powers. Usually this type of coordination is impossible because it is costly (or illegal) to enforce such agreements and, as in the monopoly case, there exist incentives to cheat (here chiseling takes the form of raising wage offers). Occasionally, however, powerful cartels can achieve a successful monopsony. An important example is provided by major league baseball teams during the period in which the "Reserve Clause" was in effect. That clause, combined with the system of player "drafts," effectively bound each player to a single team and prevented interteam competition for salaries. Even though there were 18 major league clubs (firms), their hiring was effectively cartelized—thereby creating the potential for monopsonistic exploitation.

Numerical estimates of the degree of exploitation in major league baseball were constructed by G. W. Scully in a 1974 article.[3] Because baseball players' salaries are, more or less, a matter of public record, the principal problem the author faced in measuring the effect of monopsony was to estimate the players' marginal revenue products. He adopted a two-step procedure. First, he examined the correlation between a team's winning percentage and its attendance figures. He concluded that winning did indeed produce additional revenues. Next he analyzed which aspects of individual player performance were most closely related to a team's overall performance. Two significant variables were identified: for hitters, the "slugging average" seemed most important, whereas for pitchers, the ratio of strike-outs to walks proved most relevant. Using statistics on these performance measures, Scully was then able to estimate marginal revenue products for players of differing abilities and compare these estimates to their salaries for the year 1969. A few of the author's estimates are presented in Table 14.1. These data show that most players' MRP's exceed their salaries by a substantial margin. Only for players with poor measures of performance do training and other costs result in

[3]G. W. Scully, "Pay and Performance in Major League Baseball," *American Economic Review*, LXIV, No. 6 (December 1974), pp. 915–930.

Table 14.1 / Monopsonistic Exploitation in Major League Baseball, 1969

Slugging Average	Hitters' Net[1] MRP	Estimated Salary
255	$-39,100	$ 9,700
305	103,600	14,100
350	137,800	32,700
375	156,800	39,000
427	296,500	42,200
490	350,400	60,500
525	383,700	68,000

Ratio of Strikeouts to Walks	Pitchers' Net[1] MRP	Estimated Salary
1.50	$-20,800	$ 9,000
2.00	132,000	16,500
2.30	169,200	36,900
2.79	349,600	47,200
3.09	405,300	66,800
3.54	479,700	86,300

[1]Estimated gross MRP less training and related costs. For poor players the net figure is negative.
Source: G. W. Scully, "Pay and Performance in Major League Baseball," *American Economic Review,* LXIV, No. 6 (December 1974), p. 928.

low, or even negative *MRP*'s. Hence the author concluded that, in 1969, there was significant monopsonistic exploitation of better major league players. Of course, it was only a matter of time before players came to recognize the cartelizing effect of the reserve clause and took organized action against it. A players' strike in 1972 (coupled with legal action in a suit brought by baseball outfielder Curt Flood) eventually led to the adoption of a "free agent" provision in players' contracts as a partial replacement of the reserve clause. Recent spectacular contract settlements for some star players are indicative of the bidding competition that followed the breakdown of the cartel.

Discrimination in Hiring

If a monopsony can segregate the supply of a factor into two or more distinct markets, it may be able to increase profits. For example, a monopsony may be able to discriminate in hiring between men and women. Because the firm can readily identify which market a prospective employee belongs to, it will find it profitable to pay different wages in the two markets. Such a situation is shown in Figure 14.3. The assumptions that men and women are equally productive and that the firm has a constant marginal revenue product of labor no matter how much labor is hired is shown by the horizontal MRP_L curve. The supply curves for men and women are shown in the figure as sharing the same vertical axis. Given these supply curves the firm will choose that quantity of labor in each market for which the marginal

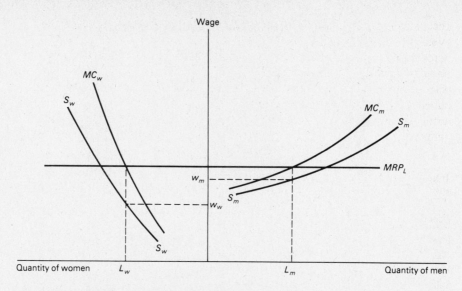

Figure 14.3 / Discrimination in Hiring by a Monopsonist

By segregating the labor market, say between men and women, a monopsonist will minimize labor costs by choosing those quantities of labor such that the marginal revenue product of labor is equal to the marginal expense in each market. In this diagram, the wages of women (w_w) will be below the wages of men (w_m) even though the marginal revenue product for both types of labor is identical.

expense (MC_L) is equal to labor's marginal revenue product. Consequently, the firm will hire L_m from the men's market and L_w from the women's. The wage rate in the two markets will be w_m and w_w, respectively. The way we have drawn Figure 14.3, men's wages will exceed women's, and this happens because women's labor supply is relatively inelastic.[4]

A similar analysis can be developed for any situation in which a monopsony can segregate the market for its inputs into two separate parts. In order to do so, it must be able to identify workers as belonging to particular markets so that its segmentation strategy will work: It must know how much of each kind of worker it is hiring. For this reason, wage discrimination among geographically distinct labor markets or among individuals with readily identifiable personal characteristics (sex, race, age) would be expected to be the types of discrimination most often encountered.

■ An Example: Racial Discrimination

There is considerable evidence of wage discrimination along racial lines in U.S. labor markets. For example, Table 14.2 shows median earnings in different

---

[4]Women may, for example, have a more inelastic supply curve because they have relatively few employment alternatives.

occupations for black and white males for the year 1969. Overall black earnings averaged about two-thirds that of whites; within occupations, ratios below 80 percent were common.[5] Although some part of these black-white differences may be explainable by "objective" characteristics (for example, age or educational differences), a number of statistical studies have found that the racial gap in earnings persists after controlling for these factors. Such findings are in general accord with the monopsony model of labor market discrimination. However, it is hard to believe that monopsony can be an important explanation for the amount of

Table 14.2 / Median Annual Earnings of Blacks and Whites in the Experienced Civilian Labor Force, 1969

Occupation	Median Earnings for Blacks	Median Earnings for Whites	Ratio: Black to White
Professional, Technical and Kindred Workers	$7,763	$10,843	0.72
Managers and Administrators	7,439	11,367	0.65
Sales Workers	5,425	8,532	0.64
Clerical and Kindred Workers	6,157	7,296	0.84
Craftspeople	5,920	8,321	0.71
Operatives, except Transport	5,582	6,894	0.81
Transport Equipment Operatives	5,431	7,149	0.76
Laborers, except Farm	4,207	4,721	0.89
Farm Laborers	1,862	2,723	0.68
Service Workers	4,359	5,249	0.83
Private Household Workers	5,194	4,837	1.06
Total	5,194	7,840	0.66

Source: Calculated from U.S. Bureau of the Census, *Statistical Abstract of the United States, 1977* (98th Edition, Washington, D.C., 1977). Table 662.

discrimination that is observed. Very few (if any) firms in the United States are the only employer in the labor market from which they draw. If we are to apply the simple monopsony model, it must be assumed that all the firms in a particular labor market are able to collude perfectly in their discriminatory hiring decisions. Since economists generally believe that such collusion is very difficult to achieve (again there are incentives to cheat on any collusive agreement that is reached), they have instead turned their attention to examining how discrimination might arise in a competitive labor market. By understanding how discrimination arises in competitive markets, economists are in a position to suggest ways to combat it.

---

[5]The overall ratio is lower than the ratio within occupations because blacks were under-represented in the more highly paid occupations.

Wage Discrimination in Competitive Markets

An initial observation to be made about discrimination in a competitive market is that it is costly to the discriminator. For example, a firm that decides not to hire black workers is raising its labor costs over what they would be if it hired workers solely on the basis of their skills. Similarly, a worker who refuses to work with black workers is lowering the possible wage he might receive if he did not foreclose some of the employment options available. Finally, consumers who refuse to buy from black-owned firms may be making their consumption choices more costly than those choices otherwise would be. Of course, discrimination does tend to persist and this fact indicates that firms, workers, and consumers are willing to pay these costs. For some reason individuals have a "taste for discrimination" and are willing to allocate resources to satisfy this taste. The importance of this observation is to demonstrate that discrimination is costly not only to those being discriminated against, but also to those doing the discriminating. Total income of both groups would be higher in the absence of discrimination.[6]

Following from this analysis is the natural policy question, what should be done about tastes for discrimination? In part, these "tastes" are based on ignorance. Employers, for example, may discriminate against black workers because they (incorrectly) believe that these workers have lower productivities. A policy of providing information to employers may alter these perceptions. More significantly, governmental "Equal Opportunity" and "Affirmative Action" programs may lead firms to make hiring decisions they would not freely make; as a result, they may gain more accurate information about true productivities. Similarly, active antimonopoly (and antimonopsony) policies may also be beneficial if they can prevent wage discrimination through market segmentation. But, to the extent wage discrimination is based on historical and deep-rooted prejudices, it is clear that additional, perhaps "non-economic" policies are also required.

Summary

Imperfect competition can affect factor pricing in three ways. First, if the firms that hire factors sell their products under imperfectly competitive conditions, those conditions will also be reflected in the firms' derived demands for inputs. In particular, firms' demands will be based on the marginal revenue obtainable from

---

[6]One of the first economists to study discrimination in detail was Gary S. Becker. In his book *The Economics of Discrimination* (Chicago: University of Chicago Press, 1957), he develops a simple model that shows that discrimination harms both the majority and minority groups. This finding is in contrast to other views that discrimination in some way benefits the discriminator. Becker shows that discrimination in employment may indeed aid white workers, but it will hurt white owners of capital and total white income will decline. For a more recent analysis with somewhat different conclusions see K. J. Arrow, "Models of Job Discrimination," in A. Pascal (ed.), *Racial Discrimination in Economic Life* (Lexington, Mass.: D. C. Heath and Company, 1972), pp. 83–102.

extra sales rather than on the market price of those sales. To take account of this, we introduced the concept of marginal revenue product as a generalization of the marginal value product concept introduced in Chapter 13.

Monopsonistic power is the second way in which imperfect competition may affect factor pricing. If a firm faces a positively sloped supply curve for the factors it rents, profits can be maximized by restricting demand for those factors. This is accomplished by hiring that quantity of a factor for which the marginal expense of hiring one more unit is equal to that unit's marginal revenue product.

Finally, although we did not explicitly examine this case here, it is possible that the suppliers of a factor may be able to form a monopoly. In this case the analysis of market pricing is similar to that for any monopoly: The supplier may choose that point on the factor's demand curve that it regards as most desirable. In the next chapter we will investigate such a possibility for the case of a labor union that possesses a monopoly in the supply of labor.

Suggested Readings

Ashenfelter, O., "Changes in Labor Market Discrimination over Time," *Journal of Human Resources* 5 (Fall 1970), pp. 1–25.

Becker, G., *The Economics of Discrimination,* 2d ed. (Chicago: University of Chicago Press, 1971).

Bordcherding, T. E., "A Neglected Social Cost of a Voluntary Military," *American Economic Review* 61 (March 1971), pp. 195–196.

Ferguson, C. E., *Microeconomic Theory,* 3d ed. (Homewood, Ill.: Richard D. Irwin, Inc., 1972), chap. 14.

Henderson, J. M., and Quandt, R. E., *Microeconomic Theory,* 2d ed. (New York: McGraw-Hill Book Company, Inc., 1971), pp. 239–251.

Malkiel, B. G., and Malkiel, J. A., "Male-Female Pay Differentials in Professional Employment," *American Economic Review* 63 (September 1973), pp. 693–705.

Pascal, A. *Racial Discrimination in Economic Life* (Lexington, Mass.: D.C. Heath and Co., 1972).

Ransom, R. L., and Sutch, R. "The Ex-Slave in the Post-Bellum South: A Study of the Economic Impact of Racism in a Market Environment," *Journal of Economic History* 33 (March 1973), pp. 131–148.

Rottenberg, S., "The Baseball Players' Labor Market," *Journal of Political Economy* 64 (June 1956), pp. 242–258.

Problems

14.1

Under what conditions would you expect the imposition of a minimum wage to:

a) have no effect on wages or on the number of workers employed?

b) increase wages and leave the number of workers unaffected?

c) increase wages and decrease the number of workers?

d) increase both wages and the number of workers?

Use your knowledge of the American economy to argue on *a priori* grounds which of these outcomes (or possibly others) seems, on the whole, the most likely.

14.2

The Ajax Coal Company is the only employer in its area. It can hire any number of female workers or male workers it wishes. The supply curve for women is given by

$$L_f = 100 \, w_f$$
$$MC_f = L_f/50$$

and for men by

$$L_m = 9 \, w_m{}^2$$
$$MC_m = \frac{1}{2} \sqrt{L_m}$$

where w_f and w_m are, respectively, the hourly wage rate paid to female and male workers. Assume that Ajax sells its coal in a perfectly competitive market at $5 per ton and that each worker hired (both men and women) can mine two tons per hour. If the firm wishes to maximize profits, how many female and male workers should be hired and what will the wage rates for these two groups be? How much will Ajax earn in profits per hour on its mining machinery? How will that result compare to one in which Ajax was constrained (say by market forces) to pay all workers the same wage based on the value of their marginal products?

14.3

Suppose the producers of fertilizer are able to form a monopoly cartel in the sale of their product to farmers.

a) How would this cartel operate to maximize the fertilizer industry's profits?

b) How would the operation of the cartel affect the quantity of fertilizer purchased by farmers and the price paid for it?

c) How would the cartel affect farmers' choices between fertilizer and other productive inputs?

d) How would the cartel affect the output of food? On what factors would the quantitative size of this effect depend?

14.4

Assume employers have no "taste for discrimination" against blacks but that the white employees do. A white employee considers his "psychic wage" to be a combination of the money wage and the percentage of blacks in the firm. That is, a white worker demands higher wages in order to work with blacks. Both blacks and whites offer their services in a perfectly competitive market and are equally productive. The wages for whites and blacks are given by

$$v = MRP \; (1 + \text{percent blacks in firm})$$
$$\text{and } w = MRP$$

respectively. How might you expect a cost-minimizing firm to adjust the racial mix of its employees?

14.5

How would you expect the merger of the National Basketball Association and the American Basketball Association to affect players' salaries? What factors might have moderated these effects?

14.6

The Federal Government is the only employer of soldiers legally permitted to recruit employees in the United States. How might hiring be done so as to minimize the costs of a volunteer army? What would determine the extent of monopsonistic exploitation in this market? What factors might mitigate this exploitation?

Chapter 15

The Labor Market

Introduction

In this chapter we will examine some aspects of factor pricing that are particularly related to the labor market. Because we have already discussed questions about the demand for labor (or any other factor) in some detail, we will in this chapter be concerned primarily with analyzing the supply of labor. There are several reasons why a chapter with this focus is presented here. First, the theory of labor supply provides another useful application of the model of individual choice that we developed in Part II. With this model it is possible to explain many of the important trends that have been observed in the United States labor market. These include the decline in the average work week since the 1890s and the marked increase in the labor force participation of women in the postwar period. A second reason for examining the economics of labor supply is to provide some insight into the job choices individuals make. The concept of compensating differentials that we will develop for this purpose also has uses that extend far beyond traditional questions of occupational choice. Finally, analyzing labor supply can provide an opportunity to examine the operation of labor unions. Because unions are important, powerful participants in the labor markets of most Western countries, any treatment of labor supply would be incomplete without such an examination. In addition, the tools used to study union behavior and bargaining can be applied to any situation in which both buyers and sellers exercise some market power. The chapter, therefore, not only applies some of the tools developed previously to new issues, but also presents additional concepts that play an important role in economists' descriptions of the market mechanism.

Allocation of Time

In Part II we analyzed the way in which an individual will choose to allocate a fixed amount of income among a variety of available goods. Individuals must make similar choices in deciding how they will spend their time. The number of hours in a day (or in a year) is absolutely fixed, and time must be used as it "passes by." It is not possible, in a strict sense, to leave some time unutilized today so that it can be used tomorrow. Given this fixed amount of time, any individual must decide how many hours to work, how many hours to spend consuming a wide variety of goods, ranging from cars and television sets to operas; how many hours to devote to self-maintenance; and how many hours to sleep. It is by studying the division of time that individuals choose to make between these activities that economists are able to understand the decision to work. By viewing work as only one of a number of choices open to individuals in the way they allocate their time, it is possible to understand why work decisions may be changed in response to changing opportunities. In the next few sections we will analyze this possiblity.

Simple Two-Good Model

For simplicity, we will assume that there are only two uses to which an individual may devote his or her time, either engaging in market work at a wage rate of w per hour or not working. We will refer to nonwork time as "leisure," but this word is not meant to carry any connotation of idleness. Time that is not spent in market work can be devoted to work in the home, to self-improvement, or to consumption (it takes time to use a television set or a bowling ball).[1] All of those activities contribute to an individual's well being, and time will be allocated to them in what might be assumed to be a utility-maximizing way.

More specifically, let us assume that utility depends on consumption of market goods (C) and on the amount of leisure time (H) available. Figure 15.1 presents an indifference curve map for this utility function. The diagram has the familiar shape we first introduced in Chapter 3, and it shows those combinations of C and H that

---

[1]This section draws on the fascinating analysis presented by S. B. Linder in *The Harried Leisure Class* (New York: Columbia University Press, 1970). The author investigates various demands on leisure time and the increasing scarcity of time in developed nations. His discussions of cooking, religion, and sexual practices are particularly recommended.

A more theoretical treatment of the allocation of time is given by G. S. Becker in "A Theory of the Allocation of Time," *The Economic Journal* 75 (September 1965), pp. 493–517. The author treats the household as both a provider of labor services and a producer of utility, which is made by combining time with goods. The household is then seen to be bound by a time constraint and must allocate available time between a number of activities. The implications drawn by Becker are far-reaching and affect most of the traditional theory of individual behavior.

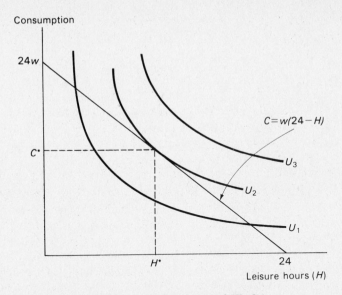

Figure 15.1 / Utility-maximizing Choice of Hours of Work

Given the budget constraint $C = w(24 - H)$, where w is the real wage rate, an individual will maximize utility by choosing to work $(24 - H^*)$ hours and to consume C^*. At this point, the rate at which he or she is willing to trade H for C (the MRS) is equal to the rate at which he or she is able to trade these in the market (w).

yield an individual various levels of utility. To discuss utility maximization we must first analyze the budget constraint that faces any individual. If the period we are studying is one day, the individual will work $24 - H$ hours. For this work she or he will earn $w(24 - H)$ and will use this to buy consumption goods (C). Consequently the budget constraint is given by

$$C = w(24 - H) \qquad [15.1]$$

This equation shows how an individual can trade hours of leisure for consumption in the market. Each additional hour of leisure taken reduces income (and consumption) by w dollars. The wage rate in equation 15.1 should be considered a "real" wage rate; that is, we are interested in how hours of work "pay off" in physical units of consumption. A money wage rate of $.25 per hour provides the same real purchasing power when the typical consumption item costs $1.00 as does a money wage of $2.00 per hour when this typical item costs $8.00. In either case, the individual must work 4 hours in order to be able to purchase the item.

Full Income and the Opportunity Cost of Leisure

An alternative way of writing the budget constraint is:

$$C + wH = 24 \cdot w \qquad [15.2]$$

Equation 15.2 records the fact that any individual has a "full income" of $24 \cdot w$. This is the income that could be earned if the individual were willing to work 24 hours a day. Full income can be devoted to two purposes: buying consumption or "buying" leisure. Equation 15.2 clearly demonstrates that leisure costs w per hour. Each hour of leisure taken reduces income available for consumption by w dollars. Economists would say that the opportunity cost of leisure is given by the wage rate. Later in this chapter we shall show how recognizing this opportunity cost can explain a number of examples of how individuals use their time.

Utility Maximization

Utility maximization can be shown by superimposing the budget constraint (equation 15.1 or 15.2) onto the indifference curve map in Figure 15.1. Given this constraint, the individual will choose to take H^* hours of leisure and to work the remaining time. With the income earned from this work $[= w(24 - H^*)]$ he or she will be able to purchase C^* units of consumption goods. At the utility-maximizing point, the slope of the budget constraint $(-w)$ is equal to the slope of indifference curve U_2. Consequently, we have:

Optimization Principle

In order to maximize utility, an individual will choose to work that number of hours for which the marginal rate of substitution of leisure hours for consumption is equal to the real wage rate he or she can earn. Mathematically, for a utility maximum it is required that

$$MRS \text{ (of } H \text{ for } C) = w \qquad [15.3]$$

In other words, the individual will choose a bundle of leisure and consumption such that the rate at which he or she is willing to trade H for C is equal to the rate at which he or she is able to trade them in the market. If this were not true, utility would not be as large as possible. For example, suppose an individual's MRS were equal to 2, indicating willingness to give up 2 units of consumption to get an additional hour of leisure. Suppose, on the other hand, that the real wage is $4 so that by working one more hour the individual is able to earn enough to buy 4 units (that is, 4 dollars' worth) of consumption. This is clearly an inefficient situation. By increasing work by 1 hour, the individual can buy 4 extra units of consumption. But compensation of only 2 units of consumption was required to make him or her as well off as before. By working the extra hour the individual earns $2 (= 4 - 2)$ units of consumption more than required. Consequently he or she could not have been maximizing utility in the initial situation. A similar proof can be constructed for any case in which the individual's psychic trade-off rate differs from the rate at which labor can be traded for consumption in the market.

Flexibility of Work

Before turning to examine how labor-leisure choices might be affected by a change in the real wage rate, it is important to ask whether the theory developed here has any relevance to the real-world decisions individuals must make. While individuals are relatively free to determine what they will do in their spare time, it might be argued that they do not have the freedom of choice in selecting their own hours of work, which is implied by the time allocation model. Most jobs require work time of approximately 40 hours per week, and this figure is not very flexible (at least in the short run) in response to individuals' desires. Nevertheless, the freedom of choice in hours of work that we have been assuming may be justified in several ways. First, the model may be taken to apply to a very long period, perhaps the individual's lifetime. Over such a period there is considerable flexibility in the number of hours to be worked since the individual may choose to work 40 hours during some weeks (or years) and 0 hours during others. By moving in and out of the labor market at different stages in his or her lifetime, the individual can adjust hours of work rather precisely. A second and similar justification for the model is to regard it as applying to the "average" person. At any one point of time, some individuals will work 40 hours and others will not work. Consequently, average hours of work will depend on how many people fall into each category. If nearly everyone works, the "average" person will work about 40 hours, whereas if no one works, the "average" person will work 0 hours. If 50 percent of all individuals work 40 hours and 50 percent do not work, the "average" person will be working 20 hours. A final way to justify the assumption of time flexibility is to note that individuals do have considerable freedom in choosing the jobs they will take. By choosing among the comforts and discomforts of particular jobs the individual can be thought of as making a "marginal" choice, even though hours of work are institutionally fixed. For example, an individual in taking a low-paying job as a surfing instructor can be regarded as choosing an occupation with a significant leisure component, and he is thereby adjusting his hours of "actual" work. We will return to examine some additional questions about occupational choice in the section of this chapter on compensating wage differentials.

Income and Substitution Effects of a Change in the Real Wage Rate

A change in the real wage rate (w) can be analyzed in a manner identical to that we used in Chapter 4. When w rises, the "price" of leisure becomes higher—the individual must give up more in lost wages for each hour of leisure he consumes. The substitution effect of an increase in w on the hours of leisure will therefore be negative. As leisure becomes more expensive there is reason to consume less of it. However, the income effect will be positive—since leisure is a normal good, the higher income resulting from a higher w will increase the demand for leisure. Hence the income and substitution effects work in the opposite direction. It is impossible to predict on *a priori* grounds whether an increase in w will increase or decrease the demand for leisure time. Since leisure and work are mutually exclusive ways to spend one's time, it is also true that it is impossible to predict what will happen to the number of hours worked. The substitution effect tends to increase hours worked when w increases; whereas the income effect, because it increases the demand for leisure time, tends to decrease the number of hours worked. Which of these two effects is the stronger is an important empirical question.[2]

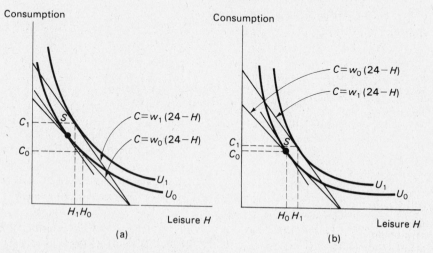

Figure 15.2 / Income and Substitution Effects of a Change in the Real Wage Rate (w)

Since the individual is a supplier of labor, the income and substitution effects of an increase in the real wage rate *(w)* work in opposite directions in their effect on the hours of leisure demanded (or on hours of work). In Figure 15.2a the substitution effect (movement to point S) outweighs the income effect, and a higher wage causes hours of leisure to decline to H_1. Hours of work therefore increase. In 15.2b, the income effect is stronger than the substitution effect, and H increases to H_1. Hours of work in this case fall.

A Graphic Analysis

Figure 15.2 illustrates two possible reactions to a change in w. In both graphs the initial wage rate is w_0, and the optimal choices of C and H are given by C_0 and H_0. When the wage rate increases to w_1 the utility maximizing combination moves to C_1, H_1. This movement can be decomposed into two effects. The substitution effect can be represented by the movement along the indifference curve U_0 from C_0, H_0 to S. This effect works to reduce the number of hours of leisure in 15.2a and 15.2b.

---

[2]If the family is taken to be the relevant decision unit, even more interesting questions arise about the income and substitution effects that changes in the wages of one family member, say the husband, will have on the labor force behavior of other family members, for example, the wife.

Individuals substitute consumption for leisure since the relative price of leisure has increased. The movement from S to C_1, H_1 represents the positive income effect of a higher real wage. It is assumed that leisure time is a normal good and that increases in income will cause more leisure to be demanded. Consequently, the income and substitution effects induced by the increase in w work in opposite directions. In Figure 15.2a the demand for leisure is reduced, that is, the substitution effect outweighs the income effect. On the other hand, in Figure 15.2b the income effect is stronger, and the demand for leisure increases in response to an increase in w. The individual actually chooses to work fewer hours when w increases. In the analysis of Part II we would have considered this result unusual—when the price of leisure rises, the individual demands more of it. For the case of consumption goods, income and substitution effects usually work in the same direction, and both cause quantity to decline when price increases. In the case of leisure and consumption, income and substitution effects work in opposite directions. An increase in w makes an individual better off because he or she is a *supplier* of labor. In the case of a consumption good, an individual is made worse off by a rise in price because she or he is a *consumer* of that good. We can therefore summarize our results by:

Optimization Principle

When the real wage rate increases a utility maximizing individual may increase or decrease hours worked. The substitution effect will tend to increase hours worked as the individual substitutes earnings for leisure. The income effect, on the other hand, will tend to reduce hours worked as the individual uses his or her increased purchasing power to "buy" more leisure time.

Individual Supply Curve for Labor

Using the analysis of the previous section, we can now discuss labor supply in detail. In Figure 15.3 we have drawn an individual's supply of labor curve by calculating the number of hours he or she is willing to work at every possible real wage rate. Such a curve might resemble that shown in Figure 15.3a. There the individual's labor supply curve is drawn with a positive slope: At higher real wage rates the individual chooses to work longer hours. The substitution effect of a higher wage outweighs the income effect. This need not always be the case, however, as 15.3b demonstrates. There the supply curve is "backward bending"—once real wages exceed a certain level, even higher wage rates induce the individual to work fewer hours. Such a curve is entirely consistent with the theory of the allocation of time we have developed. At relatively high wage rates, an increase in the wage may cause individuals to choose to work fewer hours, since the income effect may be stronger than the substitution effect. The individual uses the higher real wage rate to "buy" more leisure.

An important empirical question is whether individual labor supply curves more nearly resemble that shown in Figure 15.3a or that shown in 15.3b. Although there

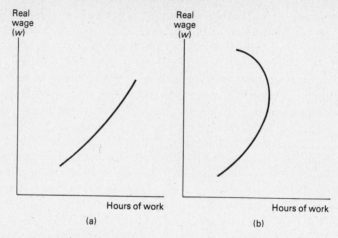

**Figure 15.3 / Two Shapes for an
Individual's Supply Curve for Labor**

In 15.3a a higher real wage induces the individual to supply more labor. The substitution effect of the
higher wage outweighs the income effect. in 15.3b, on the other hand, the supply curve of labor is
backward bending. For relatively high wage rates, the income effect of a higher wage outweighs the
substitution effect and causes the individual to demand more leisure.

is substantial evidence that short-run labor supply curves have a positive slope
(consider, for example, the positive effect on hours of work that offering higher
overtime wages has), it appears that over the long run individual supply curves may
have at times been backward bending. In 1890 the average work week in the United
States in the manufacturing industry was about 60 hours. Real wages in 1890 were
about $1.00 per hour (in terms of 1970 consumption prices). By 1929 the work
week in manufacturing had dropped to 40 hours, in spite of the fact that real wages
had risen to about $1.80 per hour. American workers chose to take some of their
increasing incomes in the form of leisure, and this is consistent with the notion of a
backward-bending supply curve. Since 1929, real wages in manufacturing have
continued to rise (to about $3.50 per hour in 1976), but the work week has not fallen
much below 40 hours per week. It appears that in recent years the substitution effect
of higher wages has almost exactly balanced the income effect—at least for
manufacturing workers.

Market Supply Curve for Labor

We can construct a market supply of labor curve from individual supply curves by
horizontal "summation." At each possible wage rate, we would add together the
quantity of labor offered by each individual in order to arrive at a market total. One
particularly interesting aspect of this procedure is that as the wage rate rises, more
individuals may be induced to enter the labor force. Figure 15.4 illustrates this
possibility for the simple case of two individuals. For a real wage below w_1 neither

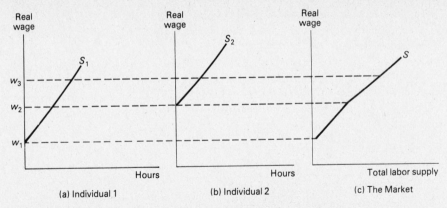

Figure 15.4 / **Construction of the Market Supply Curve for Labor**

As the real wage rises there are two reasons why the supply of labor may increase. First, higher real wages may cause each individual to work more hours. Second, higher wages may induce more individuals (for example, individual 2) to enter the labor market.

individual chooses to work. Consequently, the market supply curve of labor (Figure 15.4c) shows that no labor is supplied at real wages below w_1. A wage in excess of w_1 causes individual 1 to enter the labor market. However, so long as wages fall short of w_2, individual 2 will not work. Only at a wage rate above w_2 will both individuals participate in the labor market. In general, the possibility of the entry of new workers makes the market supply of labor somewhat more responsive to wage rate increases than would be the case if we assumed that the number of workers were fixed.

Two Examples of Labor Supply

Increasing Labor Force Participation by Married Women

The most important example of higher real wage rates inducing increased labor force participation is the labor force behavior of married women in the United States in the post-World War II period. Since about 1950 the percentage of working married women has increased from 30 percent to 46 percent; economists attribute this, at least in part, to the increasing wages that women are able to earn. In recent years a substantial portion of the annual increase in the size of the labor force has been provided by the increasing tendency for married women to work. Both recent attitudinal changes and the upward rise in real wage rates suggest that this trend will continue.

There are, however, two curious facts about the recent increases in married women's participation rates. First, the pattern for women is opposite to that of men: Increasing wage rates have induced an increase in labor supplied for women and a decrease (in the form of early retirement) for men. Are women really different from men in labor force behavior, or are there other factors (such as the alternative uses to which men and women can put their time) that explain this difference? A second anomaly derives from the findings of studies showing that wives of high-income husbands are less likely to work than are wives of low-income husbands. Over time, however, all wives have increased their working despite the fact that husbands' incomes also have increased. Economists have developed a number of theories to explain these occurrences.[3]

Supply to an Occupation: The Volunteer Army and the Draft

So far our discussion of labor supply has been concerned primarily with the question of the total supply of labor to all potential employers. In such a case it might be expected that the supply curve would be relatively inelastic because most individuals have only limited alternative uses for their time. The supply of labor to a particular occupation, however, is likely to be considerably more elastic. Rising wages in the market for one type of labor service will not only prompt an additional supply of labor through the mechanisms analyzed previously (longer hours and increased labor force participation), but, more importantly, can also attract workers from other employments. Small changes in (relative) wages may attract a substantially increased supply to an occupation.

The question of the elasticity of the supply of labor played an important role in the mid-1960s debate over the costs of establishing an all-volunteer army in the United States. If the supply of labor to the military were elastic, volunteers could be attracted with relatively small increments to existing pay schedules. An inelastic supply, on the other hand, would create sharp increases in defense costs as a result of the elimination of military conscription. To study this issue, W. Y. Oi (in a 1967 study) calculated a supply curve for military personnel.[4] His basic results are presented in Table 15.1. There is clear evidence that increases in military pay encourage enlistments. For example, Oi showed that an increase in the first term pay of enlistees from the then present level of $2,500 to a level more nearly approximating civilian wages (about $3,600 for unskilled 18-year olds in 1965) would have increased enlistments by 40 percent. Notice, however, that the supply curve tended to become more inelastic as potential wages were raised still further. Raising wages from $4,700 to $5,900 would attract only 13 percent more enlistments. This may indicate that some individuals' feelings about serving in the military vary widely across the population and those with preferences against serving can be attracted only at very high wages.

---

[3]See, for example, J. Mincer, "Labor Force Participation of Married Women," in *Aspects of Labor Economics* (New York: National Bureau of Economic Research, 1962), pp. 63–105.

[4]W. Y. Oi, "The Economic Cost of the Draft," *American Economic Review,* LVII, No. 2 (May 1967), pp. 39–62.

Table 15.1 / Supply Curve of Voluntary Enlistments in the Armed Forces in 1965

Annual First Term Pay	Enlistments (thousands)
$2,500	260
$3,600	365
$4,700	415
$5,900	470

Source: W. Y. Oi, "The Economic Cost of the Draft," *American Economic Review,* LVII, No. 2 (May 1967), pp. 39–62.

In addition to estimating the cost of a volunteer army, one of the goals of Oi's study was to calculate the economic burden of the military draft that was then in effect. Costs of the draft fell on two types of individuals: those who were actually drafted and those who were "reluctant volunteers" in that they volunteered for service only because of fear of the draft. In 1965 Oi estimated that, out of a total of 470,000 enlistments, 260,000 were "true" volunteers, 155,000 were reluctant volunteers, and 55,000 were draftees. Assuming that draftees would require a greater pay inducement to enter the armed forces voluntarily than would the reluctant volunteers, Oi conjectured that the typical individual in the latter group would have volunteered (in the absence of a draft) at a wage about halfway between $2,500 (at which level none would have volunteered) and $4,700 (at which level all 155,000 would volunteer). Hence the annual cost of the draft of reluctant volunteers was about $186 million ($3,600 required pay, less $2,500 actual pay, times 155,000).

Oi hypothesized that the wage necessary to attract actual draftees into the army was considerably above that for reluctant volunteers. Taking the rather arbitrary estimate of $5,900 as the minimum wage necessary to attract the typical draftee, he calculated a total annual cost to draftees of $138 million ($5,900 required pay, less $2,500 actual pay, times 55,000). Adding that cost to the cost that the draft imposed on reluctant volunteers, Oi concluded that the annual cost to enlistees was about $324 million. Since enlistees usually serve about 2½ years, the total cost of the draft to one year's group of enlistees was put at $810 million or over $3,800 per draft-related enlistee.[5] Even these high costs ignored other costs that the draft imposed on non-enlistees. Such costs included: taking less preferred, but draft-exempt jobs; staying in school longer to escape the draft; seeking medical exemptions or conscientious objector status; or illegal draft evasion. Political opposition to the draft in the late 1960s suggested that these costs were substantial.

---

[5]For pedagogic purposes Oi's calculations have been simplified in this example and they do not correspond exactly to those in the original article. Also, it should be pointed out that the cost figures do not include forgone rents that would be earned by "true" volunteers in moving to a volunteer army (because they would be paid more under the new pay scales than was necessary to attract them into the army).

■ Other Examples of the Time Allocation Model

Although we have applied the time allocation model only to the case of choices between labor and leisure time, the model itself is quite general. Choices that individuals must make among competing uses of time can usually be analyzed within a utility-maximization framework, and it is often possible to gain considerable insights by proceeding in this way. Here we shall briefly discuss three such additional applications: job search theory, the economics of child bearing, and transportation choices.[6] Each of those applications builds on the observation that the opportunity cost of time spent not working is given by the market wage rate.

Job Search Theory

In seeking new jobs individuals are often faced with considerable uncertainty about available openings. Consequently, they must invest some time (and possibly other resources, such as phone calls or the placing of advertisements) in finding a suitable job match. To the extent that individuals must reduce potential work time to accommodate their job search plans, the hourly cost of search can be approximated by the market wage. The higher is an individual's market wage, the more likely he or she would be to adopt search techniques that economize on time (such as using an employment agency). If, on the other hand, search time is subsidized (say, by receipt of unemployment insurance benefits), it is possible that search time may be prolonged in the hope of finding a better job. For this reason, some economists believe that the existence of unemployment insurance benefits may be one cause of unemployment.[7]

The Economics of Child Bearing

Individuals' decisions to have children are affected by a number of social, religious, and economic factors. Economists have tended to focus primarily on the costs associated with having children and how those costs vary among individuals. One of the most important of those costs is the forgone wages of parents who choose to care for their children rather than to pursue market employment. Indeed, by some estimates, this cost is far in excess of all other costs of child bearing combined. That type of calculation has led some authors to speculate that increasing real wages for women in the United States since World War II is a principal reason for the decline in the birth rate during that period. Since children have become relatively more expensive, people have chosen to "consume" fewer of them. Similarly, lower birth rates in North America and

---

[6] An additional important application of the time allocation model to examining individuals' investments in "human capital" is discussed in Chapter 16.

[7] For a summary of some studies of this effect see D. Hamermesch, *Jobless Pay and the Economy* (Baltimore: Johns Hopkins University Press, 1976).

Western Europe than in the less developed world might be attributed to wage rate differences (and hence cost of children differences) between these regions.[8]

Transportation Choices

In choosing among alternative transportation modes, individuals will take both time and dollar costs into account. Transportation planners are particularly interested in how individuals respond to differences in such costs so that they can predict the effect on demand of improvements in highways or in public transit systems. Most studies have found that individuals are quite sensitive to time costs—especially those associated with walking or waiting.[9] By examining individuals' trade-offs between time and dollar costs, those studies generally conclude that individuals value travel time at between 50 percent and 100 percent of their market wage. These findings then offer further support for the time allocation model. They can be used to put a value on the commuting time saved by better urban transit systems or to explain why individuals choose one method of getting to work rather than another. The notion that the value of time can be approximated by the market wage is therefore an indispensable tool for the development of transportation policy.

Occupational Choice and Compensating Wage Differentials

So far in this chapter we have treated the labor market as a single market. All labor was assumed to be of the same quality and all jobs were assumed to be equally attractive so we could speak of *the* wage rate as being set by supply and demand in one market. In reality, of course, wage rates differ greatly among individuals and among jobs. There are three reasons why these differentials arise. First, workers have different levels of skills. These differences in skills may cause some workers to be more productive than others; in a competitive market for labor, those with greater skills will earn higher wages. Second, some workers may receive wages that are essentially a monopoly rent. If workers can successfully limit access to certain jobs they may succeed in improving their own wages. Finally, wage rates may differ among jobs because some jobs are more pleasant than others. More enjoyable jobs will attract a large supply of applicants, and this may cause the wage rates to be lower than in less desirable ones. In this section we will restrict our attention to this third reason for wage dif-

---

[8]For a seminal contribution to the economics of fertility, see G. Becker, "An Economic Analysis of Fertility," in *Demographic and Economic Change in Developed Countries* (Princeton, N.J.: Princeton University Press, 1960).

[9]See, for example, T. A. Domencich and D. McFadden, *Urban Travel Demand* (Amsterdam: North Holland Press, 1975).

ferentials. Even though we will implicitly assume that all workers are equally skilled and that there are no monopoly elements in the wage-setting process, wage differentials can (and do) arise. We wish to examine this possibility. In Chapter 16 we will briefly discuss differential skill levels in the context of "human capital" theory. We have already (in Chapters 13 and 14) discussed the concept of monopoly rent, and we will return to this subject when we study unions later in this chapter.

The notion that differing characteristics of jobs may lead to differential wages has long been noted by economists. In *The Wealth of Nations,* for example, Smith noted that

> the whole of the advantages and disadvantages of the different employments of labour . . . must, in the same neighbourhood, be either equal or continually tending to equality. If in the same neighbourhood there is any employment either more or less advantageous than the rest, so many people would crowd into it in the one case, and so many would desert it in the other, that its advantages would soon return to the level of other employments . . .
>
> [But] pecuniary wages . . . are everywhere in Europe extremely different according to the different employments of labour . . . this difference arises partly from certain circumstances in the employments themselves, which, either really, or at least in the imaginations of men, make up for a small pecuniary gain in some and counter-balance a great one in others; . . .[10]

Smith then stresses the difference between the "whole advantages and disadvantages" of a particular job and the wages paid for the job. Even with perfect freedom of access to jobs and no skill differentials, wage rate differences can persist because of differences in the attractiveness of certain jobs. The market operates to equate the total attractiveness of jobs, not the pecuniary rewards of these jobs. To capture such effects we define:

Definition

Differences in wage rates that arise because of differing amenities of jobs are said to be *compensating wage differentials.* That is, the wage rate differences "compensate" for the differing job characteristics.

A Graphic Analysis

Figure 15.5 illustrates a simple example of the way in which compensating differentials might arise. It assumes that there are two jobs: one "pleasant," the other "unpleasant." The demand curves of firms for workers to fill those jobs are assumed to be the same for both jobs. There are no differences in the skills of workers that

---

[10]A. Smith, *The Wealth of Nations,* Cannan ed. (New York: The Modern Library, 1937), chap. 10, p. 1.

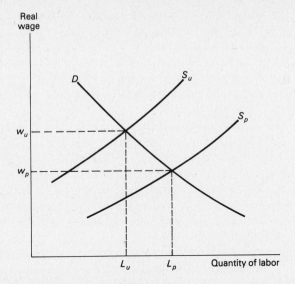

Figure 15.5 / Compensating Wage Differentials

The demand curve for labor is assumed to be the same for both a "pleasant" job and an "unpleasant" one. However, the supply curves (S_p and S_u, respectively) differ for the two types of jobs. This causes wages to differ between the jobs. The higher wage rate for the unpleasant job (w_u) is said to "compensate" for the nature of the job.

might lead to differing demand conditions. The demand curve for both jobs is represented by the curve DD. Because the jobs differ in their attractiveness, the supply of labor to them will differ. The curve S_u represents the supply curve to the unpleasant job, and the equilibrium wage is given by w_u. At this wage firms in the unpleasant industry will demand L_u hours of labor input, and this is what individuals are willing to supply. Similarly, the curve S_p represents the supply curve of workers to the pleasant job. This curve lies to the right of the S_u curve because of the differences in the jobs: At any given wage individuals are willing to supply more labor to the pleasant job. By the interaction of supply and demand, an equilibrium wage rate of w_p will be established for the pleasant job. This wage will be below w_u, and the difference between w_u and w_p is a wage differential that compensates for the unpleasantness of the first job. The equilibrium shown in Figure 15.5 is stable: There is no incentive for a worker to transfer from one job for the other. The net advantages of the two jobs have been equalized.

Examples of Compensating Differentials

It is not hard to find examples of compensating wage differentials in the real world. Probably the most important instances arise between jobs that require identical skills but differ in their riskiness. In the construction industry, for example, iron workers who work on high-rise buildings are paid more than iron workers who stay at ground level. Similarly, laborers engaged in the digging of tunnels are paid more than laborers who dig cut-and-cover trenches. Finally, as we showed in the appendix to Chapter 3, there is some evidence that, on the average, doctors and lawyers in independent professional practice earn more than those working for large firms. In this case the higher mean wage compensates for the greater risk inherent in independent practice.

Other examples of wage differentials that compensate for the disadvantages of a job are commonly encountered. Wages tend to be lower in suburban jobs than in central city jobs, and these differentials serve to compensate for the costs of the trip to work in central cities. Salaries of college professors tend to be below those for other occupations requiring similar skills probably because the academic "life-style" is regarded as being an attractive one. Anyone who has tried to get a summer job knows that lifeguarding pays less than construction work even though similar skills are required.

Obtaining numerical estimates of the size of compensating wage differentials is a difficult and controversial problem. Accurate measurement requires that other influences on wage rates (skills, monopoly or monopsony power, and so forth) be controlled for, so that observed wage differences can be correctly attributable to individuals' supply reactions to the characteristics of jobs. Tables 15.2 and 15.3 provide some very tentative estimates that are intended to capture such effects. Table 15.2 reports the results of a study by R. Thaler and S. Rosen of the way in which differences in the risk of loss of life on a job affect wages.[11] The table shows that jobs that have high mortality rates also have higher annual wages (other

Table 15.2 / Compensating Wage Differentials for Differential Death Rates, by Occupations, 1967

Occupation	Additional Annual Deaths per 100,000	Estimated Increment to Annual Salary (dollars)
Bartenders	179	$315
Boilermakers	230	405
Fire Fighters	44	77
Lumberjacks	256	451
Mine Operatives	176	310
Police and Detectives	78	137
Taxicab Drivers	182	320
Teamsters	114	201

Source: R. Thaler and S. Rosen, "The Value of Saving a Life: Evidence from the Labor Market" in N. E. Terleckyj (ed.), *Household Production and Consumption* (New York: National Bureau of Economic Research, 1975), pp. 265–298. Data computed from Tables 1 and 3.

[11]R. Thaler and S. Rosen, "The Value of Saving a Life: Evidence from the Labor Market" in N. E. Terleckyj (ed.), *Household Production and Consumption* (New York: National Bureau of Economic Research, 1975), pp. 265–298.

things being the same). Thaler and Rosen point out that their data imply that, in 1967, individuals chose among jobs as if they were putting an implicit value of about $176,000 on their own lives. In other words, employees seem willing to accept an increase in the annual probability of dying on a job of *one tenth of one percent* in exchange for $176 extra in annual salary. While that conclusion is controversial and may for a variety of reasons be too low (for instance, it disregards the costs that one person's death may impose on his or her family), there are many situations in which assigning some estimated value for a life is essential. Workplace health and safety legislation, for example, must reach some compromise between the benefits of lifesaving changes in productive techniques and the costs of such changes. Values for lives must, at least implicitly, be used in making such decisions and the Thaler-Rosen study provides a basis for devising a way to assign such values.

Because it is very difficult to define "working conditions" of jobs in objective and quantifiable ways, measuring compensating differentials for "unpleasant" jobs is even more difficult than measuring differentials associated with risk. The results of one attempt at measurement (by R. E. B. Lucas[12]) are reported in Table 15.3. These results show that, on the whole, individuals do seem to receive somewhat higher wages for taking jobs that are repetitive in nature or that require working in an unpleasant environment (that is, one characterized by heat, cold, noise, or some other unpleasant feature). As with the numbers for the death risk of jobs, however, these results should be regarded only as broadly indicative of underlying economic forces. The measurement methods used are too crude to place much faith in the precise values obtained.

Table 15.3 / Compensating Wage
Differentials for Unpleasant Working Conditions in 1967

	Percent Addition to Wage Provided by Job Attribute			
	White Males	Black Males	White Females	Black Females
Repetitive Jobs	10.3	7.7	22.3	25.6
Jobs in a Poor Work Environment	6.8	−7.7	3.3	19.5

Source: R. E. B. Lucas, "Hedonic Wage Equations and Psychic Wages in the Returns to Schooling," *American Economic Review,* Vol. 67, No. 4 (September 1977), Table 1, p. 554.

Labor Unions

Workers may at times find it advantageous to join a labor union in order to pursue goals that can more effectively be accomplished as a group. If association with a

---

[12]R. E. B. Lucas, "Hedonic Wage Equations and Psychic Wages in the Returns to Schooling," *American Economic Review,* Vol. 67, No. 4 (September 1977), Table 1, p. 554.

union were wholly voluntary, it could be assumed that every union member derives benefit from belonging. Compulsory membership (the "closed shop") is, however, frequently enforced in order to maintain the viability of the union organization. If all workers were left on their own to decide on membership, their rational decision might be not to join the union (and hence avoid dues and other restrictions). They would, however, benefit from the higher wages and better working conditions that have been won by the union. What appears to be rational from each individual worker's point of view may prove to be irrational from a group point of view, since the union is undermined by "free riders." Compulsory membership may therefore be a necessary means of maintaining an effective union coalition.[13] In this section we will examine those goals such a coalition might pursue, and how the choice of goals will affect pricing in the labor market.

Unions' Goals

As we did for our discussion of the theory of the firm, we shall start our analysis of union behavior by defining the goals toward which a union strives. A first assumption we might make is that the goals of a union are in some sense an adequate representation of the goals of its members. This assumption avoids the problem of union leadership and disregards the personal aspirations of those leaders, which may be in conflict with rank-and-file goals. Union leaders are therefore assumed to be conduits for expressing the desires of the membership. In the United States union goals have tended to be oriented toward "bread-and-butter" issues. The programs of major unions have not emphasized the promotion of radical social change, except briefly in the early 1900s. Rather, unions have attempted to exert an effect solely in the labor market to which they are suppliers, and in this they have had some success.

Strong unions can be treated in the same way as monopoly firms. The union faces a demand curve for labor; because it is the sole source of supply, it can choose at which point on this curve it will operate. The point that is actually chosen by the union will obviously depend on what particular goals it has decided to pursue. Three possible choices are illustrated in Figure 15.6. The union may, for example, choose to offer that quantity of labor that maximizes the total wage bill $(w \cdot L)$. If this is the case, it will offer that quantity for which the "marginal revenue" from labor demand is equal to zero. This quantity is given by L_1 in Figure 15.6, and the wage rate associated with this quantity is w_1. The point E_1 is therefore the preferred wage-quantity combination. Notice that at wage rate w_1 there may be an excess supply of labor and the union must somehow allocate those jobs that are available to those workers who want them.

---

[13]For a more complete discussion of the issues raised in this and later sections, see J. Dunlop. *Wage Determination Under Trade Unions* (New York: Crowell-Collier and Macmillan, Inc., 1944). A more analytical approach to many of the same issues can be found in A. M. Cartter. *The Theory of Wages and Employment* (Homewood, Ill.: Richard D. Irwin, Inc., 1959).

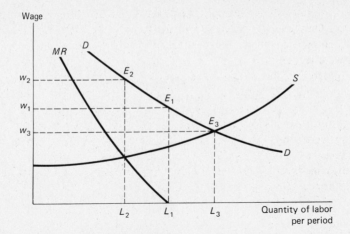

**Figure 15.6 / Three Possible Points on the
Labor Demand Curve That a Monopoly Union Might Choose**

A union has a monopoly in the supply of labor. It may therefore choose that point on the demand curve for labor that it prefers. Three such points are shown in the figure. At point E_1 total labor payments $(w \cdot L)$ are maximized; at E_2 the economic rent that workers receive is maximized; and at E_3 the total amount of labor services supplied is maximized.

Another possible goal that the union may pursue would be to choose the quantity of labor so as to maximize the total economic rent obtained by those members who are employed. This would necessitate choosing that quantity of labor for which the additional total wages obtained by having one more employed union member (the marginal revenue) is equal to the extra cost of luring that member into the market. The union should therefore choose that quantity L_2 at which the marginal revenue curve crosses the supply curve. The wage rate associated with this quantity is w_2, and the desired wage-quantity combination is labeled E_2 in the diagram. Again, this combination requires that some workers who desire to work at the prevailing wage are left unemployed. Perhaps the union may "tax" the large economic rent earned by those who do work in order to transfer income to those who don't.

A third possibility would be for the union to aim for maximum employment of its members. This would involve choosing the point w_3, L_3, which is precisely the point that would result if the market were organized in a perfectly competitive way. No employment greater than L_3 could be achieved, since the quantity of labor that union members supply would be reduced for wages less than w_3.

Other Goals: Job Security and Fringe Benefits

Although the union goals illustrated in Figure 15.6 are those that are easiest to diagram, the list is by no means exhaustive. Two other important goals that unions may seek, for example, are job security and a variety of nonwage "fringe" benefits. The issue of job security is a particularly important one in industries such as durable goods manufacturing or construction, in which there are major cyclical influences on product demand and hence on the demand for labor. Unions may seek to reduce the risks of such fluctuations for their members by establishing contractual "rights" to jobs. In that way the variability in workers' wage incomes will be reduced, and (as we showed in Chapter 3, Appendix) this reduction raises workers' utility. Fringe benefits such as pensions, vacations, insurance coverage, and generally better working conditions are also of considerable value to workers. Because such benefits are frequently of low visibility in negotiating sessions and are often nontaxable to workers, they have come to constitute an increasingly important part of firms' total labor costs.

There are two ways in which recognition of such alternative union (or for that matter, any worker's) goals should be used to modify the analysis presented previously in this chapter. First, the price of labor should be generalized to include indirect forms of compensation in addition to the usual hourly wage rate. Without this generalization it is hard to interpret many market outcomes. Related to this is a second observation: Unions may be willing to forgo wage rate goals to obtain other types of benefits. It would be necessary to introduce considerably more complex diagrams than those we have been using in order to picture these trade-offs.

■ An Example: Unionization of Fire Fighters

Our analysis so far has suggested that unions may, in the absence of effective competition, be able to exert some influence on the terms of labor contracts. In this section we shall examine a particular case: unionization of firemen by the International Association of Fire Fighters (IAFF). The market for fire fighters is one in which it is possible that union influences could be particularly pronounced. Because there is no effective private competition for the services provided by municipal fire departments, once the IAFF gains recognition as the bargaining agent with a city it does not have to be concerned about the erosion of that position. Similarly, a city's demand for fire fighters is likely to be inelastic with respect to wage changes since demand for fire prevention services is itself inelastic and there are few possibilities for substituting capital for labor.

A 1971 study by O. Ashenfelter tended to support the presumption that unionization of fire fighters can have significant labor market effects.[14] Table 15.4 summarizes Ashenfelter's findings for 1966 for small- (population 25–50,000) and moderate-size (population 50–100,000) cities. Three bargaining goals of the IAFF were examined: hourly wage rates, annual salaries, and weekly hours of work. The hours-of-work goal was included because firemen typically work long hours on duty waiting for calls (the typical work week is about 56 hours) and there is some public sympathy for reductions in those hours. Of course, a reduction in hours not

---

[14]O. Ashenfelter, "The Effect of Unionization on the Public Sector: The Case of Fire Fighters," *Industrial and Labor Relations Review*, Vol. 24, No. 2 (January 1971), pp. 191–202.

**Table 15.4 / Effects of Unionization of Fire Fighters,
All U.S. Cities, 1966 (Percent Difference between Union and Nonunion Cities)**

	Small-Size Cities	Moderate-Size Cities
Percent Difference in Weekly Hours	− 5.8	−8.5
Percent Difference in Annual Salary	+10.1	+1.0
Percent Difference in Hourly Wage	+16.0	+9.4

Source: O. Ashenfelter, "The Effect of Unionization on Public Sector Wages: The Case of Fire Fighters," *Industrial and Labor Relations Review*, Vol. 24, No. 2 (January 1971), pp. 191–202. Abstracted from Tables 2 and 3.

accompanied by a proportionate reduction in annual salary implies an increase in the hourly wage. Hence, bargaining over hours is one way in which the IAFF may have been able to achieve higher wages.

Table 15.4 shows that fire fighters represented by the IAFF tended to work 6 to 8 percent fewer hours than did nonunionized fire fighters. Those reductions in hours were not, however, matched by reductions in annual salaries in unionized cities—indeed, annual salaries tended to be slightly higher in such cities. Consequently, hourly wages paid to fire fighters represented by the IAFF were 9 to 16 percent higher than those paid to nonunion workers. Of course, the unique nature of fire fighting probably results in these data overstating by a substantial margin the economic impact of unions in the economy as a whole. The data do suggest that unionization can have a significant influence in some labor markets.

Summary

In this chapter we have examined various aspects of the theory of labor supply. Most important of these was introduction of a utility-maximizing model for an individual's allocation of time between working and not working. We showed that, in order to maximize utility, an individual should choose to work that number of hours for which the marginal rate of substitution of additional leisure time for earned income is equal to the real market wage rate. A change in that wage will induce income and substitution effects into individuals' choices. Since those effects work in opposite directions, it is impossible to predict on purely *a priori* grounds the direction of the effect of higher real wages on labor supply.

In addition to examining the time allocation model, we also analyzed the concept of compensating wage differentials and investigated possible labor market goals for unions. Our discussion of compensating differentials showed that wage rates paid to otherwise identical workers may differ if the jobs differ in their attractiveness. Such wage differences may persist in equilibrium because the "total advantages" of the job will be equalized by the market. A similar concept of the nonwage aspects of employment entered our discussion of union goals, where we showed that unions may seek many different types of benefits for their members. Recognizing the possibility of trade-offs among those benefits makes the analysis of unions' supply decisions considerably more complex than the analysis of monopoly suppliers in the goods market for which the single goal of profit maximization may be appropriate.

Suggested Readings

Becker, G. S., "An Economic Analysis of Fertility," in *Demographic and Economic Change in Developed Countries,* National Bureau Conference Series No. 11 (Princeton, N.J.: Princeton University Press, 1960).

———, "A Theory of the Allocation of Time," *Economic Journal* 75 (September 1965), pp. 493–517.

Bowen, W., and Finegan, T. A., *The Economics of Labor Force Participation* (Princeton, N.J.: Princeton University Press, 1969).

Cain, G. G., *Married Women in the Labor Force: An Economic Analysis* (Chicago: University of Chicago Press, 1966).

Marshall, A., *Principles of Economics,* 8th ed. (London: Collier-Macmillan, Ltd., 1920), book 4, chaps. 4–6.

Mincer, J., "Labor Force Participation of Married Women," in *Aspects of Labor Economics,* ed. H. G. Lewis, National Bureau Conference Series No. 14 (Princeton, N.J.: Princeton University Press, 1962).

Rees, A., "The Effects of Unions on Resource Allocation," *Journal of Law and Economics* 6 (October 1963), pp. 69–78.

———, *The Economics of Trade Unions* (Chicago: University of Chicago Press, 1962).

Problems

15.1

Suppose the supply curve for labor to a firm has the form

$$L = 100\,w$$

$$MC_L = \frac{L}{50}$$

where w is the market wage. Suppose also that the firm's demand (marginal revenue product) curve has the form

$$L = -50\,w + 450.$$

a. If the firm is a monopsonist how many workers will it hire in order to maximize profits? What wage will it pay?

b. If the supply of labor is monopolized, how many workers should be provided to the firm in order to maximize the total wage bill (wL)? What will the wage rate be?

c. If the market has both a monopsony on the demand side and a monopoly on the supply side what can you say about the "equilibrium" outcome? How will this compare to the competitive solution?

15.2

Suppose a union has a fixed supply of labor to sell. If the union desires to maximize the total wage bill, what wage rate will it demand? How would your answer change if unemployed workers were paid unemployment insurance at the rate u per worker and the union now desired to maximize the sum of the wage bill and the total amount of unemployment compensation?

15.3

Use the time allocation model in Chapter 15 to discuss the effects on an individual's hours of work of

a. the receipt of a substantial amount of outside income

b. the imposition of a tax on wages

c. an increase in the general price level with no concomitant increase in wages

d. national legislation of a maximum work week of 35 hours

15.4

Mr. Peabody has a utility function $U \ \sqrt{C \cdot H}$ and is maximizing his utility at $U = 20$ when he works 14 hours a day. Would he be willing to give up an hour of his leisure to drive Mrs. Atterby to the wrestling match if she offered him $5?

15.5

Use the concept of the opportunity cost of time to discuss:

a. whom you might expect to pay the higher fares to fly the faster Concorde to Europe;

b. who you expect would be more likely to stand in long lines and even "camp out" overnight to purchase tickets to a sporting event;

c. for whom greens fees are a larger fraction of the total cost of a golf game—a prospering physician or a peanut vendor?

d. How would the degree of traffic congestion affect who drives to work and who takes mass transit?

15.6

What factors influence families' "demand" for children? Would you expect high-income families to have more children than low-income families? Would families in less developed countries have more children than families in the United States? Would farm families have more children than city dwellers?

16   Capital

Introduction

The study of the theory of capital as a factor of production is extremely important in economics. Two areas for which we need an understanding of the nature of capital are the study of economic growth and the explanation of business cycles. Economics has traditionally assigned an important role to capital as a factor of production in the growth process. One of the major reasons for increases in per capita output over time is the increasing amount of productive equipment workers have at their disposal. To understand where this equipment comes from and the incentives that lead to its accumulation, we must develop a theory of capital. Similarly, Keynesian economic theory assigns an important role to investment as one component of aggregate demand. Since net investment comes about because firms desire to change the stock of capital they have available, it is again important to have an understanding of the factors that go into determining the desired amount of capital. For this reason capital theory is central to modern Keynesian economics.

The study of capital theory is also controversial. Primarily this controversy centers on the question of whether or not the owner of productive equipment (that is, capital) has any "right" to obtain a rent for its use. In the final analysis the answer to this question must be regarded as one aspect of the broader question of the nature and desirability of private property as a social institution. Various sections of Part VII present a brief economic discussion of this issue. In this chapter, however, we will avoid most controversial questions in order to build an understanding of the nature of capital and why the allocation of capital is an important issue. Our first step toward discussing more complex social issues would seem to be to understand the economics of the matter.

Definition of Capital

When we speak of the *capital stock* of an economy we mean the sum total of machines, buildings, and other man-made, nonlabor resources that are in existence at some point in time. These assets represent some part of an economy's output in the past that was not consumed. This output was set aside to be used for production in the future. All societies, from the most primitive to the most complex, engage in capital accumulation. A bushman's taking time off from hunting to make arrows, individuals in a modern society using part of their incomes to buy houses, or governments taxing citizens in order to purchase dams and post office buildings are all engaging in essentially the same sort of activity: Some portion of current output is being set aside for use in producing output in future periods. Present "sacrifice" for future gain is the essential aspect of capital accumulation. In the next section we will introduce the concept of a *rate of return* in order to understand why individuals are willing to engage in such an activity.

Rate of Return

The process of capital accumulation is pictured schematically in Figure 16.1. In both panels of the figure, society is initially consuming level C_0 and has been doing so for some time. At time t_1 a decision is made to withhold some output (amount s) from current consumption for one period. Starting in period t_2 this withheld

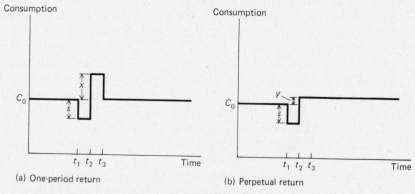

(a) One-period return   (b) Perpetual return

Figure 16.1 / Two Views of Capital Accumulation

In 16.1a society withdraws some current consumption (s) in order to gorge itself (with x extra consumption) in the next period. The one-period rate of return would be measured by $x/s - 1$. The society in 16.1b takes a more long-term view and uses s to increase its consumption perpetually by y. The perpetual rate of return would be given by y/s.

consumption is in some way put to use producing future consumption. An important concept connected with this process is the *rate of return*, which is earned on that consumption that is put aside. In 16.1a, for example, all of the withheld consumption is used to produce additional output only in period t_2. Consumption is increased by amount x in period t_2 and then returns to the long-run level C_0. Society has saved in one year in order to have an orgy in the next year. A measure of the (one-period) rate of return from this activity would be

$$r_1 = \frac{x}{s} - 1$$
[16.1]

If $x > s$ (if more consumption comes out of this process than went into it) we would say that the one-period rate of return to capital accumulation is positive. For example, if withholding 100 units from current consumption permitted society to consume an extra 110 units next year, the rate of return would be .10 (= 110/100 − 1) or 10 percent.

In 16.1b society is assumed to take a more long-term view in its consumption decisions. Again an amount s is set aside at time t_1. Now, however, this set-aside consumption is used to raise the consumption level for all periods in the future. If the permanent level of consumption is raised to $C_0 + y$, we define the perpetual rate of return to be

$$r_\infty = \frac{y}{s}$$
[16.2]

If capital accumulation succeds in raising C_0 permanently, r_∞ will be positive. For example, suppose society set aside 100 units of output in period t_1 to be devoted to capital accumulation. If this capital would permit output to be raised by 10 units for *every* period in the future (starting at time period t_2) the perpetual rate of return would be 10 percent.

When economists speak of the rate of return to capital accumulation, then, they have in mind something between these two extremes. Somewhat loosely we will define:

Definition

The *rate of return* in an economy shows the terms on which present goods that are not currently consumed can be turned into goods for consumption at some future date.

In the next section we will make this definition more precise.

Determination of the Rate of Return

We have seen that the act of capital accumulation essentially consists of withholding some output from current consumption, investing this output in some sort of equipment, and using the equipment to produce output in the future. The rate of return measures the terms on which this process can be accomplished. In a market economy the rate of return that actually prevails will depend on the technical possibilities for turning present goods into future goods, and on the preferences of individuals for present versus future goods. An equilibrium rate of return records both the return to capital accumulation that is technically feasible and the return that individuals are willing to accept.

A Supply-Demand Analysis

Determination of this equilibrium rate of return can be illustrated by considering the supply and demand for what we shall call "future goods." Such goods (which are, of course, purely fictional) are purchased today by setting aside some capital investment and are then consumed in the future. The market for future goods is pictured in Figure 16.2. As for all supply-demand graphs, the horizontal axis in the

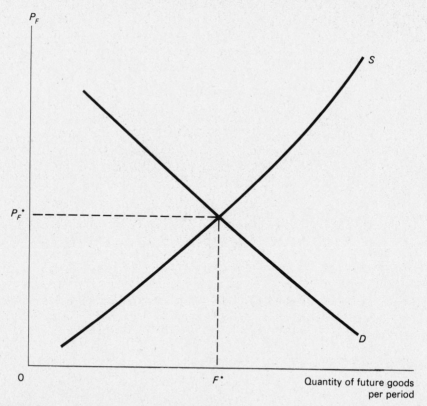

Figure 16.2 / The Market for Future Goods

The terms at which present goods trade for future goods (P_F) through capital accumulation is set by demand and supply conditions. It is likely that P_F* will be less than one. We define the rate of return (r) by the formula $\frac{1}{1+r} = P_F*$. Since $P_F* < 1$, r will be positive.

figure shows the quantity of future goods traded *(F)*. On the horizontal axis we have recorded the "price" of future goods (P_F). This price records how many current goods must be "paid" (by setting them aside as productive capital) to get one future good. The demand curve for future goods is drawn sloping downward on the assumption that the lower their price, the greater the quantity that will be demanded. In other words, the smaller the required sacrifice of present goods, the greater will be individuals' demands for goods in the future. The supply curve for future goods slopes upward because of the assumption that the process of setting aside goods for the production of future goods may run into diminishing returns. As F rises, the marginal cost (in terms of the present investment required) of producing one more unit of F rises.

Equilibrium Price of Future Goods

Equilibrium in the market shown in Figure 16.2 is at F^*, P^*. At that point individuals' supply and demand for future goods are in balance, and the required amount of current goods will be put into capital accumulation in order to produce F^* in the future.[1]

There are a number of reasons to expect that P_F^* will be less than one: that is, it will cost less than the sacrifice of one current good to "buy" one good in the future. On the demand side it might be argued that individuals require some reward for "waiting." Everyday adages ("a bird in the hand is worth two in the bush," "live for today") and more substantial realities (the uncertainty of the future and the finiteness of life) suggest that individuals are generally impatient in their consumption decisions. Hence capital accumulation such as that shown in Figure 16.2 will take place only if the current sacrifice is in some way worthwhile.

There are also supply reasons for believing P_F^* will be less than one. All of these involve the idea that capital accumulation is "productive": Sacrificing one good currently will yield more than one good in the future. Some simple examples of the productivity of capital investment are provided by such pastoral activities as the growing of trees or the aging of wine and cheese.[2] Tree owners, vineyard operators and dairymen "abstain" from selling their wares in the belief that time will make them more valuable in the future. Although it is obvious that capital accumulation in a modern industrial society is far more complex than growing trees (consider building a steel mill or an electric power system), economists believe the two processes have certain similarities. In both cases investing current goods makes the production process longer and more complex and therefore improves the overall productive power of other resources used in production.

---

[1] This is a much simplified form of an analysis originally presented by I. Fisher in *The Rate of Interest* (New York: The Macmillan Co., 1907).

[2] For a discussion of these examples in the context of "Austrian" capital theory, see M. Blaug, *Economic Theory in Retrospect* (Homewood, Ill.: Richard D. Irwin, Inc., 1962), chap. 12.

The Equilibrium Rate of Return

We can now define the relationship of the rate of return (r) to what we have called the price of future goods by the formula:

$$P_F^* = \frac{1}{1+r} \qquad [16.3]$$

Since we believe that P_F^* will be less than one, r will be positive. For example, if $P_F^* = .9$, r will equal approximately $.1$,[3] and we would say that the rate of return to capital accumulation is "ten percent." By withholding one good from current consumption, the consumption of future goods can be increased by 1.1. The rate of return and P_F are equivalent ways of measuring the terms on which present goods can be turned into future goods.[4]

In the remainder of this chapter we will assume that an equilibrium rate of return, r, has been established by the process shown in Figure 16.2. That rate provides a measure of the benefits of capital accumulation to all economic agents. We will show how these agents will take account of r in all of their decisions that concern the allocation of resources over time.

Rental Rate on Machines and the Theory of Investment

So far in this chapter we have not talked about the firm's demand for capital. It is time to do so using the concepts we have developed. Presumably a firm will rent machines in accordance with the same principles of profit maximization derived in Chapter 13. Specifically,

Optimization Principle

A profit-maximizing firm will hire that number of machines for which the marginal value product from hiring one more is equal to the machine's market rental rate (v).

---

[3]More precisely, if $P_F^* = .9$, r will be $.11111 \ldots$ since $.9 = \dfrac{1}{1 + .1111 \ldots}$

[4]It is important to make a distinction between the rate of return (r) and interest rates (R) actually observed in real-world markets (say on savings accounts or on bonds). Since we live in a world of inflation, market interest rates will reflect both the rate of return on capital accumulation and the expected change in prices (since lenders will want to be compensated for the fact that they will be repaid in devalued dollars). If the proportional change in the price level is given by P_e, R and r are related by:

$$R = r + P_e$$

For example, if $r = .05$ (five percent) and $P_e = .04$ (4 percent) the market interest rate will be $R = .09$ (nine percent).

In this section we will first investigate the determinants of this market rental rate, and we will assume that all machines are rented. Later in the section we will examine the particular problems raised because most firms buy machines, rather than rent them, and hold them until they deteriorate.

Determinants of Market Rental Rates

Consider a firm in the business of renting machines to other firms. Suppose that firm owns a machine that currently sells for P dollars in the market. How much will the firm charge its clients for the use of the machine? The owner of the machine faces two kinds of costs: depreciation on the machine, and the *opportunity cost* of having its funds tied up in a machine rather than in an investment earning the current interest rate. If it is assumed that depreciation costs per period are a constant percent (d) of the machine's market price and that the market interest rate is given by r, then the total costs to the machine owner for one period are given by

$$dP + rP = P(r + d) \qquad [16.4]$$

If we assume that the machine rental market is perfectly competitive, no pure profits can be earned by renting machines. The workings of the market will insure that the rental rate per period for the machine (v) is exactly equal to the (long-run) costs of the machine owner. Hence we have the basic result that

$$v = P(r + d) \qquad [16.5]$$

The competitive rental rate is the sum of interest and depreciation costs that the machine's owner must pay. For example, suppose that the interest rate were 5 percent (that is, .05) and that the physical depreciation rate is 4 percent (.04). Suppose also that the current market price of a particular machine is $100. Then, in this simple model, the machine would have a rental rate of $9 [$100 \times (.05 + .04)]$ per year. Five dollars of this would represent the opportunity cost of the funds invested in the machine, and the remaining $4 would reflect the physical costs of deterioration.

A Nondepreciating Machine

In the case of a machine that does not depreciate $(d = 0)$ equation 16.5 can be written in a simpler way:

$$\frac{v}{P} = r \qquad [16.6]$$

This simply says that in equilibrium an infinitely long-lived (nondepreciating) machine is equivalent to a perpetual bond and hence, must "yield" the market rate

owner must pay: interest, physical depreciation, and taxes. Consequently the rental rate on a machine will now be

$$v' = v + T = P(r + d) + T \qquad [16.7]$$

where T represents the taxes on a machine that must be paid by the owner. Obviously a higher T implies a higher rental rate and a lower T implies a lower rental. Figure 16.3 shows the effect that a reduction in T (and v') will have on the firm's desired level of capital inputs. Initially, the rental rate on capital is given by v_1'; the firm produces Q_1 by using K_1 units of capital input per period. Now suppose T declines. By Equation 16.7, this will cause a machine's rental rate to fall to v_2'. As was the case for labor, this fall in the rental rate will create both substitution and output effects, which cause more capital to be hired. In Figure 16.3a, the substitution effect causes the optimal input combination to move to point B on the Q_1 isoquant. The fall in v' also causes the firm's marginal cost curve to shift downward to MC'. Consequently, output is increased to Q_2; at this output level, the firm now wishes to hire K_2 units of capital input. Since the firm may not have a sufficient stock of capital equipment on hand to provide this level of services, it may have to buy additional equipment. In other words, it may engage in investment. This is, then, the sequence of events by which changes in governmental tax policy are related to the generation

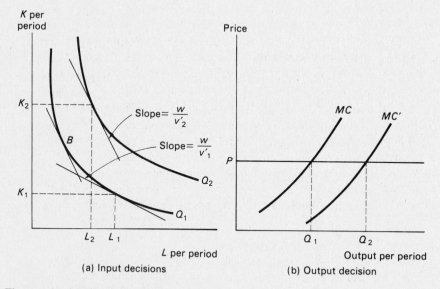

(a) Input decisions

(b) Output decision

Figure 16.3 / Effects of a Reduction in Taxes on the Demand for Capital Services

If tax policies change the rental rate on capital, this will change the demand for capital services. For example, a reduction in taxes will cause the rental rate to fall from v_1' to v_2'. This will create both substitution (from K_1, L_1 to B) and output (from B to K_2, L_2) effects, which cause the quantity of capital services demanded to increase (from K_1 to K_2). This increased demand for services may prompt firms to buy new machines.

of investment incentives. We shall now examine some specific tax measures intended to spur investment in the way illustrated in Figure 16.3.

Examples of Specific Tax Policies

Federal tax policies have been widely used to influence the overall level of investment over the past 25 years. While the general thrust of these policies has been to increase investment by lowering taxes, changes in the general tax rate have not been the primary way this has been accomplished. Rather, complex changes have been made in accounting procedures and special credits have been allowed for investment. Although it would be inappropriate to attempt to describe these changes in detail, a brief sketch of the three most important such policies may serve to indicate the ways in which investment incentives have been provided.

Accelerated Depreciation: In 1954, Federal tax policy was changed to allow firms to "write off" the costs of their investments in plant and equipment more rapidly than was previously the case. That policy had the effect of allowing firms to postpone the taxes owed on the income generated by newly purchased machinery. In essence, firms received an interest-free loan of their tax liability from the government. By one estimate this relatively subtle change in accounting principles had the effect of reducing the rental rate on capital by as much as 20 percent.[6]

Useful Lifetime Guidelines: Another provision for accelerated depreciation was instituted in 1962. Under this provision what the tax law defined to be the "useful lifetimes" of various types of equipment were shortened. For example, the minimum useful life of a car was reduced from four to three years. This made it possible for firms to gain further benefits from accelerated depreciation, and effective rental rates on capital were reduced another 2 or 3 percent.

Investment Tax Credit: An additional tax change in 1962 was the institution of an "investment tax credit" for machinery and equipment purchases. Under that policy, 7 percent of the amount firms invested could be taken as a credit against taxes due. That policy reduced effective rental rates by 7 percent: Essentially the Federal Treasury paid 7 percent of all machinery and equipment purchases.

Quantitative Effects of the Tax Policies.

Table 16.1 shows the estimated effect of each of these tax policies on firms' total gross investment in equipment in 1963. As our theoretical discussion suggested, the reduction in rental rates had a substantial effect on the demand for capital

---

[6]R.E. Hall and D.W. Jorgenson, "Tax Policy and Investment Behavior," *American Economic Review,* Vol. LVII, No. 3 (June 1967), pp. 391–414. All of the other numbers in this example are also taken from this source.

Table 16.1 / Change in Gross Investment in Equipment as a Result of Federal Tax Policy, 1963 (Billions of 1954 Dollars)

	Manufacturing Equipment	Nonmanufacturing Equipment
Total Gross Investment	$8.461	$17.982
Change due to:		
Accelerated Depreciation	$0.549	$ 1.141
Useful Lifetime Guidelines	$0.315	$ 0.656
Investment Tax Credit	$0.867	$ 1.808
Total Effect of Federal Tax Policy	$1.731	$ 3.605
Tax Effect as a Percent of Total Gross Investment	20.5%	20.0%

Source: R.E. Hall and D.W. Jorgenson, "Tax Policy and Investment Behavior," *American Economic Review,* Vol. LVII, No. 3 (June 1967), pp. 391–414. Tables 3, 4, and 5.

equipment, increasing total purchases by about 20 percent over what they would have been under older, less generous tax laws. Clearly tax policy provides a powerful lever by means of which the Federal government can affect investment and, through investment, the overall pace of economic activity. The relatively high levels of employment experienced during the mid-1960s in the United States may have been in part the result of such policies.

Present Discounted Value Criterion

The theory of firms' demand for capital is usually presented in a form rather different from that we have developed. This alternative form is termed the *present discounted value* theory of investment demand. Rather than treating the renting of machines in a way analogous to the hiring of labor and centering attention on the rental rate, this approach analyzes the decision to purchase a machine. The theory is therefore a "stock" theory of the demand for machines rather than a "flow" theory of the demand for the services of a machine. The distinction between the two theories is, however, really one of semantics, not substance. Besides discussing the present discounted value criterion, a principal purpose of this section is to show that this criterion dictates the same behavior as does the rental rate approach we have outlined.

Present Value

In order to analyze the present discounted value criterion for investment, we must first discuss the procedure that should be used to add up sums of money that are to be paid in different periods, since the purchaser of a machine will collect the net income (or, more properly, the marginal value product) from the machine over several periods into the future. Although the formal mathematical aspects of this subject are presented in the appendix to this chapter, it is possible here to provide an intuitive explanation of the logic that economists employ. The most basic observation to be made is that $1 today is worth more than a dollar that is not to be received until some later date. If a dollar is available today it can be invested and earn interest at the prevailing rate, r. Conversely, if a dollar is not received until next year, some interest must be forgone. More specifically, a dollar today will grow to $(1 + r)$ dollars next year. Alternatively, we might define:

Definition

The *present* value of $1 payable next year is $1/(1 + r)$. This is the amount which, if invested today at an annual interest rate r, will yield $1 in one year.

It is easy to generalize the idea of present value to any number of periods. If $1 is invested for 2 years, for example, it will grow to $\$1 \times (1 + r) \times (1 + r) = \$1 \times (1 + r)^2$. Similarly, the present value of $1 payable in 2 years would be $\$1/(1 + r)^2$. This is the amount that would have to be invested today in order to obtain $1 in 2 years. These results can be summarized by

$$\text{present value of \$1 payable in 1 year} \ = \frac{\$1}{(1 + r)}$$

$$\text{present value of \$1 payable in 2 years} = \frac{\$1}{(1 + r)^2}$$

$$\text{present value of \$1 payable in 3 years} = \frac{\$1}{(1 + r)^3}$$

$$\text{present value of \$1 payable in } n \text{ years} = \frac{\$1}{(1 + r)^n} \qquad \text{[16.8]}$$

In order to reinforce the implications of the present value concept, Table 16.2 shows the present value of $1 payable 1, 2, 3, 10, or 20 years in the future for five possible interest rates. For example, the table records the fact that, if r is 4 percent, the present value of $1 payable in one year is $.962. If about $.96 is invested today at 4 percent, it will grow to $1 by the end of 1 year. Similarly, the table shows that, if the interest rate is 7 percent, an investment of only $.26 will grow to $1 in 20 years. In general, the present value of a dollar available at some date in the future declines as the interest rate used increases; for a fixed interest rate, dollars payable in the distant future are worth less than those payable in the near term. Published tables are available for calculating present values for practically any interest rate or period, and these can be most helpful for economic analyses that involve sums of money payable over time.

Table 16.2 / Present Value of $1 Payable at Various Dates

Interest Rate (r)	1 Year	2 Years	3 Years	10 Years	20 Years
0.03	$0.970	$0.943	$0.915	$0.744	$0.554
0.04	0.962	0.925	0.889	0.676	0.456
0.05	0.952	0.907	0.864	0.614	0.377
0.06	0.943	0.890	0.840	0.558	0.312
0.07	0.935	0.873	0.816	0.508	0.258

Present Discounted Value
Approach to Investment Decisions

When a firm buys a machine, it is in effect buying a stream of net revenues in future periods. In order to decide whether or not to purchase the machine, the firm must compute the current value of this stream. Since the revenues will accrue to the firm in many future periods, the logic of the preceding argument suggests that the firm should compute the present discounted value of this stream. Only by doing so will the firm have taken adequate account of the effects of interest payments. This is the alternative approach we shall take to explaining the investment decision.

Consider a firm in the process of deciding whether or not to buy a particular machine. The machine is expected to last n years and will give its owner a stream of monetary returns (that is, marginal revenue products) in each of the n years. Let the return in year i be represented by R_i. If r is the present interest rate, and if this rate is expected to prevail for the next n years, the present discounted value (PDV) of the machine to its owner is given by:

$$PDV = \frac{R_1}{(1 + r)} + \frac{R_2}{(1 + r)^2} + \cdots + \frac{R_n}{(1 + r)^n}$$ [16.9]

This present discounted value represents the total value of the stream of payments that is provided by the machine, once adequate account is taken of the fact that these payments occur in different years. If the PDV of this stream of payments exceeds the price (P) of the machine, the firm should make the purchase. Even when the effects of the interest payments that the firm could have earned on its funds had it not purchased the machine are taken into account, the machine promises to return more than its prevailing price. Consequently firms would rush out to buy machines. On the other hand, if $P > PDV$, the firm would be better off to invest its funds in some alternative that promises a rate of return of r. When account is taken of forgone interest, the machine does not pay for itself. No profit-maximizing firm would buy a machine for which $P > PDV$. In a competitive market the only equilibrium that can prevail is the price of a machine being equal to the present discounted value of the net revenues from the machine. Only in this situation will there be neither an excess demand for machines nor an excess supply of machines. Hence market equilibrium requires that:

$$P = PDV = \frac{R_1}{1 + r} + \frac{R_2}{(1 + r)^2} + \cdots + \frac{R_n}{(1 + r)^n}. \qquad [16.10]$$

We shall now use this condition to show a simple situation in which the present discounted value criterion of investment reduces to the equilibrium conditions outlined previously.

Present Discounted Value and the Rental Rate

Assume first that machines are infinitely long-lived and that the marginal revenue product (that is, R_i) is the same in every year. This uniform return will also equal the rental rate for machines (v), since that is what another firm would pay for the machine's use during the period. With these simplifying assumptions we may write the present discounted value from machine ownership as:[7]

$$PDV = \frac{v}{(1 + r)} + \frac{v}{(1 + r)^2} + \cdots + \frac{v}{(1 + r)^n} + \cdots$$

$$= v \cdot \left(\frac{1}{(1 + r)} + \frac{1}{(1 + r)^2} + \cdots + \frac{1}{(1 + r)^n} + \cdots \right)$$

$$= v \cdot \left(\frac{1}{1 - 1/(1 + r)} \right) - 1 \qquad [16.11]$$

$$= v \cdot \left(\frac{1 + r}{r} \right) - 1$$

$$= v \cdot \frac{1}{r}$$

But since in equilibrium $P = PDV$, this says:

$$P = v \cdot \frac{1}{r} \qquad [16.12]$$

or

$$\frac{v}{P} = r, \qquad [16.13]$$

---

[7]The third line of this proof is derived from:

$$\frac{1}{1 - x} = 1 + x + x^2 + x^3 + \cdots$$

or

$$\frac{1}{1 - x} - 1 = x + x^2 + x^3 + \cdots$$

Here let $x = \frac{1}{1 + r}$.

as was shown in Equation 16.6. For this case the present discounted value criterion gives results identical to those outlined earlier. We have again demonstrated the algebraic relationship between a machine's price, the rental rate on the machine, and the market rate of interest. In particular, a *ceteris paribus* increase in r will decrease the machine's *PDV*, and firms will be less willing to buy machines for the same reasons as were discussed above. This result is quite general. The present discounted value approach to investment and the rental rate approach are identical. In the next two sections we will make use of the present value approach to study two additional examples of capital theory: human capital, and the use of resources that are in fixed supply.

Human Capital

One important application of the theory of capital concerns a very different kind of investment from what we have been discussing so far—the investment that a person can make in himself or herself. Individuals can invest in themselves in a variety of ways. They can acquire a formal education, they may accept apprenticeships and learn skills on the job, they can spend considerable efforts in looking for better jobs, or they can purchase various kinds of medical services that maintain them in good health. All of those activities can be looked upon as "investments" in that both time and money are sacrificed currently in the hope that this will somehow pay off in the future. By acquiring skills or buying "good health," individuals are adding to their stock of *human capital* in much the same way that the purchase of machines by firms adds to the firms' stock of physical capital. There is substantial empirical evidence that most such additions to human capital are quite productive in the sense that they serve to increase individuals' earnings in future periods. In fact, it has been found that there are many investments that individuals make in themselves that yield returns substantially in excess of the prevailing rate of interest.[8] In this section we shall briefly discuss how such calculations are made and present some empirical information on that subject. Finally, we shall analyze some of the ways in which human capital differs from physical capital.

Calculating the Yield on an Investment

Conceptually it is an easy matter to compute the rate of return (or *yield*) that an individual receives from an investment in human capital (or on any other kind of capital investment for that matter). Suppose that the cost of a proposed investment is

---

[8]For a thorough analysis of the educational aspects of human capital formation, see G.S. Becker, *Human Capital*, National Bureau of Economic Research (New York: Columbia University Press, 1964). For a recent treatment of the human capital approach to the study of medical expenditures, see. M. Grossman, *The Demand for Health*, National Bureau of Economic Research Occasional Paper 119 (New York: Columbia University Press, 1972).

given by C. Suppose also that the investment is expected to raise the individual's earnings in each period in the future and that these increments to earnings are given by $I_1, I_2, \ldots, I_n$. What we wish to know is what interest rate, i, will "discount" these earnings increments to make them exactly equal to C. Mathematically, we know C and the I's, and we wish to find that value of i that solves the equation:

$$C = \frac{I_1}{(1 + i)} + \frac{I_2}{(1 + i)^2} + \cdots + \frac{I_n}{(1 + i)^n}.$$ [16.14]

The value of i that solves Equation 16.14 would be called the "rate of return" on the particular investment. The calculation would proceed in much the same way that we would calculate the current yield on a bond from knowledge of the bond's price and the annual payments it promises (see the appendix to this chapter).

An Example: Yields on Investments in Schooling and On-the-job Training

The two most important human capital investments that individuals make are in formal schooling and in on-the-job training. Costs of investment in schooling are of two types. First are explicit costs such as tuitions and fees, transportation costs, and other incidental expenses. A second, and probably larger, component of schooling costs is the implicit opportunity costs of forgone earnings while in school. Because individuals could hold jobs instead of attending school, potential earnings on those jobs must be considered a cost of formal education. A similar opportunity cost argument suggests that if individuals forsake some earnings in order to learn skills that will be useful to them in the future, these forgone earnings are a cost of accumulating job skills. Since most skills that are specific to a particular occupation are probably learned on the job, wages will be lower during this learning period. The costs of on-the-job training are composed primarily of these (temporarily) forgone wages.

A 1970 study by T. Johnson attempted to estimate the dollar costs of these two types of human capital investments.[9] A few of the author's results for males in 1959 are presented in Table 16.3. The table shows that on-the-job training costs are about the same for individuals of differing educational levels. Most workers require about the same degree of initial preparation when starting out on a job. As would be expected, the costs of formal schooling rise rapidly for individuals with higher educational levels. Workers with less than a high school education have invested relatively little in formal schooling (less than $4,000—composed primarily of forgone earnings). More than three quarters of such workers' total human capital investments are in on-the-job training. For more highly educated

---

[9]T. Johnson, "Returns from Investment in Human Capital, *American Economic Review,* Vol. LX, No. 4 (September 1970), pp. 546–560.

individuals, formal schooling costs may be quite high. Those with education beyond the college level have a total investment that may average over $40,000 (in 1959 dollars). Again the principal component of this cost is the earnings that college graduates forgo when they attend graduate school.

The investments in human capital shown in Figure 16.3 seem to "pay off" in increasing total lifetime incomes. For example, on average, individuals with a college education earned nearly $100,000 more over their lifetimes than did those with only a high school education. The final column of Table 16.3 presents the percentage yields on total human capital investments. These yields were calculated using a formula similar to Equation 16.14. All of the yields are positive, indicating that formal schooling and on-the-job training do indeed pay off in increased earnings. The yields diminish for higher levels of formal education, however, and this suggests some kind of diminishing return to human capital investments may exist. As for any other economic activity, it appears to be possible to push investments in human capital too far. Indeed, more recent data tend to indicate that the returns to college education have fallen below those in Table 16.3, primarily because of the rapid increase in the number of college graduates over the past 20 years. All of the yields in Table 16.3 are, however, well above yields on alternative investments that individuals might make (savings accounts, bonds, and so forth) and this may reflect the unique nature of human capital investment. We will now briefly examine some of its unusual properties.

Table 16.3 / Investments in Human Capital and the Yield on Those Investments for White Males in the Northern United States, 1959

Years of Education Completed	Investment in Schooling	Investment in on-the-job Training	Total Investment in Human Capital	Total Lifetime Income	Yield Investment in Human Capital
9–11	$ 3,760	$15,316	$19,076	$220,025	24.6%
12	9,408	14,704	24,112	245,433	21.5
13–15	11,293	17,170	28,463	278,323	17.5
16	27,800	18,216	46,016	341,856	15.5
17 +	40,738	23,033	63,771	380,626	13.5

Source: T. Johnson, "Returns from Investment in Human Capital," *American Economic Review,* Vol. LX, No. 4 (September 1970), pp. 546–560, Table 3.

Limitations of the Human Capital Approach

Although the analogy between human and physical capital provides many insights into the nature of individuals' decisions, the analogy should not be pushed too far. Human capital has a number of special properties that make it unique among the assets an individual can buy. Contrary to other assets, human capital cannot (in the absence of slavery) be sold. The owner of human capital is inextricably tied to his or her investment. Although the individual may rent out this investment to employers, he or she may not sell it in the way in which a firm might sell a machine it no longer needed. Human capital also depreciates in a rather unusual way. It is totally lost upon the death of its owner, and this makes the investment rather risky. Finally, the acquisition of human capital may take substantial time. Whereas a firm seeking to buy a drill press may only have to spend five minutes in the buying process, individuals seeking to improve their skills must usually invest considerable time in doing so. The irreversibility of time makes this process of human capital investment all the more risky. Hence, there are a number of reasons to be cautious in applying the results of capital theory to the study of the acquisition of human capital.

Capital Theory and the Allocation of Exhaustible Natural Resources

As a final application of the results of basic capital theory we will consider the question of how markets will allocate nonrenewable natural resources over time. Recently much concern has been expressed about the "finiteness" of some resources (notably petroleum reserves, but concern has also been expressed about the supply of a wide variety of resources ranging from diamonds to fresh water). Our principal concern will be to examine the implications of resources being in finite supply for the pricing of those resources.

Scarcity Costs

What differentiates the production of exhaustible resources from the production of any other economic good is that current production from a finite resource stock reduces the amount of the resource available for future production. This might be contrasted to the usual economic model of production in which firms' activities during one period have no effect on their production activities next period. Hence, producers of an exhaustible resource must take an additional cost into account in their current production decisions: the opportunity cost of forgone sales in the future. To study that cost formally, we define:

Definition

The *scarcity costs* of current production of an exhaustible resource are the opportunity costs of future sales that cannot be made because of the current production.

The implications of scarcity costs for pricing are illustrated in Figure 16.4. In the absence of those costs, the industry supply curve for the resource would be given by S and that curve would, as usual, reflect the marginal costs of actually producing (that is, extracting or refining) the resource. Existence of scarcity costs (related to the finiteness of the ultimately available resource supply) shifts firms' marginal cost curves upward. The new market supply curve is S', The gap between S' and S reflects scarcity costs. Notice that current output is reduced (from Q^* to Q') by recognizing the finiteness of the resource supply. This reduction reflects firms' preference for withholding some of the resource from current supply in order to be able to sell it in the future.

Calculation of Scarcity Costs

The actual value of scarcity costs depends on firms' perceptions about what resource prices will be in the future. Knowledge of those prices is required if owners are to be able correctly to calculate the opportunity costs associated with current sales out of their resource stocks. As a simple example, suppose a firm knew that in 20 years its resources could be sold at a price of P_{20}. Then the present value of that sale would be

$$PDV = \frac{P_{20}}{(1 + r)^{20}}$$

[16.15]

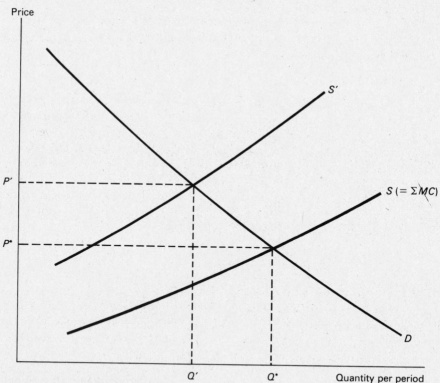

Figure 16.4 / Scarcity Costs
Associated with Exhaustible Resources

Firms that produce exhaustible resources will take into account both current marginal production costs and the opportunity costs of forgone future production. The market supply curve for such firms (S') will be above their marginal cost curves to the extent of those scarcity costs.

In equilibrium, this value must equal the present market price of the resource since only then would the firm be indifferent between selling now or selling later. If we let P_1 be the present price, equilibrium requires

$$P_1 = PDV = \frac{P_{20}}{(1 + r)^{20}}$$ [16.16]

and scarcity cost is given by the difference between P_1 and marginal production costs (see Figure 16.4).

An interesting implication of Equation 16.16 is that, in the absence of any changes in production costs, or in expectations about future prices, market prices would be expected to increase over time at the rate of return on alternative investments. If r is five percent, for example, real prices would be expected to rise at 5 percent a year.[10] Only by following that path would prices always equal the present value of P_{20}. Hence we have:

Optimization Principle

In equilibrium the competitive price of a finite natural resource will increase over time at the rate r; that is, at the rate of return on alternative investments (assuming production costs stay constant).

This result can be shown intuitively from another perspective. Any firm will evaluate its resource holdings in the same way as any other investment. Hence investments in resources should yield the same return (r) as those alternatives. Only if real natural resource prices increase at the rate r will they provide such a return to their owners. If prices were rising slower than r, natural resources would be an inferior investment and owners should put their funds elsewhere. A price rise above r is also unsustainable in the long run because investors would bid up the current price of resources to reflect their investment desirability until the possibility for future increases in excess of r were eliminated.

An Example: What Should the Price of Oil Be?   ■

As an example of this type of analysis we will investigate whether the 1978 high market price of crude oil (about $13 per barrel) reflected scarcity costs arising from the finite nature of oil reserves or more properly should have been regarded as a reflection of monopoly rents. The possibility that the price represented actual

---

[10]Since r is a "real" rate of return (that is, corrected for inflation), the prediction here is that the price of the resource relative to the price of all other goods should rise at the rate r. This result was first rigorously shown by H. Hotelling in "The Economics of Exhaustible Resources," *The Journal of Political Economy*, Vol. 39, No. 2 (April 1931), pp. 137–175.

marginal costs of production can be readily dismissed since there was general agreement that the marginal costs of the lowest cost producer (Saudi Arabia) was well below $1 per barrel. In order to assess scarcity costs in 1978 we have to assume something about the future price of oil. Although there is considerable disagreement on that subject, there is some consensus that by the year 2020 (40 years from now) energy will be generally available from new technologies (solar, fusion, tidal, geothermal, and so forth) at the equivalent of $20–$30 per barrel of oil. Taking the upper range of these numbers and assuming that r is 5 percent gives

$$PDV = \frac{P_{40}}{(1 + r)^{40}} = \frac{\$30}{(1.05)^{40}} = \$4.26 \qquad [16.17]$$

as the equilibrium present value. Hence the 1978 market price was more than three times what appeared to be dictated by the scarcity value of oil. The OPEC monopoly was therefore a far more important factor in setting the market price than was scarcity. Of course, this type of calculation is rather crude: it takes no account of substitution among fuels as prices rise nor does it allow for the substantial uncertainties involved in the development of the new technologies. More sophisticated studies[11] have, however, come up with essentially the same conclusions. As a policy guide it seemed more likely that the price of oil was too high (in relation to its scarcity value) than that it was too low.

Summary

The principal purpose of this chapter has been to integrate the theory of capital with the theory of the firm. Capital and labor can be treated symmetrically in the analysis of production decisions, and here we developed that symmetry in detail. The most important concept in that analysis is the notion of the rental rate on a machine. This is the cost per unit of capital that is relevant for the firm's choices and is directly analogous to the wage rate paid to labor. By analyzing the determinants of this rental rate, we can come to understand why the input choices of firms might change. In particular, we showed that the overall rate of return (r) is an important component of a machine's rental cost because it reflects the opportunities forgone by investing in a specific machine rather than in some alternative. An increase in r therefore increases rental rates and causes firms to reduce their demand for capital services. A fall in r would have the opposite effect.

We showed several other examples of how the rate of return can be used in economic analysis. Any decision about using resources over time (such as a decision to "invest" in an education, or a decision about how much oil to pump

---

[11]See for example W. D. Nordhaus, "The Allocation of Energy Resources," *Brookings Papers on Economic Activity,* 1973, No. 3, pp. 529–570.

currently from a fixed pool) must consider the opportunity costs involved. Those opportunity costs are best measured by the rate of return, r. In particular, we showed that individuals who are considering investing in an education or training program will compare the yield on that investment to r in making their decisions. Similarly, owners of exhaustible resources will compare r to the capital gains they are earning from the price appreciation of those resources in deciding how much to produce currently. Many other applications can be derived from these basic principles.

Our analysis in this chapter has stressed the opportunity cost of capital as a productive input and the implications of this cost for the allocation of resources. This emphasis on allocational issues is in agreement with the general focus of this book. So far we have minimized the discussion of issues of equity, and we have continued in that spirit in this chapter. We have not, therefore, asked whether the owner of a machine "deserves" to receive a payment for providing this machine to a firm, just as we paid little attention to the question of whether a highly skilled worker "deserves" the high wage rate he or she receives. Some authors (following a Marxian tradition) believe this omission is more serious in a discussion of capital pricing than it is for the labor market. Indeed, those authors would argue that capital owners do not deserve to receive any of the opportunity costs of the machines they own. As we have mentioned before, this normative aspect of capital theory can be more appropriately addressed as one aspect of the desirability of private property as an economic and social institution.

Suggested Readings

Becker, G. S., *Human Capital: A Theoretical and Empirical Analysis with Special Reference to Education,* National Bureau of Economic Research, General Series No. 80 (New York: Columbia University Press, 1964).

Bischoff, C., "Business Investment in the 1970s: A Comparison of Models," *Brookings Papers on Economic Activity* No. 1 (1971), pp. 13–58.

Blaug, M., *Economic Theory in Retrospect* (Homewood, Ill.: Richard D. Irwin, Inc., 1962), chap. 12.

Fromm, G., *Tax Incentives and Capital Spending* (Washington, D.C.: The Brookings Institution, 1971).

Harcourt, G. C., "Some Cambridge Controversies in the Theory of Capital," *Journal of Economic Literature* 7 (June 1969), pp. 369–405.

Jorgenson, D. W., "Econometric Studies of Investment Behavior: A Survey," *Journal of Economic Literature* 9 (December 1971), pp. 1111–1147.

Mincer, J., "The Distribution of Labor Incomes: A Survey with Special Reference to the Human Capital Approach," *Journal of Economic Literature* 8 (March 1970), pp. 1–26.

Samuelson, P. A., "Parable and Realism in Capital Theory: The Surrogate Production Function," *Review of Economic Studies* 39 (June 1962), pp. 193–206.

Solow, R. M., *Capital Theory and the Rate of Return* (Amsterdam: North Holland Publishing Co., 1964).

———, "The Economics of Resources or the Resources of Economics," *American Economic Review* 64 (May 1974), pp. 1–14.

Problems

16.1

Suppose J. P. Miser obtains utility from present and future consumption (C_1 and C_2) and that she has a certain amount of dollars (W) to allocate between these goods.

a. If the interest rate is r, what will the budget constraint in this problem be?

b. Using the budget constraint from part a) show graphically how W will be allocated between C_1 and C_2 so as to maximize utility. What will the tangency condition for a utility maximum be in this situation?

c. Suppose r were to increase. What will happen to the utility-maximizing choices for C_1 and C_2?

16.2

Assume that an individual expects to work for 40 years, then retire with a life expectancy of an additional 20 years. Suppose also that the individual's earnings rise at a rate of 3 percent per year and that the interest rate is also 3 percent (the overall price level is constant in this problem). What (constant) fraction of income must the individual save in each working year to be able to finance a level of retirement income equal to 60 percent of earnings in the year just prior to retirement?

16.3

The No-flite Golfball Company manufactures cut-proof golfballs and is thinking of investing in a new name. Their media personnel have come up with two suggestions: "Astro-flite" and "Jack Nickless." It's cheaper to switch to "Astro-flite" since the second name will involve legal fees for dealing with a well-known golfer who is likely to get upset by the whole thing. The second name, however, is expected to bring in more business than the first. If the costs and payoffs are as given below, and the firm expects to go out of business in five years, is it worth it to make a name switch, and if so, to which name?

	Cost	Yearly Return	Interest Rate
Astro-flite	3800	1000	10%
Jack Nickless	5000	1400	10%

Would your answer change if the interest rate were 15%?

16.4

Some foresters suggest that timber plots be managed so as to achieve "maximum sustainable yield." How might an economist evaluate this proposition?

16.5

Suppose scotch increases in value as it ages. In particular, the value of scotch at any time t is given by $V = 100t - 6t^2$ and the proportional growth rate in that value is $100 - 12t/V$. Graph this scotch function. At what value of t is V as large as possible? Is that when the scotch should be bottled? If the interest rate is .05, when should the scotch be bottled?

16.6

Why do railroad companies lay their tracks up and down hills when a level roadbed would save operating expenses and those savings would persist forever?

Compound Interest

Introduction

The purpose of this appendix is to gather some basic mathematical results of the theory of compound interest. These results are widely used in economics, and this appendix can serve as a convenient reference.

Compounding

Assume that there is a current prevailing interest rate of i per period (say, one year). This interest rate is expected to remain constant over all future periods.[1] If \$1 is invested at this rate i and the interest is compounded (that is, future interest is paid on past interest earned), then (as we showed in Chapter 16):

at the end of 1 period \$1 will be . . . $\$1 \times (1 + i)$
at the end of 2 periods \$1 will be . . . $\$1 \times (1 + i) \times (1 + i) = \$1 \times (1 + i)^2$

.

.

.

and at the end of n periods \$1 will be . . . $\$1 \times (1 + i)^n$.

---

[1] The assumption of a constant i is obviously unrealistic. Since the problems introduced by considering an interest rate that varies from period to period greatly complicate the notation without adding a commensurate degree of conceptual knowledge, such an analysis is not undertaken here.

452

Similarly, $N grows:

$$\$N \times (1 + i)$$
$$\$N \times (1 + i)^2$$

$$\cdot$$
$$\cdot$$
$$\cdot$$

$$\$N \times (1 + i)^n.$$

Present Discounted Value

The *present value* of $1 payable one period from now is

$$\frac{\$1}{(1 + i)}$$

This is simply the amount that an individual would be willing to pay now for the promise of $1 at the end of one period. Similarly, the present value of $1 payable *n* periods from now is

$$\frac{\$1}{(1 + i)^n}$$

and the present value of $N payable *n* periods from now is

$$\frac{\$N}{(1 + i)^n}$$

Table 16.2 showed the present value of $1 for various time periods and interest rates, and a review of that table may help to conceptualize the notion of present value. In general, the present value of a sum payable in the future will be smaller the higher the interest rate or the more distant the payment date.

The *present discounted value* of a stream of payments $N_0, N_1, N_2, \ldots, N_n$ (where the subscripts indicate the period in which the payment is to be made) is

$$PDV = N_0 + \frac{N_1}{(1 + i)} + \frac{N_2}{(1 + i)^2} + \ldots + \frac{N_n}{(1 + i)^n} \qquad \text{[16A.1]}$$

PDV is the amount that an individual would be willing to pay in return for a promise to receive the stream $N_0, N_1, \ldots, N_n$. It represents the amount that would have to be invested now if the person wished to duplicate the payment stream.

Annuities and Perpetuities

An *annuity* is a promise to pay N dollars in each period for n periods, starting next period. The *PDV* of such a contract is

$$PDV = \frac{N}{(1 + i)} + \frac{N}{(1 + i)^2} + \cdots + \frac{N}{(1 + i)^n} \qquad [16A.2]$$

Let $D = 1/(1 + i)$, then

$$\begin{aligned} PDV &= N(D + D^2 + \cdots + D^n) \\ &= ND(1 + D + D^2 + \cdots + D^{n-1}) \\ &= ND\left(\frac{1 - D^n}{1 - D}\right) \end{aligned}$$

Notice that D^n approaches 0 for large values of n.
Therefore, for an annuity of infinite duration,

$$PDV \text{ of infinite annuity} = ND\left(\frac{1}{1 - D}\right)$$

which, by the definition of D,

$$= N\left(\frac{1}{1 + i}\right)\left(\frac{1}{1 - [1/(1 + i)]}\right) \qquad [16A.3]$$

$$= N\left(\frac{1}{1 + i}\right)\left(\frac{1 + i}{i}\right) = \frac{N}{i}$$

This case of an infinite period annuity is sometimes called a *perpetuity,* or a *consol.* Such annuities are rare (indeed, technically illegal) in the United States but are common in Canada and the United Kingdom. The formula simply says that the amount that must be invested if an individual is to obtain $\$N$ per period forever is simply $\$N/i$, since this amount of money would earn $\$N$ in interest each period ($i \cdot \$N/i = \$N$). For example, if $N = \$10$ and $i = .05$, the *PDV* of the perpetuity would be $\$200$ ($= \$10/.05$). An investment of $\$200$ would yield $\$10$ in interest payments per year forever.

Bonds

An n period *bond* is a promise to pay N dollars each period (starting next period) for n periods. It also promises to return the principal (face) value of the bond at the end of n periods. If the principal value of the bond is P dollars (usually at least $\$1,000$ in the United States bond market), then the present discounted value of such a promise is

$$PDV = \frac{N}{(1 + i)} + \frac{N}{(1 + i)^2} + \cdots + \frac{N}{(1 + i)^n} + \frac{P}{(1 + i)^n} \qquad \text{[16A.4]}$$

We can look at equation 16A.4 in another way. Suppose we knew the price at which the bond is currently trading, say B. Then we could ask what value of i gives the bond a *PDV* equal to B. To find this i we set

$$B = PDV = \frac{N}{(1 + i)} + \frac{N}{(1 + i)^2} + \cdots + \frac{N}{(1 + i)^n} + \frac{P}{(1 + i)^n} \qquad \text{[16A.5]}$$

Since B, N, and P are known, we can solve equation 16A.5 for i.[2] The i that solves the equation is called the yield on the bond, and it is the best measure of the return actually available from the bond. The yield of a bond represents the return available from direct interest payments and from any price differential between the initial price *(B)* and the maturity price *(P)*.

Notice that as i increases, *PDV* decreases. This is a precise way of formulating the well-known concept that bond prices *(PDV's)* and interest rates (yields) are inversely correlated. Conversely, a rise in the price of a bond will reduce its yield because the buyer has to pay more for the given payment stream.

Continuous Time

So far this appendix has dealt with discrete time—the analysis has been divided into periods. Often it is more convenient to deal with continuous time. In such a case the interest on an investment is compounded "instantaneously" and growth over time is "smooth." Many financial intermediaries (for example, savings banks) have adopted continuous interest formulas in recent years.

Suppose that i is given as the (nominal) interest rate per year, but that half this nominal rate is compounded every 6 months. Then, at the end of 1 year, the investment of $1 would have grown to:

$$\$1 \times \left(1 + \frac{i}{2}\right)^2 \qquad \text{[16A.6]}$$

Notice that this is superior to investing for 1 year at the simple rate, i, because interest has been paid on interest; that is:

$$\left(1 + \frac{i}{2}\right)^2 > (1 + i) \qquad \text{[16A.7]}$$

---

[2]Since this equation is really an nth degree polynomial, there are in reality n solutions (roots). Only one of these solutions is the relevant one reported in bond tables. The other solutions are either imaginary or unreasonable. In the present example there is only one real solution.

Consider the limit of this process—for the nominal rate of i per period consider the amount that would be realized if i were in fact "compounded n times during the period"; let $n \to \infty$:

$$\lim_{n \to \infty} \left(1 + \frac{i}{n} \right)^n \qquad \text{[16A.8]}$$

This limit exists and is simply e^i, where e is the base of natural logarithms (the value of e is approximately 2.72). It is important to note that $e^i > (1 + i)$—it is much better to have continuous compounding over the period than to have simple interest.

We can ask what continuously compounded rate, r, yields the same amount at the end of one period as the simple rate i. We are looking for the value of r that solves the equation:

$$e^r = (1 + i) \qquad \text{[16A.9]}$$

Conversely, we could use Equation 16A.9 to ask what the simple interest equivalent (i) is for a continuously compounded rate r. Banks, for example, often quote an interest rate of 5 percent, but then note that interest is compounded "daily" thereby giving an "effective annual interest rate" of 5.13 percent. Table 16A.1 gives a number of such effective annual interest equivalents for continuously compounded rates between 3 and 10 percent. As we have noted, the effective annual rates are larger than the reported continuous rates because of the effects of compounding. The difference, in absolute terms, between continuous rates and their simple interest equivalents is larger for higher interest rates.

Table 16A.1 / Effective Annual Interest Rates for Selected Continuously Compounded Rates

Continuously Compounded Rate	Effective Annual Rate
3.0%	3.04%
4.0	4.08
5.0	5.13
5.5	5.65
6.0	6.18
6.5	6.72
7.0	7.25
8.0	8.33
9.0	9.42
10.0	10.52

Suggested Readings

Baumol, W. J., *Economic Theory and Operations Analysis,* 2d ed. (Englewood Cliffs, N.J.: Prentice-Hall, Inc., 1965), chap. 19.

Brigham, E. F., and J. L. Pappas, *Managerial Economics* (Hinsdale, Ill.: The Dryden Press, 1972), chap. 13 and Appen. A.

Chemical Rubber Company, *Standard Mathematical Tables* (Cleveland, Ohio: Chemical Publishing Company, Inc., 1954).

Cox, E. B., ed., *Basic Tables in Business and Economics* (New York: McGraw-Hill, Inc., 1967).

Puu, Tönu, "A Simple Graphic Method for Estimating the Yield of Bonds," in *The Theory of Interest Rates,* ed. F. G. Hahn and F. P. R. Brechling (London: Collier-Macmillan, Ltd., 1965).

Part VI   General Equilibrium and Welfare

Introduction

In previous sections of this book we have examined the operations of single markets in isolation. This simplification is necessary if we are to comprehend in any detailed way the determinants of supply and demand. In order to understand the workings of the market system, we must somewhat narrow our focus. Nonetheless, the "partial equilibrium" (single market) method of analysis has one major weakness: We can never conceptualize how the system works as a whole. Clearly, an increase in demand in one market will have an effect not only on prices in that one market; the effects of this shift in demand will also reverberate throughout the economy. For exampl, consider the effects of an increase in the demand for automobiles. Such an increase will affect pricing in the automobile market. The increased demand for cars will also create an increased demand for steel, glass, chromium, and so forth. These increased demands will similarly affect demands in other markets for goods that these industries use. But the story does not stop there; in fact, it has only begun. The increased demand for production in various industries will increase the demand for factors of production, notably labor. This increased demand for labor may raise wages, thereby increasing purchasing power and increasing the demand for all those goods that individuals buy. It is possible to extend this story indefinitely, but the essential point is clear. The economic system is tied together by a vast web of interconnected markets. A disturbance in one market generates ripples that spread through many others. In fact, by starting the discussion with an "increase in the demand for automobiles" we have probably obscured some aspects of the interwoven nature of the economic system since such "increases" do not just happen.

Rather, an ideal theory would attempt to understand the forces that caused the increase.

Economists have, naturally, been aware of the need for a *general equilibrium* approach to the economic system. At the same time that the Marshallian analysis was being developed in England, a different mode of analysis was being considered by several Continental economists. This second analytical system represented an attempt to understand the workings of the economic system as a whole. Foremost among the individuals engaged in these investigations was the French economist Léon Walras (1834–1910). In *Elements of Pure Economics,* Walras demonstrated a model for looking at the economy (in a formal way) as a set of *simultaneous equations* which determine the quantities and prices of all those goods and services that are traded among individuals. The essential concept in this analysis was that of simultaneity. Just as the solutions to two equations with two unknowns studied in high-school algebra depend simultaneously on both equations, so do the equilibrium prices and quantities determined by the economic system depend simultaneously on the workings of all markets. The Walrasian system attempts to represent this interwoven nature of the economy's allocation mechanism.

This part will not investigate the general Walrasian model in any detail. Although Walras's concepts (or their modern successors) will underlie much of the analysis, it is not necessary for us to develop a detailed general equilibrium model here. Rather, these chapters will deal with only a few simple cases, although we can easily make the results more general.

In Chapter 17 we will examine the economic concepts of efficiency and welfare. We will show what it means to say that resources are allocated "efficiently" and will demonstrate conditions which must hold if efficiency is to be obtained. Because efficiency is a property of the economic system as a whole it will be necessary for us to introduce a number of general equilibrium tools in order to discuss it adequately. Those tools will also be used in Chapter 17 to analyze briefly the question of equity and to describe what economists mean by the term "economic welfare." A principal purpose of our examination will be to show the connection, if any, between efficiency and welfare and to demonstrate how difficult it is to make utility comparisons among individuals.

In Chapter 17 efficiency and welfare are treated as goals of any economy. In Chapter 18 we examine in detail one particular means for achieving those goals: the perfectly competitive price system. We will show that there is a close relationship between economic efficiency and such a price system. Specifically, we will demonstrate that a smoothly operating, perfectly competitive price system can achieve an efficient allocation of resources. We will also show, however, that such a conclusion has two serious reservations attached to it. First there are a number of impediments that may prevent a price system from attaining efficiency and these are likely to be prevalent in the real world. Second, even though a competitive price system may, in some situations, promote efficiency, we will show that there is no mechanism which guarantees that such efficient solutions will be equitable. To achieve normative goals, additional constraints may have to be placed on the price system. Chapter 18 concludes by pointing out that these potential shortcomings of the price system do not preclude use of the relationship between pricing and efficiency to study a number of general equilibrium questions about the economy. Some applications are briefly examined.

The relationship between pricing and efficiency is examined in a slightly different way in the Appendix to Chapter 18. There we introduce a widely used mathematical tool, linear programming, and show how it can be used to solve problems in allocating resources. Particular attention is devoted to the "duality" between the solutions to such problems and the existence of prices that might bring the solutions about.

Chapter 17   Efficiency and Welfare

Introduction

In this chapter we will examine two general goals of an economic system: "efficiency" and "welfare." We will attempt to provide a definition of those goals and then show the conditions that must hold if the goals are to be achieved. Because the goal of economic efficiency can be more precisely defined and has been more intensively analyzed by economists than has welfare, the majority of the chapter will be devoted to it. The final sections of the chapter focus on the connection, if any, between efficiency and welfare and indicate some of the problems inherent in making judgments about equity among individuals.

Economic Efficiency

The word "efficiency" is used in many different economic contexts. It is frequently argued that American workers are "more efficient" than their foreign counterparts; that the steel industry is plagued by "inefficient" technology; that an electric motor is "more efficient" than a steam engine; and, perhaps, that monopolies and labor unions create "inefficiencies." Each of those notions of efficiency is important to a variety of policy issues. The tools developed in this text are useful in quantifying and understanding these issues. The concept of efficiency we will discuss in this chapter is, however, both more far-reaching and more abstract than any of those mentioned. Here we will use the term *economic efficiency* to describe a situation in which resources are allocated in an "optimal" way. To describe what economists mean by "optimal" is one principal purpose of this chapter.

Traditionally, the investigation of economic efficiency has been carried on by using a restricted model. This model examines the question of efficiency in a static context. It examines the allocation of resources at one point in time, and poses the question whether conditions might be "improved" if these resources were reallocated. This analysis is therefore one more example of the comparative statics approach. While it is possible to generalize the analysis a bit, we will not attempt such generalizations in this book. The basic static model illustrates most of the properties found in advanced models.

Definition of Efficient Allocation of Resources

A definition of an efficient allocation of resources is difficult because there is no single magnitude that is being maximized. For example, it is impossible to talk about the output of the economic system as a whole because there is no unambiguous way of adding up all the different goods that are produced. Similarly, since we have no means for making comparisons of individuals' well being, we have no way of measuring society's "utility" nor for deciding whether overall welfare is as high as is possible given existing resources. For these reasons it is clear that optimality must be a multidimensional concept; problems of aggregation can therefore be avoided. Using this multidimensional idea, we can initially introduce the concept of efficiency in an abstract setting. If there are a number of beneficial activities, a situation is said to be *efficient* if one of these activities cannot be increased without decreasing some other activity. It is perhaps easiest to see why such a situation is called efficient by observing what *inefficient* situations might be. By the definition, a situation is inefficient if some beneficial activity can be increased without necessitating a cutback on *any other* activities. In inefficient situations, conditions can be made unambiguously better. On the other hand, if we are to move from one efficient situation to another, this would require reducing one activity in order to increase other activities. Without a way of comparing these activities it is impossible to know whether or not conditions have improved.

We can make this general definition clearer by considering an example that will arise in this chapter. We will consider an *exchange economy* in which certain amounts of various goods exist and the problem is to allocate these goods among individuals in an efficient way. Among all the possible allocations of those goods we define:

Definition

An *efficient allocation* of the existing goods in an exchange economy is one in which no one individual can be made better off without making someone else worse off.

This concept of efficiency avoids the problem of interpersonal comparison of utility. Rather, individuals decide for themselves whether a particular change makes them better off or not. If one individual were made worse off by some allocational change, even if everyone else were made better off, we could not say that the change was an unambiguous improvement. Since we have no way of comparing individuals' utility levels, we cannot pass judgments on changes that make some individuals better off and others worse off. A situation in which one person could be made better off without necessarily reducing the welfare of anyone else would, however, be clearly inefficient. Conditions can be unambiguously improved by redistributing the existing goods; consequently the initial situation would, by definition, be termed inefficient.

Similar definitions of efficiency in other contexts will be introduced later in this chapter. Each of these will avoid the problem of comparing individuals (or of comparing apples and oranges for that matter) by using the approach we have just outlined. By studying each of these various definitions, we should gain an appreciation of the reasons why economists define efficiency in the way they do.

Efficiency in Exchange

In an exchange economy the quantities of all goods are fixed. By starting our discussion with this simplified case, we can, for the moment, ignore problems raised in the theory of production. Our goal is to allocate these goods among individuals in an efficient way. The necessary conditions for an efficient allocation can easily be stated:

Optimization Principle

If an allocation of goods in an exchange economy is to be efficient, the goods should be distributed among individuals so that the marginal rate of substitution[1] (*MRS*) between any two goods is the same for all individuals.

An Intuitive Proof

To show this result, let us suppose there are only two goods (say, guns and butter) and two individuals (Smith and Jones) in society. We will also assume that there are 50 guns and 100 pounds of butter to be allocated. Would an equal allocation of these commodities to each individual be efficient? The answer to this question depends on the individuals' tastes. Suppose that the *MRS* (of guns for butter) for Smith is 2/1

---

[1] Remember, in Chapter 3, we defined the *MRS* (of *X* for *Y*) to be the number of units of *Y* an individual is willing to give up to get one more *X*. It is the (negative of the) slope of an indifference curve.

when he gets 25 guns and 50 pounds of butter. Smith is willing to give up 2 pounds of butter to get 1 more gun under the proposed equal allocation. On the other hand, suppose that Jones' *MRS* (of guns for butter) is 1/1. Under the equal allocation scheme (with 25 guns and 50 pounds of butter) he would be willing to trade 1 pound of butter for 1 gun. Under these assumptions, it is easy to see that the proposed allocation is not efficient. Take 2 pounds of butter from Smith. Trade 1 of these to Jones for 1 gun (notice that Jones is willing to make this trade). Now give this gun to Smith so that he will be as well off as he was before the 2 pounds of butter were taken. We have now found a new allocation in which Smith (with 26 guns and 48 pounds of butter) and Jones (with 24 guns and 51 pounds of butter) are each as well off as they were under the original equal allocation. With this new allocation, however, there is 1 pound of butter left over. It may be given to either Smith or Jones, making the lucky recipient better off than he was before. What we have shown, therefore, is that the initial (equal) allocation was not efficient: There exists some alternative allocation in which Smith, say, could be made better off without making Jones any worse off.

Edgeworth Box Diagram

Obviously the numbers in this example were purely arbitrary. Any allocation in which the *MRS*'s of two individuals differ can be shown to be inefficient. Whenever goods are allocated so that the rates at which individuals are willing to trade one good for another differ, these goods can be reallocated in an unambiguously better way; that is, a more efficient allocation can be found. There may be many different allocations that are efficient, however, and we can most easily demonstrate these by using a graphic device known as the *Edgeworth Box*,[2] the construction of which is shown in Figure 17.1. The Edgeworth Box has dimensions given by the total (fixed) quantities of the two goods (call these goods simply X and Y). The horizontal dimension of the box represents the total quantity of X available, whereas the height of the box is the total quantity of Y. The point O_S is considered to be the origin for Smith. Quantities of X for Smith are measured along the horizontal axis rightward from O_S; quantities of Y, along the vertical axis upward from O_S. Any point in the box can then be regarded as some allocation of X and Y to Smith. For example, at the point A, Smith gets X_S^A and Y_S^A. The useful property of the Edgeworth Box is that the quantities received by Jones are also recorded by point A. Jones simply gets that part of the total quantity which is "left over." In fact, we can regard Jones' quantities as being measured from the origin O_J. The point A therefore also corresponds to the quantities X_J^A and Y_J^A for Jones. Notice that the quantities assigned to Smith and Jones in this manner exactly exhaust the total quantities of X and Y available.

---

[2]Named for F. Y. Edgeworth (1854–1926) who, in 1881, derived the concept of a contract curve in his *Mathematical Psychics: An Essay on the Application of Mathematics to the Moral Sciences* (New York: August M. Kelley, 1953).

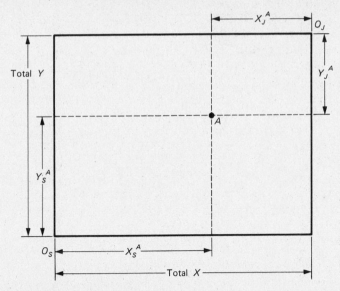

Figure 17.1 / Edgeworth Box Diagram

The Edgeworth Box diagram permits all possible allocations of two goods (X and Y) to be visualized. If we consider the corner O_S to be Smith's "origin" and O_J to be Jones's, then the allocation represented by point A would have Smith getting X_S^A and Y_S^A, and Jones would receive what is left over (X_J^A, Y_J^A). The purpose of this diagram is to discover which of the possible allocations within the box are efficient.

Finding an Efficient Point

Any point in the Edgeworth Box represents an allocation of the available goods between Smith and Jones, and all possible allocations are contained within the box. The reader may wish to choose any point in the box and demonstrate that this point represents a unique division of goods X and Y to Smith and Jones. To discover which of the points are efficient, we must introduce tastes. In Figure 17.2 Smith's indifference curve map is drawn with origin O_S. Movements in a northeasterly direction represent higher levels of utility to Smith. In the same figure, Jones' indifference curve map is drawn with the corner O_J as an origin. We have taken Jones' indifference curve map, rotated it 180°, and fit it into the northeast corner of the Edgeworth Box. Movements in a southwesterly direction represent increases in Jones' utility level.

Using these superimposed indifference curve maps it is possible to find the efficient points in the diagram. Consider any fixed utility level for Jones, say, U_J^3. The definition of efficiency requires that Smith's utility level be maximized for this given level of Jones' utility; not to do so would be inefficient. The point of maximum utility for Smith in this case is point M_2, where Smith's indifference curve (U_S^2) is just tangent to the curve U_J^3. At this point of tangency the MRS (of X for Y) for Smith is equal to that for Jones; hence the efficient conditions we discussed earlier hold.

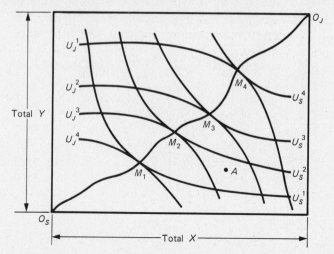

Figure 17.2 / Edgeworth Box Diagram of Efficiency in Exchange

The points on the curve O_S, O_J are efficient in the sense that at these allocations Smith cannot be made better off without making Jones worse off, and vice-versa. An allocation such as A, on the other hand, is inefficient since both Smith and Jones can be made better off (by choosing M_2, for example). Notice that along O_S, O_J the MRS for Smith is equal to that for Jones. The line O_S, O_J is called the contract curve.

Contract Curve

Within the Edgeworth Box there are a number of tangencies such as M_2. A few of these (M_1, M_3, and M_4) are labeled in Figure 17.2. Each of these points has the property that Smith's utility is as large as possible given some preassigned level for Jones' utility. Similarly, for any specific level of Smith's utility, Jones' utility is as large as possible at these points. To describe all of these efficient points we define:

Definition

The locus of all the efficient points in the Edgeworth Box diagram of an exchange economy is called the *contract curve*. It shows those allocations that individuals might attain through free bargaining. Points on the contract curve are sometimes called *Pareto optimal* allocations.[3]

In Figure 17.2 this locus is given by the line running from O_S to O_J. Every allocation on the contract curve has the property that Smith cannot be made better off without making Jones worse off. The utilities of Smith and Jones are directly in conflict at such points, as is required by the definition of efficiency. This is not true for points off the contract curve. For example, an allocation such as point A, which is off the

[3]Named for the Italian economist Vilfredo Pareto (1848–1923).

contract curve, is distinctly inefficient in that both persons can be made better off by moving to a point on the contract curve. This would be true, for instance, if the allocation M_2 were chosen rather than A. At M_2 both Smith and Jones are better off than they were at A; it is therefore obvious that point A represents an inefficient way of allocating X and Y.

The Edgeworth Box is a useful tool both for understanding the meaning of efficiency in exchange and for illustrating the requirements that MRS's be equalized. Each point in the box represents a different allocation of the same total quantities of goods. It is surprising that relatively "few" of these points are in fact efficient. Indeed, it would appear to be a very difficult task for some authority (lacking precise knowledge of individual tastes) to select allocations that just happened to be on the contract curve. It might be presumed that allocations of X and Y, which are rather arbitrarily chosen, will fail to be efficient. On the other hand, individuals, if left on their own to trade freely, may recognize the mutual benefits of being on the contract curve and may be able to choose an efficient point. We will return to this discussion on how efficient allocations might be discovered in Chapter 18.

Exchange with Initial Endowments: Gains from Trade

In our previous discussion, we assumed that fixed quantities of the two goods in question existed and that these could be allocated in any way conceivable. A somewhat different, more restricted, analysis would hold if various quantities of the goods in question started out in the possession of the individuals participating in exchange. A hypothetical example of such a situation would occur if two people were marooned on an island and each started with a supply of commodities. There is a very definite possibility that each person can benefit from voluntary trade (suppose force is ruled out by social conventions), since it is unlikely that the initial allocations would be efficient ones. On the other hand, neither person would engage in a trade that would leave him or her worse off than without trading. Hence only a portion of the contract curve can be regarded as efficient allocations that might result from exchange.

Those ideas are illustrated in Figure 17.3. The initial endowments of Smith and Jones are represented by point A in the Edgeworth Box. As before, the dimensions of the box are taken to be the total quantities of the two goods (X and Y) available. The contract curve of efficient allocations is represented by the line O_S, O_J. Let the indifference curve of Smith, which passes through point A, be called U_S^A and, similarly, let Jones's indifference curve through A be denoted by U_J^A. Notice that, at point A, the individual's indifference curves are not tangent, and therefore the initial endowments are not efficient. Neither Smith nor Jones will accept trading outcomes that give them utility levels of less than U_S^A and U_J^A, respectively. It would be preferable for an individual to refrain from trading rather than accept such an inferior outcome. Thus only those efficient allocations between M_1 and M_2 on the contract curve can occur as a result of free exchange. The range of efficient

Optimal Choice of Inputs for a Single Firm

As a starting point in our discussion of efficiency in production, let us consider a single firm that uses two inputs, capital (K) and labor (L), to produce two different goods (call these simply X and Y). In addition, suppose that the firm has fixed amounts of capital and labor[5] and must only decide how to allocate the inputs between producing either X or Y. The firm will be operating efficiently if it is not possible for it to reallocate its inputs in such a way that output of X can be increased without necessarily cutting back on Y. The condition that will bring about such an efficient allocation is quite similar to that we discussed for efficiency in exchange; presenting the condition involves reintroducing the concept of the firm's rate of technical substitution *(RTS),* first mentioned in Chapter 6. There we defined the *RTS* as the rate at which a firm can substitute one input (say, labor) for another (say, capital) while holding the output of a particular good constant. The *RTS* is simply the (negative of) the slope of a production isoquant. Using this concept we can state:

Optimization Principle

A firm with fixed resources has allocated those resources efficiently if it has them fully employed and if the *RTS* between the inputs is the same for every output the firm produces.

An Intuitive Proof

Before going on, we will present an intuitive proof of this assertion. The first part of the rule is obvious: If a firm leaves any portion of its available inputs unemployed, it is not operating efficiently. By putting the unemployed factors to work, the firm could increase its output of one good without having to cut back elsewhere. Being fully employed is not, however, sufficient to insure efficiency. It is also required that the firm allocate its resources so that the technical rate of trade-off between inputs (the *RTS*) is the same in each output the firm produces. To see this, let us assume that a firm has 100 hours of labor and 100 machine hours to devote to the production of, say, cars and trucks. Suppose that the firm (rather arbitrarily) decides to allocate half of each of the inputs to the production of cars and the other half to the production of trucks. With $50K$ and $50L$ producing cars, the *RTS* might be 2: The same number of cars could be produced with $48K$ and $51L$. Assume, alternatively, that the *RTS* in truck production is 1: The same truck output could be produced with $51K$ and $49L$. It is clear that the alternative allocation of the available inputs is superior to the initial equal allocation. The 100 labor-hours are still being used (51 in car production, 49 in truck production), but only 99 machine hours are being used (48 in car produc-

---

[5]Of course, the ultimate goal here is to analyze how much of each resource a firm should have in the first place, but for the moment it is convenient to hold input levels fixed.

tion, 51 in truck production). Even though outputs of both cars and trucks are the same under the revised allocation as under the equal allocation, there is now 1 machine hour "left over." This can be used in either car or truck production to increase output over what it initially was. The initial allocation (with unequal *RTS*'s) was therefore inefficient.

Box Diagram Proof

We can demonstrate a more precise proof by using a diagram similar to the Edgeworth Box. Figure 17.4 illustrates such a diagram. The dimensions of the box are determined by the total quantities of capital and labor available to the firm. The southwest corner of the box, O_X, is taken as the origin for an isoquant map showing alternative levels of X which might be produced using various combinations of K and L. Similarly, the northeast corner of the box, O_Y, is taken as the origin for an isoquant map for good Y. Any point within the box represents a (fully employed) allocation of the available resources between the production of X and the production of Y. As before, the locus of efficient allocations of K and L is given by the points of tangency of the various isoquants. Along the locus of these points, the inputs are allocated efficiently since X output cannot be increased without decreasing the output of Y. As required for efficiency, the RTS's are equal along the O_X, O_Y locus. Notice that allocations off this locus (such as point A) are not efficient. By moving

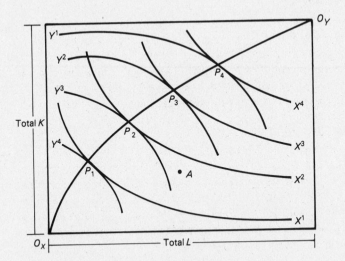

Figure 17.4 / Box Diagram of Efficiency in Production

This diagram is analogous to Figure 17.2. It shows various efficient ways in which a firm can allocate a fixed amount of K and L between the production of two outputs (X and Y). The line joining O_X and O_Y is the locus of these efficient points. Along this line the RTS (of L for K) in the production of good X is equal to the RTS in the production of Y.

from A to the efficiency locus (at a point such as P_2), the firm can produce both more $X(X^2)$ and more $Y(Y^3)$.

Production Possibility Frontier

The efficiency locus in Figure 17.4 shows the maximum output of Y that can be produced for any preassigned output of X. We can use this information to construct a *production possibility frontier,* which shows those alternative outputs of X and Y that can be produced with the fixed stocks of K and L. In Figure 17.5, the O_X, O_Y locus has been taken from Figure 17.4 and transferred onto a graph with X and Y outputs on the axes. At O_X, for example, no resources are devoted to X production; consequently Y output is as large as is possible with the existing resources. Similarly, at O_Y, the output of X is as large as possible. The other points on the production possibility frontier (say, P_1, P_2, P_3, P_4) are derived in an identical way from the efficiency locus.

The production possibility curve clearly exhibits the notion of efficiency we have been using. Any point inside the frontier is inefficient because output can be unambiguously increased. The allocation of K and L represented by point A, for example, is inefficient because output levels in the shaded area are both attainable,

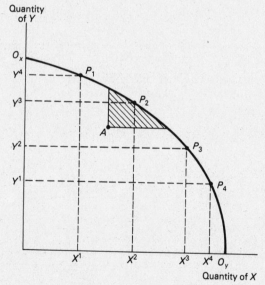

Figure 17.5 / Production Possibility Frontier Derived from Figure 17.4

The production possibility frontier shows those alternative combinations of X and Y which can be efficiently produced by a firm with fixed resources. The curve can be derived from Figure 17.4 by varying inputs between the production of X and Y while maintaining the conditions for efficiency. The slope of the production possibility curve is called the rate of product transformation (RPT).

and preferable, to A. If we look again at Figure 17.4, we can see how the available resources might be reallocated so as to obtain those more efficient points.

Rate of Product Transformation

The slope of the production possibility frontier shows how X output can be substituted for Y output when total resources are held constant. For example, for points near O_X on the production possibility frontier, the slope is a small negative number, say, $-\frac{1}{4}$, implying that by reducing Y output by 1 unit, X output could be increased by 4. Near O_Y, on the other hand, the slope is a large negative number, say -5, implying that Y output must be reduced by 5 units to permit the production of 1 more X. The slope of the production possibility frontier, then, clearly shows the possibilities that exist for trading Y for X in production. As a measure of these possibilities we define:

Definition

The *rate of product transformation* of good X for good Y (*RPT*) shows the number of units by which Y output must be reduced in order to increase X output by one unit. Graphically, the *RPT* (of X for Y) is the negative of the slope of the production possibility frontier. That is,

$$RPT \text{ (of } X \text{ for } Y) = - \text{ Slope of Production Possibility Frontier}$$

$$= - \frac{\text{change in } Y}{\text{change in } X} \text{ (along } O_X, O_Y). \qquad [17.1]$$

Increasing *RPT* and the Shape of the Production Possibility Frontier

In Figure 17.5 we have drawn the production possibility frontier so that the *RPT* increases as X output increases. In moving clockwise along the frontier, progressively greater and greater amounts of Y must be given up in order to increase X output by 1 unit. Such a shape can be justified intuitively by arguing that increases in X (or Y) output eventually run into decreasing returns. For output combinations near O_X, most resources are devoted to Y production. Some of these resources may be "more suited" to X production than they are to Y production. When X output is increased slightly, it is only reasonable to assume that these particular resources will be shifted into X output first. Such a shift will not reduce Y output very much, but it will increase X significantly. Near O_X, therefore, the *RPT* will be small. On the other hand, near O_Y, X output has been expanded greatly. To increase X further requires that resources be drawn out of Y production that are "very good" at producing Y but not good at producing X. Consequently Y will have to be cut back significantly to get only 1 more unit of X. Near O_Y, therefore, the *RPT* will be high. An increasing *RPT* therefore accords well with an intuitive idea that it is possible to push output of X "too far."

Rate of Product Transformation Is the Ratio of Marginal Costs

Much of the above argument was, of course, rather imprecise. Terms such as "too far" and "good at producing X" have no place in precise analytical economics. To show that the shape of the production possibility frontier in Figure 17.5 is rigorously justified, we must make use of the following result: The RPT (of X for Y) is equal to the ratio of the marginal cost of X (MC_X) to the marginal cost of Y (MC_Y). That is,

$$RPT \text{ (of } X \text{ for } Y) = \frac{MC_X}{MC_Y} \qquad [17.2]$$

Although we will not prove this result mathematically here, we will provide an intuitive proof. Suppose only labor is used in the production of X and Y. Assume that, at some point on the production possibility frontier, the marginal cost of producing more X is 4 (that is, assume that it takes 4 units of labor input to produce an additional unit of X output). Suppose also that the marginal cost of Y (in terms of the additional labor required to produce 1 more unit) is 2. In this situation it is clear that, since the total supply of labor is fixed, 2 units of Y must be given up in order to free enough labor to produce 1 more unit of X. We would therefore say that the RPT (of X for Y) is 2. But this is simply the ratio of the marginal cost of X to the marginal cost of Y (that is, 4/2); at least for this simple case, equation 17.2 holds. A more complete analysis would indicate that equation 17.2 holds even when there are many inputs being used to produce X and Y.

We are now in a position to show why the production possibility frontier has a concave shape. Such a shape is based on the presumption that the production of both X and Y exhibits increasing marginal costs. As either of these outputs is expanded, marginal costs are assumed to rise. Consider moving along the frontier in a clockwise direction. In so doing the production of X is being increased, whereas that of Y is being decreased. By the assumption of increasing marginal costs, then, MC_X is rising while MC_Y falls. But, by equation 17.2, this means that the RPT is rising as X is substituted for Y in production. The concave shape of the production possibility frontier is then justified by the assumption of increasing marginal costs.[6]

---

[6]This analysis might be pressed a bit further to inquire why marginal costs are assumed to increase. One obvious (but not very general) answer would be to assume that the production function for both goods exhibits diminishing returns to scale. Such an assumption would, however, be at variance with the constant returns to scale assumption we have generally used in this book. A more important explanation of increasing marginal costs rests on a "factor intensity" argument. To see the basis for this argument, suppose there are two goods, say, food and automobiles, and that food is a relatively labor-intensive good (that is, food production has a higher ratio of labor to capital than does automobile production). Now if auto production is to be expanded (and food production cut back), factors of production must be drawn from food production into car production. But as food output is cut back, a lot of labor and only a

Production Possibility Frontiers and Opportunity Cost

The reason we have spent so much space in developing the concept of the production possibility frontier is that it is the single most important tool for studying efficiency in production. The curve clearly demonstrates that there are many efficient possible combinations of goods and that producing more of one good necessitates cutting back on the production of some other good. This is precisely what economists mean by the term *opportunity cost*. The cost of producing more X can be most readily measured by the reduction in Y output that this entails. The cost of 1 more unit of X is therefore best measured as the *RPT* (of X for Y) at the prevailing point on the production possibility frontier. Although we have developed these concepts in the context of a single firm, it should be clear that they have far greater generality. In a sense the entire economy can be considered to be one giant firm (indeed, the fixed input supply assumption would seem more appropriate to this situation), and the production possibility frontier shows those combinations of goods that the economy can produce if its resources are efficiently employed. Again the slope of the frontier indicates the kinds of trade-offs possible in the economy and provides information about the opportunity costs of alternative production plans. The curve shows that as X production is expanded, the cost (in terms of forgone Y) of producing one more unit rises. In that sense the production possibility curve is a general equilibrium supply curve for the economy as a whole. In later chapters we will show how this "supply curve" can be used to study a number of important economic questions.

The requirement that individual firms choose their input mixes correctly is not all that is necessary for achieving productive efficiency. It is also important that the available factors of production be allocated efficiently among firms and that firms make efficient output choices. Our discussion of productive efficiency now turns to examining these additional conditions.

Efficient Allocation of Resources Among Firms

If society has a fixed stock of resources, these must be allocated in some efficient way among firms in order to insure overall productive efficiency. Intuitively, resources should be allocated to those firms where they can be most efficiently used. More precisely, the condition for efficient allocation is given by:

Optimization Principle

If production is to be efficient, resources should be allocated so that the marginal physical product of any resource in the production of a particular good is the same no matter which firm produces that good.

---

little capital is released. These are not the factor proportions that automobile makers need; as they try to adjust to them marginal costs progressively rise.

An Intuitive Proof

To show the necessity of this rule, we will consider a situation in which it does not hold. Suppose that the marginal physical product of labor (MP_L) in the production of corn is 3 bushels per extra labor-hour on farm A and only 1 bushel on farm B. Then a transfer of one unit of labor from farm B to farm A would increase total output by 2 bushels of corn. Clearly the initial allocation of labor was inefficient, and this transfer of labor should be continued until marginal productivities of labor are equalized. A similar result holds for any other productive input. For example, machines suitable for producing yo-yos should be allocated among producers so that their marginal productivities are identical for each user, otherwise yo-yo output could be increased. This analysis shows one more reason why the concept of *marginal* productivity is the important definition of productivity for economic problems. By examining the productivity of various inputs "at the margin," we are in a better position to understand how small reallocations of these inputs will affect output.

A Graphic Proof

Figure 17.6 provides a more precise graphic proof of the efficient allocation of inputs among firms. The figure shows the marginal productivity of labor curves for two firms, both producing the same output. Suppose that the initial allocation of labor between the firms has L_1 workers working for firm 1 and L_2 for firm 2. From

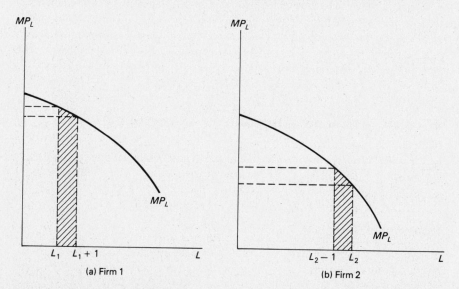

Figure 17.6 / Equality of Marginal Products is Required for Efficiency

When marginal productivities in the production of a single good differ between firms, output of the good can be increased by reallocating labor. In the figure, moving one worker from firm 2 to firm 1 increases output. Such a reallocation should continue until the marginal productivities are equal.

the figure, we can see that the marginal productivity of labor in firm 1 exceeds that in firm 2. Our discussion suggests that labor should therefore be transferred from firm 2 to firm 1. Suppose only 1 worker is so transferred. The effects of this transfer are shown in the figure. The reduction in output in firm 2 is shown by the shaded area in the Figure 17.6b. If this worker is added to the labor force for firm 1, output will expand by the shaded area in 17.6a. It is clear that output has been increased by this transfer: The shaded area in 17.6a is larger than that in 17.6b. The transfer of labor also serves to equilibrate the marginal product of labor between firms. The additional worker in firm 1 causes labor's marginal product to fall, whereas there are now fewer workers in firm 2 and the marginal productivity has consequently risen. The transfer of labor should continue until the required equality is achieved. The available stock of labor should be reallocated until a situation is reached in which marginal productivities do not differ among firms.

Efficient Choice of Output by Firms

Even though resources may be efficiently allocated both within a firm and among all firms, there is still one other condition of efficient production that must be obeyed: Firms (or nations) must produce efficient combinations of outputs. Roughly speaking, firms that are good at producing hamburgers should produce hamburgers, and those good at producing cars should produce cars. The necessary conditions for efficient choices of outputs are summarized in:

Optimization Principle

If two (or more) firms produce the same outputs, they must operate at points on their respective production possibility frontiers at which their rates of product transformation are equal if those outputs are to be produced efficiently.

Consider two firms (A and B) that each produce both cars and trucks. Let their production possibility curves be given by those in Figure 17.7. Suppose firm A chooses to produce a point P_1^A (100 cars and 50 trucks), where its RPT (of trucks for cars) is 2/1. At this point firm A must give up 2 cars if it is to produce 1 more truck. Suppose also that firm B chooses to produce 100 cars and 50 trucks but that at this point its RPT (of trucks for cars) is 1/1. In this case productive efficiency can be improved by having firm A produce more cars (since it is relatively efficient in this), and firm B produce more trucks. For example, firm A could produce 102 cars and 49 trucks, whereas B could move to producing 99 cars and 51 trucks. By this reordering of production, the total output of cars has been increased without decreasing the total output of trucks. Hence the initial choices of firms A and B were inefficient. Only if RPT's are equal is it impossible to make such a beneficial reallocation. This result is particularly interesting in that it shows that output may be increased (even if

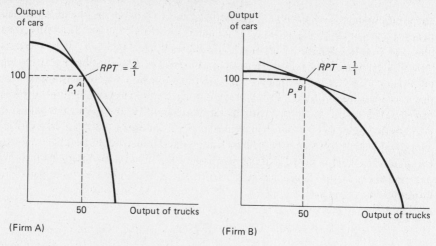

Figure 17.7 / Firms Must Produce Where Their *RPT*'s Are Equal in Order to Achieve Efficiency

If two firms' rates of product transformation differ, total output can be increased by moving these firms toward equalization of those rates. In the figure Firm A is relatively efficient at producing cars and Firm B is relatively efficient at producing trucks. If each firm were to specialize in its efficient product, total output could be increased.

the inputs to all firms are fixed) by having firms produce the "correct" output combinations.

Theory of Comparative Advantage

One of the most important applications of this principle is in the study of international trade, where it is used as the basis for the *theory of comparative advantage*. This theory was first proposed by Ricardo, who argued that countries should specialize in producing those goods of which they are relatively more efficient producers.[7] The countries then should trade with the rest of the world to obtain needed commodities. If countries do specialize in this way, total world production will be greater than it would be if each country tried to produce a balanced bundle of goods. To demonstrate this fact, let us look again at Figure 17.7. Now we can take the two production possibility curves to represent those of two different countries with fixed resources. Points P_1^A and P_1^B may represent the countries' pretrade production choices. Since the RPT differs between the two countries, world output could be increased by having country A produce more cars and country B produce more trucks. The countries should proceed to specialize in this way until their RPT's

---

[7]See D. Ricardo, *The Principles of Political Economy and Taxation* (1817; reprint ed., London: J. M. Dent and Son, 1965), pp. 81–93.

are equilibrated.[8] With country A specializing in car production, it can trade with country B to get the trucks it needs; similarly, B can trade with A for cars. Because total world output has been increased as a result of specialization, both countries will now be better off. This is the logic that provides intellectual support for the belief that "free trade is the best policy." It is important to note that the analysis uses only information about the product transformation rates between the two goods in each country, not about marginal productivity differences between countries. It is possible that a country could have an "absolute" advantage in the production of every good (in the sense that its marginal productivity of labor in the production of *every* good exceeded that of its trading partner), but such a country would still benefit from specialization and trade. The important differences are in comparative, not absolute, advantages.[9]

Summary of Efficiency in Production

We have therefore shown that efficiency in production requires that a number of conditions must hold both for the allocation of resources within a firm and for the allocation of resources among firms. These conditions can be briefly summarized as:

1. Rates of technical substitution (RTS's) between any two inputs should be equal in the production of all outputs.

---

[8] Actually in Ricardo's examples the production possibility frontiers of the two countries were assumed to be straight lines. Hence the RPT was assumed constant over all possible output combinations. However, RPT's were assumed to differ between the countries. In this situation both countries should completely specialize in production. Consider the following simple example. Suppose (following Ricardo) there are two goods, wine and cloth, produced by two countries, say, Portugal and England. Suppose the RPT (of cloth for wine) in Portugal is 2: Portugal can always trade 2 units of wine for 1 unit of cloth in production. On the other hand, suppose the RPT in England is 1. Consequently England has a comparative advantage in cloth production, whereas Portugal has a comparative advantage in wine production. Suppose, prior to trade, England produces 100 units of cloth and 100 units of wine. It is easy to show that England can be made better off by shifting its output mix toward producing more cloth. If England were to produce 1 less unit of wine and 1 more unit of cloth, it could then trade this unit of cloth with Portugal for 2 units of wine. Consumption would then be 100 units of cloth and 101 units of wine—an improvement over the pretrade position. In fact, because the RPT's are assumed to be constant, England should completely specialize in cloth production. By producing 200 units of cloth, it can trade 100 of these with Portugal for 200 units of wine. With complete specialization, then, England can consume 100 units of cloth and 200 units of wine. In the example in the text, such complete specialization would not take place because the production possibility curves are concave; that is, marginal costs begin to rise as specialization proceeds. Both countries will therefore continue to produce some of each good.

[9] Of course our discussion earlier in this chapter suggested that world output can also be increased by transferring resources from countries in which the marginal productivities of factors of production are low to those in which marginal productivities are high. While such international movements of labor and capital do take place, the flows are generally not of sufficient magnitude to equalize marginal productivities.

2. The marginal physical productivity of any input should be the same among all producers who use that input to produce a particular output.

3. Rates of product transformation (*RPT*'s) between any two goods should be the same for all producers of those goods.

It should be clear that there is a basic similarity between all of these conditions: each requires that certain technical trade-off rates be equalized. Only if all the conditions hold will production be efficient in the sense we have defined it. In Chapter 18 we will show that it is possible that under a perfectly competitive price system profit-maximizing firms may operate in a way that will bring about such an allocation. For most of that analysis (indeed for most of the remainder of this book) we will primarily use the production possibility frontier (Figure 17.5) to discuss efficiency in production. It will be assumed that this curve reflects production conditions in the economy as a whole (that is, a single large "firm") and that points on the curve represent efficient output combinations. In interpreting the "economy-wide" curve the various efficiency conditions that lie behind its construction should be kept in mind.

Efficiency in Production and Exchange

The goal of an economic system is to satisfy human wants. Being efficient in production may not be at all desirable if the "wrong" combination of goods is being produced. The definition of efficiency in a production and exchange economy we will adopt is the Pareto definition, which we used in the case of exchange:

Definition

An allocation of goods and resources among both firms and individuals is efficient if no one person can be made better off without making someone else worse off.

In this section we will examine those conditions that are required to achieve such an efficient allocation.

Exchange and Productive Efficiency Separately

It should be obvious initially that all the conditions for both exchange efficiency and productive efficiency must hold if we are to have overall efficiency. For example, if production is inefficient, then there exists some good the production of which could be increased without decreasing the production of anything else. This extra output would increase the utility of the person to whom it is given without decreasing anyone else's; thus the original situation could not have been efficient. Hence productive efficiency must hold in any allocation that is to be efficient in an overall sense. In graphic terms, we must be on the economy's production possibility frontier. Similarly, those goods that are produced must be exchanged efficiently. If this were not so, two individuals could both be made better off by trading goods among themselves. In graphic terms, individuals must be on the contract curve.

Tying Production and Exchange Together

For both production and exchange to be efficient is not a sufficient condition for overall efficiency. It must also be the case that the right goods are being produced. It does little good for an economy to be an efficient producer of yo-yos and xylophones if no one wants these goods. In order to assure overall efficiency, we need some way to tie together tastes and productive abilities. The condition necessary to insure that the right goods are produced is:

Optimization Principle

In order to achieve efficiency in production and exchange, both exchange and production must be separately efficient and individuals' marginal rates of substitution (*MRS*'s) must equal firms' rates of production transformation (*RPT*'s). That is, the rate at which individuals are willing to trade one good for another must equal the rate at which the goods can be traded in the production process.

An Intuitive Proof

For example, if individuals were willing to trade 2 apples for 1 orange, but resources were allocated so that 1 apple could be traded for 1 orange in production, conditions would not be efficient. Too few oranges are currently being produced, since individuals place a relatively higher evaluation on oranges than is their opportunity cost in production. To grow 1 additional orange, it would be necessary to cut back the apple harvest by 1. But individuals were willing to sacrifice 2 apples for another orange. Consequently, they are better off to the extent of 1 apple. As with the other example of comparing trade-off rates in this book, any time the rate at which individuals are willing to trade differs from the rate at which they can technically trade, a beneficial reallocation can be made.

A Graphic Representation

Figure 17.8 illustrates the requirement for efficiency in production and exchange for a very simple case. It assumes that there are only two goods (X and Y) being produced and that there is only one individual (perhaps Robinson Crusoe) in society. Those combinations of X and Y that can be produced are given by the production possibility frontier PP. Any point on PP represents a point of efficient production. By superimposing the individual's indifference map on Figure 17.8, however, we see that only one point on PP provides maximum utility. This point of maximum utility is at E, where the curve PP is tangent to the individual's highest indifference curve, U^2. At this point of tangency, the individual's *MRS* (of X for Y) is equal to the technical *RPT* (of X for Y), and hence this is the required condition for overall efficiency. Notice that point E is preferred to every other point that is efficient in a productive sense. In fact, for any point such as F on the curve *PP* (other than point E) there exist points that are inefficient but that are preferred to F. In Figure 17.8 the "inefficient" point G is preferred to the "efficient" point F. It would be preferable from the individual's point of view to produce inefficiently rather than be forced to produce the "wrong" combination of goods in an efficient way. Point E (which is efficiently produced) is superior to any such "second best" solutions.

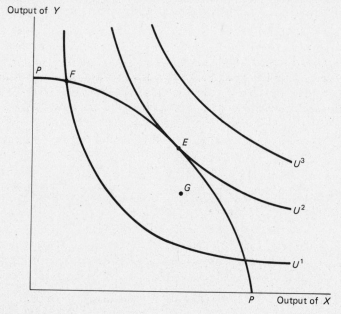

Figure 17.8 / Efficiency of Production and Exchange in a Robinson Crusoe Economy

In a single-person economy, the curve *PP* represents those combinations of X and Y that can be produced. Every point on *PP* is efficient in a production sense. However, only the output combination at point E is a true utility maximum for the individual. At E the individual's *MRS* is equal to the rate at which X can technically be traded for Y (the *RPT*).

Although we have only shown the conditions of efficiency in a simple case, they are general. By equating individuals' marginal rates of substitution to firms' rates of product transformation, we can tie together preferences and technology. Such an interconnection is necessary if resources are to be allocated in a truly efficient way. Without it, the productive system might be very efficient in producing what individuals in fact do not want. Because Figure 17.8 shows this connection in a very simple way, we will make frequent use of it in later chapters.

Welfare Economics

So far in this chapter we have talked only about the concept of economic efficiency. Although attaining efficiency is certainly a desirable goal for an economy (it seems sensible to make the best use of scarce resources), it is not the only possible goal. Perhaps equally important is the problem of attaining a fair and equitable distribution of resources among individuals. In the remainder of this chapter we will examine that problem. A principal purpose of our examination is to illustrate the connection, if any, between efficiency and equity.

Defining Equity

As was the case with our analysis of efficiency, a natural place to start our discussion of equity would seem to be with a definition of the concept. Unfortunately such a definition continues to elude philosophers and economists: There is no agreed-upon definition of the term. In comparing any two feasible allocations of resources, some individuals will prefer the first (presumably because they are better off under it) and others may prefer the second. Devising methods for weighing the preferences of one group against those of another group has proved to be an insurmountable task (unless, of course, one is willing to adopt arbitrary standard rules such as "the first group doesn't deserve anything"). We cannot therefore provide a set of "optimization principles" for achieving equity. Rather, our purpose is simply to indicate some conceptual difficulties in devising welfare criteria for achieving "equity" and to show that there are no easy answers to that problem.

Welfare Criteria in an Exchange Model

The model of efficiency in exchange we developed previously in this chapter is useful for demonstrating the problems involved in establishing welfare criteria, and we shall use that model exclusively.[10] Consider the Edgeworth Box diagram in Figure 17.9. We might first argue that only points on the contract curve should be considered in choosing a "social optimum." Points off the contract curve are dominated by points on the curve in the sense that both individuals can be made better off on the curve, and in so doing overall welfare could be improved. Along the contract curve the utilities of the two individuals (Smith and Jones) vary, and these utilities are directly competitive. Smith's utility can be increased only by decreasing Jones's. Given this set of efficient allocations, we now wish to discuss possible criteria for choosing among them. For this purpose we will assume for the moment that utilities are measurable and that they may be compared on a common

---

[10]Production can be integrated into the discussion of welfare economics. See, for example, F. M. Bator, "The Simple Analytics of Welfare Maximization," *American Economic Review* 47 (March 1957), pp. 22–59.

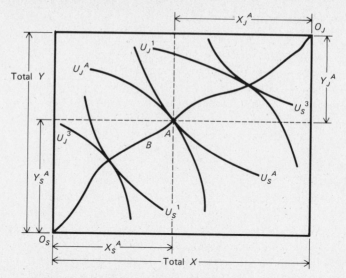

Figure 17.9 / Edgeworth Box Diagram of Exchange

This diagram is simply a redrawing of Figure 17.2. The curve O_S, O_J is the locus of efficient allocations of X and Y between Smith and Jones. Allocations off this locus are dominated by those on it in that both individuals *can be* made better off by moving to the contract curve.

scale. Obviously this assumption is in direct contradiction to the warnings expressed in Chapter 3 about the measurability of utility, but making such an assumption will permit us to conceptualize certain problems. From the assumption of measurability, we can use the possible utility combinations along the contract curve to construct the *utility possibility frontier*[11] shown in Figure 17.10. The curve O_S, O_J records those utility levels for Smith and Jones that are obtainable from the fixed quantities of available goods. Any utility combination (such as point C) that lies inside the curve O_S, O_J is inefficient in the sense that utilities *could* be unambiguously improved (for example, by moving to any point on the arc $C'C'$). This is simply a reflection of the way in which the contract curve is constructed. Using the utility possibility frontier, we can now rephrase the "problem" of welfare economics as being the development of criteria for selecting a point on this frontier. At least in this simple model, efficiency is a required condition for achieving equity. We will return later to reconsider this connection.

The Equality Criterion

Probably the most straightforward welfare criterion would be to require equality of Smith's and Jones's utilities. This criterion might be based on the homily that "the

---

[11]This construction is identical to the one we used to derive the production possibility frontier.

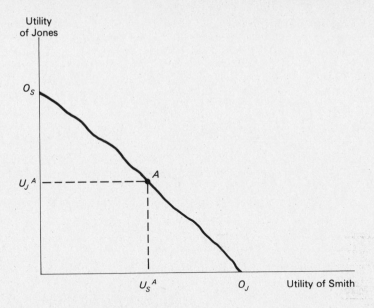

Figure 17.10 / Utility Possibility Frontier

On the assumption that utility can be measured, the utility possibility frontier can be derived from the Edgeworth Exchange Box (Figure 17.9). The curve O_S, O_J shows those combinations of utility that are achievable. One possible criterion for choosing among these points would be to require equality of utilities. This would dictate choice of point A.

only fair way to share a pie is by cutting it in half" or it might be derived from more basic philosophical beliefs about the fundamental equality of all people. Whatever the origins of the equality criterion, its implications for the allocation of goods are illustrated in Figure 17.10. Point A on the utility possibility frontier provides "equal utility" for Smith and Jones (remember the dubious nature of the assumption that utility is measurable, however). Since point A corresponds to a unique point on the contract curve, the socially optimal allocation of goods has been determined by this choice. In Figure 17.9 this allocation is seen to require that Smith gets X_S^A and Y_S^A, whereas Jones gets X_J^A and Y_J^A. Notice that the goods X and Y are not necessarily distributed equally. It is equality of utilities that is required by the criterion, not equality of goods. If individuals have rather different tastes for the two goods, these goods could be very unequally distributed at point A. It might even be the case that one of the individuals would get more of both goods at the socially optimal point. This would be true, for example, if Smith were ascetic by nature, whereas Jones were materialistic. To equalize utilities, therefore, Jones should be given more goods with which to satisfy his cravings. Notice also that point A may not be attainable solely through free exchange. If Smith, for example, started out with "most" of the goods, it might take a degree of coercion to get him to accept point A.

Social Welfare Functions

A more general approach to social welfare (which as a special case includes the equality criterion) can be obtained by examining the concept of a *social welfare function*.[12] If we assume that individual tastes are to count, this function might depend only on Smith's and Jones's utility levels:

$$\text{social welfare} = W(U_S, U_J). \tag{17.3}$$

Society's problem, then, is to allocate X and Y between Smith and Jones so as to maximize W. This procedure is pictured in Figure 17.11. The curves labeled W_1, W_2, and W_3 represent *welfare indifference curves,* because society is indifferent about which utility combination on a particular curve is chosen.[13] These indifference curves for the function W are drawn convex on the normative assumption that "society" exhibits a diminishing rate of substitution of Smith's utility for Jones's. This assumption would seem to be reasonable if society is basically egalitarian and is progressively less willing to make Smith better off at the expense of making Jones worse off.

Point E is the optimal point of social welfare, in that this is the highest level of W achievable with the given utility possibility frontier. As before, it is necessary to go from point E to the Edgeworth Box diagram in order to determine the socially optimal allocation of goods.

Conflicts between Efficiency and Equity

Figure 17.11 demonstrates the conceptually correct way of choosing a distribution of utilities to maximize social welfare. The figure again illustrates the important distinction to be made between the goals of equity and efficiency. All of the points on O_S, O_J are efficient by the Pareto criterion. However, some of the efficient points represent far more equitable distributions than do others. There are in fact many inefficient points (such as F) that are socially preferred to efficient points (such as D). It may sometimes be in society's interest to choose seemingly inefficient allocations of resources if the truly optimal allocation (point E) is unattainable. In order to satisfy societal concepts of equity, it may make sense to accept some inefficiency.

As a practical example of this sort of inconsistency between efficiency and equity, consider the debate in the United States over the desirability of adopting a guaranteed annual income. Opponents of this proposal assert that its acceptance would lead to great inefficiencies because, once the necessity to work was mitigated, individuals would withdraw from the labor force. Without examining either

---

[12] This concept was first developed by A. Bergson in "A Reformulation of Certain Aspects of Welfare Economics," *Quarterly Journal of Economics* 52 (February 1938), pp. 310–334.

[13] Under the equality criterion, the social welfare function would have L-shaped indifference curves.

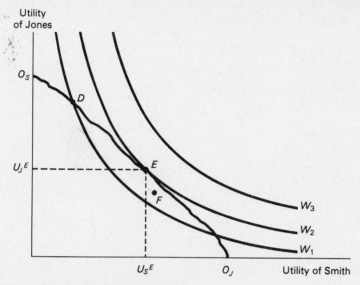

Figure 17.11 / The Social Welfare Function

If we can postulate the existence of a social welfare function having the indifference curves W_1, W_2, and W_3, it is possible to conceptualize the problem of social choice. It is clear that efficiency (being on O_S, O_J) is necessary for a welfare optimum, but this is not sufficient, as may be seen by comparing points D and F.

the logic or the actual size of this purported effect, it is possible to show on *a priori* grounds why it is not necessarily a damning assertion. For example, suppose that without income transfers only points such as D could be achieved. Perhaps initial endowments of the goods are so skewed that free, efficient trading would insure a relatively unequal outcome of utilities. On the other hand, perhaps income transfers could cause the "inefficient" point F to be achieved.[14] What has been sacrificed in efficiency has therefore more than been compensated for (in terms of social welfare) by increased equity.

Normative Economics and Political Theory

A social welfare function, then, provides a useful tool for demonstrating particular aspects of the problem of social choice. We must recognize, however, that this tool is only a conceptual one offering little guidance for the development of practical policy. The social indifference curves of Figure 17.11 are in reality nothing more than a few casually drawn lines. We have so far begged the question of how such a

---

[14]For example, the withdrawal of persons from the labor force may cause the total quantities of X and Y available to contract (not so much can be produced when income transfers are introduced). Graphically, the size of the Edgeworth Box would be contracted, and perhaps F is the "best point" that can be obtained within this new, smaller box.

function is established or what the properties of the function are likely to be. Both of these questions are at the heart of political philosophy. While a treatment of this subject is obviously far outside the scope of this book, we will, in this section, provide a brief glimpse of some of the issues raised by political theorists in attempting to define "social welfare."

A major goal of political theorists has been to propose possible definitions of "the common good." This term is usually taken to refer to a set of moral precepts about social welfare that can act as guidelines for governmental policies. Some theorists assume that there exist basic moral principles of fairness and justice with which most people would agree.[15] These "social contract" philosophers would therefore argue that the role of welfare economics is to discover these universal principles and to attempt to implement them. A wide variety of ethical postulates has been proposed, but none has proved to be both broadly acceptable and capable of pragmatic implementation. Whether there exist principles to which most people can be converted remains an open question.

A number of political theorists feel that the search for universal, pragmatic moral principles is fruitless. In any large and complex society, a wide variety of beliefs will be held; it is argued that these will ultimately prove to be irreconcilable. Economists have been most interested in those aspects of political theory that examine how these differences are accommodated by the political process. This interest derives naturally from economists' studies of the ways in which markets coordinate differences in individuals' preferences and firms' technological capabilities. The major contribution that economists have made to political theory is to demonstrate how basic economic models can be applied to political contexts as well. On a philosophical level, economists (most notably Kenneth Arrow[16]) have asked whether a consistent notion of social preferences can be derived in principle from a group of differing individual preferences. Is it possible to construct a social welfare function that adequately reflects individuals' views of what it in fact should be? The simple answer to this question seems to be no. Complex problems of inconsistency arise in attempting to "add up" different individuals' views, and it does not seem possible to define a set of rules that represent social preferences. Whatever social welfare function is decided upon, it must be either based on the preferences of a single individual (perhaps Plato's philosopher-king) or it must express preferences that are contrary to those of large segments of society. The result of these investigations is then essentially negative. There are no clearcut ways to derive ideals of social welfare from individuals' values. The basic problem of welfare economics remains unsolved.

---

[15] An interesting discussion of the concept of "fairness" and how individuals' perceptions of fairness may be divorced from their current positions in society can be found in J. Rawls, *A Theory of Justice* (Cambridge, Mass.: Harvard University Press, 1971). Rawls uses many economic tools in his analysis.

[16] See K. J. Arrow, *Social Choice and Individual Values* (New Haven, Conn.: Yale University Press, 1951).

Summary

In this chapter we have provided a theoretical analysis of two important normative economic goals for a society: efficiency and equity. We started by defining an efficient allocation of resources as being one in which no individual can be made better off without making another individual worse off. We then examined various conditions required to bring about such a situation. We showed that a necessary condition for efficiency in an exchange economy is that individuals' marginal rates of substitution should be equalized. Efficiency in production is somewhat more complex. It requires that a number of marginal conditions hold in order to insure that production will be on an economy's production possibility frontier. Finally, preferences and production possibilities are tied together by the requirement that individuals' marginal rates of substitution be equal to the rate at which firms can trade one good for another in the production process. We termed this latter trade-off rate the rate of product transformation (RPT): it is the negative of the slope of the production possibility frontier.

The reader should recognize the essential similarity in all the conditions for efficiency that we derived. The study of efficient allocations is a study in marginal trade-offs. Potential benefits and costs from any reallocation must be carefully considered. Only when trade-off rates are the same for all economic agents will resources be allocated in a truly efficient manner. That result is one of the most basic in microeconomic theory. In Chapter 18 we will examine the role of the price system in bringing about this equalization of trade-offs.

The study of welfare in this chapter provided less definitive results than did the study of efficiency. This failure derived primarily from our inability to define "equity" in a precise and unambiguous way. Situations in which one individual can gain only at the expense of others' losses pose difficult (perhaps unsolvable) problems in social decision making. Despite these ambiguities, we were able to gain two conceptual insights about the nature of social welfare. First, if all efficient allocations can be attained, one of them will be the socially preferred ("most equitable") allocation. In that sense, efficiency is a necessary condition for achieving an optimal level of social welfare. Our second insight about social welfare undercuts this conclusion somewhat, however. We pointed out that, if the efficient, socially preferred point is not attainable, efficiency is not necessarily a desirable goal. In that case, there may exist trade-offs between efficiency and equity: society may be willing to sacrifice some of the former to achieve some of the latter. It is important to keep this result in mind in evaluating the discussion of normative issues in later chapters in this book.

Suggested Readings

Arrow, K. J., *Social Choice and Individual Values,* 2d ed. (New Haven, Conn.: Yale University Press, 1963).

——— "Some Ordinalist-Utilitarian Notes on Rawls's Theory of Justice," *Journal of Philosophy* 70 (May 10, 1973), pp. 245–263.

Bator, F. M., "The Simple Analytics of Welfare Maximization," *American Economic Review* 47 (March 1957), pp. 22–59.

Baumol, W. J., "Activity Analysis and General Equilibrium," Chap. 21 in *Economic Theory and Operations Analysis,* 2d ed. (Englewood Cliffs, N.J.: Prentice-Hall, Inc. 1965).

Dorfman, R., P. A. Samuelson, and R. M. Solow, *Linear Programming and Economic Analysis* (New York: McGraw-Hill, Inc. 1958), chap. 13.

Harberger, A. C., "Three Basic Postulates for Applied Welfare Economics: An Interpretive Essay," *Journal of Economic Literature* 9 (September 1971), pp. 785–797.

Koopmans, T. C., "Efficient Allocation of Resources," *Econometrica* 19 (October 1951), pp. 455–465.

——— *Three Essays on the State of Economic Science* (New York: McGraw-Hill, Inc. 1957).

Little, I. M. D., *A Critique of Welfare Economics,* 2d ed. (London: Oxford University Press, 1957).

Mishan, E. J., *Welfare Economics: Five Introductory Essays* (New York: Random House Inc., 1964).

Quirk, J., and R. Saposnik, *Introduction to General Equilibrium Theory and Welfare Economics* (New York: McGraw-Hill, Inc. 1968).

Rawls, J., *A Theory of Justice* (Cambridge, Mass.: Harvard University Press, 1971).

——— "Some Reasons for the Maximin Criterion," *American Economic Review* 64 (May 1974), pp. 141–146.

Problems

17.1

"Jack Sprat can eat no fat, his wife can eat no lean." Construct a box diagram for this pair (assuming fixed quantities of "fat" and "lean") and indicate the contract curve.

17.2

Smith and Jones are stranded on a desert island. Each has in his possession some slices of ham (H) and cheese (C). Smith is a very choosy eater and will eat ham and cheese only in the fixed proportions of 2 slices of cheese to 1 slice of ham. His utility function is given by $U_S = \min(H, C/2)$.

Jones is more flexible in his dietary tastes and has a utility function given by $U_J = 4H + 3C$. Total endowments are 100 slices of ham and 200 slices of cheese.

a. Draw the Edgeworth Box diagram that represents the possibilities for exchange in this situation. What is the only price ratio that can prevail in any equilibrium?

b. Suppose that Smith initially had $40H$ and $80C$. What would the equilibrium position be?

c. Suppose that Smith initially had $60H$ and $80C$. What would the equilibrium position be?

d. Suppose that Smith (much the stronger of the two) decides not to play by the rules of the game. Then what could the final equilibrium position be?

17.3

The country of Extremum produces only skis *(S)* and waterskis *(W)*, using capital *(K)* and labor *(L)* as inputs. The production functions for both S and W are fixed proportions. It takes 2 units of labor and 1 unit of capital to produce a pair of skis. Waterskis, on the other hand, require 1 unit of labor and 1 unit of capital. If the total supply of labor in Extremum is 150 units and the total supply of capital is 100 units, construct the production possibility curve for this economy. Are all inputs fully employed at every point on the production possibility curve? How do you explain any unemployment that might exist?

17.4

Robinson Crusoe obtains utility from the quantity of fish he consumes in one day *(F)*, the quantity of coconuts he consumes that day *(C)*, and the hours of leisure time he has during the day *(H)* according to the utility function:

$$\text{utility} = F^{1/4} C^{1/4} H^{1/2}$$

Robinson's production of fish is given by

$$F = \sqrt{L_F}$$

(where L_F is the hours he spends fishing), and his production of coconuts is determined by

$$C = \sqrt{L_C}$$

(where L_C is the time he spends picking coconuts).

Assuming that Robinson decides to work an 8-hour day (that is, $H = 16$), graph his production possibility curve for fish and coconuts. Show his optimal choices of those goods.

17.5

There are 200 pounds of food on an island that must be allocated between two marooned sailors. The utility function of the first sailor is given by:

$$\text{utility} = \sqrt{F_1},$$

where F_1 is the quantity of food consumed by the first sailor. For the second sailor, utility (as a function of his food consumption) is given by:

$$\text{utility} = \tfrac{1}{2}\sqrt{F_2}$$

a. If the food is allocated equally between the sailors, how much utility will each receive?

b. How should food be allocated between the sailors to assure equality of utility?

c. Suppose that sailor 2 requires a utility level of at least 5 to remain alive. How should food be allocated so as to maximize the sum of utilities subject to the restraint that sailor 2 receive that minimum level of utility?

d. What other criteria might you use to allocate the available food between the sailors?

17.6

In the 1930s several authors suggested a "bribe criterion" for judging the desirability of social situations. This welfare criterion states that a movement from social state A to state B is an improvement in social welfare if those who gain by this move are able to compensate those who lose sufficiently so that they will accept the change. Compensation does not actually have to be made; it is only necessary that it could be paid. If the compensation is actually made, this criterion reduces to the Pareto definition (some individuals are made better off without making anyone worse off). Hence the criterion is novel only if that compensation is not paid by the gainers to the losers. In such a situation, does the bribe criterion seem a "value-free" one, or does the criterion seem somehow to favor those who are initially rich? Can you give some simple examples?

17.7

In this chapter we demonstrated how a "utility possibility frontier" can be constructed from an Edgeworth Box diagram on the assumption that the total quantities of the two goods being exchanged are fixed. How might a similar frontier be constructed for an economy with fixed amounts of resources but in which these resources can be shifted from the production of one good to another? Once a socially optimal distribution of utilities is chosen, what implications would this choice have for how the fixed resources are allocated?

17.8

Suppose that there are two individuals in an economy. Utilities of those individuals under five possible social states are shown in the table on page 495.

Individuals do not know which number (1 or 2) they will be assigned when the economy begins operating. Hence they are uncertain about the actual utility they will receive under the alternative social states. Which social state will be preferred if an individual adopts the following strategies in his or her voting behavior to deal with this uncertainty?

State	Utility 1	Utility 2
A	50	50
B	70	40
C	45	54
D	53	50.5
E	30	84

a. Choose that state which assures the highest utility to the least well-off person (that is, choose a maximin strategy—see Chapter 12).

b. Assume that there is a 50-50 chance of being either individual and choose that state with the highest expected utility.

c. Assume that, no matter what, the odds are always unfavorable such that there is a 60 percent chance of having the lower utility and a 40 percent chance of higher utility in any social state. Choose the state with the highest expected utility given these probabilities.

d. Assume that there is a 50-50 chance of being assigned either number, and that each individual dislikes inequality. Each will choose that state for which:

$$\text{expected utility} - \left| U_1 - U_2 \right|$$

is as large as possible (where the $\left| . . . \right|$ notation denotes absolute value).

e. What do you conclude from this problem about social choices under a "veil of ignorance" as to an individual's specific identity in society?

Chapter 18   Efficiency of Perfect Competition

Introduction

In the previous chapter we examined the notion of economic efficiency without mentioning prices. Achieving efficiency is primarily a technical problem of relating preferences and the available productive technology. Presumably this could be accomplished by an all-knowing and all-powerful central government. Such a government would need complete information about individuals' tastes and about the production possibilities for all firms. Only with this information would the government be able to make the precise marginal calculations that economic efficiency requires.

The Price System and Information

Even if it were in principle possible to gather such detailed information, it would undoubtedly be prohibitively costly to do so. Because both preferences and productive technologies are constantly changing, much of society's resources would be devoted to information gathering with little left over for the satisfaction of basic wants. Consequently, alternative, less costly allocational methods would have to be investigated. The allocational device that has received by far the greatest attention is the *price system*. By relying on the self-motivation of many decision makers, the price system permits the decentralization of allocational decisions. Relative to central planning, an interconnected market system provides a method for relating individual tastes and productive technology in a low-cost way. The natural working of the market mechanism generates information about preferences and technology in the form of prices. These prices act as signals to economic agents in guiding their supply and demand decisions. Changes in preferences or in productive techniques will require a reallocation of resources; again, the price system can quickly disseminate information relevant to this new allocation. It is clear from previous chapters that in a market economy the price system does allocate resources. The question we will investigate in this chapter is whether or not that allocation can be efficient.

Perfectly Competitive Price System

In order to study the efficiency of a price system, we must have a well-formulated model. The model we will use is the perfectly competitive price system, which we have examined throughout the earlier sections of this book. The choice of the perfectly competitive model is no accident. It will turn out that a perfectly competitive price system yields an efficient allocation of resources.

We should be aware of two things about that conclusion (which will be taken up in detail in subsequent sections) at the outset. First, we should keep in mind that we are only talking about achieving efficiency. While this is undoubtedly an important goal for any society, the goal of equity should be accorded at least as high a priority. We will see that no mechanism assures that a price system will attain an equitable allocation of resources among individuals. Second, we should be careful in drawing policy conclusions from the formal relationship between perfect competition and efficiency. Many of the requirements of the perfectly competitive model may not hold in the real world. We will discuss specific examples of such departures from the competitive model in later sections of this chapter.

Definition of the Competitive Price System

Having recorded these caveats it is now necessary to specify exactly what we mean by a *perfectly competitive price system*. The assumption is that there are in the economy under investigation some number of well-defined, homogeneous goods. Included in this list of goods are not only consumption items but also factors of production and intermediate goods. Each of these goods has an *equilibrium price,* established by the action of supply and demand.[1] At this set of prices, each market is cleared in the sense that suppliers are willing to supply that quantity that is

---

[1]One aspect of this market interaction should be made clear from the outset. The perfectly competitive market only determines relative (not absolute) prices. In this chapter, therefore, we will only speak of relative prices. It makes no difference whether the prices of apples and oranges are $.10 and $.20, respectively, or $10 and $20. The important point in either case is that 2 apples can be exchanged for 1 orange in the market.

demanded and vice versa. It is also assumed that there are no transaction or transportation charges and that both individuals and firms have perfect knowledge of these prices. Hence each good obeys the *law of one price:* A good trades at the same price no matter who buys it or which firm sells it. It is obvious why one good cannot trade at two different prices: If this were the case, individuals would rush to buy the good where it is cheaper; conversely, firms would try to sell all their output where the good was more expensive. Such actions in themselves would tend to equalize the price of the good. In the perfectly competitive model, then, each good must have only one price. This is why we may speak unambiguously of *the* price of a good.

Economic agents react to prices in specific ways:

(a) There are assumed to be a large number of individuals buying any one good. Each individual takes all prices as given. Each adjusts behavior so as to *maximize utility,* given the prices and his or her budget constraint. Individuals may also be sellers of productive services, and in such decisions they also regard prices as given.[2]

(b) There are assumed to be a large number of firms producing each good, and each firm produces only a small share of the output of any one good. In making input and output choices, firms are assumed to operate so as to *maximize profits*. The firm also treats all prices as given when making its profit-maximizing decisions. The individual firm's activities, either as a supplier of goods or as a demander of factor inputs, have no effect on market prices.

Most of the assumptions of perfect competition are, then, ones we have been making throughout this book. They can be abridged into a few simple statements:

Definition

In a perfectly competitive price system there exist equilibrium prices for each good and all economic agents take these prices as given. Using those prices, individuals are assumed to maximize utility; firms are assumed to maximize profits.

Prices and Efficiency

In this section we will show the correspondence between economic efficiency and a perfectly competitive price system. We start with a very general statement of that relationship and then examine in detail the conditions for efficiency in exchange, efficiency in production, and efficiency in production and exchange.

---

[2]Since one price represents the wage rate, the relevant budget constraint is in reality a time constraint. This is the way in which we treated individuals' labor-leisure choices in Chapter 15.

A General Summary

We can easily summarize the essence of the relationship between perfect competition and the efficient allocation of resources. In Chapter 17 we saw that the conditions of efficiency require that the rate of trade-off between any two goods, say, X and Y, should be the same for all economic agents. For a perfectly competitive market, the ratio of the price of X to the price of Y provides this common rate of trade-off to which all agents will adjust. Because prices are treated as givens both in individuals' utility-maximizing decisions and in firms' profit-maximizing decisions, all trade-off rates between X and Y will be equalized to the rate at which X and Y can be traded in the market (P_X/P_Y). Since all agents face the same prices, all trade-off rates will be equalized; an efficient allocation will be achieved. We will now examine the details of this proof.

Efficiency in Exchange

First, consider efficiency in exchange. The required condition is that the *MRS* for any two goods, X and Y, should be the same for all individuals. But utility maximization requires that each individual equate his or her *MRS* (of X for Y) to the ratio P_X/P_Y. In so doing, individuals will be equating the rate at which they are willing to trade X for Y to the rate at which these can be traded in the competitive market. Since every individual faces the same price ratio, the utility-maximizing decision of each individual will succeed in establishing the conditions for efficient exchange. Mathematically, consider any two individuals. Each faces the price ratio P_X/P_Y and will choose X and Y such that:

$$MRS \text{ (individual 1)} = \frac{P_X}{P_Y}$$

and

$$MRS \text{ (individual 2)} = \frac{P_X}{P_Y}$$

hence

$$MRS \text{ (individual 1)} = MRS \text{ (individual 2)}$$

This is the condition required for an efficient allocation of X and Y, which we derived in Chapter 17.

The simplicity of this proof may obscure some of its important features, and it is therefore worth dwelling a while on some of those aspects. First, remember that the prices P_X and P_Y are assumed to be equilibrium prices. This means that supply will be equal to demand in both markets. While it is true that any arbitrarily chosen price ratio would insure that individuals would equate their *MRS*'s to one another, such arbitrarily chosen price ratios would not assure equilibrium: Both individuals may be oversupplied with X (and undersupplied with Y) if an incorrect price ratio were arbitrarily set. For example, suppose two people were stranded on a desert island with few sources of water and that each arrived on shore with some diamonds and some water (to paraphrase an example from Chapter 2). They might initially adopt a "price ratio" of diamonds for water that approximated that in the world from which they had just come. Perhaps 1 diamond would exchange for a billion gallons of water. As time wore on, however, both individuals would find they were more than willing to trade diamonds for water at this price ratio. There would be an excess supply of diamonds and an excess demand for water at the price ratio that had been brought from the outside world. For this island society, the price ratio of 1 diamond to 1 billion gallons of water is not an equilibrium, and we would expect that some other price ratio would be decided upon by the two individuals.

A second important feature of the proof is the way in which it illustrates the remarkable information-gathering ability of the market. Not only does the market assimilate all relevant information about individuals' supply and demand functions (and with this information establish equilibrium prices), but it also creates a societal rate of trade-off of X for Y that is a correct reflection of every individual's trade-off rate. Information that would only be gathered at great cost by, say, governmental investigative bodies is costlessly generated by the interaction of supply and demand.

Conditions for Efficiency in Production

We can use proofs similar to the one we just presented to demonstrate that perfectly competitive prices will lead to efficiency in production. To show this, we will examine the three optimization principles we developed for production in Chapter 17. We first required that a firm have identical rates at which it can trade one input for another (the rate of technical substitution, RTS) in all those outputs it produces. But this is assured by the existence of perfectly competitive markets for inputs. In minimizing costs, the firm will equate the RTS between any two inputs, say labor and capital, to the ratio of their competitive rental prices (w/v). This will be true for any output the firm happens to produce, and hence the firm will be equating all its RTS's to the common price ratio w/v. In this way the firm will be led to adopt efficient input proportions in a decentralized way.

Our second requirement will hold for a similar reason. For efficiency it is necessary that every firm that produces a particular good, say X, have identical marginal productivities of labor in the production of X (MP_L^X). In Chapter 13 we saw that a profit-maximizing firm will hire additional labor up to the point at which the marginal value product $(P_X \cdot MP_L^X)$ of labor is equal to the competitive wage rate (w). Since both P_X and w are given by the market, each firm will equate its MP_L^X to w/P_X. Consequently, every firm will have the same marginal productivity of labor in the production of X. Again the competitive price system has succeeded in bringing about the conditions for an efficient allocation.

Finally, we required that the rate of product transformation (RPT—this is the rate at which one output can be traded for another in production) between any two goods, say X and Y, be the same for all firms. That a perfectly competitive price system will insure this can be most easily shown by recalling (from Chapter 17) that the RPT (of X for Y) is equal to the ratio of the marginal cost of X (MC_X) to that of Y (MC_Y). But each profit-maximizing firm will produce that output level for which marginal cost is equal to the market price. Therefore, for every firm, $P_X = MC_X$ and $P_Y = MC_Y$; hence, $MC_X/MC_Y = P_X/P_Y$ for all firms. The firms' RPT's are thereby equalized.[3] Later in this chapter we will have far more to say about the importance of the $P = MC$ condition for efficiency.

This discussion demonstrates that the profit-maximizing, decentralized decisions of many firms can achieve efficiency in production without any central direction. Competitive markets act as devices to unify the multitude of decisions that firms make into one coherent, efficient pattern. Relying on the motivations of individual entrepreneurs may be a workable and low-cost way of prompting the production sector to act efficiently. In other words, the competitive price system may permit an economy to reach its production possibility frontier.

Conditions for Efficiency in Production and Exchange

Proving that perfectly competitive markets lead to efficiency in the relationship between production and exchange is also straightforward. Since the price ratios quoted to consumers are the same ratios the market presents to firms, the MRS shared by all individuals will be identical to the RPT that is shared by all firms. This will be true for any pair of goods. Consequently, an efficient mix of goods will be produced and exchanged. Again, notice the two important functions the market performs. First, the market assures that supply and demand will be equalized for all goods. If a good were produced in too great amounts, a market reaction would set in (perhaps its price would fall) that would cut back on the production of the good and shift resources into other employment. The equilibrating of supply and demand in the market therefore assures that there will be neither excess demand nor excess supply. Second, the resulting equilibrium prices provide market trade-off rates for both firms and individuals to use as parameters in their decisions. Because these trade-off rates are identical for both firms and individuals, efficiency is assured.

Graphic Demonstration of Pricing and Efficiency

Figure 18.1 illustrates these principles. The figure shows the production possibility frontier for a two-good economy *(PP),* and the set of indifference curves represents individuals' preferences for these goods. First, consider the price ratio P_X/P_Y. At this price ratio firms will choose to produce the output combination X_1, Y_1. Only at

---

[3] An interesting example of the ability of a perfectly competitive price system to equate RPT's occurs in the theory of international trade. If world prices are set by the supply-demand mechanism, and if all markets are competitive, each country's RPT will be equated to these prevailing world prices. But this will insure that world production is allocated efficiently between countries. Each country will specialize in producing those goods of which it is a relatively efficient producer. This "theorem" forms the basis for a belief that free trade is the best policy. An additional example demonstrating this belief is taken up below.

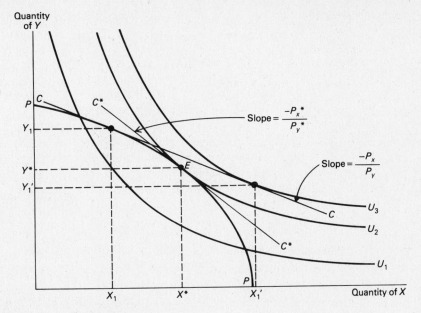

**Figure 18.1 / How Perfectly
Competitive Prices Bring About Efficiency**

With a price ratio given by P_X/P_Y, firms will produce X_1, Y_1; society's budget constraint will be given by line C. With this budget constraint, individuals demand X_1', Y_1'; that is, there is an excess demand for good X, $(X_1' - X_1)$, and an excess supply of good Y, $(Y_1 - Y_1')$. The workings of the market will move these prices toward their equilibrium levels, P_X^*, P_Y^*. At those prices, society's budget constraint will be given by line C^*, and supply and demand will be in equilibrium. The combination X^*, Y^* of goods will be chosen, and this allocation is efficient.

this point on the PP curve will the ratio of the goods be equal to the ratio of their marginal costs (and hence equal to the RPT). On the other hand, given this budget constraint[4] (line C), individuals will demand X_1', Y_1'. Consequently there is an excess demand for good X (individuals demand more than is being produced), whereas there is an excess supply of good Y. The workings of the marketplace will therefore cause P_X to rise and P_Y to fall. Consequently the price ratio P_X/P_Y will rise; the price line will take on a steeper slope. Firms will respond to these price changes by moving clockwise along the production possibility frontier. That is, they will increase their production of good X and decrease their production of good Y. Similarly, individuals will respond to the changing prices by substituting Y for X in their consumption choices. The actions of both firms and individuals, then, serve to

---

[4]It is important to recognize why the budget constraint has this location. Since P_X and P_Y are given, the value of total production is $P_X \cdot X_1 + P_Y \cdot Y_1$. This is the value of "GNP" in the simple economy pictured in Figure 18.1. It is also, therefore, the total income accruing to people in society. Individuals' budget constraint therefore passes through X_1, Y_1 and has a slope of $-P_X/P_Y$. This is precisely the line labeled C in the figure.

eliminate the excess demand for X and the excess supply of Y as market prices change.

Equilibrium is reached at X^*, Y^* with a price ratio of P_X^*/P_Y^*. With this price ratio, supply and demand are equilibrated for both good X and good Y. Firms, in maximizing their profits, given P_X^* and P_Y^*, will produce X^* and Y^*. Similarly, with a budget constraint given by C^*, individuals will demand X^* and Y^*. Not only have markets been equilibrated by the operation of the price system, but the resulting equilibrium is also efficient. As we showed in Chapter 17, the point X^*, Y^* provides the highest level of utility that can be obtained given the production possibility frontier PP. Figure 18.1 therefore provides a simple general equilibrium "proof" that the results of supply and demand interacting in competitive markets can produce an efficient allocation of resources.

Prices, Efficiency, and Laissez-Faire Policies

Consequently we have shown that a perfectly competitive price system, by relying on the self-interest of individuals and of firms, and by utilizing the information carried by prices, can produce an efficient allocation of resources. In a sense this finding provides "scientific" support for the laissez faire position taken by many economists. For example, Adam Smith's assertion that

the natural effort of every individual to better his own condition, when suffered to exert itself with freedom and security, is so powerful a principle that it is alone, and without any assistance, not only capable of carrying on the society to wealth and prosperity, but of surmounting a hundred impertinent obstructions with which the folly of human laws too often encumbers its operations . . . [5]

has been shown to have considerable validity. Again, as Smith noted, it is not the "public spirit" of the baker that provides bread for individuals' consumption. Rather, bakers (and other producers) operate in their own self-interest in responding to market signals (what Smith termed the "invisible hand"). In so doing their actions may be coordinated by the market into an efficient, overall pattern.

That efficiency "theorem" raises many important questions, which are of two rather different types. First are the relatively theoretical questions about the ability of a market to arrive at the perfectly competitive prices that the theorem requires. We have briefly discussed a few aspects of this question elsewhere; because theoretical general equilibrium analysis is quite mathematical, we will not treat the subject in any more detail here.[6] The second important set of issues raised by the theorem is whether it has any policy importance. Is the theorem a guide for governmental action or just an interesting theoretical construction? In this chapter

---

[5] A. Smith, *The Wealth of Nations* (New York: Random House, Inc., Modern Library ed., 1937), p. 508.

[6] For an important (but difficult) survey of the mathematical theory of general equilibrium see K. J. Arrow and F. H. Hahn, *General Competitive Analysis* (San Francisco: Holden-Day, Inc., 1971). Chapters 1 and 2 provide a brief survey of the field and an introduction to the mathematics used in general equilibrium analysis.

we will make a start toward answering this question, but it will generally occupy us for the remainder of the book.

When the Market System Fails to Achieve Efficiency

The efficiency of a perfectly competitive price system depends crucially on the assumptions that underlie the competitive model. When we move beyond the confines of this model and examine possible real-world allocative problems, certain difficulties become apparent. In this section we will examine some of the impediments that may prevent markets from generating an efficient allocation. We will see that many of these are quite likely in view of our knowledge of the real world. We will take up some observations about the lessons to be drawn concerning optimal resource allocation in the presence of these impediments in the next section.

The number of impediments to perfect competition that we might discuss is practically infinite. These can, however, be classed into three general groupings that include most of the cases occurring in the real world: *Imperfect competition, externalities,* and *public goods.* We will discuss each separately below.

Imperfect Competition

We will use the term "imperfect competition" in a broad sense to include all those situations in which economic agents exert some market power in determining price. Markets that are organized as oligopolies or in which there is a monopsony on the demand side are therefore also considered in this category, in addition to the usual case of monopoly. The essential aspect of all such markets is that marginal revenue (or marginal expense in the case of a monopsony) is different from market price. A profit-maximizing firm, by equating marginal revenue with marginal cost, will not produce where price is equal to marginal cost. Because of this behavior of firms, relative prices will no longer reflect relative marginal costs, and the price system no longer carries the information necessary to insure efficiency.

As an example, consider the efficiency conditions for production and exchange in the Robinson Crusoe economy diagrammed in Figure 18.2. Point E represents an efficient allocation: at that point the MRS (of X for Y) is equal to the RPT (of X for Y). A perfectly competitive price ratio of P_X^*/P_Y^* could generate this allocation. Suppose, instead, that one of the goods, say X, is produced under monopoly conditions, whereas Y is produced under conditions of perfect competition. The profit-maximizing output choice, then, is that combination of X and Y for which

$$RPT \ (X \text{ for } Y) = \frac{MC_X}{MC_Y} = \frac{MR_X}{P_Y} < \frac{P_X}{P_Y} = MRS \ (\text{of } X \text{ for } Y) \qquad [18.1]$$

where the inequality holds because $MR_X < P_X$ for the monopolist.

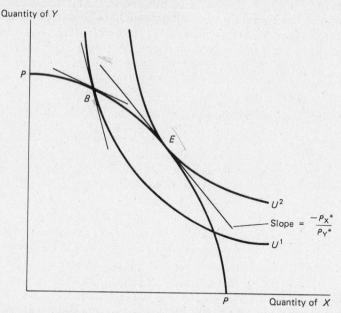

Figure 18.2 / The Production of Good X Under Monopoly Conditions Prevents Efficiency in Production and Exchange

If good X is produced in a monopoly market the profit-maximizing firm will choose that output combination for which the RPT (of X for Y) is equal to MR_X/P_Y; this will be less than the ratio of these goods' market prices (P_X/P_Y). Production will take place at a point such as B where the RPT is less than individuals' marginal rates of substitution. Too little X will be produced as a result of the monopolization of its market.

But that will entail a choice of outputs such as that represented by point B, with less X and more Y being produced than is optimal, given the existing tastes and technology.[7] The existence of a monopoly, by creating a divergence between price ratios and technical trade-off rates, has caused the efficiency of the price system to fail. No longer do individuals and firms equate their rates of trade-off to the same market-determined magnitudes. It is marginal revenue that is relevant to firms' decisions and price that is relevant to individuals' decisions; under conditions of imperfect competition these two will differ.

A similar proof would hold for other circumstances in which markets are imperfectly competitive. Market power by an agent creates a divergence between market price and the marginal figure that is relevant to the agent's decision. Because of this divergence, market prices will not carry the appropriate information about relative marginal costs. The workings of the price system will be "short-circuited," and an optimal allocation of resources cannot be achieved.

---

[7]This is a "general equilibrium" proof of the result first illustrated in Figure 11.4, where the differential effects of monopoly and perfect competition were demonstrated in a partial equilibrium framework. Figure 18.2 clearly shows that the presence of a monopoly in good X will cause resources to be directed into the production of other goods.

The importance for allocational efficiency of having market prices accurately reflect marginal costs cannot be overstated. It is this condition (or a slight generalization of it, which will be taken up shortly) that directly ties together individuals' demands and the decisions of firms. When $P = MC$, what individuals are willing to pay for a good at the margin is exactly what it costs to produce that good. When the equality fails to hold, demands and productive technologies are not properly tied together; consequently, resources are not efficiently allocated.

Externalities

The price system can also fail to allocate resources efficiently when there are interactions among firms and individuals that are not adequately represented by market prices. Examples of such occurrences are numerous. Perhaps the most common one is the case of a firm that pollutes the air with industrial smoke and other debris. To describe such "non-market" interactions, we define:

Definition

An *externality* is an effect of one economic agent's activities on another agent's well-being that is not taken into account through the normal operations of the price system.

While a more complete discussion of the nature of externalities will be presented in Chapter 20, we can here describe why the presence of such nonmarket interactions interferes with the ability of the price system to allocate resources efficiently.

The conditions for efficiency that we discussed in Chapter 17 must be redefined in a "social" sense when we recognize the possibility of externalities. In a production and exchange economy, for example, the condition for efficiency must be stated as:

Optimization Principle

A necessary condition for resources to be allocated efficiently is that the rate at which society i technically able to transform one good into another (the "social" rate of product transformation) should equal the rate at which individuals are willing to trade those goods for each other (the "social" marginal rate of substitution).

The problem that arises in the presence of externalities is that economic agents pay attention only to *private* rates of transformation and substitution in their decisions. If private and social rates diverge, the perfectly competitive price system will not generate an efficient allocation.

As an example of this possibility, suppose only two goods are produced in an economy: steel and balloons. Assume that the production of steel involves the creation of significant air pollution that reduces the utility levels of individuals by making them ill and by forcing them to dust their balloons frequently. As in the usual competitive case, firms will produce steel and balloons at the point where the RPT is equal to the ratio of these goods' equilibrium prices (say, P_S*/P_B* where P_S is the price of steel, P_B the price of balloons). If one ton of steel trades in the market for 10,000 balloons, firms will choose a point on the production possibility frontier at which reducing balloon production by 10,000 would provide the additional resources necessary for the production of one more ton of steel. Because of the externality associated with steel production, however, individuals would not be willing to make such a trade. They might, say, be only willing to give up 5,000 balloons for an extra ton of steel because of the ill health and dust that would accompany increased steel production. At least in this simple case, the price of steel does not reflect the externalities associated with steel production, and the competitive market "chooses" the wrong output combination.

This result is illustrated in Figure 18.3. Again in this figure point E records an efficient allocation of resources at which the social RPT is equal to the social MRS. Because of the externality in steel production, however, market prices do not lead

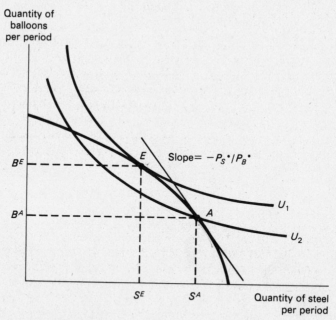

**Figure 18.3 / Externalities May
Cause an Inefficient Allocation of Resources**

With a market price ratio of P_S*/P_B* firms choose to produce S_A units of steel and B_A units of balloons. Because of externalities involved in steel production, the market prices at A do not reflect individuals' true marginal rates of substitution. The allocation A is therefore inefficient and results in a lower utility level than does the efficient allocation E.

economic agents to this point. Rather, firms choose to produce at point A where the RPT is equal to the ratio of equilibrium market prices (P_S*/P_B*). Although consumers also equate their private marginal rates of substitution to those market prices, such private demand decisions consider only the direct consumption values of steel and balloons: the steel-produced pollution is not taken into account. At point A the true social marginal rate of substitution is less than P_S*/P_B* indicating that individuals are less willing to give up balloons for steel than is indicated by the market prices of those goods. Existence of the externality therefore causes steel to be overproduced $(S^A > S^E)$ and balloons to be underproduced $(B^A < B^E)$ relative to the efficient allocation. Overall utility is reduced from U_1 to U_2 by this misallocation. In Chapter 20 we will investigate a number of additional types of externalities and we will examine several ways in which the allocational problems they cause might be corrected.

Public Goods

A third possible failure of the price system to yield an optimal allocation of resources stems from the existence of goods that must be provided on a "nonexclusive" basis. Such goods include national defense, inoculations against infectious diseases, criminal justice, and pest control. The distinguishing feature of these goods is that they provide benefits to all individuals: Once the goods are produced it is impossible (or at least very costly) to exclude anyone from benefiting from them. Consequently there is an incentive for each individual to adopt the position of a "free rider" by refusing to pay for the good in the hope that others will purchase it and thereby provide benefits to all. The pervasive nature of this incentive will ensure that resources are underallocated to nonexclusive goods. To avoid this underallocation communities (or nations) may decide to have the government produce nonexclusive goods and finance this production through compulsory taxation. For that reason nonexclusive goods are frequently termed *public goods*. In Chapter 19 we shall treat the problems raised by the existence of such goods in detail.

Theory of the Second Best

It must be admitted that the three general types of impediments we have been discussing are present in any economic system. A freely operating price system will therefore probably be incapable of generating a true Pareto optimal allocation of resources. It is tempting to reason that a competitive price system could still be advocated for those sectors of the economy in which these impediments are unimportant. By using the price system in these sectors, the Pareto rules for allocational efficiency would be satisfied there; this would be a *second-best* solution to the problem of optimal allocation. Unfortunately, this intuitive answer to the problem of finding a second-best solution is not correct. In a 1956 article R. G. Lipsey and K. Lancaster addressed themselves to this general question and reached a rather pessimistic conclusion.[8] If certain constraints within the economic system prevent some of the Pareto conditions from holding, then, given these constraints, it will generally not be desirable to have the optimum conditions hold elsewhere. It is not true that having more (but not all) of the optimum conditions hold is necessarily superior to having fewer hold. One must analyze each individual situation rather than attempt to draw such broad, all-inclusive policy recommendations.

A Graphic Demonstration

While a technical proof of the assertions made by Lipsey and Lancaster is rather difficult, the basic point can be made using a simple graphic argument. Suppose that society's production possibilities for two goods are represented by the frontier PP in Figure 18.4 and that preferences are given by the indifference curves. Assume also that there is a constraint in the economic system that makes the true optimal point (E) unattainable. Let this constraint be represented by the line AB; combinations of

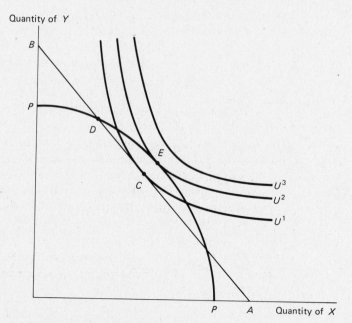

Figure 18.4 / Graphic Demonstration of the Theory of the Second Best

In the diagram the constraint AB prevents the optimal point E from being achieved. It is not true that, given this constraint, a society should strive for productive efficiency. Points such as C are preferred to those efficient points, such as D, which are obtainable. Second-best points are therefore not necessarily efficient points.

---

[8]R. G. Lipsey and K. Lancaster, "The General Theory of Second Best," *Review of Economic Studies* 24, no. 63 (1956–1957), pp. 11–32.

goods to the northeast of line *AB* cannot be achieved because of the constraint. Society's optimization problem is to maximize welfare (as represented by the indifference curves) subject to the constraint *AB*. The figure makes clear that this optimal point need not be on the *PP* frontier; the point *C* is definitely preferable to the "efficient" point *D*. This, then, demonstrates the principal negative result of the theory of the second best: If all the conditions for a Pareto optimum cannot be satisfied, it is not necessarily true that to fulfill some of them is the best policy.

This discussion of second-best choices at least casts some doubt on the advisability of advocating competitive pricing in particular sectors of the economy, when it is recognized that the Pareto conditions may not hold elsewhere. Whether or not such "partial" competitive solutions are in fact optimal will depend on the particular situation and on the nature of the constraints present in the economic system. In a theoretical sense the attainment of a Pareto optimum must be approached as a problem in constrained maximization rather than by piecemeal application of general optimal rules. It may in fact be possible to derive some optimal departures from perfectly competitive pricing.

A Note on Equity

Having summarized these negative conclusions about the normative significance of the relationship between efficiency and perfect competition, this may be an appropriate spot to remind the reader that efficiency is only one goal toward which an economy might strive. In Chapter 17 we showed that it may at times be socially optimal to sacrifice some efficiency in order to achieve an equitable distribution of utilities among the individuals in society. A perfectly operating competitive price system will not take account of such potentially desirable trade-offs and will choose an efficient allocation that, among other factors, reflects the initial endowments with which individuals start trading. Although it is impossible to make any definite statement about the extent of desirable equity-efficiency trade-offs or the specific form they might take in real-world policies, recognition of the equity problem suggests further caution in drawing normative prescriptions from the efficiency properties of the price system. As in the case of finding "second-best" solutions to the resource allocation problem, there may exist socially desirable departures from reliance on perfect competition.

So Why Study Perfect Competition?

By now you may be asking why, then, we have devoted such great attention to the optimal properties of a perfectly competitive price system if such a price system does not have unambiguously desirable properties. This is a valid question, which must be answered in a conceptual way. A study of the ideal of competitive allocation provides a pedagogic device for understanding how a price system allocates resources among alternative uses. The relationship between market trade-offs and technical trade-offs is clearly brought out by such an examination. Through a study of the competitive world we can achieve a feeling for how the economic system hangs together and gain an understanding of the notion of general equilibrium. A comprehension of the interrelationships between pricing and allocation is an integral part of any economic education.

Positive Applications

As with other economic tools, the perfectly competitive model of general equilibrium has both positive and normative applications. With regard to positive applications, there are many questions in economics for which the simple partial equilibrium models we have used will not suffice. For example, suppose that we wished to predict the effect that the imposition of a corporate profits tax would have. Clearly this is a question that cannot be answered by looking only at single markets in isolation. The tax will have effects in the capital market, in the labor market, in the output market for the taxed industry, and in the output market for untaxed industries. We might want to go even further and consider the effects that the government expenditures made possible by the tax would have. In order to encompass all these effects and to predict what new equilibria would emerge, we would need some tools with which to analyze the economic system as a whole. The perfectly competitive general equilibrium model provides such a tool and is most commonly used for that purpose. It shows the relationships between various goods markets and how economic decisions in those markets affect pricing in factor markets.[9]

■ An Example: The Corn Laws Debate

High tariffs on grain imports were imposed by the British government following the Napoleonic Wars. Debate over the effects of these "Corn Laws" dominated the analytical efforts of economists during the period 1820–1845. A principal focus of the debate concerned the effect that elimination of the tariffs would have on factor prices. In this section we present a simple general equilibrium analysis of that question.

The production possibility frontier in Figure 18.5 shows those combinations of grain (X) and manufactured goods (Y) that could be produced by English factors of production. Assuming (somewhat contrary to actuality) that the Corn Laws completely prevented trade, market equilibrium would be at E with the domestic price ratio given by P_X^*/P_Y^*. Removal of the tariffs would reduce this price ratio to P_X'/P_Y'. Given that new ratio, England would produce combination A and consume

---

[9]For an illustration of a general equilibrium model used to analyze the effects of the corporate tax, see A. C. Harberger, "The Incidence of the Corporation Income Tax," *The Journal of Political Economy* 70, No. 3 (June 1962), pp. 215–240.

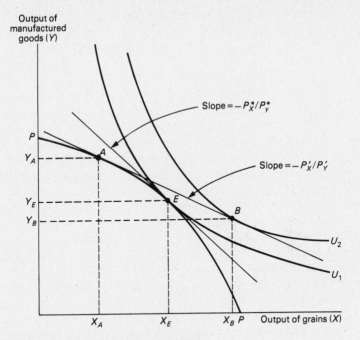

Figure 18.5 / Analysis of the Corn Laws Debate

Reduction of tariff barriers on grain would cause production to be reallocated from point E to point A. Consumption would be reallocated from E to B. If grain production is relatively capital intensive, the relative price of capital would fall as a result of these reallocations.

combination B. Grain imports would amount to $X_B - X_A$, and these would be financed by export of manufactured goods equal to $Y_A - Y_B$. Overall utility would be increased by the opening of trade. Use of the production possibility diagram therefore demonstrates the implications for production of both goods of relaxing the tariffs. By referring back to the Edgeworth production box diagram that lies behind the production possibility frontier (Figure 17.4), it is also possible to analyze the effect of tariff reductions on factor prices. The movement from point E to point A in Figure 18.5 is similar to a movement from P_3 to P_1 in Figure 17.4. Production of X is decreased and production of Y is increased by such a move and Figure 17.4 records the reallocation of capital and labor made necessary by such a move. If we assume that grain production is relatively capital intensive,[10] the movement from P_3 to P_1 causes the ratio of K to L to rise in both industries. This will in turn cause the relative price of capital to fall (and the relative price of labor to rise). Hence we conclude that repeal of the Corn Laws would be harmful to

---

[10]In the Corn Laws debate, attention centered on the factors *land* and *labor*. For convenience here we shall identify "land" as being synonymous with capital. To say that grain production is "capital intensive" means that the ratio of K to L in grain production is higher than the ratio of K to L in manufactured goods.

capital owners (that is, landlords) and helpful to laborers. It is not surprising that landed interests fought repeal of the Laws.

A Generalization: Political Support for Trade Policies

That trade policies may affect the relative incomes of various factors of production continues to exert a major influence on political debates about such policies. In the United States, for example, exports tend to be intensive in their use of skilled labor whereas imports tend to be intensive in unskilled labor input. By analogy to our discussion of the Corn Laws therefore, it might be expected that further movements toward free trade policies would result in rising relative wages for skilled workers and in falling relative wages for unskilled workers. It is not surprising therefore that unions representing skilled workers (the Machinists, certain segments of the United Auto Workers, the Petroleum and Atomic Workers) tend to favor free trade whereas unions of unskilled workers (those in textiles, shoes, and related businesses) tend to oppose it. Trade policy is clearly one area where economic interests exert a major influence on political positions taken.

A careful study of Figure 18.5 indicates another reason why workers in firms that produce imported goods may be opposed to moves toward more open world trade. The reallocation of production from point E to point A in Figure 18.5 requires that factors of production be transferred out of X (import) production into Y (export) production. Making such a reallocation may impose costs on workers. They may have to move to new communities, search for new jobs, or learn new skills.[11] All of these activities are costly to the individuals involved. Even though society as a whole benefits from trade expansion (overall utility increases from U_1 to U_2) individual workers may not be so lucky.

In order more equitably to share costs of adjusting to trade policies most countries offer some sort of governmental assistance to trade-affected workers. As part of the *Trade Expansion Act* of 1962, for example, the United States enacted a program of *Trade Adjustment Assistance* to provide jobless benefits and other services to workers in industries impacted by trade expansion. It is doubtful, however, that such ameliorated policies have a substantial effect on underlying economic interests in trade issues.

Normative Applications

Most normative applications of the general equilibrium model rely in some way on the relationship between perfect competition and efficiency. For example, some firms have adopted programs of decentralized decision making that stress the

---

[11] Notice, however, that in our model most of these costs are of a short-term nature. For example, ours is a "full-employment" model: along the production possibility frontier all inputs are employed. Hence workers transferred from X to Y production will, at most, experience some "frictional" unemployment.

necessity of correctly pricing intracompany resources such as fixed capital or sales staff. There are many similarities between the models used to study corporate efficiency and the general equilibrium models we have developed. Other applications that make use of the presumed optimal properties of the price system (most importantly, the $P = MC$ rule) include the setting of bridge tolls and airport landing fees, the use of international trade models to decide on correct tariff policies, and the institution of user charges in various social service programs. Probably the most important applications of the normative properties of the competitive price system have (surprisingly enough) centered on questions of how to ensure that a socialist economy operates efficiently. In the next section we shall discuss this application in some detail. We will then examine one particular application of the $P = MC$ rule.

An Application:
Lange Model of Socialist Pricing

One of the more interesting (and important) applications of the efficiency properties of a perfectly competitive price system has been to the problem of planning in a socialist economy. Early writers on this subject claimed that an efficient allocation of resources would be impossible to achieve in a socialist state because of the vast amount of information and infinite computations that would be necessary. It was argued that no central planning board could possibly assimilate all the information that is provided in a market economy by the price system; without the free operation of a market, resource allocation would be hopelessly inefficient. These views were challenged by the Polish economist Oscar Lange in a series of articles in the late 1930s.[12] Lange suggested that a socialist economy could achieve an efficient allocation of resources (at least in theory) by utilizing the desirable properties of markets in permitting decentralized decision making, while at the same time having social ownership of the means of production. Because an examinzation of Lange's proposals exhibits as much about the problems of resource allocation in a market economy as it does about resource allocation in a centrally planned one, we will outline his scheme in some detail.

Under Lange's system the central planning board is charged with setting prices that are to be regarded by all economic agents as fixed. Individuals are free to make consumption decisions given these prices, and presumably they will do so in a utility-maximizing way. Firm managers are under strict orders to minimize the costs of producing any level of output and are to produce that output for which price equals marginal cost. In other words, they are to approximate the decisions that managers of perfectly competitive firms would make in order to maximize profits. What Lange's model attempts to do is to approximate the efficient features of the perfectly competitive model.

---

[12]The principal article appears in edited form in O. Lange, *On the Economic Theory of Socialism* (New York: McGraw-Hill, Inc., Paperbacks, 1964), originally published by the University of Minnesota Press.

From a theoretical viewpoint there are three interesting questions that we might raise about the Lange model: How is equilibrium between supply and demand assured? How are factor supplies regulated? How are possible externalities treated?

Equilibrium Between Supply and Demand

The first of these problems is perhaps the most important. If the central planning board sets nonequilibrium prices, chaos is certain to result. A price set too high will mean that an excess supply of the good in question will be produced. Similarly, a price set below equilibrium will have the result of bringing about long shopping queues and other manifestations of excess demand. In a market economy such problems are avoided by relying on the interactions of supply and demand to establish an equilibrium price. Because this market interaction would not take place in a planned economy, the central planning board is under a strict mandate to raise prices of those goods in excess demand and lower the prices of those that are being oversupplied. Hopefully, by closely observing inventories and other indicators of market equilibrium, the central planning board would be able to adjust prices so as to respond to any possible discrepancies between supply and demand.

Factor Supplies

In the Lange model, labor is allocated in the same manner assumed to operate on a market economy. Wage rates are set by the central planning board, and individuals make their labor-leisure choices and their occupational choices based on those rates. Similarly, firms demand labor based on the marginal productivity principle because of the requirement that they "maximize profits." The board must be careful to set equilibrium wage rates.

It is in the supply of capital that Lange's solution differs markedly from the perfectly competitive model. Since capital is not privately owned in a socialist economy, no interest payments are made to individuals. At this zero interest rate there may be "insufficient" incentives to save. The central planning board is therefore charged with the responsibility of deciding how much output to withhold from current production for purposes of capital accumulation. Firms are, however, charged a rental rate for the capital equipment they use in order to insure that the supply of capital available is allocated in an optimal way. Although this procedure will (in principle) insure that capital is efficiently allocated at any one point in time, very real questions might be raised about the board's decisions regarding the total amount of capital accumulation for society as a whole. The most important of these questions is whether the decisions of the board will adequately reflect the tastes of individuals for present versus future goods. In fact, there is some evidence that planners in socialist countries may allocate too large a portion of current output to capital accumulation. The chronic "shortage" of consumer goods in the Soviet Union and some Eastern European countries is one sign of this possible misallocation. Such economies might be considered to be inefficient in an intertemporal sense.

Externalities

A final ingenious solution to the problem of achieving an efficient allocation of resources was proposed by Lange to deal with externalities. His suggestion was that external costs of production should be imposed (in the form of taxes) on the firms responsible. This would shift the firms' marginal cost curves up and would reduce the quantities they were willing to supply at the prevailing price. Then a shortage would appear in the market at the current price, and the central planning board would respond to this excess demand by raising prices. Finally, this action would presumably cut back on the demand for those products that are produced with harmful external side effects. Lange's suggestion insures an allocation of resources that adequately reflects true social costs. We will see in Chapter 21 that a similar solution might be desirable in a capitalist economy as well.

Lange's notion of "market" socialism has never been applied in practice, although recent actions in some socialist countries suggest a movement in that direction.[13] The rather lengthy discussion of Lange's ideas has been presented more because of the light it sheds on allocation in a market economy than as a practical guide to socialist planning. This model clearly exhibits the importance of relying on decentralized decision making and the central role a price system can play in unifying the actions of the decision makers. In certain circumstances these interactions may be able to achieve a socially desirable result.

Example of Marginal Cost Pricing: Congestion Tolls

In the previous example, we discussed a way in which the price system might be used to bring about an efficient allocation of resources in an entire economy. Most applications of the price system's optimal properties are not, however, on such a large scale. Rather, it has been more typical for economists to examine single prices (or a closely related set of prices) in an effort to demonstrate how a modification of these prices might bring about more desirable allocational results. Generally, economists have advocated bringing prices more nearly into line with marginal costs as a way of moving toward efficiency. Elsewhere in this chapter we have demonstrated in several contexts why such a move may represent an improvement. In this section we will analyze one specific issue, traffic congestion;

---

[13]These experiments have progressed furthest in Yugoslavia, where much of the economy is directed by (modified) Lange rules [see B. Horvat, "Survey of Yugoslavian Economic Policy," *American Economic Review,* Supplement (May 1971), for a detailed summary.] Similar experiments are being conducted in the Soviet Union under the intellectual leadership of Yevsei Liberman.

we will indicate how a system of marginal cost tolls might mitigate the allocational inefficiencies caused by this problem.

The allocational difficulties posed by traffic congestion arise because of an externality in individuals' decisions to use a particular traffic facility. When an individual decides to drive on a freeway, for example, he or she does not consider the effect that this action has on other drivers. By using the freeway, any one driver imposes costs on other individuals in the form of increased traffic congestion: Other individuals are slowed down because there is one more car on the road. During relatively slack periods of road usage, this cost may be rather small. However, during rush-hour traffic, the time-delay costs imposed by a marginal driver may (as we showed in Chapter 8) be quite high. This analysis can be rephrased by using the notion of social costs we discussed earlier in this chapter. The basic problem that arises in the use of a traffic facility is that the social marginal cost of an additional individual's using the facility during peak hours substantially exceeds the private marginal cost to the user. The time delay imposed on others is an externality that is not incorporated into the individual's calculations. As a solution to this problem, economists have proposed the imposition of "congestion" tolls that would bring private costs faced by individuals into line with true social costs. For example, it has been suggested that tolls on the bridges into New York City should be raised during rush hours. This would impose the full social costs of automobile commuting onto the individuals involved, and it might prompt some individuals to adopt methods of getting into the city that do not have such congestion costs.

Landing Fees at La Guardia Airport

One application of the concept of congestion tolls has been in the setting of landing fees at large airports. In recent years congestion has increased substantially at airports such as New York's La Guardia and Kennedy, Chicago's O'Hare, and Washington's National. This again reflects a situation in which social and private costs diverge. In deciding to use one of these airports, an airline (or a private pilot) considers only the private costs of such use; it disregards the costs (in terms of time delay) imposed on other users. In a recent study of La Guardia airport, A. Carlin and R. E. Park demonstrate that, at certain times of the day, social marginal costs may exceed private marginal costs by a wide margin.[14] For example, between 3:00 and 4:00 P.M. the delay cost imposed by an additional arrival at La Guardia (by a large jet aircraft) is estimated to be more than $1,000. The airport, on the other hand, assesses a landing fee of less than $100. An even larger divergence is found for general aviation aircraft for which marginal-delay costs of landing are put at $588 whereas the landing fee was (during 1967) only $5. Carlin and Park argue that these large differences between social and private

---

[14]A. Carlin and R. E. Park, "Marginal Cost Pricing of Airport Runway Capacity," *American Economic Review* 60, no. 3 (June 1970), pp. 310–319.

marginal costs suggest that congestion tolls should be levied during peak hours of airport use. This would force users to incorporate social costs into their decisions. In fact, the authors point out that La Guardia did (in 1968) increase its landing fees for general aviation aircraft (to $25) during peak hours, and the use of the airport by this class of carrier may have declined by as much as 70 percent during such peak hours. The savings (in terms of decreased congestion) resulting from this toll may have been substantial. Further movement toward imposing the true social costs of runway use might lead to further efficiencies.

Summary

In this chapter we showed that a perfectly competitive price system in which individuals maximize utility and firms maximize profits can achieve an efficient allocation of resources. That result is proved by noting that equilibrium competitive prices provide common trade-off rates to which economic agents adjust their behavior. These adjustments then result in satisfaction of the conditions for efficiency. The price system therefore provides a way in which resources can be efficiently allocated without relying on any sort of central direction. Recognition of this relationship between a competitive price system and the efficient allocation of resources is one of the most important results of analytical economics.

Two major caveats about the price-efficiency relationship were outlined in the chapter. First, a number of factors may interfere with the ability of a price system to achieve efficiency. These include imperfect competition, externalities, and public goods. In the presence of such impediments the normative content of perfectly competitive theory is ambiguous.

A second caveat about the efficiency of a perfectly competitive price system concerns social welfare. There is no guarantee that the efficient allocation chosen under a competitive price system will be a social welfare optimum in the sense discussed in Chapter 17. No competitive mechanism assures equity. Indeed, it is possible that some competitive outcomes may be quite inequitable if "initial endowments" are highly unequal.

There are, of course, other ways of allocating resources than by means of a price system. Detailed central planning, for example, is widely used as a substitute for the market, both within large bureaucratic organizations and for entire sectors of many national economies. Such planning generally requires substantial inputs of information, but the development of large-capacity computers and sophisticated programming techniques has reduced the costs associated with using that information considerably.[15] Other allocational methods include: love and caring (as in families and some communal organizations); first-come, first-served (the sale of World Series tickets); government discretion (the awarding of TV licenses); queuing (the infamous gasoline "crunch" of 1973); and random allocation by lot (gambling

---

[15] See the appendix to this chapter for a brief analysis of one such programming method.

winnings, the military draft, or the chance to speak to President Carter on the phone). Each of these alternatives to the price system may, in certain circumstances, be judged to be superior to the price system as an allocational device.

Despite the widespread existence of such alternatives, the price system has a remarkable degree of perseverance in its effect on allocation. Smith noted in individuals a "propensity to truck, barter, and exchange one thing for another"[16] that tends to reallocate goods from where they have low value to where they have high value regardless of how they were initially allocated. Examples of this sort of activity range from the "scalping" of World Series tickets to decisions by workers on Soviet collective farms to spend time growing food on their private "free market" garden plots. It is therefore likely that the price system will remain a dominant allocational mechanism.

Suggested Readings

Arrow, K. J., and F. H. Hahn, *General Competitive Analysis* (San Francisco: Holden-Day, Inc., 1972), chaps. 1 and 2.

Bator, F. M., "The Anatomy of Market Failure," *Quarterly Journal of Economics* 72 (August 1958), pp. 351–379.

Baumol, W. J., and D. F. Bradford, "Optimal Departures from Marginal Cost Pricing," *American Economic Review* 60 (June 1970), pp. 265–283.

Debreu, G., *Theory of Value* (New York: John Wiley & Sons, Inc., 1959).

Harberger, A. C., "The Incidence of the Corporate Profits Tax," *Journal of Political Economy* 70 (June 1962), pp. 215–240.

Henderson, J. M., and R. E. Quandt, *Microeconomic Theory,* 2d ed. (New York: McGraw-Hill, Inc., 1971), chaps. 5 and 7.

Horvat, B., "Yugoslav Economic Policy in the Post-War Period: Problems, Ideas, and Institutional Developments," *American Economic Review,* Supplement 61 (June 1971), pp. 71–169.

Johnson, H. G., *The Two-Sector Model of General Equilibrium* (Chicago: Aldine-Atherton, 1971).

Koopmans, T. C., "Is the Theory of Competitive Equilibrium with It?" *American Economic Review* 64 (May 1974), pp. 325–329.

Kuenne, R. E., *The Theory of General Economic Equilibrium* (Princeton, N. J.: Princeton University Press, 1963).

Quirk, J., and R. Saposnik, *Introduction to General Equilibrium Theory and Welfare Economics* (New York: McGraw-Hill, Inc., 1968).

Radford, R. A., "The Economic Organization of a POW Camp," *Economica* 12 (November 1945), pp. 189–201.

Shoven, J. B., and J. Whalley, "A General Equilibrium Calculation of the Effects

---

[16]A. Smith, *The Wealth of Nations* (New York: Random House, Inc., Modern Library ed., 1937), p. 13.

of Differential Taxation of Income from Capital in the U.S." *Journal of Public Economics* 1 (1972), pp. 281–321.

Walras, L., *Elements of Pure Economics,* trans. W. Jaffé (London: George Allen and Unwin, Ltd., 1954).

Problems

18.1

Consider an economy with just one technique available for the production of each good:

Good	Food	Cloth
Labor per unit output	1	1
Land per unit output	2	1

a. Supposing land is unlimited but labor equals 100, write and sketch the production possibilities frontier.

b. Supposing labor is unlimited but land equals 150, write and sketch the production possibilities frontier.

c. Supposing labor equals 100 and land equals 150, write and sketch the production possibilities frontier. (Suggestion: What are the intercepts of the production possibilities frontier? When is land fully employed? Labor? Both?)

d. Explain why the production possibility frontier of part (c) is concave.

e. Sketch the relative price of food as a function of its output in case (c).

f. If consumers insist on trading 4 units of food for 5 units of cloth, what is the relative price of food? Why?

g. Explain why production is exactly the same at a price ratio of $P_F/P_C = 1.1$ as at $P_F/P_C = 1.9$.

h. Suppose that capital is also required for producing food and clothing and that capital requirements per unit of food are 0.8 and per unit of clothing are 0.9. There are 100 units of capital available. What is the production possibilities curve in this case? Answer part (e) for this case.

18.2

In an economy with two individuals (A and B), discuss the results of exchange in the following situations:

a. Perfect competition in which A and B accept prices as given by "the market."

b. A is a monopolist and can set any price it chooses.

c. A is a perfect price discriminator and can charge a different price for each unit traded.

Does each of these lead to a Pareto efficient solution? It would be useful to work with an Edgeworth box diagram to present your solution.

18.3

The country of Podunk produces only wheat and cloth, using as inputs land and labor. Both are produced by constant returns to scale production functions. Wheat is the relatively land-intensive commodity.

a. Explain in words, or with diagrams, how the price of wheat relative to cloth *(p)* determines the land-labor ratio in each of the two industries.

b. Suppose that *p* is given by external forces (this would be the case if Podunk were a "small" country trading freely with a "large" world). Show, using the Edgeworth box, that if the supply of labor increases in Podunk, the output of cloth will rise and the output of wheat will fall.

18.4

Two types of goods that cause difficulties for the theorem of the equivalence between Pareto optimality and perfect competition are "joint products" and "public goods." These are defined as: (a) Joint products are goods like leather and beef that are produced together in fixed proportions; their production cannot be separated. (b) Public goods are consumed by everyone at the same level (for example, national defense). Once the good is produced, no one can be excluded from its use.

How must the Pareto optimal conditions be rephrased in the presence of these types of goods (think primarily about the condition $MRS_{of\ X\ for\ Y} = RPT_{of\ X\ for\ Y}$)?

Is perfect competition likely to bring about these revised conditons? Show your results graphically in a "Robinson Crusoe" economy.

18.5

Draw a production possibility frontier and a set of indifference curves representing the tastes of individuals in society.

a. Show on this diagram what the efficient production point is and what price ratio will cause it to be achieved?

b. Suppose now that this economy can trade with the rest of the world at a price ratio different from that which prevails domestically. If it continues to produce its initial output combination, how might this country trade with the rest of the world to improve welfare at this new price ratio?

c. How might the country specialize in production to take even further advantage of the possibilities for world trade?

18.6

Contrast the "general equilibrium" proof of the resource allocation effects of monopoly given in Chapter 18 to the "partial equilibrium" proof given in Chapter 11. Are the two presentations simply alternative ways of showing the same phenomenon? Explain.

Linear Programming, Pricing of Inputs, and Duality

Introduction

This appendix has two basic purposes: to introduce the mathematical tool of linear programming and to use this tool to demonstrate some additional relationships between the efficient use of resources and the pricing of those resources. Of course, a detailed treatment of linear programming is beyond the scope of this book, and therefore our analysis must be brief.[1] We will examine only one specific example of linear programming techniques. In this example, an economy is assumed to have fixed amounts of various productive inputs and must choose how to allocate these to the production of two goods, cars and trucks. In order to avoid introducing demand conditions, we will assume that the prices of the two goods remain constant throughout our analysis. More specifically, we will assume that the price of trucks (P_T) is \$4,000 each and that the price of cars (P_C) is \$5,000 each. The sole goal of the central planner in our simple economy is to allocate the available resources to car and truck production so that the total value of output is as large as possible. That is, the goal is to choose car output (C) and truck output (T) so that

$$\text{Total Value} = TV = P_T \cdot T + P_C \cdot C$$
$$= 4000 \cdot T + 5000 \cdot C \qquad \text{[18A.1]}$$

is as large as possible given available resources.

---

[1] For an interesting though fairly difficult survey of linear programming techniques see R. Dorfman, P. A. Samuelson, and R. M. Solow, *Linear Programming and Economic Analysis* (New York: McGraw-Hill, Inc., 1958).

A Graphic Solution to the Problem

Before we approach the solution to this problem through the use of linear programming, it may be useful to first demonstrate the general kind of solution we might derive by applying the tools we have presented earlier. The most direct way to proceed is by using a graphic analysis. In Figure 18A.1 we have drawn the production possibility frontier for the economy. The curve PP represents those combinations of cars and trucks that can be produced given the inputs available. Our goal now is to choose that point on the PP frontier that provides maximum revenues. This maximization process is shown in the figure. The several parallel straight lines (labeled TV_1, TV_2, TV_3) record those combinations of cars and trucks that provide equal value. The combinations lying along TV_3 provide more in total value than do those on TV_2, which in turn provide more value than do those on TV_1. The slope of these lines given by $-P_T/P_C$ ($= -4000/5000 = -4/5$) since this ratio of prices tells how cars can be traded for trucks in the market while keeping total revenue constant. The total value of cars and trucks produced is as large as possible when output combination C^*, T^* is chosen. This combination produces total revenues of TV_2, and it is the only combination that is capable of providing this amount: All other feasible output combinations on PP provide less total value than does this optimal choice. At C^*, T^* the production possibility frontier is exactly tangent to the total value line TV_2. This is the type of result that should by now be familiar. At

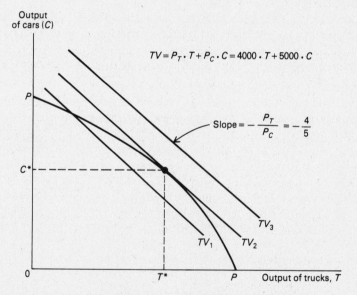

Figure 18A.1 / Value Maximization in a Hypothetical Economy

PP represents the feasible combinations of cars and trucks that can be produced with available resources. If a central planner wishes to maximize the total value of production (TV) the combination C^*, T^* should be produced. At this output combination the RPT (of trucks for cars) is equal to the ratio of these goods' prices (P_T/P_C).

the optimal point, the rate at which cars can technically be traded for trucks is equal to the rate at which these two goods can be traded in the market. In other words, the rate of product transformation (of trucks for cars) is equal to the price ratio P_T/P_C.

We will now turn to an examination of the way in which this same problem might be solved by linear programming techniques. We will see that these techniques provide not only an answer that is qualitatively very similar to what we just derived, but also additional insights into the resource allocation raised by the problem.

A Linear Programming Statement of the Problem

Linear programming is a mathematical technique that is particularly suited to solving the problem we have stated. The technique was developed as a systematic way to find the maximum values of linear functions [such as equation 18A.1] when the variables in these functions (that is, C and T) are constrained in the values they can take on by other linear functions. In order to show how this technique works, we must first examine the factors in the economy that constrain the output choices that are feasible. There are two types of constraints present in any productive economy: total quantities of various inputs are fixed, and there are certain technological rules (that is, production functions) that must be followed in turning these inputs into outputs. For the purposes of our car-truck example, we will assume that there are only three possible inputs: labor, machines, and steel. The quantities of these inputs that are assumed to be available are shown in the second column of Table 18A.1. No production plan can be implemented that uses more than 720 labor-hours, 900 machine hours, or 1800 tons of steel.

Table 18A.1 / Resources and Technology in a Hypothetical Economy

Resource	Total Available	Required to Produce 1 Truck	Required to Produce 1 Car
Labor	720 hours	1 hour	2 hours
Machines	900 hours	3 hours	1 hour
Steel	1800 tons	5 tons	4 tons

Production Functions for Cars and Trucks

Table 18A.1 also indicates the amounts of each of these inputs that are required to produce one car or one truck. It takes 1 labor-hour, 3 machine hours, and 5 tons of steel to build a truck; it takes 2 labor-hours, 1 machine hour, and 4 tons of steel to build a car. Notice that the production techniques shown in Table 18A.1 are of the fixed proportions type: No substitution between inputs is possible. This kind of "linear" technology is one characteristic of most linear programming problems.

Resource Constraints

We are now in a position to examine the constraints that the availability of inputs places on the combinations of cars and trucks that can be produced. If we again let C represent the number of cars to be produced and T the number of trucks, then the first line of Table 18A.1 records the fact that all possible choices of T and C must obey the constraint.

$$1 \cdot T + 2 \cdot C \leq 720 \qquad \text{[18A.2]}$$

That is, the quantity of labor employed in truck production (remember it takes 1 labor-hour to build one truck) plus the quantity employed in car production (that is, 2 labor-hours per car) cannot exceed the 720 labor-hours available. Equation 18A.2 might be called the "labor-hours" constraint in production.

Similar constraints exist for machines and for steel. The machine hour constraint is

$$3 \cdot T + 1 \cdot C \leq 900 \qquad \text{[18A.3]}$$

and the steel constraint is

$$5 \cdot T + 4 \cdot C \leq 1800 \qquad \text{[18A.4]}$$

These constraints record that no more machines or steel may be used than are available.

Given the constraints 18A.2, 18A.3, and 18A.4, our problem now is to find values of T and C that satisfy these constraints and make the total value of output,

$$TV = 4000 \cdot T + 5000 \cdot C \qquad \text{[18A.5]}$$

as large as possible. That, then, is our linear programming problem.

Construction of the Production Possibility Frontier

One possible (and very time-consuming) solution to the problem would be simply to enumerate all the combinations of C and T that satisfy the constraints, calculate the total value of each of these, and choose that one with the largest value. A far more efficient procedure makes use of graphic techniques. Figure 18A.2 graphs the three resource constraints. Since any feasible combination of C and T must satisfy *all* three constraints, we are only interested in those points in the diagram that fall on or below all three lines. The heavy line in Figure 18A.2 indicates the outer perimeter of such feasible choices. Points on or inside this curve can be produced.

For example, should the central planner in the economy decide to produce only cars, the heavy line indicates that 360 could be produced. In producing only cars, the economy "runs out" of labor-hours first (there is enough steel to produce 450

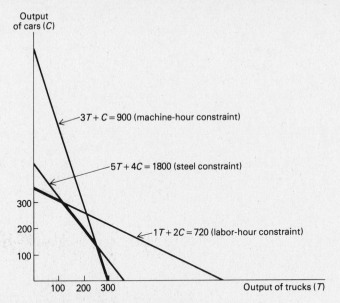

Figure 18A.2 / Construction of the Production Possibility Frontier for the Linear Programming Problem

The heavy line in this diagram is the production possibility frontier for cars and trucks implied by the input constraints. It is the perimeter of the set of output combinations that satisfies all the constraints.

cars and enough machines to produce 900 cars). For trucks, on the other hand, the binding constraint is machine availability. There are only enough machines to build 300 trucks if only trucks are built. Other combinations of cars and trucks on or inside the heavy line in Figure 18A.2 similarly satisfy all the constraints. The curve is in fact the production possibility frontier for the simple economy we have described.

Linear Programming Solution of the Problem

We can now use the production possibility frontier we derived in Figure 18A.2 to solve our maximum value problem in much the same way that the problem was solved in Figure 18A.1. Figure 18A.3 shows the production possibility frontier together with several lines of equal revenue. From the figure, we can see that the value maximizing point is that output combination C^*, T^*, where the labor-hour constraint and the steel constraint intersect.[2] (You should refer back to Figure 18A.2

---

[2]This point in a sense satisfies the rule that the RPT should equal the ratio P_T/P_C. The RPT along the labor-hour constraint is $-1/2$; along the steel constraint the RPT is $-5/4$. The vertex at C^*, T^* includes all slopes between $-1/2$ and $-5/4$. But the ratio $-P_T/P_C$ is given by $-4/5$, which lies between these two values. Hence C^*, T^* is the revenue-maximizing point. In linear programming problems the optimal solution will usually occur at corners, such as the one illustrated.

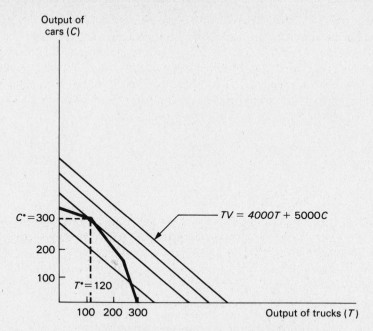

Figure 18A.3 / Maximization of Revenue in the Linear Program

By superimposing several lines of equal revenue on the production possibility frontier, the point of maximum revenue can be found. This point occurs where the labor-hour and steel constraints intersect.

to check that these are indeed the constraints that intersect at C^*, T^*.) Solving the two constraints for C^* and T^* gives:

$$1T + 2C = 720 \text{ (labor-hour constraint)}$$
$$5T + 4C = 1800 \text{ (steel constraint)} \qquad \text{[18A.6]}$$

or, from the labor-hour constraint,

$$T = 720 - 2C$$

Therefore, by substitution into the steel constraint

$$5(720) - 10C + 4C = 1800$$
$$- 6C = -1800$$

Hence our optimal solution is

$$C^* = 300 \qquad \text{[18A.7]}$$

and

$$T^* = 120$$

That means that 120 trucks should be produced along with 300 cars. The revenue provided by these outputs is \$1,980,000; this is the maximum value possible given the resource constraints. Notice that at this production level not all the available machine hours are being used. Production of 300 cars and 120 trucks requires only 660 machine hours, whereas 900 are available. The observation that, at the value-maximizing output level, there are unused machines has important implications for the pricing of machines, as we will now demonstrate.

Duality and the Pricing of Inputs

So far we have said nothing about the price of inputs in this linear programming problem. The economy had the inputs on hand and set about the task of maximizing the value of its output. A linear programming problem that is related to the *primal* problem above is the *dual* linear programming problem of finding input prices associated with the optimal choice of C and T. Formally, these dual input prices solve the following linear programming problem:

Minimize

$$M = 720\,P_L + 900\,P_K + 1800\,P_S \qquad \text{[18A.8]}$$

subject to

$$P_L + 3P_K + 5P_S \geq 4000$$
$$2P_L + P_K + 4P_S \geq 5000 \qquad \text{[18A.9]}$$

Where P_L, P_K, and P_S are the (nonnegative) per unit prices of labor, capital, and steel. This dual problem can be given an economic interpretation. We are asked to find prices for the inputs that minimize the total value of all inputs available but that also have the property that the production of neither cars nor trucks earns a pure profit [this is stated by the inequalities of equation 18A.9 of the dual]. For example, the first inequality says that the costs of producing one truck (that is, the cost of 1 labor-hour, 3 machine hours, and 5 tons of steel) should not be less than the price of a truck. If constraints such as those of equation 18A.9 were not imposed, the minimization problem of equation 18A.8 could be trivially solved by setting $P_L = P_K = P_S = 0$.

Without going into formal detail, it should be clear that the dual problem is related in some way to the original problem. All the constants that appeared in the primal problem also appear in the dual, but in different places. In particular, notice that quantities that appeared in the original constraints now appear as coefficients in the dual objective function (M) and vice versa. Also the constraints of the primal problem seem to have been "turned on their side" in the dual.

Solution to the Dual Problem

A graphic solution to the dual linear programming problem will not be presented here because it would require a three-dimensional graph. It must be taken on faith that the solution to the dual program turns out to be

$$P_L = \$1500$$
$$P_K = \$0$$
$$P_S = \$500 \qquad\qquad\qquad\qquad \text{[18A.10]}$$

These are the prices of L, K, and S that minimize 18A.8 and obey the two constraints given by equation 18A.9. The reader may wish to check to see that this is indeed true.

There are several important features to be noted about this solution.

1. With these input prices equation 18A.9 is exactly satisfied. Neither good is produced at a loss. Hence both goods can be produced in the economy.

2. The value of M with these input prices is $1,980,000. It is no coincidence that this is identical to the maximum value for TV we found in the primal problem. Such a relationship holds between the primal and the dual solutions of all linear programs. Here this equality resembles the income-output identity in the *National Income and Product Accounts*. The total value of output is equal to the total value of inputs.

3. The input that was not a binding constraint in the primal problem (machine hours) is given a price of $0 in the dual problem. This result tells economists that adding machines in this economy would have no effect on the value of output. Since labor and steel are the inputs that prevent output being increased, on the other hand, these inputs are given positive prices. The values given in equation 18A.10 for P_L and P_S indicate how much extra value would be provided by 1 more unit of these inputs. The reader may wish to show, for example, that an increase in labor by 1 unit will cause the total of output to increase by $1,500 (if we allow the economy to produce fractional parts of cars and trucks).[3]

Further Observations on Duality

These linear programming problems clearly demonstrate the relationship between the optimal choice of outputs and the correct choice of input prices. The optimal allocation of a fixed amount of inputs to the production of a variety of possible outputs has as its associated dual problem the optimal pricing of those inputs available. The solution of one problem is equivalent to the solving of the other.[4]

---

[3]The firm will produce 5/6 of an additional car in this situation but will cut truck production by 2/3 of a truck. Consequently, total revenue is changed by $5/6 \cdot 5000 - 2/3 \cdot 4000$, which is about $1,500.

[4]Linear programming problems may not always have solutions. If a linear programming problem and its associated dual have "feasible" solutions (solutions that satisfy the constraints of the problems) then they each have optimal solutions that have the qualitative properties listed above. For an elegant and concise discussion of the relationship between primal and dual linear programming problems with

This relationship has been widely used. For example, the computation of factor prices from a linear programming model can be very useful for economic planning in less developed economies. Such "shadow prices" can provide information about how important certain inputs are, and occasionally such computed prices may differ greatly from the actual prices of the inputs. For example, there are institutional reasons (labor unions, minimum wages, and so forth) why some groups of workers may have high wages even though labor is an overabundant resource in the particular country. On the other hand, linear programming models may suggest that the "real" value of labor is rather low. Planners should therefore adopt productive techniques that utilize labor to a greater extent than would seem economically warranted by looking only at market wage rates.

In a similar way linear programming has been used by corporations in order to make more efficient management decisions. One such use arises when a firm wishes to decentralize its decision making. To do so, the firm often divides its operations among several "profit centers," which are responsible for all production decisions within a specific area. One problem with which the management of such decentralized firms must contend is how to charge each profit center for the general company inputs (plant and equipment, administrative staff, advertising staff) it uses. Only by correctly choosing the bookkeeping prices of these inputs can the firm's management be sure that the decisions of the manager of each profit center will produce desirable overall results. Linear programming has been used extensively for calculating the prices of such intracompany resources.

Of course, those two examples merely hint at the huge number of applications that linear programming has had. Others include such widely different applications as the planning of natural gas pipelines and railway yards, investigating the optimal portfolio of stocks for a mutual fund to own, and studying the movement of seasonal labor forces in Africa. In many of these applications a linear program's duality features are utilized.

Suggested Readings

Baumol, W. J., *Economic Theory and Operations Analysis,* 2d ed. (Englewood Cliffs, N.J.: Prentice-Hall, Inc., 1965), chaps. 5–6.

Beals, R. E., M. B. Levy, and L. N. Moses, "Rationality and Migration in Ghana," *Review of Economics and Statistics* 49 (November 1967), pp. 480–486.

Dorfman, R., "Mathematical or 'Linear' Programming: A Nonmathematical Exposition," *American Economic Review* 43 (December 1953), pp. 797–825.

———, P. A. Samuelson, and R. M. Solow, *Linear Programming and Economic Analysis* (New York: McGraw-Hill, Inc., 1958).

---

applications to a variety of allocational problems see D. Gale, *The Theory of Linear Economic Models* (New York: McGraw-Hill, Inc., 1960).

Farrar, D. E., *The Investment Decision under Uncertainty* (Englewood Cliffs, N.J.: Prentice-Hall, Inc., 1962).

Gale, D., *The Theory of Linear Economic Models* (New York: McGraw-Hill Inc., 1960).

Glicksman, A. M., *An Introduction to Linear Programming and the Theory of Games* (New York: John Wiley & Sons, Inc., 1963).

Henderson, J. M., "Efficiency and Pricing in the Coal Industry," *Review of Economics and Statistics* 38 (February 1956), pp. 50–60.

Hicks, J. R., "Linear Theory," *Economic Journal* 70 (December 1960), pp. 671–709.

Waverman, L., "The Preventive Tariff and the Dual in Linear Programming," *American Economic Review* 62 (September 1972), pp. 620–629.

Part VII   Government

Introduction

In the previous parts of this book we have examined the way in which markets act to integrate individuals' demands with the productive techniques available to a society. Markets permit the decentralized decisions of millions of economic agents to be unified into an overall allocation of resources. In a sense, the benefits to be derived from the operation of markets are related to the differences among economic agents. If Smith and Jones have similar resources but rather different tastes, benefits will accrue to each person by trading with the other. If two firms have different productive capabilities, total output can be increased by having each firm specialize in the production of that output in which it is most efficient. Although many qualifications were expressed throughout the first six parts of this book, generally the analysis sought to demonstrate these benefits of market interactions.

There are many ways, however, in which markets may fail to produce beneficial results. Some goods that are universally desired may not be produced by the free operation of the market. For example, even though police protection and public health services may be desirable goods, free markets may not provide them in as large amounts as would be considered "optimal" by most members of society. On the other hand, the private market may overproduce other types of goods. As we discussed in Chapter 18, this would be the case if detrimental externalities were associated with the production of some good, and these externalities were not reflected in firms' output decisions. Finally, and perhaps most important, the unfettered operation of the market may produce a distribution of income that is considered to be undesirable from the point of view of overall social welfare. Some movement toward greater equality may be desired by most of the individuals in society, but the market does not provide a way to translate this desire into action.

In each of these cases it may be necessary to have governmental interference in the market system, if socially beneficial results are to be achieved. In this part we will examine the reasons for such failures, and we will develop a framework for government action. A discussion of these issues is central to our understanding modern microeconomic theory. As modern society has become more complex, examples of market failure have become more apparent. Matters that were previously treated as mildly interesting textbook examples (such as air pollution) have today become matters of major social concern. In response to these market failures, the role assigned to government in the operation of the economy has been progressively enlarged in practically all countries. For this reason it is important for us to examine the economic foundations for governmental behavior.

In Chapter 19 we will discuss the general rationale that economists have used to explain the role of government in a market economy. The central purpose of the chapter is to examine possible definitions of a "public good" and to investigate some of the problems that arise in the provision of these goods. We will also give a brief discussion of how the government might choose among several possible public goods. That discussion relies heavily on the notion of opportunity cost that we have mentioned at many other points in this book. Most of the analysis in Chapter 19 is of a normative nature: We are primarily interested in asking what a government *should* do. This is in contrast to the analysis of the first five parts of this book, where we stressed a predictive (that is, positive) approach to the study of economic phenomena. It is also possible, by using a few simple behavioral models, to produce a positive theory of government. In the final section of the chapter we will discuss some of the elements that such a theory might have.

One important function of government is in the definition of property rights for those goods that are traded in an economy. Goods are by their nature neither privately owned nor publicly owned. Rather, the government and its associated legal system must establish certain "rules of the game" that specify who owns what and outline the rights that this owner has to exchange his or her property for that of someone else. Chapter 20 examines these questions about the nature of property rights in some detail. We will see that the question of property rights and the problems raised in a market economy by the existence of externalities are closely related issues. In a sense, the existence of detrimental externalities (such as air pollution) is a manifestation of the absence of property rights (people do not own the rights to the air they breathe). The major purpose of Chapter 20 is to make this relationship more precise and to demonstrate the implications that the assignment of property rights has for the way in which resources are allocated.

All major governmental decisions affect the distribution of income among the members of society. In some situations (such as the payment of Aid to Families with Dependent Children) this effect may be a primary purpose of the program, whereas in other cases (such as the government providing for national defense) these effects may be secondary to the major purposes of the program. In either case, it is important that some attempt be made to measure these distributional effects and to judge whether or not they are desirable. In Chapter 21 we describe the distribution of income and examine some of the determinants of that distribution. We then turn to an examination of the role of government in affecting the distribution of income and present some evidence on some of these effects. Because study of the distribution of income is perhaps the central concern of normative economics, Chapter 21 provides a natural conclusion to this book.

Optimization Principle

Efficiency in the production of public goods requires that the rate at which society is willing to trade one unit of the public good for one unit of a private good (the social *MRS*—which, in this case, is the *sum* of individuals' *MRS*'s) is equal to the rate at which it is technically possible to transform these goods (the social *RPT*).[4]

A Graphic Analysis

Problems raised by the nonexclusive nature of public goods can also be demonstrated with partial equilibrium analysis by examining the demand curve associated with such goods. In the case of a private good, we found the market demand curve (see Chapter 5) by summing individuals' demands horizontally. At any price, the quantities demanded by each individual are summed to calculate the total quantity demanded in the market. The market demand curve shows the marginal evaluation that individuals place on an additional unit of output. For a public good (which is provided in the same quantity to everyone) we must add individual demand curves vertically. To find out how society values some level of public good provision, we must ask how each individual values this level of output and then sum these valuations. This idea is represented in Figure 19.1. There the total demand curve for the public good (*DD*) is the *vertical* sum of each individual's demand curve. Each point on the *DD* curve represents the social marginal evaluation of the particular level of public goods' expenditure.[5] Producing one more unit of the public good would benefit everyone. To evaluate this benefit, we must sum each individual's personal evaluation of the good. In private markets, on the other hand, the production of one more unit benefits only the individual who ultimately consumes that unit. Private markets will undervalue the benefits of public goods and underallocate resources to their production.

---

[4]These conditions are clearly demonstrated in P. A. Samuelson, "The Pure Theory of Public Expenditure," *Review of Economics and Statistics* 36 (November 1954), pp. 387–389; and in several later articles in the same journal.

[5]If MC_P and MC_G represent the marginal costs of a public and a private good, respectively, then (somewhat loosely) the conditions for optimality in the production of a private good are given by

$$MC_G = MV_G^1 = MV_G^2 = \cdots = MV_G^n$$

and for the public good by

$$MC_P = MV_P^1 + MV_P^2 + \cdots + MV_P^n$$

where MV_G^i and MV_P^i are the "marginal valuations" (that is, the amount an individual is willing to pay for one more unit of the good in question) of the two goods.

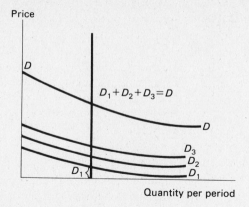

Price

$D_1 + D_2 + D_3 = D$

D

D_3
D_2
D_1

D_1

Quantity per period

Figure 19.1 / Derivation of the Demand for a Public Good

Since a public good is nonexclusive, the price that individuals are willing to pay for one more unit (their "marginal valuations") is equal to the sum of what each individual would pay. Hence, for public goods, market demand curves are derived by a vertical summation rather than the horizontal summation that we used for the case of private goods.

Problems in the Definition of Public Goods

It would be inappropriate to infer from the theory of public goods we have thus far presented that the dividing line between private and public goods is clearly drawn. Rather, the technical property of nonexclusion is only a conceptually convenient way to illustrate why markets may fail to produce certain goods. To use this technical definition as the sole criterion for government action would be misleadingly precise in an area that defies precision. There are at least three reasons why the nonexclusion principle may not be a sufficient description of those activities government should pursue:

1. There are many goods that fall between the two poles of private and public goods.

2. Leaving goods that are exclusive in nature to be produced by the free market assumes that this market will work "correctly"—this may not in fact be the case.

3. If a broader view is taken, the nonexclusion principle may become simply a matter of opinion.

Each of these difficulties will be illustrated in this section. The list of difficulties is not, however, intended to be exhaustive. Rather, it is intended only as an indication of the large dose of subjectivity which is inherent in any definition of public goods.

Goods Midway Between the Public and Private Sectors

As an example of a good that falls midway between the public and private categories, let us consider the case of education. There are many ways in which everyone in a society benefits from an educated population. Education may lead to technical progress, which benefits everyone. An educated electorate may make democracy work "better." Finally, it may just be "nice" to have educated people around to talk to. Each of these benefits is nonexclusive; it is technically infeasible to exclude some members of society from benefiting from the general educational level of their fellow citizens. On the other hand, many of the benefits of education are private in nature. An individual may, by virtue of education, obtain a higher income; he or she may derive enjoyment from the cultural aspects of education; and education may permit the individual to enter more desirable social circles. Each of these benefits has no important externalities—the individual can appropriate the entire benefits. Since it is technically feasible to exclude persons from gaining those benefits (you can keep certain people out of the schools if they do not pay for the services they receive), this aspect of education does not differ in a fundamental way from the purchase of any other private good.

The problem raised by education, then, is "how much" of it is a public good and how much a private good. If there were some way to decide this, the government could provide only that portion that is truly public.[6] In practice such a distinction is extremely difficult to make and the decision about the correct amount of government support for education is left to the political process.

Exclusive Goods and the Free Market

The suggestion that all goods that are not public in nature should be left up to the private market to produce seems, on the surface, desirable. This rule of thumb provides a way to keep the bureaucratic tentacles of government under some control. In fact, Friedman suggests that keeping government out of most activities of exchange among persons will preserve our "freedom." Without commenting on the truth of these assertions (such speculation is really a matter of opinion, which is left to the reader to decide), it is important to point out a central presumption that underlies this logic: It is implicitly assumed that the free market will function in a desirable way. This requires not only that markets be relatively free of monopolistic elements but that the other conditions of perfect competition (such as perfect knowledge on the part of all agents) also hold. To see that this may not be the case, let us examine two examples of goods that have exclusion properties but are nonetheless usually classed as public—education (again) and wilderness parks.

Consider education. Suppose all college education were left for the free market to provide; would it be provided in optimal amounts? Even if the benefits to education are regarded as exclusively private, there are reasons why individuals may not buy this good in sufficient amounts. One primary problem, not accounted for in the perfectly competitive model, is that investing in education (as for most

---

[6]It might be argued, for example, that elementary and secondary education have important public-good aspects and should therefore be provided by the government. On the other hand, the benefits of college education may be essentially private, and provision of college education should be left to the private market.

other kinds of investing) is a risky proposition. Not only is the income gained from educational expenditures subject to uncertainty, but also human capital, because it cannot be sold, is a most illiquid investment to make. Both of these features of education suggest that risk-averting individuals will not buy education in sufficient amounts and that lenders will not be willing to accommodate a borrower wishing to finance his education. The peculiar nature of the good therefore makes it dubious that the free market is totally suited for producing it.

Similar problems arise in considering the government's provision of wilderness parks. It might be argued that such parks are not truly public goods. The benefits of a park are derived almost exclusively by those who use them. Whereas it may be impossible to exclude city residents from benefiting from urban parks, the exclusion principle would seem to be operative for wilderness parks.[7] A private company could, after all, build a fence around Yellowstone and charge admission. It might thus be argued that the government should not be in the wilderness park business. Again, however, this argument assumes that the workings of the free market will produce desirable results. In particular it assumes that future demands for park land will be adequately reflected in present market interactions.[8] If this is regarded as unlikely, there is justification for governmental interference even though the principle of nonexclusive benefits is not strictly applicable.

Narrow versus Broad View of Public Goods

A final reason why a narrow definition of public goods may not be sufficient requires that a broader view be taken of the function of government. Suppose it is decided that the function of the government is to be a morally and culturally uplifting force for its citizens. In this role the government may justifiably interfere in any productive activity because every aspect of the economy has some effect on the moral virtue of the population. The government might, for example, take over motion picture production (an essentially exclusive type of good) because it determined that those motion pictures currently being produced were undermining the "moral fiber" (a nonexclusive good) of the country. Taking over the motion picture industry would be regarded as necessary to the government's mandate to produce moral fiber. Looked at in this way, the public-good definition becomes very broad indeed. It is a bit depressing (and probably far-fetched) to think of a government's taking over all productive activity in an effort to insure that goods of a proper moral and cultural tone are produced.

---

[7]This argument assumes that the benefits of just knowing that the park is there are small. For parks such as the Grand Canyon this is probably unwarranted, since virtually everyone in the country benefits from the knowledge that this park exists. On the other hand, at present, national parks exist in the United States which only a small minority of the population has ever heard of and which even fewer are likely ever to visit. The externalities of such parks are (at least to the present generation) probably insignificant.

[8]This is particularly important in the case of parks because of the irreversibility of decisions. Once it is decided, say, to strip mine an area, the possibility of using it for a park in the future is not available.

These instances of the ambiguity of the nonexclusion principle in many important cases point out the essential subjectivity of any definition of the proper
economic role of government. Instead of relying on clearly defined technical
definitions, it would seem appropriate to adopt a more flexible position in which the
government attempts to measure society's demand for potential public goods and
then develops various ethical and economic criteria to decide which should be
supplied. In the next two sections we will investigate this approach. The first of
these sections stresses the conceptual problems inherent in defining exactly what it
means to say that "society" demands som particular good. The second section
addresses the more pragmatic question of how a government might calculate the
costs and benefits from any proposed project.

Conceptual Problems in
Measuring the Demand for Public Goods

Even in the case of a well-defined public good (national defense, for example),
there are significant problems in deciding how much of this good to produce.
Efficiency considerations would suggest that additional amounts of the public good
should be produced up to the point at which the social marginal cost of production is
equal to the marginal utility evaluation placed on the good by the members of
society. Assuming that the resource costs of production can be calculated, the
problem of optimal provision of public goods then becomes one of estimating the
relevant social demand curve (see Figure 19.1). This is the problem we will be
concerned with in this section.

Measuring Output

A first difficulty with estimating the demand curve for a public good is that there is
usually no adequate measure of output: We do not know what to put on the
horizontal axis in Figure 19.1. For example, how can the quantity of national
defense be defined? The defense establishment provides something that might be
called "protection," but there seem to be no natural units in which to quantify this
concept. This problem is not unique to national defense (as another example,
consider how one might measure the quantity of education provided by a school
system). Rather, the problem is a general one for public goods because these goods
are not traded in organized markets: consequently, natural price-quantity measures
are not available.

Problem of the Free Rider

Even if a suitable quantity measure could be defined, there would still be substantial
problems in discovering the demand curve for a public good. If we decided, for
example, to ask individuals how much they value a particular public good, the
results of this poll might be extremely inaccurate. In answering the question

individuals may feel that they should understate their true preferences for fear they will ultimately have to pay what the good is worth to them in the form of taxes.[9] From the individual's point of view, the proper strategy is to understate true preferences in the hope that others will bear the burden of paying for the good. Since, for a traditional public good, no one can be excluded from enjoying its benefits, the best position to occupy is that of a "free rider." Each individual, by acting in his or her own self-interest, may insure that society underestimates the demand for public goods and hence underallocates resources to their production.

The free rider problem arises in all organizations that provide collective goods to their members. For example, labor unions are generally able to obtain better wages and working conditions in unionized plants. Workers in such plants have an incentive to enjoy the benefits of unionization while at the same time refusing to join the union. They thereby avoid the payment of dues. In order to combat such free rider problems, unions quite often insist on a "closed," or "union," shop. Similar problems arise in the United States in attempting to collect blood on a voluntary basis. Since people know that, should they be hospitalized, they will get all the blood they need, the tendency is to be a free rider and refrain from donating. As these examples illustrate, the free rider problem can only be solved by some sort of compulsion. This compulsion may arise out of a sense of group solidarity or civic pride (individuals do give blood in America—far more do in England) or it may require legal or quasi-legal force (as in the union case). For governments, the necessity to tax individuals to force them to pay for public services is inescapable.

Revealed Preferences for Public Goods

The free rider problem does not occur in markets in which ordinary goods are exchanged. There each individual has an incentive to "reveal" true preferences for the goods available: To fail to do so would result in a loss of utility. Many economists have investigated the question of whether similar incentives can be built into the process of making social decisions about the production of nonexclusive public goods. A variety of unusual voting-taxation schemes have been proposed[10] in highly abstract settings. Some of these procedures do, in certain circumstances, overcome the problem of appraising public goods demand. However, none has proved to be a general theoretical solution, let along to be capable of practical implementation.

---

[9]Taxation based on the value of benefits received has been extensively studied by economists. The determination of benefits is a difficult matter, and in practice governments often divorce expenditure decisions from taxation decisions. It should be recognized that any movement away from a system of taxation in which those who benefit from public goods also pay the costs necessarily involves some element of redistribution.

[10]For one such method and a summary of others, see T. N. Tideman and G. Tullock, "A New and Superior Process for Making Social Choices," *Journal of Political Economy* 84, No. 6 (December 1976), pp. 1145–1159.

Some economists[11] have suggested that the public goods problem may be more tractable on a local than on a national level. Because individuals are relatively mobile they may indicate their preferences for local public goods by choosing to live in communities that offer them utility-maximizing public goods-taxation packages. "Voting with one's feet" thereby provides a mechanism for revealing public goods demand in much the same way that "dollar voting" reveals private goods demand. Individuals who wish high-quality schools or a high level of police protection can "pay" for them by choosing to live in highly taxed communities. Those who prefer not to receive such benefits can choose to live elsewhere. Whether such actions can completely cope with the problem of revealing the demand for public goods (even on a local level) remains an unsettled question.

Cost-Benefit Analysis of Government Projects

In addition to making broad conceptual decisions about the types of public goods to produce, governments must also make numerous day-to-day decisions about whether to proceed with specific projects. Under the title of *cost-benefit analysis,* economists have developed a framework within which such projects can be analyzed systematically. In recent years this method of analysis has been formally adopted into United States federal government budgetary procedures under the Planning-Programming-Budgeting System (PPBS).[12] While a complete analysis of the logic underlying the PPBS system is beyond the scope of this book, we will briefly survey its major components in this section.

Discounting Benefits and Costs

Any government project will provide some benefits to citizens in any one year and (perhaps) for many years into the future. Let this stream of benefits be denoted by $B_0, B_1, B_2, \ldots, B_n$, where the subscript refers to the year in which the benefits occur. The project will also involve some costs over time; these are denoted by $C_0, C_1, C_2, \ldots, C_n$. Consequently in each year the project promises "net benefits" given by $B_0 - C_0, B_1 - C_1, B_2 - C_2 \ldots, B_n - C_n$. We might assume that in the early years of a project net benefits will be negative (costs exceed benefits) but that most projects will eventually provide positive net benefits. The government must in some way "add up" these net benefits over time in order to decide whether or not the project is desirable. If the government chooses to discount future net benefits at an

[11]See C. M. Tiebout, "A Pure Theory of Local Expenditures," *Journal of Political Economy* 64 (October 1956), pp. 416–424.

[12]For an extremely valuable survey of the theory and practices of the PPBS, see *The Analysis and Evaluation of Public Expenditures: The PPB System, Joint Economic Committee* (Washington, D. C.: U. S. Government Printing Office. 1969).

interest rate, r, then the *PDV* (present discounted value: see Chapter 16 and Appendix to Chapter 16) of the project's net benefits is given by

$$PDV = B_0 - C_0 + \frac{B_1 - C_1}{(1 + r)} + \frac{B_2 - C_2}{(1 + r)^2} + \cdots + \frac{B_n - C_n}{(1 + r)^n} \qquad [19.1]$$

If $PDV > 0$, the project promises more in benefits than it costs and might be considered for adoption. On the other hand, if $PDV < 0$, the project costs more than it returns in benefits and would in general be considered undesirable. In order to evaluate a project, then, three pieces of information are necessary: a stream of future benefits, a stream of costs, and an interest rate with which to discount future benefits and costs. We will consider each of these items separately.

Estimating Future Benefits

Computing the benefits of a proposed project poses two kinds of problems. First, many projects are characterized by benefits that occur in the distant future. To predict what these benefits will be with any accuracy is a difficult practical problem. For example, consider estimating the benefits of a job training program for high school dropouts. The chief benefits of such a program are the increased earnings that the individuals participating in the program are able to obtain in future years. These earnings gains are both highly uncertain and very difficult to predict from currently available data. Some such estimate must, however, be made if the project is to be evaluated.

An even more difficult problem arises in the evaluation of project benefits that are by their nature unquantifiable. Such benefits might include obtaining cleaner water and purer air, creating a more equal distribution of income, or saving human lives. Although economists have devised methods for assigning approximate monetary values to some of these benefits, it must be admitted that all such calculation represents a high degree of subjectivity. Because items such as clean air, human lives, or "equality" are not traded in markets, there is no "objective" basis for assigning values to them. Some value must, however, be assigned (if only implicitly) so that projects can be ranked in some rational way.

Estimating Costs

Calculating the costs of a proposed governmental project is in many ways an easier process than is the measurement of benefits. The costs of a project generally tend to occur earlier in a project's life than do benefits, and therefore some uncertainties about the future are mitigated. More importantly, many project costs can be directly evaluated by using the market prices of the resources being used in the project. The relevant notion of cost for any project, economists would argue, is *opportunity cost*—since a project employs resources that can be used elsewhere, it is the value of these resources in such alternative uses that should be included in project costs. In many instances resources are traded in competitive markets, and therefore the price of the resource is exactly equal to its marginal value product (see Chapter 13) in alternative uses. Using prevailing market prices in calculating costs is, then, in agreement with the opportunity cost doctrine.

There are situations, however, in which market prices may not accurately reflect opportunity costs. If the inputs to a project are produced under monopolistic conditions, prices of these inputs will not reflect marginal costs. When this possibility arises, input prices should be adjusted so that they more nearly reflect (marginal) opportunity costs. Similarly, when externalities are present, the logic of the opportunity cost doctrine would dictate that social rather than private costs be used in project appraisal. For example, if large amounts of coal are to be used in a proposed project, it may be inappropriate to use the market price of coal in the cost benefit calculations. Rather, adjustments should be made to costs in order to reflect the social costs inherent in coal mining and the externalities caused by the use of the coal. Finally, there may be situations in which governmental regulations have caused market prices to be inaccurate measures of opportunity costs. For example, minimum wages may dictate relatively high labor costs for a project even though the workers to be hired were previously unemployed. The logic of the opportunity cost doctrine would suggest that the costs of such workers should be specified to be very low (perhaps even 0) in cost-benefit calculations since output elsewhere will not be reduced by the employment of these workers in the project.[13]

All of the above arguments rely on the notion of opportunity cost to show why project analysts may wish to adjust market prices in measuring the costs of a project. In many practical applications of cost-benefit analysis, these adjustments are not made because it is very difficult and costly to gather the data necessary to make them. In other applications, rather crude approximations are made in order to implement the opportunity cost idea.

Choosing an Interest Rate

Besides estimating project benefits and costs, it is also necessary for a government analyst to choose an interest rate to use in equation 19.1. The proper choice of an interest rate is important for two related reasons. First, the interest rate chosen will determine which government projects can profitably be undertaken. Since the benefits of projects usually accrue over a longer time horizon than do costs, it is likely that higher interest rates will militate against the government's undertaking a project. With a high interest rate, distant benefits will be discounted to a much greater extent than are nearby costs; consequently, many projects will fail to meet the cost-benefit criterion. On the other hand, low interest rates will favor the adoption of many government projects including those with a long time-span of benefits. If a governmental policy of always undertaking those projects for which benefits exceed costs is adopted, which interest rate is used for discounting will

---

[13]This argument ignores the value of leisure to the unemployed worker. Leisure has traditionally been imputed a 0 value in most cost-benefit studies and also has a 0 value in the GNP accounts.

have a significant effect on the number of such projects to be undertaken: The choice of interest rate will affect the allocation of resources between the public and private sectors of the economy.

Second, even if the size of the governmental sector of the economy is fixed by political forces, the choice of interest rate can have an important effect in deciding what sorts of projects are favored. If a low interest rate is used, programs with a long pay-off period will be relatively more attractive, whereas the choice of a high interest rate will mean that distant benefits are discounted significantly and "fast pay-off" projects will be favored. Consequently, the choice of interest rate by which to discount benefits and costs can determine whether a government takes a long-term or a short-term view in its allocational decisions.

Choosing a proper interest rate is therefore an important policy question. In looking at the real world, a government analyst is faced with a bewildering assortment of interest rates ranging from rates on very liquid short-term assets (say 0 percent to 8 percent) through the rate of return on capital in very profitable industries (which may be higher than 40 percent). Even if these extremes are disregarded, a "reasonable" choice of interest rates would include rates from the 8 percent that is standard on government bonds through the 15–20 percent that Solow estimates as the social rate of return on business investment in the United States during the 1950s.[14] Clearly, choosing among these will have major implications for governmental allocation of resources. For this reason cost benefit calculations are frequently made using a variety of "plausible" interest rates.

In conclusion, then, there are many important choices to be made in conducting a cost-benefit analysis of a government project. Many of these choices require a substantial degree of subjective judgment on the part of the analyst. For this reason cost-benefit analysis might more properly be considered an art rather than a precise method for plugging well-defined data into a generally agreed-upon formula. Despite this degree of subjectivity, the framework of cost-benefit analysis is invaluable as an organizing device in attempts to think systematically about government projects. In the next section we will discuss a few actual cost-benefit calculations as illustrations of some of the points raised in this section.

■ Examples of Cost-Benefit Analysis

Thousands of cost-benefit analyses of government projects have been undertaken. The range of projects analyzed has extended from huge construction projects (such as the interstate highway system) to single disease control programs (for example, the federal government's syphilis control program). In this section we shall briefly discuss four cost-benefit analyses that illustrate some of the theoretical points we developed in the previous section. Because our

---

[14]R. M. Solow, *Capital Theory and the Rate of Return* (Amsterdam, North-Holland Publishing Company, 1964), pp. 92–97.

discussion of these must of necessity be brief, the interested reader is urged to refer to the original studies for a deeper understanding of the issues they raise.

Disease Control Program Studies

For many years the U.S. Department of Health, Education, and Welfare (HEW) has conducted studies of its disease control programs.[15] One of the most difficult issues that must be faced in such studies is to decide how the benefits of these programs are to be measured. Given that funds for disease control are limited, it is obviously desirable to know which programs offer the highest payoff: This problem of evaluation cannot be avoided. A simple "economic" answer to the problem of measuring benefits is to add up the dollar values of individuals' earnings saved by early disease detection and treatment. HEW does make such calculations, but it is sensitive to objections that such earnings measures may introduce biases against programs that benefit the poor and (nonworking) women. For this reason HEW also ranks programs according to "deaths averted per dollar," and this measure does not take differential earnings abilities of individuals into account. Generally, both measures of benefits tend to rank programs in more or less the same order. In particular, HEW has reported very high benefit-cost ratios for programs that stress early detection of cervical and lung cancer, syphilis, and (at least for the earnings measure) arthritis. Somewhat lower cost-effectiveness ratios have been calculated for detection and treatment programs dealing with cancer of the head, neck, colon, and rectum. HEW also finds very high payoffs to certain automobile safety programs, particularly those that stress wearing seat belts and keeping alcoholic drivers off the road.

Manpower Training Program Study

One of the best analyses of manpower training programs is a study of the Job Corps by Glen Cain.[16] The Job Corps is a work-training program for teenage men and women that involves a rather high expenditure per enrollee (more than $7000 per year). By piecing together a large amount of information about the Job Corps, Cain determined that these high expenditures also had a high payoff; his estimated ratios of benefits to costs ranged from 1.2 to more than 2. Here we shall discuss only two issues raised in the Cain paper. First, Cain uses two measures of benefits: (1) the improvement in wages experienced by Job Corps enrollees (relative to a "control" group) and (2) the improved educational attainment of the enrollees. He places a market value on the latter benefit by calculating how similar

---

[15]The HEW studies have appeared in a variety of publications. For a brief summary and partial bibliography, see R. N. Grosse, "Cost-Benefit Analysis in Disease Control Programs," in *Cost-Benefit Analysis,* ed. M. G. Kendall (New York: American Elsevier Publishing Company, 1971), pp. 17–34.

[16]Glen Cain, "Benefit-Cost Estimates for Job Corps," Discussion Paper, The Institute for Research on Poverty, University of Wisconsin, Madison, Wis., September 1967.

improved educational attainments have led to increased earnings in the population as a whole. Both of Cain's estimates of the monetary benefits from the increase in earnings of Job Corps participants are quite similar, and these are used to calculate his benefit-cost ratios. Notice that in using an earnings measure of benefits, Cain is ignoring other possible benefits (such as better health or even better "citizenship") that accrue to individuals in the Job Corps.

A second interesting issue in Cain's analysis is related to the measurement of costs. He argues that the forgone wages that Job Corps enrollees could have earned instead of participating in the program are a true program cost but that the modest stipends paid to the enrollees are not a true cost. This decision is in agreement with the basic concept of using opportunity costs in cost-benefit calculations. The fact that Job Corps participants do not have market earnings while in the program is certainly a social cost; that is, some potential output is forgone by their participation. On the other hand, the stipends paid to the enrollees are in the nature of a transfer payment—not a true social cost. Output elsewhere in the economy is not reduced as a result of paying the stipends.

Third London Airport Study

An interesting attempt at evaluating a "nonmarketable" cost can be found in the Roskill Commission Report on the desirability of five alternative sites for a third airport to serve the city of London.[17] In this report a considerable effort was made to measure the costs arising from airport noise at the sites. Many political and social commentators have suggested that the costs of "noise pollution" are quite high, and this report represents one of the few cases in which an actual attempt at evaluation has been made. The method employed was fairly simple. First, an effort was made to measure the number of households at each site that would be affected by noise nuisance. It was then necessary to estimate an average cost of noise nuisance for each of these households. This was accomplished by observing how airport noise in the vicinity of existing London airports (primarily Gatwick) had affected housing values in those areas.[18] By comparing the prices of two identical houses, one affected by airport noise and the other not, an estimate of the implicit market "price" of noise was calculated. House values were found to be about 20 percent lower in the noisy areas, and this figure was used to place a value on the cost of noise pollution at each potential site. The controversial result of this calculation was the finding that noise costs were rather low—generally less

---

[17]Commission on the Third London Airport, *Papers and Proceedings,* vol. 7 (London: H. M. Stationery Office, 1970).

[18]The report also made an attempt to evaluate lost consumer's surplus as a result of the noise from the airport, but we shall not discuss that question here. For a critical analysis of the Roskill Commission's report, see A. K. Dasgupta and D. W. Pearce, *Cost-Benefit Analysis* (London: Macmillan & Co., Ltd., 1972), chap. 9.

than 1 percent of total costs at each of the sites. It was therefore concluded that differences in the costs of noise pollution at the various sites should not have a major effect on the choice among them for the location of the airport. Government officials were apparently unconvinced by these figures, and they seem to have opted for a site that the Roskill Commission found to have the highest total costs but the lowest noise costs.

Hell's Canyon Dam

As a final example of cost-benefit analysis, we shall consider an example of a water resources project in which governmental and private investment criteria yielded different results. This project involved development of the hydroelectric potential of the Hell's Canyon area of the Snake River on the Oregon-Idaho border. A license to develop the area was granted by the Federal Power Commission to a private company (the Idaho Power Company) on the basis of a plan to build three relatively small dams along that section of the Snake. In an analysis of this decision, J. V. Krutilla and O. Eckstein demonstrate that, from a social point of view, there were two alternative plans (a single high dam and a plan involving two dams) that were superior to the plan actually chosen.[19] The question the authors address is why should the company have opted for such a second-best alternative. Krutilla and Eckstein's analysis provides three answers. First, the private company used a higher interest rate to discount the benefits and costs from the project than the federal government would have: The opportunity cost of capital to the private company was relatively high. The use of a high interest rate slanted the argument in favor of the three-dam development because the initial capital costs were a bit lower than for the other projects. Second, the private company did not opt for the alternative plans because it paid no attention to downstream developments on the Snake. The high dam would have been an important part of the entire Columbia River development project by providing downstream benefits to other (government-owned) facilities, but the private company did not take these external effects into account in its cost calculations. Finally, Krutilla and Eckstein argue that the most important influence on the power company's decision was that it had no immediate need for the power that the alternative projects could deliver. It preferred smaller increments to generating capacity as each of the three small dams were phased into operation. This example, then, clearly illustrates that the results of a cost-benefit analysis will differ according to how opportunity costs are defined and how broad a view is being taken.

In a more recent article, Krutilla, (together with A. C. Fisher and C. J. Cicchetti) suggests that the Hell's Canyon area be left in a natural state to be used for

---

[19]J. V. Krutilla and O. Eckstein, *Multiple Purpose River Development* (Baltimore: The Johns Hopkins Press, 1958).

recreational purposes.[20] In a clever (but controversial) set of numerical calculations, the authors demonstrate that refraining from the development of this area may yield the greatest net benefits of all the alternatives being considered. The argument for preservation is based on three related assumptions, which the authors assert will cause private and social decisions to differ. First, the development of Hell's Canyon is assumed to be irreversible. In many respects this is the central assumption in most arguments for preservation. If it were not true, decisions would be considerably simplified since future demand patterns would not have to be predicted so accurately in deciding on present use. A second assumption is that the demand for wilderness land is rapidly growing in the United States, and future benefits of preservation may therefore be considerably higher than present benefits. A third assumption that weights the decision toward preservation is that technological progress is occurring rapidly in electricity generation, and the Hell's Canyon hydroelectric facility may therefore quickly become obsolete. Each of those assumptions suggests that private markets will tend to underevaluate the site's value as a recreational facility (and overestimate its hydroelectric value). Preservation may therefore be a good investment from a social perspective.

Aspects of a Positive Theory of Government

In the previous discussion we have been primarily normative. We have investigated a few aspects of the question of how governments *should* behave in their economic functions. Although the answers to this question were necessarily vague, the analysis we presented did raise some interesting conceptual issues. This normative approach is rather different from that which we took in Parts II–V. In those we were more interested in developing theories to explain observed economic behavior without attaching value judgments to this behavior. Economists have recently attempted to adapt this positive methodology to the study of government and its functioning. In this section we shall examine a few of the steps that have been taken in this direction.

As we did in the case for the theory of the firm, we shall start our positive analysis by examining the motives of government leaders. It might, for instance, be proposed that government leaders act so as to maximize social welfare. At least two realities argue against assuming such benevolent motivations. First, the notion of "social welfare" is extremely ill-defined. It is just not true that everyone in society has the same view of the way things should be and is simply waiting for governmental action to bring this desirable state into being. Second, the assumption of a benevolent leadership would be in marked contrast to the self-interest assumption that underlies both the theory of the individual and the theory of the firm we

---

[20]A. C. Fisher, J. V. Krutilla, and C. J. Cicchetti, "The Economics of Environmental Preservation," *American Economic Review* 62, No. 4 (September 1972), pp. 605–619.

developed earlier. There seems no very persuasive reason why people should change their basic motivations upon elevation to political office. Consequently, in order to be consistent with the other positive theories of this book, some less socially virtuous theory is necessary.

Majority Principle and Pluralism

One interesting theory of leadership motivation has been put forward by Anthony Downs. In *An Economic Theory of Democracy,* he hypothesizes that "parties in democratic politics are analogous to entrepreneurs in a profit-seeking economy. So as to attain their private ends, they formulate whatever policies they believe will gain the most votes, just as entrepreneurs produce whatever products will gain the most profits. . . . "[21] In other words, parties act so as to *maximize political support.* In order to pursue this goal, parties must contend with uncertainty in many respects. A party is uncertain how any particular policy choice will affect political support. This is true not only because it may be hard to ascertain who benefits from government action, but also because policies must be adopted before the policies of the party (or parties) out of power are known. This strategic advantage of those out of power is significantly modified, however, by the control that the party in power has over the public's access to information.

It would be impossible to summarize the numerous insights and testable hypotheses that follow from Downs' basic assumption. Perhaps the most interesting general conclusion the author draws is that the party in power will generally adopt a *majority principle* in its policy decisions. It will pursue only those policies for which more votes are gained than are lost, and it will pursue such policies up to the point at which the marginal gain in votes from those benefiting from the policy equals the marginal loss in votes from those being hurt by the policy. The analogy between party motivation and profit maximization is quite close. It is by examining corollaries to the majority principle that Downs is able to arrive at many of his most interesting results.

It is worthwhile to contrast Downs' view of the nature of the political process with another, more commonly held view. This alternative conception examines the *pluralistic* nature of democratic government. Social decisions are assumed to be made by the interaction of many powerful special interest groups. Presumably these groups wield some influence over political leaders by virtue of campaign contributions, friendship, superior knowledge of special issues, or perhaps by direct measures of corruption. Whatever the avenues of control, it is assumed that pressure groups are the primary molders of the legal system.

Two assessments of pluralism have been put forward. The first optimistically predicts that the interaction of numerous pressure groups will, in some sense, produce a socially desirable outcome. Laws that are ultimately passed represent an equilibrium among numerous groups. Because no one group has significant power

---

[21] A. Downs, *An Economic Theory of Democracy* (New York: Harper & Row, Publishers, 1957), p. 295.

(at least not on all issues), the resultant equilibrium will generally be representative of the society as a whole.

Special-Interest and Public-Interest Pressure Groups

This beneficial assessment of pluralism has been questioned by many authors. One of the most interesting objections was put forward by Olson.[22] He pointed out that there is a systematic bias in a pluralistic society that causes only certain kinds of pressure groups to exercise political power. In particular, Olson argues, only pressure groups that represent narrow special interests will arise; pressure groups representing the "public interest" will be weak or nonexistent. The reason for this tendency, Olson explains, lies in the nature of the collective good provided by a pressure group to its members. For a close-knit group, each member can recognize the benefits of group action, and there may be strong sanctions against being a free rider. Consequently, groups such as the "oil lobby" would be expected to have considerable success because each member of the group will find it in his or her interest to engage in pressure group activity.[23] On the other hand, diffuse public-interest groups will have minimal success because individual members of such groups cannot hope to obtain for themselves any major part of the benefits of their activity. The collective goods provided by public-interest groups, say, consumer legislation, have significant nonexclusion properties (everyone will benefit whether or not they join Nader's Raiders), so the natural tendency is for such groups to be weak. Olson's assessment of pluralism is therefore not particularly positive. He foresees a serious absence of effective pressure groups to represent broad questions of public interest.

Reelection Constraint

By combining Downs's and Olson's theories of government action, we can construct an interesting third alternative. It is undoubtedly true that pressure groups exercise considerable influence over legislation, and Olson is probably right when he theorizes that the public interest will be underrepresented. However, Olson's model does not take sufficient account of the motives of political leaders. Lobby groups probably do give "utility" to political leaders in many ways, and these leaders may therefore follow the dictates of the lobbyists. But the legislator does not have an unconstrained utility-maximization problem. Rather, he or she must operate subject to the *constraint of reelection*. The legislator must therefore pay some

---

[22]See M. Olson, *Logic of Collective Action* (Cambridge, Mass.: Harvard University Press, 1965), especially chaps. 5 and 6.

[23]Other important examples of special-interest groups are found within the government. For example, the Pentagon lobby and the "welfare" lobby may be quite powerful in distorting government expenditure decisions away from those that are socially optimal. For this reason certain kinds of public goods may be overproduced.

attention to what Downs calls the majority principle, although this attention will by no means be absolute. The purpose of public-interest lobby groups can then be seen as attempting to make individual voters aware of the benefits and costs of certain governmental action. Such an awareness on the part of voters may make a legislator's reelection constraint more binding and may mitigate the void of power on public issues noted by Olson.

Bureaucracies

Although governmental policies in a representative democracy are enacted by elected officials, they are usually implemented by and operated through bureaucratic agencies. Because those agencies typically possess monopoly power in the production of the services with which they are charged, it is possible that they exercise an independent influence on the direction of policy. For example, Niskanen[24] hypothesizes that bureaus seek to maximize their budgets (perhaps because high budgets yield utility to bureaucrats). A major implication of that hypothesis is that in the bilateral monopoly bargaining between elected officials and bureaucracies, decisions will be reached that tend to overallocate resources to the public sector (relative to what would be preferred by the median voter). Several authors have attempted to estimate such allocational effects empirically.[25] They generally conclude that the data are consistent with the budget-maximization hypothesis. However, this empirical work is, of necessity, quite preliminary. More sophisticated modeling awaits the development of better data sources and more precise analytic models.

Summary

In this chapter we investigated the economic functions of government in a market economy. We showed that, in such an economy, resources will tend to be underallocated to public goods. That result derives from the nonexclusive character of public goods: Because individuals cannot be excluded from the benefits of such goods, each will find it in his or her self-interest to adopt the position of a free rider. To overcome this problem, societies (or other social groupings that provide public goods) may adopt coercive methods for financing the production of public goods.

A number of other topics related to public goods were discussed in the chapter. These included: problems in defining public goods and in measuring the demand for them; cost-benefit analysis of public goods; and a brief summary of positive theories of government. All of these subjects describe parts of a theory that is very much

---

[24]W. A. Niskanen, *Bureaucracy and Representative Government* (Chicago: Aldine Publishing Company, 1971).

[25]See, for example, T. E. Borcherding, *Budgets and Bureaucrats: The Sources of Government Growth* (Durham, N. C.: Duke University Press, 1975).

underdeveloped. Currently the allocation of resources in a market economy is far better understood than is the allocation of resources to the public sector. Perhaps this lack of development is intrinsic in the nature of "political questions."

One central message does, however, emerge from the various discursive developments of this chapter: It is in some sense desirable to have a consensus on what sorts of public goods (broadly defined) should be produced. As Olson points out, an ideal society would be one in which individuals had rather different tastes for private goods and rather similar tastes for public goods.[26] Such a society would benefit both from the markets' ability to accommodate different tastes efficiently and from a general agreement on the proper allocation between the public and private sectors. Such a normative prescription says little about how such an ideal might be achieved in practice.

Suggested Readings

Alchian, A., and Demsetz, H., "Production, Information Costs, and Economic Organization," *American Economic Review* 62 (December 1972), pp. 777–795.

Baumol, W. J., *Welfare Economics and the Theory of the State,* 2d ed. (London: G. Bell & Sons, Ltd., 1965).

Buchanan, J. M., "An Economic Theory of Clubs," *Economica* 32 (February 1965), pp. 1–14.

Friedman, M., *Capitalism and Freedom* (Chicago: University of Chicago Press, 1962).

Haveman, R., et al., *Benefit Cost Analysis* (Chicago: Aldine-Atherton, 1973). Published annually.

Margolis, J., and Guitton, H., eds., *Public Economics* (New York: St. Martin's Press, Inc., 1969).

Musgrave, R. A., *The Theory of Public Finance* (New York: McGraw-Hill Book Company, Inc., 1959).

Niskanen, W. A., *Bureaucracy and Representative Government* (Chicago: Aldine Publishing Company, 1971).

Olson, M., *The Logic of Collective Action* (Cambridge, Mass.: Harvard University Press, 1965).

Prest, A. R., and Turvey, R., "Cost-Benefit Analysis: A Survey," *Economic Journal* 75 (December 1965), pp. 683–735.

Samuelson, P. A., "The Pure Theory of Public Expenditures," *Review of Economics and Statistics* 36 (November 1954), pp. 387–389.

———, "Diagrammatic Exposition of a Theory of Public Expenditures," *Review of Economics and Statistics* 37 (November 1955), pp. 350–356.

---

[26]M. Olson, "Economics, Sociology, and the Best of All Possible Worlds," *The Public Interest,* No. 12 (Summer 1968), pp. 96–118.

Tiebout, C. M., "A Pure Theory of Local Expenditures," *Journal of Political Economy* 64 (October 1956), pp. 416–424.

Problems

19.1
The demand curve for public goods in Chapter 19 was rather casually drawn. Can you think up a way of deriving such a demand curve from more basic data on individuals' tastes? What problems would arise in such a derivation?

19.2
An investment criterion that is closely related to the present discounted value criterion we discussed in Chapters 16 and 19 is the internal rate of return criterion. In using this criterion, the present cost of an investment (P) is equated to

$$P = R_0 + \frac{R_1}{(1 + i)} + \frac{R_2}{(1 + i)^2} + \cdots + \frac{R_n}{(1 + i)^n}$$

where R_j is the net return from the investment in year j, and i is treated as an unknown. The resulting equation is then solved for i, which is termed the *internal rate of return*. This rate of return is that interest rate which, when used to discount the returns from the investment, will cause this discounted value to equal the investment's current price exactly. The investment criterion consists of undertaking the investment of $i > r$ and refusing to do so if $i < r$ (where r is the market rate of interest).

Show that this criterion is equivalent to the present discounted value criterion if all the R_i's are positive, but that these may not agree if some of the R_i's are negative.

19.3
Suppose that education provides both private benefits and (nonexclusive) public benefits to individuals. Any particular level of educational output provides equal amounts of these two types of benefits. How should resources be allocated in order to attain efficient production of this semipublic good? How might production of the good be financed?

19.4
Suppose that there are N individuals in an economy with three goods. Two of the goods are pure (nonexclusive) public goods, whereas the third is an ordinary private good.

a. What conditions must hold for resources to be allocated efficiently between either of the public goods and the private good?

b. What conditions must hold for resources to be allocated efficiently between the two public goods?

19.5

In an economy characterized by a hierarchy of governmental units (for example, federal, state, and local governments), what criteria might be used to determine which public goods are produced by which level of government? How would economies or diseconomies of scale in production affect your answer?

19.6

The government of Slobovia is considering whether or not to build a dam on the Onyz River thereby creating Lake Oscar (to be named for the current ruler). In conducting a cost-benefit analysis of this project, which of the following should be included as benefits?

a. The value of hydroelectric power produced by the dam

b. The value of the dam in controlling downstream floods

c. Profits made by resort owners when vacationers flock to the shores of Lake Oscar.

d. The pleasure individuals get from swimming in Lake Oscar

e. Employment and wages created by the project itself and by the vacation boom that follows

f. Revenues generated by the sale of Lake Oscar tee shirts and post cards

Which of the following should be included as costs?

a. Wages of workers who build the dam

b. Revenue losses of motel owners on nearby Lake Fred

c. The loss of the firm supplying concrete for the dam which miscalculates its costs

d. Social Security and Unemployment Insurance taxes paid for construction workers

e. Wildlife lost in construction of Lake Oscar

f. Reduced water skiing opportunities for those who live downriver from the dam

Chapter 20

Externalities and Property Rights

Introduction

We have discussed the idea of externalities in many places in previous chapters, and we should therefore have a general conception of what the term means. Externalities refer to interactions among economic agents that are not adequately reflected in markets. To analyze why markets may fail in this way is our purpose in the present chapter. Hopefully an explanation of why failures take place will also be indicative of the possibilities for efficient and equitable solutions. More generally, a study of externalities provides insights into the nature of and problems associated with private and public property; to examine the issue of property rights is an underlying theme of this chapter. Before launching into a detailed analysis, however, we should be more precise in defining exactly what an externality is, since there has been substantial confusion over this point in many economic investigations. To do so we repeat a definition introduced in Chapter 18:

Definition

An *externality* is an effect of one economic agent's activities on another agent's well-being that is not taken into account by the normal operations of the price system.

Hence this definition stresses the direct, nonmarket effect of one agent on another. Before examining why such effects may distort the allocation of resources, the definition may be made more concrete by giving a few examples.

Examples of Externalities

Externalities can occur between any two economic agents. Here we will briefly illustrate both negative (harmful) and positive (beneficial) externalities between firms. We will then turn to examine externalities between individuals and firms, and conclude by considering a few externalities between individuals.

Externalities Between Firms

Consider two firms—one producing good X, another producing good Y—where each uses only labor as an input. The production of Y is said to have an external effect on the production of X if the output of X depends not only on the amount of labor chosen by the X-entrepreneur but also on the level at which the production of Y is carried on. Notationally, the production function for good X can be written as

$$X = f(L_X;Y) \qquad [20.1]$$

where L_X denotes the amount of labor devoted to good X, and Y appears to the right of the semicolon in the equation to show that it is an effect on production over which the X-entrepreneur has no control.[1] As a concrete example, suppose the two firms are located on a river with firm X being downstream from Y. Suppose firm Y pollutes the river in its productive process. Then the output of firm X may depend not only on the level of inputs it uses itself but also on the amount of pollutants flowing past its factory. The level of pollutants, in turn, is determined by the output of firm Y. In the production function shown by equation 20.1, the output of firm Y would have a negative marginal physical productivity. Increases in Y output would cause less X to be produced. (In the next section we will return to analyze this case more fully as it is representative of all types of externalities.)

The relationship between two firms may also be beneficial. Most examples of such positive externalities are rather bucolic in nature. Perhaps the most famous, proposed by J. Meade,[2] involves two firms, one producing honey (raising bees) and the other producing apples. Because the bees feed on apple blossoms, an increase in apple production will improve productivity in the honey industry. The beneficial effects of having well-fed bees is a positive externality to the beekeeper. Similarly, bees pollinate apple crops and hence the beekeeper provides an external benefit to the orchard owner. Later in this chapter we will return to examine this situation in greater detail since, surprisingly enough, the beekeeper–apple grower relationship has played an important role in economic research on the significance of externalities.

---

[1] We will find it necessary to redefine the assumption of "no control" considerably as the analysis of this chapter proceeds.

[2] J. Meade, "External Economies and Diseconomies in a Competitive Situation," *Economic Journal* 62 (March 1952), pp. 54–67.

Externalities Between Firms and Individuals

Firms' productive activities may impact directly on individuals' well-being. As we showed in Chapter 18, for example, a firm that produces air pollution imposes costs on individuals living near the firm in the form of ill health and increased dust and grime. Similar effects arise from firms' pollution of water (for example, mining firms dump their waste into Lake Superior thereby reducing the lake's recreational value to individuals), misuse of land (strip mining is both an eyesore and may interfere with water supplies), and "production" of noise (the London Airport example mentioned in Chapter 19). In all of these cases, at least on first inspection, it seems that firms will not take these external costs into consideration when making decisions.

Of course, individuals may also have external effects on firms. Drivers' auto pollution harms the productivity of citrus growers, cleaning up litter and grafitti is a major expense for shopping centers, and the noise of Saturday night rock concerts on college campuses probably affects motel rentals. Again, in each of these cases there may be no simple way for the affected parties to force the producers of the externalities to take the costs of their actions into account.

Externalities Between Individuals

Finally, the activities of one individual may affect the well-being of someone else. Playing a radio too loud, smoking cigars, or choosing to drive during peak hours are all consumption activities that may negatively affect the utility of others. Planting an attractive garden or shoveling the snow off one's sidewalk may, on the other hand, provide beneficial externalities. Again, all these activities will not be reflected in market transactions among the people involved. We will now examine the implications of such failures for the allocation of resources.

Externalities, Markets, and Allocational Efficiency

It has traditionally been argued that the presence of externalities such as those we have just described can cause a market to operate inefficiently. We discussed the reasons for this in detail in Chapter 18, but we will repeat them here by using the example outlined above of the two firms located on a river. Remember, firm X is assumed to produce no externalities, but its production is assumed to be negatively affected by the level of firm Y's output (Equation 20.1). We will now show that resources will be allocated inefficiently in this situation. To do so, remember that for an efficient allocation of resources it is required that price be equal to social marginal cost in each market (see Chapter 18 for the discussion of this point).[3] If the

---

[3] The proof presented in Chapter 18 is both more elegant and formally more correct than the one presented here because it develops the analysis in terms of relative rather than absolute marginal costs.

market for X is perfectly competitive (as we will assume both markets to be), the price of X will indeed be equal to this good's private marginal cost (MC_X); that is,

$$P_X = MC_X \tag{20.2}$$

Indeed, since there are no externalities in X production, the social marginal cost of X (SMC_X) will be equal to its private marginal cost, so we have

$$P_X = MC_X = SMC_X \tag{20.3}$$

For Y production, however, the story is more complex. The producer of Y will still produce that output for which price is equal to private marginal cost. This is a direct result of the profit-maximization assumption. Therefore, as was the case for X,

$$P_Y = MC_Y \tag{20.4}$$

However, because of the external effect that production of Y has on X, it will not be true that private and social marginal costs of Y production are equal. Rather, the true social cost of Y production is equal to the private cost *plus* the cost that production of Y imposes on firm X in terms of reduced output. If MP_Y denotes the marginal productivity of Y on X production (this is a negative quantity in the present example), we have

$$SMC_Y = MC_Y - (P_X \cdot MP_Y) \tag{20.5}$$

The final term in equation 20.5, then, adjusts the private marginal cost for the effect of the externality. It records the fact that producing one more unit of Y will cause X output to decline (MP_Y) and then places a value on this decline ($P_X \cdot MP_Y$). Of course, firm Y does not recognize this effect and produces where price is equal to private marginal cost. Since $MP_Y < 0$ we have:

$$SMC_Y > MC_Y = P_Y \tag{20.6}$$

The social marginal cost of Y production exceeds the price of Y: Too much Y is being produced. Society would be made better off by reallocating labor away from good Y production and toward the production of good X. Relying on the free operation of the market (and the self-interest of firm Y) has not produced an efficient allocation of resources. Because of the existence of an externality in production, the price system no longer carries the correct information necessary to obtain efficiency.

A Graphic Demonstration

Figure 20.1 illustrates the misallocation of resources that results from the externality in Y production. Assuming firm Y is a price taker, the demand curve for its

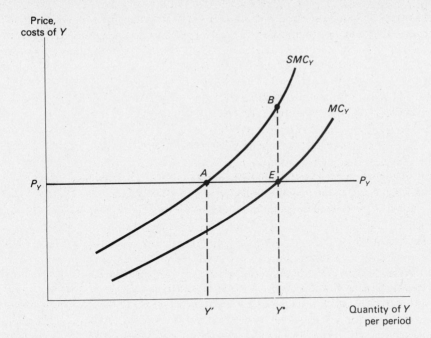

**Figure 20.1 / An Externality in
Y Production Causes an Inefficient Allocation of Resources**

Because production of Y imposes external costs on other firms, social marginal costs (SMC_Y) exceed
private marginal costs (MC_Y). In a competitive market the firm would produce Y^* at a price of P_Y. At Y^*,
however, $SMC_Y > P_Y$ and resource allocation could be improved by reducing Y output to Y'.

product is simply a horizontal line at the prevailing market price (P_Y). Profits are
maximized at Y^* where price is equal to the private marginal cost of producing Y
(MC_Y). Because of the externality that firm Y imposes on firm X, however, the social
marginal cost of Y production (SMC_Y) exceeds MC_Y as shown in the figure. At Y^*,
the social marginal cost of producing Y exceeds the price individuals are willing to
pay for Y output. Resources are hence being misallocated and production of Y
should be reduced to Y' where the social marginal cost and price are equal. Notice
that in making this reduction total social costs (area $Y'Y^*BA$) are reduced to a greater
extent than are expenditures on Y (given by area $Y'Y^*EA$). Again, that shows how
the allocation of resources is improved by such a reduction since costs are reduced
by a greater extent than is the consumers' evaluation of good Y. Now we will
examine various ways in which this reduction in Y output might be brought about.

Traditional Ways of Coping With Externalities

To investigate possible solutions to the problems that externalities pose for the
allocation of resources we must first assume that production techniques are fixed

and that the externality is a necessary fact of life.[4] Under this assumption, then, prescriptions such as "ban pollution" or "force Y to use alternative production techniques" are outside the frame of analysis. There are still two approaches that may bring about improved efficiency.

Taxation

The government could impose a suitable *excise tax* on the firm generating the external diseconomy. Presumably this tax would cause the output of Y to be cut back and would cause labor to be shifted out of the production of Y. This classic remedy to the externality problem was first lucidly put forward in the 1920s by A. C. Pigou;[5] although it has been somewhat modified, it remains the "standard" answer given by economists. The central problem for regulators becomes one of obtaining sufficient empirical information so that the correct tax structure can be enacted.

The taxation solution is illustrated in Figure 20.2. Again MC_Y and SMC_Y represent the private and social marginal costs of Y production and the market price of Y is given by P_Y. An excise tax of amount t (see Chapter 10) would reduce the net price received by the firm to $P_Y - t$ and at that price the firm would choose to produce Y'. The tax causes the firm to reduce its output by the socially optimal amount. At Y' the firm incurs private marginal costs of $P_Y - t$ and imposes external costs of t per unit. The tax paid by consumers of an extra unit of Y is therefore exactly equal to the extra costs that firm Y imposes on firm X by producing one more unit.[6]

Merger and Internalization

A second traditional cure for the allocational distortions caused by the external relationship between X and Y would be for the two firms to merge. If there were a single firm operating both plants X and Y, it would recognize the detrimental effect that Y production has on the production function for good X. In effect the firm $(X + Y)$ would now pay the full social marginal costs of Y production because it also produces X. In other words, the firm's manager would now take the marginal cost curve for Y production to be SMC_Y and would produce at the point where

$$P_Y = SMC_Y \qquad\qquad [20.7]$$

---

[4]It is also assumed that the detrimental effects of the production of Y do not affect any other agent in the economy than firm X. Similarly, the discussion of externalities usually takes place within a partial equilibrium framework in which "second-best" problems are assumed to be unimportant.

[5]A. C. Pigou, *The Economics of Welfare*, 4th ed. (London: Macmillan & Co., Ltd., 1946). Pigou also stresses the desirability of providing subsidies to firms that produce beneficial externalities.

[6]If firm Y represents an entire industry then the tax would, as in Chapter 10, raise the market price of Y. If the industry exhibited constant costs, price would rise by the exact amount of the tax and demand would be reduced to the socially optimal level by that price rise.

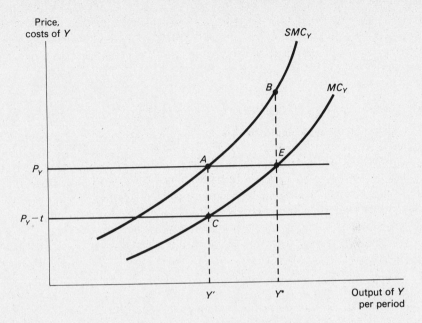

Figure 20.2 / Taxation Solution to the Externality Problem

An excise tax of amount t would reduce the net price of Y to $P_Y - t$. At that price the firm would choose to produce the socially optimal level of Y output (Y').

which is exactly what is required for efficiency. Economists would say that the externality in Y production has been *internalized* as a result of the merger.

Examples of Internalization

Attempts to internalize externalities in production are not uncommon. It is often the case that an organization will expand in size with the purpose of encompassing all the spillover effects of its activities. Firms may, for example, merge in an attempt to capture external benefits. Recreational site developers (ski areas, golf courses, resort hotels) often operate the service industries (motels, gas stations, shops) near their projects. In this way they are able to internalize the positive benefits that such developments provide to the service industries. Another important example of attempting to internalize external effects is the recent move toward the creation of regional metropolitan governments. It has been argued that geographically limited city governments cannot handle many current urban problems because these problems spill over into neighboring communities. New York's air pollution problems, for example, are not confined to the city itself but affect communities in New Jersey and Connecticut as well. New York City also provides benefits to neighboring communities by acting as a commercial and cultural center. Since many of the individuals who benefit from having such activities available do not live or work in New York City, there is no feasible way to get them to support the central city through taxes. By adopting a regional government, all such spillover effects would be internalized and policies that were optimal from a regional point of view could be pursued.

Property Rights, Allocation, and Equity

One important question we might still ask about this analysis is if firm Y's actions impose a cost on firm X, why doesn't firm X bribe firm Y to cut back on its output? Presumably the gain of such a cutback to firm X (area $ACEB$ in Figure 20.2) would exceed the loss of profits to firm Y (area ACE), and some bargaining arrangement might be worked out that would monetarily benefit both parties. Both firms would be irrational not to recognize such a possibility, and it would seem that the benefits of internalization could be obtained without the necessity of a merger.

We can make this observation more precise by introducing the concept of property rights.

Definition

Property rights are the legal specification of the ownership of a good and of the types of trades that the owner of the good might make with others.

Some goods may be defined as *common property* that are owned by "society at large"; others may be defined as *private property* that are owned personally by individuals. Private property may either be *exchangeable* or *nonexchangeable*, depending on whether the good in question may or may not be traded. In this book we have been primarily concerned with exchangeable private property,[7] and these are the type of property rights we will consider here.

Costless Bargaining and the Free Market

For the purposes of the two-firm externality example, it is interesting to consider the nature of the property right that might be attached to the river shared by the firms. Suppose property rights were defined so as to give "ownership" of the river to one of the firms, but that the firms were free to bargain over how the river might be used. It might be thought that if the ownership of the river were given to firm Y, pollution would result; whereas, if the right were given to firm X, the river would remain pure. This might not be the case, however, because such a conclusion disregards the bargains that might be reached by the two parties. Indeed, several authors have

---

[7]Two important examples of privately owned goods that are not exchangeable are an individual's human capital (this could only be sold in a society that permitted slavery) and an individual's vote (a private good that is provided by the state.)

argued that if *bargaining is costless,* the two parties left on their own will arrive at the efficient output (Y'), and this result will be independent of who "owns" the river.

Ownership by the Polluting Firm

If, for example, firm Y owns the river it must then impute some cost of this ownership into its cost function. What are the costs associated with river ownership? Again the opportunity cost doctrine provides the answer: The costs are what the river would bring in its next best alternative use. In the problem, only firm X has some alternative use for the river (to keep it clean); the amount that this firm would be willing to pay for a clean river is equal to the external damage done by the pollution. Consequently, if firm Y calculates its costs correctly its marginal cost curve (including the cost of river ownership) becomes SMC_Y in Figure 20.2. Firm Y will therefore produce Y' and sell the remaining rights of river use to firm X for a fee of some amount between ACE (Y's lost profits from producing Y' rather than Y^*) and $ACBE$ (the maximum amount X would pay to avoid having Y increased from Y' to Y^*).

Ownership by the Injured Firm

A similar allocation result would occur if firm X owned the rights to the river. In this case firm Y would be willing to pay any amount up to the total profits it earns from production for the right to pollute the river. Firm X will accept these payments so long as they exceed the costs imposed on it by the river pollution. Hence the ultimate result of bargaining will be for firm Y to offer a payment to firm X for the use of the river in dumping pollution associated with output level Y'. Firm X will not sell the rights to dump any further pollution because what firm Y would be willing to pay falls short of the cost of additional pollution to firm X. Again the efficient point can be reached by relying on free bargaining between the two firms. Notice that in both situations some production of Y takes place, and hence there will be some pollution. Having no Y output (and no pollution) would be inefficient in the same sense that producing Y^* is: Scarce resources would not be efficiently allocated. The example shows that by relying on the opportunity cost doctrine there is some "optimal" level of pollution and that this level may be achieved through bargains between the individuals involved.

The Coase Theorem

Hence we have shown that the two firms left on their own can arrive at the efficient output level (Y'). Assuming that bargaining costs are zero, both parties will recognize the advantages of striking a deal. Each will be led by the "invisible hand" to the same output level that would be achieved through an ideal merger. Interestingly, that solution will be reached no matter how property rights to river usage are assigned. The pollution-producing firm has exactly the same incentives to choose the efficient output level as does the injured firm. The ability of the two firms to bargain freely causes the true social costs to be recognized by each. This result is sometimes referred to as the *Coase Theorem* after the economist, Ronald Coase, who first proposed it in this form.[8]

Distributional Effects

There are, however, distributional effects that do depend on who is assigned ownership of the river. If both firms appear in court demanding property rights to the river, the court's decision on how these rights should be assigned will have important distributional effects. If firm Y is given ownership of the river, its owners will be better off than they would be if firm X were the owner. Because, in our example, allocation will be unaffected by the way in which property rights are assigned,[9] any assessment of the desirability of certain assignments must be made on equity grounds. For example, if the owners of firm Y were very wealthy and those of firm X poor, we might argue that ownership should be given to firm X on the basis of distributional equity. The price system may, in principle, be capable of solving certain simple externality problems of allocation but, as always, the price system cannot deal with problems of equity.[10]

It should be pointed out, however, that the issue of equity in the assignment of property rights arises in every allocational decision, not only in the study of externalities. The issue of which firm should be assigned ownership of the river is not essentially different from the question of which individual has the right of ownership to a particular house. In either case a government could decide that the prevailing system of property rights is undesirable and might therefore redefine those rights. The issue of income distribution is no more intertwined with the problem of externalities than it is with any other allocational question.

The Role of Bargaining Costs

The analysis of this section depends crucially on the assumption of zero bargaining costs. If the costs (real or psychic) of striking bargains were high, the workings of

---

[8]See R. Coase, "The Problem of Social Cost," *Journal of Law and Economics* 3 (October 1960), pp. 1–44.

[9]This conclusion requires that the changing distribution of wealth implied by different assignments of property rights has no effect on the allocation of goods. Loosely speaking, it is assumed that the demand and cost curves of Figure 21.1 will not shift in response to the changing distribution of wealth. It is assumed that "income effects" are unimportant.

[10]Matters of equity cannot be established here on *a priori* grounds but, rather, require a detailed examination of the welfare level of each agent. It would be inappropriate to argue, for example, that firm Y has an inalienable right to the use of the river or, conversely, that firm X has a basic right to clean water. Since firm Y's actions only affect firm X, no such *a priori* conclusions are possible. The desires of the two firms are strictly competitive and any arguments about the intrinsic rights of one party can symmetrically be applied to the other. For some fascinating examples of this symmetry in legal cases see Coase, "Problem of Social Cost," *op. cit.*

the free exchange system may not be capable of achieving allocational efficiency. Similarly, if bargaining costs were high the allocation of resources would probably not be independent of the way in which property rights are assigned. In the next section we will examine an important type of externality for which bargaining costs are indeed quite high—environmental externalities. We will see that for such externalities it is unlikely that the free market will attain an efficient outcome.

Bargaining Costs and Environmental Externalities

It is a commonplace observation that markets seem to have failed to cope with externalities related to the environment: Firms and individuals routinely pollute the air and water through their disposal activities; noise levels in urban areas are often so high as to be harmful to residents' health; and the array of signs and posters along most major highways creates what many individuals regard as "visual pollution." In view of the analysis of the previous section, a natural first question to ask about these externalities is why they have not been internalized through bargaining. It would seem that those who are harmed by the externalities could bargain with the individuals or firms that create them and thereby improve the allocation of resources. A principal reason this does not happen is the *high bargaining costs* that are associated with most environmental externalities. It is frequently difficult to organize these individuals into an effective bargaining unit[11] and to calculate the monetary value of the losses suffered. Finally, most legal systems have been set up primarily to adjudicate disputes between two agents, rather than to represent the rights of diffuse groups. Each of these factors makes bargaining costs extremely high in most cases of environmental spillovers. Indeed, the lack of effective group action in the real world would seem to imply that the transaction costs may exceed by a substantial amount the possible gains that can be obtained by successful action.

Bargaining Costs and Allocation

In cases characterized by high bargaining costs, the assignment of (private or common) ownership rights can have significant allocative effects. If, as is normally the case, disposal of refuse into air and water is treated as a common (and free) activity, this in effect assigns ownership rights to each agent. The agents may use the air and water around them in any way they choose, and high bargaining costs will prevent them from internalizing any external costs into their decisions. For this reason, pollution-producing activities may be operated at a higher level than would be optimal.

---

[11]Many of the problems that arise in the provision of public goods are important impediments to group antipollution action. Once pollution is abated, it is abated for everyone: The benefits are nonexclusive. Consequently, it may be to the advantage of each individual to adopt the position of a free rider.

Specification of ownership rights may also be an important determinant of the productive technology that is adopted. Because cost curves will be affected by the way in which these rights are distributed when bargaining costs are high, incentives for adopting different techniques of production can be generated. If the full social cost of pollution-producing techniques is imposed on polluters, for example, these techniques will appear less profitable than they otherwise would. When a dynamic view is taken of the economic process, the assignment of property rights may have significant effects on the evolution of productive technology. For example, it was not until strong anti-air-pollution laws were imposed on electric utility generation that low-sulfur fuels came into general use. Similarly, development of geothermal and solar electric generation may proceed more rapidly than would have been the case had the external costs of more traditional methods of generation not been imposed.

■ The Evolution of Property Rights: Some Examples

Legal assignments of property rights change over time. Some goods that were at one time commonly owned (most land, for example) have in more recent times become primarily private property. Similarly, some goods that were at one time private (roads, bridges, lighthouses, and fire companies) have increasingly come to be publicly owned. Traditionally such changes have been regarded as primarily legal or political in origin. Although economic analysis could illustrate the implications of various property rights assignments, it had little to say about how assignments were in fact made. More recently, however, several economists have argued that the definitions societies adopt for property rights are strongly motivated by economic considerations. In particular, it has been suggested that private property rights come into existence when it becomes economical for those affected by externalities to internalize them through transactions in private property: that is, when the benefits of coping with the externalities exceed the costs of enforcing private property rights.[12] In broad terms, then, the hypothesis is that legal institutions (notably property rights) evolve over time toward economically efficient outcomes. Although it would be inappropriate here to investigate the wide variety of implications for the analysis of law that stem from this hypothesis, we shall examine three specific examples of the development of private property rights as a way of internalizing externalities.

Native Americans' Land[13]

Prior to the arrival of large numbers of Europeans on the East Coast of North America, land was commonly owned. Hunting and trapping activities by one Indian

---

[12]See H. Demsetz, "Toward a Theory of Property Rights," *American Economic Review, Papers and Proceedings,* 57 (May 1967), pp. 347–359.

[13]*Ibid.*

had little effect on those of another; hence there were few incentives to adopt mechanisms for coping with externalities. Opening of trade with Europe changed that situation considerably. Because of strong European demand for fur, Indians' trapping expanded greatly both in intensity and in geographic extent. Interaction effects among tribes and among individuals within tribes came to have major importance as some animals were overhunted and productivity fell. In response to the increasing importance of these externalities, private ownership of land became more common among native Americans. By 1790 most East Coast Indian land was privately owned. In that way the problem of overhunting was mitigated, as each landowner had an incentive to manage his resources on a "sustained yield" basis.

Radio

A more recent example of the establishment of private property in what previously had been a common resource is the case of the radio spectrum.[14] Prior to a series of technical innovations in the early twentieth century, the radio spectrum had little economic value (other than for small-scale scientific experiments). Development of reliable long-distance radio transmitters altered that situation. Progressive "invasions" of the radio spectrum (through both a greater variety of wavelengths and the technical ability to discern between closer wavelengths) led to significant problems of interference among users. To cope with these externalities governments began to allocate portions of the spectrum for the unique use of specific individuals or firms. Those property rights came to be quite highly priced as they provided owners with substantial monopoly profits.

Bees and Apples

Earlier in this chapter we mentioned Meade's example of the beneficial externalities between beekeepers and apple growers. Since the costs of bargaining between these two producers are probably low, our analysis suggests that there may be incentives to internalize the externalities through private property contracts. In fact, Cheung's investigation of beekeeping in Washington state shows that such contracts are well developed.[15] Terms of the contracts typically take into account both the benefits that various crops provide to beekeepers (in the form of honey) and the benefits that farmers get from having bees pollinate their crops. For crops such as clover and alfalfa, which have high honey yields, beekeepers usually pay rent to farmers for the right to have their bees use the farmers' land. On the other hand, apple and cherry growers must

---

[14]This section draws on H. G. J. Aitken, *Syntony and Spark: The Origins of Radio* (New York: John Wiley & Sons, Inc., 1976).

[15]S. N. S. Cheung, "The Fable of the Bees: An Economic Investigation," *Journal of Law and Economics* 16 (April 1973), pp. 11–33.

"rent" bees to provide pollination because the honey yield from those crops is low. Hence, although Meade's externality example has a certain bucolic appeal, economic incentives seem to have limited its relevance in the real world.

These examples are suggestive of the relationship between externalities and the definition of property rights, but they fall short of providing a predictive theory. Additional research is required to sharpen the definition of transaction costs and to understand the ways in which legal and political institutions constrain economic outcomes.[16] In the next section we discuss a specific example of the economic benefits of property rights that illustrates the importance of the relationship between law and economics.

■ Example of the Efficiency Benefits of Property Rights: Fisheries

Fisheries provide an interesting example of a renewable natural resource for which private ownership may have different allocational consequences than does common ownership.[17] Because most ocean fisheries are treated as common property, there may be a tendency for the areas to be overfished from a long-run viewpoint. Each fisherman will adopt a policy of increasing his output up to the point at which the marginal cost of catching additional fish is equal to the price of fish. Although such a policy may lead to short-run profit maximization, it also runs the risk of so depleting the stock of fish that next year's catch may be endangered. Because the fisheries are communally owned, however, individual fishermen will not take these additional costs of their activities into account. It would not be in any one fisherman's interest to cut back on his output this year in order to aid in "conservation" since he knows others will not do so. If the fishery were owned by a single individual, however, a different logic might prevail. In that situation, the owner would undoubtedly recognize the effect that policies adopted today will have on next year's catch and would adjust his current output decision accordingly.

A Graphic Analysis

This argument is illustrated in Figure 20.3. Suppose that the price of fish is given by P^* and that the marginal cost curve for the current year's output is given by MC. Under communal ownership, each fisherman will produce output level Q_c,

---

[16]For a tongue-in-cheek analysis of externalities in a society without such institutions (that of wolves in North America), see M. C. Fredlund, "Wolves, Chimps, and Demsetz," *Economic Inquiry* 14 (June 1976), pp. 279–290.

[17]This section is based on H. S. Gordon, "The Economic Theory of a Common-Property Resource: The Fishery," *Journal of Political Economy* 62 (April 1954), pp. 124–142; and on A. Scott, "The Fishery: The Objectives of Sole Ownership," *Journal of Political Economy* 63 (April 1955), pp. 116–124.

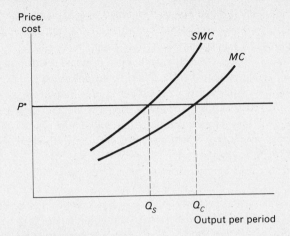

**Figure 20.3 / Differential Effects of
Common and Sole Ownership of a Fishery**

Under common ownership, fishermen will recognize only current operating costs as reflected by MC. They will therefore produce output level Q_C. If the fishery is owned by a single firm, however, the depleting effects of current operations will be taken into account. Firms would then produce at a point (Q_S) where price is equal to a comprehensive measure of marginal costs (SMC).

since this output level maximizes current profits. If the fishery were solely owned by one firm, however, that firm would consider both future and present operating costs of its actions. Since increasing the current year's catch tends to reduce the catch (and the profits), in future years, the firm will regard its marginal cost curve as being SMC. This curve reflects both current operating costs and the future costs of reduced harvests. The sole owner would therefore choose to produce output level Q_s since this provides maximum profits when full costs are taken into account.

The result of this analysis, then, is to show that whether resources are commonly or privately owned may have important effects on firms' output decisions. Under common ownership, fishermen impose an external cost on others by not recognizing the effect they have on future harvests. A firm given sole ownership of the fishery would "internalize" this externality and would operate the fishery on a "sustained yield" basis. Moves in recent years by several countries (most notably Chile, Peru, and Iceland) to expand their territorial limits can be viewed as an application of this principle. By expanding their limits, these countries are attempting to create a property right to surrounding fisheries and thereby to internalize the negative externalities created by overfishing.

Private Property
in Shellfish Beds: Oysters and Lobsters

Because shellfish are found along the continental shelf in relatively isolated beds, enforcement of property rights in such resources is less costly than for ocean fisheries. These property rights may be enforced by the state as for any other legal right or they may be enforced informally by custom and heredity. Whatever the source of the property rights our analysis suggests that shellfish producers who operate under a regime of private property will recognize the divergence between private and social marginal costs and, by so doing, will in the long run be more productive than those who fish on common property. Some direct evidence on this possibility was provided in a 1975 study of oyster production by R. J. Agnello and L. P. Donnelley.[18] In this study, the authors noted that states differ widely in the proportion of their oyster grounds that is privately owned. In Virginia, for example, about 74 percent of oysters are produced from privately owned grounds whereas in neighboring Maryland the figure is less than 17 percent. The authors found that there was clear evidence that oyster fishermen were more productive in states with a high level of private property. In Virginia, for example, the average physical productivity of oyster fishermen was nearly 60 percent higher than in Maryland. More generally, the authors found that a 10 percent increase in the proportion of oyster grounds that were privately owned led to an increase of 338 pounds in the annual oyster catch of each fisherman. They attribute this result to the greater efficiency with which private oyster beds can be managed.

A similar result was obtained by F. W. Bell in a study of lobstering.[19] In this case, however, the author found that property rights were only weakly enforced (by custom rather than by law) and that the common property nature of most production decisions led to overfishing. In 1966, for example, the author calculated that there may have been twice as many lobster traps in use as would be dictated by efficiency considerations. A reduction in the number of traps to the optimal level would have increased the catch by nearly 10 pounds per trap. The author suggested that such a reduction might be brought about through state regulation, but our analysis indicates that it might also be achieved through a more careful definition of property rights in the industry.

Summary

We began this chapter with a demonstration of the misallocation of resources that is created by the existence of an externality. That misallocation occurs because of a divergence between private and social costs that leads economic agents, acting in their own self-interest, to make choices that are nonoptimal. Traditional corrective action in such situations consists of various tax-subsidy schemes that bring social and private costs into agreement.

---

[18]R. J. Agnello and L. P. Donnelley, "Property Rights and Efficiency in the Oyster Industry," *Journal of Law and Economics* XVIII (2) (October 1975), pp. 521–533.

[19]F. W. Bell, "Technological Externalities and Common Property Resources: An Empirical Study of the U.S. Northern Lobster Industry," *Journal of Political Economy* 80 (1) (January/February 1972), pp. 148–158.

Externalities need not lead to inefficiencies, however. We showed that, if bargaining costs are low and property rights are fully specified, the parties involved in an externality can reach private agreements that internalize its effects. Existence of property rights therefore permits the efficient outcome to be obtained because both parties find it in their own interest to "bargain them away." Only recently have economists discovered (or perhaps rediscovered after a gap of nearly 100 years) those important interrelationships between the assignment of property rights and the allocation of resources. Already, however, important conceptual breakthroughs have been made as the analysis of property rights has been applied to an increasingly broad range of issues. Such questions as the authority relationships within firms, the nature of incentives on a collective farm, and the assignment of product liability can be better understood by analyzing the property rights that are being exchanged in these various situations.[20] By recognizing that property rights have a value and that these values may change over time, economists are in a better position to understand the reasons why certain exchanges do or do not take place. They may therefore judge whether a particular property rights assignment increases or impedes efficiency. It must be kept in mind, of course, that the specification of property rights can also have important implications for equity and that it may be desirable to sacrifice some efficiency to achieve this end.

Suggested Readings

Arrow, K. J., *The Limits of Organization* (New York: W. W. Norton & Company, Inc., 1974).

Alchian, A. A., and Demsetz, H., "Production, Information Costs, and Economic Organization," *American Economic Review* 62 (December 1972), pp. 777–795.

Cheung, S., "The Fable of the Bees: An Economic Investigation," *Journal of Law and Economics* 16 (April 1973), pp. 11–33.

————, "Private Property Rights and Sharecropping," *Journal of Political Economy* 76 (December 1968), pp. 1107–1122.

Coase, R. H., "The Market for Goods and the Market for Ideas," *American Economic Review* 64 (May 1974), pp. 384–391.

————, "The Problem of Social Cost," *Journal of Law and Economics* 3 (October 1960), pp. 1–44.

Demsetz, H., "Toward a Theory of Property Rights," *American Economic Review* 57 (May 1967), pp. 347–373.

Furubotn, E., and Pejovich, S., "Property Rights and Economic Theory: A Survey of the Recent Literature," *Journal of Economic Literature* 10 (December 1972), pp. 1137–1162.

---

[20]For a survey of some contemporary applications, see. E. Furubotn and S. Pejovich, "Property Rights and Economic Theory: A Survey of Recent Literature," *The Journal of Economic Literature* 10, No. 4 (December 1972), pp. 1137–1162.

Meade, J., "External Economies and Diseconomies in a Competitive Situation," *Economic Journal* 62 (March 1952), pp. 54–67.

Mishan, E. J., "The Postwar Literature on Externalities: An Interpretive Essay," *Journal of Economic Literature* 9 (March 1971), pp. 1–28.

North, D., and Thomas, R., "The Rise and Fall of the Manorial System: A Theoretical Model," *Journal of Economic History* 31 (December 1971), pp. 777–803.

Worcester, D. A., "Pecuniary and Technological Externality, Factor Rents, and Social Costs," *American Economic Review* 59 (December 1969), pp. 873–885.

Problems

20.1

On the island of Pago-Pago there are two lakes and 20 fishermen. Each fisherman gets to fish on either lake and gets to keep the average catch on his particular lake. On Lake X the total number of fish caught is given by:

$$F^X = 10L_X - \tfrac{1}{2}L_X^2,$$

where L_X is the number of men fishing on the lake. The amount an additional fisherman will catch is $MP_X = 10 - L_X$.

For Lake Y the relationship is:

$$F^Y = 5L_Y,$$

and

$$MP_Y = 5.$$

Under this organization of society, what will the total number of fish caught be?

The chief of Pago-Pago, having once read an economics book, believes that she can raise the total number of fish caught by restricting the number of men allowed to fish on Lake X. What is the correct number of men to fish on X in order to maximize the total catch of fish? What is the number of fish caught in this situation?

Being basically opposed to coercion, the chief decides to require a fishing license for Lake X. If the licensing procedure is to bring about the optimal allocation of labor, what should the cost of a license be (in terms of fish)?

Does this example prove that a "competitive" allocation of resources may not be optimal?

20.2

Suppose that the oil industry in Utopia is perfectly competitive and that all firms draw oil from a single (and practically inexhaustible) pool. Assume that each competitor believes that he can sell all the oil he can produce at a stable world price of $10 per barrel, and that the cost of operating a well for one year is $1000.

Total output per year (Q) of the oil field is a function of the number of wells (N) operating in the field. In particular,

$$Q = 500N - N^2,$$

and the amount of oil produced by each well (q) is given by:

$$q = \frac{Q}{N} = 500 - N.$$

The output from the Nth well is given by:

$$MP_N = 500 - 2N.$$

a. Describe the equilibrium output and the equilibrium number of wells in this perfectly competitive case. Is there a divergence between private and social marginal cost in the industry?

b. Suppose now that the government nationalizes the oil field. How many oil wells should it operate? What will total output be? What will the output per well be?

c. As an alternative to nationalization, the Utopian government is considering an annual license fee per well to discourage overdrilling. How large should this license fee be if it is to prompt the industry to drill the optimal number of wells?

20.3

Suppose that both the chemical and eyeglass industries in Atlantis are perfectly competitive. Smoke from the chemical industry, however, leaves particles on the grinding equipment used for making glasses that must constantly be removed. Hence chemical production raises the marginal cost of eyeglasses. Using a graphic analysis, show how usual market forces will cause resources to be misallocated in Atlantis. Illustrate the optimal allocation and use the concept of consumer's surplus to show who would gain and who would lose under such a reallocation. Explain how that reallocation might be brought about through a tax on chemical production, or through costless bargaining by the two parties. What factors might inhibit the bargaining solution?

20.4

There is currently considerable controversy concerning product safety. Two extreme positions might be termed *caveat emptor* (let the buyer beware) and *caveat vendor* (let the seller beware). Under the former scheme producers would have no responsibility for the safety of their products: buyers would absorb all losses. Under the latter scheme this liability assignment would be reversed; firms would be completely responsible under law for losses incurred from unsafe products. Using simple supply and demand analysis, discuss how the assignment of such liability might affect the allocation of resources. Would safer products be produced if firms were strictly liable under law?

20.5

Three types of contracts are used to specify the way in which tenants on a plot of agricultural land may pay rent to the landlord. Rent may be paid: (1) in money (or a fixed amount of agricultural produce); or (2) as a fixed proportionate share of the crop; or (3) in "labor dues" by agreeing to work on other plots owned by the landlord. How might these alternative contract specifications affect tenants' production decisions? What sorts of transactions costs might occur in the enforcement of each type of contract? What economic factors might affect the type of contract specified in different places of during different historical periods?

20.6

Develop an example of interpersonal externalities similar to that we used to illustrate interfirm externalities in Chapter 20. Show how the assumption of zero bargaining costs permits exchanges among the two individuals to bring about an optimal allocation of resources even in the presence of this type of externality.

20.7

Inventors are not usually able to capture all of the profits arising from their inventions. Rather, these inventions tend to become public property that can be freely used without paying royalties to the inventor. Develop a supply-demand diagram that demonstrates how this externality may cause too few inventions to be produced. How might the adoption of patent laws mitigate this problem by developing property rights to inventions? What inefficiencies might be created by patents?

Chapter **21**

Distribution of Income

Introduction

In this chapter we shall examine both positive and normative questions about the distribution of income. Although our discussion is oriented toward developed capitalist economies (particularly the United States), it has relevance to the distribution of income in any economy. Institutional details do, however, differ considerably from case to case, and a more detailed study should take these differences into account.

Our positive analysis of the distribution of income is divided into three major sections. In the first we examine the simultaneity between resource allocation and income distribution that characterizes a market economy. Next, we illustrate general features of the distribution of income and show how income inequality can be measured. Finally, we present a conceptual theory of income distribution that may provide a foundation for understanding the observed data.

Because the study of income distribution also raises a number of normative and policy issues, we conclude this chapter (and this book) by analyzing a few of them. We show that the distribution of income can be regarded as a public good and therefore redistributional policies fall within the general guidelines for governmental intervention outlined previously in this part. Using this conceptual foundation together with our positive model of the income distribution we then analyze a few redistributional policies.

Before beginning our analysis, one point of possible confusion should be clarified. As we pointed out in Chapter 17, most theoretical concepts of social

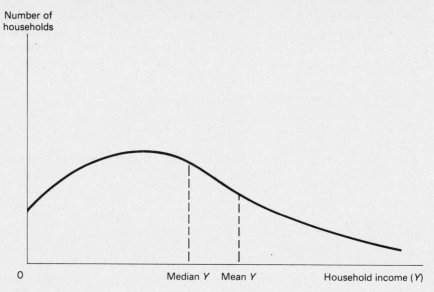

Figure 21.1 / Typical Distribution of Income in a Developed Economy

Most developed market economies have income distributions that: (1) have a large "middle class," (2) are skewed to the right so that mean income exceeds median income, and (3) obey Pareto's law in the upper tail of the distribution.

existence of very high incomes will affect location of the mean but not of the median. Finally, for income levels above the mean, the income distribution declines in a smooth way. This observation was first discovered by Pareto in the early twentieth century. Pareto's hypothesis that the upper tail of all income distributions has essentially the same form[3] has stimulated much theoretical and empirical research.

■ Measuring Inequality: An Application

Figure 21.1 illustrates the finding that most countries exhibit considerable inequality in their income distributions. Some quantitative evidence of this is provided in Table 21.1. The table shows the percentage of total national income received by the bottom 20 percent of all families and by the top 5 percent in 15 countries. Although the reader should retain some skepticism about the accuracy of these data, they clearly indicate substantial inequality. In general it appears that the top 5 percent of all families receive between 15 and 35 percent of total income in the countries listed whereas the lowest 20 percent of all families receive far less

---

[3]Specifically, Pareto's law states that $N(Y) = \alpha Y^{-B}$, where Y is income, N is the number of households having income level Y or greater, and α and B are constants.

than 10 percent. This marked degree of inequality occurs in countries of widely varying levels of per capita income: the figures for the poorest country in the table (Bangladesh) are not, in proportionate terms, very different from those for the most affluent (the United States). Some of the countries exhibited slight movements toward greater equality between 1960 and 1970, but those changes did not significantly alter the overall picture.

Table 21.1 / The Distribution of National Income in Fifteen Countries 1960, 1970

	Percent Received by Lowest 20%		Percent Received by Highest 5%		1973 GNP per capita (dollars)
	1960	1970	1960	1970	
Bangladesh	7.0	9.0	19.0	17.0	80
Colombia	3.0	4.0	36.0	33.0	440
Canada	6.5	6.4	14.0	14.0	5,450
Gabon	2.0	3.0	47.0	45.0	1,310
India	4.0	5.0	27.0	25.0	120
Israel	7.0	8.0	13.0	13.0	3,010
Korea, Republic of	7.0	10.0	17.0	15.0	400
Mexico	4.0	4.0	29.0	36.0	890
Netherlands	4.0	3.1	23.6	22.0	4,330
Peru	3.0	2.0	50.0	34.0	620
Philippines	5.0	4.0	29.0	25.0	280
Sri Lanka	5.0	7.0	27.0	19.0	120
Turkey	4.0	3.0	33.0	32.0	600
United Kingdom	6.0	6.0	15.7	15.0	3,060
United States	4.0	6.7	16.0	13.3	6,200

Source: The World Bank, *World Tables, 1976* (Baltimore, Md.: The Johns Hopkins University Press, 1976), Social Indicators Table 3, pp. 514–517.

Distribution of Income in the United States

A somewhat more detailed picture of the distribution of income in the United States is provided in Table 21.2 for the year 1974. Again, the table shows substantial inequality: the top 8.8 percent of all households received more than one-fourth of all income in 1974 whereas the lowest 12.8 percent received less than 2 percent. Any theory of the income distribution must provide some explanation for this inequality and must predict how the distribution will shift over time.

Lorenz Curve and the Gini Coefficient

Before presenting a theory of the distribution of income, it will be useful to describe a measure of inequality that provides a summary measure of income distribution

Table 21.2 / Distribution of Annual Household Income in the United States, 1974

Income ($ per year)	Percent of Households	Cumulative Percent of Households	Percent of Total Income	Cumulative Percent of Total Income
Less than $3,000	12.8	12.8	1.7	1.7
$3,000–$4,999	10.8	23.6	3.5	5.2
$5,000–$6,999	10.1	33.7	4.9	10.1
$7,000–$9,999	13.9	47.6	9.4	19.5
$10,000–$14,999	21.2	68.8	21.0	40.5
$15,000–$24,999	22.4	91.2	34.3	74.8
Over $25,000	8.8	100.0	25.2	100.0

Source: U.S. Bureau of the Census, *Current Population Reports,* series P-60.

data (such as those presented in Table 21.2). This measure is derived from the *Lorenz Curve* shown in Figure 21.2. This curve records cumulative percentages of the population (from 0 to 100 percent) along the horizontal axis and cumulative percentages of *total* income received (starting with the lowest) along the vertical axis. If income were distributed perfectly equally, the Lorenz curve would be a diagonal line showing that any (say) 10 percent of the population receives 10 percent of total income. Inequality in the actual income distribution is indicated by the curve's being bowed below the diagonal. The more unequal is the income distribution, the more extensive that bowed effect will be.

A measure of the inequality derived from the Lorenz curve is the Gini coefficient:

Definition

The *Gini Coefficient* measures inequality of the income distribution and is defined from the Lorenz Curve as:

$$\text{Gini Coefficient} = \frac{\text{area } A}{\text{area } (A + B)} \qquad [21.1]$$

The Gini coefficient hypothetically ranges from 0 (perfect equality) to 1 ("absolute" inequality—that is, one person gets all income). In the United States, Gini coefficients of 0.35–0.45 have generally been calculated for total household income, and several authors have reported that these numbers have remained relatively constant over long periods of time.[4] Gini coefficients are also widely used to compare inequality in income distributions among different population groups within a country and across countries.

---

[4]Interpretation of their constancy is, however, subject to considerable controversy. Some of the elements of that controversy are discussed in the next section.

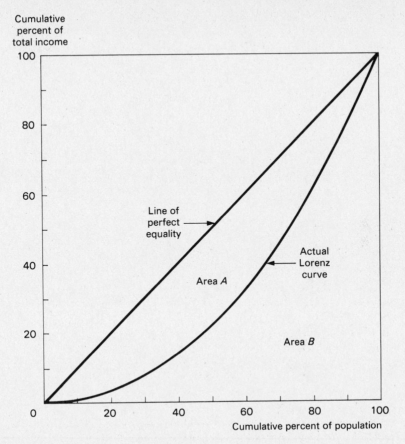

Figure 21.2 / Lorenz Curve of Cumulative Income Distribution

The Lorenz curve shows the extent to which the income distribution departs from perfect equality. A measure of inequality is given by the Gini coefficient—defined as area A ÷ area $(A + B)$. This measure ranges from 0 (perfect equality) to 1 (perfect inequality).

Theory of Income Distribution

Early studies of income distribution tended to stress the relative income shares going to different factors of production. For example, as we discussed in Chapter 19, debate over repeal of the British Corn Laws in the 1820s focused on how such a policy would affect the relative income shares of workers and landowners. Although modern income distribution theory continues to make a distinction between income from labor (earnings) and income from capital (interest, dividends, rents, and so forth), analysis no longer focuses on factor shares. Several trends account for this changed emphasis. First, most income (about 75 percent) is now labor income, and inequality in labor income is nearly as great as the inequality in total income. To focus on recipients of labor income as a homogeneous group would be to miss the principal contributor to observed inequality. Income from capital, on the other hand, is probably distributed more evenly today than in the nineteenth century. Although capital ownership remains relatively concentrated, rapid growth in savings by the middle class coupled with the growth of private and public pensions has made most families into capital owners. The distinction between workers and capitalists as separate classes is increasingly difficult to make. Finally, the observation that individuals may accumulate human capital (see Chapter 16) as well as physical capital imparts a fuzziness to the capital-labor income dichotomy. It is unclear whether a doctor's high wages should be regarded as labor income (from hard work) or as capital income (from past investments in training).

Sources of Income

Despite these warnings we shall continue to make a distinction between income from labor (Y_L) and income from capital (Y_K). Hence, a household's total income (Y) will be disaggregated as:

$$Y = Y_L + Y_K. \tag{21.2}$$

Labor income can be expressed as the product of a wage rate (w) times the number of hours worked by household members (L):[5]

$$Y_L = wL. \tag{21.3}$$

Similarly, capital income can be expressed as the product of the rental rate the household is able to earn on its capital (v) times the quantity of capital owned (K):

$$Y_K = vK. \tag{21.4}$$

Each family's income can therefore be written as:

$$Y = wL + vK. \tag{21.5}$$

Observed differences in incomes among households can arise from inequalities in any of the four variables (w, L, v, K) in Equation 21.5 or from inequalities caused by the relationships among those variables. We now turn to examine possible economic determinants of each of the principal variables.

---

[5]Obviously, if different household members earned different wage rates this result should be generalized to take those differences into account.

Distribution of Wage Rates

The wide dispersion that exists in hourly wage rates is probably the principal determinant of overall inequality in household income. For example, Blinder[6] estimates that about 40 percent of the observed Gini coefficient (0.17 out of a total of 0.43 for total annual income) can be attributed to wage rate differences. Such differences may arise from three fundamental economic causes. First, as our discussion of Chapter 13 suggests, productivity is a principal determinant of wage rates in a market economy. Productivities may differ among workers because of differences in formal education and training, on-the-job experience, or physical and mental ability. In Chapter 15 we also pointed out that wage rates may differ because nonpecuniary characteristics of various jobs lead to compensating wage differentials. Finally, wage rates may vary because of monopolistic or monopsonistic influences (such as union power or wage discrimination) in the market. Each of these causes of wage rate differences has been extensively examined by economists, but there is as yet no consensus as to their relative importance.

Distribution of Hours Worked

Hours worked by households are surprisingly varied. This occurs both because of differences in the number of individuals in a household and because of variability in hours worked by individual household members. Other than making the observation that individuals who choose to live together must obtain some benefits from doing so, economists have had little to say about possible determinants of the number of working-age adults in a household. Often the issue has been defined away by treating unrelated adults living together as separate households. Such treatment probably obscures some interesting economic questions (such as economies of scale available from such living arrangements).

Economists have had far more to say about hours-of-work decisions by individual household members. In Chapter 15 we provided a basic theoretical structure for explaining such choices through the use of the time allocation model. Two applications of that model are particularly important for explaining variations in labor supply that have a major impact for the observed distribution of income: labor supply decisions over the life cycle and labor supply decisions by married women. Students' decisions not to work at young ages and older individuals' decisions to retire cause substantial amounts of earnings to be forgone. Since any cross section of the population will contain some individuals in these life-cycle stages, inequality will be increased over what would be observed for a more homogeneous age group. Similarly, differences in decisions by married women about whether they will work can lead to large differences in income for otherwise similar families. Increasing labor force participation by married women over the past 25 years has probably had

---

[6]A. Blinder, *Toward an Economic Theory of Income Distribution* (Cambridge, Mass.: M.I.T. Press, 1974). p. 139.

the effect of reducing overall income inequality somewhat (because married women with low-wage husbands are more likely to work than are those with high-wage husbands). But the relatively recent emergence of families with two high-wage working spouses may have slowed that trend.

Capital Rent Differences

It is probable that rental rates earned on capital investments differ relatively little among households. Because capital is mobile the market will tend to equalize rates of return as capital owners reallocate their resources from low- to high-yielding investments. A number of factors may prevent this process, however. Some capital owners may be able to command a monopoly rent (consider, for example, ownership of the Polaroid patents). Imperfect information about investment alternatives may prevent some capital owners from taking advantage of desirable opportunities. Some investments may be available only to those with substantial assets. This may result either from the high transactions costs associated with selling certain investments to small investors or from discriminating policies that preclude small investors from some alternatives (for example, government ceiling rates on small savings accounts). Finally, differences in rental rates may arise because some individuals are more astute, or luckier, or more willing to take risks than are others. All in all, however, it is unlikely that rental rate differences are a major contributor to observed inequalities in the income distribution.

Distribution of Capital Ownership

The distribution of the stock of capital owned by households is highly unequal. Gini coefficients of 0.70 or higher have been calculated from survey data on financial wealth. Although there are reasons to believe that these data may overstate inequality a bit (for example, wealth in the form of houses, durable goods, or future Social Security benefits is often omitted in the surveys), there is no doubt that inequalities in capital ownership account for the major portion of observed inequalities in income from capital. Because there are only two ways in which capital stocks may be obtained, through gifts and inheritance or through accumulated savings, the observed distribution must be accounted for by variations among individuals in these methods of acquisition. Conventional opinion would suggest that inheritance is a principal cause of capital ownership differences. Parents' desires to leave bequests to their children are strong, and prevailing taxes (at least in the United States) only moderately impede that process. It should be pointed out, however, that large estates are relatively rare, and it is often the case that bequests are divided among several benefactors. In general, the total effect of inheritance on measured inequality in capital ownership is not known.

Savings behavior may be at least as important as inheritance in determining the distribution of capital ownership. Differences in savings "propensities" among households, and observing households at different stages of the life cycle both contribute to measured inequality. The latter effect is particularly important.

Younger households typically have few assets (indeed, for many, debts may exceed assets). On the other hand, older households usually have accumulated a fairly high level of assets with which to finance their retirement years. Survey results show that households in which the head is over 50 years of age have, on average, four to five times the net worth of otherwise identical households in which the head is under 30. Again, however, precise estimates of the relative contribution of this difference to observed inequality in capital ownership is not known.

This brief introduction to income distribution theory raises a number of unanswered questions. At present there is little theoretical agreement on the subject, and quantitative data that might mediate among competing hypotheses are lacking. In the remainder of this chapter we shall treat the market-determined distribution of income as a given and ask what the government can and should do to change it.

Distribution of Income as a Public Good

We shall begin our discussion of the government's role in the distribution of income by asking the normative question of whether or not the government should do anything about the distribution that comes about as a result of the private market. One way to approach this question would be to argue that the government has a "moral duty" to promote equality, or at least to eliminate abject poverty. If we adopt this principle, there is little more to be said, except perhaps to argue over how much equality is dictated by this moral imperative. For example, Plato argued that in an "ideal" society the income of the richest person would be about four times that of the poorest. A government that accepted this view as a moral absolute would not need to determine the views of its citizens toward equality. Rather, it would be faced with the conceptually easier question of deciding how to implement the degree of equality that Plato's dictum requires. If, on the other hand, we adopt the principle that any government action should be undertaken only if it is favored by "most" individuals, we have posed the question in a way that is conducive to gaining additional insights into the problem. In this section we shall show that equality is in many respects a public good and that, for reasons common to all public goods, the free market may tend to "underproduce" it.

Suppose that every individual in society is of a philanthropic nature and believes equality is a good thing. We might then ask why equality will not be achieved by the workings of the free market. After all, any individual is free to give all the money he or she wants to any other individual. Private philanthropy could therefore be relied upon to produce equality (or at least to reduce inequality to an acceptable level). Under this reasoning it might be concluded that the absence of equality is *prima facie* evidence that people are not really very philanthropic after all.

Such a conclusion would be similar to the argument that if the free market does not provide adequate public health facilities, perhaps people do not care about being healthy. The fallacy in both those arguments is that they ignore the public-good nature of the two activities. If you decide to give money to a poor person, everyone in society who favors equality will benefit. Your own personal calculations will not take this externality into account, however. Because you are not able to exclude others from gaining a psychic benefit from your generosity, you may not give as freely as would be desirable from a social point of view. By this argument, then, you, as well as everyone else, will refrain from giving; inequality will persist even though no one wants it. This is precisely the public-goods "problem" we discussed in detail in Chapter 19.

In fact, not everyone *does agree* on what the proper degree of equality should be. Some individuals have benevolent attitudes toward others and favor an egalitarian society. Other individuals may derive some utility (status) from knowing that there are persons on the economic ladder below themselves and, therefore, would prefer that inequality be maintained. We might choose to pay no attention to such malevolent preferences, but this would involve imposing a moral principle over and above those dictated by individual tastes. We might as well start out with the premise that equality is a good thing in the first place. Alternatively, a government could adopt the benefit principle of providing equality by taxing each individual to the extent he or she benefited psychically from living in a more equal society. Under this procedure, only the philanthropists of society would engage in redistributional programs; governmental coercion would ensure that no true philanthropist was a free rider. Gathering information on individuals' attitudes would be a tricky problem, however, as we mentioned in Chapter 19, since each individual would know that he or she would be taxed in accordance with professed beliefs. In short, there seems to be no easy way to base an answer to the question of redistribution on the tastes of individuals in society, just as there is no easy way to find out how much of any public good should be produced. The public good aspect of the problem does indicate, however, why governments attempt to redistribute income and why the free market might produce a distribution of income that is considered undesirable by almost everyone.

Redistributional Programs

Every activity of government will have distributional consequences. Because governmental decisions affect the allocation of resources, they cannot avoid at the same time affecting the distribution of income. In this section, however, we shall be concerned with those activities that the government undertakes with the express purpose of "improving" the distribution of income.[7] It is possible to class these activities into two different groupings: *market-oriented programs* and *tax-subsidy programs*.

---

[7]It is assumed in this section that the government's goal is to increase equality. The cynical reader could reverse many of the arguments made here to show how, in fact, real-world governments may promote inequality.

Market-Oriented Programs

In the first category would be included governmental attempts at equalizing those basic determinants of income that we discussed in the second section above. Government action to promote equal opportunity in hiring practices, for example, would be one such important activity. Many regulatory functions of government that appear based on allocational considerations (such as action against monopolistic practices) could also have important distributional effects. Finally, governments could adopt educational and work training programs with the purpose of equalizing wage rates. All of these traditional measures involve the government in trying to get the market to produce a more equitable distribution of income than would result if the market were left to operate freely.

Tax-Subsidy Programs

In addition to affecting the determinants of income, the government may also change households' incomes directly through tax or subsidy programs. To denote these effects we can rewrite total households income as:

$$Y = wL + vK - T(w,L,v,K, \ldots), \qquad [21.6]$$

where the function T may depend on the absolute level of household income, the composition of income, and other things (such as household size). A positive value for T would indicate that the household pays taxes, whereas a negative value would indicate that the household receives a subsidy. Although the function T need not differ for calculation of both positive and negative taxes (indeed, some proposals for "welfare reform" in the United States suggest moving toward identical tax and subsidy functions), in most current real-world situations the differences are substantial. Therefore we shall discuss tax and subsidy programs separately.

Tax Programs

Although the income tax is a relatively recent policy in the United States (it came into effect in 1914), general principles of income taxation were widely debated throughout most of the nineteenth century.[8] Questions raised included whether income was a suitable base for an equitable tax (consumption and wealth being the other principal contenders to serve as a base); whether income tax schedules should be proportional or progressive; whether all income should be taxed under the same schedule (it was suggested by some, for example, that income from capital should be taxed more highly because it involved less effort on the recipient's part); and whether certain expenditures (for example, gifts to charities) or other household

---

[8]For a summary of this debate, see J. S. Mill, *Principles of Political Economy* (London: J. W. Parker, 1871), book V, chap. III.

characteristics (such as the number of children) would justify special tax treatment. None of these issues is currently resolved after more than 100 years of discussion. Of course, actual income tax policies incorporate specific decisions about each of them, but widespread calls for "tax reform" are probably indicative of a failure to settle on general principles.

Subsidy Programs

Debate over government subsidy programs for households also has a long history. Only in fairly recent times, however, have such programs come to occupy a major place in governmental budgets and in public debate. In the general category of direct subsidy programs should be included both plans that subsidize the purchase of certain commodities (food stamps, low-income housing) and plans that redistribute generalized purchasing power (Aid to Families with Dependent Children, Social Security, and "negative income tax" types of proposals). Although all of these direct programs have the same general goal of redistributing income, they may differ substantially in the efficiency with which they achieve this goal. Among subsidy-type redistribution programs economists have traditionally tended to prefer cash grants rather than the provision of specific goods at below market price. For example, laypeople see low-quality housing and suggest that the obvious remedy is to build better housing for the poor. An economist's intuitive reaction, on the other hand, is to argue that poor-quality housing is simply a manifestation of low income. Rather than treating the symptom by building housing, economists would generally favor a solution that gets to the cause of the problem by supplementing incomes. Recipients may then buy better-quality housing (if they so choose), or they may purchase some other good that presumably provides more utility to them. More formally, economists would argue that "lump-sum" transfer schemes are more efficient than price subsidies at achieving any desired improvement in individuals' welfare levels.[9]

Benefits and Costs of Redistributional Programs

The principal benefit of redistributional programs[10] is, naturally enough, increased equality. If the population as a whole desires equality, this benefit will be of some value; scarce resources should be devoted to achieving it. Market-oriented redis-

---

[9]The formal proof of this assertion was presented in Chapter 3. An interesting view contrary to that expressed in the text and favoring price subsidies on specific goods is presented in J. Tobin, "On Limiting the Domain of Inequality," *The Journal of Law and Economics* 13, No. 2 (October 1970), pp. 263–277. Tobin's argument relies heavily on the idea that it is far more politically popular to provide poor people with specific (and "worthy") goods at below market prices than with general purchasing power that the recipients may "squander."

[10]We refer here to taxation as a "redistributional program" in the sense that tax payments may depart from the benefit principle of taxation (see Chapter 19). As for any program, such redistributions need not necessarily reduce inequality.

tributional programs may have the additional benefit of improving the operation of various labor markets and perhaps raising the productivity of some workers. Such programs might therefore not only ensure that the output of the economic system is distributed more equitably but also increase the total output to be distributed. Pure redistributional programs may also have this benefit—for example, eliminating malnutrition would undoubtedly have a positive effect on productivity—but this would seem to be a less important aspect of these programs than of the market-oriented programs.

The costs of redistributional plans are not the dollar costs of such programs. These dollar costs represent transfers from one member of society to another and are therefore not costs in a social sense. We should not, however, conclude that redistributional programs are costless. The raising of revenues, say, by taxes, with which to finance transfer programs can induce important distortions into the allocational process. If taxes could be imposed in some lump-sum way (so as to decrease the purchasing power of the individual taxed without biasing decisions), those distortions might be minimized. However, as we saw in Chapter 3, all existing taxation schemes violate this lump-sum principle and will in fact distort individuals' decisions. In particular, an income tax, because it affects the wage rate relevant to an individual's decisions, will cause a reaction in the labor-leisure choices of those taxed. It may be that the progressive income tax rates needed to carry out adequate redistributional programs will encourage the most highly paid (and possibly most productive) workers to choose more leisure. The concomitant reduction in output occasioned by this withdrawal from the labor force would be the true cost of any transfer program. Undertaking a redistributional program may therefore involve a very difficult choice between allocational efficiency and equity. As is always the case for any project, the relevant benefits and costs must be weighed. Subsidies may also have important effects on the behavior of recipients, and in the next section we present an example of the kind of analysis that might be used to study such behavior.

Work Disincentive Effect of Government Income Transfer Programs

In recent years there has been much discussion of the transfer system in the United States. A large portion of this discussion has centered on the issue of whether or not individuals will reduce their work efforts when they receive an income guaranteed by the government. In this section we shall discuss this specific issue in detail, since it does illustrate many of the principles of individual behavior we have developed elsewhere in this book.

Basic Features of Transfer Plans

All simple transfer plans can be characterized by two basic parameters: (1) the income guarantee (G); and (2) the reduction rate (t—also called the "tax" rate). The first of these represents the amount that the government undertakes to pay an individual with no other income. Total income therefore can never fall below G. The reduction rate indicates how governmental payments are to be reduced as the individual's other income (primarily from labor earnings) rises. As an example of these concepts, suppose that G is set at $3000 per year and that the reduction rate is 0.5 (that is, 50 percent). If an individual has no other income, he or she will therefore receive $3000 from the government. If he or she does have earnings of, say, $2000 during the year, he or she will receive $2000 (= $3000 − 0.5 × $2000). That is, the government grant is cut by one-half of what is earned. Governmental payments will decline as earnings increase. When earnings reach $6000 for the year, payments will reach 0 (since $3000 − 0.5 × $6000 = 0). Although real-world payments formulas will generally be more complex than this simple example (they may, for example, take family size into account and permit some earnings to be received before the tax rate is applied), the two parameters G and t are common to practically every program; we shall center our attention on them.

More formally, then, let E be the individual's earnings during the year and suppose that income from capital is 0. Governmental payments (P) are then given by:

$$P = G - tE. \tag{21.7}$$

Generally P cannot be negative, so $P = 0$ for $tE \geq G$. Total income earned by the individual is now given by

$$I = P + E = G + (1 - t)E, \tag{21.8}$$

and this is the basic budget constraint we shall investigate in order to determine the work disincentives brought about by the transfer program.

Disincentive Effects of Transfer Programs

The term "work disincentives" is usually taken to mean a decrease in hours of work by an individual. Here we shall expand that definition to include our interest in how an individual's hours of work will change when he or she faces the budget constraint given in Equation 21.8. Let us assume that the individual is able to earn a wage rate of w per hour. Then earnings are given by:

$$E = wL. \tag{21.9}$$

where L = hours of work. Following the theory of labor supply we developed in Chapter 15, however, we shall find it more convenient to deal with the individual's demand for hours of leisure (H). If there are T total hours in the year, $H = T - L$. Consequently,

$$E = w(T - H); \tag{21.10}$$

that is, the individual earns income for those hours he or she does not spend taking leisure.

Comparison of Budget Constraints

We are now ready to compare the budget constraint in the absence of a government transfer program to that which exists under such a program. Without the program, the individual's only source of income is earnings. Therefore the budget constraint is given by:

$$I = E = w(T - H).$$ [21.11]

Under a transfer program, total income is given by:

$$I = P + E = G + (1 - t)E = G + (1 - t)w(T - H).$$ [21.12]

These budget constraints are shown graphically in Figure 21.3. Notice that when $H = T$ the individual has no earnings since he or she is spending all the time available in leisure-time pursuits. Consequently, by Equation 21.11, earnings are 0 and income is also 0. Under a transfer program, total income would simply be G. As hours of leisure are reduced (and hours of work increase), the individual's income increases under both budget constraints. However, payments are cut back as H falls: The amount of payments is given by the distance between the two constraints. When H reaches H^*, payments drop to 0 since earnings are now relatively high.[11] To the left of H^* the individual returns to obtaining income only from earnings.

Graphic Analysis of Disincentives

In Figure 21.4 the individual's indifference curve map for H and I has been superimposed onto the budget constraints pictured in Figure 21.3. This permits us to demonstrate the work disincentives introduced by the transfer program. Initially the individual chooses the income-leisure combination I_1, H_1; this provides utility level U_1. Now when the transfer program is implemented, the individual's utility-maximizing choice moves to I_2, H_2; utility is increased to U_2. In the figure, H_2 is greater than H_1, implying that the new budget constraint under the transfer program has caused the individual to demand more leisure—that is, to reduce his or her hours of work. There are two causes of this disincentive. First, the presence of the income guarantee induces an income effect that causes more leisure to be demanded.

---

[11]From Equation 21.7 it is clear that at $H^*, G = t \cdot w(T - H^*)$. Another way of saying this is that "breakeven earnings," $w(T - H^*)$, are given by G/t. For any transfer plan, we can compute that earnings level at which payments cease by taking the ratio of G to t. In the example presented earlier in the text, $G = \$3000$ and $t = 0.5$. Therefore breakeven earnings are given by $\$3000/0.5 = \$6000$.

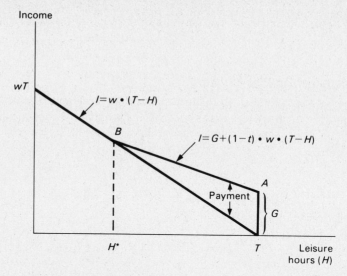

**Figure 21.3 / Budget Constraints
with and without a Transfer Program**

The line *wT, T* shows those combinations of leisure and income that are obtainable in the absence of a transfer program. With a transfer program, the budget constraint becomes *wTBA*; payments are given by the distance between the two constraints. At H^* payments become 0 since earnings have reached the "breakeven level."

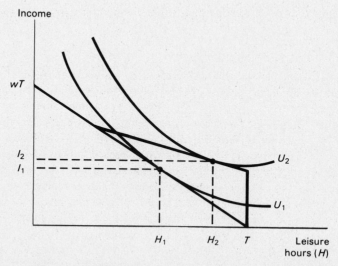

Figure 21.4 / Disincentive Effects of a Transfer Program

The result of the implementation of a governmental transfer program is to cause the individual to reduce hours of work (that is, to demand more leisure). In the absence of such a program, the individual's utility-maximizing choice is I_1, H_1. The new budget constraint introduced by the program will cause the utility-maximizing point to shift to I_2, H_2; here more leisure is demanded ($H_2 > H_1$).

Second, the effect of the imposition of the reduction rate is to reduce the marginal wage rate from w to $(1 - t)w$. In effect, the individual increases earnings by a smaller amount for each hour of work under the transfer plan than before. This, then, induces the individual to substitute leisure for hours of work.[12]

Figure 21.4 predicts an unambiguous decline in hours of work as a result of the implementation of the transfer program. Of course, the actual size of the work reduction will depend on the specific shape of the individual's indifference curve map; it is at least possible that the disincentive effects of such a program might turn out to be rather small.

An Example: Negative Income Tax Experiment ■

In order to estimate the size of the reduction in work effort brought about by a guaranteed annual income, the U.S. Office of Economic Opportunity funded a three-year experimental program in New Jersey and Pennsylvania during the period 1968–1971.[13] Families enrolled in the experiment were provided with income supplements that were calculated by a formula similar to Equation 21.7. Data on hours of work and other measures of labor market behavior were collected over the three-year period for these families and for a "control group" of families who did not receive payments. Summary results for white families in the experiment are reported in Table 21.3. Over the three years of the experiment husbands and wives in the experimental group each worked between one and two

**Table 21.3 / Effect of a Negative Income Tax on Hours Worked:
The New Jersey-Pennsylvania Graduated Work Incentive Experiment, 1968–1971**

	Hours worked per week	
	White Husbands	White Wives
Experimental Group	32.9	3.1
Control Group	34.8	4.5
Experimental—Control	−1.9	−1.4
Percent Difference	−5.6	−30.6

Source: A. Rees, "An Overview of the Labor Supply Results," *Journal of Human Resources* IX, No. 2 (Spring 1974), pp. 174, 175.

[12]It should be pointed out that the imposition of the reduction rate also introduces an income effect into the individual's labor supply decision. Essentially the individual is now "poorer" because he or she now has a lower take-home wage. This income effect would tend to decrease hours of leisure and consequently increase hours of work. However, so long as payments are positive $(G > tE)$, this income effect will be dominated by the income effect of the guarantee rate; consequently, the total effect will be to increase the number of hours of leisure chosen.

[13]The experiment is described in D. Kershaw, "A Negative-Income-Tax Experiment," *Scientific American* 227, No. 4 (October 1972), pp. 19–25.

fewer hours per week than did similar individuals in the control group. In proportional terms, however, the decrease in hours worked for wives was much larger, amounting to a 30 percent reduction. That finding is consistent with the notion that wives have better alternative uses for their time than do husbands and will therefore exhibit larger substitution effects in response to changes in their budget constraints. Because the New Jersey-Pennsylvania results are subject to a number of methodological problems, however, it is important to be careful in extrapolating them to a national program involving the whole population.

Summary

This chapter has had two purposes. The first was to present some conceptualizations about the distribution of income and its determinants. The distribution of income in a market economy is determined as part of the overall allocation of resources, and we demonstrated several interconnections between these two subjects. The distribution is, by definition, derived from the distribution of the basic determinants of income: wage rates, hours of work, rental rates on capital, and capital ownership. We demonstrated a few ways in which theories about each of these determinants might be developed. A second purpose of the chapter was to investigate the role that a government might take in modifying the income distribution that the market provides. Our discussion ranged from rather abstract questions about the problem of a government's deciding on distributional goals to practical problems related to the implementation of tax and subsidy policies. For both of these types of questions the analytical tools of economics provide considerable insights. These tools make it possible to assess alternative redistributional strategies. Deciding on such policies is just one more example of the role that a government might play in determining the allocation of resources and the distribution of welfare.

Suggested Readings

Blinder, A. S., *Toward an Economic Theory of Income Distribution* (Cambridge, Mass.: M.I.T. Press, 1974).

Bronfenbrenner, M., *Income Distribution Theory* (Chicago: Aldine-Atherton, 1971).

Fair, R. C., "The Optimal Distribution of Income," *Quarterly Journal of Economics* 75 (November 1971), pp. 551–579.

Gordon, D., *Theories of Poverty and Underemployment* (Lexington, Mass.: Lexington Books, 1972).

Harrison, B., "Ghettos Economic Development," *Journal of Economic Literature* 12 (March 1974), pp. 1–37.

Henle, P., "Exploring the Distribution of Earned Income," *Monthly Labor Review,* December 1972, pp. 16–27.

alternative combinations of productive inputs that can be used to produce a given level of output.

Long Run *See* Short Run-Long Run Distinction.

Marginal Cost (MC) The additional cost incurred by producing one more unit of output.

Marginal Expense The cost of hiring one more unit of a productive input. The marginal expense of hiring one more unit of labor, for example, is denoted by MC_L.

Marginal Physical Product (MP) The additional output that can be produced by one more unit of a particular input while holding all other inputs constant. It is usually assumed that an input's marginal productivity diminishes as additional units of the input are put into use while holding other inputs fixed.

Marginal Rate of Substitution (MRS) The rate at which an individual is willing to trade one good for another while remaining equally well off. The MRS is the absolute value of the slope of an indifference curve. It is usually assumed that the MRS (of X for Y) will diminish as X is progressively substituted for Y.

Marginal Revenue (MR) The additional revenue obtained by a firm when it sells one more unit of output.

Marginal Revenue Product (MRP) The extra revenue that accrues to a firm when it sells the output that is produced by one more unit of some input. In the case of labor, for example, $MRP_L = MR \cdot MP_L$.

Marginal Utility (MU) The extra utility that an individual receives by consuming one more unit of a particular good.

Marginal Value Product (MVP) A specific case of marginal revenue product that applies when the good being produced is sold in a perfectly competitive market. If the competitive price is given by P ($= MR$ in this case), then $MVP_L = P \cdot MP_L$.

Market Period A very short period over which quantity supplied is fixed and not responsive to changes in market price.

Monopoly An industry in which there is only a single seller of the good in question.

Monopsony An industry in which there is only a single buyer of the good in question.

Oligopoly An industry in which there are only a few sellers of the good in question.

Opportunity Cost Doctrine The simple, though far-reaching, observation that the true cost of any action can be measured by the value of the best alternative that must be forgone when the action is taken.

Output and Substitution Effects The effects that come into play when a change in the price of an input that a firm uses causes the firm to change the quantities of inputs it will demand. The substitution effect would occur even if output were held constant, and it is reflected by movements along an isoquant. Output effects, on the other hand, occur when output levels change and the firm moves to a new isoquant.

Pareto Optimality An allocation of resources in which no one individual can be made better off without making someone else worse off.

Perfect Competition The most widely used economic model in which there are assumed to be a large number of buyers and sellers for any good and in which each agent is a price taker. *See also* Price Taker.

Perfect Price Discrimination The ability of a seller to auction off each unit of output for the maximum revenue it will bring. This differs from usual market situations in which all units of a particular good are sold at the same price.

Present Discounted Value (PDV) The current value of a sum of money that is payable sometime in the future which takes into account the effect of interest payments.

Price Taker An economic agent that makes decisions on the assumption that these decisions will have no effect on prevailing market prices.

Prisoner's Dilemma A problem that was originally studied in the theory of games but that has widespread applicability. The crux of the dilemma is that each individual, faced with the uncertainty of how others will behave, may be led to adopt a course of action that proves to be detrimental for all those individuals making the same decision. A strong coalition might have led to a solution preferred by everyone in the group.

Production Function A conceptual mathematical function that records the relationship between a firm's inputs and its outputs.

Production Possibility Frontier The locus of all the alternative quantities of several outputs that can be produced with fixed amounts of productive inputs.

Profits The difference between the total

revenue a firm receives and its total economic costs.

Property Rights Legal specification of ownership and of the rights that owners have.

Rate of Product Transformation (*RPT*) The rate at which one output can be traded for another in the productive process while holding the total quantities of inputs constant. The *RPT* is the absolute value of the slope of the production possibility frontier.

Rate of Return The rate at which present goods can be transformed into future goods. For example, a one-period rate of return of 10 percent implies that forgoing 1 unit of output this period will yield 1.10 units of output next period.

Rate of Technical Substitution (*RTS*) The rate at which one input may be traded off against another in the productive process while holding output constant. The *RTS* is the absolute value of the slope of an isoquant.

Rent Payments to a factor of production that are in excess of that amount necessary to keep it in its current employment.

Rental Rate The cost of hiring one machine for one hour. Denoted by v in the text.

Returns to Scale A way of classifying production functions that records how output responds to proportional increases in *all* inputs. If a proportional increase in all inputs causes output to increase by a smaller proportion, the production function is said to exhibit *decreasing* returns to scale. If output increases by a greater proportion than the inputs, the production function exhibits *increasing* returns. *Constant* returns to scale is the middle ground where both inputs and outputs increase by the same proportions.

Scarcity Cost The opportunity cost of forgone future sales as a result of current production from a finite resource.

Second Best The best allocation of resources that is obtainable when various constraints preclude attaining true economic efficiency.

Second-Order Conditions Mathematical conditions required to ensure that points for which first-order conditions are satisfied are indeed true maximum or true minimum points. These conditions are satisfied by functions that obey certain convexity assumptions.

Shifting of a Tax Market responses to the imposition of a tax that cause the incidence of the tax to be on some economic agent other than the one who actually pays the tax.

Short Run–Long Run Distinction A conceptual distinction made in the theory of production that differentiates between a period of time over which some inputs are regarded as being fixed and a longer period in which all inputs can be varied by the producer.

Social Rates of Transformation and Substitution When externalities are present, private rates of trade-off and social rates of trade-off will differ. To study the optimal allocation of resources, it is necessary to examine social rates.

Social Welfare Function A hypothetical device that records societal views about equity among individuals.

Substitutes Two goods such that when the price of one increases, the quantity demanded of the other increases. For example, coffee and tea are substitutes. *See also* Complements.

Substitution Effects *See* Income and Substitution Effects: Output and Substitution Effects.

Supply Response Increases in production prompted by changing demand conditions and market prices. Usually a distinction is made between short-run and long-run supply responses.

Utility Function A mathematical conceptualization of the way in which individuals rank alternative bundles of commodities.

Variable Costs Those costs that change in response to changes in the level of output being produced by a firm. This is in contrast to fixed costs, which do not change.

Wage The cost of hiring one worker for one hour. Denoted by w in the text.

Author Index

Subject Index

Advertising, 335–338
Annuities, 454
Auctions, 272, 276
Average costs,
   long-run, 190–192, 194–195
   short-run, 183–184, 212–213
Average productivity, 135–138

Bargaining, 568, 570–572
Barriers to entry,
   in monopoly, 206–207
   in oligopoly, 340–342
Benefit principle of taxation, 546n
Bonds, 455
Budget constraint,
   income as, 53–54
   time as, 404–406
Bureaucracy, 557

Capital stock, 428
Cartel, 348–350
Ceteris paribus assumption, 41, 79, 101,
   121, 137

Coase Theorem, 569–570
Cobweb model, 275–278
Comparative advantage, 480–481
Comparative statics, 79
Compensated price change, 91–93
Compensating wage differentials, 415–419
Complements, 98, 102
Completeness, 43
Concentration ratio, 332–335
Congestion tolls, 517–519
Constant cost industry, 285–287
Constant elasticity curves, 118–120
Consumer surplus, 318
Continuous compounding, 455–456
Contour line, 30–32
Contract curve, 468
Cost,
   definition of, 169–172
   long-run, 188–195, 215–217
   minimization, 172–175, 181–182,
     209–210
   short-run, 179–186, 211–215
Cost-benefit analysis, 547–554
Cournot Model of Duopoly, 357–359